INTERNATIONAL LAW IN THE U.S. LEGAL SYSTEM

International Law in the U.S. Legal System

THIRD EDITION

Curtis A. Bradley

Oxford University Press is a department of the University of Oxford. It furthers the University's objective of excellence in research, scholarship, and education by publishing worldwide. Oxford is a registered trade mark of Oxford University Press in the UK and certain other countries.

Published in the United States of America by Oxford University Press
198 Madison Avenue, New York, NY 10016, United States of America.

© Oxford University Press 2021

All rights reserved. No part of this publication may be reproduced, stored in a retrieval system, or transmitted, in any form or by any means, without the prior permission in writing of Oxford University Press, or as expressly permitted by law, by license, or under terms agreed with the appropriate reproduction rights organization. Inquiries concerning reproduction outside the scope of the above should be sent to the Rights Department, Oxford University Press, at the address above.

You must not circulate this work in any other form
and you must impose this same condition on any acquirer.

Library of Congress Cataloging-in-Publication Data
Names: Bradley, Curtis A., author.
Title: International law in the U.S. legal system / Curtis A. Bradley.
  Other titles: International law in the US legal system
Description: Third edition. | New York, NY : Oxford University Press, [2021] | Includes bibliographical references and index.
Identifiers: LCCN 2020021645 (print) | LCCN 2020021646 (ebook) | ISBN 9780197525609 (hardback) |
  ISBN 9780197525616 (paperback) | ISBN 9780197525630 (epub) | ISBN 9780197525623 (updf) |
  ISBN 9780197525647 (online)
Subjects: LCSH: International and municipal law—United States.
Classification: LCC KF4581 .B73 2020 (print) | LCC KF4581 (ebook) | DDC 349.73—dc23
LC record available at https://lccn.loc.gov/2020021645
LC ebook record available at https://lccn.loc.gov/2020021646

Note to Readers
This publication is designed to provide accurate and authoritative information in regard to the subject matter covered. It is based upon sources believed to be accurate and reliable and is intended to be current as of the time it was written. It is sold with the understanding that the publisher is not engaged in rendering legal, accounting, or other professional services. If legal advice or other expert assistance is required, the services of a competent professional person should be sought. Also, to confirm that the information has not been affected or changed by recent developments, traditional legal research techniques should be used, including checking primary sources where appropriate.

(Based on the Declaration of Principles jointly adopted by a Committee of the American Bar Association and a Committee of Publishers and Associations.)

You may order this or any other Oxford University Press publication by visiting the Oxford University Press website at www.oup.com.

For Kathy, David, and Liana

Contents

Preface ix

1. Courts, Foreign Affairs, and the Structural Constitution 1
2. Treaties 33
3. Executive Agreements and Political Commitments 79
4. Decisions and Orders of International Institutions 105
5. Customary International Law 145
6. Extraterritorial Application of U.S. Law 175
7. International Human Rights Litigation 209
8. Sovereign and Individual Official Immunity 239
9. Extradition and Other Means of Criminal Law Enforcement 273
10. War Powers and the War on Terrorism 293

CONCLUSION 345
TABLE OF CASES 349
TABLE OF LEGISLATION 367
INDEX 377

Preface

THIS BOOK CONSIDERS the role of international law in the U.S. legal system. As will be shown, this role is defined by a mix of constitutional, statutory, judicial, and executive branch materials. Consequently, the international law that is applied in the United States has a distinctly American gloss. This does not mean that the role of international law in the U.S. legal system is insignificant, but it does mean that this role is mediated by a variety of domestic legal and political considerations. Much of this book is dedicated to exploring these considerations.[1]

The book is designed to be accessible by lawyers, law students, and judges who do not have any particular expertise in the subject, while also providing a starting point for more specialized research. It is hoped that non-U.S. readers with legal training will also find the book to be a useful window into how the United States processes and applies international law. Although I have written numerous academic articles concerning the topics covered in this book, the chief aim of the book is to describe the central currents of the

---

[1] This book is focused on the United States. For more general treatments of international law in domestic legal systems, with discussions of the practices of other countries, see, for example, THE OXFORD HANDBOOK OF COMPARATIVE FOREIGN RELATIONS LAW (Curtis A. Bradley ed., 2019); ANDRE NOLLKAEMPER, NATIONAL COURTS AND THE INTERNATIONAL RULE OF LAW (2011); and INTERNATIONAL LAW AND DOMESTIC LEGAL SYSTEMS: INCORPORATION, TRANSFORMATION, AND PERSUASION (Dinah Shelton ed., 2011). For comparative assessments of the specific role of treaties within domestic legal systems, see, for example, NATIONAL TREATY LAW AND PRACTICE (Duncan B. Hollis et al. eds., 2005); and THE ROLE OF DOMESTIC COURTS IN TREATY ENFORCEMENT: A COMPARATIVE STUDY (David Sloss ed., 2009).

law rather than to argue a particular position. In the places where I offer a view about a contested issue, I make clear that I am doing so and also point out contrary arguments.

While taking into account a wide range of interpretive materials, the book emphasizes considerations of constitutional structure and history. As for structure, the book focuses in particular on the Constitution's separation of powers among the three branches of the federal government and the federalism relationship between the national government and the state governments. Although these considerations have long played an important role in how international law is applied within the United States, they have sometimes been given too little attention in the academic literature. The book also emphasizes history, since it is impossible to understand international law's role in the U.S. legal system without having a sense of how particular practices by U.S. governmental institutions relating to international law have evolved and developed.

The book assesses the domestic status of all the major forms of international law. Most readers are presumably familiar with treaties, which are express agreements among nations that are intended to create obligations under international law.[2] Probably less familiar is customary international law, which is the law of the international community that results from the practices of nations followed out of a sense of legal obligation.[3] Treaties and customary international law have essentially the same weight under international law and are equally binding on nations. A small number of international norms, which are sometimes treated as a subset of customary international law, have a special status. These norms, referred to as "peremptory norms" or "*jus cogens* norms," are said to arise from nearly universal practice and to be absolute in their character, such that they do not permit any exceptions, even in times of emergency.[4] In addition to these sources, international institutions, which are typically established by treaties, sometimes have the authority to issue binding orders and decisions, and these too are part of the international law considered in this book.[5] The focus of the book is primarily on "public international

---

[2] *See* ANTHONY AUST, MODERN TREATY LAW AND PRACTICE 14–18 (3d ed. 2013). Treaties can also be concluded with, or between, international organizations. *See id.* at 15.

[3] *See, e.g.*, RESTATEMENT (THIRD) OF THE FOREIGN RELATIONS LAW OF THE UNITED STATES § 102(2) (1987) (defining customary international law as the law of the international community that "results from a general and consistent practice of states followed by them from a sense of legal obligation"); Statute of the International Court of Justice, art. 38(1), June 26, 1945, 59 Stat. 1055, 1060 (including, in the sources of international law to be applied by the International Court of Justice, "international custom, as evidence of a general practice accepted as law").

[4] *See, e.g.*, Vienna Convention on the Law of Treaties, art. 53, May 23, 1969, 1155 U.N.T.S. 331 ("For the purposes of the present Convention, a peremptory norm of general international law is a norm accepted and recognized by the international community of States as a whole as a norm from which no derogation is permitted and which can be modified only by a subsequent norm of general international law having the same character.").

[5] Legal issues associated with delegations of authority by the United States to international institutions are considered in Chapter 4. International tribunals also sometimes invoke general principles common to the major legal systems in order to help them resolve disputes. *See, e.g.*, Statute of the International Court of Justice, *supra* note 3, art. 38(1) (listing among the sources of international law "the general principles of law recognized by civilized nations").

law"—that is, the law governing the relations among nations and to some extent the relationship between nations and their citizens. Nevertheless, the book also touches on issues of "private international law"—that is, the law governing the transborder relations of private parties—such as the law concerning the enforcement of foreign judgments. Despite its name, "private international law" is primarily made up of rules of domestic law except to the extent that those rules have been incorporated into treaties.

The intersection between these sources of international law and the U.S. legal system has become increasingly important. Both treaties in general, and treaties that establish international institutions, have proliferated since the establishment of the United Nations system at the end of World War II. Moreover, these treaties, especially multilateral treaties ratified by a large number of countries, are often cited as evidence of new norms of customary international law. The scope of international law's coverage has also expanded significantly, such that it now frequently overlaps with domestic law. Nowhere is this expansion more evident than with the rise of international human rights law, which regulates how a nation (including the United States) interacts with its own citizens. Perhaps not surprisingly, therefore, U.S. courts, including the U.S. Supreme Court, have seen a surge of cases in recent years raising issues of international law. Since the publication of the first edition of this book, the Supreme Court has decided, among other things: *Kiobel v. Royal Dutch Petroleum* (2013) (concerning the territorial reach of the Alien Tort Statute, which until recently has been the principal statutory basis for human rights litigation in U.S. courts); *Bond v. United States* (2014) (concerning the effect of U.S. federalism on the interpretation of treaty-implementing legislation); *Zivotofsky v. Kerry* (2015) (concerning the president's power to recognize foreign governments and their territories); *Jesner v. Arab Bank* (2018) (concerning the ability to sue multinational corporations under the Alien Tort Statute); and *Jam v. Int'l Finance Corp.* (2019) (concerning the extent to which international organizations are immune from suit in U.S. courts).

Sometimes the heightened focus on international law by the U.S. judiciary has been controversial, as has been the case with the Supreme Court's citation of foreign and international materials in some of its constitutional interpretation decisions.[6] The "war on terrorism" following the attacks of September 11, 2001, generated additional controversies surrounding the proper role of international law in U.S. decision-making.[7] The United States has also had an uneven relationship with international institutions, as evidenced,

---

[6] *See, e.g.*, Graham v. Florida, 560 U.S. 48, 80–82 (2010) (invoking international practice and treaty provisions in support of the conclusion that imposing life sentences without parole on juvenile offenders violates the prohibition in the Eighth Amendment to the U.S. Constitution on cruel and unusual punishments); Roper v. Simmons, 543 U.S. 531, 578 (2005) (taking into account "the overwhelming weight of international opinion against the juvenile death penalty" in concluding that the execution of juvenile offenders violates the Eighth Amendment). This issue is discussed in Chapter 5.

[7] *See, e.g.*, Al-Bihani v. Obama, 590 F.3d 866, 871 (D.C. Cir. 2010) (contending, in a case involving the detention at Guantanamo Bay of an individual captured during the fighting in Afghanistan, that "[t]he international laws of war as a whole have not been implemented domestically by Congress and are therefore not a source of authority for U.S. courts"). *But cf.* Al-Bihani v. Obama, 619 F.3d 1, 1 (D.C. Cir. 2010) (declining to grant en banc

for example, by its decision not to join the International Criminal Court.[8] These and other examples reveal recurring tensions between the international legal system and the U.S. domestic legal system. It is important to be aware of these tensions in order to fully understand international law's role in the United States, and the book therefore highlights them when addressing the particular topics where they are most implicated.

In international law scholarship, the terms "monism" and "dualism" are sometimes used to describe possible relationships between international law and domestic law.[9] Although there is much uncertainty surrounding these terms, in essence the distinction is as follows: The monist view is that international and domestic law are part of the same legal order, and that international law is automatically incorporated into each nation's legal system. By contrast, the dualist view is that international law and domestic law are distinct, and that each nation determines for itself when and to what extent international law is incorporated into its legal system.[10] It is not clear how useful these categories are. In a sense, every nation is dualistic, in that one must consult the nation's domestic law in order to determine international law's status within that system. At most, the terms "monism" and "dualism" describe tendencies within particular legal systems. At first glance, the U.S. legal system might appear to have monist tendencies, in that the U.S. Constitution provides that treaties are part of the supreme law of the land,[11] and the Supreme Court has described customary international law as "part of our law."[12] As will be seen, however, in practice the U.S. legal system leans decidedly in the dualist direction. At the same time, international law has important effects in U.S. law that are not fully captured by looking only to whether international law is given direct effect in U.S. courts.

The United States' dualist tendencies likely stem from a variety of factors. There is a perception, at least in some U.S. circles, that international law can conflict with American democratic values.[13] There have also long been anxieties in the United States about

---

review of the earlier decision's treatment of international law because "the panel's discussion of that question is not necessary to the disposition of the merits"). International law issues relating to the war on terrorism are discussed in Chapter 10.

[8] *See* Curtis A. Bradley, *U.S. Announces Intent Not to Ratify International Criminal Court Treaty*, ASIL INSIGHT (May 2002), *at* http://www.asil.org/insights/volume/7/issue/7/us-announces-intent-not-ratify-international-criminal-court-treaty. The U.S. relationship with the International Criminal Court is discussed in Chapter 4.

[9] For background on the monist and dualist perspectives, *see* JAMES CRAWFORD, BROWNLIE'S PRINCIPLES OF PUBLIC INTERNATIONAL LAW 45–47 (9th ed. 2019); LOUIS HENKIN, INTERNATIONAL LAW: POLITICS AND VALUES 64–68 (1995); 1 OPPENHEIM'S INTERNATIONAL LAW 53–56 (Robert Jennings & Arthur Watts eds., 9th ed. 1992); J.G. Starke, *Monism and Dualism in the Theory of International Law*, 17 BRIT. Y.B. INT'L L. 66 (1936).

[10] *See* Curtis A. Bradley, *Breard, Our Dualist Constitution, and the Internationalist Conception*, 51 STAN. L. REV. 529, 530 (1999).

[11] *See* U.S. CONST. art. VI, cl. 2.

[12] The Paquete Habana, 175 U.S. 677, 700 (1900).

[13] *See, e.g.*, John O. McGinnis & Ilya Somin, *Should International Law Be Part of Our Law?*, 59 STAN. L. REV. 1175 (2007) (discussing "democracy deficit" in international law); Jed Rubenfeld, *Unilateralism and*

excessive entanglements with foreign powers, anxieties that were expressed as far back as President George Washington's Farewell Address in 1796, in which he stated that it was the policy of the United States to "steer clear of permanent alliances with any portion of the foreign world."[14] Furthermore, the United States has frequently thought of itself as singular—a "city on a hill"—and there have been fears that international law might erode some of the nation's unique values, such as its commitment to a particular conception of rights.[15] The superpower status of the United States has further complicated its views of both the benefits and costs of international legal constraints.[16]

None of this means that the United States has been opposed to international law. Indeed, it has often taken the lead in efforts to establish new treaty regimes and international institutions, and it has been a frequent participant throughout its history in international arbitration. It also receives many benefits from international law, on a wide range of issues, including issues relating to trade, national security, and the protection of its citizens abroad. Rather, it would be more accurate to describe the U.S. approach to international law as selective and pragmatic, an approach that looks for what international law can accomplish rather than assumes that it is desirable in the abstract. One element of this approach is a preference for political branch control over how international law operates within the U.S. legal system. Thus, although judges play a role in applying international law in the United States, they typically do so in a manner that is heavily informed by the decisions and actions of Congress and the executive branch.

It is too simplistic, however, to treat the U.S. approach to international law as a unitary phenomenon. Different institutional actors in the United States interact with international law in different ways and sometimes have divergent approaches to it. Moreover, there are sometimes variations in approach between the two major political parties and, relatedly, between different presidential administrations. Even within the

---

Constitutionalism, 79 N.Y.U. L. REV. 1971 (2004) (discussing tensions between international law and democratic constitutionalism).

[14] George Washington, *Farewell Address* (Sept. 19, 1796), *in* THE WASHINGTON PAPERS 321–22 (Saul K. Padover ed., 1955). For discussion of the historical context of the address, *see* Samuel Flagg Bemis, *Washington's Farewell Address: A Foreign Policy of Independence*, 39 AM. HIST. REV. 250 (1934).

[15] *See, e.g.*, Paul W. Kahn, *American Exceptionalism, Popular Sovereignty, and the Rule of Law*, *in* AMERICAN EXCEPTIONALISM AND HUMAN RIGHTS (Michael Ignatieff ed., 2005). The phrase "city on a hill" comes out of the New Testament, from a parable in Jesus' Sermon on the Mount. The Puritan John Winthrop used the phrase in a 1630 sermon that he wrote while sailing from England to the new Massachusetts Bay Colony. In the sermon, Winthrop advised his fellow colonists that they would be a "city upon a hill" and that "the eyes of all people are upon us." This phrase has subsequently been used by U.S. political figures, including most notably by President Ronald Reagan. *See* Steven G. Calabresi, *"A Shining City on a Hill": American Exceptionalism and the Supreme Court's Practice of Relying on Foreign Law*, 86 B.U. L. REV. 1335, 1370–73 (2006).

[16] *See* ROBERT KAGAN, OF PARADISE AND POWER: AMERICA AND EUROPE IN THE NEW WORLD ORDER 10–11 (2003) ("When the United States was weak, it practiced the strategies of indirection, the strategies of weakness; now that the United States is powerful, it behaves as powerful nations do."). *Cf.* Anu Bradford & Eric A. Posner, *Universal Exceptionalism in International Law*, 52 HARV. INT'L L.J. 1, 5 (2011) (arguing that "the United States is no more exceptional [in its treatment of international law] than any other powerful country").

executive branch, it is not unusual for different departments and agencies to vary in their approaches to international law. Sometimes this variation can be settled by the courts, but many issues concerning the relationship between international law and U.S. domestic law will rarely if ever be the subject of judicial determination.

Although the focus of this book is on the U.S. domestic legal system rather than on the substance of international law, it is worth keeping in mind that international law is affected by U.S. practices. The interpretation and application of international law by the United States can contribute to international law's development, both by adding to the state practice that is consulted in determining the content of customary international law, and by potentially influencing the actions and views of other nations. Conversely, U.S. legal doctrines that restrict the domestic status of international law may in some instances have the effect of limiting its development and enforcement more generally. This book does not take a position on the desirability of these effects on international law, but it does point out in various places that more is at stake than purely domestic considerations.

The book begins in Chapter 1 with an overview of some of the doctrines that govern the role of U.S. courts in adjudicating foreign affairs-related disputes, as well as of the U.S. constitutional system more generally. It then turns in Chapter 2 to consider the status of treaties in the U.S. legal system. Chapter 3 separately discusses the nature and domestic status of "executive agreements," as well as non-binding political commitments. The book then moves in Chapter 4 to consider the constitutional and other issues associated with delegations of authority by the United States to international institutions. Next, Chapter 5 discusses the domestic status of customary international law, and the somewhat related issue of judicial reliance on foreign and international materials in constitutional interpretation. The book then addresses the extraterritorial application of both constitutional and statutory law in Chapter 6, a topic that intersects in a variety of ways with international law, especially customary international law. Turning to a topic of considerable recent debate, the book in Chapter 7 discusses the phenomenon of international human rights litigation, especially litigation under the Alien Tort Statute. The book then addresses in Chapter 8 the immunity of foreign governments and their officials in U.S. courts. In Chapter 9, the book considers the application of extradition treaties in the U.S. legal system, as well as other forms of international criminal law enforcement. Finally, Chapter 10 addresses the relationship between international law and the war powers of Congress and the president, as well as the role of international law in the war on terrorism. Each of these chapters has been updated since the publication of the second edition to take account of new legal materials and controversies, as well as recent scholarship.

The second edition of this book was published in 2015, during the Obama administration. Actions taken during the last two years of that administration are addressed in this edition, including the administration's conclusion of the Joint Comprehensive Plan of Action (JCPOA) with Iran concerning its nuclear program, and the U.S. ratification of the Paris Agreement on climate change. The presidency of Donald Trump, which began in 2017, ushered in substantial changes in U.S. foreign relations. These changes included withdrawals from a number of international agreements (including the JCPOA and the Paris Agreement); various uses of military force, such as in Syria; the conclusion of the U.S.-Mexico-Canada trade agreement, which replaced the North American Free Trade Agreement; and changes to U.S. positions relating to Israel, including recognition of Israeli sovereignty over Jerusalem and the Golan Heights and a determination that Israeli settlements in the occupied West Bank are not inherently inconsistent with international law. This edition takes account of those and other recent developments.

During the preparation of this edition, the world was confronted with the COVID-19 pandemic, something that was causing not only severe health effects in many countries, but also significant disruptions to the global economy. This crisis likely will have important effects on international law and international relations, and it may well generate additional issues that will fall within the scope of this book's coverage. If so, those issues will be addressed in a later edition.

* * *

It seems appropriate at the outset to situate this book against the backdrop of other work on the topic. It is self-consciously written in the tradition of Louis Henkin's magisterial treatise, *Foreign Affairs and the Constitution,* which was published in 1972 and then republished in an updated form in 1996.[17] Professor Henkin, who passed away in 2010, was a towering figure in the field of U.S. foreign relations law, and I learned a tremendous amount from him, even when I sometimes reached different conclusions. Henkin's book was itself written in the tradition of work that had been done in the early twentieth century, most notably Quincy Wright's 1922 treatise, *The Control of American Foreign Relations,* and I have also benefited from that earlier work.[18] The present book, however, is somewhat narrower in focus than books on U.S. foreign relations law in that it covers only topics relating to the intersection of international law and U.S. law, not the law governing the conduct of U.S. foreign relations more generally.

Professor Henkin also served as the Chief Reporter for the American Law Institute's *Restatement (Third) of the Foreign Relations Law of the United States,* which was published in 1987. This two-volume work is an extraordinarily useful resource, and it has been highly influential with both courts and scholars, although it has increasingly been overtaken by subsequent legal developments. I had the privilege of serving as a Reporter

---

[17] *See* Louis Henkin, Foreign Affairs and the Constitution (1972); *see and compare* Louis Henkin, Foreign Affairs and the United States Constitution (2d ed. 1996).

[18] *See* Quincy Wright, The Control of American Foreign Relations (1922). In the preface to his book, Professor Henkin noted that he was "much indebted" to Quincy Wright's treatise. See Henkin (1972), *supra* note 17, at viii.

on the most recent *Restatement (Fourth) of the Foreign Relations Law of the United States*, which was published in 2018. The *Restatement (Fourth)* has to date addressed only three topics—treaties, jurisdiction, and immunity—and thus is more limited in its coverage than the *Restatement (Third)*. Where relevant, this book refers to the positions taken in these Restatements.

This book reflects ideas that I have been developing in my scholarship and teaching for over two decades. In developing these ideas, I have benefited enormously from conversations and debates with colleagues from around the country and the world. I have also learned a tremendous amount from my students, both inside and outside the classroom. To the extent that I have been able to achieve clarity of presentation in this book, it is due in large part to the refinement that comes with the give and take of teaching. My knowledge of the subject was also greatly enriched by the year I spent in 2004 in the Legal Adviser's Office of the U.S. State Department as their Counselor on International Law.

For their comments on drafts of the manuscript of the first edition of the book, I would like to thank Bill Dodge, Jean Galbraith, Larry Helfer, Suzanne Katzenstein, Julie Maupin, David Moore, Sai Prakash, David Sloss, Peter Spiro, Paul Stephan, David Stewart, Ed Swaine, Carlos Vázquez, Mark Weisburd, Ingrid Wuerth, and Ernie Young. In March 2012, Duke Law School hosted a symposium at which leading scholars of international law and U.S. foreign relations law discussed and commented on an early draft of the book manuscript for the first edition. I am grateful to the participants in that symposium for their valuable feedback, and for Duke's Center for International and Comparative Law for sponsoring it. After publication of the first edition, I received insightful comments from participants in an online symposium about the book hosted by the *Opinio Juris* blog in March 2013, and also from Ingrid Wuerth in her review of the book in the *American Journal of International Law*. For their comments on drafts of the second edition, I would like to thank Joseph Dellapenna, Bill Dodge, David Moore, Mike Ramsey, Paul Stephan, and Ingrid Wuerth.

Special thanks are due to my close friend and frequent collaborator, Jack Goldsmith. I began thinking about the topics addressed by this book in conversations with Jack in 1993, when the two of us co-taught an international litigation course at the University of Virginia. At that time, we were both working for a large law firm in Washington, D.C., and we would drive to Charlottesville on Friday afternoons, and then return to D.C. the following day. (As strange as it may seem, our students would actually come to class both Friday night and Saturday morning.) The two-hour drives each way involved nonstop dialogue—and sometimes friendly argument—about the proper interaction between U.S. law and international law. Those drives, and the course we taught, eventually led us to write our first major law review article together, on the domestic status of customary international law.[19] After a number of other collaborations, we coauthored a casebook on U.S. foreign relations law, which now (with an additional coauthor) is in its seventh

---

[19] *See* Curtis A. Bradley & Jack L. Goldsmith, *Customary International Law as Federal Common Law: A Critique of the Modern Position*, 110 HARV. L. REV. 815 (1997).

edition.[20] Inevitably, some of the ideas reflected in the present book stem from work that Jack and I have done together.

I would like to thank my former dean at Duke, David Levi, for his extensive support and encouragement during the process of writing the first edition of this book. I am also very grateful to Duke's library staff, which responded to my countless requests for books and documents with enthusiasm and good cheer. In addition, I would like to thank the student research assistants who helped me with the manuscript of the first edition, all of whom did truly excellent work: Chris Dodrill, Chris Ford, Rebecca Krefft, Tatiana Sainati, and Garrick Sevilla. Last but certainly not least, none of the editions of this book would have been possible without the long-standing support and counsel of my wife, Kathy Bradley.

---

[20] *See* CURTIS A. BRADLEY, ASHLEY S. DEEKS & JACK L. GOLDSMITH, FOREIGN RELATIONS LAW: CASES AND MATERIALS (7th ed. 2020).

1 Courts, Foreign Affairs, and the Structural Constitution

INTERNATIONAL LAW INHERENTLY concerns foreign affairs. As a result, to understand the role of international law in the U.S. legal system, it is useful first to have a sense of some of the constitutional, statutory, and common law doctrines that govern the adjudication of foreign affairs-related disputes in the United States. This chapter begins by describing the subject matter jurisdiction of the federal and state courts and some of the "justiciability" limitations on the exercise of this jurisdiction. Next, it briefly considers the requirements for U.S. courts to exercise personal jurisdiction. The chapter then discusses the issue of choice of law in the federal and state courts, especially the *Erie* doctrine that requires that the federal district courts apply the law of the state in which they sit in cases not governed by federal law.

Turning more specifically to foreign affairs, the chapter considers the common law act of state doctrine, pursuant to which U.S. courts sometimes presume the validity of foreign government acts taken within the foreign government's territory. The chapter then describes other forms of judicial deference or respect for foreign governments, as illustrated by the doctrines of *forum non conveniens* and comity-based abstention. Next, the chapter discusses the *Charming Betsy* canon of construction, which requires that courts construe statutes, where possible, to avoid violations of international law. The chapter then considers the deference that courts historically have given to the executive branch when deciding cases implicating foreign affairs.

The last part of the chapter provides a brief overview of the constitutional authority of U.S. government institutions other than the courts, and some of the considerations that courts take into account in assessing that authority. It begins by reviewing the powers of Congress and the president. It then considers the relationship between these powers, as influentially articulated by Justice Jackson in the *Youngstown* steel seizure case. Finally, it discusses federal preemption of state law.

Subject Matter Jurisdiction and Justiciability

The United States has both a federal court system and court systems in each of the states. The federal courts are courts of limited jurisdiction. They can hear a case only if it falls within the list of "Cases" and "Controversies" set forth in Article III of the Constitution.[1] In addition, except for certain cases that can be brought directly in the Supreme Court, the federal courts cannot hear a case unless it also falls within a congressional grant of subject matter jurisdiction.[2]

The two most important categories of Article III jurisdiction are federal question jurisdiction (cases "arising under this Constitution, the Laws of the United States, and Treaties") and diversity jurisdiction (controversies between parties of diverse U.S. citizenship or between U.S. citizens and foreign citizens). Congress has granted the federal courts jurisdiction in both of these categories, but its statutory grants have been construed to be substantially narrower than what would be allowed under Article III. Thus, for example, Article III federal question jurisdiction may extend to any case in which there is a federal law "ingredient,"[3] including when the federal law arises only as a defense, but statutory federal question jurisdiction has been construed to exist only when the federal law issue appears on the face of the plaintiff's well-pleaded complaint.[4]

---

[1] *See* U.S. Const. art. III, § 2 (listing the types of "Cases" and "Controversies" that fall within the judicial power of the federal courts); *see also, e.g.*, Kokkonen v. Guardian Life Ins. Co. of Am., 511 U.S. 375, 377 (1994) ("Federal courts are courts of limited jurisdiction. They possess only that power authorized by Constitution and statute ... which is not to be expanded by judicial decree."); Verlinden B.V. v. Cen. Bank of Nigeria, 461 U.S. 480, 491 (1983) ("This Court's cases firmly establish that Congress may not expand the jurisdiction of the federal courts beyond the bounds established by the Constitution.").

[2] *See, e.g.*, Kontrick v. Ryan, 540 U.S. 443, 452 (2004) ("Only Congress may determine a lower federal court's subject-matter jurisdiction."); Merrell Dow Pharms., Inc. v. Thompson, 478 U.S. 804, 807 (1986) ("Article III of the Constitution gives the federal courts power to hear cases 'arising under' federal statutes. That grant of power, however, is not self-executing...."); Owen Equipment & Constr. Co. v. Kroger, 437 U.S. 365, 372 (1978) ("[T]he jurisdiction of the federal courts is limited not only by the provisions of Art. III of the Constitution, but also by Acts of Congress.").

[3] *See* Osborn v. Bank of the United States, 22 U.S. (9 Wheat.) 738, 823 (1824).

[4] *See* Louisville & Nashville R.R. v. Mottley, 211 U.S. 149, 152 (1908). Statutory federal question jurisdiction was not conferred with any permanence until 1875.

Article III diversity jurisdiction extends to any case in which there is "minimal diversity"—that is, diversity of citizenship between any plaintiff and any defendant in the case. The diversity jurisdiction statute, however, has been construed as requiring "complete diversity"—that is, ordinarily no plaintiff can share citizenship with any defendant, even if the other parties in the case are diverse.[5] The diversity statute also requires that the amount in controversy exceed a certain amount, currently $75,000.[6] A suit between foreign parties does not satisfy even the minimal diversity requirement of Article III, even if the parties are from different countries, and thus can be heard in the federal courts only if it falls within some other category of Article III jurisdiction (such as federal question jurisdiction).[7]

Unlike the federal courts, the state courts are courts of general jurisdiction. They can hear essentially all categories of cases, whether based on state law or federal law. Even suits against foreign governments can in theory be heard in state courts, although this is rare in practice. However, certain federal laws (such as federal criminal laws) can normally be applied only in the federal courts.[8] For the most part, the state judiciaries are formally separate from the federal judiciary. The state and federal judicial systems connect at the top, though, in that the U.S. Supreme Court has the authority to review decisions from the state courts relating to federal law.[9]

When a case is filed in state court, it may ordinarily be removed by the defendant to federal court if the case could have been brought in federal court in the first instance. Removal is not allowed on the basis of diversity jurisdiction, however, if one or more of the defendants is a citizen of the state in which the suit is brought.[10] Any suit brought against a foreign state may be removed by the defendant.[11]

Even when a federal court has subject matter jurisdiction over a case, it may find that the case is "nonjusticiable"—that is, not appropriate for judicial resolution. The federal courts, for example, are not allowed to give advisory opinions.[12] Related to this limitation, courts will dismiss a case if the plaintiff lacks a sufficient stake in the case to qualify for "standing." To have standing, the plaintiff must normally have suffered (or be likely to

---

[5] *See* Strawbridge v. Curtiss, 7 U.S. (3 Cranch) 267, 367–68 (1806).
[6] *See* 28 U.S.C. § 1332.
[7] *See* Mossman v. Higginson, 4 U.S. (4 Dall.) 12, 14 (1800); *see also* Hodgson v. Bowerbank, 9 U.S. (5 Cranch) 303, 304 (1809).
[8] It is unclear whether Congress could validly require state courts to hear federal criminal cases. *See* Anthony J. Bellia, Jr., *Congressional Power and State Court Jurisdiction*, 94 Geo. L.J. 949, 992–1000 (2006); Michael G. Collins & Jonathan Remy Nash, *Prosecuting Federal Crimes in State Courts*, 97 Va. L. Rev. 243 (2011).
[9] *See* 28 U.S.C. § 1257.
[10] *See* 28 U.S.C. § 1441(b).
[11] *See* 28 U.S.C. § 1441(d).
[12] *See* Chicago & S. Air Lines, Inc. v. Waterman S.S. Corp., 333 U.S. 103, 113 (1948) ("This Court early and wisely determined that it would not give advisory opinions even when asked by the Chief Executive."). *See also* Stewart Jay, Most Humble Servants: The Advisory Role of Early Judges (1997) (discussing the historical foundations of the disallowance of advisory opinions in the federal courts).

suffer) a concrete injury, the injury must be fairly traceable to the conduct of the defendant, and it must be likely that the injury will be redressed by a favorable decision.[13]

The Supreme Court has sharply limited the circumstances under which members of Congress will be found to have standing to challenge executive branch action or inaction. Normally, the Court has held, members of Congress may not sue based on an allegation of mere institutional injury—for example, an allegation that presidential action has usurped or diminished the overall power of Congress.[14] The Court has suggested that a member of Congress might have standing to sue, however, if his or her vote on a legislative measure has been "completely nullified" by executive action, although is not clear what is required in order to properly allege such vote nullification.[15] The Court has also suggested that members of Congress might have standing in some circumstances if they are specifically authorized to sue by their chamber of the legislature, or by the full Congress.[16]

To be justiciable, a case must also be ripe, which means that the alleged harm must ordinarily be immediate rather than merely speculative,[17] and the case must not be moot, which means that it must normally still be ripe at the time of adjudication.[18] In an influential concurring opinion in a case involving the termination of a treaty, a Supreme Court justice suggested that issues relating to the distribution of authority between Congress and the executive branch should not be considered ripe until these institutions have

---

[13] *See* Clapper v. Amnesty Int'l, 568 U.S. 398, 409 (2013); Lujan v. Defenders of Wildlife, 504 U.S. 555, 560–61 (1992).

[14] Raines v. Byrd, 521 U.S. 811, 821 (1997). The Court observed that "[t]here would be nothing irrational about a system that granted standing in these cases; some European constitutional courts operate under one or another variant of such a regime. . . . But it is obviously not the regime that has obtained under our Constitution to date." *Id.* at 828.

[15] *Id.* at 823. *See also* Campbell v. Clinton, 203 F.3d 19, 22 (D.C. Cir. 2000) ("It is, to be sure, not readily apparent what the Supreme Court meant by that word. It would seem the Court used nullify to mean treating a vote that did not pass as if it had, or vice versa.").

[16] *See* 521 U.S. at 829 ("We attach some importance to the fact that appellees have not been authorized to represent their respective Houses of Congress in this action, and indeed both Houses actively oppose their suit."). *Cf.* Arizona State Legislature v. Arizona Independent Redistricting Commission, 135 S. Ct. 2652, 2664 (2015) (allowing a state legislature to challenge the actions of a state commission in setting the boundaries of election districts, and noting that, unlike in *Raines v. Byrd*, the legislature here sued "after authorizing votes in both of its chambers").

[17] *See, e.g.*, Poe v. Ullman, 367 U.S. 497, 507–508 (1961) (plurality opinion).

[18] *See, e.g.*, DeFunis v. Odegaard, 416 U.S. 312, 316 (1974). A case that would otherwise be moot can be heard if the issue raised is capable of repetition yet evades judicial review (because of timing issues, for example). *See, e.g.*, First Nat'l Bank of Boston v. Bellotti, 435 U.S. 765, 774 (1978) (election restrictions); Roe v. Wade, 410 U.S. 113, 125 (1973) (abortion restrictions). Also, a defendant's voluntary cessation of challenged activity ordinarily will not moot a case, because the defendant simply could resume the activity after the case was dismissed. *See* Friends of the Earth, Inc. v. Laidlaw Envt'l Svcs. (TOC), Inc., 528 U.S. 167, 189 (2000); United States v. W.T. Grant Co., 345 U.S. 629, 632 (1953). Voluntary cessation can moot a case, however, if it is clear that the challenged activity is unlikely to reoccur. *See* N.Y. State Rifle & Pistol Ass'n v. City of New York, 140 S. Ct. 1525 (2020) (per curiam); Already, LLC v. Nike, Inc., 568 U.S. 85, 92 (2013).

"taken action asserting [their] constitutional authority" and have reached a "constitutional impasse."[19] Some lower federal courts have invoked this "institutional ripeness" limitation when dismissing challenges to presidential actions relating to foreign affairs.[20]

Still another ground for dismissal is the political question doctrine, pursuant to which courts will decline to resolve certain issues deemed to be political in nature. In a 1962 decision, *Baker v. Carr*, the Supreme Court said that, in determining whether an issue poses a nonjusticiable political question, courts should consider whether the issue implicates one or more of the following six factors:

> [1] a textually demonstrable constitutional commitment of the issue to a coordinate political department; or [2] a lack of judicially discoverable and manageable standards for resolving it; or [3] the impossibility of deciding without an initial policy determination of a kind clearly for nonjudicial discretion; or [4] the impossibility of a court's undertaking independent resolution without expressing lack of the respect due coordinate branches of government; or [5] an unusual need for unquestioning adherence to a political decision already made; or [6] the potentiality of embarrassment from multifarious pronouncements by various departments on one question.[21]

The fourth, fifth, and sixth factors have sometimes been described as being "prudential" in character. The relative weight of these factors is unclear, although a plurality of the Supreme Court has noted that they are "probably listed in descending order of both importance and certainty."[22] In a 2012 decision declining to apply the political question doctrine, *Zivotofsky v. Clinton*, a majority of the Court referred only to the first two factors, perhaps signaling a disinclination to ground the doctrine in prudential considerations.[23]

The political question doctrine is applied only rarely in domestic cases, but it has been applied with some frequency by the lower courts in cases that implicate foreign affairs.[24] The Supreme Court has made clear, however, that "it is error to suppose that every case

---

[19] Goldwater v. Carter, 444 U.S. 996, 997 (1979) (Powell, J., concurring).
[20] *See, e.g.*, Doe v. Bush, 323 F.3d 133, 137–39 (1st Cir. 2003) (use of military force); Kucinich v. Bush, 236 F. Supp. 2d 1, 11–12 (D.D.C. 2002) (withdrawal from treaty).
[21] 369 U.S. 186, 217 (1962).
[22] Vieth v. Jubelirer, 541 U.S. 267, 278 (2004) (plurality opinion).
[23] *See* 566 U.S. 189 (2012). *See also* Rucho v. Common Cause, 139 S. Ct. 2484, 2494 (2019) (relying on second factor from *Baker v. Carr* in concluding that challenges to partisan gerrymandering of electoral districts presented a political question).
[24] *See, e.g.*, Jaber v. United States, 861 F.3d 241 (D.C. Cir. 2017); Li-Shou v. United States, 777 F.3d 175 (4th Cir. 2015); Saldana v. Occidental Petroleum Corp., 774 F.3d 544 (9th Cir. 2014). *See also Goldwater*, 444 U.S. at 1002–105 (plurality opinion) (concluding that the issue of whether the president can unilaterally withdraw the United States from a treaty is a political question). For criticism of this phenomenon, *see* THOMAS M. FRANCK, POLITICAL QUESTIONS/JUDICIAL ANSWERS (1992).

or controversy which touches foreign relations lies beyond judicial cognizance."[25] The Court has also described the political question doctrine as a "narrow exception" to the judiciary's obligation to decide cases.[26] The political question doctrine is more likely to be applied to constitutional issues concerning the distribution of authority among the federal branches of government than to other constitutional issues, or to statutory or international law issues.[27]

Because justiciability limitations stem from Article III of the Constitution, which governs only the federal courts, most of these limitations do not bind the state courts. Thus, for example, courts in some states are allowed to issue advisory opinions, and state courts can hear cases where there would not be standing to sue in federal court.[28] However, because the political question doctrine is designed in part to protect the prerogatives of the federal political branches, at least some applications of it are likely binding on state courts as well as federal courts.[29] As will be noted, the act of state doctrine, which is based on somewhat similar separation of powers considerations, has been held to be binding on state courts.

Personal Jurisdiction

Before adjudicating a case, a U.S. court must have not only subject matter jurisdiction over the case, but also personal jurisdiction over the defendant. The various states have enacted statutes or rules of court that define the personal jurisdiction of state courts. Most of these statutes provide for "long-arm" jurisdiction over defendants who are located outside the state but have certain contacts with the state. There is no general long-arm statute, however, for the federal courts. Instead, pursuant to the Federal Rules

---

[25] *Baker*, 369 U.S. at 211.

[26] *Zivotofsky*, 566 U.S. at 195.

[27] *See, e.g.*, Japan Whaling Ass'n v. Am. Cetacean Soc'y, 478 U.S. 221, 230 (1986) ("[T]he courts have the authority to construe treaties and executive agreements, and it goes without saying that interpreting congressional legislation is a recurring and accepted task for the federal courts."). As Louis Henkin noted, in many cases in which courts have labeled issues "political questions," they are really saying that a political branch—often the executive branch—has the constitutional authority to resolve the issue in a way that is dispositive for the courts. *See* Louis Henkin, *Is There a "Political Question" Doctrine?*, 85 YALE L.J. 597 (1976).

[28] *See* Asarco, Inc. v. Kadish, 490 U.S. 605, 617 (1989) ("[T]he constraints of Article III do not apply to state courts, and accordingly the state courts are not bound by the limitations of a case or controversy or other federal rules of justiciability even when they address issues of federal law....").

[29] With respect to conduct by U.S. states, even if a federal law challenge to the conduct is barred by the political question doctrine, it may be possible to bring a state law challenge. *See, e.g., Rucho*, 138 S. Ct. at 2507 (noting that, although there were insufficient standards under federal law to adjudicate challenges to state partisan gerrymandering, "[p]rovisions in state statutes and state constitutions can provide standards and guidance for state courts to apply").

of Civil Procedure, federal courts often borrow the long-arm statute of the state in which they sit, even in cases involving federal law.[30]

To be valid, an exercise of personal jurisdiction must be consistent with the due process clauses of the Constitution. The Supreme Court has held that due process requires that the defendant have certain "minimum contacts," "such that the maintenance of the suit does not offend traditional notions of fair play and substantial justice."[31] The required contacts between the defendant and the forum that are needed to satisfy due process depend on whether the jurisdiction being asserted is general or specific. Under general jurisdiction, a court may adjudicate any claim against the defendant, whereas under specific jurisdiction the court may only adjudicate claims that arise out of or relate to the defendants' contacts with the forum.[32]

General jurisdiction is proper if the defendant is a citizen or resident of the forum, or, in the case of a corporation, is incorporated or has its principal place of business there.[33] A corporation is also subject to general jurisdiction if it has connections with the forum state that "are 'so continuous and systematic' as to render [it] essentially at home" there.[34] But a foreign corporation is not subject to general jurisdiction based merely on the business contacts of its U.S. subsidiary with the forum state.[35] For a natural person, the Supreme Court has held that it is consistent with due process for a court to exercise general jurisdiction over an individual based on his or her presence in the forum state at the time of the suit, even if the presence is transitory.[36]

In order for specific jurisdiction to be proper, the defendant must have "purposefully avail[ed] itself of the privilege of conducting activities within the forum State, thus invoking the benefits and protections of its laws."[37] Because the purposeful availment inquiry

---

[30] See FED. R. CIV. P. 4(k)(1)(A). A few federal statutes, such as the antitrust and securities statutes, have personal jurisdiction provisions. The Foreign Sovereign Immunities Act, discussed in Chapter 8, also has a personal jurisdiction provision for suits against foreign states.

[31] Int'l Shoe Co. v. Washington, 326 U.S. 310, 316 (1945). In a famous nineteenth-century decision that addressed the ability of a state court to assert personal jurisdiction over an out-of-state defendant, the Supreme Court analogized to customary international law principles governing the territorial jurisdiction of nation-states. See Pennoyer v. Neff, 95 U.S. 714, 722 (1877). For cases in which personal jurisdiction is based on contacts with a state that relate to the cause of action, the Supreme Court eventually replaced the territorial approach in *Pennoyer* with the minimum contacts approach.

[32] See generally Arthur T. von Mehren & Donald T. Trautman, *Jurisdiction to Adjudicate: A Suggested Analysis*, 79 HARV. L. REV. 1121 (1966).

[33] See, e.g., Blackmer v. United States, 284 U.S. 421 (1932).

[34] Daimler AG v. Bauman, 571 U.S. 117, 127 (2014) (quoting Goodyear Dunlop Tires Operations v. Brown, 564 U.S. 915, 919 (2011)); see also Helicopteros Nacionales de Columbia, S.A. v. Hall, 466 U.S. 408, 415–16 (1984); Perkins v. Benguet Consolidated Mining Co., 342 U.S. 437, 438, 445 (1952).

[35] See *Daimler*, 571 U.S. at 138–39. In this case, the Court emphasized that its decision was supported by considerations of international comity. See id. at 141–42. The Court also explained that its shift away from the strictly territorial approach of *Pennoyer*, supra note 31, was true only for specific jurisdiction, not general jurisdiction. See id. at 132–33.

[36] See Burnham v. Superior Ct. of Cal., 495 U.S. 604, 617–18 (1990) (plurality opinion).

[37] Hanson v. Denckla, 357 U.S. 235, 253 (1958).

is to be conducted on a forum-by-forum basis, "a defendant may in principle be subject to the jurisdiction of the courts of the United States but not of any particular State."[38] Under the Federal Rules of Civil Procedure, if a case arises under federal law and the defendant does not have sufficient contacts with any one state to meet the requirements for personal jurisdiction, a federal court may assert personal jurisdiction if the defendant has sufficient contacts with the United States as a whole to satisfy due process.[39] But there is no comparable national contacts provision for cases based on state law.

Choice of Law in the Federal and State Courts

The Constitution states in Article VI that the Constitution itself, "the Laws of the United States which shall be made in Pursuance thereof," and treaties made under the authority of the United States are deemed "the supreme Law of the Land" that is binding on state judges, notwithstanding any contrary state law.[40] As a result of this Supremacy Clause, state courts are generally required to apply federal law when it is relevant to a case before them, even when it conflicts with state law.[41] Conversely, the federal courts generally must apply state law when it is relevant to a case before them and there is no controlling federal law. This is particularly likely to come up in cases based on diversity jurisdiction, since subject matter jurisdiction over those cases is not premised on the existence of a federal law claim.

For much of the nineteenth century and the early part of the twentieth century, federal and state courts also applied a body of law known as "general common law."[42] This body of law was derived from general legal principles and customary practice rather than from the pronouncements and decisions of any particular legal system. Courts did not view general common law as having the status of federal law. As a result, federal court interpretations of general common law were not binding on state courts, and the two court systems sometimes adopted differing interpretations of this law.[43]

Federal courts applied general common law even though a statute, the Rules of Decision Act, provided that federal courts were to apply the "laws of the several states" in cases not governed by the Constitution, treaties, or federal statutes. In its 1842 decision in *Swift v. Tyson*, for example, the Supreme Court applied "principles established in the

---

[38] J. McIntyre Machinery Ltd. v. Nicastro, 564 U.S. 873, 884 (2011) (plurality opinion).
[39] *See* Fed. R. Civ. P. 4(k)(2); *see also, e.g.*, Doe v. Buratai, 792 Fed. Appx. 6, 8–9 (D.C. Cir. 2019) (considering whether the defendants "have constitutionally sufficient contacts with the United States as a whole to permit the federal court's exercise of personal jurisdiction over them").
[40] *See* U.S. CONST. art. VI, cl. 2.
[41] For the obligation of state courts to hear federal law claims, see, for example, Haywood v. Drown, 556 U.S. 729 (2009); and Howlett v. Rose, 496 U.S. 356 (1990).
[42] *See generally* William A. Fletcher, *The General Common Law and Section 34 of the Judiciary Act of 1789: The Example of Marine Insurance*, 97 HARV. L. REV. 1513 (1984).
[43] *See* RESTATEMENT (THIRD) OF THE FOREIGN RELATIONS LAW OF THE UNITED STATES 41 (1987).

general commercial law," rather than New York state court decisions, to resolve a commercial dispute concerning the validity of an assignment of a negotiable instrument, even though the assignment had occurred in New York.[44] The Court reasoned that the Rules of Decision Act applied only to "the positive statutes of the state, and the construction thereof adopted by the local tribunals, and to rights and titles to things having a permanent locality," and not to state court decisions on "questions of a more general nature."[45]

In its landmark 1938 decision, *Erie Railroad v. Tompkins*, the Supreme Court overruled *Swift*, concluding that "the laws of the several states" referenced in the Rules of Decision Act included the law as determined by state courts, even for matters thought to fall within the category of "general law." The Court further announced that "there is no federal general common law," and that, henceforth, "except in matters governed by the Federal Constitution or by Acts of Congress, the law to be applied in any case is the law of the State."[46] The Court reasoned that "'law in the sense in which courts speak of it today does not exist without some definite authority behind it.'"[47] As a result, the Court denied what it called the "fallacy" that there is a "'transcendental body of law outside of any particular State but obligatory within it unless and until changed by statute.'"[48]

Despite suggestions in *Erie* that the only common law that federal courts can apply is the common law of the states, the Supreme Court has in fact allowed for the development after *Erie* of some common law in the federal courts.[49] This "federal common law" is genuine federal law that binds the states under the Supremacy Clause and potentially establishes a basis for Article III and statutory federal question jurisdiction. The Supreme Court has never provided a comprehensive explanation of its approach to federal common law after *Erie*, although when it has allowed for federal common law, it has sometimes referred to the existence of "uniquely federal" interests and a strong need for uniformity.[50] The Court has also noted that because the development of national policy is normally the prerogative of Congress rather than the courts, federal common law should be developed only in "few and restricted" instances.[51]

---

[44] Swift v. Tyson, 41 U.S. (16 Pet.) 1 (1842).

[45] *Id.* at 18, 19.

[46] Erie R.R. v. Tompkins, 304 U.S. 64, 78 (1938).

[47] *Id.* at 79.

[48] *Id.*

[49] *See* Tex. Indus., Inc. v. Radcliff Materials, Inc., 451 U.S. 630, 640 (1981) ("[T]he Court has recognized the need and authority in some limited areas to formulate what has come to be known as 'federal common law.'"). *See also* Henry Friendly, *In Praise of Erie—and of the New Federal Common Law*, 39 N.Y.U. L. REV. 383, 405 (1964) ("*Erie* led to the emergence of a federal decisional law in areas of national concern that is truly uniform because, under the supremacy clause, it is binding in every forum, and therefore is predictable and useful as its predecessor, more general in subject matter but limited to the federal courts, was not.").

[50] *See, e.g.*, Boyle v. United Techs. Corp., 487 U.S. 500, 505–506 (1988); Banco Nacional de Cuba v. Sabbatino, 376 U.S. 398, 425–26 (1964).

[51] *See, e.g.*, O'Melveny & Myers v. FDIC, 512 U.S. 79, 87 (1994); Wheeldin v. Wheeler, 373 U.S. 647, 651 (1963); *see also* Rodriguez v. FDIC, 140 S. Ct. 713, 717 (2020) ("Judicial lawmaking in the form of federal common law plays a necessarily modest role under a Constitution that vests the federal government's 'legislative

In cases in which they have jurisdiction, both federal and state courts will sometimes apply the law of other countries, pursuant to choice of law principles. For example, in an international contract dispute, it would not be unusual for a U.S. court to apply foreign contract law. A federal court, in determining foreign law, "may consider any relevant material or source, including testimony, whether or not submitted by a party or admissible under the Federal Rules of Evidence."[52] United States courts will not, however, apply the penal, revenue, or other public laws of foreign nations.[53] In explaining this limitation (sometimes called the "revenue rule"), one prominent judge noted that an evaluation of "the provisions of the public order of another state ... involves the relations between the states themselves, with which courts are incompetent to deal, and which are entrusted to other authorities," and that "[i]t may commit the domestic state to a position which would seriously embarrass its neighbor."[54]

Although the Constitution's Full Faith and Credit Clause requires each U.S. state to recognize and enforce the judgments of other states,[55] U.S. courts are not under any constitutional, federal statutory, or treaty obligation to recognize or enforce foreign judgments.[56] As early as 1895, however, the Supreme Court held that foreign judgments are generally enforceable as a matter of comity, subject to a reciprocity requirement whereby the foreign government would have to enforce similar U.S. judgments.[57] Today, the

---

Powers' in Congress and reserves most other regulatory authority to the States."). The issue of whether customary international law has the status in the U.S. legal system of federal common law, a matter of some controversy, is discussed in Chapter 5.

[52] FED. R. CIV. P. 44.1. In Animal Science Products, Inc. v. Hebei Welcome Pharmaceutical Co. Ltd., 138 S. Ct. 1865 (2018), the Supreme Court unanimously held that U.S. courts are not required to accept the representations of foreign governments about the content of their law. The Court noted that, as a matter of "international comity," courts "should carefully consider a foreign state's views about the meaning of its own laws," but it said that "the appropriate weight in each case will depend upon the circumstances; a federal court is neither bound to adopt the foreign government's characterization nor required to ignore other relevant materials." Id. at 1873.

[53] See, e.g., Att'y General of Canada v. R.J. Reynolds Tobacco Holdings, Inc., 268 F.3d 103 (2d Cir. 2001); United States v. Boots, 80 F.3d 580 (1st Cir. 1996); Her Majesty the Queen v. Gilbertson, 597 F.2d 1161 (9th Cir. 1979). Cf. Pasquantino v. United States, 544 U.S. 349 (2005) (holding that revenue rule did not apply to bar criminal prosecution, under the federal wire fraud statute, of a scheme to evade Canadian liquor taxes).

[54] Moore v. Mitchell, 30 F.2d 600, 604 (2d Cir. 1929) (Hand, J., concurring). For an argument that the ban on applying the penal, revenue, and other public laws of foreign nations should be reconsidered "because cooperation in the enforcement of public law would be mutually beneficial," see William S. Dodge, Breaking the Public Law Taboo, 43 HARV. INT'L L. J. 161, 163 (2002).

[55] See U.S. CONST. art. IV, § 1 ("Full Faith and Credit shall be given in each State to the public Acts, Records, and judicial Proceedings of every other State. And the Congress may by general Laws prescribe the Manner in which such Acts, Records and Proceedings shall be proved, and the Effect thereof.").

[56] In 2019, negotiations were concluded on the Hague Convention on the Recognition and Enforcement of Foreign Judgments in Civil or Commercial Matters, but as of the time when this edition was going to press, the Convention had not yet taken effect and the United States was not yet a party to it. For a discussion of the Convention, see David P. Stewart, Current Development, The Hague Conference Adopts a New Convention on the Recognition and Enforcement of Foreign Judgments in Civil or Commercial Matters, 113 AM. J. INT'L L. 772 (2019).

[57] See Hilton v. Guyot, 159 U.S. 113 (1895).

enforcement of foreign judgments is governed by state law, either under state common law or state codification of the Uniform Foreign Money-Judgments Recognition Act. Under most of these state laws, courts will presumptively recognize and enforce foreign judgments, even in the absence of a showing of reciprocity, as long as the foreign court had jurisdiction, the foreign proceeding was procedurally fair, and the enforcement does not offend a fundamental public policy of the state. As a result, foreign judgments are often recognized and enforced in the United States, although they receive somewhat less respect than the judgments of sister states.[58]

Act of State Doctrine

Courts in the United States apply the "act of state" doctrine, pursuant to which they will presume the validity of the acts of foreign governments taken within their own territory. Although the Supreme Court originally grounded this doctrine in considerations of international law and international comity,[59] in the seminal *Sabbatino* decision, the Court said that it did not think the doctrine was "compelled either by the inherent nature of sovereign authority ... or by some principle of international law."[60] Instead, the Court said it was based on "constitutional underpinnings" relating to the separation of powers between the three branches of the federal government.[61] In particular, the doctrine "expresses the strong sense of the Judicial Branch that its engagement in the task of passing on the validity of foreign acts of state may hinder, rather than further, this country's pursuit of goals both for itself and for the community of nations as a whole in the international sphere."[62]

---

[58] *See* RESTATEMENT (FOURTH) OF THE FOREIGN RELATIONS LAW OF THE UNITED STATES § 481 (2018). When U.S. courts decline to enforce foreign judgments because of public policy, it is often because of free speech concerns. *See, e.g.,* Louis Feraud Int'l S.A.R.L. v. Viewfinder Inc., 406 F. Supp. 2d 274 (S.D.N.Y. 2005); Matusevitch v. Telnikoff, 877 F. Supp. 1 (D.D.C. 1995). *Cf.* Yahoo! Inc. v. La Ligue Contre Le Racisme, 433 F.3d 1199 (9th Cir. 2006). In 2010, Congress enacted the Securing the Protection of our Enduring and Established Constitutional Heritage Act (the "SPEECH Act"), 28 U.S.C. § 4102, which limits the extent to which U.S. courts can enforce foreign judgments for defamation.

[59] *See* Oetjen v. Central Leather Co., 246 U.S. 297, 303–304 (1918) (noting that the act of state doctrine "rests at last upon the highest considerations of international comity and expediency"); Underhill v. Hernandez, 168 U.S. 250, 252 (1897) ("Every sovereign State is bound to respect the independence of every other sovereign State, and the courts of one country will not sit in judgment on the acts of the government of another done within its own territory.").

[60] Banco Nacional de Cuba v. Sabbatino, 376 U.S. 398, 421 (1964). The Court noted that "[m]ost of the countries rendering decisions on the subject fail to follow the [act of state doctrine] rigidly," and that whereas "[i]n English jurisprudence ... the act of state doctrine is articulated in terms not unlike those of the United States cases, ... [c]ivil law countries ... which apply the rule make exceptions for acts contrary to their sense of public order." *Id.* at 421 & n. 21.

[61] *Sabbatino*, 376 U.S. at 423.

[62] *Id.*

The *Sabbatino* case involved Cuba's expropriation, in 1960, of an American-owned sugar production company operating in Cuba. In adjudicating a dispute concerning the proceeds from a sale of the company's sugar, the Supreme Court applied the act of state doctrine and thereby presumed the validity of Cuba's title to the sugar. Even though the expropriation appeared to violate norms of customary international law concerning state responsibility to aliens, the Court held that "the act of state doctrine is applicable even if international law has been violated."[63] This is especially true for the international law governing expropriation, the Court explained, because "[t]here are few if any issues in international law today on which opinion seems to be so divided as the limitations on a state's power to expropriate the property of aliens."[64] The Court was unpersuaded by the argument that it should contribute to the development of the international law of expropriation by allowing such challenges, noting that the effectiveness of such a "patchwork approach" to the issue was "highly conjectural" and that it was unlikely that "decisions of the courts of the world's major capital exporting country and principal exponent of the free enterprise system would be accepted as disinterested expressions of sound legal principle by those adhering to widely different ideologies."[65]

The Court in *Sabbatino* did not, however, completely rule out the possibility that U.S. courts could adjudicate foreign state violations of international law. It noted that the act of state doctrine should be applied "in the absence of a treaty or other unambiguous agreement regarding controlling legal principles."[66] The Court also left room for the possibility that courts could adjudicate customary international law challenges where the "consensus as to standards is greater and which do not represent a battleground for conflicting ideologies."[67] Consistent with these statements, some lower courts have declined to apply the doctrine to treaty claims.[68] Some courts have also declined to apply the doctrine to customary international law claims relating to egregious human rights abuses, reasoning that the degree of international consensus with respect to the human rights norm is sufficiently great that *Sabbatino*'s holding does not apply.[69]

There are three requirements that must be met in order for the act of state doctrine to be triggered. First, the claim must necessarily turn on the validity of a foreign government act.[70] Second, the Supreme Court has indicated that only government acts that are

---

[63] *Id.* at 431.
[64] *Id.* at 428.
[65] 376 U.S. at 434–35. For lower court decisions applying the doctrine, see, for example, Mt. Crest SRL, LLC v. Anheuser-Busch InBev SA/NV, 937 F.3d 1067 (7th Cir. 2019); Sea Breeze Salt, Inc. v. Mitsubishi Corp., 899 F.3d 1064 (9th Cir. 2018); Von Saher v. Norton Simon Museum of Art, 897 F.3d 1141 (9th Cir. 2018); Fed. Treasury Enter. Sojuzplodoimport v. Spirits Int'l B.V., 809 F.3d 737 (2d Cir. 2016).
[66] 376 U.S. at 428.
[67] *Id.* at 430 n. 34.
[68] *See, e.g.*, Kalamazoo Spice Extraction Co. v. Provisional Military Gov't of Socialist Ethiopia, 729 F.2d 422 (6th Cir. 1984).
[69] *See, e.g.*, Filartiga v. Pena-Irala, 577 F. Supp. 860, 862 (E.D.N.Y. 1984).
[70] *See* W.S. Kirkpatrick & Co. v. Envt'l Tectonics Corp., 493 U.S. 400 (1990).

official and have a degree of formality qualify for the act of state doctrine.[71] Finally, for the doctrine to apply, the foreign government act must take place within that government's territory, a requirement that can raise complicated issues in cases involving intangible interests, such as intellectual property rights or debt obligations.[72] Courts are to apply the act of state doctrine only if each of these three requirements is met, regardless of the level of embarrassment that a particular suit might pose for a foreign government.[73] There have been calls at times for other limitations on the doctrine, such as an exception for counterclaims or claims based on commercial activity,[74] or for cases in which the executive branch expresses the view that adjudication of the case would not harm U.S. foreign relations.[75] To date, however, a majority of the Supreme Court has not endorsed any of these proposed limitations. Even when the doctrine is technically applicable, however, lower courts have assumed that they have some discretion not to apply it if they conclude that its policies are not implicated in a particular case—that is, when a case is not likely to generate foreign relations friction or interfere with the executive branch's conduct of foreign affairs.[76]

As for the status of the doctrine in the U.S. legal system, the Supreme Court went out of its way in *Sabbatino* to make clear that the doctrine is a rule of federal common law that is binding on state courts. "[W]e are constrained to make it clear," the Court stated, "that an issue concerned with a basic choice regarding the competence and function of the Judiciary and the National Executive in ordering our relationships with other members of the international community must be treated exclusively as an aspect of federal law."[77] The Court reasoned that the Court in *Erie Railroad v. Tompkins*, in relegating much of what had been treated as general common law to the status of state law, did not have in mind legal rules involving foreign affairs, such as the act of state doctrine. The Court also cited to a short essay by Professor Philip Jessup (who later served as a judge on the International Court of Justice) in which Jessup expressed the view that rules of

---

[71] *See* Alfred Dunhill of London, Inc. v. Republic of Cuba, 425 U.S. 682, 695 (1976) (declining to apply act of state doctrine where "[n]o statute, decree, order, or resolution of the Cuban Government itself was offered in evidence indicating that Cuba had repudiated its obligations in general or any class thereof or that it had as a sovereign matter determined to confiscate the amounts due three foreign importers"); *see also, e.g.*, Kashef v. BNP Paribas S.A., 925 F.3d 53, 61 (2d Cir. 2019) (rejecting application of act of state doctrine, in part because the defendants "point to no statute, decree, order, resolution, or comparable evidence of sovereign authorization for any of the actions in question").

[72] *See, e.g.*, Allied Bank Int'l v. Banco Credito Agricola de Cartago, 757 F.2d 516, 521 (2d Cir. 1985). The Supreme Court has also indicated that, in order for the doctrine to apply, the government in question must be "extant and recognized by this country at the time of suit." *Sabbatino*, 376 U.S. at 428.

[73] *See Kirkpatrick*, 493 U.S. at 409.

[74] *See* First Nat'l City Bank v. Banco Nacional de Cuba, 406 U.S. 759, 772 (1972) (Douglas, J., concurring) (counterclaim); *Dunhill*, 425 U.S. at 695–96 (plurality opinion) (commercial activity). In *Sabbatino*, the Supreme Court specifically held that the act of state doctrine applied even to counterclaims. *See* 376 U.S. at 437–38.

[75] *First Nat'l City Bank*, 406 U.S. at 768 (plurality opinion).

[76] *See, e.g.*, Grupo Protexa, S.A. v. All American Marine Slip, 20 F.3d 1224, 1236–37 (3d Cir. 1994).

[77] *Sabbatino*, 376 U.S. at 425.

international law should not be left to divergent state interpretations, a rationale that the Court said "is equally applicable to the act of state doctrine."[78]

Because it is a common law doctrine that is not required by the Constitution (albeit one with constitutional underpinnings), the act of state doctrine is probably subject to being overridden by Congress. Congress has in fact purported to override the doctrine in several select instances. It did so, for example, in the Second Hickenlooper Amendment, a statute enacted in 1964 and applied to alter the outcome of the *Sabbatino* case on remand.[79] When Congress has purported to override the doctrine, however, it has generally included a provision allowing the president to reimpose the doctrine in particular cases or otherwise block the litigation.[80]

Forum Non Conveniens and Comity-Based Abstention

Under the *forum non conveniens* doctrine, federal district courts have the discretion to dismiss a case if they determine that an alternate foreign forum has jurisdiction to hear the case and that adjudicating the case in the United States "would 'establish ... oppressiveness and vexation to a defendant ... out of all proportion to plaintiff's convenience,'" or would be "'inappropriate because of considerations affecting the court's own

---

[78] *Id.*; *see also* Philip C. Jessup, *The Doctrine of* Erie Railroad v. Tompkins *Applied to International Law*, 33 Am. J. Int'l L. 740 (1939).

[79] *See* Hickenlooper Amendment to the Foreign Assistance Act, 78 Stat. 1030 (1964), *codified as amended at* 22 U.S.C. § 2370(e)(2); Banco Nacional de Cuba v. Farr, 383 F.2d 166 (2d Cir. 1967). The Second Hickenlooper Amendment provides in relevant part:

> No court in the United States shall decline on the ground of the federal act of state doctrine to make a determination on the merits giving effect to the principles of international law in a case in which a claim of title or other right to property is asserted by any party including a foreign state (or a party claiming through such state) based upon (or traced through) a confiscation or other taking ... by an act of that state in violation of the principles of international law, including the principles of compensation.

> Although it is not an obvious requirement from the plain language of this provision, some courts have interpreted it as applying only when the property in dispute (or its proceeds) is physically present in the United States at the time of the litigation.

See, e.g., Compania de Gas de Nuevo Laredo, S.A. v. Entex, Inc., 686 F.2d 322, 327 (5th Cir. 1982).

[80] The Second Hickenlooper Amendment provides, for example, that its override of the act of state doctrine does not apply "in any case with respect to which the President determines that application of the act of state doctrine is required in that particular case by the foreign policy interests of the United States and a suggestion to this effect is filed on his behalf in that case with the court." 22 U.S.C. § 2370(e)(2); *see also, e.g.*, 22 U.S.C. § 6085(b) (allowing president to suspend operation of Helms-Burton Act provision concerning liability for trafficking in expropriated property, a provision that contains an override of the act of state doctrine). *But cf.* 9 U.S.C. § 15 ("Enforcement of arbitral agreements, confirmation of arbitral awards, and execution upon judgments based on orders confirming such awards shall not be refused on the basis of the Act of State doctrine.").

administrative and legal problems.'"[81] In making this determination, courts consider a variety of private and public interest factors. The private interest factors include the following:

> the "relative ease of access to sources of proof; availability of compulsory process for attendance of unwilling, and the cost of obtaining attendance of willing, witnesses; possibility of view of premises, if view would be appropriate to the action; and all other practical problems that make trial of a case easy, expeditious and inexpensive."[82]

The public interest factors include these considerations:

> the administrative difficulties flowing from court congestion; the "local interest in having localized controversies decided at home"; the interest in having the trial of a diversity case in a forum that is at home with the law that must govern the action; the avoidance of unnecessary problems in conflict of laws, or in the application of foreign law; and the unfairness of burdening citizens in an unrelated forum with jury duty.[83]

In weighing the various factors, courts apply a presumption in favor of the plaintiff's choice of forum, although less of a presumption is given when the plaintiff is a foreign citizen.[84] A district court is allowed to dismiss a case under the *forum non conveniens* doctrine even if it has not resolved whether it has subject matter jurisdiction over the case or personal jurisdiction over the defendant.[85]

A somewhat separate and still-evolving doctrine is one of judicial abstention based on considerations of international comity. International comity, broadly speaking, is "the recognition which one nation allows within its territory to the legislative, executive or judicial acts of another nation, having due regard both to international duty and

---

[81] American Dredging Co. v. Miller, 510 U.S. 443, 447–48 (1994) (quoting Piper Aircraft Co. v. Reyno, 454 U.S. 235, 241 (1981) (quoting Koster v. (American) Lumbermens Mut. Casualty Co., 330 U.S. 518, 524 (1947))). For a critique of the doctrine, *see* Maggie Gardner, *Retiring Forum Non Conveniens*, 92 N.Y.U. L. REV. 390 (2017).
[82] *Piper Aircraft*, 454 U.S. at 241 n.6 (quoting Gulf Oil Corp. v. Gilbert, 330 U.S. 501, 508 (1947)).
[83] *Id.* (quoting *Gulf Oil*, 330 U.S. at 509).
[84] *See id.* at 256. *See also* Sinochem Int'l Co. v. Malay. Int'l Shipping Corp., 549 U.S. 422, 430 (2007) ("A defendant invoking *forum non conveniens* ordinarily bears a heavy burden in opposing the plaintiff's chosen forum.").
[85] *See Sinochem*, 549 U.S. at 436. "If, however, a court can readily determine that it lacks jurisdiction over the cause or the defendant, the proper course would be to dismiss on that ground." *Id.* A federal district court must first determine that it has subject matter and personal jurisdiction before resolving the merits of a case. *See* Steel Co. v. Citizens for a Better Env't, 523 U.S. 83, 93–102 (1998). In some circumstances, a court may dismiss a case for lack of personal jurisdiction without first establishing subject matter jurisdiction. *See* Ruhrgas AG v. Marathon Oil Co., 526 U.S. 574, 584–85 (1999).

convenience."[86] As noted, U.S. courts often enforce foreign judgments based on considerations of international comity. These considerations may also lead a U.S. court to stay or dismiss litigation in the United States when similar or related litigation is pending in another country. Courts disagree about the precise standards for this international abstention, with some courts holding that it is appropriate only in exceptional circumstances and other courts holding that there is broad discretion to avoid such duplicative litigation.[87] Sometimes courts will dismiss a case under the international abstention doctrine even when there is no pending foreign litigation, "based on the interests of [the U.S.] government, the foreign government and the international community in resolving the dispute in a foreign forum."[88]

Charming Betsy Canon

United States courts have long followed a canon of statutory construction that is named after an 1804 Supreme Court decision, *Murray v. The Schooner Charming Betsy*.[89] The *Charming Betsy* case concerned events surrounding the undeclared war between the United States and France at the end of the eighteenth century. During that war, the United States passed a statute prohibiting trade "between any person or persons resident within the United States or under their protection, and any person or persons resident within the territories of the French Republic, or any of the dependencies thereof."[90] A U.S. navy frigate subsequently seized the schooner *Charming Betsy* on the high seas, suspecting her of engaging in trade with Guadeloupe, a French dependency, in violation of the statute. The owner of the vessel—who had been born in the United States but had moved as a child to St. Thomas, a Danish island, and had become a Danish citizen—argued that

---

[86] Hilton v. Guyot, 159 U.S. 113, 163–64 (1895). *See also* Societe Nationale Industrielle Aerospatiale v. U.S. District Court, 482 U.S. 522, 544 n. 27 (1987) ("Comity refers to the spirit of cooperation in which a domestic tribunal approaches the resolution of cases touching the laws and interests of other sovereign states."). For a comprehensive account of the various doctrines in U.S. law that incorporate considerations of international comity, see William S. Dodge, *International Comity in American Law*, 115 COLUM. L. REV. 2071 (2015).

[87] *See* Turner Ent'mt Co. v. Degeto Film GmbH, 25 F.3d 1512, 1518 (11th Cir. 1994) (describing different approaches).

[88] Ungaro-Benages v. Dresdner Bank AG, 379 F.3d 1227, 1238 (11th Cir. 2004); *see also* Bi v. Union Carbide Chems. & Plastics Co., 984 F.2d 582 (2d Cir. 1993) (deferring to India's statutory resolution of claims concerning toxic tort disaster in India). The degree of comity that U.S. courts should give to the decisions of international tribunals is discussed in Chapter 4.

[89] 6 U.S. (2 Cranch) 64 (1804). For discussion of the *Charming Betsy* canon, *see* Curtis A. Bradley, *The* Charming Betsy *Canon and Separation of Powers: Rethinking the Interpretive Role of International Law*, 86 GEO. L.J. 479 (1998); Ralph G. Steinhardt, *The Role of International Law as a Canon of Domestic Statutory Construction*, 43 VAND. L. REV. 1103 (1990); and Jonathan Turley, *Dualistic Values in an Age of International Legisprudence*, 44 HASTINGS L.J. 185 (1993). *See also* Note, *The* Charming Betsy *Canon, Separation of Powers, and Customary International Law*, 121 HARV. L. REV. 1215 (2008).

[90] *Charming Betsy*, 6 U.S. at 118.

applying the trade restriction statute to him would violate the "rights of neutrality" under customary international law.

The Court, in an opinion by Chief Justice Marshall, recited among the "principles... believed to be correct" and which "ought to be kept in view in construing the act now under consideration," the following proposition: "an act of Congress ought never to be construed to violate the law of nations if any other possible construction remains."[91] The Court then concluded that, at the time of the seizure, the owner of the vessel was neither a resident of the United States nor "under [its] protection," and thus was not within the reach of the trade statute.[92] It is not entirely clear from the opinion how international law actually influenced the Court's conclusion, particularly given that the Court reserved judgment on whether the United States had the *power* under international law to apply the trade restriction statute to the vessel's owner. Nevertheless, the *Charming Betsy* decision is often cited for the proposition that federal statutes are to be construed, where possible, so that they do not violate international law.[93]

The precise strength of the canon today is somewhat uncertain. Most courts recite the language from *Charming Betsy*: "an act of Congress ought never to be construed to violate the law of nations if any other possible construction remains." At least some courts, however, appear to interpret "possible" to mean something equivalent to "reasonable."[94] In addition, the black-letter-law formulations of the canon in the American Law Institute's *Restatements of Foreign Relations* do not precisely track the *Charming Betsy* language. In the *Restatement (Second)*, published in 1965, the canon was described as follows: "If a domestic law of the United States may be interpreted either in a manner consistent with international law or in a manner that is in conflict with international law, a court in the United States will interpret it in a manner that is consistent with international law."[95] In the *Restatement (Third)*, published in 1987, the phrasing was altered to read: "Where fairly possible, a United States statute is to be construed so as not to conflict with international law or with an international agreement of the United States."[96] The *Restatement (Fourth)* similarly uses the "fairly possible" formulation.[97] At least when

---

[91] *Id.*

[92] *Id.* at 120.

[93] Chief Justice Marshall had earlier stated in *Talbot v. Seeman*, 5 U.S. (1 Cranch) 1, 43 (1801), that "the laws of the United States ought not, if it be avoidable, so to be construed as to infract the common principles and usages of nations, or the general doctrines of national law." In the nineteenth and early twentieth centuries, courts often invoked the rule of construction associated with the *Charming Betsy* canon without citing to the decision. *See* Thomas H. Lee & David L. Sloss, *International Law as an Interpretive Tool in the Supreme Court, 1861–1900*, in INTERNATIONAL LAW IN THE U.S. SUPREME COURT: CONTINUITY AND CHANGE 124, 133 n.85 (David L. Sloss, Michael D. Ramsey & William S. Dodge eds., 2011).

[94] *See, e.g.*, United States v. Yunis, 924 F.2d 1086, 1091 (D.C. Cir. 1991); United States v. Georgescu, 723 F. Supp. 912, 921 (E.D.N.Y. 1989); Am. Baptist Churches v. Meese, 712 F. Supp. 756, 771 (N.D. Cal. 1989).

[95] RESTATEMENT (SECOND) OF THE FOREIGN RELATIONS LAW OF THE UNITED STATES § 3(3) (1965).

[96] RESTATEMENT (THIRD) OF THE FOREIGN RELATIONS LAW OF THE UNITED STATES, *supra* note 43, § 114.

[97] *See* RESTATEMENT (FOURTH) OF THE FOREIGN RELATIONS LAW OF THE UNITED STATES, *supra* note 58, § 309(1) and reporters' note 1; *id.* § 406.

applied to potential violations of customary international law, the canon applies only when a statutory provision is ambiguous.[98] For potential violations of treaties, some lower courts have suggested that Congress must evidence a clear intent to abrogate the treaty in order to overcome the canon.[99]

Sometimes the issue is not whether a statute violates international law, but rather whether the statute extends as far as international law would allow. This issue has come up in connection with suits brought under the Foreign Sovereign Immunities Act (FSIA). As discussed in Chapter 8, the FSIA provides that foreign states are immune from suit in U.S. courts unless the suit falls within one of the Act's specified exceptions to immunity. Some litigants and scholars have argued that the FSIA's exception for situations in which a foreign state has "waived its immunity . . . by implication" should be construed to include situations in which a foreign state has acted contrary to fundamental jus cogens norms of international law. Supporters of this construction sometimes invoke the *Charming Betsy* canon, reasoning that foreign states are not entitled under international law to immunity from suit for violations of jus cogens norms, and that, pursuant to the *Charming Betsy* canon, the FSIA should be construed similarly to deny immunity in this situation. Courts have consistently rejected this construction of the FSIA, reasoning that a jus cogens exception to immunity in U.S. litigation would require more explicit statutory text.[100] (As discussed in Chapter 8, the International Court of Justice has since held that there is no jus cogens exception to sovereign immunity under international law.)

There is some question about whether and to what extent the *Charming Betsy* canon should apply when the statutory interpretation in question is being advocated by the executive branch. The canon is designed, at least in part, to ensure that the United States does not breach international law without the political branches having expressly made the decision to do so. As I have explained elsewhere, the canon "is a means by which the courts can seek guidance from the political branches concerning whether and, if so, how they intend to violate the international legal obligations of the United States."[101] When the executive branch is advocating a particular interpretation of the statute, however, at least one political branch has presumably factored in the issue of international law

---

[98] *See, e.g.*, Serra v. Lappin, 600 F.3d 1191, 1198 (9th Cir. 2010); United States v. Yousef, 327 F.3d 56, 92 (2d Cir. 2003).

[99] *See, e.g.*, Owner-Operator Independent Drivers Ass'n v. U.S. Dep't of Transportation, 724 F.3d 230 (D.C. Cir. 2013). *But see* Fund for Animals, Inc. v. Kempthorne, 472 F.3d 872, 878 (D.C. Cir. 2006) ("The canon applies only to ambiguous statutes. . . .").

[100] *See, e.g.*, Sampson v. Fed. Republic of Germany, 250 F.3d 1145 (7th Cir. 2001); Smith v. Socialist People's Libyan Arab Jamahiriya, 101 F.3d 239, 244–45 (2d Cir. 1996); Princz v. Fed. Republic of Germany, 26 F.3d 1166 (D.C. Cir. 1994); Siderman de Blake v. Republic of Argentina, 965 F.2d 699, 718–19 (9th Cir. 1992). For a more expansive view of the role of the *Charming Betsy* canon, in the context of federal immigration law, *see* Beharry v. Reno, 183 F. Supp. 2d 584, 591 (S.D.N.Y. 2002) (relying on *Charming Betsy* for the proposition that "[i]mmigration statutes must be woven into the seamless web of our national and international law"), *rev'd on other grounds*, 329 F.3d 51 (2d Cir. 2003).

[101] Bradley, *supra* note 89, at 525.

compliance. Because of this, some courts have suggested that there is less basis for applying the *Charming Betsy* canon in this context.[102]

The *Charming Betsy* canon by its terms applies only to the interpretation of federal law. Although a federal court interpreting an ambiguous state law might reasonably conclude that the state would want its law to be interpreted in a manner that avoided a violation of international law, there is no categorical presumption to this effect for state law comparable to the *Charming Betsy* canon for federal law.[103] If a state law conflicts with a valid self-executing treaty, it will be subject to preemption, as discussed in Chapter 2. But the rules for interpreting state law are ultimately determined by the states, and thus there is no requirement that states adopt the federal *Charming Betsy* canon.[104]

Deference to the Executive Branch in Foreign Relations Cases

United States courts often give some level of deference to the executive branch when deciding cases that concern foreign relations. For certain issues, such as which foreign governments should be recognized by the United States, the courts treat the executive's position as dispositive. As discussed further in Chapter 8, prior to the enactment of the Foreign Sovereign Immunities Act in 1976, the executive branch would make suggestions to courts regarding whether they should grant immunity to foreign states, and these suggestions were treated by courts as binding. The executive branch continues to make

---

[102] *See* ARC Ecology v. U.S. Dep't of the Air Force, 411 F.3d 1092, 1102 (9th Cir. 2005); United States v. Corey, 232 F.3d 1166, 1179 (9th Cir. 2000). *See also Authority of the Federal Bureau of Investigation to Override International Law in Extraterritorial Law Enforcement Activities*, 13 OP. OFF. LEGAL COUNSEL 163, 171 (1989) (concluding that the *Charming Betsy* canon is not applicable to "broad authorizing statutes 'carrying into execution'" core executive powers); Eric A. Posner & Cass R. Sunstein, *Chevronizing Foreign Relations Law*, 116 YALE L.J. 1170, 1172 (2007) ("[I]f the executive wants to interpret ambiguous statutes to conflict with international law . . . it should be permitted to do so."). In the United Kingdom, the equivalent canon of construction is not applied to "statutory conferrals of executive power." Shaheed Fatima Q.C., *The Domestic Application of International Law in British Courts*, in THE OXFORD HANDBOOK OF COMPARATIVE FOREIGN RELATIONS LAW 496 (Curtis A. Bradley ed., 2019). For discussion of whether the *Charming Betsy* canon applies to the authorization of force that Congress enacted in the wake of the September 11, 2001, terrorist attacks, see Chapter 10.

[103] *See* Bradley, *supra* note 89, at 533–36. *Cf.* Daniel J. Meltzer, *Customary International Law, Foreign Affairs, and Federal Common Law*, 42 VA. J. INT'L L. 513, 535 (2002) ("[W]hether a state statute should be interpreted in this fashion is ultimately a question of state law (whether of state choice of law rules, state statutory rules, or state incorporation of CIL)."); Ernest A. Young, *Sorting Out the Debate over Customary International Law*, 42 VA. J. INT'L L. 365, 478 (2002) ("There is no obvious reason to think that state legislators are less respectful of the United States' international obligations than federal legislators, and therefore no reason to find *Charming Betsy* a less reliable guide to legislative intent in one context than the other.").

[104] *See* RESTATEMENT (FOURTH) OF THE FOREIGN RELATIONS LAW OF THE UNITED STATES, *supra* note 58, § 407 reporters' note 4 ("Although a number of States have adopted their own presumptions against extraterritoriality, . . . only a few appear to have expressly adopted a counterpart to the *Charming Betsy* canon."). Some state courts have voluntarily looked to international human rights law when interpreting state constitutions. *See, e.g.*, Johanna Kalb, *Human Rights Treaties in State Courts: The International Prospects of State Constitutionalism after Medellin*, 115 PENN. ST. L. REV. 1051, 1059 (2011).

suggestions of immunity even today with respect to whether certain foreign officials (such as heads of state) should receive immunity, and some courts have treated these suggestions as similarly dispositive.[105]

As will be discussed in Chapter 2, courts often give substantial weight to the executive branch's interpretation of treaties, although they do not treat the interpretation as binding. This deference is somewhat analogous to the deference that courts give to U.S. administrative agencies when the agencies are interpreting the statutes that they are charged with administering, which is referred to as *Chevron* deference.[106] Under the *Chevron* doctrine, courts first examine whether Congress has clearly spoken to the issue before the court. If so, courts will simply apply the statute and not defer to the agency's interpretation. If the statute is ambiguous or does not address the issue, however, courts will defer to the agency's interpretation unless it is unreasonable.[107] This strong deference is limited, however, to situations in which the circumstances suggest that Congress "expect[ed] the agency to be able to speak with the force of law when it addresses ambiguity in the statute or fills a space in the enacted law," which usually is the case only when Congress "provides for a relatively formal administrative procedure tending to foster the fairness and deliberation that should underlie a pronouncement of such force."[108] Even when an agency interpretation is not entitled to *Chevron* deference, it may be entitled to a lesser form of deference known as *Skidmore* deference. Under *Skidmore* deference, the weight to be given to the executive branch's interpretation "will depend upon the thoroughness evident in its consideration, the validity of its reasoning, its consistency with earlier and later pronouncements, and all those factors which give it power to persuade, if lacking power to control."[109]

Courts are also likely to give significant deference to the executive branch when it is exercising discretionary authority delegated to it from Congress in the area of foreign affairs. For example, in a 2018 decision, *Trump v. Hawaii*, the Supreme Court upheld a presidential proclamation that restricted entry into the United States of nationals from eight countries, despite indications that the proclamation might have stemmed from

---

[105] *See, e.g.,* Manoharan v. Rajapaksa, 711 F.3d 178, 179 (D.C. Cir. 2013); Habyarimana v. Kagame, 696 F.3d 1029 (10th Cir. 2012); Ye v. Zemin, 383 F.3d 620 (7th Cir. 2004). *But cf.* Yousuf v. Samantar, 699 F.3d 763, 773 (4th Cir. 2012) ("[W]e give absolute deference to the State Department's position on status-based immunity doctrines such as head-of-state immunity. The State Department's determination regarding conduct-based immunity, by contrast, is not controlling, but it carries substantial weight in our analysis of the issue.").

[106] For discussions of the relationship between the *Chevron* doctrine and judicial deference in the area of foreign affairs, *see* Curtis A. Bradley, Chevron *Deference and Foreign Affairs*, 86 Va. L. Rev. 649 (2000), and Posner & Sunstein, *supra* note 102. *See also* United States v. Lindh, 212 F. Supp. 2d 541, 556 (E.D. Va. 2002) ("By analogy, treaty interpretation and application warrants similar *Chevron* deference to the President's interpretation of a treaty, as American treaty-makers may be seen as having delegated this function to the President in light of his constitutional responsibility for the conduct of foreign affairs and overseas military operations.").

[107] Chevron, U.S.A., Inc. v. NRDC, Inc., 467 U.S. 837, 842–44 (1984).

[108] United States v. Mead Corp., 533 U.S. 218, 229, 230 (2001).

[109] Skidmore v. Swift & Co., 323 U.S. 134, 140 (1944).

anti-Muslim bias.[110] The president had acted under a statute that allows for the suspension of entry of aliens whenever the president "finds that the entry of any aliens or of any class of aliens into the United States would be detrimental to the interests of the United States," and the Court concluded that the president had made sufficient findings to satisfy the statute. The Court declined to conduct a searching review of the persuasiveness of these findings, explaining that such a review would be "inconsistent with the broad statutory text and the deference traditionally accorded the President in this sphere."[111]

The executive branch sometimes submits "statements of interest" expressing concerns about the foreign relations implications of particular cases. There is no settled rule concerning how much deference to give to such statements, and it presumably will vary depending on the nature of the case and legal questions involved. Such statements, however, may make it more likely that a court will find that a case presents a nonjusticiable political question or that the act of state doctrine should be applied.[112]

On some legal issues, courts give no particular deference to the executive branch, even if the issues relate to foreign affairs. In particular, courts are unlikely to defer to the executive branch when interpreting the Constitution, or when construing jurisdictional statutes that are designed to be administered by the judiciary rather than the executive.[113] They may also decline to defer to the executive branch in defining the legal contours of common law doctrines, although they may defer when making factual assessments called for by the doctrines.[114] Among other things, courts perceive that the usual arguments for deference, such as executive branch expertise, are less applicable in those contexts.

* * *

To further understand the role of the courts in foreign affairs, it is useful to have some sense of the powers of other U.S. government institutions. This chapter therefore concludes by briefly describing the powers of Congress, the president, and the state governments.

Constitutional Powers of Congress and the President

The Constitution gives Congress the authority to legislate on a wide array of subjects. Among other things, it can regulate commerce among the several states and with foreign

---

[110] 138 S. Ct. 2392 (2018).
[111] *Id.* at 2409.
[112] *See, e.g.*, Whiteman v. Dorotheum GmbH & Co. KG, 431 F.3d 57, 73–74 (2d Cir. 2006); Joo v. Japan, 413 F.3d 45, 49 (D.C. Cir. 2005).
[113] *See, e.g.*, Republic of Austria v. Altmann, 541 U.S. 677, 701 (2004) (declining to defer to the executive branch with respect to whether the Foreign Sovereign Immunities Act applied retroactively because, "[w]hile the United States' views on such an issue are of considerable interest to the Court, they merit no special deference").
[114] *See, e.g.*, W.S. Kirkpatrick & Co. v. Envtl. Tectonics Corp., 493 U.S. 400, 409 (1990) (declining to defer to executive branch with respect to standards for applying the act of state doctrine).

nations, dispose of and regulate U.S. property, impose taxes, appropriate money for national expenditures, declare war, regulate the armed forces, and define and punish offenses against the law of nations.[115] In addition, Congress has the authority to enact laws "necessary and proper" to carry into execution both its own powers and those of the other federal branches of government, an authority that has been read expansively by the Supreme Court.[116] The Supreme Court has implied some additional congressional powers, such as the power to regulate immigration, from what it perceives to be the attributes of national sovereignty.[117]

Congress's power to regulate commerce has been construed by the Supreme Court to be a particularly broad source of authority. The Court has held that Congress can use its domestic commerce power to regulate the following: the channels of interstate commerce; the instrumentalities of interstate commerce, or persons or things in interstate commerce; and activities that have a substantial effect on interstate commerce.[118] With respect to the last category, Congress can regulate even noncommercial local activities if it "concludes that failure to regulate that class of activity would undercut the regulation of the interstate market in that commodity."[119] If anything, Congress's power to regulate foreign commerce is generally assumed to be even broader than its power to regulate domestic commerce, since the regulation of foreign commerce does not implicate

---

[115] *See* U.S. CONST. art. I, § 8.

[116] *See* United States v. Comstock, 560 U.S. 126, 134 (2010) ("[I]n determining whether the Necessary and Proper Clause grants Congress the legislative authority to enact a particular federal statute, we look to see whether the statute constitutes a means that is rationally related to the implementation of a constitutionally enumerated power."); McCulloch v. Maryland, 17 U.S. (4 Wheat.) 316, 421 (1819) ("Let the end be legitimate, let it be within the scope of the constitution, and all means which are appropriate, which are plainly adapted to that end, which are not prohibited, but consist with the letter and spirit of the constitution, are constitutional.").

[117] *See* Fong Yue Ting v. United States, 149 U.S. 698, 711 (1893); The Chinese Exclusion Case (Chae Chan Ping v. United States), 130 U.S. 581, 603–06 (1889). Although the Constitution expressly gives Congress the power to establish a uniform rule of naturalization, that power does not by itself encompass the authority to exclude or deport aliens. *See also* Arizona v. United States, 567 U.S. 387, 394–95 (2012) (noting that the power to regulate immigration rests not only on Congress's authority to establish a uniform rule of naturalization but also on the national government's "inherent power as sovereign to control and conduct relations with foreign nations").

[118] *See* United States v. Lopez, 514 U.S. 549, 558 (1995); Perez v. United States, 402 U.S. 146, 150 (1971).

[119] Gonzales v. Raich, 545 U.S. 1, 18 (2005); *see also* Wickard v. Filburn, 317 U.S. 111, 128–29 (1942) (holding that Congress had the authority under the Commerce Clause to impose quotas on the local production of wheat, even for production intended for personal consumption, because "Congress may properly have considered that wheat consumed on the farm where grown, if wholly outside the scheme of regulation, would have a substantial effect in defeating and obstructing its purpose to stimulate trade therein at increased prices"). A majority of the Supreme Court has reasoned, however, that Congress's Commerce Clause authority allows it to regulate activity, not inactivity, and thus that Congress cannot use this authority to compel people to "*become* active in commerce by purchasing a product," such as, in that case, health care insurance. *See* National Federation of Independent Bus. v. Sebelius, 567 U.S. 519, 552 (2012) (opinion of Roberts, C.J.); *see also id.* at 658 (Scalia, J., dissenting) ("[I]t must be activity affecting commerce that is regulated, and not merely the failure to engage in commerce.").

the prerogatives of the U.S. states to the same degree as the regulation of domestic commerce.[120]

As compared with its treatment of Congress, the Constitution lists relatively few powers for the president. The president has the power to veto legislation. The president is also the Commander in Chief of the U.S. armed forces. In addition, the president can conclude treaties with other nations, provided that the advice and consent of two-thirds of the senators present is obtained. The president also appoints U.S. ambassadors with the advice and consent of a majority of the Senate, and the president is assigned the task of receiving ambassadors from other countries. Furthermore, the president has the power to pardon federal crimes, except in cases of impeachment. Significant additional presidential authority has developed over time. As discussed in Chapter 3, for example, presidents frequently enter into "executive agreements" with other nations without going through the two-thirds senatorial advice-and-consent process specified for treaties.

Courts have implied from the president's role in sending and receiving ambassadors, and in negotiating treaties, the power to decide whether the United States recognizes particular foreign governments.[121] This is an important power, both because it can significantly affect U.S. foreign relations and because nonrecognized governments are denied various benefits in the United States, including access to state assets held within the United States, the right to sue in U.S. courts, and the ability to invoke the act of state doctrine.[122] The Supreme Court has held that the recognition power is an exclusive power of the executive branch, which means that it cannot be limited by Congress.[123] The power to recognize may in turn imply other powers (which may or may not be exclusive), such as the power to conclude agreements to effectuate the recognition,[124] and the power

---

[120] *See* Japan Line, Ltd. v. Cnty. of Los Angeles, 441 U.S. 434, 448 (1979); Buttfield v. Stranahan, 192 U.S. 470, 492–93 (1904). The scope of Congress's ability to regulate conduct outside the United States based on its foreign commerce power is considered in Chapter 6.

[121] *See, e.g.*, Zivotofsky v. Kerry, 135 S. Ct. 2076, 2085 (2015) ("As a matter of constitutional structure, these additional powers give the President control over recognition decisions."); Banco Nacional de Cuba v. Sabbatino, 376 U.S. 398, 410 (1964) ("Political recognition is exclusively a function of the Executive."). For discussion of the original understanding of the president's authority to receive ambassadors, and an argument that this authority was expected to be a ministerial function rather than an authority to determine recognition of foreign governments, *see* David Gray Adler, *The President's Recognition Power: Ministerial or Discretionary?*, 25 PRES. STUD. Q. 267 (1995), and Robert J. Reinstein, *Recognition: A Case Study on the Original Understanding of Executive Power*, 45 RICHMOND L. REV. 801 (2011). For discussion of post-Founding historical practice relating to the recognition power, *see* Clarence A. Berdahl, *The Power of Recognition*, 14 AM. J. INT'L L. 519 (1920), and Robert J. Reinstein, *Is the President's Recognition Power Exclusive?*, 86 TEMPLE L. REV. 1 (2013).

[122] *See, e.g.*, Pfizer, Inc. v. Gov't of India, 434 U.S. 308, 319–20 (1978) ("It has long been established that only governments recognized by the United States and at peace with us are entitled to access to our courts, and that it is within the exclusive power of the Executive Branch to determine which nations are entitled to sue.").

[123] *See Zivotofsky*, 135 S. Ct. at 2094.

[124] *See* United States v. Pink, 315 U.S. 203, 229 (1942) ("Power to remove such obstacles to full recognition as settlement of claims of our nationals ... certainly is a modest implied power of the President who is the 'sole organ of the federal government in the field of international relations.'") (quoting United States v. Curtiss-Wright Export Corp., 299 U.S. 304, 320 (1936)).

to determine whether foreign government officials should receive immunity from suit in U.S. courts.[125]

The Constitution also states that the president shall "take Care that the Laws be faithfully executed."[126] Pursuant to this Take Care Clause, the president and the officers he or she appoints (along with the many employees who work for them) interpret and administer the laws enacted by Congress. In exercising this authority, presidents sometimes issue "executive orders" that set forth particular legal interpretations or directives.[127] Presidents have on occasion invoked the Take Care Clause as a source of authority to take actions beyond those specifically contemplated by Congress, but it is not clear to what extent the clause conveys such authority, and the Supreme Court has stated that the authority conferred by the Take Care Clause "allows the President to execute the laws, not make them."[128] Nor is it clear whether the word "Laws" in this clause extends beyond federal statutes to encompass international law, either treaty-based or customary (although it probably encompasses treaties, which the Constitution designates as part of the "supreme Law of the Land").[129]

In addition to listing specific powers of the president, the Constitution states that "[t]he executive Power shall be vested in a President of the United States of America," and some scholars have contended that this Vesting Clause is itself a source of presidential authority.[130] In particular, these scholars argue that all powers of the national government that are "executive" in nature (including, most notably, foreign affairs powers) implicitly rest with the president, unless those powers have been specifically assigned to another branch of the government.[131] Critics of this theory (including this author) have argued that there is little support for it in the debates over the Constitution in 1787–88, and that it would render superfluous at least some of the Constitution's specific grants of presidential authority.[132]

The Supreme Court has referred to the president as the "sole organ of the federal government in the field of international relations,"[133] and the executive branch often refers to

---

[125] The immunity of foreign government officials in U.S. courts is discussed in Chapter 8.
[126] U.S. CONST. art. II, § 3.
[127] *See* KENNETH R. MAYER, WITH THE STROKE OF A PEN: EXECUTIVE ORDERS AND PRESIDENTIAL POWER (2001); Elena Kagan, *Presidential Administration*, 114 HARV. L. REV. 2245 (2001).
[128] Medellin v. Texas, 552 U.S. 491, 532 (2008).
[129] This issue is considered in Chapters 2 and 5.
[130] *See* Saikrishna B. Prakash & Michael D. Ramsey, *The Executive Power over Foreign Affairs*, 111 YALE L.J. 231 (2001).
[131] *See id.* at 253–54.
[132] *See* Curtis A. Bradley & Martin S. Flaherty, *Executive Power Essentialism and Foreign Affairs*, 102 MICH. L. REV. 545 (2004); Julian Davis Mortenson, *Article II Vests the Executive Power, Not the Royal Prerogative*, 119 COLUM. L. REV. 1169 (2019).
[133] United States v. Curtiss-Wright Export Corp., 299 U.S. 304, 320 (1936). The Court in *Curtiss-Wright* also stated that the "investment of the federal Government with the powers of external sovereignty did not depend upon the affirmative grants of the Constitution," thus suggesting that constitutional restraints that apply to the government's exercise of domestic powers may not apply to its exercise of foreign affairs powers. The "external

this description as support for broad presidential authority in the area of foreign affairs. As discussed further in Chapter 9, the genesis of the "sole organ" language is a speech made by John Marshall in 1800 while he was a member of the House of Representatives, about a year before he became Chief Justice of the Supreme Court. President John Adams had ordered the extradition to Great Britain of an individual accused of murder while aboard a British ship. Although Adams acted pursuant to a treaty with Great Britain, he was criticized on the ground that the extradition request from Great Britain should have been processed by judicial action, not executive action. It was in this context that Marshall, defending Adams, proclaimed: "The president is the sole organ of the nation in its external relations, and its sole representative with foreign nations."[134] Marshall, in other words, was making a claim about the president's ability to execute international obligations and communicate with other countries, not about the scope of the president's independent foreign affairs powers. Moreover, while formal communications between the United States and other countries are managed by the executive branch, Congress and its members often engage in diplomatic activities.[135]

Relationship between Congress and the President

In considering the relationship between Congress and the president, a particularly important precedent is the Supreme Court's decision in *Youngstown Sheet & Tube Co. v. Sawyer*.[136] In that case, President Truman issued an executive order during the Korean War that asserted the authority to seize private steel mills in order to prevent a work stoppage that might have interfered with steel production needed for the war. The Supreme Court famously held that the president had exceeded his constitutional authority. The Court explained that, to be constitutional, the president's order had to "stem either from an act of Congress or from the Constitution itself,"[137] and the Court found that the order was not supported by either source of authority.

---

sovereignty" analysis in *Curtiss-Wright* has been heavily criticized, on historical and other grounds. *See, e.g.*, Michael J. Glennon, *Two Views of Presidential Foreign Affairs Power:* Little v. Barreme *or* Curtiss-Wright?, 13 YALE J. INT'L L. 5 (1988); David M. Levitan, *The Foreign Relations Power: An Analysis of Mr. Justice Sutherland's Theory*, 55 YALE L.J. 467 (1946); Charles A. Lofgren, United States v. Curtiss-Wright Export Corporation: *An Historical Reassessment*, 83 YALE L.J. 1 (1973); Michael D. Ramsey, *The Myth of Extraconstitutional Foreign Affairs Power*, 42 WM. & MARY L. REV. 379 (2000).

[134] John Marshall, *Address before the House of Representatives* (Mar. 7, 1800), *in* 10 ANNALS OF CONG. 596, 613 (Washington, Gales & Seaton eds., 1851). *See also* Michael P. Van Alstine, *Taking Care of John Marshall's Political Ghost*, 53 ST. LOUIS L.J. 93 (2008) (discussing historical context of Marshall's speech); Ruth Wedgwood, *The Revolutionary Martyrdom of Jonathan Robbins*, 100 YALE L.J. 229 (1990) (same).

[135] *See* Ryan M. Scoville, *Legislative Diplomacy*, 112 MICH. L. REV. 331 (2013); *see also* Kristen Eichensehr, *Courts, Congress, and the Conduct of Foreign Relations*, 85 U. CHI. L. REV. 609 (2018).

[136] Youngstown Sheet & Tube Co. v. Sawyer, 343 U.S. 579 (1952).

[137] *Id.* at 585.

Justice Jackson's concurring opinion in that case has proven to be particularly influential. In what he admitted was "a somewhat over-simplified grouping," Justice Jackson set forth the following three categories of presidential authority:

1. When the President acts pursuant to an express or implied authorization of Congress, his authority is at its maximum, for it includes all that he possesses in his own right plus all that Congress can delegate....
2. When the President acts in absence of either a congressional grant or denial of authority, he can only rely upon his own independent powers, but there is a zone of twilight in which he and Congress may have concurrent authority, or in which its distribution is uncertain....
3. When the President takes measures incompatible with the expressed or implied will of Congress, his power is at its lowest ebb, for then he can rely only upon his own constitutional powers minus any constitutional powers of Congress over the matter.[138]

Presidential power is defined under this framework not in the abstract, but rather in relationship to the intent and actions of Congress. A majority of the Supreme Court has invoked this framework in subsequent decisions.[139]

Justice Jackson's framework has the attraction of being flexible, and of avoiding abstract classifications such as "executive" and "legislative" that may be difficult to define in practice. There can be uncertainty, however, about how to classify presidential actions under Jackson's framework, especially when the classification turns on inferences about Congress's implied intent.[140] It appears that courts are more likely to find implied congressional support when the presidential action is consistent with past executive branch practice, and when the presidential action is related to what the court understands to be independent presidential authority.[141]

The Supreme Court has allowed Congress to delegate substantial regulatory authority to administrative agencies in the executive branch. These delegations of authority are in theory subject to a nondelegation doctrine, pursuant to which Congress must articulate an "intelligible principle" to guide the agencies.[142] In practice, however, the Supreme Court has upheld many broad delegations,[143] and it has applied the nondelegation

---

[138] *Id.* at 635–38 (Jackson, J., concurring).
[139] *See* Medellin v. Texas, 552 U.S. 491, 524–25 (2008); Hamdan v. Rumsfeld, 548 U.S. 557, 593 n.23 (2006); Dames & Moore v. Regan, 453 U.S. 654, 668–69 (1981).
[140] *See* HAROLD HONGJU KOH, THE NATIONAL SECURITY CONSTITUTION: SHARING POWER AFTER THE IRAN-CONTRA AFFAIR 140–42 (1990); Edward T. Swaine, *The Political Economy of* Youngstown, 83 S. CAL. L. REV. 263, 286–89 (2010).
[141] *See, e.g., Dames & Moore*, 453 U.S. at 678–79.
[142] *See, e.g.,* J.W. Hampton, Jr. & Co. v. United States, 276 U.S. 394, 409 (1928).
[143] *See, e.g.,* Gundy v. United States, 139 S. Ct. 2116 (2019); Whitman v. Am. Trucking Ass'ns, 531 U.S. 457 (2001).

doctrine to invalidate delegations in only two cases, both decided in 1935.[144] The Supreme Court has indicated that Congress has even greater latitude when delegating to the executive branch in the area of foreign affairs, in light of the president's independent constitutional authority as well as the particular need for flexibility in this area.[145] Nevertheless, the Court has insisted that changes to legislation, as opposed to regulatory implementation of legislation, must go through the legislative process. On that basis, the Court has invalidated a "one-House veto" provision that Congress included with a delegation of immigration authority to the Attorney General, and a "line-item veto" provision pursuant to which Congress purported to give the president the authority to cancel appropriations of money.[146]

In evaluating the respective constitutional authority of Congress and the president, the Supreme Court often places significant weight on historic governmental practice, especially if the practice is long-standing and has been relatively uncontested.[147] This reliance stems from a variety of considerations, including a belief that the practice may reveal how the constitutional framework was intended to operate, judicial respect for the constitutional views of the coordinate branches of the government, and a concern about expectation interests and institutional bargains that may have developed as a result of the practice.[148] Lawyers for the executive branch, such as in the Justice Department's Office

---

[144] *See* A.L.A. Schechter Poultry Corp. v. United States, 295 U.S. 495, 539–42 (1935); Panama Ref. Co. v. Ryan, 293 U.S. 388, 430 (1935). For debate over whether there should even be a nondelegation doctrine that limits the breadth of delegations, compare Eric A. Posner & Adrian Vermeule, *Interring the Nondelegation Doctrine*, 69 U. CHI. L. REV. 1721 (2002) (arguing against such a doctrine), with Larry Alexander & Saikrishna Prakash, *Reports of the Nondelegation Doctrine's Death Are Greatly Exaggerated*, 70 U. CHI. L. REV. 1297 (2003) (arguing in favor of such a doctrine). *See also* Keith E. Whittington & Jason Iuliano, *The Myth of the Nondelegation Doctrine*, 165 U. PA. L. REV. 379 (2017).

[145] *See* Loving v. United States, 517 U.S. 748, 772–73 (1996); United States v. Curtiss-Wright Export Corp., 299 U.S. 304, 319–22 (1936). Delegations of authority by the United States to international institutions are considered in Chapter 4.

[146] *See* Clinton v. City of New York, 524 U.S. 417 (1998); INS v. Chadha, 462 U.S. 919 (1983).

[147] *See, e.g.*, Zivotofsky v. Kerry, 135 S. Ct. 2076, 2091 (2015); NLRB v. Noel Canning, 573 U.S. 513, 524 (2014); Dames & Moore v. Regan, 453 U.S. 654, 686 (1981); *Curtiss-Wright*, 299 U.S. at 327–28; United States v. Midwest Oil Co., 236 U.S. 459, 474 (1915). *See also* Youngstown Sheet & Tube Co. v. Sawyer, 343 U.S. 579, 610–11 (1952) (Frankfurter, J., concurring) ("[A] systematic, unbroken, executive practice, long pursued to the knowledge of the Congress and never before questioned, engaged in by Presidents who have also sworn to uphold the Constitution, making as it were such exercise of power part of the structure of our government, may be treated as a gloss on 'executive Power' vested in the President by § 1 of Art. II."); Curtis A. Bradley & Trevor W. Morrison, *Historical Gloss and the Separation of Powers*, 126 HARV. L. REV. 411 (2012) (considering the extent to which historical practice does and should inform the interpretation of the separation of powers); Michael J. Glennon, *The Use of Custom in Resolving Separation of Powers Disputes*, 64 B. U. L. REV. 109 (1984) (same).

[148] *See* Bradley & Morrison, *supra* note 147, at 425–28. This approach to constitutional interpretation is somewhat controversial, and the Supreme Court does not invariably follow it. For a case in which the Court declined to credit longstanding practice in discerning Congress's authority, *see INS v. Chadha*, 462 U.S. 919 (1983), where the Court invalidated a legislative veto provision even though Congress had enacted hundreds of similar provisions since the 1930s.

of Legal Counsel, also frequently invoke historical practice in making arguments about the scope of presidential authority. Such invocations are especially common for claims concerning the president's foreign affairs authority because judicial precedent is often sparse or nonexistent for those issues.

Preemption of State Law

Much of U.S. law is state law. For example, states regulate most local crimes, contract law, tort law, family law, and the law governing trusts and estates. States generally have broad discretion in formulating the content of their laws.

The Constitution specifically disallows the states, however, from engaging in certain activities.[149] For example, they may not enter into treaties with foreign countries, and they may not engage in war unless invaded or in imminent danger. They are also prohibited from passing any bill of attainder, ex post facto law, or law impairing the obligation of contracts. In addition, the Supreme Court has construed the Due Process Clause of the Fourteenth Amendment to the Constitution (adopted shortly after the Civil War) as implicitly obligating states to respect many of the rights set forth in the federal Bill of Rights.[150]

As discussed earlier, the Constitution provides that the Constitution itself, federal statutes, and treaties are deemed to be the "supreme Law of the Land" that is binding on state judges, notwithstanding any contrary state law.[151] Federal common law rules, such as the act of state doctrine, also bind state courts.[152] When a state law conflicts with valid federal law, the state law is said to be "preempted" and therefore not enforceable. Courts sometimes find that state laws are preempted even when they are not directly in conflict with federal law, such as when the federal law is viewed as occupying the relevant field of regulation or when the state law poses an obstacle to the achievement of policies in the federal law.[153] A state law can also be preempted by Congress's dormant (that is, unexercised) power to regulate interstate or foreign commerce, if the state law either discriminates against commerce or imposes an excessive burden on it.[154]

---

[149] *See* U.S. CONST. art. I, § 10.
[150] *See, e.g.*, Duncan v. Louisiana, 391 U.S. 145, 147–48 (1968).
[151] *See* U.S. CONST. art. VI.
[152] See *Sabbatino*, 376 U.S. at 425–26.
[153] *See, e.g.*, Arizona v. United States, 567 U.S. 387 (2012); Crosby v. Nat'l Foreign Trade Council, 530 U.S. 363 (2000); Hines v. Davidowitz, 312 U.S. 52 (1941).
[154] *See, e.g.*, Granholm v. Heald, 544 U.S. 460, 472–73 (2005); Japan Line, Ltd. v. County of Los Angeles, 441 U.S. 434, 446–51 (1979); Pike v. Bruce Church, Inc., 397 U.S. 137, 142 (1970). *But cf.* Barclays Bank PLC v. Franchise Tax Board of California, 512 U.S. 298, 329 (1994) ("That the Executive Branch proposed legislation to outlaw a state taxation practice, but encountered an unreceptive Congress, is not evidence that the practice interfered with the Nation's ability to speak with one voice, but is rather evidence that the preeminent speaker decided to yield the floor to others.").

In *American Insurance Association v. Garamendi*, the Supreme Court concluded that a California law relating to insurance policies issued in Europe between 1920 and 1945 was preempted because the law created an obstacle to the achievement of the policies reflected in certain international agreements concluded by the president.[155] Although the decision could be viewed simply as extending "obstacle preemption" to the context of executive agreements, there are statements in the decision that could be read to suggest more broadly that the policies of the executive branch relating to foreign relations can in some instances preempt state law.[156] In this author's view, such suggestions are problematic from the perspective of the separation of powers, and they appear to be inconsistent with suggestions in other Supreme Court decisions indicating that the executive branch lacks the authority to preempt state law.[157]

In one decision, *Zschernig v. Miller*, the Supreme Court found that a state law was preempted because it conflicted with the dormant powers of the national government relating to foreign affairs more generally.[158] In that case, an Oregon statute provided that the property of a decedent would revert to the state if the decedent's heirs were nonresident aliens, unless there was a reciprocal right of U.S. citizens to take property upon the same terms as inhabitants and citizens of the country in which the aliens were citizens or inhabitants, and there was proof that the aliens had a right to receive the property without confiscation. In holding that the Oregon statute was preempted, the Court expressed the view that the statute had "a direct impact upon foreign relations and may well adversely affect the power of the central government to deal with those problems."[159] Somewhat surprisingly, the Court reached this conclusion even though the executive branch had informed the Court that the Oregon statute did not unduly interfere with U.S. foreign relations. The Supreme Court has not relied on *Zschernig* since it was decided in 1968, and the current viability of dormant foreign affairs preemption is unclear.[160]

---

[155] 539 U.S. 396 (2003).
[156] *See id.* at 413–14 (observing that "[t]here is, of course, no question that at some point an exercise of state power that touches on foreign relations must yield to the National Government's policy" and that "[n]or is there any question generally that there is executive authority to decide what that policy should be"). *See also In re* Assicurazioni Generali, S.P.A., 592 F.3d 113, 118 (2d Cir. 2010) ("The Court in *Garamendi*, however, did not find that the United States policy of encouraging resolution of Holocaust-era insurance claims through the ICHEIC depended on the existence of executive agreements. Rather, the Court viewed the executive agreements as the product of the policy.").
[157] *See, e.g.*, Medellin v. Texas, 552 U.S. 491, 532 (2008) ("This authority [of the President to take care that the laws are faithfully executed] allows the President to execute the laws, not make them."). For criticism of the possibility of executive branch foreign policy preemption, *see* Brannon P. Denning & Michael D. Ramsey, American Insurance Association v. Garamendi *and Executive Preemption in Foreign Affairs*, 46 WM. & MARY L. REV. 825 (2004).
[158] Zschernig v. Miller, 389 U.S. 429 (1968).
[159] *Id.* at 441.
[160] In *American Insurance Ass'n v. Garamendi*, the Court suggested in a footnote that dormant preemption may not be appropriate in situations in which a state is acting within an area of traditional state competence. *See* 539 U.S. 396, 420 n.11 (2003). For a lower court decision relying on *Zschernig* to preempt a state law extending

Despite the ability of the national government to preempt state law, states have some constitutional protection from federal regulation. A core principle of U.S. federalism, often recited by the Supreme Court, is that the national government has only limited and enumerated powers.[161] The limited and enumerated powers principle is implicitly reflected in the Tenth Amendment to the Constitution, which states that the powers not delegated to the federal government are reserved to the states and the people. Although the Tenth Amendment "states but a truism that all is retained which has not been surrendered,"[162] the Supreme Court sometimes uses the label "Tenth Amendment" to refer more broadly to "any implied constitutional limitation on [the federal government's] authority to regulate state activities, whether grounded in the Tenth Amendment itself or in principles of federalism derived generally from the Constitution."[163]

Since the early 1990s, the Supreme Court has expressed a renewed commitment to protecting federalism, and it has invalidated a number of legislative enactments on the ground that Congress exceeded its enumerated powers. In 1995, for example, the Court held that Congress exceeded its authority in enacting a criminal prohibition on possessing firearms near schools.[164] In 1997, the Court held that Congress had exceeded its authority in attempting to regulate religious freedom at the local level.[165] And, in 2000, the Court held that a statute that conferred a civil cause of action for local acts of violence against women exceeded Congress's powers.[166] These decisions are controversial, and some scholars have argued that enumerated power limitations should be enforced primarily through the political process rather than the courts. In any event, it is important to keep in mind that, even with these decisions, the Supreme Court continues to construe Congress's regulatory authority very broadly.[167] Moreover, the Court is likely to be even more generous in construing Congress's ability to regulate in the area of foreign affairs, such as with respect to foreign commerce.

---

the statute of limitations for insurance claims by victims of the Armenian genocide, see *Movsesian v. Victoria Verischerung AG*, 670 F.3d 1067 (9th Cir. 2012) (en banc). For a decision rejecting a dormant preemption challenge to a city's establishment of a monument to Korean "comfort women" from the World War II era, despite the possibility of creating friction with Japan, see Gingery v. City of Glendale, 831 F.3d 1222, 1234 (9th Cir. 2016) (noting that the case involved "a purely expressive, non-regulatory action").

[161] *See, e.g.*, Alden v. Maine, 527 U.S. 706, 713 (1999); City of Boerne v. Flores, 521 U.S. 507, 516 (1997); United States v. Lopez, 514 U.S. 549, 552 (1995); Gregory v. Ashcroft, 501 U.S. 452, 457 (1991). *See also* THE FEDERALIST PAPERS, *No. 45: James Madison*, at 289 (Clinton Rossiter ed., 1961) ("The powers delegated by the proposed Constitution to the federal government are few and defined. Those which are to remain in the State governments are numerous and indefinite.").

[162] United States v. Darby, 312 U.S. 100, 124 (1941).

[163] South Carolina v. Baker, 485 U.S. 505, 511 n.5 (1988).

[164] *See* United States v. Lopez, 514 U.S. 549 (1995).

[165] *See City of Boerne*, 521 U.S. at 534–35.

[166] *See* United States v. Morrison, 529 U.S. 598 (2000).

[167] *See, e.g.*, Gonzales v. Raich, 545 U.S. 1 (2005) (holding that Congress had the authority under the Commerce Clause to regulate the personal cultivation of marijuana for medicinal use).

In the context of purely domestic legislation, the Supreme Court generally presumes that, even when it has the authority to do so, Congress does not intend to preempt state law in areas of traditional state authority.[168] It has been unclear to what extent this presumption applies to legislation relating to foreign affairs.[169] However, in a 2014 decision that is discussed in Chapter 2, *Bond v. United States*, the Court applied a related presumption—that Congress does not intend to alter the traditional balance of state and federal authority—to legislation implementing a treaty.[170]

* * *

The United States has a strong and independent judiciary that plays an important role in ensuring adherence to the rule of law, even in the area of foreign affairs. At the same time, there are a variety of limitations on the ability of the courts to decide cases in this area, some of which reflect the judiciary's sense of its institutional capacity, and others of which reflect its respect for the sovereignty of other nations. Ultimately, courts appear to understand that there is an overlap between foreign relations law and foreign policy, and they seek to ensure that judicial doctrine preserves for Congress and the executive branch the lead role in formulating the latter. The federal nature of the U.S. legal system, with its separate federal and state courts, and its reservation of some powers to the state governments, further affects the way in which foreign relations law issues are addressed.

---

[168] *See, e.g.*, Rice v. Santa Fe Elevator Corp., 331 U.S. 218, 230 (1947).

[169] *See* Crosby v. Nat'l Foreign Trade Council, 530 U.S. 363, 374 n. 8 (2000) ("We leave for another day a consideration in this context of a presumption against presumption."). *See also* Jack L. Goldsmith, *Statutory Foreign Affairs Preemption*, 2000 SUP. CT. REV. 175 (arguing against any presumption in favor of or against preemption).

[170] *See* 572 U.S. 844, 858 (2014). *See also* Curtis A. Bradley, *Federalism, Treaty Implementation, and Political Process: Bond v. United States*, 108 AM. J. INT'L L. 486 (2014) (discussing the *Bond* decision).

2 Treaties

THIS CHAPTER CONSIDERS the status of treaties within the U.S. legal system. The focus here is only on international agreements concluded by the United States through the two-thirds senatorial advice-and-consent process specified in Article II of the Constitution. As explained in Chapter 3, a large majority of international agreements concluded by the United States today do not go through this process, but rather are concluded as "executive agreements." These executive agreements, like the agreements made through the senatorial advice-and-consent process, are considered "treaties" under international law. Because these agreements raise distinct issues under U.S. law, however, they will be discussed separately.[1]

At the outset, we need to take note of a particular treaty, the Vienna Convention on the Law of Treaties (VCLT).[2] The VCLT, which took effect in 1980 and has now been ratified by over 115 nations, contains detailed provisions governing the formation, interpretation, and termination of treaties. Although the United States is not a party to this treaty,[3] executive branch officials have stated that they regard much of the VCLT as

---

[1] Neither chapter discusses treaties with Native American tribes, which raise issues outside the scope of this book.
[2] Vienna Convention on the Law of Treaties, May 23, 1969, 1155 U.N.T.S. 331 [hereinafter VCLT].
[3] The Nixon administration signed the VCLT in 1970 and submitted it to the Senate, but the Senate never gave its advice and consent, in part because of a concern that provisions in the VCLT would legitimize executive agreements. *See* CONGRESSIONAL RESEARCH SERVICE, TREATIES AND OTHER INTERNATIONAL

reflecting binding norms of customary international law.[4] Moreover, U.S. courts sometimes rely on the VCLT when faced with treaty questions.[5] As a result, when referring to the rules of international law governing treaties, this chapter will use the VCLT as a rough approximation of the rules that likely apply to the United States, while also pointing out when U.S. practice appears to depart from the VCLT.

The Treaty Process

The Constitution provides, in Article II, Section 2, that the president has the power to make treaties with the "advice and consent" of the Senate, "provided two thirds of the Senators present concur."[6] The U.S. treaty-making power is therefore divided between the president and the Senate. The constitutional Founders thought it important that a unitary executive agent represent the United States in treaty negotiations, but they did not want to vest in a single elected leader the power to bind the nation to international commitments.[7] The requirement of a supermajority vote in the Senate was seen as a means of ensuring that the federal government would not favor particular sectional interests in concluding treaties.[8] In dividing the treaty power, the Founders decided not to include the House of Representatives because they thought it would be too large and its composition would change too frequently to act with the degree of secrecy, speed, and consistency of policy considered desirable in concluding treaties.[9]

Agreements: The Role of the United States Senate, S. Rpt. 106–71, 106th Cong., 2d Sess. 46–47 (2001) [hereinafter CRS Study].

[4] See Restatement (Fourth) of the Foreign Relations Law of the United States § 301, reporters' note 1 (2018); Restatement (Third) of the Foreign Relations Law of the United States, pt. III, introductory note, at 145 (1987).

[5] See, e.g., Chubb & Son, Inc. v. Asiana Airlines, 214 F.3d 301, 308–309 (2d Cir. 2000) (collecting cases). See also Maria Frankowska, The Vienna Convention on the Law of Treaties before United States Courts, 28 Va. J. Int'l L. 281, 287–88 (1988).

[6] U.S. Const. art. II, § 2, cl. 2.

[7] See The Federalist Papers, No. 75: Alexander Hamilton, at 451 (Clinton Rossiter ed., 1961) ("However proper or safe it may be in governments where the executive magistrate is an hereditary monarch, to commit to him the entire power of making treaties, it would be utterly unsafe and improper to intrust that power to an elective magistrate of four years' duration.").

[8] See, e.g., Oona A. Hathaway, Treaties' End: The Past, Present, and Future of International Lawmaking in the United States, 117 Yale L.J. 1236, 1281 (2008); Quincy Wright, The United States and International Agreements, 38 Am. J. Int'l L. 341, 350 (1944). The southern states were specifically concerned that the federal government would enter into a treaty with Spain giving up U.S. navigation rights on the Mississippi River in return for trade concessions that would benefit northern states. See Charles Warren, The Mississippi River and the Treaty Clause of the Constitution, 2 Geo. Wash. L. Rev. 271 (1934).

[9] The Federalist Papers, supra note 7, No. 75: Alexander Hamilton, at 451.

The modern U.S. treaty-making process operates essentially as follows.[10] Representatives of the president negotiate the terms of the treaty with foreign nations, and the president or the president's representative signs the completed draft. The president then transmits the treaty to the Senate. The Foreign Relations Committee of the Senate subsequently decides whether to send the treaty to the floor of the full Senate for a vote. If the treaty is sent to the full Senate and receives the required two-thirds approval, the Senate sends a resolution of advice and consent to the president in which it approves the treaty. The president has the discretion at this point to ratify or not ratify the treaty. If the president decides to ratify the treaty, the president will either exchange instruments of ratification with the other party to the treaty (in the case of a bilateral treaty) or deposit an instrument of ratification or accession with a depository such as the United Nations (in the case of a multilateral treaty).

As the reference in Article II to "advice and consent" might suggest, the Founders of the Constitution probably intended for presidents not only to seek the Senate's approval of treaties that had already been negotiated, but also to consult with the Senate during the process of negotiating treaties.[11] The first U.S. president, George Washington, appears to have understood that the Senate was to have such a consultative role.[12] Nevertheless, by the end of his administration, Washington had moved away from seeking the Senate's advice during the treaty process, relying on the Senate instead simply to approve treaties that were already negotiated.[13] This has been the practice of the United States ever since: the executive branch generally negotiates treaties without formally consulting with the Senate and then presents them to the Senate for approval.[14]

Under international law, a nation becomes a party to a treaty by expressing its "consent to be bound" by the treaty.[15] Consent to be bound can be expressed through signature of a treaty (an act known as a "definitive signature"), but under modern treaty practice, nations often express their consent to be bound by a separate act of ratification that is

---

[10] *See* CRS Study, *supra* note 3, at 6–12.
[11] *See* Curtis A. Bradley & Martin S. Flaherty, *Executive Power Essentialism and Foreign Affairs*, 102 MICH. L. REV. 545, 626–31 (2004); Jack N. Rakove, *Solving a Constitutional Puzzle: The Treatymaking Clause as a Case Study*, 1 PERSP. AM. HIST. 233, 235 (1984). *See also* LEONARD W. LEVY, ORIGINAL INTENT AND THE CONSTITUTION 30–53 (1988); Arthur Bestor, *"Advice" from the Very Beginning, "Consent" When the End Is Achieved*, 83 AM. J. INT'L L. 718, 726 (1989).
[12] *See* Bradley & Flaherty, *supra* note 11, at 631–34.
[13] *See id.* at 634–35; RALSTON HAYDEN, THE SENATE AND TREATIES, 1789–1817, at 11–16 (1920). For isolated instances since that time in which presidents have sought the advice of the Senate during the negotiating process, *see* SAMUEL B. CRANDALL, TREATIES: THEIR MAKING AND ENFORCEMENT 70–72 (2d ed. 1916).
[14] Although the president does not typically consult with the Senate as a whole when negotiating treaties, "Presidents or their Secretaries of State have often consulted with individual senators or committees prior to or during the negotiating process in order to enhance the prospects of the final treaty." CRS Study, *supra* note 3, at 107.
[15] VCLT, *supra* note 2, art. 2(1)(b); *see also* ANTHONY AUST, MODERN TREATY LAW AND PRACTICE ch. 7 (3d ed. 2013).

carried out after signature (in which case the signature is referred to as a "simple signature").[16] Because the U.S. Constitution divides the treaty power between the president and Senate, presidential signature of a treaty usually indicates (at most) that the text of the treaty is acceptable to the executive branch, not that the United States is consenting to be bound by the treaty. During the nineteenth century, when the Western world was still composed primarily of monarchies, other nations sometimes complained about the U.S. failure to ratify treaties that it had signed, and the United States had to remind them that its signature did not constitute consent to be bound by the treaty.[17] Eventually, "European governments ceased to protest against the American practice; and unratified treaties became a common feature of international relations."[18]

There are a number of reasons the United States might sign a treaty but then fail to ratify it.[19] The president might submit a treaty to the Senate and have it defeated there, although this happens only rarely.[20] More likely, a president might withhold submission of a treaty to the Senate because of perceived opposition in that body, and the president may hope that the Senate's position—or perhaps, relatedly, its composition—will change. A president might also submit a treaty to the Senate and have it languish there, once its supporters in the Senate realize that they do not have sufficient votes for advice and consent. It is also possible that a president could sign a treaty without being committed to ratification, perhaps in an effort to stay involved in subsequent negotiations related to the treaty or in the institutions established by the treaty, or for symbolic political benefits. Finally, a president might have a change of position about the desirability of a treaty after signing it, or the president may leave office while the treaty is pending in the Senate and the president's successor may have a different view of the treaty. Sometimes, however, the United States will ratify a treaty many years after signing it.[21] A long delay

---

[16] See Curtis A. Bradley, *Treaty Signature, in* OXFORD GUIDE TO TREATIES (Duncan B. Hollis ed., 2012).

[17] See J. MERVYN JONES, FULL POWERS AND RATIFICATION 76–77 (1946). *See also* 5 JOHN BASSETT MOORE, A DIGEST OF INTERNATIONAL LAW 189 (1906) (describing a treaty negotiation with Spain in 1819 in which Secretary of State John Quincy Adams explained to the Spanish minister that "by the nature of our Constitution, the full powers of our ministers never are or can be unlimited").

[18] JONES, *supra* note 17, at 77.

[19] See Curtis A. Bradley, *Unratified Treaties, Domestic Politics, and the U.S. Constitution*, 48 HARV. INT'L L.J. 307, 310 (2007).

[20] See U.S. Senate, *Treaties*, http://www.senate.gov/artandhistory/history/common/briefing/Treaties.htm (listing twenty-two treaties that have been rejected by the Senate over the course of U.S. history). *See also* W. STULL HOLT, TREATIES DEFEATED BY THE SENATE: A STUDY OF THE STRUGGLE BETWEEN PRESIDENT AND SENATE OVER THE CONDUCT OF FOREIGN RELATIONS (1933). For example, in 2012 the Obama administration failed to obtain the required two-thirds vote from the Senate in support of the Convention on the Rights of Persons with Disabilities. *See* Jennifer Steinhauer, *Dole Appears, but G.O.P. Rejects a Disabilities Treaty*, N.Y. TIMES (Dec. 4, 2012).

[21] For two especially dramatic examples, *see* Protocol for the Prohibition of the Use in War of Asphyxiating, Poisonous or Other Gases, and of Bacteriological Methods of Warfare, June 17, 1925, 26 U.S.T. 571, 94 L.N.T.S. 65 (signed by the United States in 1925 and ratified in 1975); and Convention on the Prevention and Punishment of the Crime of Genocide, Dec. 9, 1948, 102 Stat. 3045, 78 U.N.T.S. 277 (signed by the United States in 1948 and ratified in 1988). For another example, the International Labour Organization Convention

after signature therefore does not necessarily indicate that the United States is unwilling to become a party to a treaty.

The number of treaties submitted by presidents to the Senate has dropped off in recent years. During his eight years in office, President Obama submitted an average of less than five treaties per year to the Senate, which is a substantially lower number of submissions than in prior modern administrations.[22] The numbers dropped off even more sharply during the Trump administration, with only a handful of treaties submitted to the Senate during President's Trump's first three years in office.[23] This does not mean that presidents have stopped concluding binding international agreements; rather, it means (as discussed in Chapter 3) that they are largely concluding them outside of the senatorial advice-and-consent process.

Conditional Consent

On numerous occasions throughout history, the United States has sought to condition its ratification of treaties by insisting on reservations to, or particular interpretations of, treaty terms.[24] One study found that, since the constitutional Founding, the United States had included conditions with approximately 15% of all treaties that it had ratified.[25] The United States has used a variety of labels for these conditions, including "reservation," "amendment," "condition," "understanding," "declaration," and "proviso." These conditions typically appear in the Senate's resolution of advice and consent, although it is not uncommon for the executive branch to suggest conditions for the Senate to consider. The Senate's exercise of conditional consent authority is in part a response to its loss of any substantial "advice" role in the treaty process, as just discussed.[26] When the Senate includes conditions when approving a treaty, it is well established as a matter of U.S. practice that the president can proceed to ratify the treaty only if the president accepts the conditions.[27] If the president finds a condition unacceptable (or the other nation in the case of a bilateral treaty finds it unacceptable), the treaty will not be ratified.[28]

No. 87 Concerning Freedom of Association and Protection of the Right to Organize was submitted to the Senate in 1949 and was still pending before that body in 2020. *See* U.S. Dep't of State, *Treaties Pending in the Senate, at* http://www.state.gov/s/l/treaty/pending/.

[22] *See* Curtis A. Bradley & Jack L. Goldsmith, *Presidential Control over International Law*, 131 HARV. L. REV. 1201, 1210–11 (2018).

[23] *See Treaty Documents*, Congress.gov (listing dates when treaties were received by the Senate).

[24] *See generally* Curtis A. Bradley & Jack L. Goldsmith, *Treaties, Human Rights, and Conditional Consent*, 149 U. PA. L. REV. 399 (2000).

[25] *See* Kevin C. Kennedy, *Conditional Approval of Treaties by the U.S. Senate*, 19 LOY. L.A. INT'L & COMP. L.J. 89, 91, 97 (1996).

[26] *See* Bradley & Goldsmith, *supra* note 24, at 405; CRANDALL, *supra* note 13, at 79–82; HAYDEN, *supra* note 13, at 110–11.

[27] *See* CRS Study, *supra* note 3, at 124.

[28] *See* U.S. Senate, *Treaties*, http://www.senate.gov/artandhistory/history/common/briefing/Treaties.htm.

The first example of this conditional consent occurred in connection with the Jay Treaty of 1794. This treaty was designed to resolve a variety of compensation, trade, and boundary disputes between the United States and Great Britain. In giving its advice and consent to the treaty, the Senate insisted that a provision in the treaty reserving to Great Britain the right to restrict trade between the United States and the British West Indies be suspended.[29] Great Britain did not object to this reservation, and the treaty was ratified.[30]

The United States was apparently the first nation to engage in this conditional consent practice, and its treaty partners did not always respond favorably to it. In negotiating an 1803 boundary treaty with the United States, for example, Great Britain would not accept an amendment proposed by the Senate, and the treaty was never ratified. The head of the British Foreign Office at the time criticized the United States' conditional consent practice, calling it "new, unauthorized and not to be sanctioned."[31] Great Britain similarly complained about conditions proposed by the Senate in connection with an 1824 treaty concerning the slave trade.[32] In response, Secretary of State Henry Clay reminded Great Britain that the Senate's conditional consent power was a function of the constitutional division of the treaty power between the president and the Senate and that this power was something that "the government of the United States has always communicated to the foreign powers with which it treats, and none more fully than to the United Kingdom of Great Britain and Ireland."[33]

Over time, the conditional consent practice became generally accepted by the international community. The United States gave conditional consent in connection with numerous treaties during the nineteenth and early twentieth centuries, generally without controversy, as did many of its treaty partners.[34] The practice of not consenting to particular treaty terms when ratifying a treaty is now a common feature of treaty relations.

In recent years, the United States' resort to conditional consent has been particularly common with respect to human rights treaties. Since the end of World War II, a number of important human rights treaties have been developed that regulate various aspects of how nations interact with their citizens. Although the United States was initially a strong proponent of the development of international human rights standards, there were intense debates in the United States in the 1950s over whether and to what extent the nation should participate in these treaties. Among other things, critics were concerned that the treaties would undermine U.S. federalism by allowing the national government to regulate matters that Congress did not have the constitutional authority

---

[29] *See* SENATE EXEC. JOURNAL, 4th Cong., Special Sess., June 24, 1795, at 186.
[30] *See* HAYDEN, *supra* note 13, at 87.
[31] *Id.* at 150.
[32] *See* MOORE, A DIGEST, *supra* note 17, § 748, at 200.
[33] ROBERT T. DEVLIN, THE TREATY POWER UNDER THE CONSTITUTION OF THE UNITED STATES § 64, at 61–62 (1908).
[34] For examples, *see* DAVID HUNTER MILLER, RESERVATIONS TO TREATIES: THEIR EFFECT AND THE PROCEDURE IN REGARD THERETO (1919).

to regulate. There was also opposition from representatives of southern states who were concerned that the government would use treaties as a vehicle for engaging in civil rights reform that was beyond the legislative authority of Congress.[35] There were a number of proposals during this period to amend the Constitution to limit the treaty power, some of which would have prevented the United States from becoming a party to human rights treaties. This set of proposals was known collectively as the Bricker Amendment (named after a key sponsor of the proposals, Senator John Bricker of Ohio).[36] The controversy ultimately died down, but only after the Eisenhower administration promised the Senate that the United States would not join the human rights treaties being developed or otherwise use the treaty power to address matters of domestic concern.[37]

In the 1970s, President Jimmy Carter submitted a number of human rights treaties to the Senate for its advice and consent. In an effort to overcome opposition in that body, the administration proposed that the Senate condition its advice and consent with various reservations, understandings, and declarations, collectively known as "RUDs." Even with the proposed RUDs, the Senate did not begin to approve human rights treaties until the late 1980s. Each time that the United States has ratified a major human rights treaty, it has included a package of RUDs.[38] These RUDs typically do a number of things. First, they decline to agree to treaty provisions to the extent that they would violate individual rights provisions of the Constitution (such as the right of free speech). Second, they decline to agree to certain other provisions on policy grounds (such as provisions restricting the death penalty). Third, they purport to interpret some provisions that are undefined in the treaties (such as the phrase "cruel, inhuman, or degrading treatment or punishment" in the Convention against Torture). Fourth, they announce that the United States will implement the treaties in a manner consistent with its federal system of government. Finally, they declare that the terms of the treaties are non–self-executing. (The significance of the non–self-execution declaration is discussed below.)

The extensive use of RUDs has been criticized on the ground that it displays a lack of good faith by the United States in joining the relevant treaties. As Professor Louis Henkin explained, "[b]y adhering to human rights conventions subject to these reservations, the United States, it is charged, is pretending to assume international obligations but in fact is undertaking nothing."[39] Even with the RUDs, however, the United States

---

[35] See Hathaway, *supra* note 8, at 1303. For additional discussion of the reasons for U.S. resistance to the human rights treaties, see Curtis A. Bradley, *The United States and Human Rights Treaties: Race Relations, the Cold War, and Constitutionalism*, 9 CHINESE J. INT'L L. 321 (2010).

[36] See generally DUANE TANANBAUM, THE BRICKER AMENDMENT CONTROVERSY: A TEST OF EISENHOWER'S POLITICAL LEADERSHIP (1988).

[37] See Curtis A. Bradley, *The Treaty Power and American Federalism, Part II*, 99 MICH. L. REV. 98, 122–23 (2000).

[38] See, e.g., U.S. Reservations, Declarations, and Understandings, International Covenant on Civil and Political Rights, 138 CONG. REC. S4781, S4783–84 (Apr. 2, 1992).

[39] Louis Henkin, *U.S. Ratification of Human Rights Conventions: The Ghost of Senator Bricker*, 89 AM. J. INT'L L. 341, 344 (1995).

remains bound under international law to adhere to almost all of the obligations in the human rights treaties it has ratified. The United States also has enacted implementing legislation to give domestic effect to a number of these treaties. For example, to implement the Convention against Torture, Congress has enacted a criminal prohibition on torture, amendments to immigration provisions relating to deportation, and restrictions on military interrogation.[40] The United States has also agreed to subject itself to international monitoring under the human rights treaties and has submitted reports to, and appeared before, the relevant committees. Finally, it is important to keep in mind that the RUDs helped break the political logjam with respect to U.S. ratification of human rights treaties and that the United States might not have consented to these treaties at all without the RUDs.

The RUDs are also sometimes criticized on the ground that they are inconsistent with international law. Under modern international law, reservations to multilateral treaties are allowed unless they are either prohibited by the treaty or are inconsistent with the "object and purpose" of the treaty.[41] Human rights treaties generally do not prohibit reservations, and in fact many nations in addition to the United States have included reservations with their ratification of these treaties.[42] It is also unlikely that the RUDs qualify the U.S. acceptance of the treaties to a sufficient degree to run afoul of the "object and purpose" limitation, although there has been some debate about this, especially with respect to a U.S. refusal to accept a ban on the execution of juvenile offenders.[43] To date, U.S. courts have consistently given effect to the RUDs.[44]

---

[40] *See* 8 U.S.C. § 1231 Note; 18 U.S.C. § 2340A.

[41] *See* VCLT, *supra* note 2, art. 19. *See also* Int'l Law Comm'n, *Guide to Practice on Reservations* ¶ 3.1 (2011), available at https://legal.un.org/ilc/texts/instruments/english/draft_articles/1_8_2011.pdf.

[42] Some treaties prohibit reservations. When ratifying the Chemical Weapons Convention, which prohibits reservations, the United States included twenty-eight "conditions." *See* Resolution of Ratification for the Chemical Weapons Convention, S. Res. 75, 105th Cong., 143 CONG. REC. S3570, S3651 (Apr. 24, 1997).

[43] In 1995, the international committee established to monitor compliance with the International Covenant on Civil and Political Rights expressed the view that the U.S. reservation concerning the juvenile death penalty violated the object and purpose of the Covenant. *See* Curtis A. Bradley, *The Juvenile Death Penalty and International Law*, 52 DUKE L.J. 485, 501–507 (2002). The issue became moot in 2005 when the U.S. Supreme Court held that the execution of juvenile offenders violated the prohibition on "cruel and unusual punishments" in the Eighth Amendment to the U.S. Constitution. *See* Roper v. Simmons, 543 U.S. 541 (2005). There is some debate over whether the invalidity of a reservation nullifies a nation's ratification of a treaty, or whether the invalid reservation is instead severable from the ratification. *See, e.g.*, Ryan Goodman, *Human Rights Treaties, Invalid Reservations, and State Consent*, 96 AM. J. INT'L L. 531 (2002). The UN's International Law Commission has expressed the view that "[u]nless the author of the invalid reservation has expressed a contrary intention or such an intention is otherwise established, it is considered a contracting State or a contracting organization without the benefit of the reservation," but that "the author of the invalid reservation may express at any time its intention not to be bound by the treaty without the benefit of the reservation." Int'l Law Comm'n, *supra* note 41, at ¶ 4.5.3.

[44] *See, e.g.*, Auguste v. Ridge, 395 F.3d 123, 141–42 (3d Cir. 2005); Flores v. S. Peru Copper Corp., 343 F.3d 140, 168 & n.35 (2d Cir. 2003); Bannerman v. Snyder, 325 F.3d 722, 724 (6th Cir. 2003); Beazley v. Johnson, 242 F.3d 248, 263–68 (5th Cir. 2001).

After joining a treaty subject to conditions, the United States could, in theory, withdraw one or more of the conditions. If the conditions were included in the Senate's resolution of advice and consent to an Article II treaty, they presumably cannot constitutionally be withdrawn without the concurrence of two-thirds of the Senate. It is well accepted that a president cannot proceed to ratify a treaty without accepting whatever conditions are in the Senate's resolution of advice and consent, so a president should be similarly barred from withdrawing conditions without the agreement of the Senate. While it is arguable that the president has the constitutional authority to *terminate* an Article II treaty on his own authority (an issue discussed below), any such authority stems in part from the lack of any clear guidance in the constitutional text about how treaties are to be terminated. By contrast, the withdrawal of conditions insisted upon by the Senate would in effect involve making new treaty commitments, and the Constitution specifically requires two-thirds senatorial consent for the making of treaties.[45]

Treaties as Supreme Federal Law

From the onset of the Revolutionary War in 1775, until 1789, the United States operated without a constitution. Starting in 1781, it had a written agreement among the thirteen states, known as the Articles of Confederation, but the Articles were not formulated in a way to ensure strong national control of foreign relations.[46] One of the many foreign relations problems that arose in the pre-constitutional period was state violation of treaties, most notably the 1783 peace treaty between the United States and Great Britain. A provision in that treaty required that British creditors "shall meet with no lawful impediment to the recovery of the full value ... of all bona fide debts heretofore contracted,"[47] but some states were disregarding this treaty obligation and blocking recovery of debts to British creditors. Great Britain was in turn citing those violations as a reason for not complying with a provision in the treaty that required it to vacate military forts in northwestern parts of the United States.

---

[45] In 1984, President Reagan sought the Senate's advice and consent to the withdrawal of a reservation that had previously been attached to the U.S. ratification of the Patent Cooperation Treaty. *See* Letter of Transmittal from President Ronald Reagan, July 27, 1984, *in* Treaty Doc. 98-29, Request for Advice and Consent to Withdrawal of a Reservation Made to the 1975 Patent Cooperation Treaty, 98th Cong., 2d Sess. (1984). The Senate gave its advice and consent to the withdrawal two years later. *See* 132 Cong. Rec., 99th Cong., 2d Sess., S29884-85 (Oct. 9, 1986). Soon thereafter, Congress amended the patent laws to take account of the obligations that the United States would have in the absence of the reservation. *See* Act of Nov. 6, 1986, Pub. L. 99-616, 100 Stat. 3485.

[46] *See* BRADFORD PERKINS, THE CREATION OF A REPUBLICAN EMPIRE, 1776–1865, at 54–59 (1993); FREDERICK W. MARKS III, INDEPENDENCE ON TRIAL: FOREIGN AFFAIRS AND THE MAKING OF THE CONSTITUTION (1973); Jack N. Rakove, *Making Foreign Policy—The View from 1787, in* FOREIGN POLICY AND THE CONSTITUTION 1–3 (Robert A. Goldwin & Robert A. Licht eds., 1990).

[47] Treaty of Paris, Sept. 3, 1783, U.S.–Gr. Brit., art. 4, 8 Stat. 80, 82.

The constitutional Founders attempted to address the problem of state noncompliance with treaties by including treaties in the Constitution's Supremacy Clause. That Clause provides in relevant part that "all Treaties made, or which shall be made, under the Authority of the United States, shall be the supreme Law of the Land; and the Judges in every State shall be bound thereby, any Thing in the Constitution or Laws of any State to the Contrary notwithstanding."[48] The direct enforceability of treaties in the U.S. legal system distinguished it from the British approach under which treaties generally had domestic effect only after being implemented by Parliament, an approach still followed in Britain today.[49]

An early Supreme Court decision, *Ware v. Hylton*, confirmed both the supremacy of treaties over state law and the ability of the Supreme Court to enforce that supremacy.[50] In that case, the state of Virginia had allowed U.S. debtors to discharge their debts to British creditors by paying the amount of the debts to a Virginia loan office, and on that basis Virginia courts blocked actions by the creditors to recover on the debts. Because it was the practice of the Supreme Court at that time for each justice to write a separate opinion, there is no opinion for the Court. But, in reversing the Virginia courts, the justices made clear that, under the Constitution, treaties are supreme over state law. Justice Chase stated, for example, that "[a] treaty cannot be the supreme law of the land, that is of all the United States, if any act of a State Legislature can stand in its way."[51]

When the Supreme Court considers whether a federal *statute* has preempted a state law, the Court often applies a presumption against preemption.[52] This presumption is designed to ensure that Congress considers the federal-state balance when enacting legislation and that any preemption of state law is attributable to the policy judgments of Congress, where the states are represented. It is not clear whether this presumption applies when courts are interpreting treaties. Sometimes the Court has suggested that the presumption does apply even in this context,[53] but at other times the Court has suggested that it may not.[54]

---

[48] U.S. Const. art. VI, cl. 2.
[49] *See* James Crawford, Brownlie's Principles of Public International Law 59 (9th ed. 2019).
[50] Ware v. Hylton, 3 U.S. (3 Dall.) 199 (1796).
[51] *Id.* at 236 (Opinion of Chase, J.).
[52] *See, e.g.*, Gregory v. Ashcroft, 501 U.S. 452, 460 (1991); Rice v. Santa Fe Elevator Corp., 331 U.S. 218, 230 (1947).
[53] *See* United States v. Pink, 315 U.S. 203, 230 (1942); Guaranty Trust Co. v. United States, 304 U.S. 126, 143 (1938).
[54] *See* El Al Israel Airlines, Ltd. v. Tseng, 525 U.S. 155, 175 (1999) ("Our home-centered preemption analysis . . . should not be applied, mechanically, in construing our international obligations."); Nielsen v. Johnson, 279 U.S. 47, 52 (1929) ("[A]s the treaty-making power is independent of and superior to the legislative power of the states, the meaning of treaty provisions so construed is not restricted by any necessity of avoiding possible conflict with state legislation."). It is also unclear whether the presumption against preemption applies to statutory preemption when the state activities in question implicate foreign affairs. *See* Crosby v. Nat'l Foreign Trade Council, 530 U.S. 363, 374 n.8 (2000) (leaving this issue "for another day"). *Cf.* United States v. Locke, 529 U.S. 89, 108 (2000) ("The state laws now in question bear upon national and international maritime commerce, and in this area there is no beginning assumption that concurrent regulation by the State is a valid

Non-Self-Execution

Even though treaties are part of the supreme law of the land, they are not always enforceable in U.S. courts. Starting with an 1829 decision, *Foster v. Neilson*, the Supreme Court has distinguished between "self-executing" and "non–self-executing" treaty provisions. Although courts sometimes speak loosely about whether an entire treaty is self-executing, self-execution should normally be considered on a provision-by-provision basis, since it is quite possible that some provisions in a treaty will be self-executing and others will not. If a treaty provision is non–self-executing, it will not be given effect by U.S. courts unless and until it is implemented by Congress.

Foster involved an 1819 treaty between the United States and Spain in which Spain had ceded disputed territory to the United States.[55] James Foster and Pleasants Elam claimed title to a tract of land within the territory covered by the treaty, based on an 1804 grant from Spain, and on that basis sought to eject David Neilson from the tract. Before concluding the treaty, the U.S. government had taken the position that the area in which this particular tract of land was located had been ceded by Spain to France in 1800, and that France had conveyed it to the United States in 1803 as part of the Louisiana Purchase.[56] Moreover, this view was reflected in several federal statutes enacted prior to the treaty.[57]

Although a provision in the treaty purported to preserve land grants that had been made by Spain in the ceded territory, the Supreme Court concluded that the provision was non–self-executing. The Court noted that the English version of the provision, which stated that the grants "shall be ratified and confirmed," was in "the language of contract."[58] The Court further reasoned:

> [A treaty is] to be regarded in courts of justice as equivalent to an act of the legislature, whenever it operates of itself without the aid of any legislative provision. But when the terms of the stipulation import a contract, when either of the parties engages to perform a particular act, the treaty addresses itself to the political, not the judicial department; and the legislature must execute the contract before it can become a rule for the Court.[59]

---

exercise of its police powers."). *See generally* Jack Goldsmith, *Statutory Foreign Affairs Preemption*, 2000 SUP. CT. REV. 175.

[55] *See* Foster v. Neilson, 27 U.S. (2 Pet.) 253, 273–74 (1829). *See also* Carlos M. Vázquez, *The Story of* Foster v. Neilson *and* United States v. Percheman: *Judicial Enforcement of Treaties, in* INTERNATIONAL LAW STORIES (John Noyes, Mark Janis & Laura Dickinson eds., 2007).

[56] *See Foster*, 27 U.S. at 300.

[57] *Id.* at 303–305.

[58] *Id.* at 315.

[59] *Id.* at 314.

As a result, the Court upheld a dismissal of the case.

In a subsequent decision, the Court changed its mind about the treaty provision that was at issue in *Foster*. After examining the Spanish version of the provision, the English translation of which provided that the grants of land "shall remain ratified and confirmed," the Court concluded that the provision was in fact self-executing.[60] Unlike the land at issue in *Foster*, the land at issue in this subsequent case was indisputably within Spanish territory at the time of the 1819 treaty and thus the grant in question did not pose a potential conflict with preexisting statutes.

Foster stands for the proposition that a treaty provision will not be enforced by U.S. courts if its obligations are addressed to the political branches of the government rather than to the judiciary. If a treaty provision specifically calls for legislative implementation, then it is obviously non–self-executing in this sense. In many cases, however, the proper characterization of a treaty provision will be less clear, and there is significant debate and uncertainty with respect to the considerations that should govern this determination. The term "non–self-executing" has also been used in a variety of different, and not always consistent, ways.[61] The result is a highly complex doctrine that has been described as "perhaps one of the most confounding in treaty law."[62]

A number of difficult questions surround the self-execution issue. First, whose intent should courts consider in discerning whether a treaty provision is self-executing—the collective intent of the parties to the treaty, or just the intent of the U.S. treaty-makers? When interpreting the meaning of the substantive terms of a treaty, courts attempt to discern the intent of the parties. Self-execution, however, concerns a matter of domestic implementation, an issue that is not normally the focus of international law or negotiation. Moreover, in some countries, treaties are always non–self-executing, making it unlikely that there will be a shared intent concerning whether a treaty is self-executing in the United States. Both the *Restatement (Third) of Foreign Relations Law* and the *Restatement (Fourth)* therefore emphasize the intent or understanding of the United States.[63] Some lower courts and commentators have suggested, however, that the intent of the parties should be considered.[64]

Second, what factors should courts look to in discerning whether a treaty provision is self-executing? Without much explanation, courts have tended to treat mandatory, present-tense provisions in bilateral treaties as self-executing, especially if the provisions

---

[60] *See* United States v. Percheman, 32 U.S. (7 Pet.) 51, 88–89 (1833).
[61] *See* Carlos Manuel Vázquez, *The Four Doctrines of Self-Executing Treaties*, 89 AM. J. INT'L L. 695 (1995).
[62] United States v. Postal, 589 F.2d 862, 876 (5th Cir. 1979).
[63] *See* RESTATEMENT (THIRD) OF THE FOREIGN RELATIONS LAW OF THE UNITED STATES, *supra* note 4, § 111, cmt. h; RESTATEMENT (FOURTH) OF THE FOREIGN RELATIONS LAW OF THE UNITED STATES, *supra* note 4, § 310, reporters' note 8.
[64] *See, e.g., Postal*, 589 F.2d at 876; Diggs v. Richardson, 555 F.2d 848, 851 (D.C. Cir. 1976); Vázquez, *supra* note 61, at 708.

concern the rights of individuals.⁶⁵ Courts have been less likely to treat multilateral treaties as self-executing, especially when the treaties overlap with federal statutes.⁶⁶ Some multilateral treaties, however, such as the Warsaw Convention for the Unification of Certain Rules Relating to International Transportation by Air (which governs the liability of international air carriers), and the Convention on Contracts for the International Sale of Goods (which provides contractual default rules for international sales agreements) have been held to be directly enforceable by U.S. courts.⁶⁷ Also, as will be discussed in Chapter 8, treaty provisions governing the immunity of diplomats and consular officials have been assumed to be self-executing.

Starting in the 1970s, some lower courts adopted multifactored balancing tests for determining whether a treaty provision was self-executing.⁶⁸ The following list of factors is illustrative: "the purposes of the treaty and the objectives of its creators, the existence of domestic procedures and institutions appropriate for direct implementation, the availability and feasibility of alternative enforcement methods, and the immediate and long-range consequences of self—or non-self-execution."⁶⁹ Some of these factors, it should be noted, do not seem directly related to the intent of the parties, but rather appear to be focused on the domestic consequences of finding self-execution. Courts may also give weight to the executive branch's view of whether a treaty is self-executing,⁷⁰ again a factor that is not necessarily tied to the collective intent of the parties. In its 2008 decision in *Medellin v. Texas*, which will be discussed, the Supreme Court was not receptive to a multifactored approach whereby a particular treaty provision could be self-executing in some cases and not in others, but it nevertheless took into account a number of considerations in making its self-execution determination.

Third, should courts apply a presumption in favor of self-execution, a presumption against self-execution, or no presumption at all? Some commentators have argued that, in light of the inclusion of treaties in the Supremacy Clause, there should be a strong presumption in favor of self-execution.⁷¹ Other commentators have challenged this position,

---

⁶⁵ *See, e.g.*, Clark v. Allen, 331 U.S. 503, 507–508 (1947); Asakura v. City of Seattle, 265 U.S. 332, 341–43 (1924); United States v. Rauscher, 119 U.S. 407, 418–19 (1886).
⁶⁶ *See, e.g., Postal*, 589 F.2d at 878–80.
⁶⁷ *See, e.g.*, Trans World Airlines, Inc. v. Franklin Mint Corp., 466 U.S. 243, 252 (1984) (observing that the Warsaw Convention "is a self-executing treaty" and that "no domestic legislation is required to give the Convention the force of law in the United States"); Delchi Carrier Spa v. Rotorex Corp., 71 F.3d 1024, 1027 (2d Cir. 1995) (describing the Convention on Contracts for the International Sale of Goods as "a self-executing agreement between the United States and other signatories").
⁶⁸ *See, e.g.*, Frolova v. Union of Soviet Socialist Republics, 761 F.2d 370, 373 (7th Cir. 1985); *Postal*, 589 F.2d at 877; People of Saipan v. U.S. Dep't of Interior, 502 F.2d 90, 97 (9th Cir. 1974).
⁶⁹ *Postal*, 589 F.2d at 877 (quoting *Saipan*, 502 F.2d at 97).
⁷⁰ *See* Republic of the Marshall Islands v. United States, 865 F.3d 1187, 1199 (9th Cir. 2017); Doe v. Holder, 763 F.3d 251, 256 (2d Cir. 2014); More v. Intelcom Support Servs., Inc., 960 F.2d 466, 471–72 (5th Cir. 1992).
⁷¹ *See, e.g.*, LOUIS HENKIN, FOREIGN AFFAIRS AND THE UNITED STATES CONSTITUTION 201 (2d ed. 1996); Martin S. Flaherty, *History Right?: Historical Scholarship, Original Understanding, and Treaties as "Supreme*

arguing, among other things, that a presumption against self-execution would promote democratic values by requiring the involvement of the House of Representatives in treaty implementation.[72] It does not appear that lower courts in recent years have applied a presumption in favor of self-execution; indeed, in some cases they appear to have presumed that treaties are not generally enforceable by the courts.[73]

Fourth, what is the precise domestic status of a non–self-executing treaty? Some commentators have argued that non–self-executing treaties simply lack a private right of action and thus can be enforced by courts when such a right of action is not necessary, such as when a treaty is invoked defensively in a criminal proceeding or when there is some other source for the cause of action.[74] Other commentators, including this author, have argued that non–self-executing treaties do not confer any judicially enforceable rights.[75] Some lower courts have gone even further, suggesting that non–self-executing treaties have no status whatsoever as domestic law.[76]

The VCCR Litigation

The Supreme Court addressed the self-execution doctrine at some length in its 2008 decision, *Medellin v. Texas*,[77] which sheds light on some of the above questions even if it does

---

Law of the Land," 99 COLUM. L. REV. 2095 (1999); Carlos M. Vázquez, *Laughing at Treaties*, 99 COLUM. L. REV. 2154 (1999).

[72] *See* John C. Yoo, *Treaties and Public Lawmaking: A Textual and Structural Defense of Non–Self-Execution*, 99 COLUM. L. REV. 2218 (1999).

[73] *See, e.g.*, ESAB Group, Inc. v. Zurich Ins. PLC, 685 F.3d 376, 387 (4th Cir. 2012) (noting "an emerging presumption against finding treaties to be self-executing"); United States v. Emuegbunam, 268 F.3d 377, 389 (6th Cir. 2001) ("As a general rule . . . international treaties do not create rights that are privately enforceable in the federal courts."); United States v. Jimenez-Nava, 243 F.3d 192, 195 (5th Cir. 2001) (noting that treaties "do not generally create rights that are enforceable in the courts"); Goldstar (Panama) S.A. v. United States, 967 F.2d 965, 968 (4th Cir. 1992) ("International treaties are not presumed to create rights that are privately enforceable.").

[74] *See* David Sloss, *Ex parte Young and Federal Remedies for Human Rights Treaty Violations*, 75 WASH. L. REV. 1103 (2000).

[75] *See* Curtis A. Bradley, *The Military Commissions Act, Habeas Corpus, and the Geneva Conventions*, 101 AM. J. INT'L L. 322, 337–38 (2007). *See also Republic of the Marshall Islands*, 865 F.3d at 1193 ("Because non–self-executing treaty provisions are not judicially enforceable, claims seeking to enforce them are nonjusticiable."); Auguste v. Ridge, 395 F.3d 123, 132 & 133 n.7 (3d Cir. 2005) ("Treaties that are not self-executing do not create judicially-enforceable rights unless they are first given effect by implementing legislation."); Flores v. Southern Peru Copper Corp., 343 F.3d 140, 163 (2d Cir. 2003) ("Non-self-executing treaties 'require implementing action by the political branches of government or . . . are otherwise unsuitable for judicial application.' ").

[76] *See, e.g.*, ITC Ltd. v. Punchgini, Inc., 482 F.3d 135, 161 n.21 (2d Cir. 2007) ("Non-self-executing treaties do not become effective as domestic law until implementing legislation is enacted."); Renkel v. United States, 456 F.3d 640, 643 (6th Cir. 2006) ("'[N]on–self-executing' treaties do require domestic legislation to have the force of law.").

[77] Medellin v. Texas, 552 U.S. 491 (2008).

not conclusively resolve them.[78] The *Medellín* case concerned the Vienna Convention on Consular Relations (VCCR). The VCCR, which the United States ratified in 1969, regulates the establishment and functions of consulates and the immunity of consular officials.[79] Article 36 of the VCCR provides that when one party country arrests a national of another party country, the arrested individual shall have the right to have his or her consulate notified of the arrest and the right to communicate with that consulate.[80] It further provides that the arresting authorities "shall inform the person concerned without delay" of these rights.[81] When it ratified the VCCR, the United States also became a party to an Optional Protocol to the VCCR that gives the International Court of Justice (ICJ) jurisdiction to hear disputes arising under the Convention.[82]

In 1994, a Mexican national, Jose Ernesto Medellín, was convicted of murder in a Texas state court and sentenced to death. At that time, he was not advised of his rights under Article 36. Ten years later, in *Case Concerning Avena and Other Mexican Nationals*, the ICJ ruled that the United States was legally obligated to provide "review and reconsideration" of the convictions and sentences of fifty-one Mexican nationals on death row throughout the United States, including Medellín, because of violations of Article 36.[83]

Although the U.S. executive branch took the position that the ICJ's decision did not have direct effect in the U.S. legal system, it acknowledged that the United States was bound under international law to comply with that decision. Under Article 94 of the United Nations Charter, which the United States has been a party to since 1945, each member of the United Nations "undertakes to comply with the decision of the [ICJ] in any case to which it is a party."[84] Article 94 also provides that if a party to an ICJ case fails to perform the obligations imposed on it by an ICJ judgment, "the other party may have recourse to the [United Nations] Security Council, which may, if it deems necessary, make recommendations or decide upon measures to be taken to give effect to the judgment."[85] In an effort to comply with the *Avena* decision, President George W. Bush

---

[78] For discussion of the *Medellín* decision and its implications for treaty self-execution, *see* Curtis A. Bradley, *Intent, Presumptions, and Non–Self-Executing Treaties*, 102 AM. J. INT'L 540 (2008); Curtis A. Bradley, *Self-Execution and Treaty Duality*, 2008 SUP. CT. REV. 131; David H. Moore, *Do U.S. Courts Discriminate against Treaties?: Equivalence, Duality, and Non–Self-Execution*, 110 COLUM. L. REV. 2228 (2010); Carlos Manuel Vázquez, *Treaties as Law of the Land: The Supremacy Clause and the Judicial Enforcement of Treaties*, 122 HARV. L. REV. 599 (2008).
[79] *See* Vienna Convention on Consular Relations, Apr. 24, 1963, 21 U.S.T. 77, 596 U.N.T.S. 261.
[80] *Id.*, art. 36(1).
[81] *Id.*, art. 36(1)(b).
[82] *See* Optional Protocol Concerning the Compulsory Settlement of Disputes, Apr. 24, 1963, 21 U.S.T. 77, 169, 596 U.N.TS 487, 488.
[83] *See* Case Concerning Avena and Other Mexican Nationals (Mexico v. United States), 2004 I.C.J. No. 128 (Judgment), Mar. 31, 2004, 43 I.L.M. 581.
[84] United Nations Charter, June 26, 1945, art. 94(1), 59 Stat. 1051, T.S. No. 933.
[85] *Id.*, art. 94(2).

issued a memorandum directing state courts to provide review and reconsideration in the fifty-one cases addressed by the ICJ.[86]

Despite the ICJ's decision and the president's memorandum, the Texas Court of Criminal Appeals denied Medellin review and reconsideration, reasoning that he had not met the requirements under state law for obtaining a new hearing. The U.S. Supreme Court upheld this decision. The Court did not decide whether Article 36 of the VCCR is self-executing because the Court had already held in an earlier case that even if Article 36 is self-executing, it should not be interpreted to override state procedural default rules.[87] Although the Court acknowledged that the United States was obligated by Article 94 of the UN Charter to comply with the ICJ's decision, the Court agreed with the executive branch that this particular obligation was not self-executing. The Court noted that Article 94 "does not provide that the United States 'shall' or 'must' comply with an ICJ decision, nor indicate that the Senate that ratified the U.N. Charter intended to vest ICJ decisions with immediate legal effect in U.S. courts."[88] The Court further reasoned that the provision in Article 94 for enforcement of ICJ decisions through the UN Security Council "is itself evidence that ICJ judgments were not meant to be enforceable in domestic courts."[89]

Although the Court was not entirely clear, it appears to have viewed the intent of the U.S. treaty-makers as dispositive on the question of self-execution. The Court stated that "[o]ur cases simply require courts to decide whether a treaty's terms reflect a determination *by the President who negotiated it and the Senate that confirmed it* that the treaty has domestic effect."[90] The Court also noted that "we have held treaties to be self-executing when the textual provisions indicate that *the President and Senate* intended for the agreement to have domestic effect."[91] And, in summarizing its finding of non–self-execution, the Court explained that "[n]othing in the text, background, negotiating and drafting history, or practice among signatory nations suggests that the *President or Senate* intended the improbable result of giving the judgments of an international tribunal a higher status than that enjoyed by 'many of our most fundamental constitutional protections.' "[92] In addition to these statements, the Court relied on the U.S. ratification history

---

[86] *See* George W. Bush, Memorandum for the Attorney General, *Compliance with the Decision of the International Court of Justice in Avena* (Feb. 28, 2005), *at* http://georgewbush-whitehouse.archives.gov/news/releases/2005/02/20050228-18.html. Shortly thereafter, the United States informed the Secretary-General of the United Nations that it was withdrawing from the Optional Protocol to the VCCR, a move presumably designed to preclude additional cases from being filed against the United States for breaches of the VCCR. *See* Adam Liptak, *U.S. Says It Has Withdrawn from World Judicial Body*, N.Y. TIMES (Mar. 10, 2005).

[87] *See* Sanchez-Llamas v. Oregon, 548 U.S. 331 (2006).

[88] Medellin v. Texas, 552 U.S. 491, 508 (2008).

[89] *Id.* at 509.

[90] *Id.* at 521 (emphasis added).

[91] *Id.* at 519 (emphasis added).

[92] *Id.* at 523 (emphasis added) (quoting *Sanchez-Llamas*, 548 U.S. at 360).

for the UN Charter rather than on the collective negotiating history. Furthermore, the Court explained its heavy reliance on the treaty text by stating, "That is after all what the Senate looks to in deciding whether to approve the treaty."[93]

As for the factors that should be considered in discerning this intent, the Court, as noted, placed significant emphasis on treaty text. In particular, the Court suggested that future-oriented treaty language that is directed generically at the states parties rather than at their courts, such as the phrase "undertakes to comply" in Article 94 of the UN Charter, is indicative of non–self-execution.[94] The Court also looked at the understanding of the executive branch at the time the president submitted the Charter to the Senate for its advice and consent. The Court rejected a multifactored approach suggested by the dissent in that case, pursuant to which courts would rely on "practical, context-specific criteria" in determining whether a treaty provision was self-executing.[95] The Court explained that such an approach would be too indeterminate and would improperly "assign to the courts—not the political branches—the primary role in deciding when and how international agreements will be enforced."[96] The Court did not rule out more categorical references to contextual factors, however, and it seems likely that considerations such as the subject matter of a treaty and whether it addresses individual rights will continue to have a bearing on the self-execution analysis.

The Court in *Medellin* implicitly rejected any strong presumption in favor of self-execution. It did not mention such a presumption, and, in concluding that the treaties in question were non–self-executing, it did not require clear evidence of an intent to preclude domestic judicial enforcement. Instead, it examined the text, structure, and ratification history of the treaties to discern whether they were self-executing. The Court also emphasized that "Congress is up to the task of implementing non–self-executing treaties."[97] Nevertheless, the Court did not appear to adopt a presumption against self-execution. Rather, the Court made clear that self-execution should be considered on a treaty-by-treaty basis. The Court stated, for example, that "under our established precedent, some treaties are self-executing and some are not, depending on the treaty."[98] In addition, the Court observed that prior decisions that have found treaties to be self-executing "stand only for the unremarkable proposition that some international

---

[93] *Id.* at 514. *But cf.* David L. Sloss, *Executing* Foster v. Neilson: *The Two-Step Approach to Analyzing Self-Executing Treaties*, 53 HARV. INT'L L.J. 135 (2012) (arguing that there will generally not be any genuine "intent" concerning self-execution).

[94] *Medellin*, 552 U.S. at 508–509. In a concurrence, Justice Stevens agreed with the majority on this point, concluding that the phrase "undertakes to comply" in Article 94(1) of the UN Charter, especially when read in context, is best construed as "contemplat[ing] future action by the political branches." *Id.* at 534 (Stevens, J., concurring).

[95] *See id.* at 549 (Breyer, J., dissenting).

[96] *Id.* at 516.

[97] *Id.* at 521.

[98] *Id.* at 520.

agreements are self-executing and others are not."[99] No "talismanic words" are required for self-execution,[100] the Court continued. The Court's invocation of deference to the executive branch with respect to self-execution was also formulated in treaty-specific terms.[101]

The most ambiguous part of the Court's decision concerns the domestic status of a non–self-executing treaty. The Court appeared to reject the argument that had been made by some commentators that a non–self-executing treaty merely fails to provide a private right of action. A non–self-executing treaty, said the Court, "does not by itself give rise to domestically enforceable federal law."[102] The Court also expressly distinguished the issue of self-execution from the issue of private rights of action. The opinion leaves unclear, however, whether a non–self-executing treaty is simply judicially unenforceable, or whether it more broadly lacks the status of domestic law. On the one hand, the opinion contains numerous statements equating non–self-execution with lack of domestic law status.[103] On the other hand, the opinion also contains statements that equate non–self-execution simply with lack of judicial enforceability,[104] and the Court's test for self-execution appears to focus on whether a treaty is a "directive to domestic courts,"[105] not whether it has the status of domestic law. This distinction between mere judicial unenforceability and lack of domestic law status might be particularly relevant to the authority and obligation of the executive branch to take actions to enforce treaty obligations.

Even if a treaty provision is self-executing, it might not provide particular remedies. This proposition is illustrated by the Supreme Court's 2006 decision in *Sanchez-Llamas v. Oregon*.[106] In that case, one of the claimants sought to have incriminating statements excluded from his state court criminal case because of a violation of Article 36 of the

---

[99] *Id.* at 518.
[100] *Id.* at 521.
[101] *See id.* at 513 ("The Executive Branch has unfailingly adhered to its view *that the relevant treaties* do not create domestically enforceable federal law.") (emphasis added).
[102] *Id.* at 505 n.2.
[103] *See, e.g., id.* at 504 ("This Court has long recognized the distinction between treaties that automatically have effect as domestic law, and those that—while they constitute international law commitments—*do not by themselves function as binding federal law*.") (emphasis added); *id.* at 505 n.2 ("What we mean by 'self-executing' is that the treaty has automatic domestic effect as federal law upon ratification. Conversely, a 'non–self-executing' treaty does not by itself give rise to domestically enforceable federal law."); *id.* at 520 ("[T]he particular treaty obligations on which Medellín relies do not of their own force create domestic law.").
[104] *See, e.g., id.* at 504 ("[N]ot all international law obligations automatically constitute binding federal law *enforceable in United States courts*.") (emphasis added); *id.* ("The question we confront here is whether the *Avena* judgment has automatic *domestic* legal effect *such that the judgment of its own force applies in state and federal courts*.") (second emphasis added); *id.* at 513 ("The pertinent international agreements, therefore, do not provide for implementation of ICJ judgments *through direct enforcement in domestic courts* . . .") (emphasis added).
[105] *See id.* at 508 (stating that Article 94 of the UN Charter is not self-executing because it is not such a directive).
[106] Sanchez-Llamas v. Oregon, 548 U.S. 331 (2006).

VCCR. The Court held that, even if Article 36 is judicially enforceable at the behest of private parties, it does not confer the remedy of suppression of evidence. The Court further stated that it would be "entirely inconsistent with the judicial function" for a U.S. court to create a remedy not contemplated by the treaty.[107]

More generally, even when a treaty is self-executing and thus can in theory provide a rule of decision for the courts, the treaty might not confer a private right to sue for affirmative relief, such as damages or an injunction. Indeed, in *Medellín*, the Court said that there is a presumption that treaties do not confer privately enforceable rights.[108] This limitation on private rights of action further reduces the extent to which treaties are subject to enforcement by the judiciary.[109]

Exclusive Congressional Power and Non–Self-Execution

If a treaty regulates a matter falling with an area of exclusive congressional authority, it will be treated as non–self-executing. When this happens, implementing legislation is required before the treaty will be given domestic effect.

The Supreme Court has not made clear which, if any, congressional powers are exclusive for this purpose. Many are not. Thus, for example, the United States has often entered into treaties regulating international trade, even though Congress has the power to regulate international trade through its foreign commerce power. Probably the strongest candidate for exclusive congressional authority concerns the appropriation of money. The Constitution provides that "[n]o Money shall be drawn from the Treasury, but in Consequence of Appropriations made by Law,"[110] and it has generally been assumed in practice that a treaty does not constitute "Law" for this purpose. Consequently, a treaty

---

[107] *Id.* at 346. *See also* The Amiable Isabella, 19 U.S. (6 Wheat.) 1, 71 (1821) ("[T]o alter, amend, or add to any treaty, by inserting any clause, whether small or great, important or trivial, would be on our part an usurpation of power, and not an exercise of judicial functions.").

[108] *See Medellín*, 552 U.S. at 506 n.3.

[109] *See, e.g.*, McKesson Corp. v. Islamic Republic of Iran, 539 F.3d 485, 488–89 (D.C. Cir. 2008) (concluding that a treaty of amity between the United States and Iran was self-executing but did not confer a private right of action). For a discussion of private rights of action under treaties, and various ways that treaties can be enforced in the United States even when they do not confer a private right of action, *see* Oona A. Hathaway, Sabria McElroy, & Sara Aronchick Solow, *International Law at Home: Enforcing Treaties in U.S. Courts*, 37 YALE J. INT'L L. 51 (2012). As the authors note, before World War II, "the Supreme Court treated the issues of self-execution, private rights, and private rights of action as essentially indistinguishable," in part because the private rights being asserted were traditional common law rights that had long been assumed to be judicially enforceable. *Id.* at 60. By contrast, in the post–World War II era many rights asserted under treaties concern relations between states or between states and individuals, and courts have been more skeptical of the propriety of direct judicial enforcement of such rights. *See id.* at 63.

[110] U.S. CONST. art. I, § 9, cl. 7.

provision calling for the expenditure of money normally will not be given effect in the United States until implemented by Congress.[111]

Another congressional power that has in practice been treated as exclusive is the imposition of federal criminal liability. Since early in U.S. history, it has been settled that there is no federal common law of crimes, and that federal criminal liability therefore requires a statute.[112] Since then, it has generally been assumed that a treaty is not an adequate substitute for a statute, perhaps because concerns about notice and democratic accountability are particularly high in this context.[113] In practice, when a treaty calls for imposing criminal liability, the United States typically waits to ratify the treaty until Congress enacts the necessary legislation.[114]

Yet another congressional power that is a candidate for exclusivity involves the imposition of taxes and duties. The Constitution provides that "[a]ll Bills for raising Revenue shall originate in the House of Representatives."[115] Since the House does not participate in treaty-making, it can be argued that a treaty should not be able to levy taxes or impose duties. Although some judicial dicta support such a limitation,[116] U.S. treaty practice has not consistently reflected it.[117]

---

[111] *See, e.g.*, The Over the Top, 5 F.2d 838, 845 (D. Conn. 1925) ("All treaties requiring the payment of money have been followed by acts of Congress appropriating the amount."); Turner v. Am. Baptist Missionary Union, 24 F. Cas. 344, 345 (C.C.D. Mich. 1852) ("[M]oney cannot be appropriated by the treaty-making power."). There has sometimes been debate over whether Congress has a duty to make appropriations called for by a treaty, an issue that arose as early as the 1794 Jay Treaty. *See* DAVID P. CURRIE, THE CONSTITUTION IN CONGRESS: THE FEDERALIST PERIOD, 1789–1801, at 211–17 (1997). In practice, Congress has reserved to itself independent judgment about whether to make treaty-related appropriations, and the issue is probably a nonjusticiable political question.

[112] *See* United States v. Hudson & Goodwin, 11 (7 Cranch) U.S. 32, 34 (1812); United States v. Coolidge, 14 U.S. (1 Wheat.) 415, 416–17 (1816). This is true of prosecutions in the regular federal courts. Prosecutions of enemy belligerents for violations of the laws of war have been allowed before military tribunals, even in the absence of a statute specifically defining the crimes. *See, e.g.*, Ex parte Quirin, 317 U.S. 1 (1942).

[113] *See* RESTATEMENT (FOURTH) OF THE FOREIGN RELATIONS LAW OF THE UNITED STATES, *supra* note 4, § 310, reporters' note 11; Robert E. Dalton, *National Treaty Law and Practice: United States, in* NATIONAL TREATY LAW AND PRACTICE 788 (Duncan B. Hollis et al. eds., 2005); *see also* Hopson v. Kreps, 622 F.2d 1375, 1380 (9th Cir. 1980); The Over the Top, 5 F.2d 838, 845 (D. Conn. 1925).

[114] Even if domestic criminal liability cannot be imposed by a treaty, a treaty may be able to validly affect the reach of criminal statutes—for example, by regulating the extent of U.S. territorial jurisdiction. *See, e.g.*, Cook v. United States, 288 U.S. 102, 120–21 (1933). *See also* Edwin D. Dickinson, *Are the Liquor Treaties Self-Executing?*, 20 AM. J. INT'L L. 444 (1926).

[115] U.S. CONST. art. I, § 7, cl. 1.

[116] *See, e.g.*, Edwards v. Carter, 580 F.2d 1055, 1058 (D.C. Cir. 1978); Swearingen v. United States, 565 F. Supp. 1019, 1022 (D. Colo. 1983). In *Edwards*, the D.C. Circuit held that Congress's power to "dispose of and make all needful Rules and Regulations respecting the Territory or other Property belonging to the United States," U.S. CONST. art. IV, § 3, cl. 2, was not an exclusive congressional power and thus could be accomplished by treaty.

[117] *See* CRANDALL, *supra* note 13, at 183–99 (discussing the history of treaties addressing revenue). *See also* Retfalvi v. United States, 930 F.3d 600, 608 (4th Cir. 2019) (upholding treaty authorizing the United States to collect unpaid income taxes on behalf of Canada because the treaty "merely facilitates collection of an already existing debt").

A final candidate for exclusivity concerns Congress's authority to declare war. Although the language of the Declare War Clause is not written in exclusive terms, it is arguable that the power to declare war was given to Congress as an important check on the president and as a guarantee that there would be democratic deliberation before the nation committed itself to war, and that a treaty would not adequately serve these purposes.[118] In practice, all declarations of war by the United States have been issued by Congress rather than by treaty.[119]

Non–Self-Execution Declarations

As discussed, the Senate and president sometimes condition U.S. ratification of treaties with various qualifications or interpretive statements. A common declaration that has been included with U.S. ratification of human rights treaties, as well as certain other treaties, is a declaration of non–self-execution, which purports to render all of the substantive terms of the treaty to be non–self-executing and thus judicially unenforceable in the absence of implementing legislation.[120] These declarations are a relatively modern phenomenon. Although there were instances in the nineteenth century in which the United States consented to treaties on the condition that they not take effect until Congress enacted legislation implementing them,[121] non–self-execution declarations do not prevent the treaties from taking effect. Rather, they simply prevent them from

---

[118] *See Edwards*, 580 F.2d at 1058 n.7. For discussion of whether UN Security Council resolutions can provide a constitutional substitute for congressional authorizations of war, see Chapter 10.

[119] *See* Jennifer K. Elsea & Matthew C. Weed, *Declarations of War and Authorizations for the Use of Military Force: Historical Background and Legal Implications* 1 (Cong. Res. Serv., Apr. 14, 2014) ("From the Washington Administration to the present, there have been 11 separate formal declarations of war against foreign nations enacted by Congress and the President, encompassing five different wars—the War of 1812 with Great Britain, the War with Mexico in 1846, the War with Spain in 1898, the First World War, and the Second World War."), *at* https://www.fas.org/sgp/crs/natsec/RL31133.pdf. For an argument that Congress's power to vest jurisdiction in the lower federal courts is also exclusive and thus cannot be exercised by treaty, *see* John T. Parry, *No Appeal: The U.S.–U.K. Supplementary Extradition Treaty's Effort to Create Federal Jurisdiction*, 25 Loy. L.A. Int'l & Comp. L. Rev. 543 (2003).

[120] Most courts have concluded that non–self-execution declarations preclude any judicial enforcement of the treaty. *See, e.g.*, Auguste v. Ridge, 395 F.3d 123, 133 n.7 (3d Cir. 2005) (collecting cases). This is also how the Supreme Court described one of the declarations. *See* Sosa v. Alvarez-Machain, 542 U.S. 692, 735 (2004) (noting that the United States ratified the International Covenant on Civil and Political Rights "on the express understanding that it was not self-executing *and so did not itself create obligations enforceable in the federal courts*") (emphasis added). Some scholars have nevertheless argued that the declarations simply preclude a "private right of action" for damages or other affirmative relief and do not preclude other forms of reliance on the treaties—for example, as a defense to a criminal prosecution, or as a source of law that can be combined with some other law that provides a cause of action. *See, e.g.*, David Sloss, *The Domestication of International Human Rights: Non–Self-Executing Declarations and Human Rights Treaties*, 24 Yale J. Int'l L. 129 (1999).

[121] *See* Bradley & Goldsmith, *supra* note 24, at 408.

being enforced in U.S. courts. These declarations have been criticized by some scholars as being in tension with the Supremacy Clause,[122] but courts consistently have given effect to them.

In the 1950s, in *Power Authority of New York v. Federal Power Commission*, the U.S. Court of Appeals for the D.C. Circuit suggested that a declaration reserving domestic implementation of a treaty for Congress might be unconstitutional.[123] That case concerned a treaty between the United States and Canada concerning the use of the waters of the Niagara River. In giving its advice and consent to the treaty, the Senate included what it referred to as a "reservation" stating that the United States "expressly reserves the right to provide by Act of Congress for redevelopment, for the public use and benefit, of the United States' share of the waters of the Niagara River made available by the provisions of the Treaty, and no project for redevelopment of the United States' share of such waters shall be undertaken until it be specifically authorized by Act of Congress." In order to avoid what it perceived to be significant constitutional concerns, a 2–1 majority of the D.C. Circuit construed the reservation merely to be "an expression of the Senate's desires and not a part of the treaty."[124] In doing so, the court suggested that the treaty power of the president and Senate may not extend to matters of purely domestic concern. For reasons that will be discussed, it is not clear whether there is in fact any such subject matter limitation on the treaty power. In any event, even if there is such a limitation, it is doubtful that it should apply to a non–self-execution declaration, which does not seek to increase the regulatory power of the U.S. treaty-makers, but instead simply seeks to involve the full Congress in the implementation of treaties.[125] Although occasionally invoked by commentators, the *Power Authority* decision has not been a significant precedent in the courts.

---

[122] *See, e.g.*, Henkin, *supra* note 39, at 346 (invoking the Supremacy Clause and arguing that non–self-execution declarations are "against the spirit of the Constitution").

[123] Power Auth. of N.Y. v. Fed. Power Comm'n, 247 F.2d 538 (D.C. Cir. 1957), *vacated and remanded with directions to dismiss as moot sub nom.* Am. Pub. Power Ass'n v. Power Auth., 355 U.S. 64 (1957).

[124] 247 F.2d at 543.

[125] *See* Bradley & Goldsmith, *supra* note 24, at 452–53. *See also* Louis Henkin, *The Treaty Makers and the Law Makers: The Niagara Reservation*, 56 COLUM. L. REV. 1151, 1182 (1956) ("The power exercised in this case by the President and the Senate does not impinge on powers which might otherwise be exercised by the states; it does not limit rights which might otherwise be preserved for the individual citizen; it does not encroach on the legislative power of Congress—it would seem to enable the legislative power to operate more effectively."). The reservation in *Power Authority*, if enforced, would have limited the operation of a preexisting federal statute concerning the Federal Power Commission's licensing authority, and it is possible that the court was concerned about the Senate's use of a reservation to override a statute. This concern would not apply to the non–self-execution declarations included with U.S. ratification of human rights treaties, which do not purport to override statutes.

Last-in-Time Rule

The Constitution states that both federal statutes and treaties are part of the supreme law of the land and thus preempt inconsistent state law, but it does not specify the relationship between these statutes and treaties. On the one hand, it is arguable that, because treaties are concluded through a supermajority process, they should not be subject to being overridden (even domestically) by a mere majority of the legislature. On the other hand, one could argue that, because it takes two houses of Congress to make legislation and the full Congress is more democratic than the Senate acting by itself, statutes should not be subject to being overridden by a treaty.

The Supreme Court has to some extent split the difference between these arguments, adopting what is called the "last-in-time" or "later-in-time" rule: when there is a conflict between a self-executing treaty and a federal statute, U.S. courts are to apply whichever is last in time. When the Court has applied this rule, it has generally been in the context of giving effect to a statute that is inconsistent with an earlier treaty.[126] The Court has explained that to the extent that a treaty has domestic effect and concerns a subject within Congress's power, "it can be deemed in that particular only the equivalent of a legislative act, to be repealed or modified at the pleasure of Congress" and that, "[i]n either case the last expression of the sovereign will must control."[127] In at least one modern decision, the Court has applied the last-in-time rule to give effect to a treaty that was inconsistent with an earlier statute.[128] In addition, lower courts have found provisions in

---

[126] *See* Breard v. Greene, 523 U.S. 371, 376 (1998); Chinese Exclusion Case (Chae Chan Ping v. United States), 130 U.S. 581, 600–601 (1889); Whitney v. Robertson, 124 U.S. 190, 194 (1888); Edye v. Robertson (Head Money Cases), 112 U.S. 580, 597–99 (1884). *See also* The Cherokee Tobacco, 78 U.S. (11 Wall.) 616, 621 (1871); Memorandum for Alan J. Kreczko, Special Assistant to the President and Legal Adviser to the National Security Council, from Christopher Schroeder, Acting Assistant Attorney General, Office of Legal Counsel, *Validity of Congressional-Executive Agreements That Substantially Modify the United States' Obligations under an Existing Treaty* (Nov. 25, 1996), 20 Op. Off. Legal Counsel 389 (1996).

[127] *Chinese Exclusion Case*, 130 U.S. at 600; *see also* Dred Scott v. Sandford, 60 U.S. 393, 629 (1857) (Curtis, J., dissenting) ("[T]hat a treaty with a foreign nation can deprive the Congress of any part of the legislative power conferred by the people, so that it no longer can legislate as it was empowered by the Constitution to do, I more than doubt."); Taylor v. Morton, 23 F. Cas. 784, 786–87 (C.C.D. Mass. 1855) ("To refuse to execute a treaty, for reasons which approve themselves to the conscientious judgment of the nation, is a matter of the utmost gravity and delicacy; but the power to do so, is prerogative, of which no nation can be deprived, without deeply affecting its independence. That the people of the United States have deprived their government of this power in any case, I do not believe. That it must reside somewhere, and be applicable to all cases, I am convinced. I feel no doubt that it belongs to congress.").

[128] *See* Cook v. United States, 288 U.S. 102, 118–19 (1933); *see also* United States v. Schooner Peggy, 5 U.S. (1 Cranch) 103, 110 (1801) ("[W]here a treaty is the law of the land, and as such affects the rights of parties litigating in court, that treaty as much binds those rights and is as much to be regarded by the court as an act of congress."); Hon. Caleb Cushing, *Copyright Convention with Great Britain* (Feb. 16, 1854), 6 Op. Att'y Gen. 291, 293 (1854) ("A treaty, assuming it to be made conformably to the Constitution, in substance and form, has the effect of repealing, under the general conditions of the legal doctrine that '*leges posteriores priores contrarias*

Mutual Legal Assistance Treaties to be self-executing and to supersede an earlier federal statute with respect to the standards for discovery requests made by foreign governments relating to criminal proceedings abroad.[129] Although the last-in-time rule is reasonably well settled in the courts, scholars continue to debate it, with some asserting that statutes should always override treaties,[130] and others asserting that treaties should always override statutes.[131]

The last-in-time rule does not relieve the United States of responsibility under international law for complying with a treaty. As a result, if a court applies a statute to override an earlier treaty, the United States may be placed in breach of its international obligations.[132] Because of the potential foreign relations consequences of such action, courts generally presume that Congress does not intend to override treaties. This presumption is a subset of the "*Charming Betsy*" canon of construction, discussed in Chapter 1, pursuant to which U.S. courts will attempt to construe statutes, where possible, so that they do not conflict with international law (either treaty-based or customary).[133] Since the canon is

---

abrogant,' all pre-existing federal law in conflict with it,—whether unwritten, as law of nations, of admiralty, and common law—or written, as acts of Congress."). In *Cook*, the Supreme Court applied a treaty with Great Britain to limit the authority of the Coast Guard to enforce a liquor-smuggling statute outside of U.S. territorial waters. The Court noted that "in a strict sense the Treaty was self-executing, in that no legislation was necessary to authorize executive action pursuant to its provisions." 288 U.S. at 119.

[129] *See, e.g.*, In re Search of the Premises Located, 634 F.3d 557, 568 (9th Cir. 2011); *In re* Commissioner's Subpoenas, 325 F.3d 1287, 1305–06 (11th Cir. 2003); *In re* Erato, 2 F.3d 11, 15–16 (2d Cir. 1993). Mutual Legal Assistance Treaties are discussed further in Chapter 9.

[130] For an argument, based on Founding intent, that statutes should always take precedence in U.S. courts over treaties, and that treaties that conflict with statutes should be treated as non–self-executing, *see* Vasan Kesavan, *The Three Tiers of Federal Law*, 100 Nw. U. L. Rev. 1479, 1486 (2006). *See also* Akhil Reed Amar, America's Constitution 303 (2005) (similar conclusion); John C. Yoo, *Treaties and Public Lawmaking: A Textual and Structural Defense of Non–Self-Execution*, 99 Colum. L. Rev. 2210, 2243 (1999) (questioning ability of treaties to override federal statutes).

[131] *See, e.g.*, Louis Henkin, *The Constitution and United States Sovereignty: A Century of Chinese Exclusion and Its Progeny*, 100 Harv. L. Rev. 853, 870–72 (1987); Jules Lobel, *The Limits of Constitutional Power: Conflicts between Foreign Policy and International Law*, 71 Va. L. Rev. 1071 (1985). For a defense of the last-in-time rule as currently applied by the courts, *see* Julian G. Ku, *Treaties as Laws: A Defense of the Last-in-Time Rule for Treaties and Federal Statutes*, 80 Ind. L.J. 319 (2005).

[132] *See, e.g.*, Pigeon River Improvement, Slide & Boom Co. v. Charles W. Cox, Ltd., 291 U.S. 138, 160 (1934) (noting that although a federal statute that conflicted with a treaty provision "would control in our courts as the later expression of our municipal law . . . the international obligation [would] remain[] unaffected").

[133] *See* Murray v. The Schooner Charming Betsy, 6 U.S. (2 Cranch) 64, 118 (1804) ("an act of Congress ought never to be construed to violate the law of nations if any other possible construction remains"); Restatement (Third) of the Foreign Relations Law of the United States, *supra* note 4, § 114 ("Where fairly possible, a United States statute is to be construed so as not to conflict with international law or with an international agreement of the United States."); Restatement (Fourth) of the Foreign Relations Law of the United States, *supra* note 4, § 309(1) ("Where fairly possible, courts in the United States will construe federal statutes to avoid a conflict with a treaty provision."). *See also* Curtis A. Bradley, *The* Charming Betsy *Canon and Separation of Powers: Rethinking the Interpretive Role of International Law*, 86 Geo. L.J. 479 (1998) (discussing the history and purposes of this canon of construction).

designed in part to avoid unintended breaches of international law, it probably does not matter whether the treaty is self-executing.[134] The precise strength of the presumption is unclear, with some courts suggesting that it applies only if a statute is ambiguous,[135] and others suggesting that it applies unless Congress has made clear its intent to override the treaty in question.[136] In some cases, the Supreme Court has suggested that there is also in effect a reverse-*Charming Betsy* canon whereby treaties will be construed, where possible, to avoid conflicts with a statute.[137] A conflict between a treaty and an earlier statute may also be a reason to construe the treaty as non–self-executing.[138]

Treaties and the President

The Constitution states that the president "shall take Care that the Laws be faithfully executed." Although the issue has not been resolved by the Supreme Court, it seems likely that the word "Laws" in this clause includes treaties. As noted earlier, treaties are listed

---

[134] *See, e.g.*, Ma v. Ashcroft, 257 F.3d 1095, 1114 (9th Cir. 2001) (applying the canon to avoid a violation of the International Covenant on Civil and Political Rights, even though it has been declared to be non–self-executing). *See also* Bradley, *supra* note 133, at 483 ("[T]he *Charming Betsy* canon presumably applies to *all* international obligations of the United States, regardless of whether they are viewed as enforceable domestic law."); Rebecca Crootoff, Note, *Judicious Influence: Non–Self-Executing Treaties and the* Charming Betsy *Canon*, 120 YALE L.J. 1784, 1790 (2011) (arguing that "ambiguous statutes may be construed in light of all non–self-executing treaties"). *But see* Fund for Animals, Inc. v. Kempthorne, 472 F.2d 872, 880 (D.C. Cir. 2006) (Kavanaugh, J., concurring) ("There is little authority squarely analyzing whether [the *Charming Betsy* canon] should extend to non–self-executing treaties, which have no force as a matter of domestic law.").

[135] *See, e.g., Fund for Animals*, 472 F.3d at 879 ("The canon applies only to ambiguous statutes . . ."). *See also* Trans World Airlines, Inc. v. Franklin Mint Corp., 466 U.S. 243, 252 (1984) ("There is, first, a firm and obviously sound canon of construction against finding implicit repeal of a treaty in ambiguous congressional action.").

[136] *See, e.g.*, Owner-Operator Independent Drivers Association v. United States Department of Transportation, 724 F.3d 230, 234 (D.C. Cir. 2013) ("[A]bsent some clear and overt indication from Congress, we will not construe a statute to abrogate existing international agreements even when the statute's text is not itself ambiguous."). *See also* Cook v. United States, 288 U.S. 102, 120 (1933) ("A treaty will not be deemed to have been abrogated or modified by a later statute unless such purpose on the part of Congress has been clearly expressed.").

[137] *See* Johnson v. Browne, 205 U.S. 309, 321 (1907); United States v. Lee Yen Tai, 185 U.S. 213, 222 (1902).

[138] *See* Bradley, *Self-Execution and Treaty Duality, supra* note 78, at 162–63; Timothy Wu, *Treaties' Domains*, 93 VA. L. REV. 571, 595–96 (2007). Because of Congress's last-in-time authority, as well as its authority to regulate the jurisdiction of the federal courts, Congress probably has the authority to enact legislation that precludes judicial enforcement of an otherwise self-executing treaty. As a possible illustration, Section 5(a) of the Military Commissions Act of 2006 provided that: "No person may invoke the Geneva Conventions or any protocols thereto in any habeas corpus or other civil action or proceeding to which the United States, or . . . agent of the United States is a party as a source of rights in any court of the United States or its States or territories." Pub. L. No. 109–366, 120 Stat. 2600, § 5(a). For discussion of this provision, *see* Curtis A. Bradley, *The Military Commissions Act, Habeas Corpus, and the Geneva Conventions*, 101 AM. J. INT'L L. 322, 339–40 (2007), and Carlos Manuel Vázquez, *The Military Commissions Act, the Geneva Conventions, and the Courts: A Critical Guide*, 101 AM. J. INT'L L. 73, 86 (2007). *See also* Noriega v. Pastrana, 564 F.3d 1290, 1296 (11th Cir. 2009) (applying this provision to bar a Geneva Convention claim).

as part of the "supreme Law of the Land" in the Supremacy Clause. Moreover, there is no question that "Laws" includes federal statutes, and, as discussed, the status of treaties in the U.S. legal system (at least when they are self-executing) is similar to that of statutes. The records of the drafting of the U.S. Constitution are at least suggestive that "Laws" was meant to include treaties,[139] and in a famous early debate between Alexander Hamilton and James Madison about presidential power, both agreed that treaties were encompassed by the Take Care Clause.[140]

To say that treaties are part of the "Laws" in the Take Care Clause does not mean that they are judicially enforceable against the president. As discussed, treaties are judicially enforceable only if they are self-executing. In addition, the justiciability limitations discussed in Chapter 1 (such as the political question doctrine) may be particularly likely to apply to claims brought against the president. Furthermore, it is possible that, despite the Take Care Clause, the president has some constitutional authority to violate treaties. The last-in-time rule is premised on the assumption that one of the sovereign powers of the United States is the power not to comply with a treaty (and accept whatever international consequences may follow). Sometimes, however, only the president can exercise the sovereignty of the United States. This may be true, for example, when carrying out certain functions as Commander in Chief.[141]

Judicial enforceability of a treaty against the president is more likely if Congress has incorporated the treaty into U.S. law. As discussed in Chapter 10, this was the case in *Hamdan v. Rumsfeld*, a 2006 decision in which the Supreme Court held invalid the military commission system that President Bush had established after the September 11, 2001, attacks.[142] The Court in that case applied a treaty provision—Common Article 3 of the Geneva Conventions—because it found that Congress had implicitly incorporated the treaty provision in statutory provisions governing military commissions.[143]

The Take Care Clause may operate not only as a restriction on the president, but also as a source of presidential authority. The Clause was invoked in this way in the

---

[139] *See* Curtis A. Bradley, *The Alien Tort Statute and Article III*, 42 Va. J. Int'l L. 587, 602 n.65 (2002).

[140] *See* Alexander Hamilton, *Pacificus No. 1* (1793), *reprinted in* 15 The Papers of Alexander Hamilton 33, 38 (Harold C. Syrett ed., 1969); James Madison, *Helvidius Number 1* (1793), *reprinted in* 15 The Papers of James Madison 66, 69 (Thomas Mason et al. eds., 1985).

[141] *Cf.* Derek Jinks & David Sloss, *Is the President Bound by the Geneva Conventions?*, 90 Cornell L. Rev. 97 (2004). For a historically based argument that the scope of the president's exclusive commander-in-chief authority is limited to superintending the military chain of command, *see* David J. Barron & Martin S. Lederman, *The Commander in Chief at the Lowest Ebb—Framing the Problem, Doctrine, and Original Understanding*, 121 Harv. L. Rev. 689 (2008), and David J. Barron & Martin S. Lederman, *The Commander in Chief at the Lowest Ebb—A Constitutional History*, 121 Harv. L. Rev. 941 (2008). For discussion of additional issues concerning the relationship between non–self-executing treaties and presidential authority, see Restatement (Fourth) of the Foreign Relations Law of the United States, *supra* note 4, § 310, reporters' note 13.

[142] *See* Hamdan v. Rumsfeld, 548 U.S. 557 (2006).

[143] *See id.* at 629–31.

above-mentioned debate between Hamilton and Madison over a controversial neutrality proclamation issued by President Washington in 1793.[144] John Marshall also invoked the Clause in this way when defending President John Adams's extradition of a criminal suspect pursuant to an extradition treaty.[145] In the modern era, President Truman invoked the Take Care Clause to support the seizure of U.S. steel mills during the Korean War, although this invocation of the Clause was famously repudiated by the Supreme Court in the *Youngstown* case.[146]

In the *Medellin* case described earlier, the Court held that President Bush did not have the authority under the Take Care Clause to implement a judgment of the International Court of Justice by preempting state law, even though the United States had a treaty obligation to comply with the judgment. The Court had concluded earlier in its opinion that the treaty obligation to comply with the judgment was non–self-executing and thus did not of its own force preempt state law. The Take Care Clause did not give the president the authority to create such preemptive effect, reasoned the Court, because this Clause "allows the President to execute the laws, not make them."[147] Although the Court did not elaborate on this point, it did make clear that the president could comply with non–self-executing treaty obligations "by some other means, so long as they are consistent with the Constitution."[148]

Prohibition of State Treaty-Making

Article I, Section 10 of the Constitution prohibits the states from engaging in certain activities, including entering into "any Treaty." The treaty power is therefore an exclusive power of the national government. But the states are allowed to enter into an "Agreement or Compact" if they obtain congressional approval. The Constitution does not, however, explain the difference between treaties and agreements or compacts.[149]

In a nineteenth-century extradition case, the Supreme Court suggested that treaties impose ongoing obligations, whereas agreements and compacts address temporary

---

[144] *See* Hamilton, *supra* note 140, at 40.
[145] *See* 10 ANNALS OF CONG. 613–14 (1800).
[146] *See* Youngstown Sheet & Tube Co. v. Sawyer, 343 U.S. 579, 587–88 (1952). *See also* Edward T. Swaine, *Taking Care of Treaties*, 108 COLUM. L. REV. 331, 402 (2008) (arguing that the Take Care Clause "confers limited authority on the President as a function of his duty to enforce treaty obligations").
[147] Medellin v. Texas, 552 U.S. 491, 532 (2008).
[148] *Id.* at 530.
[149] *See generally* CRANDALL, *supra* note 13, at 141. *See also* Abraham C. Weinfeld, *What Did the Framers of the Federal Constitution Mean by "Agreements or Compacts?,"* 3 CHI. L. REV. 453, 464 (1936) ("To summarize, 'agreements or compacts' as intended by the framers of the Constitution included (1) settlements of boundary lines with attending cession or exchange of strips of land, (2) regulation of matters connected with boundaries as for instance regulation of jurisdiction of offenses committed on boundary waters, of fisheries or of navigation.").

matters.[150] A somewhat different theory, advocated by the prominent nineteenth-century Supreme Court justice and scholar, Joseph Story, is that treaties concern military and political accords, whereas agreements and compacts concern "mere private rights of sovereignty; such as questions of boundary; interests in land, situate in the territory of each other; and other internal regulations for the mutual comfort, and convenience of states, bordering on each other."[151]

Some arrangements between states and foreign nations are not even considered agreements or compacts and thus have been permitted even without Congress's consent. For example, states have often engaged in sister-city relationships with foreign cities and have formed nonbinding understandings concerning trade or investment with foreign countries.[152] In referring to agreements between U.S. states, the Supreme Court has stated that the distinction between agreements that require congressional consent and those that do not turns on whether the agreement tends to "increase [the] political power in the States, which may encroach upon or interfere with the just supremacy of the United States."[153] In recent years, some states and localities have unilaterally adopted international standards, such as standards governing antidiscrimination and environmental protection, even though the federal government has not ratified treaties containing these standards.[154] These local acts of incorporation are probably valid as long as they do not conflict with existing treaty commitments or federal statutes.[155]

Relationship of Treaties to U.S. Federalism

As noted in Chapter 1, although Congress has broad regulatory authority, this authority is not unlimited, and the Supreme Court has occasionally invalidated federal legislation

---

[150] *See* Holmes v. Jennison, 39 U.S. (14 Pet.) 540, 572 (1840) (opinion of Taney, C.J.).

[151] 3 JOSEPH STORY, COMMENTARIES ON THE CONSTITUTION OF THE UNITED STATES § 1397, at 272 (Fred B. Rothman & Co. 1999) (1833).

[152] *See* EARL H. FRY, THE EXPANDING ROLE OF STATE AND LOCAL GOVERNMENTS IN U.S. FOREIGN AFFAIRS 90 (1998).

[153] Virginia v. Tennessee, 148 U.S. 503, 519 (1893). *See also* United States Steel Corp. v. Multistate Tax Comm'n, 434 U.S. 452, 471 (1978) (applying the test from *Virginia v. Tennessee*); New Hampshire v. Maine, 426 U.S. 363, 369 (1976) (same).

[154] For discussion of this phenomenon, see, for example, Catherine Powell, *Dialogic Federalism: Constitutional Possibilities for Incorporation of Human Rights Law in the United States*, 150 U. PA. L. REV. 245 (2001); Judith Resnik, *Rethinking Horizontal Federalism and Foreign Affairs Preemption in Light of Translocal Internationalism*, 57 EMORY L.J. 31 (2007); and Lesley Wexler, *Take the Long Way Home: Sub-Federal Integration of Unratified and Non–Self-Executing Federal Treaty Law*, 28 MICH. J. INT'L L. 1 (2006).

[155] In 2019, the federal government sued the state of California concerning a "cap-and-trade" agreement that California had entered into with the provincial government of Quebec, Canada, in an effort to combat climate change. The federal government alleged that California was violating Article I, Section 10 of the Constitution. For a rejection of this argument by a federal district court, see United States v. California, No. 2:19-cv-02142 WBS EFB (E.D. Cal. Mar. 12, 2020).

as invading the reserved powers of the states. The Court has held, however, that the treaty power is not limited to the scope of Congress's powers. In a 1920 decision, *Missouri v. Holland*, the Court considered the constitutionality of a migratory bird protection statute, which implemented a treaty between the United States and Great Britain.[156] Two federal district courts had held that a similar statute that had been enacted prior to the conclusion of the treaty was unconstitutional because it invaded the reserved power of the states to control natural resources within their borders.[157] In an opinion authored by Justice Holmes, the Supreme Court reasoned that, even if those decisions were correct, their reasoning was no longer valid once a treaty was in place. The Court noted that the Tenth Amendment merely reserves powers to the states that have not been delegated to the national government, whereas the treaty power has been so delegated, and that the Constitution also precludes states from engaging in treaties.[158] In addition, the Court observed that the treaty in question did not "contravene any prohibitory words" in the Constitution, and so the only question was whether it was "forbidden by some invisible radiation from the general terms of the Tenth Amendment."[159] This decision thus makes clear that the national government has more authority to regulate state and local matters when using the treaty power than when acting solely pursuant to Congress's legislative authority.[160]

Some of Justice Holmes's reasoning could be questioned. For example, the mere fact that the treaty power is an exclusive national government power does not necessarily mean that it is unconstrained by federalism.[161] One could also question as being unduly formalistic Holmes's distinction between a lack of power and a prohibition on the exercise of power. Perhaps a better argument for the holding in *Holland* is that the constitutional requirement of supermajority senatorial approval of treaties provides an adequate process protection for state interests, making judicial protection unnecessary. It has been suggested at times that the courts should not enforce federalism limitations on Congress because the legislative process adequately protects the states, and the Supreme Court has sometimes embraced that argument.[162] Although this process argument has

---

[156] Missouri v. Holland, 252 U.S. 416 (1920).

[157] *See* United States v. McCullagh, 221 F. 288 (D. Kan. 1915); United States v. Shauver, 214 F. 154 (E.D. Ark. 1914).

[158] *Holland*, 252 U.S. at 432.

[159] *Id.* at 433–34. For discussion of *Holland*, see Curtis A. Bradley, *The Treaty Power and American Federalism*, 97 MICH. L. REV. 390 (1998); Bradley, *supra* note 37; David M. Golove, *Treaty-Making and the Nation: The Historical Foundations of the Nationalist Conception of the Treaty Power*, 98 MICH. L. REV. 1075 (2000). *See also* Charles A. Lofgren, Missouri v. Holland *in Historical Perspective*, 1975 SUP. CT. REV. 77 (1975).

[160] *See also* United States v. Lara, 541 U.S. 193, 201 (2004) ("[A]s Justice Holmes pointed out, treaties made pursuant to [the treaty] power can authorize Congress to deal with 'matters' with which otherwise 'Congress could not deal.'" (citing *Holland*, 252 U.S. at 433)).

[161] *See* William E. Mikell, *The Extent of the Treaty-Making Power of the President and Senate of the United States (Pt. II)*, 57 U. PA. L. REV. 528, 539–40 (1909).

[162] *See* Herbert Wechsler, *The Political Safeguards of Federalism: The Role of the States in the Composition and Selection of the National Government*, 54 COLUM. L. REV. 543 (1954); Jesse H. Choper, *The Scope of the National Power* vis-à-vis *the States: The Dispensability of Judicial Review*, 86 YALE L.J. 1552 (1977). *See also*

been challenged and does not appear to be the view of the current Supreme Court, the argument is probably stronger for treaties than for legislation. Certainly it is easy to think of examples in which the Senate has either opposed treaties or has insisted on conditions to treaties in an effort to protect state interests. It should be noted, however, that treaty provisions are often vague, in which case their federalism implications might not be apparent at the time of ratification. Perhaps more importantly, this process argument would apply only to Article II treaties, not to the much larger number of executive agreements concluded by the United States.[163]

Another significant holding of *Holland* concerns the Constitution's Necessary and Proper Clause. This Clause provides that Congress has the power "[t]o make all Laws which shall be necessary and proper for carrying into Execution" both its own powers and the powers vested in the other branches of the government. The Supreme Court has interpreted this power broadly to allow Congress to enact any legislation "rationally related to the implementation of a constitutionally enumerated power."[164] In *Holland*, Congress had implemented the migratory bird treaty, and the Court reasoned that, as long as the treaty was constitutionally valid, the statute was also valid under the Necessary and Proper Clause, even if Congress would have lacked the authority to enact the statute in the absence of the treaty.[165]

In 2014, the Supreme Court had an opportunity to revisit these issues, in *Bond v. United States*, but it resolved the case on other grounds.[166] *Bond* involved a criminal

---

Garcia v. San Antonio Metro. Transit Auth., 469 U.S. 528, 552 (1985) ("State sovereign interests ... are more properly protected by procedural safeguards inherent in the structure of the federal system than by judicially created limitations on federal power."). *But cf.* John C. Yoo, *The Judicial Safeguards of Federalism*, 70 S. CAL. L. REV. 1311, 1312 (1997) (arguing that, since *Garcia*, the Supreme Court has "reasserted the applicability of judicial review to questions concerning state sovereignty and the proper balance between the national and state governments").

[163] *See* David Sloss, *International Agreements and the Political Safeguards of Federalism*, 55 STAN. L. REV. 1963 (2003).

[164] United States v. Comstock, 560 U.S. 126, 134 (2010). *See also* McCulloch v. Maryland, 17 U.S. 316, 421 (1819) ("Let the end be legitimate, let it be within the scope of the constitution, and all means which are appropriate, which are plainly adapted to that end, which are not prohibited, but consist with the letter and spirit of the constitution, are constitutional.").

[165] *Holland*, 252 U.S. at 432; *see also* Neely v. Henkel, 180 U.S. 109, 121 (1901) (stating that Congress's authority under the Necessary and Proper Clause "includes the power to enact such legislation as is appropriate to give efficacy to any stipulation which it is competent for the President by and with the advice and consent of the Senate to insert in a treaty with a foreign power"); United States v. Park, 938 F.3d 354, 363–64 (D.C. Cir. 2019). For a critique of *Holland*'s Necessary and Proper Clause holding, *see* Nicholas Quinn Rosenkranz, *Executing the Treaty Power*, 118 HARV. L. REV. 1867 (2005) (arguing that the Necessary and Proper Clause gives Congress only the power to enact legislation to facilitate the making of treaties, not the implementation of treaties already made). *But see* Jean Galbraith, *Congress's Treaty-Implementing Power in Historical Practice*, 56 WM. & MARY L. REV. 59 (2014) (arguing that historical practice supports Congress's authority to use the Necessary and Proper Clause to implement treaties).

[166] *See* 572 U.S. 844 (2014).

prosecution under legislation that implements the Chemical Weapons Convention.[167] In that case, the defendant had stolen chemicals from her employer and used them in an effort to poison a romantic rival. Although the defendant's conduct fell within a literal reading of the legislation (i.e., the use of "toxic chemicals" for other than a "peaceful purpose"), the Court expressed concern that such a reading "would transform the statute from one whose core concerns are acts of war, assassination, and terrorism into a massive federal anti-poisoning regime that reaches the simplest of assaults."[168]

In rejecting such a broad reading of the statute, the Court in *Bond* applied a presumption that Congress does not intend to intrude on traditional areas of state authority, such as the prosecution of local crime, absent a clear indication that Congress intended that result.[169] Although the Court had previously applied that presumption to purely domestic legislation, the *Bond* decision is significant in extending the presumption to treaty implementation legislation. Instead of a literal reading of the statute, the Court applied what it described as the "natural meaning" of the term "chemical weapon," which it said involved a consideration of "both the particular chemicals that the defendant used and the circumstances in which she used them."[170] In concluding that the defendant's conduct did not fall within that natural meaning, the Court noted that the chemicals at issue there were "not of the sort that an ordinary person would associate with instruments of chemical warfare."[171] Several justices concurred in the judgment, arguing for various constitutional limitations on the treaty power.[172]

Even if the Supreme Court would fully reaffirm its analysis today, *Holland* does not address all of the possible federalism limitations on the national government. For example, the Supreme Court has held that Congress may not "commandeer" state legislative and executive officials to carry out federal programs.[173] The basis for this limitation is

---

[167] The Court had previously held in the case that the defendant had standing to argue that the statute exceeds federalism limits on Congress's authority. *See* Bond v. United States, 564 U.S. 211 (2011). In reaching this conclusion, the Court emphasized the importance of federalism to the protection of individual liberty. *See id.* at 221–22.

[168] 572 U.S. at 863. In implementing the Chemical Weapons Convention, Congress largely copied language from the Convention. While that language may be perfectly adequate for purposes of international relations, it lacks some of the specificity and precision that is appropriate for domestic criminal legislation. *See* Curtis A. Bradley, *Federalism, Treaty Implementation, and Political Process: Bond v. United States*, 108 AM. J. INT'L L. 486 (2014); Kevin L. Cope, *Lost in Translation: The Accidental Origins of Bond v. United States*, 112 MICH. L. REV. FIRST IMPRESSIONS 133 (2014).

[169] *See* 572 U.S. at 860.

[170] *Id.* at 861.

[171] *Id.*

[172] *See id.* at 876 (Scalia, J., concurring in the judgment) (arguing for limits on Congress's Necessary and Proper Clause authority to implement treaties); *id.* at 892 (Thomas, J., concurring in the judgment) (arguing for subject matter limits on the treaty power).

[173] *See* Murphy v. NCAA, 138 S. Ct. 1461 (2018); Printz v. United States, 521 U.S. 898 (1997); New York v. United States, 505 U.S. 144 (1992). *See also* Reno v. Condon, 528 U.S. 141, 149 (2000) ("In *New York* and *Printz*, we held federal statutes invalid, not because Congress lacked legislative authority over the subject matter, but because those statutes violated the principles of federalism contained in the Tenth Amendment.").

the "dual sovereignty" structure of the U.S. constitutional system rather than enumerated power limitations on Congress, so there is a reasonable argument that it applies to the treaty power as well as to legislation.[174] In addition, the Court has held that states have broad sovereign immunity from private lawsuits, and that Congress has only limited authority to override that immunity.[175] The Court has reasoned that sovereign immunity protects the "dignity" of states "as residuary sovereigns and joint participants in the governance of the Nation."[176] Again, this reasoning would seem to be applicable to treaties as well as statutes, and, indeed, the Court has suggested that this limitation does apply even to claims based on treaties.[177]

Notwithstanding *Holland*, it is not uncommon for the executive branch in the treaty process to invoke constitutional concerns relating to federalism. Sometimes the executive branch invokes federalism concerns as a reason for declining to enter into particular treaties, or as a reason for insisting on changes to proposed ones.[178] At other times, it has insisted on "federal clauses" that limit the extent to which a treaty applies to constituent states.[179] In addition, one of the understandings commonly included in the RUDs attached to U.S. ratification of human rights treaties (discussed earlier) is a federalism understanding that provides that the United States will implement the treaty in a manner consistent with its federal system of government.[180] Federalism reservations and understandings are increasingly being used in connection with the ratification of other treaties as well.[181]

---

[174] *See Printz*, 521 U.S. at 918–99; *compare* HENKIN, *supra* note 71, at 467 (assuming that the anti-commandeering restriction limits the treaty power), *with* Martin Flaherty, *Are We to Be a Nation? Federal Power vs. "States' Rights" in Foreign Affairs*, 70 U. COLO. L. REV. 1277 (1999) (arguing that the anti-commandeering restriction does not limit the treaty power); *see also* Carlos Manuel Vázquez, *Breard, Printz, and the Treaty Power*, 70 U. COLO. L. REV. 1317, 1321 (1999) (arguing that "there is little reason for exempting the treaty power from the anticommandeering principle if that principle were understood narrowly to encompass only the sort of directives involved in the *Printz* and *New York* cases"); Janet R. Carter, Note, *Commandeering under the Treaty Power*, 76 N.Y.U. L. REV. 598, 601 (2001) (arguing that "Congress's need to commandeer the states is greater when it acts pursuant to the treaty power than when it exercises its domestic lawmaking powers").

[175] *See* Alden v. Maine, 527 U.S. 706 (1999); Seminole Tribe of Fl. v. Florida, 517 U.S. 44 (1996).

[176] *Alden*, 527 U.S. at 748.

[177] *See* Breard v. Greene, 523 U.S. 371, 377–78 (1998); *see also* Carlos Manuel Vázquez, *Treaties and the Eleventh Amendment*, 42 VA. J. INT'L L. 713, 741 (2002) (arguing that "state sovereign immunity doctrine is fully applicable to exercises of the Treaty Power").

[178] *See* Duncan B. Hollis, *Executive Federalism: Forging New Federalist Constraints on the Treaty Power*, 79 S. CAL. L. REV. 1327, 1372–78 (2006).

[179] *See id.* at 1374–77. For example, Article 11 of the United Nations Convention on the Recognition and Enforcement of Foreign Arbitral Awards, June 10, 1958, 21 U.N.T.S. 2517, provides that "[w]ith respect to those articles of this Convention that come within the legislative jurisdiction of constituent states or provinces which are not, under the constitutional system of the federation, bound to take legislative action, the federal Government shall bring such articles with a favourable recommendation to the notice of the appropriate authorities of constituent states or provinces at the earliest possible moment." *Id.*, art. XI(b).

[180] *See, e.g.*, 138 CONG. REC. S4781, S4784 (Apr. 2, 1992).

[181] *See* Hollis, *supra* note 178, at 1361–63.

Subject Matter Scope of the Treaty Power

It is unclear whether the Constitution restricts the subject matters that may properly be addressed by treaty. When discussing treaties, the constitutional Founders appear to have had in mind particular treaty subjects such as "war, peace, and commerce,"[182] but this does not necessarily mean that they intended to preclude treaty-making on other subjects. The Supreme Court has described the subject matter scope of the treaty power in broad, although not unlimited, terms. In an 1890 decision, *Geofroy v. Riggs*, for example, the Court stated:

> That the treaty power of the United States extends to all proper subjects of negotiation between our government and the governments of other nations, is clear. . . . It would not be contended that it extends so far as to authorize what the Constitution forbids, or a change in the character of the government or in that of one of the States, or a cession of any portion of the territory of the latter, without its consent. . . . But with these exceptions, it is not perceived that there is any limit to the questions which can be adjusted touching any matter which is properly the subject of negotiation with a foreign country.[183]

Although the Court in *Missouri v. Holland* rejected the argument that the treaty power is limited to the scope of Congress's legislative authority, it did not necessarily rule out subject matter limitations on the treaty power. Indeed, the Court in *Holland* specifically noted that the protection of migratory birds involved "a national interest of very nearly the first magnitude," and that the birds could be protected "only by national action in concert with that of another power."[184]

In 1929, shortly before becoming Chief Justice of the Supreme Court, Charles Evans Hughes suggested that the treaty power might be limited to "matters of international concern" and thus might not allow for the regulation of matters "which normally and appropriately were within the local jurisdiction of the States."[185] In the 1950s, in responding

---

[182] THE FEDERALIST PAPERS, *supra* note 7, *No. 64: John Jay*, at 390. *See also* WILLIAM RAWLE, A VIEW OF THE CONSTITUTION OF THE UNITED STATES OF AMERICA 65 (2d ed. 1829) ("[A treaty] is a compact entered into with a foreign power, and it extends to all matters which are generally the subjects of compact between independent nations. Such subjects are peace, alliance, commerce, neutrality, and others of a similar nature.").

[183] Geofroy v. Riggs, 133 U.S. 258, 267 (1890); *see also* Santovincenzo v. Egan, 284 U.S. 30, 40 (1931) (describing the scope as "all subjects that properly pertain to our foreign relations"); Asakura v. City of Seattle, 265 U.S. 332, 341 (1924) (describing the scope as "proper subjects of negotiation with foreign governments"). *But cf.* 3 STORY, COMMENTARIES ON THE CONSTITUTION, *supra* note 151, § 1502, at 356 ("A treaty to change the organization of the government, or annihilate its sovereignty, to overturn its republican form, or to deprive it of its constitutional powers, would be void; because it would destroy, what it was designed merely to fulfil: the will of the people.").

[184] Missouri v. Holland, 252 U.S. 416, 435 (1920).

[185] Statement of Charles Evans Hughes, 1929 AM. SOC. INT'L L. PROC. 194, 194–96.

to the proposed Bricker Amendment (discussed earlier), Secretary of State John Foster Dulles maintained that a treaty could not regulate matters "which do not essentially affect the actions of nations in relation to international affairs, but are purely internal."[186] Similarly, as discussed earlier in this chapter, the D.C. Circuit's *Power Authority* decision from the 1950s suggested that the treaty power could not be used for matters "of purely domestic concern."[187] And the original *Restatement of Foreign Relations Law*, published in 1965, stated that the treaty power was limited to matters "of international concern" and that treaties "must relate to external concerns of the nation as distinguished from matters of a purely internal nature."[188]

Today, however, many commentators maintain that, as long as a treaty involves a genuine agreement with one or more other nations, it is valid regardless of subject matter. The *Restatement (Third) of Foreign Relations Law*, for example, argued that, "[c]ontrary to what was once suggested, the Constitution does not require that an international agreement deal only with 'matters of international concern.'"[189] One possible reason for the *Restatement*'s change of position is that an "international" limitation might pose an obstacle to U.S. ratification of human rights treaties, which concern how nations treat their own citizens and thus do not involve traditional interstate obligations.[190] The *Restatement (Fourth) of Foreign Relations Law*, however, does not take a position on whether there is a subject matter limitation on the treaty power.[191]

In any event, even if there is some sort of "international" subject matter limitation, it seems doubtful that the courts would feel competent to overturn the considered judgment of the president and Senate that a particular treaty was sufficiently related to U.S. foreign relations.[192] Nevertheless, in *Bond v. United States*, discussed earlier, three

---

[186] Treaties and Executive Agreements: Hearings on S.J. Res. 1 Before a Subcomm. of the Senate Comm. on the Judiciary, 84th Cong. 183 (1955).

[187] *See* Power Auth. of N.Y. v. Fed. Power Comm'n, 247 F.2d 538 (D.C. Cir. 1957), *vacated as moot*, 355 U.S. 64 (1957).

[188] RESTATEMENT (SECOND) OF FOREIGN RELATIONS LAW § 117(1)(a) & cmt. b (1965).

[189] RESTATEMENT (THIRD) OF THE FOREIGN RELATIONS LAW OF THE UNITED STATES, *supra* note 4, § 302, cmt. c.

[190] *See id.* § 302, reporters' note 2 ("Early arguments that the United States may not adhere to international human rights agreements because they deal with matters of strictly domestic concern were later abandoned."). *Cf.* Louis Henkin, *The Constitution, Treaties, and International Human Rights*, 116 U. PA. L. REV. 1012, 1025 (1968) ("If there is a constitutional requirement that a treaty deal with a matter of 'international concern,' that it be an act of American foreign policy in the conduct of American foreign relations, surely human rights conventions today amply satisfy that requirement.").

[191] *See* RESTATEMENT (FOURTH) OF THE FOREIGN RELATIONS LAW OF THE UNITED STATES, *supra* note 4, § 312, reporters' notes 4, 8.

[192] Many scholars assume that the national government may not enter into treaties merely as a pretext for expanding its domestic legislative authority. *See, e.g.*, HENKIN, *supra* note 71, at 185; Golove, *supra* note 159, at 1090 n.41; Hathaway, *supra* note 8, at 1344. Given the difficulty of assessing governmental motives, the possibility of mixed motives, and the generally deferential posture of courts in the foreign affairs area, it seems unlikely that such a limitation would be judicially enforceable. *But see* Oona A. Hathaway et al., *The Treaty Power: Its*

Justices on the Supreme Court expressed support for limiting the treaty power to matters of "international intercourse" and disallowing its use for "purely domestic matters."[193]

Relationship of Treaties to Individual Rights

When the Supremacy Clause refers to federal statutes, it refers to "the laws of the United States which shall be made *in pursuance [of the Constitution]*." When it refers to treaties, however, it refers to "treaties made, or which shall be made, *under the authority of the United States*."[194] In *Holland*, the Court took note of this difference and observed that "[i]t is open to question whether the authority of the United States means more than the formal acts prescribed to make the convention."[195]

If it were true that the only requirement for treaties to operate as supreme federal law is that they follow the procedure set forth in Article II, it might mean that treaties could be used to override the individual rights protections of the Constitution. As one commentator noted at the time of the *Holland* decision, the Court's "hint that there may be no other test to be applied than whether the treaty has been duly concluded indicates that the court might hold that specific constitutional limitations in favor of individual liberty and property are not applicable to deprivations wrought by treaties."[196] In subsequent decisions, however, the Supreme Court made clear that treaties cannot override the individual rights protections of the Constitution.

In *Reid v. Covert*, civilian wives of U.S. military personnel had been tried by military courts-martial for murdering their husbands on overseas bases.[197] Despite the fact that such military trials were contemplated by international agreements that purportedly had been implemented by Congress,[198] the Court held that the trials were invalid because they did not comply with the grand jury and jury trial provisions of the Constitution. A plurality of the Court stated that "no agreement with a foreign nation can confer power on the Congress, or on any other branch of Government, which is free from the restraints of the Constitution."[199] The plurality correctly pointed out that the reason the Supremacy Clause refers to treaties made under the authority of the United States rather than in pursuance of the Constitution is not because the Founders wanted to exempt

---

History, Scope, and Limits, 98 CORNELL L. REV. 239 (2013) (proposing a pretext limitation that the authors contend would be judicially enforceable).
[193] 572 U.S. at 886 (Thomas, J., concurring in the judgment, with Justices Scalia and Alito).
[194] U.S. CONST. art. VI, cl. 2 (emphasis added).
[195] Missouri v. Holland, 252 U.S. 416, 433 (1920).
[196] Thomas Reed Powell, *Constitutional Law in 1919–20*, 19 MICH. L. REV. 1, 13 (1920).
[197] Reid v. Covert, 354 U.S. 1 (1957).
[198] The agreements in question were executive agreements rather than Article II treaties, but the Court did not rest its decision on that distinction.
[199] *Reid*, 354 U.S. at 16 (plurality opinion).

treaties from constitutional limitations, but rather because they wanted the treaties that had been concluded by the United States prior to the Constitution, most notably the peace treaty with Britain, to operate as supreme federal law.[200] The plurality further noted that the last-in-time rule (discussed earlier in this chapter) is premised on the assumption that treaties have no higher status in U.S. law than federal statutes, which are subject to constitutional limits.[201]

The plurality in *Reid* did not, however, retreat from the federalism holding in *Holland*. The plurality distinguished *Holland* as a case in which the treaty "was not inconsistent with any specific provision of the Constitution."[202] The plurality further repeated the argument from *Holland* that "[t]o the extent that the United States can validly make treaties, the people and the States have delegated their power to the National Government and the Tenth Amendment is no barrier."[203]

A majority of the Court confirmed that treaties are subject to the individual rights limitations of the Constitution, in *Boos v. Barry*.[204] That case concerned legislation that, among other things, prohibited the display of signs within 500 feet of a foreign embassy if the sign tended to bring the foreign government into "public odium" or "public disrepute." Despite the fact that the legislation was designed to implement treaty obligations, the Court held that it was invalid because it violated the right of free speech protected by the First Amendment to the Constitution. Under the Court's First Amendment jurisprudence, the Court did leave open the possibility, however, that a governmental interest in fulfilling obligations under international law could be a "compelling" interest that would justify content-based limitations on speech.[205]

If a treaty violates a constitutional right, this does not mean that it is invalid as a matter of international law. A violation of domestic law will not invalidate a treaty unless the domestic law concerns the "competence to conclude treaties," and the violation of that law was "manifest."[206] The individual rights protections of the Constitution, however, do not concern the competence to conclude treaties. As a result, if the United States agrees by treaty to do something that would violate an individual constitutional right, the United States will be obligated under international law to fulfill that obligation, even though U.S. courts will decline to enforce it absent an amendment to the Constitution.

---

[200] *See id.* at 16–17.
[201] *Id.* at 18.
[202] *Id.*
[203] *Id.*
[204] Boos v. Barry, 485 U.S. 312 (1988).
[205] *See id.* at 324. *Cf.* Gonzales v. O Centro Espirita Beneficente Uniao do Vegetal, 546 U.S. 418, 438 (2006) ("The fact that *hoasca* [tea] is covered by the [Convention on Psychotropic Substances] … does not automatically mean that the Government has demonstrated a compelling interest in applying the Controlled Substances Act [to religious use of the tea]."). (Chapter 6 discusses the extent to which constitutional rights apply outside the United States.)
[206] *See* VCLT, *supra* note 2, arts. 27, 46.

The only constitutional restrictions that concern the competence to conclude treaties are the process requirements set forth in Article II—that is, that the treaty be concluded by the president with the advice and consent of two-thirds of the Senate. As discussed in Chapter 3, however, it is not clear when, if ever, the failure to follow the senatorial consent part of that restriction would result in a manifest violation.

Interpretation of Treaties

Although treaties sometimes operate in the U.S. legal system like federal legislation, they differ from legislation in that they involve not only domestic law, but also commitments to other nations. Recognizing this difference, U.S. courts attempt to construe treaties "'consistent with the shared expectations of the contracting parties.'"[207] To discern these shared expectations, U.S. courts commonly look not only to the text of a treaty, but also to its structure, purpose, and negotiating and drafting history. Courts also consider evidence of the post-ratification understandings of the contracting parties, such as decisions of foreign courts construing the treaty.[208]

As in the area of statutory interpretation, there have been debates among justices on the Supreme Court about the extent to which the Court should look at extratextual materials when interpreting treaties,[209] and the Court has indicated that it will not consider these materials when the text of the treaty is clear.[210] Even so, a number of commentators have suggested that U.S. courts tend to rely more heavily on the drafting history of treaties than is appropriate under the VCLT. The VCLT provides that "supplementary means of interpretation," such as drafting history, may be relied on only to confirm the meaning of the treaty that is suggested by textual materials or to inform the treaty's meaning when the textual materials leave the meaning ambiguous or obscure.[211]

---

[207] Olympic Airways v. Husain, 540 U.S. 644, 650 (2004) (quoting Air France v. Saks, 470 U.S. 392, 399 (1985)). *See also* Curtis J. Mahoney, Note, *Treaties as Contracts: Textualism, Contract Theory, and the Interpretation of Treaties*, 116 YALE L.J. 824 (2007) (arguing that courts should apply contract principles when interpreting treaties).

[208] *See* Abbott v. Abbott, 560 U.S. 1, 16–17 (2010); Zicherman v. Korean Air Lines Co., 516 U.S. 217, 226 (1996); Air France v. Saks, 470 U.S. 392, 404 (1985).

[209] *See, e.g.*, United States v. Stuart, 489 U.S. 353, 371–72 (1989) (Scalia, J., dissenting).

[210] *See* Chan v. Korean Airlines, 490 U.S. 122, 134 (1989).

[211] *See* VCLT, *supra* note 2, art. 32. *See also* Evan Criddle, *The Vienna Convention on the Law of Treaties in U.S. Treaty Interpretation*, 44 VA. J. INT'L L. 431 (2004). For an argument that the VCLT in fact allows for broader consideration of supplementary materials than is commonly assumed, *see* Julian Davis Mortenson, *The Travaux of Travaux: Is the Vienna Convention Hostile to Drafting History?*, 107 AM. J. INT'L L. 780 (2013). *Cf.* RESTATEMENT (FOURTH) OF THE FOREIGN RELATIONS LAW OF THE UNITED STATES, *supra* note 4, 306, reporters' note 3 ("In interpreting treaties, the Supreme Court generally has considered the same interpretive sources as those addressed in the Vienna Convention on the Law of Treaties, without necessarily invoking the Convention's precise ordering or methodology.").

The Supreme Court's 2010 decision in *Abbott v. Abbott* provides an example of how the Court approaches treaty interpretation.[212] That case concerned the Hague Convention on the Civil Aspects of International Child Abduction, which provides that a child abducted in violation of "rights of custody" must be returned to the child's country of habitual residence, subject to certain exceptions.[213] The United States ratified the Convention in 1988 and implemented it by statute.[214] The issue in the case was whether a parent has a "right of custody" by reason of that parent's *ne exeat* right under local law—that is, the authority to consent before the other parent may take the child to another country. In concluding that there is a right of custody in this situation, the Court explained that its "inquiry is shaped by the text of the Convention; the views of the United States Department of State; decisions addressing the meaning of 'rights of custody' in courts of other contracting states; and the purposes of the Convention."[215]

Treaties are sometimes written in more than one authoritative language. When this is the case, there can be interpretive difficulties created by discrepancies in the terms used in the different languages. As noted earlier in this chapter, the Supreme Court in *Foster v. Neilson* relied on the English version of a treaty in concluding that it was not self-executing, but then changed its mind about the treaty after reviewing the Spanish version.[216] According to the VCLT, when there is a discrepancy between two or more authoritative languages that is not resolved by the normal rules of interpretation, "the meaning which best reconciles the texts, having regard to the object and purpose of the treaty, shall be adopted."[217]

The Supreme Court has stated the judiciary is to accord "great weight" to the executive branch's interpretation of treaties.[218] This deference stems from a variety of factors, including the lead role of the executive branch in negotiating treaties, its status as the principal "organ" of the United States in international communications, its expertise in

---

[212] Abbott v. Abbott, 560 U.S. 1 (2010).
[213] *See* Hague Convention on the Civil Aspects of International Child Abduction art. 1, Oct. 25, 1980, T.I.A.S. No. 11,670, 1343 U.N.T.S. 49.
[214] *See* International Child Abduction Remedies Act, 102 Stat. 437, *codified at* 42 U.S.C. § 11601 *et seq.*
[215] *Abbott*, 560 U.S. at 9–10. *See also* Lozano v. Montoya Alvarez, 572 U.S. 1, 11 (2014) (noting that "our 'duty [i]s to ascertain the intent of the parties' by looking to the document's text and context").
[216] *See* United States v. Percheman, 32 U.S. (7 Pet.) 51, 88–89 (1833).
[217] VCLT, *supra* note 2, art. 33. Sometimes English is not an authoritative language for a treaty. For the Warsaw Convention for the Unification of Certain Rules Relating to International Transportation by Air, for example, French is the only authoritative language. In that situation, U.S. courts will look not only at the official foreign text but also the English translation of the text that was before the Senate when it gave its advice and consent. *See, e.g.*, Olympic Airways v. Husain, 540 U.S. 644, 649 n.4 (2004); Air France v. Saks, 470 U.S. 392, 397 (1985).
[218] *See, e.g., Abbott*, 560 U.S. at 15; Medellin v. Texas, 552 U.S. 491, 513 (2008); Sumitomo Shoji Am., Inc. v. Avagliano, 457 U.S. 176, 184–85 (1982); Kolovrat v. Oregon, 366 U.S. 187, 194 (1961). At times, the Court has used somewhat different terms to describe this deference—see El Al Israel Airlines, Ltd. v. Tsui Yuan Tseng, 525 U.S. 155, 168 (1999) ("[r]espect"); Factor v. Laubenheimer, 290 U.S. 276, 295 (1933) ("of weight")—but it is not clear that the Court has intended these terms to reflect a different standard.

treaty matters and foreign affairs more generally, and its special access to information concerning the likely effect of particular treaty interpretations.[219] One study concluded that judicial deference to the executive "may be the single best predictor of interpretive outcomes in American treaty cases."[220] Nevertheless, such deference does not appear to be inevitable. For example, as discussed in Chapter 10, the Supreme Court in a 2006 decision appeared to give little deference to the executive branch's interpretation of a provision in the Geneva Conventions (which concerns the treatment of various classes of people during armed conflict).[221]

Because the treaty power is divided between the Senate and president, courts will presumably attempt to give effect to the shared understandings of these institutions at the time of ratification.[222] Deference to the executive branch's post-ratification treaty interpretation can sometimes be in tension with this proposition—for example, when the executive branch seeks to interpret a treaty in a way that is different from either the executive's or Senate's interpretation at the time of ratification. This tension became evident when the Reagan administration proposed to "reinterpret" the 1972 Treaty on the Limitation of Anti-Ballistic Missile Systems (ABM Treaty) between the United States and the Soviet Union to permit the development of anti-ballistic missile systems that used technologies not in existence in 1972.[223] Although the Reagan administration ultimately decided not to rely on this new interpretation, the proposed reinterpretation caused substantial concern in the Senate because it appeared to contradict the shared understanding of the

---

[219] *See, e.g.*, Coplin v. United States, 6 Cl. Ct. 115, 135–36 (1984) (majority opinion of Chief Judge Kozinski), *rev'd on other grounds*, 761 F.2d 688 (Fed. Cir. 1985). These rationales for deference probably also apply to executive branch interpretations of customary international law, although there are few decisions addressing the issue. *See* RESTATEMENT (THIRD) OF THE FOREIGN RELATIONS LAW OF THE UNITED STATES, *supra* note 4, § 112, cmt. c (arguing that deference is appropriate with respect to issues of customary international law). This point is discussed further in Chapter 5.

[220] David J. Bederman, *Revivalist Canons and Treaty Interpretation*, 41 UCLA L. REV. 953, 1015 (1994).

[221] *See* Hamdan v. Rumsfeld, 548 U.S. 557, 629–31 (2006). For an argument that the lack of deference in *Hamdan* is consistent with the approach of the Supreme Court to treaty cases in the early years of U.S. constitutional history, *see* David Sloss, *Judicial Deference to Executive Branch Treaty Interpretations: A Historical Perspective*, 62 N.Y.U. ANN. SURV. AM. L. 497 (2007). For a functional critique of the lack of deference in *Hamdan*, *see* Julian Ku & John Yoo, Hamdan v. Rumsfeld: *The Functional Case for Foreign Affairs Deference to the Executive Branch*, 23 CONST. COMM. 179 (2006). In *Medellin v. Texas*, the Court gave deference to the executive branch's view that the treaties at issue were non-self-executing, but it did not appear to give deference to the executive branch's view that the treaties implicitly delegated authority to the president to implement the treaties by preempting state law, in part because of what the Court described as "the fundamental constitutional principle that '[t]he power to make the necessary laws is in Congress; the power to execute in the President.'" 552 U.S. at 526 (citations omitted).

[222] *See generally* Memorandum from Charles J. Cooper, Assistant Attorney General, Office of Legal Counsel, to Abraham D. Sofaer, Legal Adviser, Department of State, *Relevance of Senate Ratification to Treaty Interpretation*, 11 OP. ATT'Y. GEN. 28 (Apr. 9, 1987).

[223] *See* Abram Chayes & Antonia Handler Chayes, *Testing and Development of "Exotic" Systems under the ABM Treaty: The Great Reinterpretation Caper*, 99 HARV. L. REV. 1956 (1986); John Yoo, *Politics as Law?: The Anti-Ballistic Missile Treaty, the Separation of Powers, and Treaty Interpretation*, 89 CAL. L. REV. 851 (2001).

Senate and president concerning the treaty at the time of ratification. In giving its advice and consent to a subsequent treaty, the Senate included a condition that states that treaties shall be interpreted "in accordance with the common understanding of the Treaty shared by the President and the Senate at the time the Senate gave its advice and consent to ratification."[224] And then, in giving its advice and consent to yet another treaty, the Senate affirmed "the applicability to all treaties of the constitutionally-based principles" in the aforementioned condition.[225]

At times, the Supreme Court has stated that treaties should be interpreted "liberally" or in "good faith."[226] The precise import of these terms is unclear, and they may simply confirm the need to discern the shared understandings of the treaty parties. In any event, the Supreme Court has not placed significant reliance on these terms in modern treaty interpretation cases.[227]

Terminating Treaty Commitments

The Constitution describes how treaties are to be made, but it does not describe how they are to be unmade. Under international law, a treaty can be terminated for various reasons. For example, a party to a bilateral treaty may terminate the treaty in response to a material breach of the treaty by the other party.[228] A nation may also withdraw from a treaty if the parties to the treaty intended to allow for withdrawal or a right of withdrawal can be implied from the nature of the treaty.[229] International law does not address, however, which institutional actors within a nation may exercise the right of termination or withdrawal.

---

[224] *See* Resolution of Advice and Consent of May 27, 1988 to the U.S.–U.S.S.R. Treaty on the Elimination of Their Intermediate-Range and Shorter-Range Missiles, 134 CONG. REC. 12,849 (1988).

[225] *See* Resolution of Advice and Consent of Nov. 25, 1991 to the Treaty on Conventional Armed Forces in Europe, 137 CONG. REC. S17,845, 17,846 (Nov. 23, 1991); *adopted id.* at S18,038 (Nov. 25, 1991).

[226] *See, e.g.*, Factor v. Laubenheimer, 290 U.S. 276, 294 (1933) ("Considerations which should govern the diplomatic relations between nations, and the good faith of treaties, as well, require that their obligations should be liberally construed so as to effect the apparent intention of the parties to secure equality and reciprocity between them. For that reason if a treaty fairly admits of two constructions, one restricting the rights which may be claimed under it, and the other enlarging it, the more liberal construction is to be preferred."); Geofroy v. Riggs, 133 U.S. 258, 271 (1890) ("It is a general principle of construction with respect to treaties that they shall be liberally construed, so as to carry out the apparent intention of the parties to secure equality and reciprocity between them.").

[227] *See generally* Michael P. Van Alstine, *The Death of Good Faith in Treaty Jurisprudence and a Call for Resurrection*, 93 GEO. L.J. 1885 (2005).

[228] *See* VCLT, *supra* note 2, art. 60.

[229] *See id.*, arts. 54, 56. *See also* Laurence R. Helfer, *Exiting Treaties*, 91 VA. L. REV. 1579, 1581–82 (2005). The VCLT provides that when a treaty does not contain a withdrawal provision, a party must give at least twelve months' notice before withdrawing. It is not clear, however, whether this twelve-month default period is required as a matter of customary international law.

It is arguable that, under U.S. law, treaties should be terminated pursuant to the same process that is required for making them—that is, with two-thirds senatorial consent. By analogy, it is well settled that federal statutes can be terminated only pursuant to the bicameralism and presentment process required for making statutes.[230] Treaties, however, are not precisely like statutes. For example, although statutes can be enacted over a president's veto, treaties can never be concluded without presidential approval. Moreover, some actions that require senatorial advice and consent, such as the appointment of federal officers, can be terminated unilaterally by the president.[231]

During the nineteenth century, it seems generally to have been understood that presidents needed to obtain the agreement of either the Senate or the full Congress before terminating a treaty.[232] In the twentieth century, however, this understanding appears to have shifted, such that unilateral presidential termination of treaties became the norm.[233] One such unilateral termination—President Carter's termination of a mutual defense treaty with Taiwan in the late 1970s as part of the United States' recognition of mainland China—generated substantial controversy.[234] For the most part, however, presidential termination of treaties has not been a source of significant conflict between the executive and legislative branches.[235] Since taking office in 2017, President Trump has withdrawn the United States from a number of treaties without seeking senatorial or congressional approval, including the Intermediate-Range Nuclear Forces (INF) Treaty with Russia and the Optional Protocol to the Vienna Convention on Diplomatic Relations. Although these withdrawals have generated policy concerns, they have not generated significant constitutional controversy.[236]

---

[230] *See, e.g.*, Clinton v. New York, 524 U.S. 417, 421 (1998).

[231] *See, e.g.*, Myers v. United States, 272 U.S. 52, 176 (1926). *Cf.* Morrison v. Olson, 487 U.S. 654, 696–97 (1988) (allowing Congress to impose a "good cause" limitation on the president's ability to remove independent counsel). Advocates of the Vesting Clause theory of presidential power, discussed in Chapter 1, maintain that because the termination of treaties is an executive function that has not been expressly delegated to Congress, it rests with the president. *See* Saikrishna B. Prakash & Michael D. Ramsey, *The Executive Power over Foreign Affairs*, 111 YALE L.J. 231, 324–27 (2001).

[232] *See* Curtis A. Bradley, *Treaty Termination and Historical Gloss*, 92 TEX. L. REV. 773, 788–801 (2014). For additional discussion of the relevant historical practice, *see* DAVID GRAY ADLER, THE CONSTITUTION AND THE TERMINATION OF TREATIES 149–247 (1986); CRANDALL, *supra* note 13, §§ 178–86; and 5 GREEN HAYWOOD HACKWORTH, DIGEST OF INTERNATIONAL LAW § 509 (1943).

[233] *See* Bradley, *supra* note 232, at 801–20.

[234] *See id.* at 810–14.

[235] In 2002, President George W. Bush unilaterally terminated the ABM Treaty. *See* U.S. Dep't of State, *ABM Treaty Fact Sheet* (Dec. 13, 2001), http://georgewbush-whitehouse.archives.gov/news/releases/2001/12/20011213-2.html. The termination of the ABM Treaty was unsuccessfully challenged in court by members of the House of Representatives. *See* Kucinich v. Bush, 236 F. Supp. 2d 1, 2 (D.D.C. 2002); *see also* Bruce Ackerman, *Editorial: Treaties Don't Belong to Presidents Alone*, N.Y. TIMES (Aug. 29, 2001), at A23 (questioning President Bush's authority to terminate the ABM treaty unilaterally).

[236] Alarmed by suggestions from President Trump that he might consider withdrawing the United States from the North Atlantic Treaty Organization (NATO), bills were proposed in Congress that would have attempted to restrict his ability to do so. *See, e.g.*, Karoun Demirjian, *Bipartisan Bill Would Prevent Trump from Exiting*

In light of the historical practice, *the Restatement (Fourth) of Foreign Relations Law*, like the earlier *Restatement (Third)*, has taken the position that the president has the unilateral authority to terminate treaties whenever such termination is permitted under international law and is not disallowed either by the Senate in its resolution of advice and consent to the treaty or by Congress in a statute.[237] This issue is not fully settled, however, and some commentators have argued against a general presidential power of treaty termination.[238]

Even if the president does not have a general power of treaty termination, he or she might have the authority to terminate treaties in some circumstances. For example, the president may have the authority to terminate a treaty when the termination is related to the exercise of some other presidential power, such as the recognition of a foreign government.[239] In addition, as "sole organ" for the United States in foreign affairs, perhaps the president can properly decide if there is a legal justification for termination, such as a material breach, even if the president does not have the authority to withdraw from a treaty on purely policy grounds.[240]

Whatever the scope of the president's authority to terminate treaties unilaterally, historical practice does not suggest that this authority is an exclusive presidential power. If, as seems likely, it is merely a concurrent power shared with either the full Congress or the Senate, then either Congress or the Senate could potentially place limitations on it.[241] As stated in the reporters' notes to the *Restatement (Fourth) of Foreign Relations Law*, "[i]f treaty termination is a concurrent, rather than exclusive, power, it is possible that it could

---

NATO Without Senate Consent, WASH. POST (July 26, 2018). In a budgetary statute enacted in December 2019, Congress included a provision stating that if the president provided a notice of withdrawal from the North Atlantic Treaty, "during the one-year period beginning on the date of such notice, no funds authorized to be appropriated by this Act may be obligated, expended, or reprogrammed for the withdrawal of the United States Armed Forces from Europe." S. 1790, National Defense Authorization Act for Fiscal Year 2020, § 1242, 116th Cong. (Dec. 20, 2019). This statute also included a provision requiring the president to give advance notice to Congress before attempting to withdraw the United States from the Treaty on Open Skies, a multilateral agreement that allows for unarmed observational flights over member countries. *Id.*, § 1234.

[237] *See* RESTATEMENT (FOURTH) OF THE FOREIGN RELATIONS LAW OF THE UNITED STATES, *supra* note 4, § 313; RESTATEMENT (THIRD) OF THE FOREIGN RELATIONS LAW OF THE UNITED STATES, *supra* note 4, § 339.

[238] *See, e.g.*, Harold Hongju Koh, *Presidential Power to Terminate International Agreements*, 128 YALE L.J.F. 432 (2018); Catherine Amirfar & Ashika Singh, *The Trump Administration and the "Unmaking" of International Agreements*, 59 HARV. INT'L L.J. 443 (2018).

[239] *See* Goldwater v. Carter, 444 U.S. 996, 1007 (1979) (Brennan, J., dissenting) (arguing that President Carter had the authority to terminate a treaty with Taiwan as part of his recognition of mainland China).

[240] *See, e.g.*, Charlton v. Kelly, 229 U.S. 447, 473–76 (1913) (suggesting that it is for the executive branch to decide whether to terminate a treaty in response to a breach by the other party).

[241] *See, e.g.*, MICHAEL J. GLENNON, CONSTITUTIONAL DIPLOMACY 156 (1990) (arguing that the Constitution compels the president to follow any termination procedure prescribed by the Senate); Kristen E. Eichensehr, *Treaty Termination and the Separation of Powers*, 53 VA. J. INT'L L. 247, 279–86 (2013) (arguing that "for cause" limitations imposed by the Senate on the president's treaty-termination power would be constitutional).

be limited by the Senate in its advice and consent to a particular treaty, and possibly also by Congress through statute."[242]

In any event, the issue of how treaties are to be terminated for the United States may be a nonjusticiable political question that courts will decline to resolve. In *Goldwater v. Carter*, some members of Congress challenged President Carter's termination of a mutual defense treaty with Taiwan as part of the U.S. recognition of mainland China.[243] The Supreme Court declined to address the merits of the challenge, and four justices specifically concluded that the case posed a nonjusticiable political question.[244] These justices reasoned that the text of the Constitution provides insufficient guidance for the courts regarding the process for terminating treaties, and that "different termination procedures may be appropriate for different treaties."[245] These justices also expressed a more general reluctance "to settle a dispute between coequal branches of our Government, each of which has resources available to protect and assert its interests."[246] A federal district court relied on this plurality decision in dismissing a challenge to President Bush's termination of the ABM treaty based on the political question doctrine.[247] While the Supreme Court has more recently emphasized that the political question doctrine is a "narrow exception" to the judiciary's duty to decide cases,[248] it did so in the context of a direct conflict between Congress and the president, a situation that is not typically presented in the context of treaty termination.

Treaty termination is distinct from the issue of "unsigning" a treaty, an issue that generated substantial controversy in connection with U.S. actions relating to the treaty establishing the International Criminal Court. In 2000, the Clinton administration signed the treaty—the Rome Statute of the International Criminal Court—shortly before President Clinton left office. This was a "simple signature" that did not indicate consent by the United States to be bound by the treaty. In 2002, the Bush administration sent a letter to the Secretary-General of the United Nations stating that the United States did not intend to become a party to the Rome Statute, an action that some have referred to as "unsigning" the treaty (although there was no attempt to physically remove the earlier U.S. signature).[249]

---

[242] RESTATEMENT (FOURTH) OF THE FOREIGN RELATIONS LAW OF THE UNITED STATES, *supra* note 4, § 313, reporters' note 6.

[243] *See* Goldwater v. Carter, 444 U.S. 996 (1979). This case was brought before the Supreme Court's decision in *Raines v. Byrd*, 521 U.S. 811 (1997), in which the Court substantially restricted the circumstances under which legislators have standing to challenge actions of the executive branch.

[244] *See Goldwater*, 444 U.S. at 1002–105 (Rehnquist, J., concurring).

[245] *Id.* at 1003.

[246] *Id.* at 1004.

[247] *See* Kucinich v. Bush, 236 F. Supp. 2d 1 (D.D.C. 2002).

[248] Zivotofsky v. Clinton, 566 U.S. 189, 195 (2012). For additional discussion of the political question doctrine, see Chapter 1.

[249] *See* Letter from John R. Bolton, Under Sec'y for Arms Control & Int'l Sec., U.S. Dept. of State, to Kofi Annan, Sec'y Gen., United Nations (May 6, 2002), *at* https://2001-2009.state.gov/r/pa/prs/ps/2002/9968.htm; *see also* Curtis A. Bradley, *U.S. Announces Intent Not to Ratify International Criminal Court Treaty*,

Article 18 of the VCLT states that a nation that signs a treaty is "obliged to refrain from acts which would defeat the object and purpose" of the treaty.[250] Although the United States is not a party to the VCLT, U.S. officials have suggested at times that Article 18 reflects customary international law.[251] Even so, there appears to be little question that a nation may announce after signing a treaty that it does not intend to ratify the treaty, thereby relieving itself of any obligations associated with its signature of the treaty. Indeed, Article 18 of the VCLT appears to contemplate precisely this scenario, stating that the signing obligation applies "until [the signing nation] shall have made its intentions clear not to become a party to the treaty."[252] In addition, the president would appear to be the most logical actor for carrying out this "unsigning" for the United States, since it is the president who signs treaties for the United States, and a treaty cannot be ratified without presidential approval. In this sense, the unsigning issue is an easier constitutional one than the issue of treaty termination. For these reasons, the controversy over the U.S. unsigning of the Rome Statute appears primarily to have concerned the policy wisdom of this action rather than its legal validity.[253] In 2019, President Donald Trump "unsigned" a multilateral arms trade agreement, which had been signed by the Obama administration in 2013, by announcing that the United States had no intention of ratifying it.[254] The Treaty was pending before the Senate at the time, and President Trump asked the Senate to return it to him.

* * *

The president and Senate have broad authority to conclude international agreements on behalf of the United States. The relationship between this authority and the United States' federal system of government has sometimes been a topic of controversy, and has

---

ASIL INSIGHTS, May 2002, http://www.asil.org/insights/volume/7/issue/7/us-announces-intent-not-ratify-international-criminal-court-treaty. This was not the first time that a presidential administration had announced that it did not intend to ratify a treaty that had been signed by the United States, but it was apparently the first time that the announcement was made through a formal letter to the United Nations.

[250] *See* VCLT, *supra* note 2, art. 18. For a discussion of constitutional issues raised for the United States by this provision, *see generally* Bradley, *supra* note 19; and David H. Moore, *The President's Unconstitutional Treatymaking*, 59 UCLA L. REV. 598 (2012).

[251] *See* Bradley, *supra* note 19, at 315 n.36.

[252] *See* AUST, *supra* note 15, at 107–109.

[253] Since a president can unilaterally both sign and "unsign" a treaty, a president presumably can also unilaterally reverse the effect of an unsigning, by announcing that the United States is rescinding its earlier announcement and now considers itself bound by any obligations associated with being a signatory. While not quite going that far, the State Department's Legal Adviser in the Obama administration stated on various occasions that, as a policy matter, the United States would not attempt to frustrate the object and purpose of the Rome Statute. *See, e.g.*, Remarks of Harold Hongju Koh, Panel Discussion at NYU Center for Global Affairs, *The Challenges and Future of International Justice* (Oct. 27, 2010), *at* https://2009-2017.state.gov/s/l/releases/remarks/150497.htm.

[254] Katie Rogers, *Trump Pulls Out of Arms Treaty During Speech at NRA Convention*, N.Y. TIMES (Apr. 26, 2019).

never been entirely resolved, but in general the desire for national control over foreign affairs has prevailed over considerations of states' rights. Nevertheless, all branches of the federal government have been attentive to federalism concerns associated with how treaties, especially modern multilateral treaties, are implemented within the U.S. legal system. Stronger constitutional arguments can be made for separation-of-powers limitations on the treaty power, although these arguments have generally been accommodated by deeming certain types of treaties (such as those that call for the expenditure of funds or the imposition of criminal liability) to be non–self-executing. It is also settled that treaties are subject to the individual rights limitations of the Constitution. Despite the status of treaties as "supreme Law of the Land," a number of doctrines limit the extent to which treaties can be invoked in judicial proceedings, including the doctrine of non–self-execution and the last-in-time rule for conflicts between treaties and federal statutes. Moreover, when courts do apply treaties, they typically give substantial deference to the views of the executive branch about how the treaties should be interpreted.

3   Executive Agreements and Political Commitments

THE PRIOR CHAPTER discussed what are sometimes referred to as "Article II treaties"—that is, agreements that are concluded by the president with the advice and consent of two-thirds of the Senate, pursuant to the process specified in Article II of the Constitution. This chapter considers "executive agreements," which are international agreements concluded by the United States without resort to the two-thirds senatorial advice-and-consent process. The distinction between treaties and executive agreements is one of U.S. law, not international law. Under international law, all international agreements between nations that are intended to be legally binding and governed by international law are referred to as treaties.[1] As a result, even though they are concluded by a different process, executive agreements are just as binding on the United States internationally as are Article II treaties. This chapter also considers "political commitments," which are not binding under international law but which can nevertheless be very consequential.

---

[1] *See* Vienna Convention on the Law of Treaties, May 23, 1969, art. 1(a), 1155 U.N.T.S. 331 [hereinafter VCLT].

The Rise of Executive Agreements

The phenomenon of executive agreements is a particularly good illustration of how historical practice can shape and define the authority of the three branches of the federal government. Although executive agreements were relatively rare early in U.S. history, today they constitute the vast majority of international agreements entered into by the United States. In the first fifty years of its constitutional history, the United States concluded sixty treaties and only twenty-seven executive agreements. Between 1939 and 1989, however, it concluded 11,698 executive agreements and only 702 treaties.[2] In the last few decades, the United States has concluded an average of several hundred executive agreements per year, but only about twenty treaties per year, and the use of the treaty process dropped even further during the Obama and Trump administrations.[3] Since the 1940s, well over 90% of the international agreements concluded by the United States have been executive agreements rather than treaties.

There are a number of reasons for the rise of executive agreements. The defeat of the Versailles Treaty in the Senate after World War I highlighted the difficulty of concluding treaties through the Article II process and prompted supporters of international agreements to seek alternatives. Moreover, as the United States' role in the world increased during the twentieth century, it began concluding a much larger number of international agreements. The United Nations system, established at the end of World War II, also prompted a substantial growth in international agreements, as did changes in travel and communications. In addition, globalization revealed, and in many instances created, problems that could be addressed effectively only through international cooperation. The executive branch found that it was much easier to conclude the growing number of international agreements without submitting them for approval by two-thirds of the Senate, and the Senate acquiesced to some extent in this development. At the same time, there was increasing overlap between international agreements and Congress's regulatory authority, prompting a shift from having treaties approved by a supermajority of the Senate to having them authorized or approved by a majority of the full Congress.[4]

---

[2] *See* CONGRESSIONAL RESEARCH SERVICE, TREATIES AND OTHER INTERNATIONAL AGREEMENTS: THE ROLE OF THE UNITED STATES SENATE, S. Prt. 106–71, 106th Cong., 2d Sess. 39 (2001) [hereinafter CRS Treaty Study]; Curtis A. Bradley & Jack L. Goldsmith, *Presidential Control over International Law*, 131 HARV. L. REV. 1201, 1210 (2018).

[3] *See* Robert E. Dalton, *National Treaty Law and Practice: United States, Annex I, in* NATIONAL TREATY LAW AND PRACTICE 820 (Duncan B. Hollis et al. eds., 2005); Oona A. Hathaway, *Treaties' End: The Past, Present, and Future of International Lawmaking in the United States*, 117 YALE L.J. 1236, 1237–38 (2008); *see also* Curtis Bradley, Oona Hathaway & Jack Goldsmith, *The Death of Article II Treaties?*, LAWFARE (Dec. 13, 2018), *at* https://www.lawfareblog.com/death-article-ii-treaties.

[4] CRS Treaty Study, *supra* note 2, at 22. For additional discussion of the growth in the number of executive agreements, *see* GLEN S. KRUTZ & JEFFREY S. PEAKE, TREATY POLITICS AND THE RISE OF EXECUTIVE AGREEMENTS (2011).

There are four basic types of executive agreements: executive agreements concluded pursuant to authorization in a prior treaty; "ex ante congressional–executive agreements," which are agreements authorized in advance by statute and concluded by the executive branch without subsequent congressional review or approval; "ex post congressional–executive agreements," which are approved by a majority of Congress after they are negotiated; and "sole executive agreements," which are concluded by presidents on their own constitutional authority without any express congressional authorization or approval. The vast majority of executive agreements—probably well over 80%—are ex ante congressional–executive agreements.[5]

The U.S. State Department authorizes the negotiation of international agreements on behalf of the United States pursuant to what is referred to as the "Circular 175 procedure" (named after a State Department circular first issued in 1955).[6] In determining the proper form for an international agreement, the State Department considers eight factors:

(1) The extent to which the agreement involves commitments or risks affecting the nation as a whole;
(2) Whether the agreement is intended to affect state laws;
(3) Whether the agreement can be given effect without the enactment of subsequent legislation by Congress;
(4) Past U.S. practice as to similar agreements;
(5) The preference of the Congress as to a particular type of agreement;
(6) The degree of formality desired for the agreement;
(7) The proposed duration of the agreement, the need for prompt conclusion of an agreement, and the desirability of concluding a routine or short-term agreement; and
(8) The general international practice as to similar agreements.[7]

These factors obviously leave substantial room for discretion.[8] Nevertheless, they confirm the importance of both historical practice (factor 4) and interbranch dialogue (factor 5) in this area.

Both the Senate and the full Congress have sometimes either resisted, or attempted to monitor, the use of executive agreements. For example, in the early 1970s, a central reason

---

[5] *See* Bradley & Goldsmith, *supra* note 2, at 1213; Oona A. Hathaway, *Presidential Power over International Law: Restoring the Balance*, 119 YALE L.J. 140, 145 (2009).
[6] *See* U.S. Dep't of State, *Treaty Procedures*, https://www.state.gov/treaty-procedures/.
[7] U.S. Dep't of State, *Foreign Affairs Manual*, 11 FAM 723.3, https://fam.state.gov/FAM/11FAM/11FAM0720.html.
[8] *See, e.g.*, Phillip R. Trimble & Jack S. Weiss, *The Role of the President, the Senate and Congress with Respect to Arms Control Treaties Concluded by the United States*, 67 CHI.-KENT L. REV. 645, 648 (1991) ("The Circular 175 factors are rather general and may sometimes suggest inconsistent choices, and probably do not have much impact on actual Executive branch decisions.").

that the Senate did not give its advice and consent to the Vienna Convention on the Law of Treaties (discussed in Chapter 2) was a concern that a provision in the Convention would further legitimize the use of executive agreements.[9] In 1972, Congress enacted the Case-Zablocki Act, which requires the Secretary of State to transmit to Congress the text of any international agreement concluded by the United States, other than an Article II treaty, within sixty days of its entry into force for the United States.[10] Pursuant to regulation, these agreements are transmitted to Congress with a background statement that is supposed to include "information explaining the agreement and a precise citation of legal authority."[11] The executive branch's reporting under the Case-Zablocki Act has often been late and incomplete, and Congress has amended the statute at various times in an effort to prompt better compliance.[12] As described in the next section, the Senate has sometimes successfully insisted that particular agreements be concluded pursuant to the Article II treaty process.

Executive Agreements Pursuant to Treaty

Some Article II treaties either expressly or implicitly authorize the conclusion of executive agreements. For example, a treaty allowing the United States to operate a military base in another country might authorize the conclusion of additional agreements relating to employment at the base or the trial of U.S. service personnel stationed there.[13] The U.S. naval base at Guantánamo Bay, Cuba—the subject of much controversy in the post–September 11, 2001, "war on terrorism"—was acquired pursuant to an executive

---

[9] Article 46 of the Convention precludes a nation from invoking a violation of its internal law as a basis for invalidating a treaty unless the violation was "manifest and concerned a rule of its internal law of fundamental importance." The Senate Foreign Relations Committee was concerned that this article might bind the United States to international agreements made by the president without the two-thirds Senate consent required by Article II of the Constitution, because that requirement might not be considered "manifest" given the extensive U.S. practice of concluding agreements outside of this process. See CRS Treaty Study, *supra* note 2, at 46–47; Maria Frankowska, *The Vienna Convention on the Law of Treaties before United States Courts*, 28 VA. J. INT'L L. 281, 296–98 (1988).

[10] See 1 U.S.C. § 112b(a). When the president determines that public disclosure of the agreement would be prejudicial to U.S. national security, the agreement is transmitted to the Senate Foreign Relations Committee and the House International Relations Committee under a security classification. See id. The Case-Zablocki Act has been implemented by federal regulations. See 22 C.F.R. §§ 181.1–181.9. Between 1978 and 1999, over seven thousand agreements were reported to Congress pursuant to the Case-Zablocki Act. See CRS Treaty Study, *supra* note 2, at 227.

[11] 22 C.F.R. § 181.7(c).

[12] See Bradley & Goldsmith, *Presidential Control*, *supra* note 2, at 1273–75; *see also* Oona A. Hathaway, Curtis A. Bradley & Jack L. Goldsmith, *The Failed Transparency Regime for Executive Agreements: An Empirical and Normative Analysis*, 134 HARV. L. REV. (forthcoming 2020).

[13] See, e.g., Wilson v. Girard, 354 U.S. 524 (1957) (applying executive agreement with Japan, made pursuant to an Article II treaty, concerning jurisdiction over criminal offenses by U.S. service personnel).

agreement authorized by a 1903 treaty with Cuba.[14] Administrative details of treaty implementation are also often handled by executive agreement.[15]

The principal limitation on this category of executive agreements is that these agreements must fall within the scope of the underlying treaty. It is possible that there is also a requirement that the treaty provide some guidance about the nature of the agreements it is authorizing, in order to avoid an unduly broad delegation of authority, but any such requirement is likely to be modest. Assuming that an executive agreement authorized by a treaty falls within the scope of the treaty, it will have the same status in the U.S. legal system as the treaty.[16] Thus, for example, if it is self-executing, it will preempt inconsistent state law. Like the underlying treaty, it can also override an earlier inconsistent treaty or federal statute, although courts will likely attempt to construe it in a way that will avoid this outcome if possible.

While there have occasionally been concerns that particular agreements were not within the scope of a treaty, in general this category of executive agreements has not generated significant controversy, probably because by definition a supermajority of the Senate is viewed as authorizing these agreements. In the late nineteenth and early twentieth centuries, however, the Senate resisted delegating by treaty a certain type of executive agreement power to the president, partly on constitutional grounds. During this period, presidents sought ratification of a series of bilateral arbitration treaties, pursuant to which the president would have had the subsequent authority to agree with other nations about which particular disputes would be submitted to the arbitration body. The Senate objected that such a delegation to the president would improperly dilute the treaty-making power, and it successfully insisted that any subsequent agreements to arbitrate under the treaties had themselves to be approved by the Senate.[17] It seems unlikely that such delegations would be viewed as constitutionally problematic today, given that, as discussed in the next chapter, the U.S. Supreme Court has shown little inclination since the 1930s to enforce constitutional restraints on legislative delegations of authority to the executive branch even in the domestic arena, and the Court has been even more

---

[14] *See* Treaty on Relations with Cuba, art. VII, May 22, 1903, 33 Stat. 2248 ("To enable the United States to maintain the independence of Cuba, and to protect the people thereof, as well as for its own defense, the Government of Cuba will sell or lease to the United States lands necessary for coaling or naval stations, at certain specified points, to be agreed upon with the President of the United States.").

[15] *See* SAMUEL B. CRANDALL, TREATIES: THEIR MAKING AND ENFORCEMENT 117–19 (2d ed. 1916) (describing a series of executive agreements entered into by the United States and other countries to address the administration or implementation of treaties in force).

[16] *See* RESTATEMENT (THIRD) OF THE FOREIGN RELATIONS LAW OF THE UNITED STATES § 303, cmt. 4 (1987).

[17] *See* Chandler P. Anderson, *The Senate and Obligatory Arbitration Treaties*, 26 AM. J. INT'L L. 328, 329 (1932). For criticism of the Senate's position, see, for example, 1 WESTEL WOODBURY WILLOUGHBY, THE CONSTITUTIONAL LAW OF THE UNITED STATES § 203, at 474–76 (1910); John Bassett Moore, *Treaties and Executive Agreements*, 20 POL. SCI. Q. 385, 417–20 (1905); Quincy Wright, *Treaties and the Constitutional Separation of Powers in the United States*, 12 AM. J. INT'L L. 64, 91–93 (1918).

reluctant to limit Congress's authority to delegate in the area of foreign affairs. Moreover, as discussed in the next section, presidents have on a number of occasions entered into agreements calling for arbitration of claims even in the absence of a delegation of authority in a treaty.

Congressional–Executive Agreements

There have been congressional–executive agreements since early in U.S. history. In 1792, for example, Congress authorized the postmaster general to conclude international agreements concerning the exchange of mail.[18] Congressional–executive agreements have been particularly common in the area of international trade, in part because of the perception that this area falls within the prerogatives of the full Congress to regulate foreign commerce and raise revenues.[19] The Dingley Tariff Act of 1897, for example, authorized the president to negotiate reciprocal trade concessions with countries exporting certain goods to the United States.[20] Earlier trade statutes that allowed the president to suspend or impose duties based on reciprocity but did not specifically call for the conclusion of agreements, such as the McKinley Tariff Act of 1890, were also construed as authorizing executive agreements.[21]

Most congressional–executive agreements before World War II involved *ex ante* delegations of authority from Congress—that is, Congress authorized the executive agreements in advance. Since World War II, however, a number of congressional–executive agreements have involved *ex post* approval from Congress, whereby the president has negotiated the agreement and then concluded it only after obtaining majority approval from both houses of Congress. The North American Free Trade Agreement (NAFTA) and the agreements associated with the World Trade Organization (WTO), for example,

---

[18] *See* Act of Feb. 20, 1792, ch. 7, § 26, 1 Stat. 232, 239. In concluding many years later that the postal agreements were constitutional, William Howard Taft, while serving as Attorney General, reasoned: "where long usage, dating back to a period contemporary with the adoption of the Constitution, sanctions an interpretation of that instrument different from that which would be reached by the ordinary rules of construction were the question a new one, the usage will be followed." *Postal Conventions with Foreign Countries*, 19 Op. Att'y Gen. 513, 515 (1890).

[19] *See* Detlev F. Vagts, *The Exclusive Treaty Power Revisited*, 89 Am. J. Int'l L. 40, 41 (1995); Jane N. Smith, Daniel T. Shedd & Brandon J. Murrill, *Why Certain Trade Agreements Are Approved as Congressional–Executive Agreements Rather Than as Treaties* (Cong. Res. Serv., April 15, 2013), *available at* https://fas.org/sgp/crs/misc/97-896.pdf.

[20] *See* Act of July 24, 1897, ch. 11, § 3, 30 Stat. 151, 203.

[21] *See* 5 John Bassett Moore, A Digest of International Law § 753, at 218–19 (1906); Crandall, *supra* note 15, at 122; Bruce Ackerman & David Golove, *Is NAFTA Constitutional?*, 108 Harv. L. Rev. 799, 821–22 (1995). *See also* Field v. Clark, 143 U.S. 649, 694 (1892) (upholding delegation of authority to president, in McKinley Tariff Act, to suspend the free importation of certain goods); J.W. Hampton v. United States, 276 U.S. 394, 409 (1928) (upholding delegation of authority to president, in 1922 Tariff Act, to adjust tariff rates).

were concluded with the *ex post* approval by Congress, as was the recently concluded United States-Mexico-Canada trade agreement (USMCA).

Since the 1970s, Congress has sometimes granted the president "fast-track" trade authority, also known more recently as "trade promotion" authority.[22] Under this legislation, Congress commits in advance that it will either approve or reject a trade agreement, without attempting to amend it, and that it will act quickly, typically within ninety days.[23] This type of authority is thought to enhance the negotiating position of the United States because it allows the president to make more credible commitments.

Congressional–executive agreements have been used for many subjects other than trade. For example, through such agreements the United States has joined a number of international institutions, such as the International Labour Organization, the International Monetary Fund, and the World Bank.[24] Although normally Article II treaties have been used for extradition of criminal suspects, in the mid-1990s, congressional–executive agreements were concluded allowing for the extradition of suspects to the international criminal tribunals for the former Yugoslavia and Rwanda.[25] While not constituting agreements per se, the United States annexed both Texas and Hawaii by means of statutes rather than treaties after proposed annexation treaties encountered opposition in the Senate.[26]

Despite the fact that the use of congressional–executive agreements is now widespread, questions have sometimes been raised about their constitutionality. The Constitution does not mention executive agreements, and they do not involve the supermajority senatorial consent specified in Article II. Nevertheless, the Founders of the Constitution appeared to recognize that some international agreements would not be "treaties." As noted in Chapter 2, the Constitution distinguishes between "treaties" and "agreements and compacts," disallowing states from entering into the former altogether but permitting them to enter into the latter if they receive congressional authorization. It seems unlikely that the constitutional Founders would have wanted states, but not the federal government, to be able to conclude non-treaty international agreements.

---

[22] *See* Harold Hongju Koh, *The Fast Track and United States Trade Policy*, 18 BROOK. J. INT'L L. 143 (1992); Committee on Finance, *Trade Promotion Authority Annotated*, 110th Cong., 1st Sess., S. Prt. 110-10, at 32–33 (Feb. 2007); William H. Cooper, *Trade Promotion Authority (TPA) and the Role of Congress in Trade Policy* (Cong. Res. Serv., Jan. 13, 2014), *available at* http://www.fas.org/sgp/crs/misc/RL33743.pdf.

[23] This trade promotion authority has lapsed at various times and has been periodically revived by Congress, most recently in 2015. *See* Congressional Research Service, *Trade Promotion Authority (TPA): Frequently Asked Questions* (June 21, 2019), *at* https://fas.org/sgp/crs/misc/R43491.pdf.

[24] 22 U.S.C. § 271 (International Labour Organization); 22 U.S.C. § 286 (International Monetary Fund and World Bank).

[25] *See* National Defense Authorization Act for Fiscal Year 1996, Pub. L. No. 104–106, § 1342, 110 Stat. 186, 486; Ntakirutimana v. Reno, 184 F.3d 419, 422 (5th Cir. 1999).

[26] *See* Ackerman & Golove, *supra* note 21, at 832–36; CRANDALL, *supra* note 15, at 135–38.

Although the Supreme Court has not expressly addressed the validity of congressional–executive agreements, it has stated in dicta that one of the sovereign powers of the United States is "the power to make such international agreements as do not constitute treaties in the constitutional sense."[27] It has also interpreted the word "treaty" in a statute as referring to congressional–executive agreements as well as Article II treaties.[28] In addition, as discussed in the next section, the Court has specifically upheld the validity of certain sole executive agreements, which do not involve any approval by Congress, let alone supermajority approval by the Senate.

In the 1940s, when the number of executive agreements began to increase substantially, there was an intense scholarly debate over their constitutionality.[29] Critics argued that they improperly evaded the requirements for making treaties specified in the Constitution and increased the likelihood that the United States would become bound by commitments that were not in its best interests. Defenders replied that executive agreements were functionally necessary and that congressional–executive agreements were more democratic than Article II treaties because they involved the full Congress and could not be blocked by a minority of legislators. Proposed constitutional amendments were introduced in the mid-1940s that would have substituted approval by a simple majority in Congress rather than two-thirds of the Senate in order for the United States to conclude treaties, but the amendments were not adopted.[30] Later proposed amendments in the 1950s would have disallowed the use of executive agreements in lieu of treaties, but these proposals also were not adopted.[31] The constitutional debate receded after the 1950s but was revived in the mid-1990s when the United States entered into the NAFTA and WTO trade agreements through the congressional–executive agreement process.[32]

The constitutionality of NAFTA was challenged in court in *Made in the USA Foundation v. United States*. In rejecting the constitutional challenge, a federal district

---

[27] United States v. Curtiss-Wright Export Corp., 299 U.S. 304, 318 (1936).
[28] *See* B. Altman & Co. v. United States, 224 U.S. 583, 601 (1912); *see also* Weinberger v. Rossi, 456 U.S. 25, 36 (1982) (interpreting term "treaty" in employment discrimination statute as encompassing executive agreements).
[29] *Compare* Edwin Borchard, *Shall the Executive Agreement Replace the Treaty?*, 53 YALE L.J. 664 (1944), *and* Edwin Borchard, *Treaties and Executive Agreements—A Reply*, 54 YALE L.J. 616 (1945), *with* Myers S. McDougal & Asher Lans, *Treaties and Congressional–Executive or Presidential Agreements: Interchangeable Instruments of National Policy (Pt. I)*, 54 YALE L.J. 181, 246 (1945), *and* Myres McDougal & Asher Lans, *Treaties and Congressional–Executive or Presidential Agreements: Interchangeable Instruments of National Policy (Pt. II)*, 54 YALE L.J. 534 (1945); *see also* WALLACE MCCLURE, INTERNATIONAL EXECUTIVE AGREEMENTS (1941).
[30] *See* Ackerman & Golove, *supra* note 21, at 886–95.
[31] *See* DUANE TANANBAUM, THE BRICKER AMENDMENT CONTROVERSY: A TEST OF EISENHOWER'S POLITICAL LEADERSHIP 36–37 (1988).
[32] *Compare* Ackerman & Golove, *supra* note 21, *and* David M. Golove, *Against Free-Form Formalism*, 73 N.Y.U. L. REV. 1791 (1998), *with* Laurence H. Tribe, *Taking Text and Structure Seriously: Reflections on Free-Form Method in Constitutional Interpretation*, 108 HARV. L. REV. 1221 (1995); *see also* Memorandum from Walter Dellinger, Assistant Attorney General, to Ambassador Michael Kantor, U.S. Trade Representative, *Whether the GATT Uruguay Round Must be Ratified as a Treaty* (July 29, 1994), *reprinted at* 140 CONG. REC. 19492 (Aug. 4, 1994).

court reasoned that Congress's authority under both the Commerce Clause and the Necessary and Proper Clause, combined with the president's foreign relations authority, provided a sufficient basis for concluding a commercial agreement such as NAFTA as a congressional–executive agreement.[33] On appeal, the U.S. Court of Appeals for the Eleventh Circuit did not address the merits of this issue, instead concluding that the case presented a nonjusticiable political question.[34] In reaching this determination, the Eleventh Circuit noted that there was a lack of textual and other materials to guide the courts in determining which commercial agreements must be concluded as Article II treaties, that a judicially imposed limitation on such agreements could seriously undermine U.S. foreign relations, and that there was no "impasse" between the political branches over the issue that necessitated judicial intervention.[35]

Like Article II treaties, valid congressional–executive agreements will preempt inconsistent state law, and they can also override earlier inconsistent treaties or federal statutes.[36] As with Article II treaties, when U.S. courts are asked to enforce congressional–executive agreements, they will need to determine whether and to what extent the agreements were intended to be judicially enforceable. For congressional–executive agreements approved by Congress after they are negotiated, however, there is a greater likelihood that Congress will have addressed issues of domestic implementation, including judicial enforceability. In the legislation implementing the WTO agreements, for example, Congress stated that "[n]o provision [in the agreements] . . . that is inconsistent with any law of the United States shall have effect" and that no state law could be declared invalid because of a conflict with the agreements "except in an action brought by the United States for the purpose of declaring such law or application invalid."[37] Similarly, in implementing the United States-Mexico-Canada trade agreement (USMCA) in 2020, Congress provided that "[n]o State law, or the application thereof, may be declared invalid as to any person or circumstance on the ground that the provision or application is inconsistent with the USMCA, except in an action brought by the United States for the purpose of declaring such law or application invalid."[38]

---

[33] *See* Made in the USA Foundation v. United States, 56 F. Supp. 2d 1226, 1317–22 (N.D. Ala. 1999).

[34] Made in the USA Foundation v. United States, 242 F.3d 1300, 1302 (11th Cir. 2001). (The political question doctrine is discussed in Chapter 1.)

[35] *See id.* at 1312–19. In *Zivotofsky v. Clinton*, 566 U.S. 189 (2012), the Supreme Court emphasized that the political question doctrine is a "narrow exception" to the judiciary's obligation to decide cases. *Id.* at 195.

[36] *See* Memorandum for Alan J. Kreczko, Special Assistant to the President and Legal Adviser to the National Security Council, from Christopher Schroeder, Acting Assistant Attorney General, Office of Legal Counsel, *Validity of Congressional–Executive Agreements That Substantially Modify the United States' Obligations under an Existing Treaty* (Nov. 25, 1996), 20 OP. OFF. LEGAL COUNSEL 389 (1996).

[37] 19 U.S.C. § 3512(a)(1) & (b)(2)(A).

[38] United States-Mexico-Canada Agreement Implementation Act § 102(b), H.R. 5430 (signed by President Trump on Jan. 29, 2020).

Partial Interchangeability of Treaties and Congressional–Executive Agreements

Although congressional–executive agreements are probably valid as a general matter, this does not necessarily mean that they are completely interchangeable with Article II treaties. Neither the district court nor the court of appeals in the *Made in the USA Foundation* case expressed the view that congressional–executive agreements were freely interchangeable with Article II treaties.[39] Although the *Restatement (Third) of Foreign Relations Law*, published in 1987, states that "[t]he prevailing view is that the Congressional–Executive agreement may be used as an alternative to the treaty method in every instance,"[40] a number of scholars have questioned this proposition.[41]

As a matter of historical practice, it does not appear that presidents have treated congressional–executive agreements as a complete alternative to the Article II treaty process. Presidents generally have used the Article II treaty process for significant treaties within certain subject areas, such as human rights, arms control, military alliances, and environmental protection. Moreover, although congressional–executive agreements have been used to join some international institutions, especially institutions relating to trade and finance, the Article II treaty process has generally been used for joining political and security organizations, such as the United Nations and NATO.[42] Importantly, presidents have used the Article II treaty process for some agreements even when this process has reduced the likelihood that the agreement will be approved. For example, in seeking approval of the Comprehensive Nuclear Test Ban Treaty, which

---

[39] *See Made in the USA Foundation*, 242 F.3d at 1302 ("We . . . affirm the principle, as enunciated by the U.S. Supreme Court, that certain international agreements may well require Senate ratification as treaties through the constitutionally-mandated procedures of Art. II, § 2."); *Made in the USA Foundation*, 56 F. Supp. 2d at 1323 n.364 ("[T]here may exist circumstances where the procedures outlined in the Treaty Clause must be adhered to in order to adopt an international agreement.").

[40] RESTATEMENT (THIRD) OF THE FOREIGN RELATIONS LAW OF THE UNITED STATES, *supra* note 16, § 303, cmt. e. Professor Louis Henkin, who served as the Chief Reporter for the *Restatement*, similarly contended that "it is now widely accepted that the Congressional–Executive agreement is available for wide use, even general use, and is a complete alternative to a treaty." LOUIS HENKIN, FOREIGN AFFAIRS AND THE UNITED STATES CONSTITUTION 217 (2d ed. 1996). In a footnote, Henkin added the qualification that "doubts might spark if it were used for an agreement traditionally dealt with by treaty and that seems to ask for the additional 'dignity' of a treaty, for example, a major alliance or disarmament arrangement." HENKIN at 217 n.*.

[41] *See* John C. Yoo, *Laws as Treaties: The Constitutionality of Congressional–Executive Agreements*, 99 MICH. L. REV. 757, 773 (2001); Peter J. Spiro, *Treaties, Executive Agreements, and Constitutional Method*, 79 TEX. L. REV. 961 (2001); Joel R. Paul, *The Geopolitical Constitution: Executive Expediency and Executive Agreements*, 86 CAL. L. REV. 671 (1998). *Cf.* Steve Charnovitz, *Using Framework Statutes to Facilitate U.S. Treatymaking*, 98 AM. J. INT'L L. 696, 703 (2004) (arguing that the United States should conclude more international agreements pursuant to framework statutes rather than as Article II treaties, without arguing that congressional–executive agreements are completely interchangeable with treaties).

[42] In 1999, Congress enacted a statute providing that, if the United States ever joins the International Criminal Court, it must do so through an Article II treaty. *See* 22 U.S.C. § 7401(a).

the Senate ultimately rejected, President Clinton apparently never contemplated using the congressional–executive agreement process. Similarly, President Clinton supported U.S. ratification of human rights agreements relating to discrimination against women and the rights of children, and environmental agreements such as the Kyoto Protocol relating to climate change, but he apparently did not contemplate overcoming resistance in the Senate by seeking approval of these agreements from a simple majority of Congress. To take another example, a number of recent presidents have sought to have the United States join the Law of the Sea Convention, but, despite encountering resistance in the Senate, have not attempted to bypass the Article II process. Similarly, President Obama unsuccessfully sought Senate approval of the UN Convention on the Rights of Persons with Disabilities, and, despite the existence of majority (but not two-thirds) support in the Senate, he did not appear to contemplate trying to conclude the Convention as a congressional–executive agreement.

At times, the Senate has specifically insisted that particular agreements go through the Article II treaty process. Such insistence has been particularly common in the area of arms control. Although the 1972 Interim Agreement on Strategic Offensive Arms (a component of the first Strategic Arms Limitation Agreement between the United States and the Soviet Union) was concluded as a congressional–executive agreement, every major arms control treaty since that time has been concluded through the Article II process.[43] This pattern is not a mere fortuity. In giving its advice and consent to a number of arms control treaties, the Senate has included a declaration stating that agreements "that would obligate the United States to reduce or limit the Armed Forces or armaments of the United States in a militarily significant manner" could be concluded "only pursuant to the treaty power as set forth in Article II, Section 2, Clause 2 of the Constitution."[44] In 1997, in response to Senate pressure, President Clinton agreed to submit an update of the Treaty on Armed Conventional Forces in Europe to the Senate for its advice and consent, thereby abandoning an earlier decision to seek only congressional majority approval for the agreement.[45] In 2001, President Bush suggested that he and Russian President Vladimir Putin could achieve large cuts in nuclear weapons through an informal agreement.[46] After the Secretary of State confirmed that the president intended to conclude a

---

[43] *See* Yoo, *supra* note 41, at 804–805. This is true even though the 1961 Arms Control and Disarmament Act contemplated that arms control agreements could be concluded either through the Article II treaty process or as congressional–executive agreements. *See* Pub. L. No. 87-297, § 33, 75 Stat. 631, 634 (1961) (stating that "no action shall be taken . . . that will obligate the United States to disarm or to reduce or to limit the Armed forces or armaments of the United States, except pursuant to the treaty making power of the President under the Constitution *or unless authorized by further affirmative legislation of the Congress of the United States*") (emphasis added).

[44] *See* Spiro, *supra* note 41, at 997.

[45] *See* Phillip R. Trimble & Alexander W. Koff, *All Fall Down: The Treaty Power in the Clinton Administration*, 16 BERKELEY J. INT'L L. 55, 56 (1998).

[46] *See* Presidential News Conference (Nov. 19, 2001), *in* 37 PUBLIC PAPERS OF THE PRESIDENT NO. 46 (2001).

legally binding agreement with Russia, the senior Democratic and Republican members of the Senate Foreign Relations Committee sent the Secretary of State a letter stating that because the agreement "would most likely include significant obligations by the United States regarding deployed U.S. strategic nuclear warheads," they were "convinced that such an agreement would constitute a treaty subject to the advice and consent of the Senate."[47] President Bush subsequently submitted the agreement to the Senate for its advice and consent.[48]

It is debatable whether this continuing practice of using the Article II process for certain types of agreements has, or should have, constitutional significance. As Professor Oona Hathaway has explained, it is difficult to find logical justifications for the distinctions in this practice.[49] Instead, the limited areas in which the Article II process is still treated as exclusive may be the product of particular historical developments and episodes of controversy. It also seems likely, however, that expectation interests have now formed around this practice, such that it would be politically difficult to conclude certain types of agreements (such as high-profile arms control and human rights agreements) outside of the Article II process. Moreover, if it is necessary to show that the Senate has acquiesced in full interchangeability between Article II treaties and congressional–executive agreements in order to show that such interchangeability has become constitutionally acceptable (as some theories about the role of historical practice in constitutional interpretation would suggest), modern historical practice does not provide clear support for a finding of such acquiescence.[50]

Even if congressional–executive agreements may constitutionally be used for the same subjects as Article II treaties, they are probably not entitled to the benefit of the holding in *Missouri v. Holland*, discussed in Chapter 2. According to that decision, neither Article II treaties nor legislation implementing them are subject to the enumerated power limitations that apply to Congress. One common justification for this proposition is that state interests are sufficiently protected in the Article II treaty process as a result of the requirement of supermajority advice and consent, so judicially imposed limitations are unnecessary to protect state interests. Another justification is that the Treaty Clause in Article II is textually separate from the list of Congress's powers in Article I and thus

---

[47] *See* CURTIS A. BRADLEY, ASHLEY S. DEEKS & JACK L. GOLDSMITH, FOREIGN RELATIONS LAW: CASES AND MATERIALS 389–90 (7th ed. 2020) (excerpting the letter).

[48] *See id.* The pattern continued under the Obama administration. For example, the New Strategic Arms Reduction Treaty between the United States and the Russian Federation, which President Obama signed in April 2010, was concluded as an Article II treaty. The Senate gave its advice and consent to the treaty in December 2010, subject to a variety of conditions, understandings, and declarations. *See* U.S. Dep't of State, *Press Release: New START Treaty: Resolution of Advice and Consent to Ratification* (Dec. 22, 2010), https://2009-2017.state.gov/t/avc/rls/153910.htm.

[49] Hathaway, *supra* note 3, at 1240.

[50] *See* Curtis A. Bradley & Trevor W. Morrison, *Historical Gloss and the Separation of Powers*, 126 HARV. L. REV. 411, 472–76 (2012).

should not be subject to the limitations that apply to those powers. Those arguments are inapplicable to congressional–executive agreements, which do not require supermajority consent by the Senate and are not concluded under Article II. As a result, congressional–executive agreements probably cannot regulate matters within the United States that fall outside of Congress's legislative authority, such as certain intrastate activities not involving commerce.[51]

The termination of congressional–executive agreements presents a more complicated question than for Article II treaties. Congressional–executive agreements involve a statute enacted by both houses of Congress, and the president ordinarily does not have the constitutional authority to terminate a statute unilaterally. When a statute simply provides *ex ante* authority to conclude an agreement, presumably the president has at least the same authority to terminate the agreement as he or she would have if it were an Article II treaty. Similarly, when Congress has approved an agreement *ex post* but has done nothing more, the president is likely to have whatever withdrawal authority he or she would have had if the agreement had been approved by the Senate instead of the full Congress.[52] When Congress has implemented the terms of an agreement into U.S. federal law, however, presidential withdrawal might not by itself undo the implementation, unless Congress has made the implementation subject to the continuing effect of the treaty.[53] Moreover, if Congress places statutory limitations on U.S. withdrawal when it authorizes or approves an agreement, and the president ratifies the agreement in light of those limitations, the president's domestic authority to withdraw may be subject to the limitations unless they are modified by a subsequent statute.[54]

---

[51] *See* Hathaway, *supra* note 3, at 1343; Bradford R. Clark, *Separation of Powers as a Safeguard of Federalism*, 79 TEX. L. REV. 1321, 1442 (2001); David Sloss, *International Agreements and the Political Safeguards of Federalism*, 55 STAN. L. REV. 1963, 1975 (2003); Carlos Manuel Vázquez, *Treaties and the Eleventh Amendment*, 42 VA. J. INT'L L. 713, 725 (2002).

[52] *Compare* Curtis A. Bradley, *Exiting Congressional-Executive Agreements*, 67 DUKE L.J. 1615, 1617 (2018) ("If one accepts presidential authority to terminate Article II treaties . . . there is no persuasive reason to conclude differently with respect to congressional–executive agreements."), *with* Joel Trachtman, *Power to Terminate U.S. Trade Agreements: The Presidential Dormant Commerce Clause Versus an Historical Gloss Half Empty*, 51 INT'L LAW. 445 (2018) (arguing that presidents do not have the unilateral authority to terminate congressional–executive agreements relating to trade).

[53] In the legislation implementing the United States-Mexico-Canada trade agreement (USMCA), Congress provided that, if the agreement ceases to be in force with respect to the United States, the implementing legislation "shall cease to have effect." USMCA Implementation Act, § 621(b).

[54] *See* Hathaway, *supra* note 3, at 1332–34. The United States joined the World Health Organization (WHO) in 1948 pursuant to a congressional-executive agreement. The statute authorizing the president to join the Organization stated that the United States was reserving the right to withdraw from the WHO "on a one-year notice," and that, in the event of such withdrawal, "the financial obligations of the United States to the Organization shall be met in full for the Organization's current fiscal year." In July 2020, the Trump administration notified the WHO that the United States was withdrawing from the Organization, but it indicated that the withdrawal would not become effective for a year, thereby appearing to comply with the notice provision.

Sole Executive Agreements

As with congressional–executive agreements, there have been sole executive agreements since early in U.S. history. In 1799, for example, President John Adams used a sole executive agreement to resolve claims against the Dutch government by American citizens who had lost their cargo on the *Wilmington Packet*, a schooner that had been seized by Dutch privateers in 1793.[55] In 1813, during the War of 1812 between the United States and Great Britain, President James Madison used a sole executive agreement to address the treatment and exchange of prisoners of war.[56]

The Supreme Court has considered the legal effect of sole executive agreements in four cases, and in each case has both treated the agreements as valid and has given them domestic effect. In two decisions during the 1930s and 1940s, the Court considered the effect of the Litvinov Assignment, an executive agreement entered into by President Franklin Roosevelt as part of his recognition of the Soviet Union. In the agreement, the United States waived claims against the Soviet Union relating to Soviet nationalization of American property, and in return the Soviet Union assigned to the U.S. government all Soviet claims to property located in the United States that had been held by Russian nationals at the time of the nationalization.[57]

In *United States v. Belmont*, the Supreme Court considered the effect of the Litvinov Assignment on property located in New York that had been owned by a Russian company at the time of the Soviet nationalization.[58] The Court held that the Assignment effectively validated the Soviet nationalization, which meant that the Soviet Union had lawful title to the property and could therefore transfer the property to the U.S. government under the Assignment. The Court declined to consider whether New York law would recognize the Soviet Union's title to the property, concluding that the Assignment preempted any contrary state law concerning the validity of title. The Court explained that "an international compact . . . is not always a treaty which requires the participation of the Senate. There are many such compacts, of which a protocol, a modus vivendi, a postal convention, and agreements like that now under consideration are illustrations."[59]

---

[55] *See* Exchange of Notes Regarding the "Wilmington Packet," Dec. 7 & 12, 1799, U.S.–Neth., T.I.A.S. No. 151, *reprinted in* 5 TREATIES AND OTHER INTERNATIONAL ACTS OF THE UNITED STATES OF AMERICA 1075–1104 (Hunter Miller ed., 1931–48).

[56] Cartel for the Exchange of Prisoners of War, May 12, 1813, U.S.–Gr. Brit., *reprinted in* 2 TREATIES AND OTHER INTERNATIONAL ACTS, *supra* note 2, at 557–65.

[57] For discussion of this and other agreements between Roosevelt and the Soviet Union, *see* DONALD G. BISHOP, THE LITVINOV AGREEMENTS: THE AMERICAN VIEW (1965).

[58] United States v. Belmont, 301 U.S. 324 (1937). *See also* STEPHEN M. MILLETT, THE CONSTITUTIONALITY OF EXECUTIVE AGREEMENTS: ANALYSIS OF UNITED STATES V. BELMONT (1990).

[59] *Belmont*, 301 U.S. at 330–31.

In a later decision, *United States v. Pink*, the Court reaffirmed both the validity and domestic effect of the Assignment, this time emphasizing the president's power to determine which governments are recognized by the United States:

> The powers of the President in the conduct of foreign relations included the power, without consent of the Senate, to determine the public policy of the United States with respect to the Russian nationalization decrees.... That authority is not limited to a determination of the government to be recognized. It includes the power to determine the policy which is to govern the question of recognition.[60]

The Court further stated that "[a] treaty is a 'Law of the Land' under the supremacy clause (Art. VI, Cl. 2) of the Constitution. Such international compacts and agreements as the Litvinov Assignment have a similar dignity."[61]

The Supreme Court also gave legal effect to a sole executive agreement in *Dames & Moore v. Regan*.[62] That case involved the Algiers Accords, an agreement entered into by President Carter with Iran in order to resolve the Iranian hostage crisis, in which U.S. embassy personnel were held hostage in Tehran for over a year. In the Algiers Accords, the United States agreed to transfer claims against Iran from U.S. courts to a new arbitral tribunal to be established in The Hague. A company that had a claim against Iran for breach of contract challenged the authority of the president to transfer the claim out of U.S. courts. In upholding the transfer, the Court relied primarily on a determination that Congress had acquiesced in presidential claims settlement of the sort addressed by the Accords.[63] The Court further stated, however, that "prior cases of this Court have also recognized that the President does have some measure of power to enter into executive agreements without obtaining the advice and consent of the Senate."[64]

Most recently, in *American Insurance Ass'n v. Garamendi*, the Supreme Court found that a state law was preempted by the policies reflected in sole executive agreements that were designed to settle war-related claims against private companies.[65] In that case, California had enacted a statute requiring insurance companies doing business in California to report on any policies they issued in Europe between 1920 and 1945, and

---

[60] United States v. Pink, 315 U.S. 203, 229 (1942).

[61] *Id.* at 230. For an argument, based on the original understanding of the constitutional Founders, that sole executive agreements should not have domestic legal effect, *see* Michael D. Ramsey, *Executive Agreements and the (Non)Treaty Power*, 77 N.C. L. REV. 133, 136–37 (1998). See also Bradford R. Clark, *Domesticating Sole Executive Agreements*, 93 VA. L. REV. 1573, 1655 (2007) (arguing that "courts should uphold sole executive agreements purporting to alter preexisting legal rights only when the President has independent constitutional or statutory authority to do so").

[62] Dames & Moore v. Regan, 453 U.S. 654 (1981).

[63] *See id.* at 674.

[64] *Id.* at 682.

[65] American Ins. Ass'n v. Garamendi, 539 U.S. 396 (2003).

also extending the statute of limitations for recovering under such policies. The Clinton administration subsequently entered into agreements with Germany, Austria, and France stating that, in return for their establishment of voluntary compensation funds, the executive branch would ask U.S. courts, and state and local governments, to defer to the funds as the means for resolving World War II–era claims against private companies. In a 5–4 decision, the Supreme Court held that the California statute was preempted because it created an obstacle to the achievement of the policies embodied in the agreements.

The Court in *Garamendi* reasoned that "at some point an exercise of state power that touches on foreign relations must yield to the National Government's policy," and that generally "there is executive authority to decide what that policy should be."[66] The Court also noted more specifically that its decisions "have recognized that the President has authority to make 'executive agreements' with other countries, requiring no ratification by the Senate or approval by Congress," and that "[m]aking executive agreements to settle claims of American nationals against foreign governments is a particularly longstanding practice."[67] Finally, the Court held that "[g]enerally . . . valid executive agreements are fit to preempt state law, just as treaties are."[68] Although the four dissenting justices disagreed with the majority that the California statute was preempted, they agreed that the president had the authority to conclude executive agreements to settle international claims and that, "in settling such claims . . . an executive agreement may preempt otherwise permissible state laws or litigation."[69]

Despite these decisions, the Supreme Court has not held that the president's power to enter into sole executive agreements is unlimited. In *Dames & Moore*, for example, the Court merely observed that the president has "some measure of power" to enter into such agreements. Most legal scholars, including those who maintain that congressional-executive agreements are interchangeable with Article II treaties, believe that the president's authority to enter into sole executive agreements is substantially narrower than the president's authority to enter into Article II treaties. Professor Louis Henkin, for example, described the proposition that sole executive agreements are completely interchangeable with Article II treaties as "unacceptable, for it would wholly remove the 'check' of Senate consent which the Framers struggled and compromised to write into the Constitution."[70]

---

[66] *Id.* at 413.
[67] *Id.* at 415.
[68] *Id.* at 416.
[69] *Id.* at 436 (Ginsburg, J., dissenting). For criticism of the Court's finding of preemption, *see* Brannon P. Denning & Michael D. Ramsey, American Insurance Association v. Garamendi *and Executive Preemption in Foreign Affairs*, 46 WM. & MARY L. REV. 825, 869–98 (2004). For a decision applying *Garamendi* to preempt state law claims relating to Holocaust-era insurance policies, despite the absence of a relevant executive agreement, *see* In re *Assicurazioni General*, 592 F.3d 113 (2d Cir. 2010).
[70] HENKIN, *supra* note 40, at 222; *see also* 1 LAURENCE H. TRIBE, AMERICAN CONSTITUTIONAL LAW 649 (3d ed. 2000) ("That the power to conclude executive agreements coincides perfectly with the treaty power is untenable . . . since such a conclusion would emasculate the structurally crucial senatorial check on executive discretion that the Framers so carefully embodied in the Constitution.").

There is significant uncertainty, however, about how to discern the limits of the sole executive agreement power, and about whether any such limits are judicially enforceable.[71]

There is little doubt that presidents have some authority to conclude sole executive agreements when the agreements relate to an independent presidential power. The president's commander-in-chief power, for example, has been the basis for numerous sole executive agreements.[72] It was the basis for President Madison's executive agreement concerning prisoners of war, mentioned earlier. It was also the basis for the Rush–Bagot agreement of 1817 limiting naval forces on the Great Lakes (which President Monroe eventually submitted to the Senate almost a year after it had taken effect).[73] Important armistice agreements have also been concluded unilaterally by the president under the commander-in-chief power, such as the peace protocol with Spain in 1898 that established the conditions for ending the Spanish–American War.[74] In 1940, before the United States became directly involved in World War II, President Roosevelt controversially entered into a sole executive agreement with Great Britain whereby the United States provided Great Britain with decommissioned destroyers in return for military bases.[75] "Status of forces agreements" (which establish a framework for the operation of U.S. troops stationed in another country and the exercise of jurisdiction over them) have also sometimes been concluded as sole executive agreements.[76]

---

[71] *See* Memorandum from Teresa Wynn Roseborough, Deputy Assistant Attorney General, to Conrad K. Harper, Legal Adviser, Department of State, *Waiver of Claims Arising Out of Cooperative Space Activity*, 19 Op. Off. Legal Counsel 140, 152 (1995) ("Although the President's authority to enter into sole executive agreements is well established, the precise limitations that may exist on the proper scope of those agreements is far from settled.").

[72] *See* Restatement (Second) of the Foreign Relations Law of the United States § 121, cmt. b (1965) ("A large proportion of the international agreements made under the powers of the President and intended to create legal relationships under international law have been based on his power as commander-in-chief and have provided for the conduct of military operations with allies of the United States.").

[73] *See* James F. Barnett, International Agreements Without the Advice and Consent of the Senate 29–30 (1906); *see also* McClure, *supra* note 29, at 49 (describing the Rush–Bagot agreement as "[b]y far the most famous and significant of the early executive agreements"). President Monroe ultimately decided to submit the agreement to the Senate "as an act of prudence." Crandall, *supra* note 15, at 103.

[74] *See* Protocol—Spain, Aug. 12, 1898, 30 Stat. 1742; *see also* Moore, *supra* note 17, at 391–92.

[75] Agreement between the United States and Great Britain Respecting Naval and Air Bases, U.S.–Gr. Brit., Sept. 2, 1940, 54 Stat. 2405. For discussion of the legality of the agreement, compare Opinion of Attorney General Robert H. Jackson, *Acquisition of Naval and Air Bases in Exchange for Over-Age Destroyers*, 39 Op. Att'y Gen. 484 (1940), with Edwin Borchard, *The Attorney General's Opinion on the Exchange of Destroyers for Naval Bases*, 34 Am. J. Int'l L. 690, 691 (1940). For additional discussion of the historical and legal context of the agreement, *see* William R. Casto, *Advising Presidents: Robert Jackson and the Destroyers-for-Bases Deal*, 52 Am. J. Legal Hist. 1 (2012).

[76] *See* R. Chuck Mason, *Status of Forces Agreement (SOFA): What Is It, and How Has It Been Utilized?* (Cong. Res. Serv., Mar. 15, 2012), *available at* https://fas.org/sgp/crs/natsec/RL34531.pdf. Even for issues connected to the commander-in-chief power, there have sometimes been questions about whether a sole executive agreement is proper. In 2008, for example, there was controversy surrounding President George W. Bush's decision to conclude security agreements with Iraq as sole executive agreements. *See, e.g.*, Bruce Ackerman, *Bush Can't Act Alone*, L.A. Times (Nov. 29, 2007). *See also* Michael John Garcia, R. Chuck Mason & Jennifer K. Elsea,

The Algiers Accords agreement that was at issue in *Dames & Moore* arguably related to the commander-in-chief power, because it resolved a national security crisis, and one might even make this claim as well about the agreements at issue in *Garamendi*, because they related to conduct during World War II. The *Belmont* and *Pink* decisions, by contrast, related to the president's implied recognition power, because they concerned the recognition of the Soviet Union. It is worth noting, however, that in connection with the agreement at issue in those cases, there was also a resolution of claims by the Soviet Union relating to military activities by the United States during the Russian Revolution, something connected to the president's commander-in-chief power.[77]

Sole executive agreements may also be appropriate for short-term or one-time commitments. As noted in Chapter 2, the Supreme Court suggested in a nineteenth-century extradition decision that "treaties" impose ongoing obligations, whereas "compacts" and "agreements" address one-time or temporary matters.[78] The Court based this distinction on the writings of the influential Swiss publicist Emmerich Vattel, who explained the distinction as follows:

> Compacts which have for their object matters of temporary interest are called agreements, conventions, arrangements. They are fulfilled by a single act and not by a continuous performance of acts. When the act in question is performed these compacts are executed once and for all; whereas treaties are executory in character and the acts called for must continue as long as the treaty lasts.[79]

Congressional Oversight and Related Issues Concerning the Prospective Security Agreement between the United States and Iraq (Cong. Res. Serv., Apr. 1, 2008), *available at* http://www.fas.org/sgp/crs/mideast/RL34362.pdf; Michael J. Glennon & Garth Schofield, *Tacit Commitments, Constitutional Limits, and the Iraq Security Arrangement*, 49 HARV. INT'L L.J. ONLINE 56 (2008).

[77] For accounts of the U.S. military activities in Russia during the Russian revolution, *see* DAVID S. FOGLESONG, AMERICA'S SECRET WAR AGAINST BOLSHEVISM: U.S. INTERVENTION IN THE RUSSIAN CIVIL WAR, 1917–1920 (1995), and GEORGE F. KENNAN, THE DECISION TO INTERVENE: SOVIET–AMERICAN RELATIONS, 1917–1920 (1958).

[78] *See* Holmes v. Jennison, 39 U.S. (14 Pet.) 540, 572 (1840) (Opinion of Taney, C.J.); *see also* United States Steel Corp. v. Multistate Tax Comm'n, 434 U.S. 452, 462 n.12 (1978) ("This distinction between supposedly ongoing accords, such as military alliances, and instantaneously executed, though perpetually effective, agreements, such as boundary settlements, may have informed the drafting in Art. I, § 10."); David M. Levitan, *Executive Agreements: A Study of the Executive in the Control of the Foreign Relations of the United States*, 35 ILL. L. REV. 365, 369 (1940) ("[O]ther questions, such as boundary disputes, had long been settled by agreements. It was the right to resort to these agreements that the framers sought to leave open for future use, providing only for Congressional consent as a guarantee against the abuse of this prerogative."). *Cf.* Ramsey, *supra* note 61, at 236 (arguing that the original understanding of the constitutional Founders was that sole executive agreements could be used only for "minor and temporary (or nonexecutory) agreements").

[79] 2 EMMERICH DE VATTEL, THE LAW OF NATIONS OR THE PRINCIPLES OF NATURAL LAW, ch. 12, § 153 (1758) (Charles G. Fenwick trans., 1916); *see also* Paul, *supra* note 41, at 737 ("While treaties would bind the nation in perpetuity, agreements and compacts functioned like contemporaneous exchanges which imposed no future obligations on any party; agreements and treaties were not interchangeable.").

A common short-term commitment is a *modus vivendi*, which is "an instrument recording an international agreement of temporary or provisional nature intended to be replaced by an arrangement of a more permanent and detailed character."[80] These instruments have been used by the United States on subjects ranging from fishing rights to international boundaries to import duties.[81] A presidential power to enter into such agreements may stem in part from the president's constitutional authority to negotiate treaties, since these agreements are designed to facilitate negotiation.[82]

In 2011, the Obama administration signed the Anti-Counterfeiting Trade Agreement (ACTA), which addresses the domestic enforcement of intellectual property rights, without seeking congressional or senatorial approval. Initially, the administration suggested that it was proper to conclude ACTA as a sole executive agreement because it would not require changes to U.S. law.[83] The Obama administration subsequently seemed to argue that the agreement was implicitly authorized by existing legislation and thus was a congressional–executive agreement rather than a sole executive agreement.[84] In May 2012, over fifty legal scholars sent a letter to the Senate's Committee on Finance arguing that ACTA could not constitutionally be concluded as a sole executive agreement and that existing statutes did not authorize the conclusion of the agreement.[85] ACTA is not the only instance in which the executive branch has attempted to justify its conclusion of an international agreement by reference to statutes that do not specifically authorize the conclusion of agreements, and this phenomenon may become more common going forward.[86]

---

[80] UN Treaty Collection, *Treaty Reference Guide* (1999), http://treaties.un.org/Pages/Overview.aspx?path=overview/treatyRef/page1_En.xml; *see also* Moore, *supra* note 17, at 397 ("As the name indicates, a *modus vivendi* is in its nature a temporary or working arrangement, made in order to bridge over some difficulty, pending a permanent settlement.").

[81] *See* CRANDALL, *supra* note 15, at 112–14; Charles Cheney Hyde, *Agreements of the United States Other than Treaties*, 17 GREEN BAG 229, 233–34 (1905); Moore, *supra* note 17, at 398. Some *modi vivendi* have likely been concluded as non-binding political commitments rather than as legally binding agreements.

[82] *See* CRS Treaty Study, *supra* note 2, at 90.

[83] For critiques of this claim, *see* Oona A. Hathaway & Amy Kapczynski, *Going It Alone: The Anti-Counterfeiting Trade Agreement as a Sole Executive Agreement*, ASIL INSIGHTS (Aug. 24, 2011), http://www.asil.org/pdfs/insights/insight110824.pdf; and Jack Goldsmith & Lawrence Lessig, *Anti-Counterfeiting Agreement Raises Constitutional Concerns*, WASH. POST (Mar. 26, 2010), at A23.

[84] *See* Letter from Harold Hongju Koh, Legal Adviser, U.S. Department of State, to Senator Ron Wyden (Mar. 6, 2012), *at* http://infojustice.org/wp-content/uploads/2012/03/84365507-State-Department-Response-to-Wyden-on-ACTA.pdf; Remarks of Harold Hongju Koh, *Twenty-First Century Lawmaking* (Oct. 17, 2012), *at* https://2009-2017.state.gov/s/l/releases/remarks/199319.htm. For a critical evaluation of the claim, *see* Jack Goldsmith, *The Doubtful Constitutionality of ACTA as an Ex Ante Congressional-Executive Agreement*, LAWFARE (May 21, 2012), *at* http://www.lawfareblog.com/2012/05/the-doubtful-constitutionality-of-acta-as-an-ex-ante-congressional-executive-agreement/.

[85] *See* Law Professor Letter to Senate Finance Committee (May 16, 2012), *at* http://infojustice.org/senatefinance-may2012.

[86] *See, e.g.*, U.S. State Department, Media Note, *United States Joins Minamata Convention on Mercury* (Nov. 6, 2013) (noting that the executive branch had ratified a convention to reduce exposure to mercury and that

Settlement of Claims

A particularly well-established subject for sole executive agreements has been the settlement of monetary claims—both claims by private U.S. citizens against foreign governments and intergovernmental claims between the United States and another country. Early in U.S. history, these agreements often related to maritime disputes, such as the dispute at issue in the *Wilmington Packet* settlement, discussed earlier. By the second half of the nineteenth century, these settlements came to encompass a broader range of claims, including claims of damage to or seizure of U.S. property abroad and false imprisonment of U.S. citizens. One example is the Boxer Indemnity Protocol of 1901, in which China agreed to indemnify the United States for losses arising out of the Boxer Rebellion, and which President McKinley joined without submitting to the Senate.[87] Presidents during the late nineteenth century also increasingly settled claims by having them referred to international arbitration.[88] The four Supreme Court decisions that have considered the effect of sole executive agreements—*Belmont, Pink, Dames & Moore*, and *Garamendi*—all involved, in part, the settlement of claims.[89]

The president's authority to settle claims has been thought to stem from specific presidential powers as well as from the president's lead role in representing the United States in international relations. It is also worth noting that private claimants have often consented to have the president act on their behalf, in part because this has been their only opportunity to obtain redress. As discussed in Chapter 8, until the 1950s, foreign governments had essentially absolute immunity in U.S. courts from private lawsuits. In addition, international law often required that an individual with a claim against a foreign

---

the United States would "implement Convention obligations under existing legislative and regulatory authority"), *at* https://2009-2017.state.gov/r/pa/prs/ps/2013/11/217295.htm. For a defense of what the authors call "Executive Agreements+," which are agreements not specifically authorized by Congress but which "complement" or are "consistent with" existing law, *see* Daniel Bodansky & Peter Spiro, *Executive Agreements+*, 49 VAND. J. TRANSNAT'L L. 885 (2016). For a critique of this phenomenon, *see* Bradley & Goldsmith, *Presidential Control, supra* note 2, at 1260–61. *See also* Harold Hongju Koh, *Triptych's End: A Better Framework to Evaluate 21st Century International Lawmaking*, 126 YALE L.J.F. 338, 343 (2017) (arguing that the executive branch can conclude international agreements whenever it "determine[s] that the negotiated agreement fit[s] within the fabric of existing law, [is] fully consistent with existing law, and [does] not require any further legislation to implement").

[87] *See* BARNETT, *supra* note 73, at 36–37.

[88] *See* Ingrid Brunk Wuerth, *The Dangers of Deference: International Claims Settlement by the President*, 44 HARV. INT'L L.J. 1, 26 (2003); CRANDALL, *supra* note 15, at 109–11. For an example, see 5 MOORE, *supra* note 21, at 215–16 (describing 1871 agreement with Spain to arbitrate claims of U.S. citizens arising out of insurrection in Cuba).

[89] *See also* Ozanic v. United States, 188 F.2d 228, 231 (2d Cir. 1951) (opinion of Hand, J.) ("The constitutional power of the President extends to the settlement of mutual claims between a foreign government and the United States, at least when it is an incident to the recognition of that government; and it would be unreasonable to circumscribe it to such controversies.").

government have their government "espouse" the claim on the individual's behalf.[90] Both of these limitations have been relaxed: foreign governments can sometimes be sued by private parties in U.S. courts, especially for commercial claims, and private parties now sometimes have legal claims that they can pursue without their government's espousal. In part because of these changes, the claimants in *Dames & Moore* opposed presidential resolution of their claim.

Most executive claims settlements have involved claims against foreign governments. In *Garamendi*, however, the Court concluded that the president's settlement authority extended even to claims against private entities. The Court explained that "insisting on [a line between public and private acts] in defining the legitimate scope of the Executive's international negotiations would hamstring the President in settling international controversies."[91] The Court also noted that in the context of war-related settlements, "untangling government policy from private initiative ... is often so hard that diplomatic action settling claims against private parties may well be just as essential in the aftermath of hostilities as diplomacy to settle claims against foreign governments."[92]

Congress appears to have accepted a presidential power to settle claims. In 1949, it enacted the International Claims Settlement Act, which established a procedure whereby funds from such settlements could be distributed.[93] The Act created the International Claims Commission, which is now the Foreign Claims Settlement Commission, and gave it jurisdiction to make final and binding decisions with respect to claims by U.S. nationals against settlement funds. The Act has been amended numerous times to address particular foreign settlements. Although the Act did not apply to the particular settlement in *Dames & Moore*, the Court in that case relied on the Act for the proposition that Congress had "placed its stamp of approval" on the general practice of executive claims settlement.[94] In *Garamendi*, the Court noted that, "[g]iven the fact that the practice goes back over 200 years, and has received congressional acquiescence throughout its history, the conclusion '[t]hat the President's control of foreign relations includes the settlement of claims is indisputable.' "[95] Nevertheless, this authority is not unlimited. In fact, in a 2008 decision, *Medellin v. Texas*, the Court described the president's claims settlement authority as "involv[ing] a narrow set of circumstances: the making of executive agreements to settle civil claims between American citizens and foreign governments or foreign nationals."[96]

---

[90] *See* Wuerth, *supra* note 88, at 20–21; Clark, *supra* note 61, at 1626–29.
[91] American Ins. Ass'n v. Garamendi, 539 U.S. 396, 416 (2003).
[92] *Id.*
[93] *See* 22 U.S.C. § 1621 *et seq.*
[94] Dames & Moore v. Regan, 453 U.S. 654, 680 (1981).
[95] *Garamendi*, 539 U.S. at 415 (quoting United States v. Pink, 315 U.S. 203, 240 (1942) (Frankfurter, J., concurring)).
[96] Medellin v. Texas, 552 U.S. 491, 531 (2008). In practice, claims settlement agreements have been broader than the Court's description in *Medellin* and have involved, for example, the settlement or waiving of claims between the U.S. government and foreign governments. *Cf.* Memorandum from Roseborough, *supra* note 71,

Legal Effect and Termination of Sole Executive Agreements

The Supreme Court's decisions clearly establish that a valid sole executive agreement can preempt inconsistent state law. Presumably, the self-execution analysis that is applicable to treaties (see Chapter 2) will also apply to sole executive agreements, although there are few decisions addressing this issue.[97] Unlike for Article II treaties, lower courts have held that sole executive agreements cannot override even an earlier-in-time federal statute.[98] This proposition is consistent with the influential framework for assessing presidential authority set forth by Justice Jackson in the *Youngstown* steel seizure case, discussed in Chapter 1, pursuant to which the president's authority is at its lowest when the president is acting contrary to the express or implied will of Congress.[99] There may be instances, however, in which a sole executive agreement relates to an area of exclusive presidential authority that cannot validly be regulated by Congress, and in such an instance the agreement would take precedence over the statute (because that application of the statute would be unconstitutional). Although the Supreme Court gave effect to a sole executive agreement in *Dames & Moore* that had the effect of limiting an otherwise-applicable federal statute (the Foreign Sovereign Immunities Act), the Court rested its decision primarily on legislative acquiescence and authorization rather than on the agreement. Like Article II treaties, executive agreements are subject to the individual rights protections of the Constitution.[100]

Because sole executive agreements are concluded unilaterally by the president, as a matter of U.S. constitutional law they can presumably also be terminated unilaterally by the president.[101] Such a presidential termination will prevent the agreement from having any further domestic effect. Whether such a termination also ends the international law obligations of the United States will depend on the international law governing the termination of treaties rather than on U.S. constitutional law.

---

at 140 (concluding that "the President may waive claims, including subrogated claims, against foreign governments, in exchange for a reciprocal waiver from the foreign government").

[97] For a rare decision addressing the issue of self-execution for executive agreements, see *Islamic Republic of Iran v. Boeing Co.*, 771 F.2d 1279, 1283 (9th Cir. 1985).

[98] *See, e.g.*, United States v. Guy W. Capps, Inc., 204 F.2d 655, 659–60 (4th Cir. 1953), *aff'd on other grounds*, 348 U.S. 296 (1955); Swearingen v. United States, 565 F. Supp. 1019, 1021 (D. Colo. 1983).

[99] *See* Youngstown Sheet & Tube Co. v. Sawyer, 343 U.S. 579, 637–38 (1952) (Jackson, J., concurring) ("When the President takes measures incompatible with the expressed or implied will of Congress, his power is at its lowest ebb, for then he can rely only upon his own constitutional powers minus any constitutional powers of Congress over the matter. Courts can sustain exclusive presidential control in such a case only by disabling the Congress from acting upon the subject."); *see also Medellín*, 552 U.S. at 529–30 (2008) ("[T]he authority of the President to represent the United States before such [international] bodies speaks to the President's *international* responsibilities, not any unilateral authority to create domestic law.").

[100] *See* Reid v. Covert, 354 U.S. 1, 16–17 (1957) (plurality opinion).

[101] *See, e.g.*, JOHN MABRY MATHEWS, THE CONDUCT OF AMERICAN FOREIGN RELATIONS 251 (1922).

Finally, it should be noted that, even when not constitutionally required, there may be good legal or policy reasons for a president to seek senatorial or congressional approval for an international agreement. As discussed, agreements approved by the Senate or the full Congress generally will have a higher status in U.S. law than sole executive agreements. They may also signal a higher degree of commitment by the United States, since they reflect the support of more than just a particular presidential administration.[102] Some international agreements may also require congressional involvement for their implementation—for example, if the implementation involves an appropriation of funds or changes to U.S. criminal law.

Political Agreements

It has become common for nations to enter into what are known as "political" or "soft law" agreements—that is, agreements that are not intended to be legally binding under international law. These agreements can take a variety of forms, including joint statements and declarations, communiqués, and exchanges of notes. Also common are memoranda of understanding between administrative agencies and their counterparts in other countries concerning cooperation in addressing regulatory issues. Political agreements can be an attractive vehicle for coordinating action and fostering dialogue when nations are reluctant to bind themselves legally.[103] When the executive branch enters into these political agreements on behalf of the United States, they are not submitted to either the Senate or the full Congress for approval. Nor are they reported to Congress under the Case-Zablocki Act.

A prominent example of a political commitment was the Atlantic Charter, a joint declaration issued by President Franklin Roosevelt and Prime Minister Winston Churchill in 1941 announcing "certain common principles in the national policies of their respective countries on which they base their hopes for a better future for the world."[104] Another example is the 1975 Helsinki Accords, a non-binding declaration in which the United States and other western nations pledged to respect the Soviet Union's territorial boundaries and the Soviet Union in turn pledged to respect human rights.[105]

---

[102] *Cf.* Julian Nyarko, *Giving the Treaty a Purpose: Comparing the Durability of Treaties and Executive Agreements*, 113 AM. J. INT'L L. 54 (2019) (finding that Article II treaties are more durable than executive agreements).

[103] For discussion of the international attractions of political agreements, *see* Andrew T. Guzman & Timothy L. Meyer, *International Soft Law*, 2 J. LEG. ANALYSIS 171 (2010), and Gregory C. Shaffer & Mark A. Pollack, *Hard vs. Soft Law: Alternatives, Complements, and Antagonists in International Governance*, 94 MINN. L. REV. 706 (2010). *See also* Kenneth W. Abbott & Duncan Snidal, *Hard and Soft Law in International Governance*, 54 INT'L ORG. 421 (2000).

[104] Joint Declaration by the President and Prime Minister, Signed in Placentia Bay, Newfoundland, Aug. 14, 1941.

[105] *See* Conference on Security and Co-operation in Europe Final Act, Helsinki 1975, *at* http://www.osce.org/mc/39501?download=true.

Although these political agreements—unlike Article II treaties and executive agreements—are not binding under international law, they can affect the expectations that other nations have about U.S. actions going forward. Moreover, given the weak enforcement machinery that often exists under international law, the differences between the sanctions associated with breaching legally binding agreements and breaching political agreements may not be substantial. Political agreements also have the potential to harden into more binding obligations under customary international law (the status of which in the U.S. legal system is discussed in Chapter 5), and to erode opposition to the formation of binding treaties. For these reasons, they might be a means through which presidents could create some of the effects of binding international agreements without obtaining the approval of either Congress or two-thirds of the Senate, even in areas in which presidents lack authority to conclude sole executive agreements. Nevertheless, it is difficult to discern constitutional constraints on executive authority to enter into these agreements.[106]

President Barack Obama controversially invoked his authority to make political commitments when concluding two high-profile agreements: the Joint Comprehensive Plan of Action (JCPOA) with Iran concerning its nuclear program, which the United States joined in 2015; and the Paris Agreement on climate change, which the United States joined in 2016.

Under the JCPOA, an agreement that included not only the United States and Iran but also China, France, Germany, Russia, and the United Kingdom, the Obama administration promised to reduce U.S. sanctions against Iran and to support the lifting of international sanctions in return for Iran taking steps to limit its development of nuclear materials. The Obama administration claimed that the entire agreement was non-binding and thus did not require congressional approval, and that the executive branch could use authority previously delegated by Congress to carry out the U.S. obligations under the agreement. Congress responded by enacting a statute that delayed U.S. implementation of the agreement until Congress had an opportunity to review it, but ultimately there were insufficient votes in Congress to block it.[107]

For the Paris Agreement, at least some of the agreement was likely authorized by a prior agreement that the United States had previously joined as an Article II treaty—the 1992 UN Framework Convention on Climate Change. But the Framework Convention did not appear to authorize binding emissions reductions. As a result, the Obama

---

[106] For an argument that Congress should become more involved in monitoring and regulating political agreements, *see* Duncan B. Hollis & Joshua J. Newcomer, *"Political" Commitments and the Constitution*, 49 VA. J. INT'L L. 507 (2009). For an argument that courts should give deference to non-binding agreements made between U.S. administrative agencies and regulators in other countries, *see* Jean Galbraith & David Zaring, *Soft Law as Foreign Relations Law*, 99 CORNELL L. REV. 735 (2014).

[107] *See* Iran Nuclear Agreement Review Act of 2015, Pub. L. No. 114-117, 129 Stat. 201; *see also* Bradley & Goldsmith, *Presidential Control*, *supra* note 2, at 1295–96.

administration insisted that the emissions reduction provision in the Paris Agreement be framed as a non-binding political commitment ("should" rather than "shall"). Because the provision was framed this way, the administration maintained that it did not need to obtain congressional approval.[108] As with the JCPOA, President Obama relied on preexisting regulatory authority to implement the agreement. The U.S. involvement in these agreements turned out to be short lived, as President Donald Trump subsequently acted to withdraw the United States from both of them.[109]

* * *

The phenomenon of executive agreements provides a vivid illustration of how historical practice can inform the powers of the legislative and executive branches of the U.S. government. The constitutional text offers little guidance about the proper scope of executive agreements, so the law in this area has largely been worked out over time by interactions between the political branches, conducted against the backdrop of the functional needs of the country in conducting foreign relations. The courts have played only a relatively minor role, primarily in upholding certain sole executive agreements that involved the recognition of foreign governments or the settlement of claims. The historical practice, which continues to evolve, suggests that there are at least modest constraints on the use of congressional–executive agreements in certain subject areas, and that there are more robust (but still vaguely defined) constraints on the use of sole executive agreements. Absent greater judicial involvement in policing executive agreements, the effectiveness of such constraints will depend on some combination of political resistance—by the Senate, the full Congress, or the public—and self-policing by the executive. The same can be said of political commitments.

---

[108] *See* Bradley & Goldsmith, *Presidential Control*, *supra* note 2, at 1251.
[109] The U.S. withdrawal from the JCPOA was effective immediately in 2018. But the U.S. withdrawal from the Paris Agreement will not become effective until November 2020.

4 Decisions and Orders of International Institutions

THIS CHAPTER CONSIDERS some of the constitutional issues that are implicated by delegations of authority from the United States to international institutions.[1] Despite sometimes having an isolationist reputation, the United States has often been at the forefront of establishing international institutions, and it participates in numerous such institutions, ranging from the Universal Postal Union to the International Atomic Energy Association to the Organisation for the Prohibition of Chemical Weapons. By joining these institutions, the United States has delegated various forms of authority to international actors, including in some instances the authority to issue binding adjudicatory decisions, enact legislative or regulatory provisions, and take enforcement actions. These delegations are typically embodied in treaties or executive agreements.

The chapter begins by describing the general proliferation of international institutions during the twentieth century. It then considers some of the general constitutional

---

[1] For other general treatments of this topic, see, for example, George A. Bermann, *Constitutional Implications of U.S. Participation in Regional Integration*, 46 AM. J. COMP. L. SUPP. 463 (1998); Curtis A. Bradley, *International Delegations, the Structural Constitution, and Non–Self-Execution*, 55 STAN. L. REV. 1557 (2003); Julian G. Ku, *The Delegation of Federal Power to International Organizations: New Problems with Old Solutions*, 85 MINN. L. REV. 71 (2000); and Edward T. Swaine, *The Constitutionality of International Delegations*, 104 COLUM. L. REV. 1492 (2004).

doctrines and provisions that might be implicated by U.S. delegations of authority to international institutions. After laying this groundwork, the chapter proceeds to discuss various types of international delegations and the constitutional issues they implicate. It first considers the constitutional issues associated with delegations of judicial authority to international arbitral and adjudicatory institutions. It then reviews an important series of decisions by the International Court of Justice (ICJ) directing the United States to reopen domestic proceedings in certain criminal cases. The chapter next considers the particular constitutional issues associated with U.S. participation in international criminal tribunals, including issues that might arise were the United States to join the International Criminal Court.

Shifting to legislative and regulatory delegations, the chapter examines constitutional issues associated with delegating to international institutions the authority to make amendments to U.S. treaty commitments. The chapter then turns to enforcement delegations, focusing in particular on the constitutional issues associated with delegations of inspection authority to international bodies as part of arms control agreements. The chapter concludes by considering the extent to which potential constitutional issues can be avoided by treating international orders and decisions as presumptively "non–self-executing" in the U.S. legal system.

Rise of International Institutions

International leagues and alliances have existed since antiquity. It was not until the nineteenth century, however, that nations began to establish international governance institutions.[2] Participants in the 1815 Congress of Vienna, held after the Napoleonic Wars, envisioned that a group of nations would meet regularly to conduct diplomacy. The Congress of Vienna also established the Central Commission for Navigation on the Rhine, which some consider to be the world's oldest international institution.[3] A number of other river commissions were subsequently established. By the mid-to-late nineteenth century, additional institutions were set up relating to areas of technological and economic cooperation. These institutions include the International Telegraphic Union, established in 1865; the Universal Postal Union, established in 1874; and the International Copyright Union, established in 1886.

After World War I, the League of Nations was established, as part of the Versailles Treaty. The League was the first international institution designed not simply to organize cooperation, but to guarantee peace and establish a system of collective security.

---

[2] *See generally* DAVID MACKENZIE, A WORLD BEYOND BORDERS: AN INTRODUCTION TO THE HISTORY OF INTERNATIONAL ORGANIZATIONS 4 (2010); BOB REINALDA, ROUTLEDGE HISTORY OF INTERNATIONAL ORGANIZATIONS: FROM 1815 TO THE PRESENT DAY 17–20 (2009).

[3] *See* REINALDA, *supra* note 2, at 28–30.

Eventually, over fifty nations joined the League. Another institution established under the Versailles Treaty was the Permanent Court of International Justice, which was given jurisdiction to resolve international law disputes between consenting nations as well as to issue advisory opinions. As discussed in the next section, the United States never joined these institutions because the Versailles Treaty failed to obtain the required two-thirds approval by the Senate.

The end of World War II saw the establishment of the United Nations, and the United States played a leading role in its formation.[4] The United Nations has six main organs, including the Security Council, which can issue binding directives relating to peace and security, and the ICJ, which can adjudicate certain disputes between nations. Today, essentially all nations are members of the United Nations. In addition to its various substantive activities, the United Nations is a forum for communication and negotiation and, as such, it has facilitated a substantial growth in the number of treaties, including treaties establishing new international institutions.

Other major international institutions established during and after World War II include economic institutions such as the World Bank and the International Monetary Fund, which were established at the Bretton Woods Conference in 1944; collective self-defense institutions such as the North Atlantic Treaty Organization, which was established in 1949; the International Atomic Energy Agency, which was established in 1957; and the World Trade Organization, which was established in the mid-1990s. A variety of regional international institutions were also established in the post–World War II period. Particularly powerful institutions have developed in Europe, as part of the European Union, but there are also regional institutions in most other parts of the world. There has also been a proliferation of international adjudicatory institutions.[5] In addition to the ICJ, notable examples include the Dispute Settlement Body of the World Trade Organization; the International Criminal Court; and regional adjudicatory institutions such as the European Court of Justice, the European Court of Human Rights, and the Inter-American Court on Human Rights.

---

[4] *See generally* STANLEY MEISLER, UNITED NATIONS: A HISTORY ch. 1 (2d ed. 2011); STEPHEN SCHLESINGER, ACT OF CREATION: THE FOUNDING OF THE UNITED NATIONS (2003).

[5] *See, e.g.,* Chester Brown, *The Proliferation of International Courts and Tribunals: Finding Your Way through the Maze*, 3 MELB. J. INT'L L. 453 (2002); Cesare P.R. Romano, *The Proliferation of International Judicial Bodies: The Pieces of the Puzzle*, 31 INT'L L. & POL'Y 709 (1999); *see also* Laurence R. Helfer & Anne-Marie Slaughter, *Why States Create International Tribunals: A Response to Professors Posner and Yoo*, 93 CALIF. L. REV. 899, 910 (2005) ("Within the past decade, the world has witnessed an explosion of international adjudication."). For a chart showing a wide variety of international judicial and quasi-judicial bodies and mechanisms, *see* The Project on International Courts and Tribunals, *Synoptic Chart*, https://elaw.org/system/files/intl%20tribunals%20synoptic_chart2.pdf?_ga=2.42601061.194946393.1582219185-1208667513.1582219185. For a general account of the relations between national courts and international courts, *see* YUVAL SHANY, REGULATING JURISDICTIONAL RELATIONS BETWEEN NATIONAL AND INTERNATIONAL COURTS (2007).

Like other nations, the United States derives a number of benefits from participation in international institutions. Among other things, such institutions can help facilitate international cooperation through monitoring, oversight, and dispute resolution, and they can allow for the development of specialization and expertise to address complex international issues.[6] At the same time, because participation in these institutions entails delegations of authority to non-U.S. actors, they can raise legal concerns relating to the distribution of authority within the United States.

Background Constitutional Principles

There are a variety of constitutional doctrines and provisions that might be relevant to delegations of authority by the United States to international institutions. Before turning to them, it may be instructive to consider some of the general concerns that have been raised in the United States about the phenomenon of international delegations.[7] One concern relates to democratic accountability. By transferring legal authority from U.S. actors to international actors—actors that are physically and culturally more distant from, and not directly responsible to, the U.S. electorate—there is a worry that the delegations will dilute domestic political accountability. This accountability concern is heightened by the lack of transparency and public awareness associated with some international decision-making.

Another concern relates to the separation of powers between the three branches of the federal government. The worry here is that transfers of authority to international institutions will increase the power of one branch of the federal government relative to the other branches. In particular, the concern is that these transfers of authority will enhance the power of the executive branch, both because they often delegate the powers of the legislative and judicial branches, and because the United States is represented in these international institutions by executive branch agents. A third concern is that delegations of authority to international institutions have the potential to erode U.S. federalism by further shifting authority away from local decision-making. Even if these effects seem relatively modest with respect to particular delegations, the worry is that their cumulative effect will be more problematic.

---

[6] *See* Curtis A. Bradley & Judith G. Kelley, *The Concept of International Delegation*, 71 LAW & CONTEMP. PROBS. 1, 25–26 (2008).

[7] For a discussion of these and other concerns, see, for example, John O. McGinnis, Medellin *and the Future of International Delegation*, 118 YALE L.J. 1712 (2009); Jed Rubenfeld, *The Two World Orders*, 27 WILSON Q. 22 (2003); Eric Stein, *International Integration and Democracy: No Love at First Sight*, 95 AM. J. INT'L L. 489 (2001); and Paul B. Stephan, *Accountability and International Lawmaking: Rules, Rents, and Legitimacy*, 17 NW. J. INT'L L. & BUS. 681 (1996–97). For a discussion of U.S. ambivalence about international institutions during the twentieth century, see EDWARD C. LUCK, MIXED MESSAGES: AMERICAN POLITICS AND INTERNATIONAL ORGANIZATION 1919–1999 (1999).

These concerns, it should be emphasized, are primarily hypothetical, and there is substantial disagreement about the extent to which they are likely to materialize in practice.[8] Nevertheless, the concerns are not eliminated, as some commentators have suggested,[9] either by Congress's ability to override international decisions and orders within the U.S. legal system or by the ability of the United States to withdraw from many international institutions.[10] Political and resource constraints, and institutional inertia more generally, often make it difficult for Congress to override particular actions or decisions. This is particularly true if Congress must overcome a presidential veto in order to do so. Furthermore, even if Congress succeeds in enacting legislation to override an international decision or order for purposes of U.S. law, it has no ability to overturn the effect of such a decision or order on the international plane. As for withdrawing from an international institution, treaties often condition the ability to withdraw on periods of notice or other requirements, and, in any event, because international delegations are often embedded within broader treaty frameworks, withdrawal is a blunt and costly tool for responding to an exercise of delegated authority. In addition, any such withdrawal would operate only prospectively and thus would not affect decisions or orders already issued.[11]

None of this means, of course, that international delegations are unconstitutional. The following are some constitutional doctrines that could in theory be implicated by particular delegations, but in most instances they are unlikely to pose significant barriers to U.S. participation in international institutions.

Nondelegation doctrine. One potentially relevant principle of U.S. constitutional law that might be implicated by international delegations is the nondelegation doctrine. The Supreme Court has stated that "Congress generally cannot delegate legislative power to the President."[12] Under this doctrine, when Congress delegates authority (such as to

---

[8] For an argument that, with a few notable exceptions, delegations of authority to international institutions have been modest in scope and importance, *see* Andrew T. Guzman & Jennifer Landsidle, *The Myth of International Delegation*, 96 CALIF. L. REV. 1693 (2008). For the view that "there are good reasons to doubt that international delegations will have the negative effects that critics suggest" and that "[e]ven if these effects are confirmed . . . critics have not shown that those costs outweigh the potential benefits of international delegation," *see* Note, *International Delegation as Ordinary Delegation*, 125 HARV. L. REV. 1042, 1063 (2012). For the claim that international delegations do not pose greater concerns than domestic delegations because "[t]he economic, political, and military power of the United States makes it uniquely well placed to influence *ex ante* the design and structure of the international institutions to which it might choose to delegate binding authority, and shape *ex post* the product of those international institutions," *see* Daniel Abebe, *Rethinking the Costs of International Delegations*, 34 U. PA. J. INT'L L. 491, 494 (2013).

[9] *See, e.g.*, LOUIS HENKIN, FOREIGN AFFAIRS AND THE UNITED STATES CONSTITUTION 262 (2d ed. 1996); David M. Golove, *The New Confederalism: Treaty Delegations of Legislative, Executive, and Judicial Authority*, 55 STAN. L. REV. 1697, 1741 (2003).

[10] *See* Bradley, *supra* note 1, at 1585, 1595 n.186; Swaine, *supra* note 1, at 1540–44.

[11] Congress can, however, use its power over appropriations and other tools in an effort to influence both how international institutions operate and the U.S. relationship with them. *See, e.g.*, Kristina Daugirdas, *Congress Underestimated: The Case of the World Bank*, 107 AM. J. INT'L L. 517 (2013) (describing Congress's longstanding and persistent efforts to affect the policies of the World Bank).

[12] Mistretta v. United States, 488 U.S. 361, 372 (1989).

administrative agencies), it must "lay down by legislative act an intelligible principle to which the person or body authorized to [act] is directed to conform."[13] The Supreme Court has explained that this "intelligible principle" requirement "seeks to enforce the understanding that Congress may not delegate the power to make laws and so may delegate no more than the authority to make policies and rules that implement its statutes."[14]

As noted in Chapter 1, the Supreme Court has nevertheless allowed Congress to delegate substantial interpretive and regulatory authority to the executive branch and the judiciary, and it has not found a violation of the intelligible principle requirement since the mid-1930s. The Court has explained that its nondelegation doctrine "has been driven by a practical understanding that in our increasingly complex society, replete with ever changing and more technical problems, Congress simply cannot do its job absent an ability to delegate power under broad general directives."[15] Some justices on the current Supreme Court appear to be willing to reinvigorate nondelegation constraints, but so far a majority of the Court has not done so.[16] In any event, the Court has suggested that the nondelegation doctrine applies even less strictly in the foreign affairs area, explaining that "congressional legislation which is to be made effective through negotiation and inquiry within the international field must often accord to the President a degree of discretion and freedom from statutory restriction which would not be admissible were domestic affairs alone involved."[17]

---

[13] J.W. Hampton, Jr. & Co. v. United States, 276 U.S. 394, 409 (1928).

[14] Loving v. United States, 517 U.S. 748, 758 (1996).

[15] *Mistretta*, 488 U.S. at 372.

[16] *See, e.g.*, Gundy v. United States, 139 S. Ct. 2116 (2019) (upholding delegation to Attorney General to apply sex offender registration requirements to individuals convicted prior to the statute's enactment); Whitman v. Am. Trucking Assn's, 531 U.S. 457 (2001) (finding that broad delegation of authority to the Environmental Protection Agency satisfied the "intelligible principle" requirement). *But cf. Gundy*, 139 S. Ct. at 2130–31 (Alito, J., concurring) ("[S]ince 1935, the Court has uniformly rejected nondelegation arguments and has upheld provisions that authorized agencies to adopt important rules pursuant to extraordinarily capacious standards.... If a majority of this Court were willing to reconsider the approach we have taken for the past 84 years, I would support that effort."). Some commentators have called for abandoning the nondelegation doctrine altogether. *See, e.g.*, Eric A. Posner & Adrian Vermeule, *Interring the Nondelegation Doctrine*, 69 U. CHI. L. REV. 1721 (2002). Others have defended the doctrine. *See, e.g.*, Larry Alexander & Saikrishna Prakash, *Reports of the Nondelegation Doctrine's Death Are Greatly Exaggerated*, 70 U. CHI. L. REV. 1297 (2003).

[17] United States v. Curtiss-Wright Export Corp., 299 U.S. 304, 320 (1936). It is arguable that delegations to international institutions are more analogous to delegations to private parties than to delegations to the executive or judiciary. Even delegations of regulatory authority to private parties are often allowed under U.S. law, especially when they involve only the exercise of advisory authority subject to the approval of the regulated parties or a government body, or when the outcome triggered by the private action has been specified in advance by the government. *See, e.g.*, Sunshine Anthracite Coal Co. v. Adkins, 310 U.S. 381, 399 (1940); United States v. Rock Royal Co-operative, Inc., 307 U.S. 533, 577–78 (1939). Courts have indicated, however, that these delegations raise greater concerns than delegations to the executive branch. *See, e.g.*, Carter v. Carter Coal Co., 298 U.S. 238, 310–11 (1936); Ass'n of Am. Railroads v. U.S. Dep't of Transp., 721 F.3d 666, 670–71 (D.C. Cir. 2013), *cert. granted*, 134 S. Ct. 2685 (2014); *see also* 1 LAURENCE H. TRIBE, AMERICAN CONSTITUTIONAL LAW 992 (3d ed. 2000) ("[D]elegations to private groups continue to be viewed with understandable, and perhaps justifiable, suspicion.").

The current state of the nondelegation doctrine is such, therefore, that it is unlikely to pose much of a barrier to U.S. delegations of authority to international institutions. Nevertheless, some commentators have argued that the doctrine should be applied more vigorously with respect to international institutions than with respect to delegations of authority to domestic administrative agencies within the executive branch.[18] They note, for example, that unlike the executive branch, international institutions do not have a direct electoral connection to U.S. voters. Moreover, they point out that international institutions are not subject to the public notice and comment, congressional oversight, and judicial review applicable to U.S. administrative agencies. Regardless of the merits of these arguments, it is worth keeping in mind that, even in the domestic arena, the Supreme Court sometimes takes account of delegation concerns when interpreting the *scope* of congressional delegations.[19] As discussed in the next section, such an interpretive use of the nondelegation doctrine may make sense for some international delegations as well.[20]

Constitutional process. Separate from the general nondelegation doctrine are considerations of constitutional process that might be implicated by some delegations of authority. The Supreme Court has held that the constitutionally prescribed process for making legislation precludes Congress from delegating its lawmaking function. In its 1983 decision, *INS v. Chadha*, for example, the Court held that a statutory provision that allowed one house of Congress to veto certain actions by the Attorney General was unconstitutional because it allowed for legislative changes without going through the bicameralism and presentment process for legislation specified in Article I of the Constitution.[21] Similarly, in a 1998 decision, *Clinton v. New York*, the Supreme Court invalidated a statute that allowed the president to cancel items in appropriations laws, on the ground that it unconstitutionally delegated legislative authority to the president.[22] As with federal legislation, there are procedural requirements specified in the Constitution for making treaties—most notably the requirements of senatorial consent and presidential ratification—and (as will be discussed) it is arguable that these requirements similarly impose limits on delegation.

Appointments Clause. Delegations of authority may also raise issues under the Appointments Clause in Article II of the Constitution. This Clause gives the president

---

[18] *See, e.g.*, Ku, *supra* note 1, at 121; McGinnis, *supra* note 7, at 1714. *Cf.* Oona A. Hathaway, *Presidential Power over International Law: Restoring the Balance*, 119 YALE L.J. 140, 219–24 (2009) (explaining that the usual checks on administrative agencies do not apply to delegations of authority to the president in foreign affairs).

[19] *See* John F. Manning, *The Nondelegation Doctrine as a Canon of Avoidance*, 2000 SUP. CT. REV. 223; Cass R. Sunstein, *Nondelegation Canons*, 67 U. CHI. L. REV. 315 (2000).

[20] By analogy, the Supreme Court has held that interpretive principles designed to protect federalism in the context of purely domestic legislation also apply to legislation implementing treaties. *See* Bond v. United States, 572 U.S. 844, 859–60 (2014). This decision is discussed in Chapter 2.

[21] INS v. Chadha, 462 U.S. 919 (1983).

[22] Clinton v. New York, 524 U.S. 417 (1998).

the power to appoint, with the advice and consent of the Senate, ambassadors, other public ministers and consuls, Supreme Court justices, and all other "Officers of the United States" whose appointment is not otherwise provided for in the Constitution.[23] It also states that Congress may vest the appointment of "inferior Officers" in the president, the courts, or in the heads of departments.[24] The Supreme Court has made clear that "[u]nless their selection is elsewhere provided for [in the Constitution], all Officers of the United States are to be appointed in accordance with the Clause."[25] The Court also has stated that "any appointee exercising significant authority pursuant to the laws of the United States is an 'Officer of the United States,' and must, therefore, be appointed in the manner prescribed" by the Clause.[26] These requirements, the Court has explained, are designed both to prevent aggrandizement of power by one branch at the expense of another and to ensure public accountability in the appointments process.[27] The Justice Department's Office of Legal Counsel has issued conflicting opinions about whether the Appointments Clause can apply to individuals who are not employees of the federal government.[28] If it can, the Clause might limit some delegations of authority to international actors, since they are not appointed pursuant to the process specified in Article II.

Article III. Some delegations of adjudicative authority may also implicate Article III of the Constitution. This Article provides that "[t]he judicial Power of the United States, shall be vested in one supreme Court, and in such inferior Courts as the Congress may from time to time ordain and establish," and it also specifies that the federal judicial power is to be exercised by judges who "shall hold their Offices during good Behaviour, and [who] shall, at stated Times, receive for their Services a Compensation, which shall not be diminished during their Continuance in Office."[29] This language has been interpreted

---

[23] U.S. CONST. art. II, § 2, cl. 2.

[24] *Id.* Whether an officer is "inferior" turns on the extent to which he or she is "directed and supervised" by persons "appointed by Presidential nomination with the advice and consent of the Senate." Edmond v. United States, 520 U.S. 651, 663 (1997).

[25] Buckley v. Valeo, 424 U.S. 1, 132 (1976).

[26] *Id.* at 126. The Clause does not apply, however, to "lesser functionaries subordinate to officers of the United States." *Id.* at 126 n.162. *Cf.* Financial Oversight and Management Bd. for Puerto Rico v. Aurelius Investment, LLC, 140 S. Ct. 1649, 1657, 1658 (2020) (holding that the requirements of the Appointments Clause apply to "all exercises of federal power" but not to individuals exercising "primarily local powers and duties").

[27] *See, e.g., Edmond*, 520 U.S. at 660.

[28] *Compare* Memorandum from Walter Dellinger, Assistant Attorney General, for the General Counsels of the Federal Government, *The Constitutional Separation of Powers between the President and Congress*, 20 OP. OFF. LEG. COUNSEL 124, 142 (May 7, 1996) (concluding that the Appointments Clause is limited to individuals who "hold positions in the public service of the United States"), *with* Memorandum from Steven G. Bradbury, Assistant Attorney General, Office of Legal Counsel, to the General Counsels of the Executive Branch, *Officers of the United States Within the Meaning of the Appointments Clause*, at 1 (Apr. 16, 2007) (concluding that the Clause extends to officials who exercise a continuing function and are "invested by legal authority with a portion of the sovereign powers of the federal Government"), *available at* http://www.justice.gov/sites/default/files/olc/opinions/2007/04/31/appointmentsclausev10.pdf.

[29] U.S. CONST. art. III, § 1.

as at least sometimes precluding the vesting of the judicial power of the United States in domestic tribunals that are not ordained and established by Congress and that do not have the Article III tenure and salary protections.[30]

The Supreme Court has not provided clear guidance, however, about when non-Article III tribunals are disallowed. Such tribunals have historically been used for certain types of proceedings, such as military courts-martial, adjudications in U.S. territorial possessions, and consular courts established in foreign countries. The Supreme Court has also indicated that such tribunals are allowed for disputes involving "public rights"—that is, noncriminal cases involving the interaction of the government and individuals concerning "matters that historically could have been determined exclusively by [the legislative and executive branches]."[31] In addition, the Court has suggested that greater use of non-Article III tribunals is permissible when the parties consent to the tribunal's exercise of jurisdiction, when the tribunal addresses only a narrow range of specialized issues, and when the tribunal's decisions are subject to review by an Article III federal court.[32] The limitation on the use of non-Article III tribunals might affect U.S. participation in some international adjudicatory institutions.

In addition to restricting the use of non-Article III tribunals, Article III's reference to the "judicial Power" precludes at least some forms of review of federal court decisions by non-Article III officials. An early Supreme Court decision, *Hayburn's Case*, has come to stand for the proposition that Congress may not vest review of the decisions of Article III courts in officials of the executive branch.[33] That case involved a 1792 statute that authorized pensions for disabled veterans of the Revolutionary War. The statute provided that the federal circuit courts were to determine the appropriate disability payments, but that the Secretary of War had the discretion either to adopt or reject the courts' findings. The Supreme Court did not address the constitutionality of this arrangement, but the views of several circuit courts (reflecting the views of five of the six Supreme Court justices) were reported with the case, and these courts reasoned that the statute was unconstitutional because it asked the federal courts to do something that was not judicial in nature, and because, by subjecting judicial determinations to executive branch review, it

---

[30] *See, e.g.,* Stern v. Marshall, 564 U.S. 462 (2011) (holding that non-Article III bankruptcy courts could not constitutionally adjudicate certain state-law counterclaims); Northern Pipeline Const. Co. v. Marathon Pipe Line Co., 458 U.S. 50 (1982) (plurality opinion) (holding that bankruptcy courts could not adjudicate certain state-law contract claims).

[31] *Northern Pipeline*, 458 U.S. at 68; *see also* Oil States Energy Servs., LLC v. Greene's Energy Grp., LLC, 138 S. Ct. 1365 (2018); Crowell v. Benson, 285 U.S. 22 (1932); Ex parte Bakelite Corp., 279 U.S. 438 (1929); Murray's Lessee v. Hoboken Land & Improvement Co., 59 U.S. (18 How.) 272 (1856).

[32] *See* Wellness Int'l Network, Ltd. v. Sharif, 135 S. Ct. 1932 (2015); Peretz v. United States, 501 U.S. 923 (1991); Commodity Futures Trading Comm'n v. Schor, 478 U.S. 833 (1986); Thomas v. Union Carbide Agric. Prods. Co., 473 U.S. 568 (1985).

[33] Hayburn's Case, 2 U.S. (2 Dall.) 408 (1792).

threatened the independence of the federal judiciary.³⁴ One can imagine similar concerns being raised with respect to the review of U.S. judicial decisions by international institutions, where the only U.S. representative is an executive branch agent.

The Supreme Court also has held, in *Plaut v. Spendthrift Farm, Inc.*, that Congress does not have the power to reopen, retroactively, a federal court's final judgment in a civil case.³⁵ In *Plaut*, Congress had authorized the reinstitution of certain lawsuits that had been dismissed on statute-of-limitations grounds. Analogizing to *Hayburn's Case*, the Court held that Congress's reopening of a final judgment unconstitutionally interferes with the power of the federal courts to decide cases, in violation of Article III of the Constitution and principles of separation of powers. The Constitution, reasoned the Court,

> gives the Federal Judiciary the power, not merely to rule on cases, but to decide them, subject to review only by superior courts in the Article III hierarchy—with an understanding, in short, that "a judgment conclusively resolves the case" because "a 'judicial Power' is one to render dispositive judgments."³⁶

---

³⁴ *Id.* at 410–14. The views of the remaining Supreme Court justice (Johnson) were not reported with the case, but he too had ruled that he could not "constitutionally take Cognizance of and determine on the said Petitions." *See* Susan Low Bloch, *The Early Role of the Attorney General in Our Constitutional Scheme: In the Beginning There Was Pragmatism*, 1989 DUKE L.J. 561, 592 n.102 (describing and citing Johnson's decision); *see also* Miller v. French, 530 U.S. 327, 343 (2000) (stating that *Hayburn's Case* "'stands for the principle that Congress cannot vest review of the decisions of Article III courts in officials of the Executive Branch'" (quoting Plaut v. Spendthrift Farm, Inc., 514 U.S. 211, 218 (1995))). *Hayburn's Case* is also frequently cited for the broader proposition that the federal courts may not issue advisory opinions. Some of the justices in the decisions reported in *Hayburn's Case* suggested that nonjudicial duties could be assigned to federal judges acting individually rather than as part of an Article III court. *See Hayburn's Case*, 2 U.S. (2 Dall.) at 410 n.1 (Opinion of Jay, C.J. & Cushing, J.). The full Court later endorsed that suggestion in a case involving a claims settlement procedure established by Congress as part of its implementation of a treaty with Spain. *See* United States v. Ferreira, 54 U.S. (13 How.) 40, 50–51 (1851). Based in part on that reasoning, the Court held in 1989 that it was not unconstitutional for federal judges to serve on the U.S. Sentencing Commission, which promulgated the U.S. Sentencing Guidelines. *See* Mistretta v. United States, 488 U.S. 361, 402–08 (1989); *see also* Lo Duca v. United States, 93 F.3d 1100 (2d Cir. 1996) (upholding constitutionality of the federal extradition statute, pursuant to which federal judges and magistrate judges issue certificates of extraditability that are reviewable by the Secretary of State).

³⁵ Plaut v. Spendthrift Farm, Inc., 514 U.S. 211 (1995); *see also, e.g.*, Chicago & S. Air Lines, Inc. v. Waterman, 333 U.S. 103, 113–14 (1948) ("It has also been the firm and unvarying practice of Constitutional Courts to render no judgments not binding and conclusive on the parties and none that are subject to later review or alteration by administrative action."); Gordon v. United States, 69 U.S. (2 Wall.) 561 (1865), *reported in full* 117 U.S. 697, app. at 704 ("[T]his Court has no jurisdiction in any case where it cannot render judgment in the legal sense of the term. . . .").

³⁶ *Plaut*, 514 U.S. at 218–19 (quoting Frank Easterbrook, *Presidential Review*, 40 CASE W. L. REV. 905, 926 (1990)).

Again, this concern with protecting the integrity of the federal judicial process is potentially relevant to international delegations.

Federalism. Principles of federalism might also be implicated by some international delegations. The Supreme Court has held that, although Congress's legislative authority is broad, it is not unlimited. In 1995, for example, the Supreme Court invalidated a federal statute that criminalized the possession of firearms near schools on the ground that the statute exceeded Congress's authority to regulate interstate commerce, and in 2000 it invalidated on a similar ground a federal statute that created civil remedies for violence against women.[37] In the latter case, the Court explained that "[t]he regulation and punishment of intrastate violence that is not directed at the instrumentalities, channels, or goods involved in interstate commerce has always been the province of the States."[38] The Court has also disallowed Congress from "commandeering" state legislatures and executive branches to carry out federal programs, reasoning that when state governments are compelled by the federal government to legislate or regulate, the accountability of both state and federal officials is diminished, and the "dual sovereignty" structure of the U.S. constitutional system is impermissibly compromised.[39] Regardless of whether these federalism limitations operate as constraints on the treaty power—an issue discussed in Chapter 2—they may at least reflect constitutional values that should inform how treaties, and international delegations made pursuant to treaties, should be construed.[40]

Individual rights. Finally, the Constitution's individual rights provisions might also be implicated by certain international delegations. As discussed in Chapter 1, the U.S. Constitution contains a variety of individual rights protections, including the rights listed in the Bill of Rights (such as freedom of speech, protection against unreasonable searches and seizures, and entitlement to a jury trial). Furthermore, as noted in Chapter 2, the Supreme Court has held that U.S. treaty commitments are subject to the individual rights constraints of the Constitution. With respect to delegations of authority to international institutions, individual rights issues generally will arise only for those institutions with the direct ability to regulate individuals. The most obvious example would be an international criminal tribunal, although, as will be discussed, treaties that delegate certain types of enforcement authority (such as authority to conduct inspections) can also potentially implicate individual rights considerations.

---

[37] *See* United States v. Lopez, 514 U.S. 549 (1995); United States v. Morrison, 529 U.S. 598 (2000).

[38] *Morrison*, 529 U.S. at 618.

[39] Murphy v. NCAA, 138 S. Ct. 1461 (2018); Printz v. United States, 521 U.S. 898 (1997); New York v. United States, 505 U.S. 144 (1992). For discussion of the implications of international delegations for U.S. federalism, see, for example, Swaine, *supra* note 1; and Neil S. Siegel, *International Delegations and the Values of Federalism*, 70 LAW & CONTEMP. PROBS. 93 (2008). *See also* Barry Friedman, *Federalism's Future in the Global Village*, 47 VAND. L. REV. 1441 (1994) (discussing more generally the effect of globalization on U.S. federalism).

[40] As discussed in Chapter 2, the Supreme Court held in *Bond v. United States*, 572 U.S. 844 (2014), that "it is appropriate to refer to basic principles of federalism embodied in the Constitution to resolve ambiguity in a federal statute," even if the statute is implementing a treaty. *Id.* at 859.

International Adjudication and Arbitration

From early in its history, the United States has participated in international arbitration. That is, the United States has agreed, typically by treaty, to have particular legal disputes with other nations resolved by panels of arbitrators. In the Jay Treaty of 1794 between the United States and Great Britain, for example, the United States agreed to the establishment of three arbitral commissions—one designed to resolve a boundary issue, a second to resolve claims by British creditors for alleged debts owed by U.S. citizens, and a third to resolve claims by U.S. citizens for British interference with shipping between the United States and France.[41] Under the terms of the treaty, the United States and Great Britain would each have the right to select a certain number of arbitrators, and the selected arbitrators would then have the right to choose the final arbitrator. For the individuals selected by the United States to serve on these commissions, the treaty specified that they would be appointed by the president with the advice and consent of the Senate.

Opponents of the Jay Treaty argued that, in order to comply with the Appointments Clause, *all* of the arbitral commissioners would have to be appointed by the president and confirmed by the Senate. Alexander Hamilton famously responded that the Appointments Clause was inapplicable in this context because the commissioners "are not in a strict sense officers" and because historical practice suggested that "it has not been deemed a violation of the [Appointments Clause] to appoint Commissioners or special Agents for special purposes in a different mode."[42] Ultimately, the Senate gave its advice and consent to the treaty. The British debts commission became mired in procedural and jurisdictional controversy, however, and never decided any cases. Instead, the debts issue was eventually settled by means of a lump-sum payment, combined with an assurance that creditors on both sides would not meet with lawful impediments to the recovery of debts.[43] The other two arbitral commissions operated successfully, however, with the boundary commission reaching a unanimous decision and the commission focused on U.S. claims eventually making over five hundred awards, for a total of over eleven million dollars in compensation.[44]

---

[41] *See* Treaty of Amity, Commerce and Navigation, Nov. 19, 1794, U.S.–Gr. Brit., 8 Stat. 116. For discussion of the Jay Treaty, *see* SAMUEL FLAGG BEMIS, JAY'S TREATY: A STUDY IN COMMERCE AND DIPLOMACY (rev. ed. 1962), and JERALD A. COMBS, THE JAY TREATY: POLITICAL BATTLEGROUND OF THE FOUNDING FATHERS (1970).

[42] Alexander Hamilton, *The Defence No. 37* (Jan. 6, 1796), *reprinted in* 20 THE PAPERS OF ALEXANDER HAMILTON 13, 20 (Harold C. Syrett ed., 1974); *see also* DAVID P. CURRIE, THE CONSTITUTION IN CONGRESS: THE FEDERALIST PERIOD, 1789–1801, at 212 n.46 (1997) (describing the constitutional debate).

[43] *See* BEMIS, *supra* note 41, at 438–39.

[44] *See* Charles H. Brower, II, *The Functions and Limits of Arbitration and Judicial Settlement under Private and Public International Law*, 18 DUKE J. COMP. & INT'L L. 259, 267–69 (2008).

The United States continued to participate in international arbitration throughout the nineteenth century.[45] One noteworthy example was the establishment of a U.S.–Mexico Claims Commission in 1868 to resolve both claims by U.S. citizens against Mexico and claims by Mexican citizens against the United States, for property damage, personal injury, and wrongful detention.[46] This Commission eventually resolved more than two thousand claims.[47] Another important example is the 1871 Treaty of Washington between the United States and Great Britain, which provided for arbitral commissions to resolve various matters, including the Alabama Claims dispute (concerning alleged breaches of neutrality by Britain during the U.S. Civil War).[48] The Alabama Claims commission consisted of five commissioners, with one commissioner appointed each by the U.S. president, the queen of England, the king of Italy, the president of the Swiss Confederation, and the emperor of Brazil, and the commission ended up awarding the United States over fifteen million dollars, a very large sum for the time.[49]

There were calls in the international community for greater use of international arbitration in the late nineteenth century. In 1899, a treaty was developed to establish a Permanent Court of Arbitration in The Hague, and the United States joined the treaty in 1900.[50] Despite its name, the Permanent Court of Arbitration is not a standing court;

---

[45] *See* JOHN BASSETT MOORE, THE UNITED STATES AND INTERNATIONAL ARBITRATION 6–21 (1896). During the nineteenth century, Great Britain entered into a series of bilateral treaties that allowed for the search and seizure of vessels suspected of engaging in the slave trade and the establishment of international tribunals that would adjudicate the seizures. *See* Farida Shaikh, *Judicial Diplomacy: British Officials and the Mixed Commission Courts*, *in* SLAVERY, DIPLOMACY AND EMPIRE 42 (Keith Hamilton & Patrick Salmon eds., 2009). For differing accounts of the constitutional concerns raised by some U.S. officials about participation in such tribunals, *see* Eugene Kontorovich, *The Constitutionality of International Courts: The Forgotten Precedent of Slave Trade Tribunals*, 158 U. PA. L. REV. 39 (2009); and Jenny S. Martinez, *International Courts and the U.S. Constitution: Reexamining the History*, 159 U. PA. L. REV. 1069 (2011). The United States finally entered into a treaty with Great Britain in 1862 to establish anti-slave-trade tribunals, but the slave trade was largely eradicated soon thereafter and these Anglo-American tribunals never adjudicated any cases. For a fascinating account of an 1822 arbitration by the Czar of Russia of a dispute between the United States and Great Britain over compensation for U.S. slaves that had fled to the British lines during the War of 1812, *see* Bennett Ostdiek & John Fabian Witt, *The Czar and the Slaves: Two Puzzles in the History of International Arbitration*, 113 AM. J. INT'L L. 535 (2019).

[46] Convention Between the United States of America and the Republic of Mexico for the Adjustment of Claims, July 4, 1868, U.S.–Mex., 115 Stat. 679.

[47] *See* A.H. FELLER, MEXICAN CLAIMS COMMISSIONS, 1923–1934, at 6 (1935). In 1923, the United States and Mexico agreed to set up another claims commission to resolve claims of U.S. and Mexican citizens arising after 1868. *See id.* at 23.

[48] *See* ADRIAN COOK, THE ALABAMA CLAIMS: AMERICAN POLITICS AND ANGLO–AMERICAN RELATIONS, 1865–1872 (1975); CALEB CUSHING, THE TREATY OF WASHINGTON (1873); 1 JOHN BASSETT MOORE, HISTORY AND DIGEST OF THE INTERNATIONAL ARBITRATIONS TO WHICH THE UNITED STATES HAS BEEN A PARTY 495–682 (1898); Tom Bingham, *The Alabama Claims Arbitration*, 54 INT'L & COMP. L.Q. 1 (2005).

[49] *See* Brower, *supra* note 44, at 272–73.

[50] *See* CALVIN DEARMOND DAVIS, THE UNITED STATES AND THE FIRST HAGUE PEACE CONFERENCE ch. 14 (1962); David D. Caron, *War and International Adjudication: Reflections on the 1899 Peace Conference*, 94 AM. J. INT'L L. 4 (2000).

rather, it is an administrative institution designed to assist nations that have entered into agreements to arbitrate.[51] Among other things, the Court maintains a list of potential arbitrators that countries can select from when designating arbitration panels. The United States used the services of this institution when arbitrating a number of disputes in the early twentieth century.

As noted in Chapter 3, there were controversies in the United States in the late nineteenth and early twentieth centuries about whether it was constitutional to delegate to the president the authority to decide which disputes to submit to standing arbitral bodies. Even though many academic commentators concluded that such a delegation posed no constitutional problem, the Senate successfully insisted during this period that any agreements to submit particular disputes to arbitration had to separately receive the advice and consent of the Senate. A different delegation dispute arose concerning arbitral treaties with Great Britain and France submitted by President Taft to the Senate in 1911. Under these treaties, if the parties disagreed about whether a particular matter fell within the scope of the arbitration clause, an arbitral commission would have had jurisdiction to decide this issue. The Senate objected that this arrangement would entail an unconstitutional delegation of the treaty-making power, and it therefore made its advice and consent to the treaty conditional on having this particular provision stricken from the treaty. The Senate's condition was unacceptable to Taft, who argued that "[t]he agreement to abide a judgment as to jurisdiction in future is no more a delegation of control over foreign affairs than is agreement to abide a judgment of an existing controversy in respect to such relations," and he therefore declined to proceed with ratification of the treaty.[52]

Constitutional issues also arose in connection with a proposed international prize court in the early 1900s. Under the Twelfth Hague Convention of 1907, an international court would have had jurisdiction to review and potentially reverse prize decisions from the national courts of the parties to the treaty. As one commentator noted, this arrangement would have created a "novelty" for the United States in that "[c]ases originating in the courts of the United States will be capable of removal by appeal to a court located on foreign soil, not forming a part of our judiciary system, and not subject to the control or supervision of the United States Government or any Department thereof."[53] Because of

---

[51] *See* Brower, *supra* note 44, at 277–78.

[52] *See* 5 GREEN HAYWOOD HACKWORTH, DIGEST OF INTERNATIONAL LAW 67–68 (1927); Chandler P. Anderson, *The Senate and Obligatory Arbitration Treaties*, 26 AM. J. INT'L L. 328, 331–32 (1932); Editorial Comment, *The Pending Treaty of Arbitration between the United States and Great Britain*, 6 AM. J. INT'L L. 167 (1912).

[53] Thomas Raeburn White, *Constitutionality of the Proposed International Prize Court—Considered from the Standpoint of the United States*, 2 AM. J. INT'L L. 490, 490–91 (1908). This commentator nevertheless thought that the arrangement would be constitutional because, in his view, "the grant of the judicial power of the United States does not include the power to decide finally the rights of foreigners involved in prize cases." *Id.* at 499. One of the arbitral commissions established by the 1871 Treaty of Washington resolved claims by British citizens against the United States, and this commission felt free to disregard prize decisions by U.S. courts in reaching its judgments. *See* Henry Paul Monaghan, *Article III and Supranational Judicial Review*, 107 COLUM.

constitutional concerns raised about such direct review, the United States negotiated an additional protocol to the Convention in 1910 that provided that countries "which are prevented by difficulties of a constitutional nature from accepting the said Convention in its present form" had the right to limit recourse against them in the international court to actions for damages rather than direct review of national court decisions. Submitting the "question" but not the "judgment" to the international court was thought to alleviate constitutional doubts about having an international body reverse or revise a federal court prize judgment.[54] The Convention was never ratified by any of the signatories, however, and thus the proposed international court was never established.

After World War I, the Permanent Court of International Justice (PCIJ) was established, pursuant to a directive in the League of Nations Covenant.[55] The PCIJ was a standing international judicial tribunal that had the authority to both decide contentious disputes between states and to issue advisory opinions. As noted earlier, because of opposition in the Senate, the United States did not join the League of Nations, and it never became a party to the Court.[56] It did cooperate with the Court, however, by sending it judges and other personnel, and the Court in fact always had an American judge.

The United States did of course join the United Nations, established at the end of World War II. One of the organs of the United Nations is the ICJ, a successor to the Permanent Court of International Justice. The ICJ is a fifteen-judge court that sits in The Hague, and it can both hear contentious cases between nations and issue advisory opinions when requested to do so by certain organs of the United Nations. For the ICJ to have jurisdiction over a contentious case, both parties to the case must have consented

---

L. REV. 833, 861–62 (2007). The commission did not, however, directly review or overturn U.S. prize decisions. *See* A. Mark Weisburd, *Medellín, The President's Foreign Affairs Power and Domestic Law*, 28 PENN. ST. INT'L L. REV. 595, 610 (2010) ("[N]ot only did the arbitration not require American courts to revisit cases that had been finally decided; it likewise had no effect against successful participants in such cases who had not consented to the tribunal's authority.").

[54] *See* SAMUEL B. CRANDALL, TREATIES: THEIR MAKING AND ENFORCEMENT 243–44 (2d ed. 1916); 2 CHARLES CHENEY HYDE, INTERNATIONAL LAW CHIEFLY AS INTERPRETED AND APPLIED BY THE UNITED STATES § 504, at 25–26 (1922); James Scott Brown, *The International Court of Prize*, 5 AM. J. INT'L L. 302 (1911). For an argument that the constitutional concern could also have been addressed by creating a specialized non–Article III prize court in the United States and having the international court review decisions from that specialized court, *see* QUINCY WRIGHT, THE CONTROL OF AMERICAN FOREIGN RELATIONS 118 (1922).

[55] *See* Brower, *supra* note 44, at 284–86; *see also* MANLEY O. HUDSON, THE PERMANENT COURT OF INTERNATIONAL JUSTICE, 1920–1942 (1943) (describing the history and jurisprudence of the PCIJ).

[56] At various times in the 1920s, the United States considered joining the PCIJ subject to certain reservations. *See* Quincy Wright, *The United States and the Permanent Court of International Justice*, 21 AM. J. INT'L L. 1 (1927). The United States finally signed the treaty for the PCIJ in 1935, but the Senate declined to give its advice and consent to it. *See* Signature and Ratification of the Protocol of the Permanent Court of International Justice (PCIJ) Member States, http://www.indiana.edu/~league/pcijmemberstates.htm. The vote in the Senate was 52 votes in favor and 36 against, which was 7 votes short of the two-thirds majority needed for the Senate's approval of a treaty. *See* 79 CONG. REC. 1147 (1935).

in some fashion to its jurisdiction. This consent can occur in advance, either through a general acceptance of the ICJ's compulsory jurisdiction or in a treaty, or at the time of the dispute. Under Article 94 of the UN Charter, each party to the Charter (including the United States) "undertakes to comply with the decision of the International Court of Justice in any case to which it is a party."[57]

When joining the ICJ in 1945, the United States filed a declaration accepting the ICJ's compulsory jurisdiction. This acceptance, however, was subject to several limitations, including the "Connally Reservation," which excluded from the jurisdiction of the ICJ "disputes with regard to matters which are essentially within the domestic jurisdiction of the United States of America as determined by the United States of America."[58] In 1985, after the ICJ exercised jurisdiction over a case brought against the United States by Nicaragua concerning U.S. covert activities in that country, the United States withdrew its consent to compulsory jurisdiction.[59] The Legal Adviser for the U.S. Department of State explained that "the hopes originally placed in compulsory jurisdiction by the architects of the Court's Statute have never been realized and will not be realized in the foreseeable future."[60] The Legal Adviser also expressed concern that "for the first time in its history, the Court [in the *Nicaragua* case] has sought to assert jurisdiction over a controversy concerning claims related to an ongoing use of armed force."[61]

As a result of its withdrawal from the Court's compulsory jurisdiction, the United States currently can be sued in the Court only if it has consented to the ICJ's jurisdiction in a particular treaty with the complaining party or if it gives its specific consent to jurisdiction at the time the suit is filed. The United States continues to be a party, however, to dozens of treaties that contain clauses authorizing the ICJ to resolve disputes arising under the treaties. This helps explain the series of cases brought against the United States, which will be discussed, concerning breaches of the Vienna Convention on Consular Relations, as well as other recent cases. Since the 1980s, however, the United States has declined to accept any additional treaty clauses providing for ICJ jurisdiction.[62]

The United States participates in a number of other adjudicatory bodies. For example, along with over 150 other countries, the United States is a party to the World Trade Organization (WTO), which was established in 1995 to administer the General

---

[57] United Nations Charter, June 26, 1945, art. 94(1), 59 Stat. 1051, T.S. No. 933.
[58] *See* U.S. Declaration Accepting the Compulsory Jurisdiction of the ICJ (Aug. 26, 1946), 61 Stat. 1218.
[59] *See* United States: Department of State Letter and Statement Concerning Termination of Acceptance of I.C.J. Compulsory Jurisdiction, 24 I.L.M. 1742 (1985).
[60] Testimony of Abraham D. Sofaer, U.S. Dep't of State Legal Adviser, to the Senate Foreign Relations Committee (Dec. 4, 1985), *reprinted in* 86 DEP'T OF STATE BULL. 67, 68 (1986).
[61] *Id.* at 70.
[62] For a thoughtful discussion of the U.S. relationship with the ICJ, *see* Sean D. Murphy, *The United States and the International Court of Justice: Coping with Antinomies, in* THE SWORD AND THE SCALES: THE UNITED STATES AND INTERNATIONAL COURTS AND TRIBUNALS (Cesare P.R. Romano ed., 2009).

Agreement on Tariffs and Trade and related treaties.[63] The WTO includes a dispute settlement process, in which adjudicatory panels can adjudicate trade disputes, and the panel decisions can be appealed to a standing WTO Appellate Body.

The dispute settlement decisions are binding, and, if the losing party does not comply with a decision, the WTO may authorize the prevailing party to impose trade sanctions on the losing party. The United States has participated in a number of cases in the WTO, both as a complaining party and as a respondent, and it has prevailed in some cases and lost in others. As a respondent, the United States has lost a number of significant cases, including a case challenging clean air regulations issued by the Environmental Protection Agency, a case challenging U.S. limits on shrimp imports designed to protect sea turtles, and a case challenging U.S. tax treatment of foreign sales corporations.[64] WTO decisions are not given direct effect in the U.S. legal system and thus must be implemented by Congress or the executive branch before they are enforceable domestically.[65] The U.S. relationship with the WTO became more fractious during the Trump

---

[63] For discussions of the relationship between the United States and the WTO dispute settlement system, see, for example, Robert Z. Lawrence, *The United States and the WTO Dispute Settlement System* (Council on Foreign Relations, March 2007); and Paul B. Stephan, *Sheriff or Prisoner? The United States and the World Trade Organization*, 1 CHI. J. INT'L L. 49 (2000).

[64] *See* WTO Appellate Body, *Report: United States—Tax Treatment for "Foreign Sales Corporations" (Recourse to Article 21.5 of the DSU by the European Communities)* (Jan. 14, 2002), *reprinted in* 41 I.L.M. 447 (2002); WTO Appellate Body, *Report: United States—Import Prohibition of Certain Shrimp and Shrimp Products (Recourse to Article 21.5 of the DSU by Malaysia)* (Oct. 22, 2001), *reprinted in* 41 I.L.M. 149 (2002); WTO Appellate Body, *Report: United States—Standards for Reformulated and Conventional Gasoline* (May 20, 1996), *reprinted in* 35 I.L.M. 603 (1996); *see also* Jeanne J. Grimmett, *WTO Dispute Settlement: Status of U.S. Compliance in Pending Cases* (Cong. Res. Serv., Apr. 23, 2012).

[65] A Statement of Administrative Action, which was submitted by the executive branch to Congress along with the WTO agreements, states that "[r]eports issued by panels or the Appellate Body under the [WTO's Dispute Settlement Understanding] have no binding effect under the law of the United States and do not represent an expression of U.S. foreign or trade policy. . . . If a report recommends that the United States change federal law to bring it into conformity with a [WTO] agreement, it is for the Congress to decide whether any such change will be made." Statement of Administrative Action to Uruguay Round Agreements Act, H.R. Doc. No. 103–316, 103d Cong., 2d Sess. 1032–33 (1994). The implementing legislation for the WTO agreements provides that this Statement "shall be regarded as an authoritative expression by the United States concerning the interpretation and application of the [WTO agreements] and this Act in any judicial proceeding in which a question arises concerning such interpretation or application." 19 U.S.C. § 3512(d). The implementing legislation also states that "[n]o provision of any of the [World Trade Organization agreements], nor the application of any such provision to any person or circumstance, that is inconsistent with any law of the United States shall have effect," and that "[n]o State law, or the application of such a State law, may be declared invalid as to any person or circumstance on the ground that the provision or application is inconsistent with any of the Uruguay Round Agreements, except in an action brought by the United States for the purpose of declaring such law or application invalid." 19 U.S.C. § 3512(a)(1) & (b)(2)(A). Congress also considered but did not enact legislation that would establish a "WTO Dispute Settlement Review Commission," made up of U.S. judges, to review WTO decisions adverse to the United States. *See* NAFTA Renegotiation and WTO Dispute Settlement Review Commission Act, H.R. 78, 105th Cong., 1st Sess. (1997); WTO Dispute Settlement Review Commission Act, S. 1438, 104th Cong., 1st Sess. (1995).

administration, as the United States proceeded to block appointments to the WTO's Appellate Body.[66]

Another example of a dispute resolution institution that the United States participates in is the Iran–United States Claims Tribunal. In 1981, in the wake of the Iran hostages crisis, the United States and Iran agreed to establish an arbitral tribunal in The Hague that would resolve various claims, including commercial claims by U.S. citizens against Iran and its state-owned enterprises.[67] The tribunal has nine arbitrators, three appointed by the United States, three appointed by Iran, and three appointed by the six others. As of 2020, the tribunal had resolved all the private claims but still had before it certain claims directly between Iran and the United States.

For the most part, the arbitral and adjudicatory institutions the United States has participated in have not had the authority to review U.S. judicial decisions. Arbitration under the North American Free Trade Agreement (NAFTA), and now under its successor—the United States-Mexico-Canada Agreement (USMCA)—is to some extent an exception to this pattern. The United States became a party to NAFTA in 1993, along with Canada and Mexico.[68] Chapter 19 of NAFTA, the substance of which has been continued in Chapter 10 of the USMCA,[69] allows import decisions of the member countries concerning antidumping and countervailing duties to be reviewed by binational arbitral panels. These panels apply the standard of review and substantive law that would be applied by the importing country's own courts, and the panels' decisions are final and binding.[70] In the case of the United States, the panels exercise review over the application of U.S. trade law by the Commerce Department and the International Trade Commission, whose decisions otherwise would be subject to review by the Court of International Trade, an Article III court. By statute, U.S. agencies are required to comply with decisions of the panels, and no judicial review of the panel decisions is allowed.[71] These panels are unique in that they apply U.S. law and exercise direct review over U.S. administrative decisions.

---

[66] *See* Ana Swanson, *Trump Cripples WTO as Trade War Rages*, N.Y. TIMES (Dec. 8, 2019).
[67] *See* CHARLES N. BROWER & JASON D. BRUESCHKE, THE IRAN–UNITED STATES CLAIMS TRIBUNAL (1998). As discussed in Chapter 3, the tribunal was established pursuant to a "sole executive agreement."
[68] *See* North American Free Trade Agreement, Dec. 8, 1992, Can.–Mex.–U.S., 32 I.L.M. 289 [hereinafter NAFTA].
[69] *See* United States-Mexico-Canada Agreement Implementation Act, Pub. L. No. 116-113, § 421.
[70] NAFTA, *supra* note 68, art. 1904.
[71] *See* 19 U.S.C. § 1516a(g)(7)(A). The panel decisions can be reviewed by an "extraordinary challenge committee" on certain narrow grounds, such as gross misconduct, bias, or conflict of interest. *See* NAFTA, *supra* note 68, art. 1904(13), annex 1904.13. Also, although the panel decisions cannot be challenged in a U.S. court, the constitutionality of the binational panel scheme itself can be challenged in the U.S. Court of Appeals for the D.C. Circuit. *See* 19 U.S.C. § 1516a(g)(2), (g)(4)(A). Even if the scheme is found to be unconstitutional, however, the president has statutory discretion "to accept, as a whole, the decision of a binational panel," in which case the International Trade Commission shall "take action not inconsistent with such decision." *Id.* § 1516a(g)(7)(B).

Constitutional challenges have been raised about this type of review, but to date the challenges have been dismissed for lack of jurisdiction and standing.[72]

NAFTA also provided for more traditional investor-state arbitration, and even this aspect of NAFTA was used to conduct a type of review of U.S. judicial proceedings. Chapter 11 of NAFTA required each country to afford investors of the other two countries certain minimum standards of treatment, including protection against uncompensated expropriation, as well as nondiscriminatory treatment. Investors who alleged a violation of Chapter 11 could submit claims to a panel of three private arbitrators who could award monetary damages but not injunctive relief. In an important decision in 2001, a NAFTA arbitration panel held, in a case filed by a Canadian company against the United States, that a decision by a Mississippi trial court could itself constitute an expropriation and thus could be challenged under Chapter 11.[73] In a similar case, a Canadian company filed an action against the United States for alleged expropriation after a Massachusetts court dismissed its breach-of-contract suit against the City of Boston on sovereign immunity grounds. Although the arbitral panel eventually held in favor of the United States in this second case, it did so only after carefully reviewing the Massachusetts court's reasoning.[74] As a result, NAFTA arbitration was used in these cases, at least indirectly, to conduct international review of the fairness and outcome of U.S. judicial decisions. (The USMCA substantially cut back on this investor-state arbitration, eliminating it entirely as between Canada and the United States and narrowing its scope as between Mexico and the United States.)

As a general matter, U.S. participation in international arbitration and adjudication does not appear to raise serious constitutional concerns. Typically, these institutions apply international law, not U.S. law, and they do not ordinarily exercise any direct review of U.S. judicial decisions. Moreover, as we have seen, the United States has participated in international arbitration and international claims settlement procedures throughout

---

[72] *See* Coalition for Fair Lumber Imports v. United States, 471 F.3d 1329 (D.C. Cir. 2006); America Coalition for Free Trade v. Clinton, 128 F.3d 761 (D.C. Cir. 1997). For discussion of the constitutionality of this scheme, *see* Ethan Boyer, *Article III, the Foreign Relations Power, and the Binational Panel System of NAFTA*, 13 INT'L TAX & BUS. LAWYER 101 (1996); Matthew Burton, Note, *Assigning the Judicial Power to International Tribunals: NAFTA Binational Panels and Foreign Affairs Flexibility*, 88 VA. L. REV. 1529 (2002); Jim C. Chen, *Appointments with Disaster: The Unconstitutionality of Binational Arbitral Review under the United States–Canada Free Trade Agreement*, 49 WASH. & LEE L. REV. 1455 (1992); William J. Davey, *The Appointments Clause and International Dispute Settlement Mechanisms: A False Conflict*, 49 WASH. & LEE L. REV. 1315 (1992).

[73] *See* Decision on Hearing of Respondent's Objection to Competence and Jurisdiction, Loewen Group, Inc. v. United States, Case No. ARB(AF)/98/3 (Jan. 5, 2001), https://2009-2017.state.gov/documents/organization/3921.pdf. For a list of the cases filed by and against the United States under NAFTA Chapter 11, and links to materials concerning those cases, *see* U.S. Dep't of State, *NAFTA Investor–State Arbitrations*, https://2009-2017.state.gov/s/l/c3439.htm.

[74] *See* Award, Mondev Int'l Ltd v. United States, Case No. ARB(AF)/99/2 (Oct. 11, 2002), https://2009-2017.state.gov/documents/organization/14442.pdf.

its history, dating back to the 1794 Jay Treaty. The unusual Chapter 19 NAFTA panels present a closer question because their decisions have direct effect in U.S. law and displace Article III judicial review.[75] Nevertheless, because these panels address only a narrow range of specialized trade issues, and these issues concern what could reasonably be described as "public rights," they are probably constitutional.[76]

The Vienna Convention Cases

A series of cases brought against the United States in the ICJ starting in the 1990s implicated additional constitutional issues.[77] These cases, which are also discussed in Chapter 2, concerned Article 36 of the Vienna Convention on Consular Relations, which provides that when foreign nationals from other party countries are arrested, they are to be informed without delay that they have the right to have their consulate notified of the arrest and to communicate with the consulate.[78] It also provides that these rights "shall be exercised in conformity with the laws and regulations of the receiving State, subject to the proviso, however, that the said laws and regulations must enable full effect to be given to the purposes for which the rights accorded under this article are intended."[79] The United States ratified the Vienna Convention in 1969. At the same time, it ratified an "optional protocol" to the Convention providing that disputes between nations arising under the treaty could be heard in the ICJ.[80]

---

[75] *Cf.* A. Mark Weisburd, *International Courts and American Courts*, 21 MICH. J. INT'L L. 877, 900 (2000) (concluding that "a treaty permitting an international tribunal to effectively reverse the judgments of federal courts in cases involving some question of international law ... would be unconstitutional").

[76] *See, e.g.*, HENKIN, *supra* note 9, at 272 ("The Constitution does not require that determinations of import duties be subject to review at all, and review by an international body (rather than a U.S. court, or no review at all), therefore, raises no constitutional issues."); Boyer, *supra* note 72, at 133 ("Claims arising under antidumping and countervailing duty law are quintessentially public rights since they are matters that could be conclusively determined by the executive or legislative branch."); Monaghan, *supra* note 53, at 842 (arguing that "NAFTA-like trade tribunals raise no serious problems under Article III and are sanctioned by an ancient lineage"). *Cf.* James E. Pfander, *Article I Tribunals, Article III Courts, and the Judicial Power of the United States*, 118 HARV. L. REV. 643, 768 (2004) ("Unlike Article I tribunals, the NAFTA panels are not in a legal sense the creatures of Congress, they do not act as agents of the United States in resolving litigated disputes, and they do not answer to the Supreme Court in the interpretation of the Agreement or in the resolution of disputes. Rather, NAFTA panels are the creatures of the parties to an international agreement—the United States, Canada, and Mexico.").

[77] The discussion in this section draws from Curtis A. Bradley, *Self-Execution and Treaty Duality*, 2009 SUP. CT. REV. 131; and Curtis A. Bradley, *The Federal Judicial Power and the International Legal Order*, 2006 SUP. CT. REV. 59.

[78] Vienna Convention on Consular Relations art. 36(1), Apr. 24, 1963, 21 U.S.T. 77, 596 U.N.T.S. 261.

[79] *Id.*, art. 36(2).

[80] *See* Optional Protocol Concerning the Compulsory Settlement of Disputes, Apr. 24, 1963, 21 U.S.T. 77, 169, 596 U.N.T.S. 487, 488.

The vast majority of criminal cases in the United States are handled at the state and local levels rather than by the federal government. For a long time after U.S. ratification of the Vienna Convention, state and local police often failed to inform foreign nationals of their rights under Article 36 when arresting them, in part because the police were unaware of the treaty obligation. Before the mid-1990s, however, these violations were rarely the subject of U.S. court litigation. This changed with the *Breard* case. There, a Paraguayan citizen on death row in Virginia filed a habeas corpus action in a U.S. federal court arguing that he should receive either a new trial or sentencing proceeding because he had never been advised of his right to have his consulate notified of his arrest. As the lower courts began to deny him relief, and as his execution date approached, the nation of Paraguay initiated a proceeding against the United States in the ICJ, seeking to have the Court order a new trial for Breard. About five days before the scheduled execution, the ICJ issued a provisional order stating that the United States should "take all measures at its disposal" to ensure that Breard was not executed while the Court considered the case.[81]

At this point, Breard's case had also reached the U.S. Supreme Court, which declined to grant a stay of execution, concluding that Breard's Vienna Convention claim had been procedurally defaulted because he had failed to raise it in a timely manner in the state courts.[82] While recognizing that it should give "respectful consideration to the interpretation of an international treaty rendered by an international court with jurisdiction to interpret such," the Court reasoned that absent "a clear and express statement to the contrary, the procedural rules of the forum State govern the implementation of the treaty in that State."[83] One such procedural rule in the United States, explained the Court, is that "assertions of error in criminal proceedings must first be raised in state court in order to form the basis for relief in habeas."[84] Although the U.S. government took the position that the ICJ's provisional order was not binding, the Secretary of State at that time, Madeline Albright, wrote a letter to Virginia's governor, asking him voluntarily to stay the execution.[85] The governor declined, however, and Breard was executed. Paraguay subsequently withdrew its case from the ICJ.

A similar case, *LaGrand*, was initiated in the ICJ by Germany in 1999. *LaGrand* concerned two brothers of German citizenship on death row in Arizona, one of whom was executed shortly before Germany brought its case. The Court issued a provisional order directing the United States to take all measures at its disposal to stay the execution of the

---

[81] Vienna Convention on Consular Relations (Paraguay v. United States), Provisional Measures, 1998 I.C.J. Rep. 248, ¶ 41 (Apr. 9).
[82] *See* Breard v. Greene, 523 U.S. 371, 375 (1998).
[83] *Id.*
[84] *Id.*
[85] *See* Letter from Madeleine K. Albright, U.S. Secretary of State, to James S. Gilmore III, Governor of Virginia (Apr. 13, 1998), *reprinted in part in* 92 AM. J. INT'L L. 671–72 (1998).

other brother. Once again, however, the execution was carried out on schedule. Unlike Paraguay in the *Breard* case, however, Germany did not abandon its case at this point, but rather pressed on for a judgment. Subsequently, in June 2001, the ICJ issued a final decision, concluding that Article 36 of the Vienna Convention confers not only state-to-state rights but also individual rights, that the United States had violated these individual rights with respect to the German brothers, and that U.S. court application of procedural default rules had prevented "full effect" from being given to the rights under Article 36.[86] The ICJ also concluded that, in the future, when German nationals are sentenced to severe penalties in the United States without their Article 36 rights being respected, the United States would be obligated to provide for "review and reconsideration" of their convictions and sentences in light of the violation.[87] The ICJ noted, however, that this "obligation can be carried out in various ways" and that the "choice of means must be left to the United States."[88]

LaGrand set the stage for the *Avena* case. In early 2003, Mexico initiated a proceeding against the United States in the ICJ on behalf of fifty-four Mexican nationals on death row throughout the United States, alleging that they had not been notified of their rights under Article 36 of the Vienna Convention. This was a particularly significant case, since it resembled a class action rather than just a challenge to a particular execution. In February 2003, the Court issued a provisional order relating to three of the individuals who appeared to be at greatest risk of execution in the coming months, directing the United States to "take all measures necessary to ensure" that the individuals were not executed "pending final judgment in these proceedings."[89] This time, none of the individuals were executed while the Court considered the case. In March 2004, the ICJ issued its judgment on the merits. The Court held that the United States had violated the Vienna Convention rights of fifty-one Mexican nationals, and that it was required to provide these Mexican nationals with review and reconsideration of their convictions and sentences as a result of having failed to notify them of their consular rights. In its opinion, the Court reasoned that Article 36 confers individual rights, and that the proper remedy for a violation of these rights is "review and reconsideration of these nationals' cases by the United States courts ... with a view to ascertaining whether in each case the violation of Article 36 ... caused actual prejudice to the defendant in the process of administration of criminal justice."[90] The ICJ further suggested that procedural default rules should not

---

[86] *See* LaGrand (Federal Republic of Germany v. United States) ¶¶ 67, 73, 77, 91, 2001 I.C.J. Rep. 466 (June 27).
[87] *Id.*, ¶ 125.
[88] *Id.*
[89] Case Concerning Avena and Other Mexican Nationals (Mexico v. United States), Provisional Measures ¶ 59 (I.C.J. Feb. 5, 2003).
[90] Case Concerning Avena and Other Mexican Nationals (Mexico v. United States), Judgment ¶ 121, 2004 I.C.J. No. 128 (Mar. 31).

be applied to bar this review and reconsideration because the application of such rules would prevent full effect from being given to the rights.[91]

After the *Avena* decision, the executive branch took the position that the ICJ had erred in its construction of the Convention. Nevertheless, in February 2005, President Bush sent a memorandum to the U.S. Attorney General stating that the United States, "in accordance with general principles of comity," would discharge its obligations under *Avena* by having its state courts provide review and reconsideration in the fifty-one cases covered by the decision.[92] About a week later, the U.S. Secretary of State, Condoleezza Rice, sent a letter to the UN Secretary-General stating that the United States was withdrawing from the optional protocol that gives the ICJ jurisdiction over Vienna Convention disputes.[93] (The authority of the executive branch to terminate U.S. treaty commitments is discussed in Chapter 2.)

The Supreme Court subsequently decided *Sanchez-Llamas v. Oregon*, which involved two consolidated state cases, one from Oregon and one from Virginia.[94] In each case, state police had failed to advise a foreign citizen of his rights under Article 36 of the Vienna Convention. In the Oregon case, a Mexican citizen was seeking suppression of incriminating statements as a remedy for the treaty violation, and in the Virginia case a Honduran citizen was seeking to overcome state rules of procedural default that would otherwise prevent him from raising the treaty violation for the first time in state post-conviction proceedings. In an opinion authored by Chief Justice Roberts, a majority of the Court rejected the claims of both petitioners. The Court did not take a position on whether Article 36 confers judicially enforceable individual rights. The Court reasoned that even if Article 36 does confer such rights, suppression of evidence is not an appropriate remedy for violations of that article, and that the article does not require the disregard of state rules of procedural default.[95]

The Court in *Sanchez-Llamas* emphasized the federal judicial power under Article III of the Constitution in both its analysis of the suppression issue and its analysis of the procedural default issue. In concluding that there was no suppression-of-evidence remedy for violations of Article 36, the Court rejected the argument that it could use its remedial authority to promote state court compliance with Article 36. The Court explained that "our authority to create a judicial remedy applicable in state court must lie, if anywhere, in the treaty itself."[96] Imposing a remedy not provided for by the Convention, the Court noted, would be "enlarging the obligations of the United States under the

---

[91] *Id.*, ¶ 113.
[92] *See* Memorandum for the Attorney General, Compliance with the Decision of the ICJ in Avena (Feb. 28, 2005), https://georgewbush-whitehouse.archives.gov/news/releases/2005/02/20050228-18.html.
[93] *See* Adam Liptak, *U.S. Says It Has Withdrawn from World Judicial Body*, N.Y. TIMES (Mar. 10, 2005).
[94] Sanchez-Llamas v. Oregon, 548 U.S. 331 (2006).
[95] *See id.* at 350, 356.
[96] *Id.* at 346.

Vienna Convention," which would be "entirely inconsistent with the judicial function."[97] The Court concluded that "where a treaty does not provide a particular remedy, either expressly or implicitly, it is not for the federal courts to impose one on the States through lawmaking of their own."[98] In other words, regardless of whether fashioning a suppression remedy would promote U.S. compliance with Article 36, limitations on the judicial power meant that this was not an appropriate task for the federal courts.

In concluding that Article 36 did not require the disregard of state rules of procedural default, despite the ICJ's view that it did have this effect, the Court in *Sanchez-Llamas* similarly focused on the judicial power—this time as something to be protected rather than kept in check. The Court rejected the argument, advanced by a group of international law professors in an amicus curiae brief, that the Court was obligated to accept as "authoritative" the ICJ's interpretation of the Vienna Convention. The Court explained that, although the ICJ's interpretation deserves "respectful consideration," when treaties are being applied as federal law, the ultimate authority to interpret them must rest with the domestic U.S. court system, not an international tribunal.[99] Citing its famous 1803 decision in *Marbury v. Madison*, the Court stated that "[i]f treaties are to be given effect as federal law under our legal system, determining their meaning as a matter of federal law 'is emphatically the province and duty of the judicial department,' headed by 'one Supreme Court' established by the Constitution."[100] Importantly, the Court in *Sanchez-Llamas* did not suggest that the United States' delegation of judicial authority to the ICJ to resolve disputes under the Vienna Convention (through the Optional Protocol) was constitutionally problematic. The Court's Article III concern, rather, related to the *domestic effect* of the ICJ decision—the determination of the meaning of treaties "as a matter of federal law."

Neither of the two petitioners in *Sanchez-Llamas* was among the fifty-one Mexican nationals named in the *Avena* decision. In *Medellin v. Texas*, however, the Supreme Court considered a habeas petition brought by one of those Mexican nationals, Jose Ernesto Medellin.[101] Medellin was convicted of murder and sentenced to death in a Texas state court in 1994. He first raised a Vienna Convention claim in state post-conviction proceedings, and the state courts held that the claim was procedurally defaulted because it had not been raised on direct appellate review. After the *Avena* decision and President Bush's issuance of the February 2005 memorandum, Medellin once again initiated state post-conviction proceedings. The relevant state court denied relief, concluding that

---

[97] *Id.*
[98] *Id.* at 347.
[99] *Id.* at 355.
[100] *Id.* at 353–54. For additional discussion of *Sanchez-Llamas, see* Mark L. Movsesian, *Judging International Judgments*, 48 VA. J. INT'L L. 65 (2007); Paper Symposium, *Domestic Enforcement of Public International Law after* Sanchez-Llamas v. Oregon, LEWIS & CLARK L. REV. 1–98 (2007) (articles from Julian Ku, Janet Levit, Margaret McGuinness, John Parry, Paul Stephan, and Melissa Waters).
[101] Medellin v. Texas, 552 U.S. 491 (2008).

neither *Avena* nor the president's memorandum operated to displace state law restrictions on the filing of a subsequent post-conviction application.[102]

The U.S. Supreme Court affirmed. The Court explained that "[t]he question we confront here is whether the *Avena* judgment has automatic *domestic* legal effect such that the judgment of its own force applies in state and federal courts."[103] In concluding that the judgment did not have this effect, the Court reasoned that the phrase "undertakes to comply" in Article 94 of the UN Charter does not constitute "a directive to domestic courts" but rather a commitment to take future political branch action.[104] The Court further observed that the requirement of compliance with ICJ decisions was situated within an international legal system that emphasized political rather than judicial enforcement—in particular, enforcement through the Security Council, where the United States holds a veto.[105] The Court also appears to have been influenced by the federalism implications of giving direct effect to ICJ judgments. It stated, for example, that "[g]iven that ICJ judgments may interfere with state procedural rules, one would expect the ratifying parties to the relevant treaties to have clearly stated their intent to give those judgments domestic effect, if they had so intended."[106]

As the dissenting justices charged in *Medellin*, this decision probably means that ICJ judgments issued pursuant to jurisdictional clauses in other treaties will also be deemed to be non–self-executing in the United States.[107] Importantly, though, the Court made clear that it was "not suggest[ing] that treaties can never afford binding domestic effect to international tribunal judgments."[108]

International Criminal Tribunals

The United States played a leading role in the establishment of the international criminal tribunals at Nuremberg and Tokyo at the end of World War II. It also supported the creation during the 1990s of the ad hoc international criminal tribunals for the former Yugoslavia and Rwanda, and it has provided a variety of forms of support to those

---

[102] Ex parte Medellin, 223 S.W.3d 315 (Tex. Ct. Crim. App. 2006).
[103] *Medellin*, 552 U.S. at 504.
[104] *Id.* at 508.
[105] *Id.* at 509–10.
[106] *Id.* at 517.
[107] *See id.* at 541 (Breyer, J., dissenting) ("[H]ere (and presumably in any other ICJ judgment entered pursuant to any of the approximately 70 U.S. treaties in force that contain similar provisions for submitting treaty-based disputes to the ICJ for decisions that bind the parties). Congress must enact specific legislation before ICJ judgments entered pursuant to our consent to compulsory ICJ jurisdiction can become domestic law.").
[108] *Id.* at 519. In the absence of domestic judicial enforcement of the ICJ's decision in *Avena*, the executive branch has made various efforts to persuade U.S. states to grant hearings to individuals covered by the decision, with mixed success.

tribunals. It has further supported the creation of "hybrid" international criminal tribunals, such as for Sierra Leone and Cambodia.

In the 1990s, the United States actively participated in the negotiations to establish a permanent International Criminal Court (ICC).[109] The United States sought to have ICC prosecutions limited to situations in which either the Security Council or a state party has referred a case to the Court, but it was unable to persuade the other delegates to accept this approach.[110] For this and other reasons, when the treaty establishing the Court (the Rome Statute) was finalized in 1998, the United States voted against it. At that time, the United States expressed concerns about the ability of the ICC to assume jurisdiction over nonparty nationals in some circumstances, as well as the danger of politicized prosecutions. These concerns could not be addressed through reservations to the treaty because the Rome Statute expressly prohibits reservations.[111] Despite the U.S. vote against the Statute, the United States participated in the Preparatory Commissions that followed the Rome Conference and, in 2000, joined consensus on the Court's Draft Elements of Crimes and the Draft Rules of Evidence and Procedure.

The Rome Statute took effect in July 2002. As of 2020, over 120 countries were parties to the Statute. The ICC has jurisdiction under the Statute to hear cases involving the crimes of genocide, crimes against humanity, and war crimes, and it may in the future have jurisdiction to hear cases involving the crime of aggression.[112] The ICC can assume jurisdiction over a case in several different ways: the Security Council can refer cases to the ICC, parties to the Rome Statute can also refer cases to the Court, and the ICC's prosecutor can initiate cases independently. The ICC's exercise of jurisdiction, however, is subject to the principle of "complementarity," pursuant to which the ICC can exercise jurisdiction only when a state that has jurisdiction over the alleged offense is "unwilling or unable genuinely to carry out the investigation or prosecution."[113]

Despite its concerns about the Rome Statute, the Clinton administration signed the Statute in late 2000, shortly before the end of President Clinton's time in office. President

---

[109] For an account of the history of efforts to establish a permanent international criminal tribunal, *see* Paul D. Marquardt, *Law without Borders: The Constitutionality of an International Criminal Court*, 33 COLUM. J. TRANSNAT'L L. 73 (1995). For a description of the U.S. relationship to the International Criminal Court, both before and after conclusion of the Rome Statute, *see* Task Force Report, *U.S. Policy toward the International Criminal Court: Furthering Positive Engagement* (Mar. 2009), https://iccobservers.files.wordpress.com/2009/03/asil-08-discpaper2.pdf.

[110] *See* David J. Scheffer, *The United States and the International Criminal Court*, 93 AM. J. INT'L L. 12 (2017); William A. Schabas, *United States Hostility to the International Criminal Court: It's All About the Security Council*, 15 EUR. J. INT'L L. 701 (2004).

[111] *See* Rome Statute of the International Criminal Court, art. 120, July 17, 1998, 2187 U.N.T.S. 90 [hereinafter Rome Statute].

[112] Article 5(2) of the Rome Statute made jurisdiction over the crime of aggression contingent on the adoption of a definition of the crime. That occurred in the Review Conference in 2010. The States Parties to the Rome Statute voted in 2017 to activate the ICC's jurisdiction over the crime of aggression, effective as of July 17, 2018.

[113] Rome Statute, *supra* note 111, art. 17.

Clinton explained that although the United States continued to believe that there were "significant flaws" in the treaty, with signature, the United States would "be in a position to influence the evolution of the Court."[114] The subsequent president, George W. Bush, opposed U.S. participation in the ICC. In 2002, the United States sent a letter to the Secretary-General of the United Nations making clear that the United States had no intention of ratifying the treaty.[115] As noted in Chapter 2, some commentators referred to this notice as an "unsigning" of the Rome Statute, but that characterization is somewhat misleading since the United States did not attempt to physically remove its earlier signature.

After announcing its intent not to ratify the Rome Statute, the United States proceeded to conclude bilateral agreements with nations pursuant to which these nations would commit not to deliver U.S. personnel to the ICC. In doing so, the United States sought to take advantage of Article 98(2) of the Rome Statute, which provides that the ICC

> may not proceed with a request for surrender which would require the requested State to act inconsistently with its obligations under international agreements pursuant to which the consent of a sending State is required to surrender a person of that State to the Court, unless the Court can first obtain the cooperation of the sending State for the giving of consent for the surrender.[116]

Eventually, the United States concluded these "Article 98 agreements" with over one hundred nations.[117]

Congress has also been opposed to the ICC. In 1999, it enacted a law that prohibits the use of U.S. funds to assist the ICC.[118] In 2001, it went even further in the American Servicemembers' Protection Act. This Act limits U.S. government support and assistance to the ICC and authorizes the president to use "all means necessary and appropriate to bring about the release of any US or allied personnel being detained or imprisoned by, on behalf of, or at the request of the International Criminal Court."[119] Because of the latter provision, the Act is sometimes referred to colloquially as the "Hague Invasion Act,"

---

[114] William J. Clinton, *Statement on the Rome Treaty on the International Criminal Court*, 37 WEEKLY COMP. PRES. DOC. 4 (Dec. 31, 2000).

[115] *See* Letter of John R. Bolton, Under Secretary of State for Arms Control and International Security, to U.N. Secretary General Kofi Annan (May 6, 2002), *available at* http://2001-2009.state.gov/r/pa/prs/ps/2002/9968.htm.

[116] Rome Statute, *supra* note 111, art. 98(2).

[117] *See* International Criminal Court—Article 98 Agreements Research Guide, https://guides.ll.georgetown.edu/article_98.

[118] Admiral James W. Nance and Meg Donovan Foreign Relations Authorization Act, Fiscal Years 2000 and 2001, §§ 705–706, *app. to* Pub. L. 106–113, 113 Stat. 1501 (1999).

[119] Pub. L. No. 107–206, § 2008, 116 Stat. 899 (2002).

by virtue of the fact that it could be read to allow for the use of military force to obtain the release of prisoners held by the ICC in The Hague. The American Servicemembers' Protection Act also requires the president to certify, as a condition of having U.S. military personnel participate in certain United Nations peacekeeping or peace enforcement operations, that the personnel are not subject to a risk of prosecution or other assertion of jurisdiction by the ICC.[120]

For a time, however, the United States became more supportive of the ICC.[121] In 2005, the Bush administration decided not to oppose a referral by the UN Security Council of the atrocities in Darfur, Sudan, to the ICC, and in 2008 it supported the ICC's arrest warrant for Sudanese President Omar Hassan al-Bashir. In 2009, under the Obama administration, the United States resumed its observer status in the ICC's Assembly of States Parties, and in 2010 it took part in negotiations over the definition of the crime of aggression.[122] In 2014, it supported an unsuccessful effort in the UN Security Council to have the ICC investigate alleged crimes committed in the civil war in Syria.[123] The U.S. relationship with the ICC deteriorated, however, during the Trump administration, especially after the ICC allowed for the investigation of U.S military actions in Afghanistan.[124]

Despite its uneven relationship with the ICC, it is conceivable that the United States would consider joining the Rome Statute at some point in the future. In order to do so, the president and the Senate would need to satisfy themselves that U.S. participation in the ICC is constitutional. (As discussed in Chapter 3, U.S. accession to the Rome Statute would almost certainly take the form of an Article II treaty rather than an executive agreement and thus would require the advice and consent of two-thirds of the Senate.) If at some point the United States did become a party to the treaty, the Court would have jurisdiction to try U.S. citizens for the covered offenses, even if committed in the United States. In trying these offenses, the Court would apply the terms of the treaty, other applicable treaties, "rules of international law, including the established principles of the international law of armed conflict," and, as a last resort, "general principles of law derived by the Court from national laws of legal systems of the world including, as

---

[120] *See* 22 U.S.C. § 7424(b), (c). *See also, e.g.*, Presidential Memorandum, *Certification Concerning U.S. Participation in the United Nations Multidimensional* (Jan. 31, 2014) (making a certification with respect to U.S. forces participating in a UN mission in Mali), *at* http://www.whitehouse.gov/the-press-office/2014/01/31/presidential-memorandum-certification-concerning-us-participation-united.

[121] *See* WILLIAM A. SCHABAS, AN INTRODUCTION TO THE INTERNATIONAL CRIMINAL COURT 28–29 (5th ed. 2017).

[122] *See* Beth Van Schaack, *Negotiating the Interface of Power and Law: The Crime of Aggression*, 49 COLUM. J. TRANSNAT'L L. 507 (2011).

[123] *See* Somini Sengupta, *China and Syria Block Referral of Syria to Court*, N.Y. TIMES (May 22, 2014).

[124] *See, e.g.*, Lara Jakes & Michael Crowley, *U.S. to Penalize War Crimes Investigators Looking Into American Troops*, N.Y. TIMES (June 11, 2020); Susannah George, *International Criminal Court Approves Investigation of Possible War Crimes in Afghanistan Involving U.S. Troops*, WASH. POST (Mar. 5, 2020); Matt Apuzo & Marlise Simons, *U.S. Attack on I.C.C. Seen as Bolstering World's Despots*, N.Y. TIMES (Sept. 13, 2018).

appropriate, the national laws of States that would normally exercise jurisdiction over the crime."[125] As a party to the treaty, the United States would be required to "cooperate fully with the Court in its investigation and prosecution of crimes within the jurisdiction of the Court," and to "comply with requests for arrest and surrender."[126]

Several constitutional concerns have been raised about U.S. ratification of the Rome Statute.[127] It has been argued that if the United States participated in the ICC, the Court would in effect be applying the federal judicial power specified in Article III without the tenure, salary, and appointment protections specified in the Article. This argument is not compelling. Although it is true that adjudication of U.S. criminal law is a core part of the federal judicial power, the ICC applies international criminal law, not U.S. criminal law. It does not matter that there is some overlap between international criminal law and U.S. criminal law; there is also overlap between U.S. criminal law and the criminal law of other countries, and yet (as will be discussed in Chapter 9) that is no barrier to extraditing suspects to be tried in foreign courts.

Concerns also have been raised about the ICC's lack of a jury trial and certain other procedural protections that would be available in criminal trials in the United States. Again, however, this is also true in the extradition context, and yet it does not stop the U.S. government from sending suspects to be tried in foreign courts. Indeed, as discussed in Chapter 9, pursuant to the "rule of non-inquiry," U.S. courts in extradition cases generally do not consider the fairness of the foreign legal system.

To be sure, extradition to a foreign country is not precisely analogous to extradition to an international court. If the United States were a party to the Rome Statute, the ICC would be connected to the United States in ways that a foreign sovereign is not. Moreover, one reason for the rule of non-inquiry is respect for the sovereignty of other countries, a consideration that has less force when the focus is an international institution. As a result, it is arguable that U.S. courts considering an extradition request to an international tribunal should satisfy themselves that the tribunal contains basic protections of what is considered in the United States to be due process. As will be explained in Chapter 6, the Supreme Court held in the early 1900s that, although the Constitution did not apply

---

[125] Rome Statute, *supra* note 111, art. 21.

[126] *Id.*, art. 86.

[127] For constitutional objections to U.S. participation in the ICC, see, for example, Lee A. Casey, *The Case against the International Criminal Court*, 25 FORDHAM INT'L L.J. 840 (2002). *See also* Senate Comm. on Foreign Relations, *International Criminal Court*, S. Rep. No. 71, 103d Cong., 1st Sess. (1993) (containing report from the Judicial Conference of the United States raising constitutional concerns); ABA Task Force on an Int'l Criminal Court, *Establishment of an International Criminal Court, reprinted in* 27 INT'L LAW 257 (1993) (raising constitutional concerns). For commentators who have concluded that these constitutional objections are ultimately unpersuasive, see, for example, Diane Marie Amann & M.N.S. Sellers, *The United States of America and the International Criminal Court*, 50 AM. J. COMP. L. 381 (2002); Audrey I. Benison, *International Criminal Tribunals: Is There a Substantive Limit on the Treaty Power?*, 37 STAN. J. INT'L L. 75 (2001); and David Scheffer & Ashley Cox, *The Constitutionality of the Rome Statute of the International Criminal Court*, 98 J. CRIM. L. & CRIMINOLOGY 983 (2008).

in full to U.S. territorial possessions, basic requirements of due process were applicable. Importantly, those cases make clear that basic due process does not require a jury trial. Putting that aside, the ICC would seem to satisfy a due process analysis, because it has most of the features required in U.S. criminal proceedings, including a right to counsel, a right against self-incrimination, and protection from double jeopardy. The ICC also has pretrial procedures that are somewhat comparable to presentment and indictment by a grand jury in the United States.

The U.S. Court of Appeals for the Fifth Circuit upheld an extradition to the International Criminal Tribunal for Rwanda, in *Ntakirutimana v. Reno*.[128] The main focus of the decision was on whether it was constitutional for the United States to extradite someone pursuant to a congressional–executive agreement rather than an Article II treaty, and a majority of the court held that it was. But the court also rejected the petitioner's argument that the procedures of the Rwandan tribunal were insufficient to protect constitutional rights, reasoning that such considerations were beyond the proper bounds of what a court could review in an extradition case. The court therefore treated an extradition to an international criminal tribunal the same way that it would treat an extradition to a foreign country. The dissenting judge, while arguing that an Article II treaty is required for extradition, did not contend that an extradition to the tribunal was otherwise constitutionally problematic.[129]

Treaty Amendments

Some international institutions have been delegated the authority to make changes to treaties that become binding on the parties to the treaty without the expectation of a national act of ratification of the changes.[130] These treaty changes are often concluded

---

[128] Ntakirutimana v. Reno, 184 F.3d 419 (5th Cir. 1999). The United States has statutorily committed itself to extradite suspects to the ad hoc international criminal tribunals established for former Yugoslavia and for Rwanda. *See* National Defense Authorization Act for Fiscal Year 1996, Pub. L. No. 104-106, 1342, 110 Stat. 186, 486.

[129] In a footnote, the dissenting judge observed: "Whether executive and legislative actions such as those giving rise to this case reflect, as political commentator George Will has suggested, a disturbing trend of 'dilution of American democracy,' I leave for others to judge." *Ntakirutimana*, 184 F.3d at 438 n.35 (citing George Will, *See You in Congress...*, WASH. POST, May 20, 1999, at A29).

[130] *See generally* Robin R. Churchill & Geir Ulfstein, *Autonomous Institutional Arrangements in Multilateral Environmental Agreements: A Little Noticed Phenomenon in International Law*, 94 AM. J. INT'L L. 623 (2000); Kristina Daugirdas, *International Delegations and Administrative Law*, 66 MD. L. REV. 707 (2007); Frederic L. Kirgis, Jr., *Specialized Law-Making Processes*, in 1 UNITED NATIONS LEGAL ORDER 109 (1995); Richard B. Stewart, *U.S. Administrative Law: A Model for Global Administrative Law?*, 68 LAW & CONTEMP. PROBS. 63 (2004-05). For more general accounts of these and other features of international institutions, *see* BOWETT'S LAW OF INTERNATIONAL INSTITUTIONS (Philippe Sands & Pierre Klein eds., 6th ed. 2009); JAN KLABBERS, AN INTRODUCTION TO INTERNATIONAL INSTITUTIONAL LAW (3d ed. 2015); HENRY G. SCHERMERS & NIELS M. BLOKKER, INTERNATIONAL INSTITUTIONAL LAW: UNITY WITHIN DIVERSITY (5th ed. rev. 2011).

pursuant to a "tacit" amendment process, whereby the changes are adopted by an international institution and automatically take effect for a party unless the party objects within a specified period of time. One common justification given for tacit amendment procedures is that they allow for the regular updating of technical or administrative provisions in a treaty, without the need for potentially lengthy and unwieldy national ratifications. In explaining why a tacit amendment process has been incorporated into many of the conventions adopted under the auspices of the International Maritime Organization, for example, the Organization's website notes that this process "has greatly speeded up the amendment process."[131]

Although often described as technical or administrative in nature, unratified treaty amendments can substantially affect a party's treaty obligations. Consider, for example, the International Convention for the Regulation of Whaling, which the United States ratified in 1948. In an effort to "establish a system of international regulation for the whale fisheries to ensure proper and effective conservation and development of whale stocks,"[132] this Convention establishes an International Whaling Commission, which is composed of one representative from each party country.[133] The Convention also includes an attached "Schedule," which the Convention describes as an "integral part" of the Convention.[134] The Commission is given the authority, upon a three-fourths vote, to amend the Schedule with respect to such basic issues as the species subject to protection; the open and closed waters and seasons; the time, methods, and intensity of whaling; and the types of gear that can be used.[135] These amendments to the Schedule become effective for all parties to the Convention except those that object during a specified period of time.[136]

Another example of a treaty containing a tacit amendment procedure is the Chemical Weapons Convention, which the United States ratified in 1997. Parties to the Convention have agreed, among other things, never to develop, produce, acquire, stockpile, retain, transfer, or use chemical weapons.[137] They have also agreed to be subject to international inspections to verify their compliance. The Convention's definition of chemical weapons

---

[131] *See* International Maritime Organization, http://www.imo.org/About/Conventions/Pages/Home.aspx.

[132] International Convention for the Regulation of Whaling pmbl., Dec. 2, 1946, 62 Stat. 1716, 1718, 161 U.N.T.S. 72.

[133] *See id.*, art. III(1).

[134] *See id.*, art. I(1).

[135] *See id.*, art. V(1).

[136] *Id.*, art. V(3). The amendments take effect ninety days after the parties are notified of them if there is no objection. If there is an objection, then the amendments take effect after an additional ninety days for the parties that have not objected, or thirty days after the last objection is received, whichever is later. In *Japan Whaling Ass'n v. Am. Cetacean Soc'y*, 478 U.S. 221 (1986), the Supreme Court referred to the Commission's ability to amend the Schedule.

[137] United Nations Convention on the Prohibition of the Development, Production, Stockpiling and Use of Chemical Weapons and on Their Destruction art. I(1), Jan. 13, 1993, S. Treaty Doc. No. 103–21, 1974 U.N.T.S. 317 [hereinafter Chemical Weapons Convention].

refers to "toxic chemicals," and that term is defined as "[a]ny chemical which through its chemical action on life processes can cause death, temporary incapacitation or permanent harm to humans or animals."[138] The schedules contained in an Annex on Chemicals attached to the Convention then list the toxic chemicals subject to the Convention's verification measures. The Convention provides for tacit amendments to these schedules "if proposed changes are related only to matters of an administrative or technical nature."[139] Under this process, "[i]f the Executive Council [which consists of forty-one nations with rotating membership] recommends to all States Parties that the proposal be adopted, it shall be considered approved if no State Party objects to it within 90 days after receipt of the recommendation."[140]

In the above examples, the United States can prevent itself from being bound by the treaty amendments by lodging an objection to them. Some treaty amendment procedures, however, allow for amendments to take effect for a party even over its objection. If there is an objection to a proposed change to the Chemical Weapons Convention's Annexes, for example, the proposed change is referred for decision to the Conference of the States Parties, where, as long as the change is found to involve a "matter[] of an administrative or technical nature," it can be adopted by a two-thirds vote and thereby bind dissenting countries.[141] A similar procedure exists under the Montreal Protocol on Substances that Deplete the Ozone Layer, which the United States ratified in 1988. The Protocol requires that parties reduce and ultimately eliminate the use of certain substances that degrade the ozone layer, in accordance with agreed-upon timetables. Certain changes to the annexes to this Convention can be adopted by a two-thirds majority vote and thereby take effect for all the parties, including those that voted against the amendments.[142]

Yet another example is the Protocol Additional to the Safeguards Agreement between the United States and the International Atomic Energy Agency (IAEA), which the United States ratified in 2004.[143] The Protocol allows the IAEA's Board of Governors to amend the annexes to the Protocol (which set forth definitions of nuclear activities, equipment, and material subject to declaration under the Protocol) "upon the advice of an open-ended working group of experts established by the Board," and such amendments take effect four months after being adopted by the Board.[144] Although the IAEA

---

[138] *Id.*, art. II(2).
[139] *Id.*, art. XV(4).
[140] *Id.*, art. XV(5)(d). For additional examples of tacit amendment provisions, *see* Swaine, *supra* note 1, at 1512 n.71.
[141] Chemical Weapons Convention, *supra* note 137, art. XV(4) & (5)(e), art. VIII(18); *see also* Note, *Discretion and Legitimacy in International Regulation*, 107 HARV. L. REV. 1099, 1102 n.18 (1994).
[142] *See* Montreal Protocol on Substances That Deplete the Ozone Layer, art. 2(9)(c), (d), Sept. 16, 1987, S. Treaty Doc. No. 100–10, 1522 U.N.T.S. 29 [hereinafter Montreal Protocol]. *See also* Stewart, *supra* note 126, at 90–91.
[143] *See* Protocol Additional to the Agreement between the United States of America and the International Atomic Energy Agency (IAEA) for the Application of Safeguards in the United States of America, June 12, 1998, U.S.–IAEA, S. Treaty Doc. No. 107–7.
[144] *Id.*, art. 16(b).

Board (which is composed of representatives from thirty-five member states, including the United States) generally takes action on the basis of consensus, it has the authority to take action even when there is dissent.

Constitutional concerns have sometimes been raised about this sort of treaty amendment authority. For example, in negotiating the structure of the proposed International Labour Organization in 1919, U.S. delegates argued against granting the organization the power to create binding labor standards, on the ground that this power would improperly allow the organization to impose new treaty obligations on the United States without going through the treaty process specified in the U.S. Constitution.[145] Ultimately, the Organization was given the authority only to promulgate proposed conventions that its members were free to accept or reject (although members are obligated to submit the conventions to their national authorities for consideration).[146]

The U.S. Court of Appeals for the D.C. Circuit expressed doubts about the constitutionality of treaty amendment authority in *Natural Resources Defense Council v. Environmental Protection Agency*.[147] The case concerned the Montreal Protocol, discussed earlier in this section. After the United States ratified the Protocol, Congress incorporated its terms into U.S. domestic law and directed the U.S. Environmental Protection Agency (EPA) to comply with them. The Protocol allows "adjustments" to be made to its terms without formal amendment and ratification. In incorporating the Protocol into domestic law, Congress defined the Protocol to include "adjustments adopted by the Parties thereto and amendments that have entered into force."[148]

In 1997, the parties to the Protocol "adjusted" it to require developed-country parties to cease production and consumption of methyl bromide by 2005, except "to the extent that the Parties decide to permit the level of production or consumption that is necessary to satisfy uses agreed by them to be critical uses."[149] The parties subsequently issued "decisions" regulating critical-use exemptions to the ban on methyl bromide. Relying on those decisions, the Natural Resources Defense Council sought to challenge regulations issued by the EPA relating to methyl bromide. In rejecting this challenge, the court reasoned that "[h]olding that the Parties' post-ratification side agreements were 'law' would raise serious constitutional questions in light of the nondelegation doctrine, numerous constitutional procedural requirements for making law, and the separation of powers."[150] The court further expressed the view that, "[w]ithout congressional action ... side agreements

---

[145] *See* Pittman B. Potter, *Inhibitions upon the Treaty-Making Power of the United States*, 28 AM. J. INT'L L. 456, 456–57 (1934). Despite not joining the League of Nations, the United States eventually joined the ILO in the 1930s. *See* 48 Stat. 1182 (1934) (authorizing the president to accept membership for the United States).

[146] *See* Swaine, *supra* note 1, at 1503–505; *see also* Laurence R. Helfer, *Monitoring Compliance with Unratified Treaties: The ILO Experience*, 71 LAW & CONTEMP. PROBS. 193, 197 (2008).

[147] NRDC v. EPA, 464 F.3d 1 (D.C. Cir. 2006).

[148] 42 U.S.C. § 7671c(9).

[149] Montreal Protocol, *supra* note 142, art. 2H(5).

[150] *NRDC*, 464 F.3d at 9.

reached after a treaty has been ratified are not the law of the land; they are enforceable not through the federal courts, but through international negotiations."[151]

The constitutionality of at least some treaty amendment procedures may be supported by the general phenomenon of executive agreements, discussed in Chapter 3. In particular, it is well accepted that the Senate and president in a treaty may delegate to the president the authority to conclude executive agreements relating to the treaty.[152] Treaty amendments that can take effect only with the consent of the U.S. representative in the international institution may be analogous to such treaty-authorized executive agreements. This argument would not apply, however, to treaty amendments that can be adopted over the objection of the United States. Treaty amendment authority might also be constitutionally defensible on the ground that it is analogous to administrative authority that has long been delegated by Congress to U.S. administrative agencies. The analogy is not perfect, however, in that international institutions are not subject to some of the checks applicable to U.S. administrative agencies (such as public notice and comment procedures, congressional oversight, and judicial review). In any event, this analogy probably works best when treaty amendments are limited to technical or administrative matters rather than the core substantive terms of the treaty.[153]

In general, the Senate appears to have accepted the phenomenon of unratified treaty amendments. At times, however, it has insisted that the treaty amendment authority be limited to technical or administrative matters.[154] It has also sometimes "requested or required the executive branch to advise the Senate of such amendments prior to their entry into force."[155]

---

[151] *Id.* at 10. For criticism of the decision, see Daugirdas, *supra* note 130, at 719–20.

[152] *See* Wilson v. Girard, 354 U.S. 524, 528–29 (1957).

[153] For additional discussion of constitutional issues relating to the delegation of treaty amendment authority to international institutions, see Curtis A. Bradley, *Unratified Treaty Amendments and Constitutional Process* (unpublished manuscript, Feb. 6, 2006), http://www.law.duke.edu/publiclaw/pdf/workshop06sp/bradleyc.pdf; Oona Hathaway et al., *Tacit Amendments* (unpublished manuscript, Nov. 15, 2011), https://law.yale.edu/sites/default/files/documents/pdf/cglc/TacitAmendments.pdf; David A. Koplow, *When Is an Amendment Not an Amendment?: Modification of Arms Control Agreements without the Senate*, 59 U. CHI. L. REV. 981 (1992); Swaine, *supra* note 1, at 1506–15. For a signing statement issued by President Bush raising delegation concerns about legislation that would take effect and remain in place only if international institutions took certain actions, see *Statement on Signing the Clean Diamond Trading Act* (Apr. 25, 2003), http://www.presidency.ucsb.edu/ws/index.php?pid=65039#axzz1nDmFzwH4. Similarly, in 2004, the Bush administration objected on delegation grounds to proposed legislation that would tie the timing of notice-and-comment procedures in the United States (concerning the regulation of "persistent organic pollutants") to the actions of an international body. *See* Daugirdas, *supra* note 130, at 720–23.

[154] *See* S. Exec. Rep. No. 108-12, at 34 (2004) ("The Senate has also at times specifically limited its acceptance of future tacit amendments to those of a technical or administrative nature.").

[155] CONGRESSIONAL RESEARCH SERVICE, TREATIES AND OTHER INTERNATIONAL AGREEMENTS: THE ROLE OF THE UNITED STATES SENATE, S. Prt. 106-71, 106th Cong., 2d Sess. 183 (2001); *see also* 1 S. Exec. Rep. No. 96-36, at 2 (1980) ("The Committee expects the Administration to inform it of any proposed amendments subject to this procedure prior to the time for tacit acceptance. This will enable the Committee to voice an objection to tacit acceptance in appropriate cases, before the issue becomes moot.").

Arms Control Inspection

The United States has long participated in treaties designed to prohibit or limit the use of certain armaments.[156] For example, the United States concluded a number of nuclear arms reduction treaties with the Soviet Union, and then later with Russia. The United States is also a party to a variety of other arms control agreements, such as the Nuclear Test Ban Treaty, the Nuclear Non-Proliferation Treaty, and the Biological Weapons Convention.

Arms control agreements sometimes contain mechanisms for verifying compliance with the terms of the agreements, such as through on-site inspections. Consider, for example, the Chemical Weapons Convention, which the United States ratified in 1997.[157] The Convention prohibits the development, retention, and use of chemical weapons. The Convention also established a new international organization, the Organization for the Prohibition of Chemical Weapons, which has the power to verify Convention compliance by ordering inspections of public and private facilities in the party countries. Inspections are conducted by the organization's Technical Secretariat, members of which are not appointed by or removable by U.S. officials. The Secretariat conducts two types of inspections: "routine" inspections and "challenge" inspections.

Some commentators have suggested that, as applied to the United States, the inspection provisions in the Convention violate the Appointments Clause of the Constitution. One scholar makes the argument as follows:

> First, the [Chemical Weapons Convention (CWC)] grants the power to search American facilities and sites to officials of an international organization who are not appointed pursuant to the Appointments Clause, who are not members of the executive branch, and who are not accountable to the President. Second, the treaty grants the authority to select the locations to be inspected to the Technical Secretariat. Their decisions neither are made by officers of the United States subject to standards established by federal law, nor are they reviewable by an American official appointed by, and accountable to, the President. In other words, the CWC establishes an entity that exercises public authority upon American citizens without the constitutional safeguards designed to preserve government accountability.[158]

---

[156] *See, e.g.*, Louis Henkin, Arms Control Inspection and American Law (1958); David A. Koplow, *Arms Control Inspection: Constitutional Restrictions on Treaty Verification in the United States*, 63 N.Y.U. L. Rev. 229 (1988).

[157] *See* Chemical Weapons Convention, *supra* note 137.

[158] See John C. Yoo, *The New Sovereignty and the Old Constitution: The Chemical Weapons Convention and the Appointments Clause*, 15 Const. Comment. 87 (1998). *Cf.* Kevin C. Kennedy, *The Constitution and On-Site Inspection*, 14 Brook. J. Int'l L. 1, 25 (1988) ("[S]earches conducted by Soviet inspectors within the territory of the United States at private premises arguably constitute the exercise of an Executive Branch function—the

There are a number of problems with this argument. Although it seems reasonable to characterize the power to carry out a nonconsensual search of a private facility on U.S. territory as the exercise of a government function that is subject to the requirements of the Appointments Clause, the legislation that Congress enacted to implement the Chemical Weapons Convention makes clear that this function is not to be exercised directly by international officials. Under that legislation, all nonconsensual private searches require a warrant—either an administrative warrant or a criminal warrant—to be issued by a U.S. judicial official. Moreover, the U.S. government must approve the inspection, and U.S. government officials accompany the international inspectors.[159] As a result of these limitations, international inspectors are not themselves exercising direct compulsory authority over private facilities.

There is, however, a more serious constitutional question relating to the Chemical Weapons Convention, which is its compatibility with the Fourth Amendment to the Constitution. The Fourth Amendment protects against "unreasonable searches and seizures" and often requires the government to obtain a search warrant before entering private facilities without the owner's consent. When inspectors from the Technical Secretariat attempt to enter private facilities in the United States, there is a strong argument that the Fourth Amendment should apply.[160] Although the Fourth Amendment does not require warrants for the inspection of pervasively regulated industries,[161] many private facilities subject to inspection under the Convention probably do not fall within that category.[162]

Both the Senate and the full Congress have sought to address this Fourth Amendment issue. Although the Convention prohibits reservations, in giving its advice and consent to the Convention, the Senate included twenty-eight "conditions." The twenty-eighth condition requires that, before ratifying the Convention, the president shall certify to Congress that a warrant shall be obtained prior to allowing any nonconsensual search (a criminal warrant in the case of a challenge inspection, and an administrative warrant in the case of a routine inspection).[163] Congress's implementing legislation for the

---

execution of a Fourth Amendment search—by persons who are not Executive Branch officers, agents, or employees.").

[159] *See* 22 U.S.C. § 6723(a), (b)(2).

[160] *See, e.g.*, HENKIN, *supra* note 9, at 266; David A. Koplow, *Back to the Future and Up to the Sky: Legal Implications of "Open Skies" Inspection for Arms Control*, 79 CAL. L. REV. 421, 453 (1991).

[161] *See* Jonathan P. Hersey & Anthony F. Ventura, *Challenging Challenge Inspections: A Fourth Amendment Analysis of the Chemical Weapons Convention*, 25 FLA. ST. U. L. REV. 570 (1998); Kennedy, *supra* note 158.

[162] *See* Ronald D. Rotunda, *The Chemical Weapons Convention: Political and Constitutional Issues*, 15 CONST. COMMENT. 131 (1998).

[163] *See* U.S. Senate's Conditions to the Ratification of the Chemical Weapons Convention, http://www.cwc.gov/cwc_authority_ratification_text.html.

Convention further provides for various safeguards in connection with the inspections, including procedures for obtaining warrants.[164]

Non-Self-Execution

As we have seen, although the Constitution generally does not impose serious obstacles to U.S. participation in international institutions, some delegations of authority to such institutions can pose constitutional concerns. Many of these concerns can be avoided by treating the output of international institutions as "non–self-executing"—that is, as not operating as judicially enforceable domestic law without some act of incorporation by the political branches. This is true regardless of whether the terms of treaties themselves should be presumed to be non–self-executing, an issue discussed in Chapter 2. By requiring political branch implementation, this non–self-execution approach subjects international orders and decisions to the filter of the U.S. democratic process while preserving the traditional role of the U.S. judiciary to interpret and apply existing domestic law. At the same time, it does not restrict U.S. participation in international institutions and thus preserves the flexibility that is often thought essential in foreign policy.[165]

In practice, U.S. courts have tended to follow this approach. Consider, for example, the 1976 decision by the U.S. Court of Appeals for the D.C. Circuit in *Diggs v. Richardson*.[166] In that case, the Security Council had issued a resolution calling upon all nations to cease certain relationships with South Africa because of its occupation of the former UN territory of Namibia. Relying on this resolution, a group of plaintiffs sought declaratory and injunctive relief prohibiting the U.S. government from continuing to deal with South Africa concerning the importation of seal furs from Namibia. The D.C. Circuit upheld dismissal of the lawsuit, concluding that the UN resolution was not self-executing. The

---

[164] *See* Chemical Weapons Convention Implementation Act of 1998, Pub. L. No. 105–277, 112 Stat. 2681, *codified at* 22 U.S.C. §§ 6701–71. Another example of international inspection authority that potentially implicated Fourth Amendment and other issues is the Optional Protocol to the Convention against Torture and Other Cruel, Inhuman and Degrading Treatment or Punishment, which allows international monitors to inspect places of detention in party countries. In declining to support the Protocol, a U.S. representative stated that the "overall approach and certain specific provisions [of the Protocol] are contrary to our Constitution, particularly with respect to matters of search and seizure," and that "in view of our Federal system of government, the regime established by the draft would be overly intrusive." UNITED STATES PRACTICE IN INTERNATIONAL LAW, 2002–2004, at 194 (Sean D. Murphy ed., 2005); *see also* Barbara Crossette, *U.S. Fails in Effort to Block Vote on U.N. Convention on Torture*, N.Y. TIMES (July 25, 2002), at A7.

[165] For arguments along these lines, *see generally* Bradley, *supra* note 1. *See also* John Harrison, *International Adjudicators and Judicial Independence*, 30 HARV. J.L. & PUB. POL'Y 127, 127 (2006) (arguing, on structural constitutional grounds, that "adjudicatory tribunal decisions . . . have, of their own force, no effect in domestic law, even when they are made pursuant to international agreements to which the United States is a party"); McGinnis, *supra* note 7, at 1719 (arguing that an international delegation "raises serious questions of legality under domestic law" only if it has domestic legal effect).

[166] Diggs v. Richardson, 555 F.2d 848 (D.C. Cir. 1976).

court noted, among other things, that the resolution was not addressed to the judicial branch, did not by its terms confer individual rights, addressed foreign relations issues within the discretion of the executive branch, and did not provide specific standards. As the court also noted, by treating the resolution as non–self-executing, the court was able to "avoid the larger questions raised by this case: under what circumstances a Security Council resolution can create a binding international obligation on the United States; whether Article 25 of the UN Charter, in which nations agree to carry out the resolutions of the Council, can ever give rise to a self-executing resolution; and so on."[167]

Other decisions by the D.C. Circuit have followed a similar approach. In *Committee of United States Citizens Living in Nicaragua v. Reagan*, for example, the court concluded that an ICJ decision prohibiting the United States from assisting rebel forces in Nicaragua was non–self-executing because the relevant treaty provisions evidenced "no intent to vest citizens who reside in a UN member nation with authority to enforce an ICJ decision against their own government."[168] Similarly, in the *Natural Resources Defense Council* decision discussed earlier, the court held that decisions of the parties under the Montreal Protocol did not have the status of "judicially enforceable domestic law."[169]

Even more significantly, this is the approach followed by the Supreme Court in the litigation over the Vienna Convention on Consular Relations. In its 2008 decision in *Medellin v. Texas*, the Court reasoned that the ICJ's decision in *Avena* directing the United States to provide review and reconsideration to the fifty-one Mexican nationals did not operate as a "directive to domestic courts."[170] The Court's conclusion was influenced in part by the federalism implications of giving direct effect to ICJ decisions: "Given that ICJ judgments may interfere with state procedural rules, one would expect the ratifying parties to the relevant treaties to have clearly stated their intent to give those judgments domestic effect, if they had so intended."[171] As a number of commentators (including this author) have noted, whatever *Medellin* may suggest about the circumstances under which treaty obligations in general will be treated as self-executing

---

[167] *Id.* at 850 n.9. For additional discussion of the status of Security Council resolutions in the United States, *see* James A.R. Nafziger & Edward M. Wise, *The Status in United States Law of Security Council Resolutions under Chapter VII of the United Nations Charter*, 46 Am. J. Comp. L. 421 (1998). The issue of whether resolutions of the Security Council can provide domestic authority for presidential uses of military force is considered in Chapter 10.

[168] Committee of United States Citizens Living in Nicaragua v. Reagan, 859 F.2d 929, 938 (D.C. Cir. 1988).

[169] NRDC v. EPA, 464 F.3d 1, 10 (D.C. Cir. 2006).

[170] Medellin v. Texas, 552 U.S. 491, 508 (2008).

[171] *Id.* at 517; *see also id.* at 518 (expressing concern that, under the petitioner's interpretation of the relevant treaties, "there is nothing to prevent the ICJ from ordering state courts to annul criminal convictions and sentences, for any reason deemed sufficient by the ICJ").

within the U.S. legal system, the decision is consistent with a presumption against giving self-executing effect to the decisions of international institutions.[172]

Since it is a general presumption, this non–self-execution approach operates more broadly than is strictly required by the Constitution (the relationship of which to international delegations is, as already discussed, highly uncertain).[173] Moreover, since it is only a presumption, it will not avoid constitutional issues when the treaty or implementing legislation has expressly provided that the output of the international institution has domestic effect. This was the case, for example, with the Chapter 19 NAFTA arbitration system. In addition, even when the output of an international institution is treated as non–self-executing, there may still be some constitutional issues. Thus, for example, if treaty amendments adopted by international institutions are constitutionally problematic because they bypass the constitutionally specified process for making treaties, this problem would not be eliminated merely by treating the amendments as non–self-executing. Nevertheless, the non–self-execution approach, combined with other limitations typically imposed by the U.S. treaty-makers and Congress on international delegations, substantially reduces the potential conflict between the Constitution and U.S. participation in international institutions.[174] This approach is also likely to be much easier for courts to administer than imposing direct constitutional restraints on international delegations.

A potential downside of the non–self-execution approach is that there might be situations in which the lack of direct enforceability of international decisions or orders will make it more likely that the United States will end up breaching its international commitments. At least so far, however, it does not appear that non–self-execution has created any generalized compliance problems, even if one can think of isolated instances in which there have been difficulties (such as in connection with the ICJ's *Avena* decision). Moreover, non–self-execution in this context is only a presumption, so if there is undue tension between this approach and the need for compliance, Congress and the treaty-makers have options to reduce that tension. It is also worth remembering that non–self-execution simply precludes direct judicial enforcement of a treaty, and that the

---

[172] *See* Bradley, *Self-Execution and Treaty Duality*, *supra* note 77, at 172; Julian G. Ku, *Medellín's Clear Statement Rule: A Solution for International Delegations*, 77 FORDHAM L. REV. 609 (2008); McGinnis, *supra* note 7, at 1730–33.

[173] *See* Swaine, *supra* note 1, at 1553–54.

[174] Arbitral decisions involving private parties are often enforceable directly in U.S. courts, pursuant to the New York Convention for the Recognition and Enforcement of Foreign Arbitral Awards and its implementing legislation. There is no such clear directive for the domestic enforcement of interstate decisions such as *Avena*, however, and their application in the U.S. legal system raises a number of distinct issues. *See* Mark L. Movsesian, *International Commercial Arbitration and International Courts*, 18 DUKE J. COMP. & INT'L L. 423 (2008). Similarly, although U.S. courts often enforce foreign court judgments involving private parties, the U.S. relationship with international adjudicatory bodies is distinguishable from the comity relationship that exists between U.S. courts and other national courts. *See* Paul B. Stephan, *Open Doors*, 13 LEWIS & CLARK L. REV. 11 (2009).

United States can comply with many treaty obligations without such enforcement, such as through administrative or other executive action.

* * *

In our complex and interdependent world, international institutions play a vital role in helping nations work together in addressing pressing issues of mutual concern, and in resolving disputes between them fairly and peacefully. Participation in such institutions can raise constitutional questions for the United States, however, as it seeks to ensure that its constitutional framework for distributing authority is not undermined by these new arrangements. In general, U.S. constitutional law is sufficiently flexible that it can accommodate international delegations, just as it accommodated the rise of administrative agencies domestically, but this does not mean that such delegations are always unproblematic. International delegations create the most significant constitutional difficulties for the United States when they entail the ability to effectuate direct changes in U.S. domestic law. This phenomenon is still rare, however, in part because both the courts and the political branches of the government have generally sought to ensure that the country retains some measure of control over how the decisions and orders of international institutions are implemented.

5 Customary International Law

THE FOCUS OF this chapter is the domestic status of customary international law (CIL), which is the law of the international community that results from the general and consistent practices of nations that are followed out of a sense of legal obligation.[1] CIL has long been an important source of international law. Indeed, before the mid-nineteenth century, it was the principal form of international law, because there were relatively few treaties, and almost no multilateral treaties. Even today, CIL is regularly applied by international tribunals, such as the International Court of Justice.

Unlike with treaties, nations do not need to affirmatively agree to rules of CIL in order to become bound by them. Instead, it is generally accepted that, if there is the requisite national practice, a rule of CIL will bind all nations except for those that have persistently

---

[1] *See, e.g.*, RESTATEMENT (THIRD) OF THE FOREIGN RELATIONS LAW OF THE UNITED STATES § 102(2) (1987) ("Customary international law results from a general and consistent practice of states followed by them from a sense of legal obligation."); Statute of the International Court of Justice, art. 38(1), June 26, 1945, 59 Stat. 1055, 1060 (including, in the sources of international law to be applied by the International Court of Justice, "international custom, as evidence of a general practice accepted as law"); International Law Commission, Draft Conclusions on Identification of Customary International Law, Conclusion 2 (2018) ("To determine the existence and content of a rule of customary international law, it is necessary to ascertain whether there is a general practice that is accepted as law (*opinio juris*)."), *at* https://legal.un.org/ilc/texts/instruments/english/draft_articles/1_13_2018.pdf.

objected to the rule before it developed.[2] Even the limited right of opting out through persistent objection is not available for a small set of customary norms referred to as "peremptory norms" or "*jus cogens* norms," which are generally thought to prohibit all nations from engaging in egregious human rights practices such genocide, war crimes, slavery, and torture.[3]

Given its decentralized nature, it is not surprising that the international legal system would rely on custom, which can reflect shared expectations and fill in gaps in formal written rules. The treatment of international custom as law, however, can create tensions when it intersects with the U.S. legal system, which has formal procedures for making law and institutions with limited powers. This chapter explores some of those tensions and describes how courts and other actors in the United States have treated CIL, both historically and in the modern era.

Text of the U.S. Constitution

At the time that the U.S. Constitution was drafted and ratified, CIL was referred to as part of the "law of nations," a category that included both public international law (rights and duties between nations) and private international law (rules governing international relationships and disputes involving private parties).[4] Issues regulated by the public law component of the law of nations included rights on the seas, conduct during wartime, and diplomatic immunity. Issues regulated by the private law component included conflict-of-laws principles; rules for the enforcement of foreign judgments; and the "law merchant," which consisted of general principles applicable to cross-border commerce.

Although the constitutional Founders were very familiar with the law of nations, it is mentioned only once in the constitutional text: among the various powers granted to Congress in Article I of the Constitution is the power to "define and punish ... Offences against the Law of Nations."[5] By contrast, the Constitution mentions treaties four

---

[2] For discussion of the persistent objector doctrine, see, for example, David A. Colson, *How Persistent Must the Persistent Objector Be?*, 61 WASH. L. REV. 957 (1986); and Ted L. Stein, *The Approach of the Different Drummer: The Principle of the Persistent Objector in International Law*, 26 HARV. INT'L L.J. 457 (1985).

[3] *See* RESTATEMENT (THIRD) OF THE FOREIGN RELATIONS LAW OF THE UNITED STATES, *supra* note 1, § 702 & reporters' note 11 (listing human rights norms that qualify as jus cogens norms); *see also, e.g.*, Siderman de Blake v. Republic of Argentina, 965 F.2d 699, 715–16 (9th Cir. 1992) (discussing the jus cogens category); Vienna Convention on the Law of Treaties, art. 53, May 23, 1969, 1155 U.N.T.S. 331 (defining a jus cogens norm as a "norm accepted and recognized by the international community of States as a whole as a norm from which no derogation is permitted and which can be modified only by a subsequent norm of general international law having the same character").

[4] *See* Curtis A. Bradley & Jack L. Goldsmith, *Customary International Law as Federal Common Law: A Critique of the Modern Position*, 110 HARV. L. REV. 815, 822 (1997); Stewart Jay, *The Status of the Law of Nations in Early American Law*, 42 VAND. L. REV. 819, 821–22 (1989).

[5] U.S. CONST. art. I, § 8, cl. 10. For discussions of the scope of the define-and-punish power, see, for example, Sarah H. Cleveland & William S. Dodge, *Defining and Punishing Offenses Under Treaties*, 124 YALE L.J. 2202 (2015); J. Andrew Kent, *Congress's Under-Appreciated Power to Define and Punish Offenses against the Law of*

times: Article I, Section 10 denies states the ability to enter into treaties. Article II grants the president the power to make treaties, with the advice and consent of two-thirds of the Senate. Article III grants the federal courts the power to hear cases arising under treaties. And Article VI states that treaties are part of the supreme law of the land.

A possible inference from this differential treatment of CIL and treaties is that, unlike treaties, CIL cannot operate as self-executing federal law in the United States. Under this reading of the Constitution, in order for CIL to be applied as federal law, it would need to be incorporated into law by the federal political branches, such as through a statute or treaty. Such a reading might draw additional support from considerations of constitutional structure. For example, an incorporation requirement would have the structural advantage of ensuring that democratically accountable institutions in the United States are involved in deciding which CIL norms are applicable domestically, and how these norms should be defined. In addition, to the extent that CIL norms are applied to override the law of the U.S. states, a requirement that the CIL be incorporated into a statute or treaty would ensure that a process is utilized in which representatives from the states have a voice.

Some scholars have suggested, however, that the phrase "Laws of the United States" in Articles III and VI of the Constitution was intended to encompass CIL.[6] For a number of reasons, this seems unlikely. Article VI refers to the "Laws of the United States . . . made in Pursuance [of the Constitution]," and CIL is not made pursuant to the U.S. Constitution. At the time of the constitutional Founding, CIL was understood as stemming either from principles of natural law or the customs of the international community, and judges applying this law were seen as involved in a process of discovery rather than creation.[7] Moreover, in an early Supreme Court decision, *Ware v. Hylton*, two of the seriatim opinions specifically reasoned (without objection from the other justices) that,

---

Nations, 85 TEX. L. REV. 843 (2007); and Beth Stephens, *Federalism and Foreign Affairs: Congress's Power to "Define and Punish . . . Offenses against the Law of Nations,"* 42 WM. & MARY L. REV. 447 (2000). In *United States v. Arjona*, 120 U.S. 479 (1887), the Supreme Court held that this power gave Congress the authority to punish counterfeiting of foreign currency in the United States. The Court reasoned: "The law of nations requires every national government to use 'due diligence' to prevent a wrong being done within its own dominion to another nation with which it is at peace, or to the people thereof; and because of this the obligation of one nation to punish those who within its own jurisdiction counterfeit the money of another nation has long been recognized." *Id*. at 484. As discussed in Chapter 6, the scope of the define-and-punish power affects the extent to which Congress has the authority to regulate conduct outside the United States. *See, e.g.*, United States v. Bellaizac-Hurtado, 700 F.3d 1245 (11th Cir. 2012) (holding that Congress did not have authority under its define-and-punish power to criminalize drug trafficking in the territorial waters of another country).

[6] *See, e.g.*, Jordan J. Paust, *Customary International Law and Human Rights Treaties Are Law of the United States*, 20 MICH. J. INT'L L. 301 (1998); *see also* David M. Golove & Daniel J. Hulsebosch, *The Law of Nations and the Constitution: An Early Modern Perspective*, 106 GEO. L.J. 1593, 1607 (2018) (discussing "evidence from the Founding era that demonstrates the understanding of leading Founders, government officials, judges, lawyers, and jurists that the Constitution adopted the law of nations as part of the law of the United States").

[7] *See* Curtis A. Bradley, *The Alien Tort Statute and Article III*, 42 VA. J. INT'L L. 587, 603 (2002); Jay, *supra* note 4, at 822–24, 832–33; *see also* Michael D. Ramsey, *International Law as Part of Our Law: A Constitutional Perspective*, 29 PEPPERDINE L. REV. 187, 195 (2001) ("Whether or not international law is part of 'the laws

unlike treaties, CIL did not preempt inconsistent state law.[8] Nor are there any reported decisions from either the eighteenth or nineteenth centuries in which CIL was held to preempt state law, and prominent commentators of the period denied that the law of nations would have this effect.[9]

Article III does not have the "made in Pursuance" phrase, so it could be argued that CIL is part of the "Laws of the United States" for purposes of federal court jurisdiction even if not part of the supreme law of the land under Article VI.[10] Numerous statements from the Founding period suggest, however, that the phrase "Laws of the United States" in Article III was understood as referring only to federal statutes.[11] As Justice Joseph Story would later explain in his influential constitutional law treatise, "cases arising under the laws of the United States, are such as grow out of the legislation of Congress."[12] In

---

of the United States,' it is in any event, not 'made in Pursuance' of the Constitution, for the parochial U.S. Constitution is not within international law's contemplation.").

[8] *See* Ware v. Hylton, 3 U.S. (3 Dall.) 199, 229 (1796) (Opinion of Chase, J.); *id.* at 265–66 (Opinion of Iredell, J.); *see also* DAVID P. CURRIE, THE CONSTITUTION IN THE SUPREME COURT: THE FIRST HUNDRED YEARS, 1789–1888, at 37–38 (1985) ("[B]oth Chase and Iredell agreed that it was immaterial whether Virginia's confiscation offended the law of nations: if it did, that was a matter for international sanctions, but the courts were bound by Virginia law."); MICHAEL D. RAMSEY, THE CONSTITUTION'S TEXT IN FOREIGN AFFAIRS 353 (2007) ("[T]hese opinions indicate that these Justices did not place the law of nations within supreme law nor think federal courts could use the law of nations to disregard conflicting state laws.").

[9] *See, e.g.*, CHARLES PERGLER, JUDICIAL INTERPRETATION OF INTERNATIONAL LAW IN THE UNITED STATES 19 (1928) (noting that, if a state statute "violates an established principle of international law . . . clearly there would be only one course open to the courts, viz., to enforce the state statute, always assuming its constitutionality and that it does not contravene any valid federal enactment, or any treaty"); QUINCY WRIGHT, THE CONTROL OF AMERICAN FOREIGN RELATIONS 161 (1922) (noting that a "state constitution or legislative provision in violation of customary international law is valid unless in conflict with a Federal constitutional provision or an act of Congress").

[10] *See, e.g.*, William S. Dodge, *The Constitutionality of the Alien Tort Statute: Some Observations on Text and Context*, 42 VA. J. INT'L L. 687 (2002) (arguing that the phrase "Laws of the United States" in Article III was intended to encompass the law of nations).

[11] *See* Bradley, *supra* note 7, at 606–608; *see also* Anthony J. Bellia, Jr. & Bradford R. Clark, *The Federal Common Law of Nations*, 109 COLUM. L. REV. 1, 35 (2009) ("The framing and ratification of [Articles III and VI] lend support to the argument that 'Laws' meant acts of Congress, not forms of customary law, including the customary law of nations."); John Harrison, *The Constitution and the Law of Nations*, 106 GEO. L.J. 1659 (2018) (arguing that the constitutional Founders understood references to the "Laws of the United States" in the Constitution as encompassing only federal statutes and thus as not including the law of nations).

[12] 3 JOSEPH STORY, COMMENTARIES ON THE CONSTITUTION OF THE UNITED STATES 1641, at 508 (1833); *see also, e.g.*, PETER S. DUPONCEAU, A DISSERTATION ON THE NATURE AND EXTENT OF THE JURISDICTION OF THE COURTS OF THE UNITED STATES 99 (1824) (observing that in adopting the phrase "Laws of the United States" in Article III, "the framers of the Constitution only meant the statutes which should be enacted by the national Legislature"). Some of the proposed drafts of the Constitution would have included a general reference to cases arising under the law of nations as part of the federal courts' jurisdiction, but that proposed language was never adopted. Instead, the constitutional drafters decided to list specific cases and controversies, some of which, such as admiralty cases and controversies involving ambassadors, would be likely to involve the law of nations. *See* Bradley, *supra* note 7, at 597–98; *see also* Bellia & Clark, *supra* note 11, at 37–38 ("Certain Framers favored going further and giving federal courts jurisdiction over all cases arising under the law of nations. The Convention, however,

addition, the Supreme Court held in the early nineteenth century that a case involving the application of admiralty law—part of the law of nations—does "not in fact, arise under the Constitution or Laws of the United States."[13] Finally, as noted in this section, the law of nations at that time also encompassed the law merchant, so if the "Laws of the United States" in Article III included all of the law of nations, it would have meant that the federal courts potentially could hear all cases involving general commercial law, even in disputes between citizens of the same state. Such expansive federal court jurisdiction, however, would have been highly controversial,[14] and is therefore unlikely to represent the Founders' intent.

Part of Our Law

Even though CIL was probably not considered part of the "Laws of the United States" for constitutional purposes, it was still applied by U.S. courts in a variety of contexts. The United States inherited British legal traditions, and in Great Britain the law of nations was historically viewed as incorporated into the common law. As Blackstone noted in his *Commentaries on the Laws of England*, "the law of nations . . . is here adopted in its full extent by the common law, and is held to be a part of the law of the land."[15] Similarly, prior to the adoption of the Constitution, state courts in the United States treated the law of nations as part of state common law. A prominent example was the Pennsylvania Supreme Court's decision in *Respublica v. DeLongchamps*, which involved the criminal

---

chose instead to extend the judicial power to several types of cases in which the law of nations was likely to apply."); Michael G. Collins, *The Diversity Theory of the Alien Tort Statute*, 42 VA. J. INT'L L. 649, 657 (2002) ("[O]ne might even explain the rationale for listing these other party-based grants and admiralty as grounded in part in the recognition that the unwritten law of nations would not be federal law giving rise to jurisdiction pursuant to the federal question provisions of Article III."); David M. Golove & Daniel J. Hulsebosch, *A Civilized Nation: The Early American Constitution, the Law of Nations, and the Pursuit of International Recognition*, 85 N.Y.U. L. REV. 932, 1001 (2010) ("[T]he framers focused not on declaring the law of nations to be the supreme law of the land, but instead on extending the judicial power to every kind of justiciable controversy that could be expected to raise questions under the law of nations—or at least those that might implicate foreign affairs.").

[13] Am. Ins. Co. v. Canter, 26 U.S. (1 Pet.) 511, 545 (1828). In that case, the Supreme Court held that a territorial court in Florida could not hear a claim of maritime salvage because the claim did not fall within a statutory provision allowing the territorial courts to exercise jurisdiction over cases "arising under the laws and Constitution of the United States." For additional discussion of the decision, *see* A.M. Weisburd, *State Courts, Federal Courts, and International Cases*, 20 YALE J. INT'L L. 1, 30–31 (1995).

[14] *See* Jay, *supra* note 4, at 832.

[15] 4 WILLIAM BLACKSTONE, COMMENTARIES ON THE LAWS OF ENGLAND 67 (1769); *see also* Triquet v. Bath, 3 Burr. 1478, 1481, 97 Eng. Rep. 936, 938 (K.B. 1764) (Mansfield, J.) (stating that "[t]he law of nations, in its full extent was part of the law of England"); Bellia & Clark, *supra* note 11, at 27–28 (explaining that "English courts assumed a common law power to adopt the law of nations as part of English municipal law . . . [but] they did not necessarily imply that it took priority over other parts of the law of the land, including not only acts of Parliament but also (in some instances) local custom").

prosecution of a French citizen for his assault upon the French Consul-General to the United States, an offense considered at that time to be a violation of the law of nations.[16] The Pennsylvania court explained that the law of nations "in its full extent, is part of the law of this State, and is to be collected from the practice of different Nations, and the authority of writers."[17]

After the Constitution took effect, courts and government officials often referred to the law of nations as part of U.S. law. In criminal cases involving alleged breaches of the international law of neutrality during the late 1700s, for example, judges instructed juries that the law of nations was "part of the laws of the United States" or "part of the law of the land."[18] Similarly, in a decision concerning the confiscation of goods on a vessel captured by American privateers during the War of 1812, the Supreme Court observed that in the absence of a federal statute to the contrary, it was "bound by the law of nations which is a part of the law of the land."[19] Early opinions from the U.S. Attorney General also contain statements along these lines. For example, in response to a diplomatic protest over a raid into Spanish Florida by private U.S. citizens seeking to retrieve runaway slaves, Attorney General Charles Lee observed that "the common law has adopted the law of nations in its full extent, and made it a part of the law of the land."[20]

---

[16] Respublica v. DeLongchamps, 1 U.S. (1 Dall.) 113 (1784).

[17] *Id.* at 119.

[18] *See* Henfield's Case, 11 F. Cas. 1099, 1100–101 (C.C.D. Pa. 1793) (No. 6360) (Grand Jury charge of Jay, C.J.); *id.* at 1117 (Grand Jury charge of Wilson, J.); James Iredell's Charge to the Grand Jury of the Circuit Court for the District of South Carolina (May 12, 1794), *in* 2 THE DOCUMENTARY HISTORY OF THE SUPREME COURT, 1789–1800, at 467 (Maeva Marcus ed., 1988); Charge to the Grand Jury for the District of New York (Apr. 4, 1790), in New Hampshire Gazette (Portsmouth 1790) (Jay, C.J.). Subsequently, in the early nineteenth century, the Supreme Court held that nonwritten common law (including, presumably, customary international law) could not serve as the basis for a criminal prosecution in the federal courts. *See* United States v. Hudson & Goodwin, 11 U.S. (7 Cranch) 32, 34 (1812); United States v. Coolidge, 14 U.S. (1 Wheat.) 415, 416–17 (1816). Edmund Randolph, who was Attorney General during the neutrality prosecutions and who later became the Secretary of State, expressed the view that these prosecutions were based on a combination of treaties (such as the peace treaty with Great Britain) and state common law. *See* MONCURE DANIEL CONWAY, OMITTED CHAPTERS OF HISTORY DISCLOSED IN THE LIFE AND PAPERS OF EDMUND RANDOLPH 185 (1888) (quoting letter from Randolph to James Madison); *see also Edmund Randolph's Opinion on the Case of Gideon Henfield, May 30, 1793, in* 26 THE PAPERS OF THOMAS JEFFERSON 145–46 (John Catanzariti ed., 1995) (expressing the view that a common law criminal prosecution was proper for a breach of neutrality because the conduct constituted a "disturbing of the Peace of the United States" and because it was inconsistent with treaty commitments to Great Britain and other countries at war with France, commitments that "are the Supreme law of the land").

[19] The Nereide, 13 U.S. (9 Cranch) 388, 423 (1815).

[20] 1 Op. ATT'Y GEN. 69, 69 (1797); *see also, e.g.,* 1 OP. ATT'Y GEN. 26, 27 (1792) (Attorney General Randolph) ("The law of nations, although not specially adopted by the constitution or any municipal act, is essentially a part of the law of the land."); 5 OP. ATT'Y GEN. 691, 692 (1802) (Attorney General Lincoln) (finding "no provision in the Constitution, in any law of the United States, or in the treaty with Spain, which reaches the case" but observing that the "law of nations is considered as a part of the municipal law of each State").

The most famous case in which the Supreme Court referred to the law of nations as part of U.S. law is *The Paquete Habana*, which was decided in 1900. That case concerned the seizure by the U.S. Navy of two fishing vessels off the coast of Cuba during the Spanish-American War. The owners of the vessels argued that the seizure violated CIL, and the Supreme Court agreed. After reviewing extensive historical practice since the 1400s, the Court concluded that a rule of CIL had developed prohibiting the capture of unarmed coastal fishing vessels.[21] In a frequently quoted passage, the Court stated that "[i]nternational law is part of our law, and must be ascertained and administered by the courts of justice of appropriate jurisdiction, as often as questions of right depending upon it are duly presented for their determination."[22] The Court also noted that the "customs and usages of civilized nations" should be applied "where there is no treaty, and no controlling executive or legislative act or judicial decision."[23]

To understand what these references to the law of nations meant for its status in U.S. law, it is necessary to understand a type of law in the United States that was neither federal law nor what we would regard today as state law: general common law.

General Common Law

In the nineteenth century and early twentieth century, U.S. courts applied a body of law that has come to be referred to as general common law.[24] General common law was not viewed as emanating from any one sovereign source, but rather from "common practice and consent among a number of sovereigns."[25] Importantly, general common law was not understood to be part of the "Laws of the United States" for purposes of Articles III or VI of the Constitution, and thus did not have the same status as a federal statute or treaty.[26] General common law did not, for example, preempt inconsistent state law, and state courts were free to interpret the general common law differently from the federal courts. Nor did claims arising under the general common law constitute federal questions for purposes of the jurisdiction of the federal courts. To hear general common law claims,

---

[21] *See* The Paquete Habana, 175 U.S. 677, 708 (1900). Three justices dissented, arguing that there was no established custom requiring an exemption from capture for fishing vessels and that any restraint from capture in past conflicts had been "an act of grace, not a matter of right." *See id.* at 719 (Fuller, J., dissenting).

[22] *Id.* at 700.

[23] *Id.; see also id.* at 708 ("This rule of international law is one which prize courts, administering the law of nations, are bound to take judicial notice of, and to give effect to, in the absence of any treaty or other public act of their own government in relation to the matter.").

[24] *See* William A. Fletcher, *The General Common Law and Section 34 of the Judiciary Act of 1789: The Example of Marine Insurance*, 97 HARV. L. REV. 1513 (1984).

[25] *Id.* at 1517.

[26] *See* Bradford R. Clark, *Federal Common Law: A Structural Reinterpretation*, 144 U. PA. L. REV. 1245, 1276–92 (1996); Fletcher, *supra* note 24, at 1521–27; Stewart Jay, *Origins of Federal Common Law: Part Two*, 133 U. PA. L. REV. 1231, 1274–75 (1985).

therefore, the federal courts needed to have some other basis for jurisdiction, such as diversity of citizenship or a claim in admiralty.

Although the proposition has occasionally been disputed, there is substantial evidence that CIL was treated in the nineteenth and early twentieth centuries as having the status of general common law. The Supreme Court's most famous application of general common law, in *Swift v. Tyson*,[27] involved the law merchant, which, as noted earlier, was then a component of the law of nations. Furthermore, the Supreme Court during the nineteenth and early twentieth centuries consistently declined to review state court decisions concerning the law of nations, on the ground that the cases did not arise under federal law. In an 1875 decision, for example, the Court held that it lacked jurisdiction to review issues concerning "the general laws of war, as recognized by the law of nations" because such issues did not involve "the constitution, laws, treaties, or executive proclamations, of the United States" but rather concerned only "principles of general law alone."[28]

Numerous scholars who disagree about the contemporary status of CIL nevertheless agree that it was treated as general common law in the nineteenth and early twentieth centuries.[29] Similarly, the *Restatement (Third) of Foreign Relations Law*, which is

---

[27] Swift v. Tyson, 41 U.S. (16 Pet.) 1 (1842). As the Court noted: "The law respecting negotiable instruments may be truly declared in the language of Cicero, adopted by Lord Mansfield in Luke v. Lyde, to be in a great measure, not the law of a single country only, but of the commercial world." *Id.* at 19; *see also* 1 WILLIAM BLACKSTONE, COMMENTARIES ON THE LAWS OF ENGLAND 264 (1765) ("[T]he affairs of commerce are regulated by a law of their own, called the law merchant, or *lex mercatoria*, which all nations agree in and take notice of.").

[28] New York Life Ins. Co. v. Hendren, 92 U.S. 286, 286–87 (1876). The Court reached this conclusion over Justice Bradley's dissent, in which he argued that a claim under "unwritten international law" is made under the "laws of the United States." *Id.* at 288 (Bradley, J., dissenting); *see also* Oliver Am. Trading Co. v. Mexico, 264 U.S. 440, 442–43 (1924) (holding that the Court did not have jurisdiction to review an issue concerning foreign sovereign immunity—an issue governed by the law of nations—because that issue was one of "general law" over which the Court had no jurisdiction); Ker v. Illinois, 119 U.S. 436, 444 (1886) (holding that the question whether forcible seizure of a criminal defendant in a foreign country is grounds to resist trial in state court is "a question of common law, or of the law of nations" that the Court has "no right to review"); Julian G. Ku, *Customary International Law in the State Courts*, 42 VA. J. INT'L L. 265, 291 (2001) (describing "a regime [in the nineteenth century and early twentieth century] where state courts often controlled the interpretation, application, and development of CIL").

[29] *See, e.g.*, Bradley & Goldsmith, *supra* note 4, at 824 (explaining that "the law of nations . . . had the legal status of general common law"); William S. Dodge, *Bridging* Erie: *Customary International Law in the U.S. Legal System after* Sosa v. Alvarez-Machain, 12 TULSA J. COMP. & INT'L L. 87, 89 (2004) ("There is widespread agreement that, when the Constitution was adopted and the First Judiciary Act was passed, the law of nations was understood to be general common law, which was binding on both federal and state courts."); Ryan Goodman & Derek P. Jinks, Filartiga's *Firm Footing: International Human Rights and Federal Common Law*, 66 FORDHAM L. REV. 463, 470 (1997) ("For most of the nation's history, CIL—or the 'law of nations'—was indisputably part of the general common law."); Jay, *supra* note 4, at 83 ("The law of nations was classified as 'general law' in the sense that *Swift v. Tyson* later employed the term."); Gerald L. Neuman, *Sense and Nonsense About Customary International Law: A Response to Professors Bradley and Goldsmith*, 66 FORDHAM L. REV. 371, 374 (1997) ("[C]ustomary international law came to be treated as part of the 'general common law,' assertable in both State and federal courts, but not specifically federal in character."); Ernest A. Young, *Sorting Out the Debate over Customary International Law*, 42 VA. J. INT'L L. 365, 374 (2002) ("Almost all participants in

otherwise supportive of a broad domestic role for CIL, acknowledges that "during the reign of *Swift v. Tyson* . . . State and federal courts respectively determined international law for themselves as they did common law, and questions of international law could be determined differently by the courts of various States and by the federal courts."[30] The Supreme Court eventually put an end, however, to the body of law known as general common law.

Erie Railroad v. Tompkins

As noted in Chapter 1, the Supreme Court held in 1938, in *Erie Railroad Co. v. Tompkins*, that it was no longer appropriate for federal courts to apply general common law.[31] *Erie* concerned the use of general common law in the context of domestic tort law, not international law. Tompkins was injured by a passing freight train while walking at night alongside a railroad track in Pennsylvania. He sued the railroad in a federal court in New York, and the issue was whether the federal court should decide the case in the way it likely would have been decided by the Pennsylvania state courts or, instead, apply its own view of general common law. Expressing concern about the forum shopping that was invited by the general common law regime, and describing as a "fallacy" the idea that there is law in a state that does not stem from a sovereign source, the Court overturned *Swift v. Tyson* and declared that "there is no federal general common law."[32] As a result, said the Court, "[e]xcept in matters governed by the Federal Constitution or by Act of Congress, the law to be applied in any case is the law of the State."[33]

When cases involving CIL are not governed by either the Constitution or a federal statute, *Erie* might suggest that the federal courts are obligated to apply state law in resolving them. A year after *Erie*, Philip C. Jessup, a professor of international law at Columbia who would later serve as a judge on the International Court of Justice, wrote

---

current debates over customary international law appear to agree that, prior to the Supreme Court's [1938] decision in *Erie Railroad Co. v. Tompkins*, that law had the status of 'general' law."); *see also* INTERNATIONAL LAW IN THE U.S. SUPREME COURT: CONTINUITY AND CHANGE 27–32 (David L. Sloss, Michael D. Ramsey & William S. Dodge eds., 2011) (suggesting that the law of nations was treated as general common law in the nineteenth century); William A. Fletcher, *International Human Rights in American Courts*, 93 VA. L. REV. 653, 671–72 (2007) ("[C]ustomary international law in the nineteenth century was general rather than federal law."); *Leading Case—Alien Tort Statute*, 118 HARV. L. REV. 446, 451 (2004) ("In 1789, the law of nations clearly was considered part of the general common law, that 'brooding omnipresence' recognized rather than created by federal and state judges alike.").

[30] RESTATEMENT (THIRD) OF THE FOREIGN RELATIONS LAW OF THE UNITED STATES, *supra* note 1, ch. 2; *id.* at 41 (introductory note).
[31] Erie R.R. Co. v. Tompkins, 304 U.S. 64 (1938).
[32] *Id.* at 78.
[33] *Id.*

a short essay addressing this issue.³⁴ In his essay, Jessup noted that, if *Erie* were "applied broadly, it would follow that hereafter a state court's determination of a rule of international law would be a finding regarding the law of the state and would not be reviewed by the Supreme Court of the United States."³⁵ But Jessup argued against this construction of *Erie*. He reasoned that the Court in *Erie* was not thinking about international law, and that it "would be as unsound as it would be unwise" to bind federal courts to state court interpretations of customary international law.³⁶

The one judicial decision to address the domestic status of CIL in the quarter century after *Erie* reached a conclusion contrary to Jessup's. In *Bergman v. De Sieyes*, the U.S. Court of Appeals for the Second Circuit considered whether an ambassador passing through New York on his way to another country was entitled under international law to immunity from service of process.³⁷ At that time, there was no federal statute or treaty governing the question. The court, in an opinion by the eminent jurist Learned Hand, explained that "[the New York state courts'] interpretation of international law is controlling upon us, and we are to follow them so far as they have declared themselves."³⁸ After analyzing three New York decisions and a variety of international sources, the court concluded that "the courts of New York would today hold" that an ambassador in transit is immune under CIL from service of process.³⁹ The court did, however, add the following caveat: "Whether an avowed refusal to accept a well-established doctrine of international law, or a plain misapprehension of it, would present a federal question we need not consider, for neither is present here."⁴⁰

Federal Common Law and *Sabbatino*

Erie did not end up precluding all federal court development of common law. Instead, the Supreme Court held in a series of cases that it is appropriate for the federal courts to develop common law to resolve certain issues, such as boundary and water allocation issues in disputes between U.S. states,⁴¹ and some of the rights and duties of the U.S. government.⁴² Federal court development of common law is also appropriate when expressly

---

³⁴ *See* Philip C. Jessup, *The Doctrine of* Erie Railroad v. Tompkins *Applied to International Law*, 33 Am. J. Int'l L. 740 (1939).
³⁵ *Id.* at 742.
³⁶ *Id.* at 743.
³⁷ Bergman v. De Sieyes, 170 F.2d 360 (2d Cir. 1948).
³⁸ *Id.* at 361.
³⁹ *Id.* at 363.
⁴⁰ *Id.* at 361.
⁴¹ *See, e.g.*, Hinderlider v. La Plata River & Cherry Creek Ditch Co., 304 U.S. 92, 110 (1938) ("For whether the water of an interstate stream must be apportioned between the two States is a question of 'federal common law' upon which neither the statutes nor the decisions of either State can be conclusive.").
⁴² *See, e.g.*, Clearfield Trust Co. v. United States, 318 U.S. 363, 366 (1943) ("The rights and duties of the United States on commercial paper which it issues are governed by federal rather than local law.").

or implicitly authorized by federal statute.[43] This post-*Erie* "federal common law" differs from the pre-*Erie* general common law in that it is truly federal law. As a result, claims arising under this federal common law will fall within the federal question jurisdiction of the federal courts, and this federal common law can potentially preempt inconsistent state law.[44]

The Supreme Court applied federal common law to an international dispute in *Banco Nacional de Cuba v. Sabbatino*.[45] As discussed in Chapter 1, the *Sabbatino* case involved an expropriation of American-owned property by the Cuban government after Fidel Castro came to power. In declining to consider the legality of the expropriation, the Court applied the "act of state doctrine," pursuant to which "the courts of one country will not sit in judgment on the acts of the government of another, done within its own territory."[46] The Court in *Sabbatino* made clear that this doctrine was not required by international law and that it instead had "constitutional underpinnings" stemming from "the basic relationships between branches of government in a system of separation of powers."[47] In particular, the Court was concerned that judicial determinations of the validity of foreign government acts would undermine the ability of the executive branch to conduct U.S. foreign relations.[48]

Importantly for present purposes, the Court held that the act of state doctrine was a rule of federal common law binding on state courts. "[W]e are constrained to make it clear," said the Court "that an issue concerned with a basic choice regarding the competence and function of the Judiciary and the National Executive in ordering our relationships with other members of the international community must be treated exclusively as an aspect of federal law."[49] The Court explained that the act of state doctrine concerns issues that "are uniquely federal in nature," and that if state courts were not bound to follow the federal rule, "the purposes behind the doctrine could be as effectively undermined as if there had been no federal pronouncement on the subject."[50] As for *Erie*, the Court said that it "seems fair to assume that the Court did not have rules like the act of state doctrine in mind" in deciding *Erie*.[51] Invoking Jessup's essay, the Court further stated:

---

[43] *See, e.g.*, Textile Workers Union v. Lincoln Mills, 353 U.S. 448, 456–57 (1957) (interpreting labor statute as implicitly conferring federal common lawmaking power).

[44] *See, e.g.*, Boyle v. United Techs. Corp., 487 U.S. 500 (1988) (preemption of state tort law by federal common law of government contractor immunity); Illinois v. Milwaukee, 406 U.S. 91, 100 (1972) (concluding that federal "arising under" jurisdiction "will support claims founded upon federal common law as well as those of a statutory origin").

[45] Banco Nacional de Cuba v. Sabbatino, 376 U.S. 398 (1964).

[46] Underhill v. Hernandez, 168 U.S. 250, 252 (1897).

[47] *Sabbatino*, 376 U.S. at 423.

[48] *See id.* at 432–33.

[49] *Id.* at 425.

[50] *Id.* at 424.

[51] *Id.* at 425.

Soon [after *Erie*], Professor Philip C. Jessup . . . recognized the potential dangers were *Erie* extended to legal problems affecting international relations. He cautioned that rules of international law should not be left to divergent and perhaps parochial state interpretations. His basic rationale is equally applicable to the act of state doctrine.[52]

The Court in *Sabbatino* proceeded to apply the act of state doctrine to bar a challenge to Cuba's expropriation, notwithstanding the argument that the expropriation violated CIL. The Court made clear that "the act of state doctrine is applicable even if international law has been violated."[53] The Court also emphasized the contentious nature of the CIL concerning expropriation: "There are few if any issues in international law today on which opinion seems to be so divided as the limitations on a state's power to expropriate the property of aliens."[54] Finally, the Court noted that "[t]here are, of course, areas of international law in which consensus as to standards is greater and which do not represent a battleground for conflicting ideologies," and it stressed that it was not "intimat[ing] that the courts of this country are broadly foreclosed from considering questions of international law."[55]

The implications of *Sabbatino* for the domestic status of CIL remain unclear. On the one hand, the Court seemed to endorse Jessup's contention that *Erie* should not be applied to CIL, and the justifications that the Court gave for treating the act of state doctrine as federal common law—the uniquely federal nature of the issue and the need for a uniform rule—arguably apply to CIL. On the other hand, the Court made clear that the act of state doctrine was not required by CIL, and it declined to apply CIL governing the expropriation of alien property, prompting Justice White to complain in a dissent that the Court had "with one broad stroke, declared the ascertainment and application of international law beyond the competence of the courts of the United States in a large and important category of cases."[56]

In its *Restatement (Second) of the Foreign Relations Law of the United States*, published one year after *Sabbatino*, the American Law Institute took a cautious approach.

---

[52] *Id.*
[53] *Id.* at 431.
[54] *Id.* at 429.
[55] *Id.* at 430 n.34.
[56] *Id.* at 439 (White, J., dissenting); *see also, e.g.*, Michael J. Bazyler, *Abolishing the Act of State Doctrine*, 134 U. Pa. L. Rev. 325, 329 (1986) ("The [act of state] doctrine is probably the single most important reason for the arrested development of international law in the United States."); Harold Hongju Koh, *Transnational Public Law Litigation*, 100 Yale L.J. 2347, 2362–63 (1991) (noting that the Court in *Sabbatino* "declined even to apply international law to review the validity of the act of a recognized foreign sovereign fully executed within its own territory" and that the decision "cast a profound chill upon the willingness of United States domestic courts to interpret or articulate norms of international law—both customary and treaty-based—in both private and public cases").

In its recitations of black-letter law, the *Restatement (Second)* did not address the issue of CIL's domestic legal status. A reporters' note, contrasting Jessup's essay with *Bergman*, observed that the status of CIL as state or federal law was "not settled."[57] The note added without further explanation, however, that "the holding of the *Sabbatino* case that Erie v. Tompkins does not apply to the act of state doctrine would appear to apply a fortiori to questions of international law."[58]

Some commentators in the 1960s and 1970s were more confident than the *Restatement (Second)* about the impact of *Sabbatino* on the legal status of CIL. Emphasizing the importance of CIL to U.S. foreign relations and the desirability of having one interpretation of CIL for the United States, these scholars argued that it was implicit in *Sabbatino* that, just as with the act of state doctrine, CIL should be treated as federal common law.[59] This position received two significant endorsements in 1980.

Filartiga and the Restatement (Third)

The first major endorsement of a federal law status for CIL came from the U.S. Court of Appeals for the Second Circuit, in *Filartiga v. Pena-Irala*.[60] In that case, two Paraguayan citizens were suing another Paraguayan citizen for the torture and killing of a member of their family in Paraguay. As support for federal court jurisdiction over the case, the plaintiffs relied on the Alien Tort Statute, which provides that "[t]he district courts shall have original jurisdiction of any civil action by an alien for a tort only, committed in violation of the law of nations or a treaty of the United States."[61] (The Alien Tort Statute is discussed at length in Chapter 7.)

One of the issues in *Filartiga* was whether the case fell within the list of cases and controversies that federal courts are permitted to hear as set forth in Article III of the Constitution. It has long been settled that a suit between aliens does not fall within Article III diversity jurisdiction, so that was not an option. Nor did the case concern any claim under the Constitution, a federal statute, or a treaty. The court in *Filartiga* nevertheless concluded that there was Article III jurisdiction over the case because it concerned an alleged violation of the law of nations, and, said the court, "the law of nations ... has always been part of the federal common law."[62] In support of that proposition, the court

---

[57] RESTATEMENT (SECOND) OF THE FOREIGN RELATIONS LAW OF THE UNITED STATES § 3, reporters' note 2 (1965).

[58] *Id.*

[59] *See, e.g.,* LOUIS HENKIN, FOREIGN AFFAIRS AND THE CONSTITUTION 223 (1972); Alfred Hill, *The Law-Making Power of the Federal Courts: Constitutional Preemption*, 67 COLUM. L. REV. 1024, 1065–67 (1967); John Norton Moore, *Federalism and Foreign Relations*, 1965 DUKE L.J. 248, 268–75.

[60] Filartiga v. Pena-Irala, 630 F.2d 876 (2d Cir. 1980).

[61] 28 U.S.C. § 1350.

[62] *Filartiga*, 630 F.2d at 885.

relied primarily on pre-*Erie* decisions such as *The Paquete Habana*. As already discussed, however, CIL appears to have been treated as general common law, not federal law, prior to *Erie*.

The second major endorsement came from the American Law Institute's issuance of a new *Restatement of Foreign Relations Law*. Although the *Restatement (Third) of the Foreign Relations Law of the United States* was not published in final form until 1987, the Tentative Draft was first circulated in 1980.[63] While acknowledging that CIL had not been considered federal law prior to *Erie* and that the *Restatement (Second) of Foreign Relations Law* had considered the status of CIL to be an open question, the Tentative Draft contended that CIL's status as federal law "had now been established."[64] Without citing any cases, the draft also stated that "courts have declared that ... interpretations of customary international law are ... supreme over state law."[65]

The final version of the *Restatement (Third)* refined and provided additional support for the Tentative Draft's assertion that CIL was federal law.[66] In the reporters' notes, the *Restatement (Third)* reasons that *United States v. Belmont*, in which the Supreme Court held that a sole executive agreement between the United States and the Soviet Union preempted state law, "would apply" to CIL as well.[67] The notes also quote from the paragraph in *Sabbatino* that cites Jessup, and states: "Based on the implications of *Sabbatino*, the modern view is that customary international law in the United States is federal law and its determination by the federal courts is binding on the State courts."[68] In addition, the reporters' notes cite to a law review article published in 1984 by Professor Louis Henkin, the *Restatement (Third)*'s Chief Reporter.[69] In arguing that "there is now general agreement" that CIL is federal law, however, Henkin's article simply cited back to the Tentative Draft of the *Restatement (Third)*.[70] Of course, the *Restatement (Third)*

---

[63] *See* RESTATEMENT (THIRD) OF THE FOREIGN RELATIONS LAW OF THE UNITED STATES (Tentative Draft No. 1, 1980).

[64] *Id.*, § 131 reporters' note 8.

[65] *Id.*, introductory note at 7; *see also id.*, pt. I, ch. 2, introductory note at 41 (contending that CIL "has come to be regarded as federal common law").

[66] *See* RESTATEMENT (THIRD) OF THE FOREIGN RELATIONS LAW OF THE UNITED STATES, *supra* note 1, §§ 111, 115. In an apparent concession to the Chief Reporter, Professor Henkin, the final draft maintained that CIL was "like" federal common law rather than actually federal common law. *See id.* § 111 cmt. d; *see also* Louis Henkin, *International Law as Law in the United States*, 82 MICH. L. REV. 1555, 1561–62 (1984) (stating that CIL is "like federal common law"). Henkin maintained that, like federal common law, CIL preempted inconsistent state law and provided a basis for federal jurisdiction, but that unlike federal common law it was not subservient to federal legislation and that, as a result, when there is a conflict between CIL and federal legislation, "the more recent of the two governs." Louis Henkin, *The Constitution and United States Sovereignty: A Century of Chinese Exclusion and Its Progeny*, 100 HARV. L. REV. 853, 878 (1987).

[67] RESTATEMENT (THIRD) OF THE FOREIGN RELATIONS LAW OF THE UNITED STATES, *supra* note 1, § 111 reporters' note 2.

[68] *Id.* § 111 reporters' note 3.

[69] *See id.* pt. I, ch. 2, introductory note at 42 (citing Henkin, *International Law as Law*, *supra* note 66).

[70] *See* Henkin, *International Law as Law*, *supra* note 66, at 1559; *see also* Henkin, *The Constitution and U.S. Sovereignty*, *supra* note 66, at 878 & n.103 (citing the Tentative Draft of the Restatement for the proposition

could have cited to the *Filartiga* decision, but it did not do so, perhaps because the court in *Filartiga* had reasoned that CIL was historically treated as federal law whereas the *Restatement (Third)* argued that the federal law status of CIL was a modern development based on the implications of *Sabbatino*.

CIL as Federal Common Law

In *Filartiga*, the proposition that CIL has the status of federal common law was invoked to support the exercise of federal court jurisdiction over a case involving aliens. *Filartiga*'s federal common law holding, however, has other potential implications. Post-*Erie* federal common law is normally regarded as preemptive of conflicting state law, so if CIL is federal common law, it too might have this preemptive effect. In fact, the *Restatement (Third)* and a number of commentators claim that it should have this effect.[71] If CIL is federal common law, it might also be regarded as part of the "Laws" that the president is obligated to faithfully execute in the Take Care Clause of Article II of the Constitution.[72] It is even arguable that CIL, if it is self-executing federal law, should override earlier inconsistent federal statutes, since (as we saw in Chapter 2) self-executing treaties can have this effect. As the *Restatement (Third)* explains in a reporters' note: "Since international customary law and an international agreement have equal authority in international law, and both are law of the United States, arguably later customary law should be given effect as law of the United States, even in the face of an earlier law or agreement, just as a later international agreement of the United States is given effect in the face of an earlier law or agreement."[73]

To date, U.S. courts have not endorsed any of these applications of CIL. There are no post-*Filartiga* decisions relying on CIL to preempt state law.[74] In addition, almost all

---

that CIL "has now been declared to be United States law within the meaning of both article III and the supremacy clause").

[71] *See, e.g.*, RESTATEMENT (THIRD) OF THE FOREIGN RELATIONS LAW OF THE UNITED STATES, *supra* note 1, § 111(1); JORDAN J. PAUST, INTERNATIONAL LAW AS LAW OF THE UNITED STATES 6–7 (1996); Lea Brilmayer, *Federalism, State Authority, and the Preemptive Power of International Law*, 1994 SUP. CT. REV. 295, 295, 302–304; Henkin, *International Law as Law, supra* note 66, at 1560–62; Harold Hongju Koh, *Is International Law Really State Law?*, 111 HARV. L. REV. 1824 (1998).

[72] For discussion of these and other issues concerning the relationship between CIL and the executive branch, *see* Essays, Agora: *May the President Violate Customary International Law?*, 80 AM. J. INT'L L. 913 (1986); Essays, Agora: *May the President Violate Customary International Law? (Cont'd)*, 81 AM. J. INT'L L. 371 (1987); *The Authority of the United States Executive to Interpret, Articulate or Violate the Norms of International Law*, 80 AM. SOC'Y INT'L L. PROC. 297 (1986); Michael J. Glennon, *Raising* The Paquete Habana: *Is Violation of Customary International Law by the Executive Unconstitutional?*, 80 NW. U. L. REV. 321 (1985); Arthur M. Weisburd, *The Executive Branch and International Law*, 41 VAND. L. REV. 1205 (1988).

[73] RESTATEMENT (THIRD) OF THE FOREIGN RELATIONS LAW OF THE UNITED STATES, *supra* note 1, § 115, reporters' note 4.

[74] One state court decision prior to *Filartiga* might be read to support this proposition. In *Republic of Argentina v. City of New York*, 250 N.E.2d 698 (N.Y. Ct. App. 1969), the New York Court of Appeals held that the City

courts have held that the president and other high-level executive officers (such as the Attorney General) have the domestic legal authority to violate CIL.[75] Not surprisingly, lawyers in the executive branch have also endorsed that proposition.[76] Finally, courts have consistently held that CIL is subordinate in the U.S. legal system to federal legislation, and, unlike what they do for conflicts with treaties, they have not looked to see which is later in time.[77]

Even the jurisdictional implication of CIL's purported status as federal common law has had only limited application in the courts. In Alien Tort Statute cases, the few courts that have addressed the issue have concluded, like the court in *Filartiga*, that suits between aliens for violations of CIL fall within the Article III jurisdiction of the federal courts.[78] As discussed more fully in Chapter 7, however, the jurisdictional holding of *Filartiga* became less relevant as a result of the Supreme Court's 2004 decision in *Sosa v. Alvarez-Machain*, which treated the Alien Tort Statute as providing statutory authority for the development of whatever federal common law claims are allowed in this litigation.[79] Such statutorily-authorized federal common law provides a sufficient basis for

---

of New York could not assess taxes against Argentina's consulate property because the assessment would violate CIL. The court did not explain its views about the precise status of customary international law, but the court might have implicitly been accepting Argentina's argument that CIL had the status of preemptive federal law.

[75] *See, e.g.*, Barrera-Echavarria v. Rison, 44 F.3d 1441, 1451 (9th Cir. 1995); Gisbert v. U.S. Attorney General, 988 F.2d 1437, 1448 (5th Cir. 1993); Garcia-Mir v. Meese, 788 F.2d 1446, 1454–55 (11th Cir. 1986). These decisions rely heavily on the statement from *The Paquete Habana* that the law of nations is to be applied by U.S. courts "only 'where there is no treaty and no controlling executive or legislative act or judicial decision.'"

[76] *See, e.g.*, Memorandum from Jay S. Bybee, Assistant Attorney Gen., U.S. Dep't of Justice, to Alberto R. Gonzales, Counsel to the President, and William J. Haynes II, Gen. Counsel, U.S. Dep't of Defense, *Application of Treaties and Laws to al Qaeda and Taliban Detainees*, at 32 (Jan. 22, 2002) ("Customary international law . . . cannot bind the executive branch under the Constitution because it is not federal law."), *available at* http://www.washingtonpost.com/wp-srv/nation/documents/012202bybee.pdf.

[77] *See, e.g.*, United States v. Yousef, 327 F.3d 56, 93 (2d Cir. 2003); United States v. Yunis, 924 F.2d 1086, 1091 (D.C. Cir. 1991). For a rare decision suggesting that CIL can supersede a federal statute if it develops after the enactment of the statute, *see* Beharry v. Reno, 183 F. Supp. 2d 584 (E.D.N.Y. 2002), *rev'd on other grounds*, 329 F.3d 51 (2d Cir. 2003). *But see* Guaylupo-Moya v. Gonzales, 423 F.3d 121 (2d Cir. 2005) ("[T]o the extent that *Beharry* purports to declare that international law should override the plain language and effect of the relevant statutes, that reasoning was in error; clear congressional action trumps customary international law and previously enacted treaties.").

[78] *See, e.g.*, In re Estate of Marcos Human Rights Litig., 978 F.2d 493, 502–503 (9th Cir. 1992); Xuncax v. Gramajo, 886 F. Supp. 162, 193 (D. Mass. 1995).

[79] *See* 542 U.S. 692, 731, 732 (2004) (describing "indications that the [Alien Tort Statute] was meant to underwrite litigation of a narrow set of common law actions derived from the law of nations" and concluding that "federal courts should not recognize private claims under federal common law for violations of any international law norm with less definite content and acceptance among civilized nations than the historical paradigms familiar when [the Alien Tort Statute] was enacted"). *Cf.* Kiobel v. Royal Dutch Petroleum Co., 569 U.S. 108, 124 (2013) ("Nothing about this historical context suggests that Congress also intended federal common law under the ATS to provide a cause of action for conduct occurring in the territory of another sovereign."); *see also* Curtis A. Bradley, Jack L. Goldsmith & David H. Moore, Sosa, *Customary International Law, and the Continuing Relevance of* Erie, 120 HARV. L. REV. 869, 906 n.204 (2007).

federal question jurisdiction, regardless of CIL's status. Outside the context of the Alien Tort Statute, there are essentially no decisions holding that CIL operates as federal law for jurisdictional purposes.[80] Moreover, in *Sosa*, the Supreme Court denied that its decision to allow certain CIL claims to be brought under the Alien Tort Statute would mean that the general federal question jurisdiction statute could be used to adjudicate claims under CIL,[81] and the lower courts have subsequently declined to entertain CIL claims under that statute.[82]

Challenges to the Federal Common Law Claim

The leading academic view following *Filartiga* was that CIL has the status in the United States of self-executing federal common law. Starting in the mid-1980s, however, some scholars began questioning this proposition.[83] In 1997, this author, along with Professor Goldsmith, published a critique of the federal common law claim that received particular attention.[84] This critique was referred to as "revisionist," in that it appeared to be challenging conventional wisdom. Since then, however, a number of additional scholars have challenged the claim that CIL has the status of self-executing federal common law. Some of these scholars have argued for an intermediate position pursuant to which CIL would be applied by U.S. courts, but not as preemptive federal law.[85] Other scholars have argued

---

[80] The federal question jurisdiction statute provides that the district courts shall have "original jurisdiction of all civil actions arising under the Constitution, laws, or treaties of the United States." 28 U.S.C. § 1331. For pre-*Sosa* decisions concluding that CIL was not part of the "laws of the United States" for purposes of this statute, *see* Princz v. Fed. Republic of Germany, 26 F.3d 1166, 1176 (D.C. Cir. 1994); Xuncax v. Gramajo, 886 F. Supp. 162, 193–94 (D. Mass. 1995); Handel v. Artukovic, 601 F. Supp. 1421, 1426 (C.D. Cal. 1985). *But see* Forti v. Suarez-Mason, 672 F. Supp. 1531, 1544 (N.D. Cal. 1987) (concluding that federal question jurisdiction was available as an alternative to jurisdiction under the Alien Tort Statute).

[81] *See Sosa*, 542 U.S. at 731 n.19 ("[The Alien Tort Statute] was enacted on the congressional understanding that courts would exercise jurisdiction by entertaining some common law claims derived from the law of nations; and we know of no reason to think that federal-question jurisdiction was extended subject to any comparable congressional assumption.").

[82] *See, e.g.*, Mohamad v. Rajoub, 634 F.3d 604, 609–10 (D.C. Cir. 2011), *aff'd on other grounds*, 132 S. Ct. 1702 (2012); Serra v. Lappin, 600 F.3d 1191, 1197–98 & n.7 (9th Cir. 2010); *see also* McKesson v. Islamic Republic of Iran, 672 F.3d 1066, 1076 (D.C. Cir. 2012) (concluding that the commercial activities exception in the Foreign Sovereign Immunities Act did not authorize courts to create a cause of action under customary international law).

[83] *See generally* Phillip R. Trimble, *A Revisionist View of Customary International Law*, 33 UCLA L. REV. 665 (1986); Weisburd, *supra* note 13.

[84] *See* Bradley & Goldsmith, *supra* note 4; *see also* Curtis A. Bradley & Jack L. Goldsmith, *The Current Illegitimacy of International Human Rights Litigation*, 66 FORDHAM L. REV. 319 (2007). For responses to these articles, see, for example, Goodman & Jinks, *supra* note 29; Koh, *supra* note 71; Neuman, *supra* note 29; and Beth Stephens, *The Law of Our Land: Customary International Law as Federal Law after Erie*, 66 FORDHAM L. REV. 393 (1997).

[85] *See, e.g.*, T. Alexander Aleinikoff, *International Law, Sovereignty, and American Constitutionalism: Reflections on the Customary International Law Debate*, 98 AM. J. INT'L L. 91 (2004); Young, *supra* note 29. For a lengthy

that only some rules of CIL should apply as federal law.[86] In the wake of *Sosa,* some courts have also concluded that CIL does not operate as self-executing federal common law.[87]

The revisionist scholars have argued, among other things, that it is difficult to reconcile treating all of CIL as federal common law with the usual limitations on post-*Erie* federal common law. Although there is scholarly debate about the proper contours of federal common law, many scholars have reasoned that it must have its source in extant federal law: the Constitution, a federal statute, or a treaty.[88] It is not clear, however, what federal law source exists to support the wholesale incorporation of CIL into federal common

---

description and critique of the intermediate positions, *see* Carlos M. Vázquez, *Customary International Law as U.S. Law: A Critique of the Revisionist and Intermediate Positions and a Defense of the Modern Position,* 86 NOTRE DAME L. REV. 1495, 1554–617 (2011).

[86] *See, e.g.,* David J. Bederman, *Law of the Land, Law of the Sea: The Lost Link between Customary International Law and the General Maritime Law,* 51 VA. J. INT'L L. 299, 301 (2011) (arguing that CIL should, like general maritime law, be "regarded as federal law for some purposes, but not for others"); Bellia & Clark, *supra* note 11, at 7 (arguing that, historically, "certain principles derived from the law of nations" relating to "the Constitution's allocation of foreign affairs powers to Congress and the President" have been treated as federal law); Daniel J. Meltzer, *Customary International Law, Foreign Affairs, and Federal Common Law,* 42 VA. J. INT'L L. 513, 536 (2002) (suggesting that "at least some matters—head of state immunity is, again, a good example—should not be left to the vagaries of state decision making"); *see also* Dodge, *supra* note 29, at 97 ("[T]he [Supreme] Court seems to prefer a more particularized approach that looks at the incorporation of customary international law into the U.S. legal system issue-by-issue.").

[87] *See* Sarei v. Rio Tinto, PLC, 671 F.3d 736, 752 (9th Cir. 2011) (en banc) ("Thus, it is by now widely recognized that the norms *Sosa* recognizes as actionable under the ATS *begin* as part of international law—which, without more, would not be considered federal law for Article III purposes—but they *become* federal common law once recognized to have the particular characteristics required to be enforceable under the ATS."); In re Xe Servs. Alien Tort Litig., 665 F. Supp. 2d 569, 579 (E.D. Va. 2009) ("It is clear, then, that *Sosa* does not incorporate customary international law ('CIL') into the body of federal common law in a wholesale manner."); *see also* Al-Bihani v. Obama, 619 F.3d 1, 19 (D.C. Cir. 2010) (Kavanaugh, J., concurring in denial of rehearing en banc) ("*Sosa* thus confirmed that international-law principles are not automatically part of domestic U.S. law and that those principles can enter into domestic U.S. law only through an affirmative act of the political branches."); Sampson v. Fed. Republic of Germany, 250 F.3d 1145, 1153 n.4 (7th Cir. 2001) (noting, in a pre-*Sosa* decision, "the present uncertainty about the precise domestic role of customary international law").

[88] *See, e.g.,* Martha A. Field, *Sources of Law: The Scope of Federal Common Law,* 99 HARV. L. REV. 881, 887 (1986) ("[T]he only limitation on courts' power to create federal common law is that the court must point to a federal enactment, constitutional or statutory, that it interprets as authorizing the federal common law rule."); Henry J. Friendly, *In Praise of* Erie—*And of the New Federal Common Law,* 39 N.Y.U. L. REV. 383 (1964) ("Just as federal courts [after *Erie*] now conform to state decisions on issues properly for the states, state courts must conform to federal decisions in areas where Congress, acting within powers granted to it, has manifested, be it ever so lightly, an intention to that end."); Daniel J. Meltzer, *Forfeitures of Federal Rights,* 99 HARV. L. REV. 1128, 1168 (1986) (noting that, after *Erie,* "some more specialized source must be found for each example of judicial lawmaking"); Thomas Merrill, *The Common Law Powers of Federal Courts,* 52 U. CHI. L. REV. 1, 17 (1985) ("Federal courts should *not* . . . promulgate federal common law rules that intrude upon [the traditional domain of the states] unless they have been authorized to do so by an enacting body in which the states are represented."). *Cf.* Larry Kramer, *The Lawmaking Power of the Federal Courts,* 12 PACE L. REV. 263, 269 (1992) ("[A]s the connection between a judicial rule and some source of statutory authorization becomes more attenuated, the question of legitimacy becomes more problematic.").

law.[89] In addition, because "federal courts, unlike state courts, are not general common-law courts and do not possess a general power to develop and apply their own rules of decision,"[90] the post-*Erie* federal common law is supposed to be "interstitial"—that is, courts are supposed to develop it only in a retail fashion to fill in the gaps, or interstices, of federal statutory or constitutional regimes.[91] Incorporating all of the diverse norms of CIL into federal common law does not appear to be consistent with this limitation. Furthermore, because federal common law is a derivative form of lawmaking rather than an independent judicial power to make policy decisions, it is supposed to be applied in a manner that is consistent with the policy choices reflected in existing federal law.[92] A wholesale federalization of CIL is unlikely to reflect such consistency. As we saw in Chapter 2, for example, the political branches have suggested through non–self-execution declarations that they do not want the norms in human rights treaties to operate as judicially enforceable federal law.[93]

Another argument made by the revisionist scholars is that treating CIL as automatically part of federal law is anomalous in light of the limitations on the domestic status of the other major form of international law—treaties. Treaties are expressly negotiated by the executive branch and are subject to the approval of the Senate. They are also specifically mentioned in Articles III and VI of the Constitution. Nevertheless, as discussed in Chapter 2, the doctrine of "non–self-execution" limits the circumstances under which courts can apply treaties as preemptive federal law. In its 2008 decision, *Medellin v. Texas*, the Supreme Court confirmed that this doctrine is a significant limitation on the

---

[89] For an argument that the Constitution implicitly authorizes the courts to apply rules of CIL where necessary to uphold certain foreign relations powers of the president and Congress, *see* Anthony J. Bellia, Jr. & Bradford R. Clark, *The Law of Nations as Constitutional Law*, 98 VA. L. REV. 729 (2012). *See also* ANTHONY J. BELLIA, JR. & BRADFORD R. CLARK, THE LAW OF NATIONS AND THE UNITED STATES CONSTITUTION (2017).

[90] City of Milwaukee v. Illinois, 451 U.S. 304, 312 (1981) (citing Erie R.R. Co. v. Tompkins, 304 U.S. 64, 78 (1938)).

[91] *See, e.g.*, Meltzer, *supra* note 88, at 549 (referring to the "limited and interstitial quality of federal common law"); Ernest A. Young, *Preemption at Sea*, 67 GEO. WASH. L. REV. 273, 287 (1999) ("Federal common law is generally viewed as interstitial in character, devoted primarily to filling in the gaps in federal statutory and constitutional law."). *See also* Sosa v. Alvarez-Machain, 542 U.S. 692, 726 (2004) (noting that "this Court has thought it was in order to create federal common law rules in interstitial areas of particular federal interest").

[92] *See* D'Oench, Duhme & Co. v. FDIC, 315 U.S. 447, 472 (1942) (Jackson, J., concurring) ("[F]ederal common law implements the federal Constitution and statutes, and is conditioned by them."); *see also* Paul Lund, *The Decline of Federal Common Law*, 76 B.U. L. REV. 895, 968 (1986) ("[A] federal court's primary responsibility in deriving an appropriate federal common law rule is to attempt to give effect to the underlying federal policy found in federal statutes, the Constitution, or another federal text.").

[93] *See generally* Curtis A. Bradley & Jack L. Goldsmith, *Treaties, Human Rights, and Conditional Consent*, 149 U. PA. L. REV. 399, 419–22 (2000) (discussing non–self-execution declarations attached to U.S. ratification of human rights treaties). *See also Sosa*, 542 U.S. at 735 (noting that "the United States ratified the [International Covenant on Civil and Political Rights] on the express understanding that it was not self-executing and so did not itself create obligations enforceable in the federal courts").

domestic enforceability of treaties.[94] If CIL is automatically self-executing federal common law, it would mean that the form of international law that has less direct support from the political branches of the government and less support in the constitutional text is easier to apply as federal law. This anomaly is even more significant when one considers that claims about the content of CIL are often based on multilateral treaties.[95]

Whatever one may think of these arguments, it is worth noting that the Supreme Court has not been receptive in recent years to recognizing new federal common law claims. The Court has, for example, emphasized that the instances in which it is appropriate to develop federal common law are "few and restricted."[96] It has also sharply limited the circumstances under which courts are allowed to develop common law remedies under statutory and constitutional provisions.[97] In the *Sosa* decision just referred to, the Court recited these developments and seemed to indicate that they were relevant to the domestic status of CIL.[98] Citing *Sabbatino*, for example, the Court noted that "although we have even assumed competence to make judicial rules of decision of particular importance to foreign relations, such as the act of state doctrine, . . . the general practice has been to look for legislative guidance before exercising innovative authority over substantive law."[99]

---

[94] *See* Medellin v. Texas, 552 U.S. 491, 504 (2008) ("This Court has long recognized the distinction between treaties that automatically have effect as domestic law, and those that—while they constitute international law commitments—do not by themselves function as binding federal law."). For discussion of the potential relevance of *Medellin* to the domestic status of CIL, *see* David H. Moore, Medellin, *The Alien Tort Statute, and the Domestic Status of International Law*, 50 VA. J. INT'L L. 485 (2010); *see also* David H. Moore, *An Emerging Uniformity for International Law*, 75 GEO. WASH. L. REV. 1, 4 (2006) (arguing that "[i]n *Sosa*, the Court suggested that questions as to whether treaties and CIL may be applied as rules of decision by federal courts are governed by the same doctrine").

[95] *See, e.g.*, JACK L. GOLDSMITH & ERIC A. POSNER, THE LIMITS OF INTERNATIONAL LAW 23 (2005) ("Treaties, especially multilateral treaties, but also bilateral ones, are often used as evidence of customary international law, but in an inconsistent way."); R.R. Baxter, *Multilateral Treaties as Evidence of Customary International Law*, 41 BRIT. Y.B. INT'L L. 275, 275 (1965–66) ("Both multilateral and bilateral treaties are not infrequently cited as evidence of the state of customary international law.").

[96] *See* O'Melveny & Myers v. FDIC, 512 U.S. 79, 87 (1994) (observing that the instances in which it is appropriate to create a federal common law rule are "few and restricted" (quoting Wheeldin v. Wheeler, 373 U.S. 647, 651 (1963))); *see also* Rodriguez v. FDIC, 140 S. Ct. 713, 717 (2020) ("Judicial lawmaking in the form of federal common law plays a necessarily modest role under a Constitution that vests the federal government's 'legislative Powers' in Congress and reserves most other regulatory authority to the States.'").

[97] *See, e.g.*, Hernandez v. Mesa, 140 S. Ct. 735, 742 (2020) ("With the demise of federal general common law, a federal court's authority to recognize a damages remedy must rest at bottom on a statute enacted by Congress . . ."): Alexander v. Sandoval, 532 U.S. 275, 286 (2001) ("Like substantive federal law itself, private rights of action to enforce federal law must be created by Congress.").

[98] *See Sosa*, 542 U.S. at 726–27.

[99] *Id.* at 726.

Political Branch Authorization for Federalizing CIL

Even if CIL is not self-executing federal common law, it could still operate as federal law in select instances pursuant to express or implicit authorization from the political branches of the government. Some statutes specifically reference CIL and thus invite courts to incorporate and interpret CIL as part of the statutory scheme. For example, the federal piracy statute provides that "whoever, on the high seas, commits the crime of piracy *as defined by the law of nations*, and is afterwards brought into or found in the United States, shall be imprisoned for life."[100] This statute clearly authorizes courts to ascertain and apply as federal law the CIL prohibition on piracy.[101] Similarly, the Foreign Sovereign Immunities Act (FSIA), which is discussed in Chapter 8, provides an exception to foreign governmental immunity for certain situations in which "rights in property taken in violation of international law are in issue."[102] The phrase "international law" in this exception refers primarily to the CIL governing the expropriation of alien property.[103]

Sometimes courts develop federal common law not pursuant to an express reference in a statute, but rather in order to interpret statutory terms or fill gaps in a statutory scheme, and this approach might in some instances involve a consideration of CIL. For example, some courts have looked to CIL in interpreting aspects of the FSIA, even where the statute does not expressly incorporate CIL, based on indications in the FSIA's legislative history that this is what Congress intended.[104] Similarly, in a decision in 1983, *First National City Bank v. Banco Para El Comercio Exterior de Cuba*, the Supreme Court looked in part to CIL in an effort to fill in a gap in the FSIA.[105] In that case, the issue was what body of

---

[100] 18 U.S.C. § 1651 (emphasis added).

[101] In an early decision involving a predecessor to this statute, the Supreme Court held that Congress's definition of piracy by reference to the law of nations was sufficiently precise. The Court reasoned that piracy had a definite meaning in international law and that "Congress may as well define by using a term of a known and determinate meaning, as by an express enumeration of all the particulars included in that term." United States v. Smith, 18 U.S. (5 Wheat.) 153, 162 (1820). For a decision concluding that the piracy statute implicitly "incorporates a definition of piracy that changes with advancements in the law of nations," *see* United States v. Dire, 680 F.3d 446, 469 (4th Cir. 2012). The court noted, among other things, that it is accepted that evolving CIL can be applied under the Alien Tort Statute, and the court reasoned that "there is no reason to believe that the 'law of nations' evolves in the civil context but stands immobile in the criminal context." *Id.* at 467.

[102] 28 U.S.C. § 1605(a)(3).

[103] *See, e.g.*, Republic of Austria v. Altmann, 541 U.S. 677, 685–86 (2004) (claim under CIL to recover works of art allegedly stolen by the Nazis and acquired by an Austrian state-owned art gallery); Agudas Chasidei Chabad of United States v. Russian Fed'n, 528 F.3d 924, 943 (D.C. Cir. 2008) (claim under CIL to recover library collection allegedly expropriated by the Soviet Union).

[104] *See, e.g.*, Aquamar S.A. v. Del Monte Fresh Produce N.A., Inc., 179 F.3d 1279, 1294 (11th Cir. 1999) ("We may look to international law as a guide to the meaning of the FSIA's provisions."). *Cf.* Permanent Mission of India to the U.N. v. City of New York, 551 U.S. 193, 199 (2007) (describing as one of the purposes of the FSIA the "codification of international law at the time of the FSIA's enactment").

[105] 462 U.S. 611 (1983).

law should apply in determining whether to pierce the veil between a foreign government and its state-owned corporation for purposes of attributing the government's actions to the corporation (and thereby allowing a counterclaim of expropriation to be brought against the corporation). The FSIA, which provided the basis for subject matter jurisdiction and the potential abrogation of sovereign immunity, did not address this issue. In resolving the question, the Supreme Court developed a rule based on what it described as "principles . . . common to both international law and federal common law, which in these circumstances is necessarily informed both by international law principles and by articulated congressional policies."[106]

Courts also sometimes look to CIL principles to resolve ambiguities in treaties. In doing so, they often rely on the Vienna Convention on the Law of Treaties, which (as noted in Chapter 2) sets forth a variety of general rules governing the formation, interpretation, and termination of treaties.[107] The United States has not ratified the Convention and thus it cannot bind the United States as a treaty, but the U.S. government has stated that it accepts many of the Convention's terms as reflective of CIL.[108] Perhaps not surprisingly, therefore, courts sometimes invoke the CIL of treaty law as embodied in the Vienna Convention.[109]

In some circumstances, the executive branch may be able to provide the authorization for courts to draw upon CIL in developing federal common law. As discussed in Chapter 8, a possible example is the way in which courts have addressed the immunity of foreign heads of state. For most of U.S. history, head-of-state immunity was viewed as a component of foreign sovereign immunity. Prior to *Erie*, and consistent with the view that CIL was treated as nonfederal general common law, federal and state courts alike applied the CIL of foreign sovereign immunity without authorization from Congress or the executive.[110] Around the time of *Erie*, however, the Supreme Court stopped applying the CIL of immunity on its own authority and began to justify its application, at least in part, on the basis of executive branch authorization.[111] In 1976, the FSIA transferred

---

[106] *Id.* at 263.
[107] *See* Vienna Convention on the Law of Treaties, May 23, 1969, 1155 U.N.T.S. 331.
[108] *See* RESTATEMENT (THIRD) OF THE FOREIGN RELATIONS LAW OF THE UNITED STATES, *supra* note 1, pt. III, at 145 n.2 (documenting executive branch statements).
[109] *See, e.g.*, Avero Belg. Ins. v. Am. Airlines, Inc., 423 F.3d 73, 79 n.8 (2d Cir. 2005); Gonzalez v. Gutierrez, 311 F.3d 942, 949 & n.15 (9th Cir. 2002); *see generally* Evan Criddle, *The Vienna Convention on the Law of Treaties in U.S. Treaty Interpretation*, 44 VA. J. INT'L L. 431 (2004).
[110] Thus, for example, in The Schooner Exchange v. McFaddon, 11 U.S. (7 Cranch) 116 (1812), the Supreme Court applied the CIL of sovereign immunity without bothering to consider domestic authorization to do so. Similarly, in Hatch v. Baez, 14 N.Y. Sup. Ct. 596 (Gen. Term 1876), a New York court relied on an English precedent but no domestic authorization in holding that the former president of the Dominican Republic was entitled to immunity for his official acts. *See id.* at 599–600.
[111] In Compania Espanola de Navegacion Maritima S.A. v. The Navemar, 303 U.S. 68 (1938), decided on the day that *Erie* was argued, the Supreme Court intimated for the first time that courts were bound by executive suggestions of immunity. *See id.* at 74. Subsequently, in Ex parte *Republic of Peru*, 318 U.S. 578 (1943), the Court squarely held that because immunity determinations implicated important foreign relations interests, courts

the political branch authorization for judicial application of foreign sovereign immunity from executive suggestion to congressional statute. The FSIA did not address head-of-state immunity, however, and most courts have held that this immunity continues to be tied to executive branch authorization.[112]

Finally, even if CIL does not have direct application in U.S. law, it can affect the interpretation of federal statutes pursuant to the well-accepted *Charming Betsy* canon of construction discussed in Chapter 1. That canon directs that courts should attempt to construe federal statutes, where possible, so that the statutes do not violate international law, and the canon applies to potential conflicts with CIL as well as with treaties.[113] As discussed in Chapter 6, this canon is sometimes applied, for example, as a justification for limiting the extraterritorial application of federal statutes.

International Law and Constitutional Interpretation

In the early 2000s, there was significant debate over the Supreme Court's reference to foreign and international materials in its interpretation of some provisions of the U.S. Constitution.[114] These references appeared most frequently in connection with the

---

were bound to follow executive suggestions of immunity. *See id.* at 587. Two years later, in Republic of Mexico v. Hoffman, 324 U.S. 30 (1945), the Court went further, stating that even in the face of executive branch silence, U.S. courts should look to "the principles accepted by the [executive branch]." *Id.* at 35. As a result, the Court explained that "it is ... not for the courts to deny an immunity which our government has seen fit to allow, or to allow an immunity on new grounds which the government has not seen fit to recognize." *Id.; see also* Curtis A. Bradley & Jack L. Goldsmith, *Pinochet and International Human Rights Litigation*, 97 MICH. L. REV. 2129, 2163–64 (1999) (suggesting a connection between this shift in approach to immunity and *Erie*).

[112] *See, e.g.*, Manoharan v. Rajapaksa, 711 F.3d 178, 180 (D.C. Cir. 2013); Habyarimana v. Kagame, 696 F.3d 1029, 1032–33 (10th Cir. 2012); Ye v. Zemin, 383 F.3d 620, 624–25 (7th Cir. 2004); United States v. Noriega, 117 F.3d 1206, 1212 (11th Cir. 1997). For the argument that the executive branch has the authority to determine head-of-state immunity in U.S. litigation, based on the president's constitutional powers relating to diplomacy, *see* Lewis S. Yelen, *Head of State Immunity as Sole Executive Lawmaking*, 44 VAND. J. TRANSNAT'L L. 911 (2011).

[113] *See* RESTATEMENT (THIRD) OF THE FOREIGN RELATIONS LAW OF THE UNITED STATES, *supra* note 1, § 114 ("Where fairly possible, a United States statute is to be construed so as not to conflict with international law or with an international agreement of the United States."). *See also* Murray v. The Schooner Charming Betsy, 6 U.S. (2 Cranch) 64, 118 (1804) (stating that "an act of Congress ought never to be construed to violate the law of nations if any other possible construction remains"); Curtis A. Bradley, *The* Charming Betsy *Canon and Separation of Powers: Rethinking the Interpretive Role of International Law*, 86 GEO. L.J. 479, 525 (1998) (arguing that the canon, among other things, "is a means by which the courts can seek guidance from the political branches concerning whether and, if so, how they intend to violate the international legal obligations of the United States").

[114] For articles supporting this practice, see, for example, Sarah H. Cleveland, *Our International Constitution*, 31 YALE J. INT'L L. 1 (2006); Vicki C. Jackson, *Constitutional Comparisons: Convergence, Resistance, Engagement*, 119 HARV. L. REV. 109 (2005); Harold Hongju Koh, *International Law as Part of Our Law*, 98 AM. J. INT'L L. 43 (2004); Gerald L. Neuman, *The Uses of International Law in Constitutional Interpretation*, 98 AM. J. INT'L L. 82 (2004); and Jeremy Waldron, *Foreign Law and the Modern* Ius Gentium, 119 HARV. L. REV. 129 (2005). For articles critical of this practice, see, for example, Roger P. Alford, *Misusing International Sources to Interpret the Constitution*, 98 AM. J. INT'L L. 57 (2004); Robert J. Delahunty & John Yoo, *Against Foreign Law*, 29

Court's interpretation of the Eighth Amendment's ban on "cruel and unusual punishments." For example, in a 2005 decision, *Roper v. Simmons*, the Court held that the execution of juvenile offenders violates the Eighth Amendment, and in reaching this conclusion the Court took account of the fact that the United States was "the only country in the world that continues to give official sanction to the juvenile death penalty."[115] The Court also cited various treaties that prohibited the execution of juvenile offenders, including the Convention on the Rights of the Child, which had been ratified by almost all nations, although not by the United States.[116] "The opinion of the world community," the Court explained, "while not controlling our outcome, does provide respected and significant confirmation for our own conclusions."[117] Similarly, in a 2010 decision, *Graham v. Florida*, the Court held that it violated the Eighth Amendment to sentence a juvenile offender to life imprisonment without possibility of parole for a nonhomicide offense, and in doing so the Court took account of "the global consensus against the sentencing practice in question."[118]

The Court's invocation of foreign and international materials has not been limited to the context of the Eighth Amendment. Most notably, in a 2003 decision, *Lawrence v. Texas*, the Court held that a state law that criminalized consensual sex between homosexual couples violated a liberty right protected by the Due Process Clause of the Fourteenth Amendment, and in its reasoning the Court emphasized that the right in question "has been accepted as an integral part of human freedom in many other countries."[119] In support of this proposition, the Court referred both to decisions by the European Court of Human Rights and to decisions and actions of foreign governments.[120]

These references to foreign and international materials are distinct from the *Charming Betsy* canon of construction.[121] The issue in the Eighth Amendment cases, for example, is

---

HARV. J.L. & PUB. POL'Y 291 (2005); John O. McGinnis, *Foreign to Our Constitution*, 100 NW. U. L. REV. 303 (2006); and Ernest A. Young, *Foreign Law and the Denominator Problem*, 119 HARV. L. REV. 148 (2005); *see also* Roger P. Alford, *In Search of a Theory for Constitutional Comparativism*, 52 UCLA L. REV. 639 (2005) (considering how reliance on foreign and international materials relates to various theories of constitutional interpretation); Stephen G. Calabresi & Stephanie Dotson Zimdahl, *The Supreme Court and Foreign Sources of Law: Two Hundred Years of Practice and the Juvenile Death Penalty Decision*, 47 WM. & MARY L. REV. 743, 756 (2005) (arguing that "in the overwhelming majority of non-Fourth and non-Eighth Amendment cases, it is inappropriate for the Court to cite foreign law").

[115] Roper v. Simmons, 543 U.S. 551, 575 (2005).
[116] *See id.* at 576.
[117] *Id.* at 578.
[118] Graham v. Florida, 560 U.S. 48 (2010).
[119] Lawrence v. Texas, 539 U.S. 558, 577 (2003).
[120] *See id.* at 573, 576–67.
[121] *See* Curtis A. Bradley, *The Juvenile Death Penalty and International Law*, 52 DUKE L.J. 484, 555–56 (2002); *see also* McGinnis, *supra* note 114, at 307 n.23 (arguing that "the [*Charming Betsy*] canon should not be applied to the Constitution because its application would interpret the Constitution to accord with international law and thus tend to deprive the political branches of the opportunity to decide whether they want to violate international law").

not whether a particular construction of the Eighth Amendment will place the United States in breach of international law. Instead, the issue is simply whether the Eighth Amendment prohibits a practice that might violate international law. Even if the Eighth Amendment does not do so, the practice would not be allowed unless authorized by some other U.S. law. It would be that other U.S. law, not the Eighth Amendment, that would potentially create a violation of international law. (Indeed, the United States would not be in violation of international law even if it had no Eighth Amendment, and, indeed, even if it had no written constitution.) Moreover, if the law that authorized the practice in question were unambiguous (as it presumably would be for an authorization of criminal punishment), the *Charming Betsy* canon would be inapplicable even to that law, since the canon only applies in situations of ambiguity.

The Supreme Court's reliance on foreign and international materials is also distinct from the claim, discussed earlier, that CIL has the status of federal common law.[122] The materials referenced in the constitutional interpretation cases are broader than the materials thought to establish CIL, and the Supreme Court has made clear in these cases that it is not claiming that the constitutional interpretation it is adopting is necessary to avoid a violation of international law. In *Graham v. Florida*, for example, the Court noted that "[t]he question before us is not whether international law prohibits the United States from imposing the sentence at issue in this case."[123] The Court further explained that it:

> has treated the laws and practices of other nations and international agreements as relevant to the Eighth Amendment not because those norms are binding or controlling but because the judgment of the world's nations that a particular sentencing practice is inconsistent with basic principles of decency demonstrates that the Court's rationale has respected reasoning to support it.[124]

However, a constitutional interpretation informed by foreign and international materials will bind Congress and can be overturned only through a constitutional amendment, so in that sense the foreign and international materials in these cases can potentially have more significance in the U.S. legal system than application of CIL as federal common law.[125]

The Supreme Court's reliance on foreign and international materials prompted criticism by some members of Congress, and bills were proposed that would have attempted

---

[122] *See* Bradley, Goldsmith & Moore, *supra* note 79, at 934.
[123] *Graham*, 560 U.S. at 81.
[124] *Id.*
[125] *See* Bradley, Goldsmith & Moore, *supra* note 79, at 934; *see also* David Sloss, *Using International Law to Enhance Democracy*, 47 Va. J. Int'l L. 1 (2006) (criticizing the use of international law in constitutional interpretation as being the least democratic way of incorporating international law into the U.S. legal system).

to restrict this practice, although none were enacted.[126] Senators also specifically asked potential appointees to the Supreme Court about their views on this issue.[127] In a somewhat related development, some U.S. states enacted laws that purported to restrict state courts from relying on foreign law, international law, and Sharia law.[128] These laws are presumably invalid at least to the extent that they disallow state courts from applying self-executing treaties, since, as we saw in Chapter 2, such treaties are constitutionally part of the supreme law of the land that is binding on the states.[129]

Notwithstanding these controversies, judicial reference to international law in constitutional interpretation is not a new phenomenon. Some provisions of the Constitution, such as the provisions relating to war and hostilities, were written against the backdrop of international law principles and thus invite some consideration of those principles. (The relationship between international law and the government's war powers is explored further in Chapter 10.) Moreover, courts have also long taken account of international law when considering the relationship between the Constitution and issues of territoriality and sovereignty, a point discussed in Chapter 6. What has potentially changed, due in part to the rise of international human rights law, is the extent to which international materials are being invoked as a basis for resolving divisive issues of domestic social policy.

Uncertainties Surrounding CIL

Although not the focus of this chapter, it is worth noting that there are many uncertainties today concerning CIL as a source of international law.[130] CIL is supposed to result

---

[126] *See, e.g.*, Constitution Restoration Act of 2005, S. 520, 109th Cong., 1st Sess., § 201 (2005) ("In interpreting and applying the Constitution of the United States, a court of the United States may not rely upon any constitution, law, administrative rule, Executive order, directive, policy, judicial decision, or any other action of any foreign state or international organization or agency, other than English constitutional and common law up to the time of the adoption of the Constitution of the United States.").

[127] *See, e.g.*, Confirmation Hearing on the Nomination of John G. Roberts, Jr. To Be Chief Justice of the United States: Hearing Before the S. Comm. on the Judiciary, 109th Cong. 293 (2005) (Sen. Coburn) ("My question to you is, relying on foreign precedent and selecting and choosing a foreign precedent to create a bias outside of the laws of this country, is that good behavior?").

[128] *See* Aaron Fellmeth, *U.S. State Legislation to Limit Use of International and Foreign Law*, 106 AM. J. INT'L L. 107 (2012).

[129] A federal court enjoined the Sharia law portion of such a restriction in Oklahoma on the ground that it violated the religious freedom protections of the Constitution. *See* Awad v. Ziriax, 747 F. Supp. 2d 1298 (W.D. Okla. 2010), *aff'd*, 670 F.3d 1111 (10th Cir. 2012).

[130] For discussion of some of the uncertainties surrounding CIL, *see* Curtis A. Bradley & Mitu Gulati, *Withdrawing from International Custom*, 120 YALE L.J. 202, 210–15 (2010); Jack L. Goldsmith & Eric A. Posner, *A Theory of Customary International Law*, 66 U. CHI. L. REV. 1113, 1117–118 (1999); Andrew T. Guzman, *Saving Customary International Law*, 27 MICH. J. INT'L L. 115, 124–28 (2005); Daniel H. Joyner, *Why I Stopped Believing in Customary International Law*, 9 ASIAN J. INT'L L. 31 (2019). *See also* Hamdan v. United States, 696 F.3d 1238, 1250 (D.C. Cir. 2012) ("It is often difficult to determine what constitutes customary international law, who defines customary international law, and how firmly established a norm has to be to qualify as a customary international law norm.").

from the practice of nations, but it is not clear precisely what counts as practice for these purposes. There is much debate, for example, over the extent to which treaties and the pronouncements and decisions of international institutions qualify as evidence of CIL. Nor is it clear how widespread the practice must be, or for how long it must be followed. There is also uncertainty about what constitutes evidence of a nation's sense of legal obligation (referred to by international lawyers as *opinio juris*), and even how such a sense develops. More generally, there is substantial disagreement about the extent to which the binding force of CIL is, or should be, tied to national consent.[131]

Although some of these uncertainties are long-standing, they are particularly salient with respect to certain modern claims about CIL.[132] The traditional view of CIL was that it developed inductively from widespread and long-standing patterns of national behavior. By contrast, modern claims about the content of CIL, especially in the area of international human rights law, are often more deductive in character and involve reliance on treaties, international resolutions, scholarly opinion, and similar materials. The emphasis under this approach tends to be on the "sense of legal obligation" component of CIL rather than on the national practice component, with inconsistent national practices treated as breaches of the norms, rather than as evidence against their existence. Claims about the content of this modern CIL are therefore more normative, and less empirical, than with respect to traditional CIL.

The expanded ability today to make international law through multilateral treaties—which has been facilitated by the United Nations and other international institutions, as well as by technological changes in travel and communications—has also raised new questions about the need for CIL as a distinct source of international law.[133] Most of the major areas that were historically regulated by CIL are now regulated, to one degree or another, by treaties. Treaties also have a variety of attractive qualities compared to CIL, in

---

[131] *See, e.g.*, MICHAEL BYERS, CUSTOM, POWER AND THE POWER OF RULES: INTERNATIONAL RELATIONS AND CUSTOMARY INTERNATIONAL LAW 142–46 (1999) (discussing different views about the relationship between consent and CIL); Guzman, *supra* note 130, at 141–45 (same); *see also* C.L. Lim & Olufemi Elias, *Withdrawing from Custom and the Paradox of Consensualism in International Law*, 21 DUKE J. COMP. & INT'L L. 143, 145 (2010) (noting that "[a] number of conceptions of the role of consent in customary international law have been expressed").

[132] *See* Bradley & Goldsmith, *supra* note 4, at 838–42 (describing the "New CIL"). For differing views about the legitimacy of this modern CIL, compare, for example, Richard B. Lillich, *The Growing Importance of Customary International Human Rights Law*, 25 GA. J. INT'L & COMP. L. 1, 12–21 (1995) (arguing in favor of recent changes in the process of CIL formation), with Bruno Simma & Philip Alston, *The Sources of Human Rights Law: Custom, Jus Cogens, and General Principles*, 12 AUST'L Y.B. INT'L L. 82, 83 (1992) (arguing against these changes); *see also* Anthea Elizabeth Roberts, *Traditional and Modern Approaches to Customary International Law: A Reconciliation*, 95 AM. J. INT'L L. 757 (2006) (attempting to reconcile traditional and modern approaches to CIL).

[133] For discussion of some of these uncertainties concerning the relationship between CIL and treaties, *see* Curtis A. Bradley & Mitu Gulati, *Customary International Law and Withdrawal Rights in an Age of Treaties*, 21 DUKE J. COMP. & INT'L L. 1 (2010). *See also* Joel P. Trachtman, *The Growing Obsolescence of Customary International Law*, in CUSTOM'S FUTURE (Curtis A. Bradley ed., 2016).

that they provide more direct evidence of what nations want (since they are the product of express negotiation), they can provide for greater specificity (since they are typically in writing), and they can establish concrete institutional mechanisms to promote monitoring, adjudication, and enforcement of the norms.

Perhaps not surprisingly in light of these uncertainties, CIL has been the subject of a wide range of academic criticism in recent years, especially in the United States. Some scholars have questioned whether CIL can meaningfully operate as law.[134] Others have questioned its usefulness and legitimacy.[135] Still others have questioned its normative attractiveness—from the perspectives, for example, of efficiency and democratic accountability.[136] Questions have also been raised about how international and domestic adjudicators actually discern purported rules of customary international law.[137] Regardless of the merits of these critiques, the very fact that CIL is a more uncertain and contested form of international law as compared with treaties is potentially relevant when considering CIL's domestic status.

* * *

There is still significant academic debate concerning the status of CIL in the U.S. legal system. Importantly, however, there are also significant points of agreement. Most scholars now agree that, before *Erie v. Tompkins*, CIL had the status in the United States of general common law, not federal law. Most scholars also agree that it can be appropriate for courts to take account of CIL, along with other materials, when developing certain

---

[134] *See, e.g.*, GOLDSMITH & POSNER, *supra* note 95, at 43 (arguing that CIL "is not an exogenous influence on state behavior").

[135] *See, e.g.*, J. Patrick Kelly, *The Twilight of Customary International Law*, 40 VA. J. INT'L L. 449 (2000).

[136] *See, e.g.*, Eugene Kontorovich, *Inefficient Customs in International Law*, 48 WM. & MARY L. REV. 859, 889–94 (2006) (efficiency); John O. McGinnis & Ilya Somin, *Should International Law Be Part of Our Law?*, 59 STAN. L. REV. 1175 (2007) (democratic accountability); *see also* David J. Bederman, *Acquiescence, Objection and the Death of Customary International Law*, 21 DUKE J. COMP. & INT'L L. 31, 43 (2010) (noting that this is a "time when customary international law is coming under attack by both extreme positivists (who suggest that its processes are illegitimate and non-transparent) and by those of a naturalist bent (who regard it as merely pandering to state interests)"); Guzman, *supra* note 130, at 116 (noting that "CIL is under attack from all sides"); George Norman & Joel P. Trachtman, *The Customary International Law Game*, 99 AM. J. INT'L L. 541, 541 (2005) ("[CIL] is under attack as behaviorally epiphenomenal and doctrinally incoherent.").

[137] *See, e.g.*, Stephen J. Choi & Mitu Gulati, *Customary International Law: How Do Courts Do It?*, *in* CUSTOM'S FUTURE, *supra* note 133, at 146–47 (finding that "international courts do not come anywhere close to engaging in the type of analysis the officially stated two-part rule for the evolution of CIL sets up"); Ryan M. Scoville, *Finding Customary International Law*, 101 IOWA L. REV. 1893, 1948 (2016) (finding that U.S. courts "depend heavily on portrayals of CIL in other U.S. government sources, rarely consider direct evidence of foreign state practice, focus almost exclusively on the advanced democracies of the West even when they do look abroad, and cite to Western academics who exhibit a similar tendency to focus on the laws and policies of the West"); *see also* Curtis A. Bradley, *Customary International Law Adjudication as Common Law Adjudication*, *in* CUSTOM'S FUTURE, *supra* note 133 (arguing that adjudication of CIL, including by the International Court of Justice, is analogous to the judicial development of common law).

rules of post-*Erie* federal common law. There is also broad agreement that CIL can in some instances inform the interpretation of ambiguous federal statutes. Although some scholars continue to support the claim of the *Restatement (Third) of Foreign Relations Law* that CIL has the status of self-executing federal law,[138] that claim appears to have lost force in both the academic community and the courts. The uncertainties surrounding CIL as a source of international law, described here, provide further grounds for U.S. courts to proceed cautiously before incorporating it into domestic law.

---

[138] *See, e.g.*, Vázquez, *supra* note 85; Ralph G. Steinhardt, *Laying One Bankrupt Critique to Rest:* Sosa v. Alvarez-Machain *and the Future of International Human Rights Litigation in U.S. Courts*, 57 VAND. L. REV. 2241 (2004).

6   Extraterritorial Application of U.S. Law

THIS CHAPTER DISCUSSES the application of federal and state law to conduct that takes place at least partially outside the territory of the United States, a topic that intersects with U.S. obligations under international law, especially customary international law. The chapter begins with a discussion of the extraterritorial application of constitutional rights, including the right of habeas corpus. Although the judicial decisions relating to such rights ultimately concern U.S. constitutional law, they have often taken account of international law and practice, as well as functional considerations relating to the ability of the United States to operate effectively as a sovereign nation. Next, the chapter discusses the extraterritorial application of federal statutory provisions in light of several considerations: the long-standing presumption in U.S. law against extraterritoriality, the customary international law limitations on the exercise of prescriptive jurisdiction, and possible constitutional limitations on congressional authority. Finally, the chapter briefly addresses the ability of U.S. states to apply their laws extraterritorially.[1]

---

[1] Although not addressed here, important issues have also arisen concerning the extraterritorial scope of U.S. obligations under human rights treaties, such as the obligation in the Convention against Torture not to engage in "cruel, inhuman or degrading treatment."

Territorial Scope of the Constitution

The Constitution imposes a variety of limitations on the national government, including a number of limitations designed to protect individual liberties. Many of these limitations are set forth in the first ten amendments to the Constitution, known as the Bill of Rights. These limitations, among other things, disallow the government from abridging freedom of speech and religion; prohibit unreasonable searches and seizures; allow individuals subjected to criminal prosecution to be tried by a jury of their peers; and condition deprivations of life, liberty, and property on the observance of due process of law.

The Supreme Court's approach to the extraterritorial application of constitutional rights has evolved over time. Although early decisions resisted or sharply limited application of the Constitution abroad, the Court appeared to become more receptive to an extraterritorial approach in the modern era.[2] The extent to which particular constitutional rights will be applied abroad remains unclear, however, and a number of contextual considerations tend to affect the result in litigated controversies, such as the citizenship of the person whose rights are in question, the nature of the U.S. control over the foreign location, and the functional difficulties associated with applying the right to that location.

In a decision from the late 1800s, *In re Ross*, the Supreme Court suggested that the Constitution did not apply outside of U.S. territory. In that case, Ross, a British citizen who was serving as a member of the crew of a U.S.-flagged vessel, was tried and convicted in a U.S. consular court in Japan for murdering a fellow seaman while the ship was anchored in a Japanese harbor. In rejecting Ross's argument that the trial violated his constitutional rights to a grand jury indictment and a trial by jury, the Supreme Court reasoned that "[b]y the Constitution a government is ordained and established 'for the United States of America,' and not for countries outside of their limits," and stated flatly that "[t]he Constitution can have no operation in another country."[3] The Court in *Ross* also noted that the use of a consular court such as the one in this case was consistent with

---

[2] *See generally* GERALD L. NEUMAN, STRANGERS TO THE CONSTITUTION: IMMIGRANTS, BORDERS, AND FUNDAMENTAL LAW chs. 5, 6 (1996); KAL RAUSTIALA, DOES THE CONSTITUTION FOLLOW THE FLAG? THE EVOLUTION OF TERRITORIALITY IN AMERICAN LAW (2009).

[3] 140 U.S. 453, 464 (1891). During the nineteenth and early twentieth centuries, the United States had treaties allowing it to operate consular courts in a number of non-Western countries, such as China and Japan. *See* SAMUEL CRANDALL, TREATIES: THEIR MAKING AND ENFORCEMENT 234–35 (2d ed. 1916). These courts would, among other things, adjudicate criminal prosecutions of U.S. citizens for acts committed in the foreign country. In 1906, the United States established a Court for China in Shanghai, which operated until 1943. This court had jurisdiction over both civil and criminal cases involving U.S. citizens, and appeals from the court were heard in the U.S. Court of Appeals for the Ninth Circuit. *See* Crawford M. Bishop, *American Extraterritorial Jurisdiction in China*, 20 AM. J. INT'L L. 281 (1926); *see also* Teemu Ruskola, *Canton Is Not Boston: The Invention of American Imperial Sovereignty*, 57 AM. Q. 859 (2005); Tahirih V. Lee, *The United States Court for China: A Triumph of Local Law*, 52 BUFFALO L. REV. 923 (2004).

"the uniform practice of civilized governments for centuries to provide consular tribunals in other than Christian countries, or to invest their consuls with judicial authority, which is the same thing, for the trial of their own subjects or citizens for offences committed in those countries, as well as for the settlement of civil disputes between them."[4]

Subsequently, in a series of decisions in the early 1900s, referred to collectively as the *Insular Cases*, the Court considered the applicability of the Constitution to the U.S. territorial possessions in the Philippines, Puerto Rico, and Guam. The Court held that various constitutional rights, including the right to a grand jury indictment and the right to a jury trial, did not apply in these possessions.[5] The Court reasoned that although certain "fundamental rights" apply wherever the United States exercises jurisdiction over a territory, some rights, such as the right to a grand jury indictment and the right to a jury trial, do not qualify as such fundamental rights. Otherwise, explained the Court, the United States would be compelled to disregard local customs and preferences and impose "a system of trial unknown to [the local population] and unsuited to their needs."[6] The Court also referred to "the power of the United States, like other sovereign nations, to acquire, by the methods known to civilized people, additional territory," and suggested that this right would be unduly undermined if jury trial rights automatically applied to any acquired territory.[7]

In a 1957 decision, *Reid v. Covert*, the Court was more receptive to extraterritorial application of the Constitution.[8] *Reid* concerned the trials by courts-martial of two wives of U.S. servicemembers who were accused of murdering their husbands on foreign military bases. The Court held that the military trial violated the wives' constitutional rights to an indictment by a grand jury and to a jury trial. Writing for a four-justice plurality, Justice Black reasoned that the U.S. government is "entirely a creature of the Constitution" and that "[i]t can only act in accordance with all the limitations imposed by the Constitution."[9] When the U.S. government acts against U.S. citizens abroad, therefore, the plurality reasoned that the government is subject to constitutional limitations, including the grand jury and jury trial requirements. The plurality dismissed *Ross* as a "relic from a different era."[10] It also distinguished the *Insular Cases* on the ground that territories present a special case in which there may be a temporary need to tailor procedures to the local cultures and traditions. The Court reached this conclusion notwithstanding executive agreements that authorized the United States to exercise criminal

---

[4] 140 U.S. at 462.
[5] *See, e.g.*, Balzac v. Porto Rico, 258 U.S. 298 (1922); Dorr v. United States, 195 U.S. 138 (1904); Hawaii v. Mankichi, 190 U.S. 197 (1903). *See generally* BARTHOLOMEW H. SPARROW, THE INSULAR CASES AND THE EMERGENCE OF AMERICAN EMPIRE (2006).
[6] *Dorr*, 195 U.S. at 148.
[7] *Id.* at 146.
[8] 354 U.S. 1 (1957).
[9] *Id.* at 6.
[10] *Id.* at 12.

jurisdiction in these cases, reasoning that "no agreement with a foreign nation can confer power on the Congress, or on any other branch of Government, which is free from the restraints of the Constitution."[11]

Because Justice Black's opinion in *Reid* did not reflect the views of a majority of the Court, its reasoning is not binding on the Court in subsequent cases. In an important concurrence in *Reid*, Justice John Marshall Harlan reasoned more narrowly that the right to a jury trial applied abroad when a U.S. citizen is being tried for a capital offense. Citing *Ross* and the *Insular Cases*, Harlan said that he could not agree "with the suggestion that every provision of the Constitution must always be deemed automatically applicable to American citizens in every part of the world."[12] With respect to the right of a jury trial, he explained that "what *Ross* and the *Insular Cases* hold is that the particular local setting, the practical necessities, and the possible alternatives are relevant to a question of judgment, namely, whether jury trial *should* be deemed a necessary condition of the exercise of Congress' power to provide for the trial of Americans overseas."[13] Under Harlan's analysis, a jury trial is considered a necessary condition for trying capital offenses because, he contended, in this context "the law is especially sensitive to demands for that procedural fairness which inheres in a civilian trial where the judge and trier of fact are not responsive to the command of the convening authority," and "[t]he number of such cases would appear to be so negligible that the practical problems of affording the defendant a civilian trial would not present insuperable problems."[14]

More recently, in a 1990 decision, *United States v. Verdugo-Urquidez*, the Court held that the Fourth Amendment to the Constitution, which protects against unreasonable searches and seizures, does not apply when the U.S. government searches a foreign citizen's residence abroad, at least when the foreign citizen does not have what the Court referred to as a "significant voluntary connection with the United States."[15] The Court noted that the Fourth Amendment, like the First, Second, and Tenth Amendments but unlike other Bill of Rights provisions, refers to "the people," which the Court construed as a reference to "a class of persons who are part of a national community or who have otherwise developed sufficient connection with this country to be considered part of that community."[16] The Court also observed that there would be "deleterious consequences for the United States in conducting activities beyond its boundaries," including activities involving U.S. armed forces, if the U.S. government were subjected to Fourth Amendment requirements when acting abroad.[17] The Court concluded by observing that

---

[11] *Id.* at 16. This aspect of the decision is discussed further in Chapter 2.
[12] *Id.* at 74 (Harlan, J., concurring).
[13] *Id.* at 75.
[14] *Id.* at 77, 78. The Court extended the holding in *Reid* to noncapital cases in *Kinsella v. Singleton*, 361 U.S. 234 (1960).
[15] *See* 494 U.S. 259 (1990).
[16] *Id.* at 265.
[17] *Id.* at 273.

"[f]or better or for worse, we live in a world of nation-states in which our Government must be able to 'function effectively in the company of sovereign nations.'"[18]

In a concurrence in *Verdugo-Urquidez*, Justice Anthony Kennedy cited favorably to the *Insular Cases* and to Justice Harlan's concurrence in *Reid* and expressed the view that the Court "must interpret constitutional protections in light of the undoubted power of the United States to take actions to assert its legitimate power and authority abroad."[19] He concluded that, even if the Fourth Amendment applied to the U.S. government's actions in this case, it did not require the issuance of a search warrant, given "the absence of local judges or magistrates available to issue warrants, the differing and perhaps unascertainable conceptions of reasonableness and privacy that prevail abroad, and the need to cooperate with foreign officials."[20] Kennedy also emphasized that a foreign national being tried in a U.S. court is still entitled to the protections of due process, but he noted that "[n]othing approaching a violation of due process has occurred in this case."[21]

Based on these decisions, there is no categorical rule with respect to the extraterritorial application of the Constitution. At least some constitutional rights apply abroad to protect U.S. citizens. The extent to which constitutional rights also protect aliens abroad in their interactions with the U.S. government is less clear. As discussed in the next section, the Supreme Court has confirmed that at least one constitutional right—the right to seek habeas corpus review—applies to aliens abroad in some circumstances.[22] But in a more recent decision, the Court seemed to suggest that, except in U.S. territorial possessions or other places where the United States exercises jurisdiction and control, constitutional rights do not apply to non-U.S. citizens abroad.[23]

When someone has a constitutional right, they are generally allowed to seek injunctive relief against government officials to stop an ongoing violation of the right. The ability to seek damages, however, is more constrained. The federal government generally has

---

[18] *Id.* at 275 (citing Perez v. Brownell, 356 U.S. 44, 57 (1958)).

[19] *Id.* at 277 (Kennedy, J., concurring).

[20] *Id.* at 278.

[21] *Id.*

[22] For decisions holding that the warrant requirement of the Fourth Amendment does not apply to searches abroad conducted by U.S. agents, even of U.S. citizens, and that such searches are simply subject to a requirement of reasonableness, see, for example, United States v. Odeh, 548 F.3d 276 (2d Cir. 2008); and United States v. Stokes, 726 F.3d 880 (7th Cir. 2013). For a decision holding that a foreign citizen with no connection to the United States has no right to compensation under the Fifth Amendment of the Constitution for a taking of property that occurs in a foreign country, *see* Atamirzayeva v. United States, 524 F.3d 1320 (Fed. Cir. 2008). For a decision holding that a foreign citizen's study at a U.S. university gave her a significant voluntary connection to the United States that allowed her to bring a constitutional challenge against being included on U.S. terrorist watchlists, *see* Ibrahim v. Dep't of Homeland Security, 669 F.3d 983 (9th Cir. 2012).

[23] *See* Agency for Int'l Development v. Alliance for Open Society Int'l, Inc., 207 L. Ed. 2d 654, 658 (2020) (stating that it is "settled as a matter of American constitutional law that foreign citizens outside U.S. territory do not possess rights under the U.S. Constitution"). But *see id.* at 674 (Breyer, J., dissenting) ("At most, one might say that they are unlikely to enjoy very often extraterritorial protection under the Constitution. Or one might say that the matter is undecided.").

immunity from damage suits except to the extent that it has waived its immunity. For tort suits, the government has waived its immunity to an extent in the Federal Tort Claims Act, but the Act contains a number of limitations.[24] One limitation that is especially important in the foreign affairs context is that suits are not allowed under the Act for claims "arising in a foreign country."[25] The Court has construed this limitation to mean that, "claims that would otherwise permit the recovery of damages are barred if the injury occurred abroad."[26]

In some situations, damage suits may be brought directly against federal officials, rather than the government itself, for constitutional violations.[27] These "*Bivens* suits" (named after the main Supreme Court decision allowing them) are not subject to the constraints of the Federal Tort Claims Act, although the defendant officials can assert their own "qualified immunity" defense, which will limit their liability to violations of clearly established law.[28] The Supreme Court has viewed such *Bivens* suits with disfavor in recent years, and it has indicated that courts should be reluctant to allow damage suits against federal officials for harm that occurs outside the United States, even when the harm stems from actions taken within the United States.[29]

The Reach of Habeas Corpus

When someone is being detained in the United States, the traditional means by which they can challenge the lawfulness of their detention is through petitioning a court for a writ of habeas corpus. A habeas proceeding is brought against the detainee's custodian, such as the warden of a prison, and it is separate from any criminal proceeding concerning the detainee.

The Constitution provides that "[t]he Privilege of the Writ of Habeas Corpus shall not be suspended, unless when in Cases of Rebellion or Invasion the public Safety may require it."[30] The Supreme Court has interpreted the Suspension Clause as, at minimum, protecting the right of habeas corpus as it existed at common law in 1789 when the Constitution took effect.[31] The Court has also observed that "[a]t its historical core,

---

[24] *See generally* 28 U.S.C. §§ 1346(b), 2671–80; *see also* Cong. Res. Serv., *The Federal Tort Claims Act: A Legal Overview* (updated Nov. 20, 2019), *at* https://fas.org/sgp/crs/misc/R45732.pdf.

[25] 28 U.S.C. § 2680(k).

[26] Hernandez v. Mesa, 140 S. Ct. 735, 748 (2020); *see also* Sosa v. Alvarez-Machain, 542 U.S. 692, 700–12 (2004) (disallowing suit under Federal Tort Claims Act for foreign tort even where the "headquarters" for planning the tort was in the United States).

[27] *See, e.g.*, Bivens v. Six Unknown Named Agents of the Federal Bureau of Narcotics, 403 U.S. 388 (1971).

[28] *See* Harlow v. Fitzgerald, 457 U.S. 800, 818 (1982).

[29] *See Hernandez*, 140 S. Ct. at 747 (disallowing a *Bivens* claim for a cross-border shooting by a U.S. border patrol agent and noting the need for "hesitation in deciding whether to extend a judge-made cause of action beyond our borders").

[30] U.S. Const. art. I, § 9.

[31] *See* INS v. St. Cyr, 533 U.S. 289, 301 (2001).

the writ of habeas corpus has served as a means of reviewing the legality of executive detention, and it is in that context that its protections have been strongest."[32] Although President Abraham Lincoln controversially suspended the writ of habeas corpus on his own authority during the Civil War, the modern Supreme Court appears to assume that only Congress can suspend the writ of habeas corpus, probably because this Suspension Clause is contained in Article I of the Constitution, which addresses Congress's powers.[33]

Ever since the federal courts were first established, Congress has provided by statute for a right to seek habeas corpus review. Until after the Civil War, the federal habeas statute applied only to persons being detained by the federal government. In 1867, the statute was amended to apply to state prisoners as well. The current habeas corpus statute applicable to federal detainees provides in relevant part:

> Writs of habeas corpus may be granted by the Supreme Court, any justice thereof, the district courts and any circuit judge within their respective jurisdictions ... [for a prisoner] in custody under or by color of the authority of the United States ... [or] in custody in violation of the Constitution or laws or treaties of the United States.[34]

In a 1950 decision, *Johnson v. Eisentrager*, the Supreme Court held that a group of German nationals who were being held by U.S. military authorities in occupied Germany after World War II did not have the right to seek habeas corpus review in the United States.[35] The German nationals had been apprehended in China in 1945 and were alleged to have violated the laws of war by providing military intelligence to the Japanese armed forces after Germany had surrendered. They were tried before a U.S. military commission in China and, after they were convicted, they were transferred to a prison in Germany to serve their sentences. In seeking habeas review in U.S. courts, the German nationals argued that their trial, conviction, and imprisonment violated various U.S. constitutional guarantees as well as international law.

In directing a dismissal of their habeas petition, the Supreme Court in *Eisentrager* began by noting that "[w]e are cited to no instance where a court, in this or any other

---

[32] *Id.*

[33] *See* Hamdi v. Rumsfeld, 542 U.S. 507, 525 (2004) (plurality) ("Only in the rarest of circumstances has Congress seen fit to suspend the writ. ... At all other times, it has remained a critical check on the Executive, ensuring that it does not detain individuals except in accordance with law."); *id.* at 554 (Scalia, J., dissenting) ("[T]he Constitution's Suspension Clause, Art. I, § 9, cl. 2, allows Congress to relax the usual protections temporarily."); *see also* Ex parte Merryman, 17 F. Cas. 144, 148 (C.D. Md. 1861) ("The clause of the constitution, which authorizes the suspension of the privilege of the writ of habeas corpus, is in the 9th section of the first article [of the Constitution]. This article is devoted to the legislative department of the United States, and has not the slightest reference to the executive department."). For an argument that the president has a concurrent authority to suspend the writ of habeas corpus in the absence of contrary action by Congress, *see* Daniel Farber, Lincoln's Constitution 158–63 (2003).

[34] 28 U.S.C. § 2241(a), (c)(1).

[35] 339 U.S. 763 (1950).

country where the writ is known, has issued it on behalf of an alien enemy who, at no relevant time and in no stage of his captivity, has been within its territorial jurisdiction."[36] The Court proceeded to hold that a prisoner of the U.S. military is not constitutionally entitled to seek habeas corpus review when the prisoner:

> (a) is an enemy alien; (b) has never been or resided in the United States; (c) was captured outside of our territory and there held in military custody as a prisoner of war; (d) was tried and convicted by a Military Commission sitting outside the United States; (e) [was tried and convicted] for offenses against laws of war committed outside the United States; (f) and is at all times imprisoned outside the United States.[37]

The Court also reasoned that "the Constitution does not confer a right of personal security or an immunity from military trial and punishment upon an alien enemy engaged in the hostile service of a government at war with the United States."[38]

The Supreme Court has distinguished *Eisentrager* in two decisions concerning the detention of terrorist suspects at the Guantanamo Bay naval base in Cuba. The United States has occupied the base since the Spanish-American War at the end of the nineteenth century. Under lease and treaty arrangement with Cuba, the United States has exclusive jurisdiction and control over the base and has the right to remain there indefinitely, but Cuba retains "ultimate sovereignty" over the area. After the September 11, 2001, terrorist attacks, the United States detained various foreign citizens at the base as "enemy combatants" in the war on terrorism.

In a 2004 decision, *Rasul v. Bush*, the Court held that the habeas corpus statute could be invoked by the Guantanamo detainees.[39] The Court distinguished the Guantanamo detainees from the petitioners in *Eisentrager* as follows:

> [The petitioners here] are not nationals of countries at war with the United States, and they deny that they have engaged in or plotted acts of aggression against the United States; they have never been afforded access to any tribunal, much less charged with and convicted of wrongdoing; and for more than two years they have been imprisoned in territory over which the United States exercises exclusive jurisdiction and control.[40]

---

[36] *Id.* at 768.
[37] *Id.* at 777.
[38] *Id.* at 785. Justice Black (who later wrote the plurality opinion in *Reid v. Covert*) dissented and was joined by two other justices.
[39] 542 U.S. 466 (2004).
[40] *Id.* at 476.

The Court also concluded that applying the habeas statute to Guantanamo would not be inconsistent with the presumption (discussed in the next section) against applying statutes outside the United States. "Whatever traction the presumption against extraterritoriality might have in other contexts," the Court explained, it does not apply to a place such as Guantanamo where the United States exercises "complete jurisdiction and control."[41] In a concurrence, Justice Kennedy expressed the view that Guantanamo "is in every practical respect a United States territory, and it is one far removed from any hostilities."[42]

In response to *Rasul*, Congress amended the habeas statute to provide that "no court, justice, or judge shall have jurisdiction to hear or consider . . . an application for a writ of habeas corpus filed by or on behalf of an alien detained by the Department of Defense at Guantanamo Bay, Cuba."[43] Congress further provided that, instead of filing an application for a writ of habeas corpus, each detainee could appeal, to the federal appellate court in Washington, D.C., the military's determination that the detainee qualified as an enemy combatant. After the Supreme Court concluded that this statutory amendment did not apply to the many habeas cases brought on behalf of Guantanamo detainees that were already pending in the courts at the time the amendment was enacted,[44] Congress amended the habeas statute again, this time making clear that the disallowance of habeas review applied "to all cases, without exception, pending on or after the date of the [amendment]."[45] Congress also broadened the habeas restriction to apply to any alien determined by the government to be an enemy combatant, regardless of the location of the detention.[46] This eliminated all statutory grounds upon which a detainee could seek habeas relief, leaving only an assertion of a constitutional right to such relief.

In *Boumediene v. Bush*, the Supreme Court held, in a closely divided decision, that this attempt by Congress to restrict habeas review was unconstitutional as applied to Guantanamo, even though Guantanamo was not technically part of U.S. territory.[47] The Court identified what it described as a "common thread" running throughout the decisions in the *Insular Cases*, *Reid*, and *Eisentrager*, which is "the idea that questions of extraterritoriality turn on objective factors and practical concerns, not formalism."[48] Thus, although the Court accepted the government's argument that Cuba retains "legal sovereignty" over the Guantanamo base, it said that it was appropriate to look also to the

---

[41] *Id.* at 480.
[42] *Id.* at 487 (Kennedy, J., concurring).
[43] Detainee Treatment Act of 2005, Pub. L. No. 109–148, 119 Stat. 2739, § 1005(e), codified at 28 U.S.C. § 2241(e).
[44] *See* Hamdan v. Rumsfeld, 548 U.S. 547, 575–84 (2006).
[45] *See* Military Commissions Act of 2006, Pub. L. No. 109–366, 120 Stat. 2600, § 7(b), codified at 28 U.S.C. § 2241(e).
[46] *Id.* § 7(a).
[47] *See* Boumediene v. Bush, 553 U.S. 723 (2008).
[48] *Id.* at 764. For a discussion of the Court's functional approach and its potential implications, *see* Gerald L. Neuman, *The Extraterritorial Constitution after* Boumediene v. Bush, 92 S. CAL. L. REV. 259 (2009).

degree of actual control the United States has over the base, which the Court concluded gave the United States in effect "de facto" sovereignty there. The Court stated that "[i]n every practical sense Guantanamo is not abroad; it is within the constant jurisdiction of the United States."[49] The Court expressed concern that if the Constitution had no application to a place such as Guantanamo, the government could too easily evade the Constitution's restraints, and it stated that the government should not "have the power to switch the Constitution on or off at will."[50]

Based on its prior decisions, the Court in *Boumediene* identified "at least three factors" that are relevant in determining the reach of the Suspension Clause:

> (1) the citizenship and status of the detainee and the adequacy of the process through which that status determination was made; (2) the nature of the sites where apprehension and then detention took place; and (3) the practical obstacles inherent in resolving the prisoner's entitlement to the writ.[51]

The Court found that these factors supported the application of the habeas right to Guantanamo. In doing so, the Court distinguished *Eisentrager* on a number of grounds. It noted that the affiliation of the detainees as enemy aliens in *Eisentrager* was not in dispute, whereas the status of the detainees at Guantanamo was very much in dispute. It also noted that the detainees in *Eisentrager* had received an adversarial military trial, whereas the detainees here had not been tried in any tribunal. In addition, the Court observed that in *Eisentrager* the United States did not have complete jurisdiction and control over occupied Germany, whereas here the United States did have complete and indefinite jurisdiction and control over Guantanamo. Finally, the Court noted that the security, resource, and disruption concerns that troubled the Court in *Eisentrager* were less significant in this case.[52] The Court acknowledged, however, that if the United States were "answerable to [another] sovereign for its acts . . . or if the detention facility were located in an active theater of war, arguments that issuing the writ would be 'impracticable or anomalous' would have more weight."[53]

---

[49] 553 U.S. at 769.
[50] *Id.* at 765.
[51] *Id.* at 766.
[52] *See* 553 U.S. at 768–70.
[53] *Id.* at 770. The "impractical and anomalous" standard was suggested by Justice Harlan in *Reid v. Covert* (see 354 U.S. at 74) based on his reading of *Ross* and the *Insular Cases*, and it was endorsed by Justice Kennedy in his concurrence in *Verdugo* (see 494 U.S. at 277–78). For criticism of this standard, *see* Christina Duffy Burnett, *A Convenient Constitution? Extraterritoriality after* Boumediene, 109 COLUM. L. REV. 973 (2009). For an argument that "*Boumediene*'s functional test, which focuses the inquiry of whether the Suspension Clause applies to an executive detention abroad primarily on practical concerns, is in considerable tension with the fundamental norms jurisprudence that underlies and pervades the Court's opinion," *see* Jules Lobel, *Fundamental Norms, International Law, and the Extraterritorial Constitution*, 36 YALE J. INT'L L. 307, 309

On the same day that it issued its decision in *Boumediene*, the Court decided another case involving habeas corpus petitions filed by two U.S. citizens being detained by U.S. military forces that were operating as part of a multinational force in Iraq.[54] The Court concluded that the petitioners were "in custody" for purposes of the habeas corpus statute because they were U.S. citizens being held by soldiers who were subject to a U.S. chain of command.[55] The Court also held, however, that U.S. courts exercising their habeas jurisdiction did not have the authority to enjoin the U.S. military from transferring the petitioners to Iraqi custody. "[H]abeas," the Court explained, "is not a means of compelling the United States to harbor fugitives from the criminal justice system of a sovereign with undoubted authority to prosecute them."[56]

It is uncertain to what extent the right of habeas corpus review extends to aliens detained in extraterritorial locations other than Guantanamo. In 2010, the U.S. Court of Appeals for the D.C. Circuit held that foreign citizens being detained by U.S. forces in Afghanistan had no statutory or constitutional right to habeas review.[57] Because the detainees there had been determined by the government to be alien enemy combatants, the habeas statute was inapplicable as a result of the same statutory restriction considered in *Boumediene*. The court proceeded to conclude that, unlike in *Boumediene*, application of the statutory restriction in this case did not violate any constitutional right of habeas corpus review. The court emphasized that, unlike the detention facility at Guantanamo, the Afghanistan facility was in a "theater of war," and the host government exercised both de facto and de jure sovereignty over the territory where the facility was located.[58] The court considered this issue again in 2013, in light of arguments about changed circumstances in Afghanistan, and reached the same conclusion.[59] (Other issues concerning the war on terrorism are explored in Chapter 10.)

(2011). For a critique of the extraterritoriality analysis in *Boumediene*, especially its treatment of the *Insular Cases*, see Andrew Kent, *Boumediene, Munaf, and the Supreme Court's Misreading of the Insular Cases*, 97 IOWA L. REV. 101 (2011).

[54] *See Munaf v. Geren*, 553 U.S. 674 (2008).
[55] *Id*. at 686–88.
[56] *Id*. at 697.
[57] *See Maqaleh v. Gates*, 605 F.3d 84 (D.C. Cir. 2010).
[58] *See id*. at 364–66. For a discussion of this and other post-*Boumediene* decisions, see Note, *Extraterritoriality and the War on Terror*, 124 HARV. L. REV. 1258 (2011).
[59] *See Al Maqaleh v. Hagel*, 738 F.3d 312 (D.C. Cir. 2013). *But cf.* Doe v. Mattis, 889 F.3d 745 (D.C. Cir. 2018) (disallowing forcible transfer of U.S. citizen from one foreign country to another, despite allegation that the citizen was an Islamic State fighter, unless he was first given an opportunity to contest his status as an enemy combatant).

186 | International Law in the U.S. Legal System

Presumption against Extraterritoriality

Since early in U.S. history, the Supreme Court has stated that it will presume that Congress does not intend to regulate conduct that occurs outside the United States. In an 1818 decision, for example, the Court held that the federal piracy statute did not apply to a robbery committed on the high seas by foreign citizens on board a foreign ship. The Court, in an opinion by Chief Justice Marshall, began by observing that Congress had the constitutional power, pursuant to its authority to "define and punish...Offenses against the Law of Nations," to regulate the conduct in question.[60] The Court also acknowledged that the words of the statute, which purported to cover "any person or persons," were "broad enough to comprehend every human being."[61] The Court nevertheless concluded that the statute did not apply to the defendants' conduct, explaining that such "general words" should not be construed "to embrace [offenses] when committed by foreigners against a foreign government."[62]

The regulation of foreign citizens outside the United States would have been problematic under international law, so the application of a presumption against such extraterritorial regulation was related to the *Charming Betsy* canon of construction, discussed in Chapter 1 and throughout this book, pursuant to which ambiguous federal statutes are construed to avoid violations of international law. As the Supreme Court explained in another early decision:

> The laws of no nation can justly extend beyond its own territories, except so far as regards its own citizens. They can have no force to control the sovereignty or rights of any other nation, within its own jurisdiction. And, however general and comprehensive the phrases used in our municipal laws may be, they must always be restricted in construction, to places and persons, upon whom the Legislature have authority and jurisdiction.[63]

Over time, the Supreme Court broadened the presumption to encompass the extraterritorial regulation of U.S. citizens and corporations as well. It was applied this way, for example, in a famous antitrust law decision in the early 1900s, *American Banana Co. v. United Fruit Co.*[64] In that case, the Supreme Court held that the Sherman Antitrust Act, which declares illegal "[e]very contract, combination in the form of trust or otherwise, or conspiracy, in restraint of trade or commerce among the several States, or with

---

[60] United States v. Palmer, 16 U.S. (3 Wheat.) 610, 630 (1818).
[61] *Id.* at 631.
[62] *Id.* at 632–33.
[63] The Apollon, 22 U.S. (9 Wheat.) 362, 371 (1824).
[64] *See* Am. Banana Co. v. United Fruit Co., 213 U.S. 347 (1909).

foreign nations," did not extend to anticompetitive conduct allegedly committed by a U.S. company in Panama and Costa Rica. The Court said that "in case of doubt," a federal statute should be construed "to be confined in its operation and effect to the territorial limits over which the lawmaker has general and legitimate power."[65] As a result, explained the Court, even statutes with provisions that are "universal [in] scope," such as "every contract," or "every person," will be construed as applying only to conduct within U.S. territory.[66]

After *American Banana*, the Supreme Court applied the presumption against extraterritoriality in a number of cases involving labor-related statutes.[67] In other cases, however, the Supreme Court declined to apply the presumption. The Court held, for example, that the presumption was inapplicable to criminal statutes that "are, as a class, not logically dependent on their locality for the Government's jurisdiction, but are enacted because of the right of the Government to defend itself against obstruction, or fraud wherever perpetrated."[68] The Court also declined to apply the presumption in the context of admiralty law, instead considering a variety of choice-of-law factors.[69] In addition, the Court construed the Lanham Trade-Mark Act to apply to foreign acts of counterfeiting by a U.S. citizen that had effects within the United States.[70] Finally, despite the *American*

---

[65] *Id.* at 357.

[66] *Id.*

[67] *See* Sandberg v. McDonald, 248 U.S. 185, 195–96 (1918) (Seaman's Act); New York Cent. R.R. v. Chisholm, 268 U.S. 29, 31–32 (1925) (Employers' Liability Act); Foley Bros., Inc. v. Filardo, 336 U.S. 281, 285 (1949) (Eight Hour Law); Benz v. Compania Naviera Hidalgo, S.A., 353 U.S. 138, 143–46 (1957) (Labor Management Relations Act); McCulloch v. Sociedad Nacional de Marineros de Honduras, 372 U.S. 10, 19–22 (1963) (National Labor Relations Act).

[68] United States v. Bowman, 260 U.S. 94, 98 (1922). For lower court decisions applying this limitation on the presumption against extraterritoriality, see, for example, United States v. Lawrence, 727 F.3d 386 (5th Cir. 2013) (drug smuggling); United States v. Leija-Sanchez, 602 F.3d 797 (7th Cir. 2010) (violent crimes committed abroad in connection with racketeering in the United States); United States v. Frank, 599 F.3d 1221 (11th Cir. 2010) (purchasing of a minor for sexual conduct); United States v. Delgado-Garcia, 374 F.3d 1337 (D.C. Cir. 2004) (attempted smuggling of aliens into the United States); *see also* United States v. Vilar, 729 F.3d 62, 73 (2d Cir. 2013) ("In other words, the presumption against extraterritoriality *does* apply to criminal statutes, except in situations where the law at issue is aimed at protecting 'the right of the government to defend itself.' "). *Cf.* United States v. Sota, 948 F.3d 356 (D.C. Cir. 2020) (requiring a "high probability that the criminalized conduct would occur abroad" as a prerequisite for applying this limitation on the presumption against extraterritoriality). For a general discussion of the extraterritorial application of U.S. criminal law, *see* Charles Doyle, *Extraterritorial Application of American Criminal Law* (Cong. Res. Serv., Oct. 31, 2016), *available at* http://www.fas.org/sgp/crs/misc/94-166.pdf.

[69] In a case involving the Jones Act (which governs personal injury claims by seamen), the Supreme Court treated the issue of extraterritoriality as if it were simply a matter of weighing modern choice-of-law factors, without referring to the presumption against extraterritoriality. *See* Lauritzen v. Larsen, 345 U.S. 571, 583 (1953); *see also* Romero v. Int'l Terminal Operating Co., 358 U.S. 354, 381–84 (1959) (applying *Lauritzen* test to claims under both Jones Act and general maritime law, with respect to injury in U.S. waters).

[70] *See* Steele v. Bulova Watch Co., 344 U.S. 280, 285 (1952); *see also* McBee v. Delica Co., 417 F.3d 107, 118 (1st Cir. 2005) ("The *Steele* Court concluded that an American citizen could not evade the thrust of the laws of the United States by moving his operations to a 'privileged sanctuary' beyond our borders."). For additional

Banana decision, the Court has moved away from the presumption against extraterritoriality in the area of antitrust law.[71]

By the early 1990s, a number of scholars had questioned whether the presumption against extraterritoriality still made sense in the modern era.[72] Critics of the presumption pointed out that (as discussed in the next section) the acceptable grounds under international law for national regulation have expanded and now include the ability to regulate extraterritorial conduct that has effects within a nation's territory. The critics also noted that the general approach to choice of law, both in the United States and in other countries, had become more flexible, and less territorial, than when cases such as *American Banana* were decided. Furthermore, the critics contended that Congress is now more globally focused than in the past, making a presumption against extraterritoriality a poor predictor of likely congressional intent.

Despite these arguments, the Supreme Court strongly reaffirmed the presumption against extraterritoriality in a 1991 decision, *EEOC v. Arabian American Oil Co.*[73] In that case, the Court held that Title VII of the Civil Rights Act, which prohibits various types of employment discrimination, did not apply to the employment practices of a U.S. company overseas, even with respect to a U.S.-citizen employee. The Court explained that the presumption against extraterritoriality is a "longstanding principle of American law" that "serves to protect against unintended clashes between our laws and those of other nations which could result in international discord."[74] The Court also noted that it assumes that

---

discussion of *Steele*, *see* Curtis A. Bradley, *Territorial Intellectual Property Rights in an Age of Globalism*, 37 VA. J. INT'L L. 505, 526–29 (1997).

[71] *See* United States v. Sisal Corp., 274 U.S. 268, 276 (1927) (applying Sherman Antitrust Act to "deliberate acts, here and elsewhere, [that] brought about forbidden results within the United States"); United States v. Pacific & Arctic Ry., 228 U.S. 87, 105–106 (1913) (applying Sherman Act to combination formed in United States to monopolize certain transportation partly within and partly without the United States). In 1945, the U.S. Court of Appeals for the Second Circuit, in a case referred to it by the Supreme Court because the Court could not obtain a quorum of disinterested justices, held that U.S. antitrust law applies to agreements made abroad "if they were intended to affect imports and did affect them." United States v. Aluminum Co. of Am., 148 F.2d 416, 444 (2d Cir. 1945) (en banc). The Supreme Court appeared to endorse this idea in subsequent cases. *See* Matsushita Elec. Indus. Co. v. Zenith Radio Corp., 475 U.S. 574, 582 n.6 (1985); Continental Ore Co. v. Union Carbide & Carbon Corp., 370 U.S. 690, 704 (1962). In 1982, Congress enacted the Foreign Trade Antitrust Improvements Act (FTAIA) in order to clarify the application of U.S. antitrust laws to foreign conduct. The FTAIA provides that the Sherman Act "shall not apply to conduct involving trade or commerce . . . with foreign nations (other than import trade or import commerce)" unless the conduct has "a direct, substantial and reasonably foreseeable effect" on domestic commerce, U.S. imports, or U.S. exports, and "such effect gives rise to a claim" under the Sherman Act.

[72] *See, e.g.*, Gary B. Born, *A Reappraisal of the Extraterritorial Reach of U.S. Law*, 24 LAW & POL'Y INT'L BUS. 1 (1992); Larry Kramer, *Vestiges of Beale: Extraterritorial Application of American Law*, 1991 SUP. CT. REV. 179; Jonathan Turley, *"When in Rome": Multinational Misconduct and the Presumption against Extraterritoriality*, 84 NW. U. L. REV. 598 (1990).

[73] EEOC v. Arabian Am. Oil Co., 499 U.S. 244 (1991).

[74] *Id.* at 248.

Congress "'is primarily concerned with domestic conditions.'"[75] Congress legislates "against the backdrop" of the presumption against extraterritoriality, said the Court, and it found insufficient indications in Title VII that Congress intended to overcome the presumption.[76] If Congress wished to apply Title VII extraterritorially, the Court explained, it could amend the statute "and in doing so will be able to calibrate its provisions in a way that we cannot."[77]

The Court continued to endorse the presumption in subsequent decisions.[78] In those decisions, it made clear that the presumption is applicable even when there is no risk of a clash with the laws of foreign nations, because the presumption is also based on "the commonsense notion that Congress generally legislates with domestic concerns in mind."[79] The Court also confirmed, however, that antitrust law was not subject to the presumption. In *Hartford Fire Insurance Co. v. California*, the Court explained that "[a]lthough the proposition was perhaps not always free from doubt, see *American Banana Co. v. United Fruit Co. . . .*, it is well established by now that the Sherman Act applies to foreign conduct that was meant to produce and did in fact produce some substantial effect in the United States."[80] In that case, the Court held that the Act could be applied to an alleged conspiracy among foreign insurance companies to affect the U.S. insurance market.

Justice Scalia dissented in *Hartford Fire*, but he did not argue for application of the presumption against extraterritoriality. While noting that "if the question were not governed by precedent, it would be worth considering whether that presumption controls the outcome here," he conceded that "it is now well established that the Sherman Act applies extraterritorially."[81] Instead, he argued that the Court had neglected to consider the *Charming Betsy* canon of construction, which, as noted earlier, requires U.S. courts to construe statutes, where reasonably possible, so that they do not violate international law. He noted that, according to the *Restatement (Third) of Foreign Relations Law*, international law requires nations to take account of various "reasonableness" or "comity" factors when applying laws extraterritoriality, and he complained that the majority in *Hartford Fire* had failed to do so.[82]

---

[75] *Id.* at 248 (quoting *Foley Bros.*, 336 U.S. at 285).
[76] *Id.*
[77] *Id.* at 259. In response to the decision, Congress amended Title VII to make clear that it applied to the treatment of U.S. citizens overseas by U.S.-controlled employers but that it did not require the employers to violate the law of the country in which the workplace is located. *See* Civil Rights Act of 1991, Pub. L. No. 102–166, 105 Stat. 1071 (*codified at* 42 U.S.C. § 2000e(f)).
[78] *See* Microsoft Corp. v. AT&T Corp., 550 U.S. 437, 455 (2007); Sale v. Haitian Ctrs. Council, Inc., 509 U.S. 155, 173–74 (1993); Smith v. United States, 507 U.S. 197, 204 (1993).
[79] *Smith*, 507 U.S. at 204 n.5.
[80] Hartford Fire Ins. Co. v. California, 509 U.S. 764, 795–96 (1993).
[81] *Id.* at 814 (Scalia, J., dissenting).
[82] In antitrust cases before *Hartford Fire*, some lower courts had adopted multifactored "comity" tests designed to take account of the interests of foreign nations. *See, e.g.*, Mannington Mills v. Congoleum, 595 F.2d 1287 (3d Cir. 1979); Timberlane Lumber Co. v. Bank of America, 549 F.2d 597 (9th Cir. 1976). It is unclear to

In a subsequent antitrust decision, *Hoffman-La Roche Ltd. v. Empagran S.A.*, the Court moved toward Justice Scalia's position.[83] In that case, purchasers of vitamins filed a class action suit alleging that various vitamin manufacturers and distributors had engaged in a conspiracy to raise vitamin prices in the United States and foreign countries, in violation of U.S. antitrust law. The issue before the Supreme Court was whether foreign purchasers of the vitamins could maintain an action under the Sherman Act for their foreign harm. In concluding that the Act does not apply to the foreign effects of foreign anticompetitive conduct, the Court explained that "this Court ordinarily construes ambiguous statutes to avoid unreasonable interference with the sovereign authority of other nations.... This rule of construction reflects principles of customary international law—law that (we must assume) Congress ordinarily seeks to follow."[84] The Court cited to the *Charming Betsy* decision, the *Restatement*, and Justice Scalia's dissent in *Hartford Fire*.[85]

The Court again affirmed the presumption against extraterritoriality in an important 2010 decision, *Morrison v. National Australia Bank*.[86] The issue there was whether the federal securities fraud statute—Section 10(b) of the Securities Exchange Act of 1934—applied to allegedly fraudulent activities in the United States that affected only securities listed on foreign exchanges. For many years, the lower federal courts had applied the statute when there were either substantial effects or significant conduct in the United States, on the theory that Congress would have wanted the statute to apply in those situations.[87] The Supreme Court, in an opinion by Justice Scalia, firmly rejected that approach, explaining that "[r]ather than guess anew in each case [about Congress's intent], we apply the presumption in all cases, preserving a stable background against which Congress can legislate with predictable effects."[88] The Court then proceeded to find that the allegations

---

what extent the majority in *Hartford Fire* disapproved of such comity analysis. Some commentators construed the decision as limiting comity analysis to situations involving a "true conflict"—that is, to situations in which compliance with U.S. law would violate foreign law. *See, e.g.*, Roger P. Alford, *The Extraterritorial Application of Antitrust Laws: A Postscript on* Hartford Fire Insurance Co. v. California, 34 VA. J. INT'L L. 213, 220 (1993); Larry Kramer, *Extraterritorial Application of American Law after the Insurance Antitrust Case: A Reply to Professors Lowenfeld and Trimble*, 89 AM. J. INT'L L. 750, 754 (1995); Robert C. Reuland, Hartford Fire Insurance Co., *Comity, and the Extraterritorial Reach of United States Antitrust Laws*, 29 TEX. INT'L L.J. 159, 161 (1994). *But see* Bradley, *supra* note 70, at 557–60 (contesting that interpretation).

[83] F. Hoffman-La Roche, Ltd. v. Empagran S.A., 542 U.S. 155 (2004).

[84] *Id.* at 164.

[85] The Court rejected an approach, however, whereby courts could take account of comity factors on a case-by-case basis, reasoning that such an approach was "too complex to prove workable." *Id.* at 168.

[86] Morrison v. Nat'l Australian Bank Ltd., 561 U.S. 247 (2010).

[87] *See, e.g.*, Itoba Ltd. v. LEP Group PLC, 54 F.3d 118, 121–22 (2d Cir. 1995); Bersch v. Drexel Firestone, Inc., 519 F. 2d 974, 985 (2d Cir. 1975); Schoenbaum v. Firstbrook, 405 F.2d 200, 208–209, *rev'd on other grounds*, 405 F.2d 215 (2d Cir. 1968) (en banc). *But cf.* Zoelsch v. Arthur Andersen & Co., 824 F. 2d 27, 32 (D.C. Cir. 1987) ("Were it not for the Second Circuit's preeminence in the field of securities law, and our desire to avoid a multiplicity of jurisdictional tests, we might be inclined to doubt that an American court should ever assert jurisdiction over domestic conduct that causes loss to foreign investors.").

[88] 561 U.S. at 261.

in this case did not satisfy the presumption against extraterritoriality. "The focus of the Exchange Act is not upon the place where the deception originated," the Court reasoned, "but upon purchases and sales of securities in the United States."[89] The Court concluded that, because "[t]his case involves no securities listed on a domestic exchange, and all aspects of the purchases complained of by those petitioners who still have live claims occurred outside the United States," the petitioners had failed to state a claim under the Act.[90]

As discussed in more detail in Chapter 7, the Alien Tort Statute (ATS), which was first enacted in 1789, provides that "[t]he district courts shall have original jurisdiction of any civil action by an alien for a tort only, committed in violation of the law of nations or a treaty of the United States."[91] In *Kiobel v. Royal Dutch Petroleum Co.*, the Supreme Court held that the presumption against extraterritoriality applies to claims brought under the ATS.[92] Even though the statute is jurisdictional and does not directly prescribe conduct, the Court explained that "the danger of unwarranted judicial interference in the conduct of foreign policy is magnified in the context of the ATS, because the question is not what Congress has done but instead what courts may do."[93] The Court also noted that, even though the ATS may seem to have a transnational focus in referring to torts committed against aliens in violation of international law, "that does not imply extraterritorial reach—such violations affecting aliens can occur either within or outside the United States."[94]

Despite these decisions, the presumption against extraterritoriality continues to be controversial among academic commentators. Some commentators have called for refashioning the presumption—for example, by limiting it to situations in which the conduct in question does not have substantial effects within the United States,[95] or by aligning it more closely to international law principles of prescriptive jurisdiction.[96] As

---

[89] *Id.* at 266.

[90] Congress quickly responded to *Morrison* by amending the Securities Exchange Act to provide that the federal courts have jurisdiction to hear actions brought by the Justice Department and Securities and Exchange Commission (SEC) under the Act based on either: "(1) conduct within the United States that constitutes significant steps in furtherance of the violation, even if the securities transaction occurs outside the United States and involves only foreign investors; or (2) conduct occurring outside the United States that has foreseeable substantial effect within the United States." The statute does not, however, authorize private suits for these situations. Rather, in a separate provision, Congress directed the SEC to solicit public comment and "conduct a study to determine the extent to which private rights of action" under the Exchange Act should apply extraterritorially, and to report the results of its study to Congress. *See* Dodd-Frank Wall Street Reform and Consumer Protection Act, Pub. L. No. 111–203, 124 Stat. 1376, § 929P(b).

[91] 28 U.S.C. § 1350.

[92] 569 U.S. 108 (2013).

[93] *Id.* at 109.

[94] *Id.* at 118.

[95] *See* William S. Dodge, *Understanding the Presumption against Extraterritoriality*, 16 BERKELEY J. INT'L L. 85 (1998).

[96] *See* John H. Knox, *A Presumption against Extrajurisdictionality*, 104 AM. J. INT'L L. 351 (2010).

this author has argued, however, one potential virtue of the Supreme Court's approach to the presumption is that it provides a fairly bright-line backdrop against which Congress can legislate and parties can plan their activities.[97] Some critics of the presumption point out that Congress quickly responded to *Arabian American Oil* by amending Title VII to make clear that it applied extraterritorially, a development that shows, the critics contend, that the presumption does not reflect likely congressional intent.[98] Instead of being seen as an indictment of the presumption, however, this development could be seen as a vindication of it. In amending Title VII, Congress made clear that it wanted Title VII to apply extraterritorially only to U.S.-controlled firms, and that it did not want the statute to compel firms to take actions that would violate foreign law. This sort of calibration of the extraterritorial scope of a statute is what the presumption is designed to elicit, and the policy judgment that such calibration requires is arguably better exercised by the elected legislature than by unelected judges.[99]

Even if the presumption against extraterritoriality provides a brighter line than a more contextual approach, its application will not always be obvious merely by looking at the text of a statute. The Supreme Court in *Morrison* explained that, although Congress must provide a "clear indication" of extraterritorial intent to overcome the presumption, it is appropriate for a court to consult the "context" of a statutory provision as well as its text in determining whether Congress has provided such an indication.[100] In addition, as *Morrison* itself illustrates, in some cases in which conduct has occurred both within and outside the United States, it will be necessary to determine which type of conduct Congress intended to regulate in order to know whether the plaintiff is seeking extraterritorial application of the statute, and that determination may require some judicial judgment about the statute's purposes. That is, it will be necessary to determine the "focus" of the statute. In *Morrison*, the Court concluded that the focus of the securities fraud statute was "not upon the place where the deception originated, but upon purchases and sales of securities in the United States,"[101] and thus that the application of the statute would still

---

[97] *See* Bradley, *supra* note 70, at 551–57.
[98] *See, e.g.*, RAUSTIALA, *supra* note 2, at 113, 172, 177.
[99] *See* EINER ELHAUGE, STATUTORY DEFAULT RULES: HOW TO INTERPRET UNCLEAR LEGISLATION 205 (2008) (defending the decision on these grounds); *see also* Bradley, *supra* note 70, at 550–54 (making similar argument); Austen Parrish, *The Effects Test: Extraterritoriality's Fifth Business*, 61 VAND. L. REV. 1455, 1497 (2008) ("The idea [behind the presumption against extraterritoriality] is based much more on notions of legislative primacy and the practical considerations of avoiding foreign resentment."); Cass R. Sunstein, *Interpreting Statutes in the Regulatory State*, 103 HARV. L. REV. 405, 477 (1989) ("Courts should construe statutes so that those who are politically accountable and highly visible will make regulatory decisions.").
[100] 561 U.S. at 265. *See also, e.g.*, United States v. Delgado-Garcia, 374 F.3d 1337, 1345 (D.C. Cir. 2004) ("[I]n examining the statute for congressional intention of extraterritorial application, we consider both contextual and textual evidence.").
[101] 561 U.S. at 266.

be extraterritorial in that case despite the fact that certain deceptive acts had allegedly taken place in the United States.[102]

In a subsequent decision, *RJR Nabisco, Inc. v. European Community*, the Court made clear that this "focus" inquiry comes into play only if the presumption against extraterritoriality has not been overcome.[103] In that case, the Court found that the presumption had been rebutted with respect to some applications of the Racketeer Influenced and Corrupt Organizations Act (RICO) because RICO incorporated by reference other statutes that were extraterritorial. "While the presumption can be overcome only by a clear indication of extraterritorial effect," the Court explained, "an express statement of extraterritoriality is not essential."[104] And for these extraterritorial applications of RICO, the Court made clear, no additional consideration of the "focus" of the statute was required.[105]

International Law Limits on Prescriptive Jurisdiction

It is generally thought that customary international law imposes limitations on "prescriptive jurisdiction"—that is, on the authority of each nation to apply its criminal and other regulatory laws to persons and activities. According to most international law commentators, there are five basic categories of prescriptive jurisdiction: territoriality, nationality, the protective principle, passive personality, and universality.[106] (The territoriality category is sometimes divided into two categories, one covering conduct within a territory and the other covering effects within a territory.) United States courts regularly refer to these bases (each of which will be discussed) in considering the extraterritorial

---

[102] For an argument that the Court in *Morrison* "introduced a new factor into the treatment of extraterritoriality that will give rise to new levels of unpredictability, as lower courts try to guess what the Supreme Court would consider to be the focus of the statutes at issue," see John H. Knox, *The Unpredictable Presumption against Extraterritoriality*, 40 SW. L. REV. 635, 645 (2011).

[103] 136 S. Ct. 2090 (2016).

[104] *Id.* at 2102.

[105] *Id.* at 2103–204. The Court concluded, however, that the presumption against extraterritoriality was not overcome with respect to the private cause of action provision in RICO. The Court explained: "we separately apply the presumption against extraterritoriality to RICO's cause of action despite our conclusion that the presumption has been overcome with respect to RICO's substantive prohibitions" because "providing a private civil remedy for foreign conduct creates a potential for international friction beyond that presented by merely applying U.S. substantive law to that foreign conduct." *Id.* at 2106. For an argument that *Morrison* articulated a new, more flexible version of the presumption against extraterritoriality and that this was confirmed in *RJR Nabisco*, see William S. Dodge, *The New Presumption Against Extraterritoriality*, 133 HARV. L. REV. 1582 (2020).

[106] *See, e.g.*, JAMES CRAWFORD, BROWNLIE'S PRINCIPLES OF PUBLIC INTERNATIONAL LAW 441–48 (9th ed. 2019); I.A. SHEARER, STARKE'S INTERNATIONAL LAW ch. 8 (11th ed. 1994); RESTATEMENT (FOURTH) OF THE FOREIGN RELATIONS LAW OF THE UNITED STATES § 407 (2018). *See also* Harvard Research in International Law, *Jurisdiction with Respect to Crime*, 29 AM. J. INT'L L. 474 (1935).

application of federal statutes. Another circumstance under which the exercise of prescriptive jurisdiction is permissible is when one nation specifically agrees with another nation (for example, in a treaty) to allow the other nation to regulate within the first nation's territory. If nothing else, this category follows from the proposition that nations can override customary international law by agreement.

Some commentators have argued that, in addition to falling within one of the above categories, exercises of prescriptive jurisdiction (other than universal jurisdiction) must also be reasonable. The *Restatement (Third) of Foreign Relations Law* endorsed such a limitation, and listed the following factors that should be considered in determining whether the exercise of jurisdiction is reasonable:

(a) the link of the activity to the territory of the regulating state, i.e., the extent to which the activity takes place within the territory, or has substantial, direct, and foreseeable effect upon or in the territory;
(b) the connections, such as nationality, residence, or economic activity, between the regulating state and the person principally responsible for the activity to be regulated, or between that state and those whom the regulation is designed to protect;
(c) the character of the activity to be regulated, the importance of regulation to the regulating state, the extent to which other states regulate such activities, and the degree to which the desirability of such regulation is generally accepted;
(d) the existence of justified expectations that might be protected or hurt by the regulation;
(e) the importance of the regulation to the international political, legal, or economic system;
(f) the extent to which the regulation is consistent with the traditions of the international system;
(g) the extent to which another state may have an interest in regulating the activity; and
(h) the likelihood of conflict with regulation by another state.[107]

There has been debate, however, over whether these considerations are in fact required by international law,[108] and the *Restatement (Fourth)* has taken the position that the

---

[107] RESTATEMENT (THIRD) OF THE FOREIGN RELATIONS LAW OF THE UNITED STATES § 403(2) (1987).
[108] *Compare* Philip R. Trimble, *The Supreme Court and International Law: The Demise of Restatement Section 403*, 89 AM. J. INT'L L. 53 (1995) (arguing that international law does not contain reasonableness limitation), *with* ANDREAS F. LOWENFELD, INTERNATIONAL LITIGATION AND THE QUEST FOR REASONABLENESS (1996) (defending reasonableness limitation on jurisdiction to prescribe). *See also* David B. Massey, Note, *How the American Law Institute Influences Customary Law: The Reasonableness Requirement of the Restatement of Foreign Relations Law*, 22 YALE J. INT'L L. 419 (1997).

reasonableness considerations are merely matters of "prescriptive comity"—that is, something that U.S. courts voluntarily consider when interpreting statutes.[109]

To understand the effect of the international law of prescriptive jurisdiction on U.S. law, it is important to recall the status of customary international law within the U.S. legal system, a topic addressed in Chapter 5. As discussed there, it is well settled that, when there is a clear conflict between a federal statute and customary international law, U.S. courts will apply the statute. This means that, as a matter of U.S. law, Congress can exceed the limitations on prescriptive jurisdiction described earlier.[110] Nevertheless, U.S. courts also apply the *Charming Betsy* canon of construction, pursuant to which ambiguous federal statutes are construed, where fairly possible, so that they do not violate international law.[111] As a result, the customary international law governing prescriptive jurisdiction can influence how U.S. courts construe the extraterritorial reach of federal statutes.[112] These international law considerations will arise, however, only if the presumption against extraterritoriality, discussed in this section, is either overcome or is inapplicable.

Prescriptive jurisdiction over conduct or persons within a nation's territorial boundaries has long been uncontroversial. Indeed, the view during the nineteenth century was that a nation had essentially absolute regulatory control over what happened in its borders and essentially no control over what happened outside its borders (except perhaps with respect to the actions of its citizens).[113] In the twentieth century, the concept of territorial jurisdiction expanded to include conduct outside of a nation's territory that had certain effects within the territory. The Permanent Court of International Justice endorsed such effects-based jurisdiction in the widely discussed 1927 decision, *The Case of the S.S. Lotus*.[114] In *Lotus*, a French steamship and a Turkish steamship collided on the high seas, causing eight Turkish nationals to die. The international court held that Turkey

---

[109] *See* RESTATEMENT (FOURTH) OF THE FOREIGN RELATIONS LAW OF THE UNITED STATES, *supra* note 106, § 405.

[110] *See, e.g.*, Lea Brilmayer, *International Law in American Courts: A Modest Proposal*, 100 YALE L.J. 2277, 2287 n.54 (1991) ("It seems well established that Congress may, if it chooses, specify greater extraterritorial scope than international law would allow, since Congress generally is held to have the power to violate international law."); Harold G. Maier, *Extraterritorial Jurisdiction at a Crossroads: An Intersection between Public and Private International Law*, 76 AM. J. INT'L L. 280, 291 (1982) ("Whenever Congress acts within its broad constitutional powers and clearly intends that the statute in question shall be applied in the situation before the court, the court must apply the legislation even though that application would violate international law.").

[111] *See* F. Hoffman-La Roche Ltd. v. Empagran S.A., 542 U.S. 155, 164 (2004); McCulloch v. Sociedad Nacional de Marineros de Honduras, 372 U.S. 10, 21 (1963); *see also* Hartford Fire Ins. Co. v. California, 509 U.S. 764, 814–16 (1993) (Scalia, J., dissenting).

[112] *See, e.g.,* United States v. Ali, 718 F.3d 929, 934 (D.C. Cir. 2013) ("Because international law itself limits a state's authority to apply its laws beyond its borders, . . . *Charming Betsy* operates alongside the presumption against extraterritorial effect to check the exercise of U.S. criminal jurisdiction."); United States v. Weingarten, 632 F.3d 60, 64 (2d Cir. 2011) (noting that "our review of the statutory text occurs against the backdrop of [these] two well-established presumptions").

[113] *See, e.g.*, JOSEPH STORY, COMMENTARIES ON THE CONFLICT OF LAWS 19, 21–22 (2d ed. 1841).

[114] 1927 PCIJ, Ser. A, No. 10.

could apply its criminal laws to a French officer on the French ship, on the theory that his negligence had caused the collision. This was true even though a ship is treated like the territory of the nation to which it is registered, which meant that the French officer's negligence technically occurred on the equivalent of French territory.

Although effects-based jurisdiction is generally accepted, its proper scope is unclear, and there is often dispute about how direct, substantial, and intended the effects need to be. Such controversy has been evident, for example, with respect to U.S. application of its antitrust laws to foreign conduct.[115] In that area, controversies over U.S. extraterritoriality have sometimes become sufficiently intense that other countries have issued diplomatic protests and even enacted retaliatory legislation such as blocking provisions (disallowing enforcement of U.S. judgments) and clawback remedies (allowing lawsuits to recover the damages awarded in U.S. proceedings).[116] In an effort to reduce tensions, the United States has entered into cooperation agreements with a number of countries and the European Union concerning the application of antitrust law.[117]

Somewhat similar conflicts over the scope of the effects doctrine arose in connection with the U.S. enactment of the Cuban Liberty and Democratic Solidarity Act of 1996, also known as the "Helms-Burton Act."[118] Title III of that Act gives U.S. citizens a cause of action against anyone "trafficking" in property confiscated by Cuba since 1959. Trafficking is defined broadly to include not only trading in the confiscated property, but also engaging in commercial activity using the property or otherwise benefiting from the property. This law generated significant foreign protest, and the European Union and some individual countries enacted blocking statutes and clawback provisions.[119] Notably, Title III contains a clause allowing the president to suspend the cause of action for renewable six-month terms, and presidents repeatedly invoked this waiver clause. In 2019, however, President Donald Trump announced that he would end the suspension and allow suits to begin.[120] Commentators have debated whether the statute can be justified under the effects doctrine.[121]

---

[115] *See, e.g.*, Roger P. Alford, *The Extraterritorial Application of Antitrust Laws: The United States and European Community Approaches*, 33 VA. J. INT'L L. 1 (1992).

[116] *See* GARY B. BORN & PETER B. RUTLEDGE, INTERNATIONAL CIVIL LITIGATION IN UNITED STATES COURTS 665–67 (6th ed. 2018) (describing foreign protests and other resistance to extraterritorial applications of U.S. antitrust law).

[117] *See* U.S. Department of Justice, *Antitrust Cooperation Agreements*, available at http://www.justice.gov/atr/public/international/int-arrangements.html.

[118] *See* Pub. L. No. 104–114, § 302, 110 Stat. 785, 815–18 (1996) (*codified at* 22 U.S.C. §§ 6081–85).

[119] For a description of some of the foreign protests against the Act, *see* Steven Lee Myers, *Clinton Troubleshooter Discovers Big Trouble from Allies on Cuba*, N.Y. TIMES (Oct. 23, 1996), at A1.

[120] *See* Peter Baker, *To Pressure Cuba, Trump Plans to Lift Limits on American Lawsuits*, N.Y. TIMES (Apr. 16, 2019).

[121] *Compare* Andreas F. Lowenfeld, *Congress and Cuba: The Helms-Burton Act*, 90 AM. J. INT'L L. 419 (1996) (arguing that the statute cannot be justified under the effects doctrine), *with* Brice M. Clagett, *Title III of the Helms-Burton Act Is Consistent with International Law*, 90 AM. J. INT'L L. 434 (1996) (arguing that the statute can be justified under the effects doctrine).

The effects doctrine overlaps with what is sometimes referred to as the *objective territorial principle*, which concerns situations in which the harmful consequences of an activity occur within the regulating nation's borders. This can be distinguished from the *subjective territorial principle*, which involves situations in which activities are carried out in the regulating nation's territory but the harm from the activities occurs elsewhere. The subjective territorial principle appears to be an accepted basis in international practice for exercising jurisdiction over at least some crimes, such as counterfeiting, drug trafficking, and terrorism, and a number of U.S. criminal laws are premised on the idea that U.S. territory should not serve as a haven for criminal activities consummated elsewhere.[122]

Separate from territoriality, it has long been accepted that nations have broad authority to regulate the conduct of their own nationals around the world. The Supreme Court invoked this principle in a 1932 decision, *Blackmer v. United States*.[123] The issue there was whether the federal contempt statute could be applied to a U.S. citizen living in France who had failed to respond to a subpoena directing him to appear as a witness in a criminal case in the United States. The Court noted that "there is no question of international law" being violated because "[b]y virtue of the obligations of citizenship, the United States retained its authority over him, and he was bound by its laws made applicable to him in a foreign country."[124] An example of an expansive regulation of U.S. nationals, involving the criminalization of "sex tourism," will be discussed in connection with a consideration of Congress's constitutional authority to regulate foreign commerce.

In some circumstances, the United States has sought to regulate companies incorporated under the law of foreign nations when those companies are "owned or controlled" by U.S. citizens or corporations, including foreign subsidiaries of U.S. companies and banks. This has occurred, for example, in connection with economic sanctions and export restrictions imposed under statutes such as the International Emergency Economic Powers Act.[125] Regulations adopted by the executive branch at various times have taken the position that foreign corporations that are owned or controlled by U.S. corporations are "subject to the jurisdiction of the United States" for purposes of these statutes. Such regulations have often generated foreign protests and sometimes overt efforts by foreign governments to assist the foreign companies in flouting the U.S. restrictions.[126] There

---

[122] *See, e.g.*, 18 U.S.C. § 956(a)(1) ("Whoever, within the jurisdiction of the United States, conspires with one or more other persons, regardless of where such other person or persons are located, to commit at any place outside the United States an act that would constitute the offense of murder, kidnapping, or maiming if committed in the special maritime and territorial jurisdiction of the United States shall, if any of the conspirators commits an act within the jurisdiction of the United States to effect any object of the conspiracy, be punished....").

[123] *See* 284 U.S. 421 (1932).

[124] *Id.* at 437.

[125] *See, e.g.*, KENNETH A. RODMAN, SANCTIONS BEYOND BORDERS: MULTINATIONAL CORPORATIONS AND U.S. ECONOMIC STATECRAFT (2001).

[126] *See* Harry L. Clark, *Dealing with U.S. Extraterritorial Sanctions and Foreign Countermeasures*, 25 U. PA. J. INT'L ECON. L. 455 (2004).

is nothing definitive in international law regarding the legality of these types of regulations,[127] but European countries have often alleged that these regulations violate international law, as being neither within the nationality category nor the effects doctrine.

Nationality-based jurisdiction was also part of the basis for Congress's enactment of the Foreign Corrupt Practices Act (FCPA).[128] Originally enacted in 1977, the FCPA (among other things) makes it a criminal offense for U.S. citizens and companies, and certain foreign issuers of securities, to pay bribes to foreign officials for the purpose of obtaining or retaining business. In response to concerns that the FCPA imposed an unfair burden on U.S. companies vis-à-vis their foreign competitors, Congress in 1988 added certain affirmative defenses that could be invoked by those charged under the Act, including that the payment was lawful under the written laws of the foreign country.[129] Eventually, the United States led the way in developing a treaty relating to bribery, under the auspices of the Organization for Economic Cooperation and Development (OECD). This OECD Convention, which has been ratified by over forty countries, provides that:

> Each Party shall take such measures as may be necessary to establish that it is a criminal offence under its law for any person intentionally to offer, promise or give any undue pecuniary or other advantage, whether directly or through intermediaries, to a foreign public official, for that official or for a third party, in order that the official act or refrain from acting in relation to the performance of official duties, in order to obtain or retain business or other improper advantage in the conduct of international business.[130]

Congress amended the FCPA in 1999 to implement the Convention.[131]

Another fairly well-recognized basis for prescriptive jurisdiction is the protective principle, which allows for jurisdiction over foreign conduct that threatens the security of a state or the integrity of its government operations. Examples include acts, and intended acts, of espionage, counterfeiting of currency, and falsification of official documents. This category could be seen as a special subset of the effects doctrine. It may be treated separately because, as already noted, the effects test may require substantial effects (or intended effects) in the regulating nation's territory, whereas the protective principle may

---

[127] Section 414 of the *Restatement (Third) of Foreign Relations Law* states that "ordinarily" a state may not engage in such regulations, but it also notes that the regulations may be allowable in "exceptional cases," and it defines exceptional cases to include situations in which compliance by the subsidiaries is needed for effective implementation of a national program. *See also* RESTATEMENT (FOURTH) OF THE FOREIGN RELATIONS LAW OF THE UNITED STATES, *supra* note 106, § 410.

[128] *See* 15 U.S.C. §§ 78dd–1 *et seq.*

[129] *See id.* § 78dd–2(c).

[130] Convention on Combating Bribery of Foreign Public Officials in International Business Transactions, art. I(1), Dec. 18, 1997, S. TREATY DOC. No. 105–43, 37 ILM 1 (entered into force Feb. 15, 1999).

[131] *See* International Anti-Bribery and Fair Competition Act of 1998, Pub. L. No. 105–366, 112 Stat. 3302.

not.¹³² In some of its drug trafficking provisions, the United States has referred to the protective principle, although this is a somewhat controversial use of the doctrine.¹³³

Yet another category of prescriptive jurisdiction is the passive personality category, which would allow nations to assert jurisdiction, especially criminal jurisdiction, over aliens who injure their nationals abroad. Historically, the United States disputed the validity of this category of jurisdiction. For example, in the *Cutting Case* in 1887, the Secretary of State protested when Mexico arrested a U.S. citizen for libeling a Mexican citizen in the United States.¹³⁴ In recent years, however, the United States and other countries have increasingly relied on this category of jurisdiction as a basis for regulating terrorist and other attacks directed at their citizens.¹³⁵

Finally, there is substantial support today for the concept of "universal jurisdiction," which allows all nations to regulate certain heinous crimes, regardless of where the crimes are committed or the nationality of the perpetrator.¹³⁶ The historical roots of the universal jurisdiction concept are said to lie with the criminal prosecution of pirates in the eighteenth and nineteenth centuries on the theory that they were *hostis humani generis*— enemies of all mankind. The United States has had a federal piracy statute since 1790.¹³⁷ The current statute provides that "Whoever, on the high seas, commits the crime of piracy as defined by the law of nations, and is afterwards brought into or found in the United States, shall be imprisoned for life."¹³⁸ In an early decision involving a predecessor to this statute, the Supreme Court held that Congress's definition of piracy by reference to the law of nations was sufficiently precise.¹³⁹ The Court reasoned that the crime of piracy had

---

[132] *See, e.g.,* United States v. Saac, 632 F.3d 1203, 1211 (11th Cir. 2011) ("'The protective principle does not require that there be proof of an actual or intended effect inside the United States.'") (quoting United States v. Gonzalez, 776 F.2d 931, 939 (11th Cir. 1985)).

[133] *See, e.g., Saac*, 632 F.3d at 1211; United States v. Cardales, 168 F.3d 548, 553 (1st Cir. 1999). *See also* 21 U.S.C. § 959(c) (making clear that the drug statute "is intended to reach acts of manufacture or distribution committed outside the territorial jurisdiction of the United States").

[134] *See* 2 JOHN BASSETT MOORE, INTERNATIONAL LAW DIGEST 232–40 (1906); *see also* RESTATEMENT (SECOND) OF FOREIGN RELATIONS LAW OF THE UNITED STATES § 30(2) (1965) (rejecting passive personality principle).

[135] *See, e.g.,* United States v. Yousef, 327 F.3d 56, 96 (2d Cir. 2003); United States v. Yunis, 924 F.2d 1086, 1091 (D.C. Cir. 1991). For a broader application of the passive personality concept, *see* United States v. Neil, 312 F.3d 419 (9th Cir. 2002) (reasoning that extraterritorial application of statute criminalizing sexual conduct with a minor was justified under the passive personality doctrine where the victim was a U.S. citizen passenger on a foreign cruise ship).

[136] For a general discussion of universal jurisdiction, *see* Kenneth C. Randall, *Universal Jurisdiction under International Law*, 66 TEX. L. REV. 785 (1988).

[137] *See, e.g.,* United States v. Furlong, 18 U.S. (5 Wheat.) 184, 197 (1820) ("Robbery on the seas is considered as an offense within the criminal jurisdiction of all nations."); United States v. Klintock, 18 U.S. (5 Wheat.) 144, 152 (1820) ("[G]eneral piracy, or murder, or robbery . . . by persons on board of a vessel not at the time belonging to the subjects of any foreign power, but in possession of a crew acting in defiance of all law, and acknowledging obedience to no government whatever . . . are proper objects for the penal code of all nations.").

[138] 18 U.S.C. § 1651.

[139] *See* United States v. Smith, 18 U.S. (5 Wheat.) 153, 162 (1820).

a definite meaning in international law and that "Congress may as well define by using a term of a known and determinate meaning, as by an express enumeration of all the particulars included in that term."[140] There has been a resurgence of piracy in recent years, especially off the coast of Africa, and cases involving the prosecution of these pirates have come to U.S. courts.[141]

These piracy cases have raised a number of interesting issues. One issue is whether, in applying the piracy statute, courts should look to understandings of what constituted piracy at the time the statute was enacted, or to modern understandings. In *United States v. Dire*, the U.S. Court of Appeals for the Fourth Circuit concluded that, in referring to piracy "as defined by the law of nations," Congress had intended to allow for application of evolving understandings of piracy.[142] In reaching this conclusion, the court analogized to the Alien Tort Statute, which (as discussed in Chapter 7) has been interpreted by the Supreme Court as allowing for application of the modern law of nations in certain civil cases. "[T]here is no reason to believe that the 'law of nations' evolves in the civil context but stands immobile in the criminal context," reasoned the court.[143]

Another issue that has arisen is whether it is proper for U.S. courts to exercise universal jurisdiction not only over acts of piracy abroad, but also over foreign acts of aiding and abetting piracy or conspiracy to commit acts of piracy. In considering this issue in *United States v. Ali*, the U.S. Court of Appeals for the D.C. Circuit applied the *Charming Betsy* canon of construction.[144] Looking to the modern understanding of piracy under international law (most notably, as set forth in the UN Convention on the Law of the Sea), the court concluded that this understanding extended to facilitative acts and thus supported the exercise by U.S. courts of universal jurisdiction over aiders and abettors.[145] By contrast, the court did not find support in modern international law for exercising universal jurisdiction over conspiracy to commit piracy. Because exercising such jurisdiction would violate customary international limitations on prescriptive jurisdiction, and because there was no clear intent in the conspiracy statute to override such limitations, the court concluded that the *Charming Betsy* canon required that the statute be construed not to provide for universal jurisdiction.[146]

Today, a number of treaties that direct parties to "prosecute or extradite" offenders are thought to implicitly sanction universal jurisdiction. This is how the British House of Lords construed the Convention against Torture in the famous *Pinochet* case, for

---

[140] *Id.* at 159.
[141] For discussion of some of the legal difficulties associated with prosecuting pirates, *see* Eugene Kontorovich, *"A Guantanamo on the Sea": The Difficulties of Prosecuting Pirates and Terrorists*, 98 CAL. L. REV. 243 (2010).
[142] 680 F.3d 446 (4th Cir. 2012).
[143] *Id.* at 467.
[144] 718 F.3d 929 (D.C. Cir. 2013).
[145] *See id.* at 936. *See also* United States v. Shibin, 722 F.3d 233 (4th Cir. 2013) (concluding that aiders and abettors of piracy need not have acted on the high seas in order to be prosecuted).
[146] *See* 718 F.3d at 941.

example.¹⁴⁷ Even outside of the treaty frameworks, however, it is generally thought that customary international law allows for universal jurisdiction with respect to certain international crimes such as genocide, war crimes, crimes against humanity, slavery, and torture.¹⁴⁸ A number of European countries have enacted criminal provisions founded on universal jurisdiction. These provisions have sometimes generated friction with other countries, including the United States. The use of Belgium's universal jurisdiction statute to initiate investigations and charges against high-level U.S. officials, for example, led to vigorous protests by the United States and an eventual overhaul of the Belgian statute.¹⁴⁹

Most U.S. criminal statutes expressly or implicitly require a connection to the United States or a U.S. national and thus do not assert universal jurisdiction. Until fairly recently, this was true even of the federal genocide statute, which required that the offense occur in the United States or that the offender be a U.S. national. In 2007, however, the statute was amended to allow for prosecution of non-U.S. citizens who commit genocide outside the United States and are "brought into, or found in" the United States.¹⁵⁰ The federal torture statute, enacted in 1994, also allows for universal jurisdiction over official acts of torture committed outside the United States.¹⁵¹ The statute has been rarely used, however. Apparently the first time that federal prosecutors charged someone with violating the statute was in 2006, when they sought and obtained an indictment against Charles McArthur Emmanuel, the son of former Liberian president Charles Taylor. In that case, prosecutors alleged that Emmanuel, who was born in the United States, participated in the torture of a man in Liberia in 2002. Emmanuel, also known as "Chuckie Taylor," was subsequently convicted under the torture statute and sentenced to ninety-seven years in prison.¹⁵² There has been some disagreement in the courts over whether certain acts of terrorism might qualify for universal jurisdiction.¹⁵³ In any event, the United States has

---

¹⁴⁷ *See* Regina v. Bow Street Metro. Stipendiary Magistrate, Ex parte Pinochet Ugarte, 2 WLR 827 (HL 1999).

¹⁴⁸ *See* RESTATEMENT (FOURTH) OF THE FOREIGN RELATIONS LAW OF THE UNITED STATES, *supra* note 106, § 414; THE PRINCETON PRINCIPLES ON UNIVERSAL JURISDICTION 29 (2001).

¹⁴⁹ *See* Steven R. Ratner, *Belgium's War Crimes Statute: A Postmortem*, 97 AM. J. INT'L L. 888 (2003).

¹⁵⁰ *See* 18 U.S.C. § 1091(d)(5).

¹⁵¹ *See* 18 U.S.C. § 2340A.

¹⁵² The U.S. Court of Appeals for the Eleventh Circuit upheld the conviction in *United States v. Belfast*, 611 F.3d 783 (11th Cir. 2010). For another example of universal jurisdiction, *see* 18 U.S.C. § 2442(c)(3). This statute, the Child Soldiers Accountability Act, was enacted in 2008 and makes it a federal crime to knowingly recruit, enlist, or conscript a person under fifteen years of age into an armed force or group or to knowingly use a person under fifteen years of age to participate actively in hostilities. The Act applies even to conduct by non-U.S. nationals abroad as long as they are present in the United States when charged. For a general discussion of the relationship between U.S. law and universal jurisdiction, *see* Curtis A. Bradley, *Universal Jurisdiction and U.S. Law*, 2001 CHI. LEG. FORUM 323.

¹⁵³ *Compare* United States v. Yousef, 327 F.3d 56, 103 (2d Cir. 2003) ("[T]he indefinite category of 'terrorism' is not subject to universal jurisdiction."), *with* United States v. Yunis, 924 F.2d 1086, 1092 (D.C. Cir. 1991) ("Aircraft hijacking may well be one of the few crimes so clearly condemned under the law of nations that states may assert universal jurisdiction to bring offenders to justice, even when the state has no territorial connection to the hijacking and its citizens are not involved.").

tended to prosecute acts of terrorism only when they are connected in some fashion to the United States or U.S. nationals.

Constitutional Limits on Statutory Extraterritoriality

There are probably at least modest constitutional limits on the extent to which Congress can regulate conduct outside the United States. Congress has broad regulatory authority, and some of this authority clearly allows it to regulate extraterritorially. For example, Congress has the power to regulate commerce with foreign nations. In addition, it has the power to define and punish offenses against the law of nations, as well as felonies and piracies committed on the high seas. Furthermore, as discussed in Chapter 2, it has the authority to enact laws that are "necessary and proper" to implement U.S. treaty commitments.

Although expansive, these powers are presumably not unlimited. The Supreme Court has interpreted Congress's domestic commerce authority as allowing it to regulate in only three categories: "the use of the channels of interstate commerce"; "the instrumentalities of interstate commerce, or persons or things in interstate commerce"; and intrastate activities "having a substantial relation to interstate commerce . . ., i.e., those activities that substantially affect interstate commerce."[154] To be sure, the Court has broadly interpreted what it means to "substantially affect" interstate commerce.[155] Moreover, courts have suggested that the scope of the foreign commerce power is even broader than the domestic commerce power because the foreign commerce power does not implicate the interests of U.S. states to the same degree as does the domestic commerce power.[156] Nevertheless, the foreign commerce power presumably does not allow Congress to regulate (for example) purely noncommercial conduct by aliens abroad.[157]

The reach of the foreign commerce power has been an issue in cases brought under a 2003 statute, the Prosecutorial Remedies and Other Tools to End the Exploitation of Children Today (PROTECT) Act. This statute provides that "[a]ny United States

---

[154] United States v. Lopez, 514 U.S. 549, 558–59 (1995). *See also* United States v. Morrison, 529 U.S. 598, 608 (2000) ("*Lopez* emphasized . . . that even under our modern, expansive interpretation of the Commerce Clause, Congress' regulatory authority is not without effective bounds.").

[155] *See, e.g.*, Gonzales v. Raich, 545 U.S. 1 (2005) (holding that Congress could regulate the personal cultivation of marijuana for medicinal use under its commerce power because Congress could rationally conclude that such personal cultivation could affect the (illegal) interstate market for marijuana).

[156] *See* Buttfield v. Stranahan, 192 U.S. 470 (1904); Champion v. Ames (The "Lottery Case"), 188 U.S. 321, 373 (1903); *see also* Japan Line, Ltd. v. Cnty. of Los Angeles, 441 U.S. 434, 448 (1979) ("Although the Constitution, Art. I, § 8, cl. 3, grants Congress power to regulate commerce 'with foreign Nations' and 'among the several States' in parallel phrases, there is evidence that the Founders intended the scope of the foreign commerce power to be the greater.").

[157] For an extensive consideration of the scope of the Foreign Commerce Clause, *see* Anthony J. Colangelo, *The Foreign Commerce Clause*, 96 VA. L. REV. 949 (2010).

citizen or alien admitted for permanent residence who travels in foreign commerce, and engages in any illicit sexual conduct with another person shall be fined under this title or imprisoned not more than 30 years, or both."[158] Illicit sexual conduct is in turn defined as either a sexual act with a person under eighteen years of age that would violate U.S. law if it occurred within the United States, any commercial sex act with a person under eighteen years of age, or the production of child pornography. To date, courts have held that the statute falls within Congress's commerce clause authority, either because the defendants will have traveled in the channels of foreign commerce before engaging in the covered sexual conduct, or because Congress could reasonably conclude that the conduct is likely to affect foreign commerce.[159] Some dissenting judges have argued, however, that the connection to commerce is too thin in these cases.[160]

Since 2002, the United States has been a party to a treaty—the Optional Protocol to the United Nations Convention on the Rights of the Child on the Sale of Children, Child Prostitution, and Child Pornography—that commits nations to protect against the sexual exploitation of children. As a result, even if the PROTECT Act exceeds the scope of Congress's authority to regulate foreign commerce, it might be constitutional as an exercise of Congress's authority to implement treaties.[161]

There have also been questions raised about the scope of Congress's define-and-punish power. In order to find that a criminal statute falls within the scope of this power, a court may need to satisfy itself that the conduct regulated by the statute is, in fact, a violation of the "law of nations."[162] In addition, it is unclear to what extent Congress can use the define-and-punish power to enact civil legislation. Although the term "punish" might suggest only a criminal lawmaking power, Congress has invoked its define-and-punish authority as a basis for enacting important civil legislation relating to foreign relations, including the Torture Victim Protection Act (discussed in Chapter 7) and the Foreign Sovereign Immunities Act (discussed in Chapter 8).[163] With respect to the Torture Victim

---

[158] Pub. L. No. 108–21, 117 Stat. 650 (2003).

[159] *See, e.g.*, United States v. Durham, 902 F.3d 1180 (10th Cir. 2018); United States v. Baston, 818 F.3d 651 (11th Cir. 2016); United States v. Bollinger, 798 F.3d 201 (4th Cir. 2015); United States v. Pendleton, 658 F.3d 299 (3d Cir. 2011); United States v. Clark, 435 F.3d 1100 (9th Cir. 2006).

[160] The PROTECT Act was amended in 2013 to cover not only citizens who engage in the prohibited sexual conduct after traveling in foreign commerce but also those who engage in such conduct after residing in a foreign country. *See* 18 U.S.C. § 2423(c). *See* United States v. Pepe, 895 F.3d 679 (9th Cir. 2018) (concluding that, in light of this amendment, the earlier version of the statute must have applied only to those citizens who had traveled abroad for a temporary stay).

[161] For a decision relying on Congress's treaty implementation authority as support for the statute, *see* United States v. Park, 938 F.3d 354 (D.C. Cir. 2019). For additional discussion of Congress's treaty implementation authority, see Chapter 2.

[162] *See, e.g.*, United States v. Bellaizac-Hurtado, 700 F.3d 1245 (11th Cir. 2012).

[163] For an argument that the clause authorizes civil as well as criminal enactments, *see* Beth Stephens, *Federalism and Foreign Affairs: Congress's Power to "Define and Punish . . . Offenses against the Law of Nations,"* 42 WM. & MARY L. REV. 447 (2000). *But cf.* Charles D. Siegal, *Deference and Its Dangers: Congress' Power to*

Protection Act, which confers a cause of action for damages arising from acts of torture and "extrajudicial killing" committed under color of foreign law, some commentators have questioned whether the define-and-punish clause gives Congress the authority to regulate violations of international law committed by non-U.S. citizens on foreign soil.[164]

As discussed in the next section, the Due Process Clause of the Fourteenth Amendment to the Constitution probably imposes modest limits on the ability of U.S. states to apply their laws extraterritorially. It is not clear whether the national government is similarly restrained by the Due Process Clause of the Fifth Amendment.[165] This issue has arisen in cases brought under the Maritime Drug Law Enforcement Act (MDLEA), which makes it a federal crime to engage in drug trafficking on board "a vessel subject to the jurisdiction of the United States."[166] Vessels subject to the jurisdiction of the United States for purposes of this statute include stateless vessels and vessels "registered in a foreign nation if that nation has consented or waived objection to the enforcement of United States law by the United States."[167]

Courts have generally assumed that applications of this statute are subject to due process limitations but that these limitations simply require that the law not be applied in an "arbitrary or fundamentally unfair" manner.[168] Courts have also generally held that applications of the MDLEA are not arbitrary or fundamentally unfair, even without a nexus to the United States, if they comport with the international law principles of prescriptive jurisdiction discussed earlier (such as the protective principle), or if the vessel's flag state consents to the exercise of jurisdiction.[169]

"*Define . . . Offenses against the Law of Nations*," 21 Vand. J. Transnat'l L. 865, 866–67 (1988) (stating that the clause permits "Congress to define violations of customary international law as domestic crimes").

[164] *See* Eugene Kontorovich, *The "Define and Punish" Clause and the Limits of Universal Jurisdiction*, 103 Nw. U. L. Rev. 149 (2009) (arguing, based on historical materials, that the Define and Punish Clause allows Congress to punish purely foreign conduct only in the case of piracy). For additional discussion of the clause, *see* Sarah H. Cleveland & William S. Dodge, *Defining and Punishing Offenses Under Treaties*, 124 Yale L.J. 2202 (2015); J. Andrew Kent, *Congress's Under-Appreciated Power to Define and Punish Offenses against the Law of Nations*, 85 Tex. L. Rev. 843 (2007); and Note, *The Offences Clause after* Sosa v. Alvarez-Machain, 118 Harv. L. Rev. 2378 (2005). For a decision holding that the Torture Victim Protection Act falls within Congress's authority to implement the Convention against Torture, a treaty ratified by the United States two years after the TVPA's enactment, *see United States v. Belfast*, 611 F.3d 783, 806 (11th Cir. 2010).

[165] *Compare* Lea Brilmayer & Charles Norchi, *Federal Extraterritoriality and Fifth Amendment Due Process*, 105 Harv. L. Rev. 1217 (1992) (arguing that the national government is restrained in its assertions of extraterritoriality by the Due Process clause), *with* A. Mark Weisburd, *Due Process Limits on Federal Extraterritorial Legislation*, 35 Colum. J. Transnat'l L. 379 (1997) (arguing that the national government is not so restrained). *See also* Anthony T. Colangelo, *Constitutional Limits on Extraterritorial Jurisdiction: Terrorism and the Intersection of National and International Law*, 48 Harv. Int'l L.J. 121 (2007) (arguing for a due process limitation that incorporates elements of international law).

[166] 46 U.S.C. § 70503(a), (e).

[167] 46 U.S.C. § 70502(c).

[168] *See, e.g.*, United States v. Van Der End, 943 F.3d 98 (2d Cir. 2019); United States v. Suerte, 291 F.3d 366 (5th Cir. 2002); United States v. Cardales, 168 F.3d 548 (1st Cir. 1999).

[169] *See, e.g.*, United States v. Dávila-Reyes, 937 F.3d 57, 62–63 (1st Cir. 2019); United States v. Ibarguen-Mosquera, 634 F.3d 1370, 1378 (11th Cir. 2011); *Cardales*, 168 F.3d at 553.

Cases under the MDLEA have also implicated other constitutional issues. In an important decision in 2012, *United States v. Bellaizac-Hurtado,* the U.S. Court of Appeals for the Eleventh Circuit held that an application of the MDLEA to drug trafficking in a foreign country's territorial waters exceeded Congress's constitutional authority.[170] In that case, the United States was seeking to prosecute several individuals under the MDLEA, after drugs were discovered on their vessel in Panamanian waters. The government argued that this application of the MDLEA was supported by Congress's authority to "define and punish . . . Offenses against the Law of Nations," but the court disagreed. The court reasoned that Congress is limited under the Define and Punish Clause to punishing conduct that actually violates the law of nations, which the court said was synonymous with customary international law. With that in mind, the court concluded that, regardless of whether it should look to the customary international law that existed at the time of the Founding or contemporary customary international law, the result would be the same: "Drug trafficking was not a violation of customary international law at the time of the Founding, and drug trafficking is not violation of customary international law today."[171]

Extraterritorial Application of State Law

Issues sometimes arise concerning attempts by U.S. states to apply their laws to conduct occurring in foreign countries. The presumption against extraterritoriality, already discussed, applies only to federal statutes, and it is up to each state to decide what presumption, if any, to apply to its own laws.[172] In some instances, however, federal law will disallow the extraterritorial application of state law.

To be valid, an extraterritorial state law will need to avoid federal preemption. As discussed in Chapter 1, when there is a conflict between a valid federal law and a state law, the federal law will preempt (that is, override) the state law. The preemptive federal law can be the Constitution, a federal statute, or a self-executing treaty. Moreover, the

---

[170] United States v. Bellaizac-Hurtado, 700 F.3d 1245 (11th Cir. 2012).
[171] *Id.* at 1253–54. While agreeing with the majority opinion, one judge argued in a special concurrence that, when foreign conduct has no connection to the United States or U.S. citizens, Congress should be able to regulate it under the Define and Punish Clause only if there is a basis in international law for exercising universal jurisdiction over the conduct. *See id.* at 1258–59 (Barkett, J., specially concurring). For drug trafficking on the high seas, as opposed to in the territorial waters of another nation, the application of the MDLEA can potentially be supported by another congressional power: the power to "define and punish . . . Felonies committed on the high seas." *See, e.g.,* United States v. Nueci-Pena, 711 F.3d 191 (1st Cir. 2013).
[172] Some state courts apply their own version of a presumption against extraterritoriality to state law. *See, e.g.,* Global Reinsurance Corp. U.S. Branch v. Equitas Ltd., 969 N.E.2d 187, 195 (N.Y. 2012); Sullivan v. Oracle Corp., 51 Cal. 4th 1191, 1207 (Cal. 2011); Citizens Ins. Co. of America v. Daccach, 217 S.W.3d 430, 443 (Tex. 2007).

conflict between the federal law and the state law need not always be direct. Courts will also find preemption when federal law has "occupied the field" in question and when state law "stands as an obstacle" to achievement of the policies of the federal law.[173] In some instances, courts may even find that judicial preemption of state law is warranted to protect the dormant powers of the national government in foreign affairs.[174] Some state laws with an extraterritorial focus have been invalidated on these various preemption grounds.[175]

There are also probably some modest due process limits on the extraterritorial application of state law. In addressing the ability of U.S. states to apply their laws to conduct in the territory of other U.S. states, the Supreme Court has interpreted the Due Process Clause of the Fourteenth Amendment (along with the Full Faith and Credit Clause, which applies to relations among the U.S. states) to require that the regulating state have "a significant contact or significant aggregation of contacts, creating state interests, such that choice of its law is neither arbitrary nor fundamentally unfair."[176] Courts have generally assumed that this standard also applies to the application of state law to conduct in foreign countries.[177]

* * *

Perhaps not surprisingly, as the power and role of the United States in the world have increased, so have its assertions of regulatory and enforcement authority abroad. A less territorially confined conception of jurisdiction has also been a natural outgrowth of globalization. At the same time, assertions of extraterritorial authority can generate

---

[173] *See, e.g.*, Arizona v. United States, 567 U.S. 387 (2012) (field and obstacle preemption); Crosby v. Nat'l Foreign Trade Council, 530 U.S. 363 (2000) (obstacle preemption); Hines v. Davidowitz, 312 U.S. 52 (1941) (field and obstacle preemption).

[174] *See* Zschernig v. Miller, 389 U.S. 429 (1968).

[175] *See, e.g.*, Am. Ins. Ass'n v. Garamendi, 539 U.S. 396, 421–24 (2003) (finding California statute designed to facilitate recovery on insurance policies issued in Europe to be preempted because it was an obstacle to the achievement of policies reflected in executive agreements); *Crosby*, 530 U.S. at 374–82 (finding Massachusetts statute that barred state entities from buying goods or services from persons and firms doing business with Burma to be preempted because it was an obstacle to the achievement of policies reflected in a federal statute).

[176] Phillips Petroleum v. Shutts, 472 U.S. 797, 837 (1985); Allstate Ins. Co. v. Hague, 449 U.S. 302, 312–13 (1981) (plurality opinion). *See also* Home Ins. Co. v. Dick, 281 U.S. 397, 410 (1930) ("[A state] may not abrogate the rights of parties beyond its borders having no relation to anything done or to be done within them.").

[177] *See, e.g.*, Gerling Global Reinsurance Corp. of Am. v. Gallagher, 267 F.3d 1228 (11th Cir. 2001) (holding that a Holocaust insurance recovery statute enacted by Florida had an insufficient nexus with the state to satisfy due process). *Cf.* Skiriotes v. Florida, 313 U.S. 69, 77 (1941) ("If the United States may control the conduct of its citizens upon the high seas, we see no reason why the State of Florida may not likewise govern the conduct of its citizens upon the high seas with respect to matters in which the State has a legitimate interest and where there is no conflict with acts of Congress.").

friction with other countries, as well as concerns about bypassing legal protections that apply within the United States. The courts have been attentive to both of these issues, through limiting doctrines such as the presumption against extraterritoriality and the *Charming Betsy* canon, and through extraterritorial application of certain constitutional rights.

7 International Human Rights Litigation

THIS CHAPTER CONSIDERS the phenomenon of international human rights litigation in U.S. courts. Its focus in particular is on litigation brought under a statute that dates back to the country's founding, the Alien Tort Statute (ATS), which allows aliens to sue in U.S. courts for torts committed in violation of international law. Most of this litigation has concerned alleged violations of customary international law (which, as we have seen, was historically referred to as part of the "law of nations") rather than violations of treaties. This is due in part to limitations that the president and Senate have placed on the domestic status of human rights treaties. As discussed in Chapter 2, to the extent that the United States has ratified the major human rights treaties, it has consistently attached non–self-execution declarations to its ratifications, and these declarations have been construed by courts as disallowing the invocation of the treaties as a source of rights in U.S. litigation.

The chapter begins by exploring the early history of the ATS. It then considers how, starting in 1980, the ATS became the fount of international human rights litigation in U.S. courts. Next, it discusses the scope and limitations of a statute that Congress enacted in 1992, the Torture Victim Protection Act, which provides an express cause of action for human rights claims relating to torture and "extrajudicial killing." The chapter then describes the growth of ATS litigation during the last several decades, and the Supreme

Court's 2004 decision in *Sosa v. Alvarez-Machain*, which set forth certain requirements for claims to be brought under the statute. Finally, the chapter considers the implications of the Supreme Court's 2013 decision in *Kiobel v. Royal Dutch Petroleum Co.*, which sharply restricted the extraterritorial reach of the ATS, and the Court's 2018 decision in *Jesner v. Arab Bank*, which disallowed ATS suits against non-U.S. corporations.

Alien Tort Statute

The ATS originated as a provision in the Judiciary Act of 1789, a statute enacted shortly after the United States began operating under its Constitution.[1] The Judiciary Act established the federal courts and regulated their jurisdiction and structure. Section 9 of the Act addressed the jurisdiction of the federal district courts. In addition to giving these courts the authority to hear certain criminal cases, admiralty cases, common law suits brought by the U.S. government, and suits against consuls and vice-consuls, Section 9 provided that the district courts "shall also have cognizance, concurrent with the courts of the several States, or the circuit courts, as the case may be, of all causes where an alien sues for a tort only in violation of the law of nations or a treaty of the United States."[2] This alien tort provision has been recodified by Congress several times, with minor alterations.[3] The current version of the ATS dates back to a 1948 revision of the Judicial Code and provides that the district courts "shall have original jurisdiction of any civil action by an alien for a tort only, committed in violation of the law of nations or a treaty of the United States."[4]

The original purposes of the ATS are uncertain, and there is essentially no legislative history for this portion of the Judiciary Act. Many scholars have reasonably speculated that the ATS was designed to reduce potential friction with foreign countries by allowing sensitive tort cases to be heard in the national courts, particularly cases in which the

---

[1] For discussions of the historical origins of the ATS, see, for example, Anthony J. Bellia, Jr. & Bradford R. Clark, *The Alien Tort Statute and the Law of Nations*, 78 U. CHI. L. REV. 445 (2011); Curtis A. Bradley, *The Alien Tort Statute and Article III*, 42 VA. J. INT'L L. 587 (2002); Anne-Marie Burley, *The Alien Tort Statute and the Judiciary Act of 1789: A Badge of Honor*, 83 AM. J. INT'L L. 461 (1989); William R. Casto, *The Federal Courts' Protective Jurisdiction over Torts Committed in Violation of the Law of Nations*, 18 CONN. L. REV. 467 (1986); Thomas H. Lee, *The Safe-Conduct Theory of the Alien Tort Statute*, 106 COLUM. L. REV. 830, 883 (2006); Kenneth C. Randall, *Federal Jurisdiction over International Law Claims: Inquiries into the Alien Tort Statute*, 18 N.Y.U. J. INT'L L. & POL. 1 (1985).

[2] 1 Stat. 73, 77, § 9 (1789).

[3] The Statute was modified in 1873 to read: "The district courts shall have jurisdiction as follows: . . . Of all suits brought by any alien for a tort 'only' in violation of the law of nations, or of a treaty of the United States." Revised Statutes tit. 13, ch. 3, § 563, para. 16 (1873). It was slightly altered in a 1911 codification to read: "The district courts shall have original jurisdiction as follows: . . . Of all suits brought by any alien for a tort only, in violation of the laws of nations or a treaty of the United States." Act of March 3, 1911, ch. 231, § 24, 36 Stat. 1087, 1093 (1911).

[4] 28 U.S.C. § 1350.

United States would have had an obligation to provide redress.[5] The state courts would have been open to hear tort cases involving aliens, but Congress understandably might not have wanted to rely entirely on such courts when the interests of the nation were at stake, as would be the case when the tort implicated international law. As far as scholars have been able to ascertain, the decision to give the federal courts jurisdiction over these alien tort cases was uncontroversial.

The relationship between the ATS and Article III of the Constitution is unclear. As discussed in Chapter 1, Article III lists the types of cases that can be heard in the federal courts, and Congress is not allowed to give the federal courts jurisdiction over any cases that do not fall within this list. Although the list includes cases arising under treaties, it does not contain any general category for cases arising under the law of nations. There is a category for cases arising under the "Laws of the United States," but, as discussed in Chapter 5, it seems unlikely that the law of nations was viewed as encompassed within this category.[6]

Some scholars (including this author) have suggested that the law of nations portion of the ATS may have been an implementation of the category in Article III for "alienage diversity jurisdiction"—that is, for controversies between U.S. citizens and foreign citizens.[7] This is admittedly not obvious from the text of the ATS: although the ATS requires that the plaintiff be an alien, it does not specifically say that there must be a U.S. citizen on the other side of the case. That is also true, however, of other provisions in the Judiciary Act that have been interpreted as implementations of alienage diversity

---

[5] *See, e.g.*, Bellia & Clark, *supra* note 1, at 448–49; Lee, *supra* note 1, at 883; John M. Rogers, *The Alien Tort Statute and How Individuals "Violate" International Law*, 21 VAND. J. TRANSNAT'L L. 47, 48–60 (1988); *see also* Ali Shafi v. Palestinian Authority, 642 F.3d 1088, 1099 (D.C. Cir. 2011) (Williams, J., concurring) ("The concern was that U.S. citizens might engage in incidents that could embroil the young nation in war and jeopardize its status or welfare in the Westphalian system. Similarly, foreign violators, if sufficiently linked to the United States, could create an incident threatening the United States's peace."); Tel-Oren v. Libyan Arab Republic, 726 F.2d 774, 782 (D.C. Cir. 1984) (Edwards, J., concurring) ("There is evidence ... that the intent of [the ATS] was to assure aliens access to federal courts to vindicate any incident which, if mishandled by a state court, might blossom into an international crisis.").

[6] For an argument that the ATS was intended as an admiralty provision that would address torts committed in connection with the taking of prize vessels, *see* Joseph Modeste Sweeney, *A Tort only in Violation of the Law of Nations*, 18 HASTINGS INT'L & COMP. L. REV. 445 (1995). For a rebuttal, *see* William S. Dodge, *Historical Origins of the Alien Tort Statute: A Response to the Originalists*, 19 HASTINGS INT'L & COMP. L. REV. 221 (1995). *See also* Bradley, *supra* note 1, at 617 (noting "several reasons to believe that the First Congress was not thinking of admiralty jurisdiction when enacting the Alien Tort Statute").

[7] *See* Bellia & Clark, *supra* note 1, at 525–26; Bradley, *supra* note 1, at 619–36; Arthur M. Weisburd, *The Executive Branch and International Law*, 41 VAND. L. REV. 1205, 1224–26 (1988). *But see* William S. Dodge, *The Constitutionality of the Alien Tort Statute: Some Observations on Text and Context*, 42 VA. J. INT'L L. 687 (2002) (contesting the alienage diversity interpretation). *Cf.* Michael G. Collins, *The Diversity Theory of the Alien Tort Statute*, 42 VA. J. INT'L L. 649, 651 (2002) (suggesting a "friendly amendment" to the alienage diversity interpretation, whereby the ATS would be understood as implementing "those Article III provisions designed to implement the law of nations, including admiralty jurisdiction, the provision for jurisdiction over ambassadors, other public ministers and consuls, as well as alienage diversity jurisdiction").

jurisdiction. Section 11 of the Act, for example, gave the federal circuit courts jurisdiction over cases in which "an alien is a party," and the Supreme Court construed this provision as implicitly requiring a U.S. citizen on the other side of the case.[8]

Section 11 had a $500 amount in controversy requirement, a large sum for the time that would have precluded most tort claims. This limitation was probably included in part to limit the ability of British creditors to pursue claims for Revolutionary War–era debts in the federal courts, a potential application of alienage diversity jurisdiction that was particularly controversial when the Judiciary Act was being considered.[9] The concern about debt claims would not have been an issue under the ATS, however, because it was limited to "torts only," and, perhaps for that reason, it contains no amount in controversy requirement. It was in theory possible for a tort claim to be over $500, however, and this helps explain why jurisdiction under the ATS was expressly made concurrent with the jurisdiction of the circuit courts.

This alienage diversity construction of the ATS is consistent with the law of international responsibility in the late 1700s, when the ATS was enacted. Under that law, the United States would have had a duty to ensure that torts committed by its citizens in violation of international law were redressed. Vattel explained in his influential international law treatise, for example, that "[a] sovereign who refuses to repair the evil done by one of his subjects, or to punish the criminal, or, finally, to deliver him up, makes himself in a way an accessory to the deed, and becomes responsible for it."[10] Blackstone in his *Commentaries* similarly stated that "where the individuals of any state violate this general law [of nations], it is then the interest as well as duty of the government under which they live, to animadvert upon them with a becoming severity, that the peace of the world may be maintained."[11] Blackstone also noted that there were three principal offenses against the law of nations that were "animadverted on as such by the municipal laws of England": "1. Violations of safe-conducts; 2. Infringement of the rights of ambassadors;

---

[8] *See* Hodgson v. Bowerbank, 9 U.S. (5 Cranch) 303 (1809); Mossman v. Higginson, 4 U.S. (4 Dall.) 12, 14 (1800). There is evidence that Oliver Ellsworth, the chief draftsman of the Judiciary Act, believed that Section 11 would require a U.S. citizen in the case. *See* Bradley, *supra* note 1, at 628. His failure to note this explicitly in the language of the statute would not have been out of character with his writing style. As one biographer noted, "Ellsworth . . . possessed a peculiar style of condensed statement." WILLIAM GARROTT BROWN, THE LIFE OF OLIVER ELLSWORTH 41 (1905).

[9] *See* Bradley, *supra* note 1, at 625; William R. Casto, *The First Congress's Understanding of Its Authority over the Federal Courts' Jurisdiction*, 26 B.C. L. REV. 1101, 1113 (1985). For a more general discussion of the relationship between the British debts controversy and the First Judiciary Act, *see* Wythe Holt, *"To Establish Justice": Politics, the Judiciary Act of 1789, and the Invention of the Federal Courts*, 1989 DUKE L.J. 1421.

[10] EMMERICH DE VATTEL, THE LAW OF NATIONS, OR THE PRINCIPLES OF THE NATURAL LAW, APPLIED TO THE CONDUCT AND TO THE AFFAIRS OF NATIONS AND OF SOVEREIGNS 137 (1758) (Charles G. Fenwick trans., 1916).

[11] 4 WILLIAM BLACKSTONE, COMMENTARIES ON THE LAWS OF ENGLAND 68 (1769).

and 3. Piracy."[12] The views of these commentators were well known in the United States, and heavily relied upon, in the pre-constitutional and Founding periods.[13]

The Marbois Controversy

One event that is frequently mentioned as a catalyst for the ATS, the Marbois controversy, might cast doubt on the alienage diversity theory. The Marbois controversy occurred in 1784, during the period between the end of the Revolutionary War and the adoption of the Constitution. The Consul General of France and Secretary of the French Legation, Francois Barbé-Marbois, was assaulted by a French citizen, Charles Julian de Longchamps, on a public street in Philadelphia. Marbois insisted that Longchamps be arrested and prosecuted. At that time, there was neither a national judiciary nor any national criminal law, so the prosecution would have to occur in a Pennsylvania state court. Marbois initially expressed concern, however, that Pennsylvania might not adequately address the incident. It did not help matters that, after being apprehended by Pennsylvania authorities, Longchamps briefly escaped. Ultimately, Longchamps was tried and convicted before a Pennsylvania court, and he was sentenced to approximately two years in jail. The Pennsylvania courts declined, however, to turn Longchamps over to French authorities, notwithstanding a demand to this effect from Marbois.[14]

The Marbois controversy involved a tort in violation of the law of nations, so it is possible that Congress had it in mind when drafting the alien tort provision in Section 9 of the Judiciary Act.[15] If so, it might suggest that the ATS was intended to reach disputes between aliens, at least when the dispute concerns a tort committed in the United States. It should be noted, however, that the controversy involved a criminal rather than civil case, whereas the ATS provides for jurisdiction only over civil tort claims. To address the need for federal criminalization of offenses such as the one in the Marbois controversy, the Framers of the Constitution gave Congress the power to "define and punish Piracies and Felonies committed on the high Seas, and Offences against the Law of Nations," and Congress relied on this authority in 1790, a year after the enactment of the ATS, in

---

[12] *Id*. For an argument that the ATS was designed exclusively to address violations of safe conducts, see Lee, *supra* note 1.

[13] For Blackstone's influence, *see* Dennis R. Nolan, *Sir William Blackstone and the New American Republic: A Study of Intellectual Impact*, 51 N.Y.U. L. Rev. 731 (1976). For Vattel's influence, *see* Daniel George Lang, Foreign Policy in the Early Republic: The Law of Nations and the Balance of Powers 15–16 (1985).

[14] *See* Respublica v. De Longchamps, 1 US (1 Dall.) 111, 116 (Pa. Ct. Oyer & Terminer 1784). For accounts of the Marbois–Longchamps affair, *see* Alfred Rosenthal, *The Marbois–Longchamps Affair*, 63 Penn. Mag. of Hist. & Biog. 294 (1939); and G.S. Rowe & Alexander W. Knott, *Power, Justice, and Foreign Relations in the Confederation Period: The Marbois–Longchamps Affair, 1784–1786*, 104 Penn. Mag. of Hist. & Biog. 275 (1980).

[15] *See, e.g.*, Casto, *supra* note 1, at 491–93; Randall, *supra* note 1, at 24–26.

criminalizing assaults on ambassadors. Moreover, Article III of the Constitution contemplates that civil cases involving ambassadors could be filed directly in the Supreme Court, and, consistent with this authority, Section 13 of the Judiciary Act gave the Supreme Court "original, but not exclusive jurisdiction of all suits brought by ambassadors, or other public ministers, or in which a consul, or vice consul, shall be a party."[16] The ATS, by contrast, addresses the jurisdiction of the district courts.[17] As a result, although it is conceivable that the drafters of the ATS had the Marbois episode in mind, there is no direct evidence indicating that they did, and there are a number of reasons to think that concerns about the episode were addressed in different ways.[18]

The *Filartiga* Decision

Whatever its original purposes, the ATS was an insignificant source of federal court jurisdiction until late in the twentieth century. For 190 years after the ATS's enactment, it was relied upon by courts as a basis for jurisdiction in only two reported decisions, one in a case involving the seizure of a vessel in 1795, and the other involving a child custody dispute in 1961.[19] The ATS was invoked unsuccessfully as a basis for jurisdiction in

---

[16] Judiciary Act, § 13. *See also* Burley, *supra* note 1, at 473 (contending that "all foreign plenipotentiaries worth worrying about were provided for" in other portions of the Judiciary Act).

[17] *See also* Bellia & Clark, *supra* note 1, at 536 ("There are strong reasons grounded in the structure of Article III and the Judiciary Act to suggest that the ATS would have been most reasonably understood in 1789 not to include claims by ambassadors."); Lee, *supra* note 1, at 853–66 (explaining that the Constitution and Congress addressed the issue of protection of ambassadors in provisions other than the ATS).

[18] For a number of years before the adoption of the Constitution, national affairs in the United States were managed by the Continental Congress, and some scholars have suggested that a resolution issued by that body in 1781 might have been a precursor to the Alien Tort Statute. *See* Burley, *supra* note 1, at 476–77; Casto, *supra* note 1, at 490–91, 495. In that resolution, Congress called on the states to criminally punish various international law offenses, and also to "authorize suits to be instituted for damages by the party injured, and for compensation to the United States for damage sustained by them from an injury done to a foreign power by a citizen." 21 JOURNALS OF THE CONTINENTAL CONGRESS 1136–37 (Gaillard Hunt ed., 1912) (Nov. 23, 1781). Some early commentators appear to have understood this provision as requiring a U.S. citizen perpetrator. *See, e.g.*, THOMAS SERGEANT, CONSTITUTIONAL LAW: BEING A VIEW OF THE PRACTICE AND JURISDICTION OF THE COURTS OF THE UNITED STATES, AND OF CONSTITUTIONAL POINTS DECIDED 16 (2d ed. 1830); 3 JOSEPH STORY, COMMENTARIES ON THE CONSTITUTION OF THE UNITED STATES § 1654, at 523 n.3 (1833). For discussion of whether this is a correct interpretation of the resolution, compare Bradley, *supra* note 1, at 632–33 (arguing that it is), and Collins, *supra* note 7, at 654 n.21 (same), with Casto, *supra* note 1, at 499 n.179 (contesting this interpretation), and Dodge, *supra* note 6, at 228 (same). *Cf.* Scott A. Rosenberg, Note, *The Theory of Protective Jurisdiction*, 57 N.Y.U. L. REV. 933, 1016–18 (1982) (noting that the 1781 resolution "seems to bear out the suggestion that Congress primarily envisioned suits against citizens of the United States," but nevertheless arguing that the ATS should be interpreted more broadly).

[19] *See* Adra v. Clift, 195 F. Supp. 857 (D. Md. 1961); Bolchos v. Darrel, 3 F. Cas. 810 (D.S.C. 1795) (No. 1607); *see also* Yen v. Kissinger, 528 F.2d 1194, 1202 n.13 (9th Cir. 1975) (suggesting, in a suit by Vietnamese citizens against U.S. officials, that jurisdiction under the Alien Tort Statute "may be available").

a relatively small number of additional reported decisions.[20] In 1975, a prominent federal judge (and expert on federal jurisdiction) referred to the ATS as an "old but little used section" and described it as "a kind of legal Lohengrin ... no one seems to know whence it came."[21] One reason that the ATS did not play a more significant role, even after World War II, is that courts generally held that the "law of nations" referred to in the ATS did not encompass a government's treatment of its own citizens—that is, it did not encompass modern international human rights law.[22]

This all changed in 1980, with the decision by the U.S. Court of Appeals for the Second Circuit in *Filartiga v. Pena-Irala*.[23] In that case, two Paraguayan citizens, Joel and Dolly Filartiga, brought suit in a federal court in New York against Pena-Irala, another Paraguayan citizen who was residing in Brooklyn, New York, with an expired visa. The Filartigas alleged that Pena-Irala, while serving as a police inspector in Paraguay, had been involved in the kidnapping, torture, and killing of a member of their family. For federal court jurisdiction, the Filartigas relied on the ATS, contending that Pena-Irala's conduct constituted a tort in violation of the law of nations. The district court dismissed the case, concluding that the law of nations referred to in the ATS did not include modern international law governing how nations treat their own citizens.

In a landmark decision, the Court of Appeals reversed. The court first concluded that an act of torture committed by a state official against someone held in detention violates the "established norms of the international law of human rights."[24] In reaching this conclusion, the court considered a wide variety of sources, including resolutions from the UN General Assembly, general references to human rights in the UN Charter, human rights treaties that had not at that point been ratified by the United States, and academic opinion. The court also reasoned that, in applying the ATS, "courts must interpret international law not as it was in 1789, but as it has evolved and exists among the nations of the world today."[25] In looking to modern practice, the court acknowledged that official

---

[20] *See, e.g.*, O'Reilly de Camara v. Brooke, 209 U.S. 45 (1908); Anh v. Levi, 586 F.2d 625 (6th Cir. 1978); Benjamins v. British European Airways, 572 F.2d 913 (2d Cir. 1978); IIT v. Vencap, Ltd., 519 F.2d 1001 (2d Cir. 1975); Abiodun v. Martin Oil Serv., Inc., 475 F.2d 142 (7th Cir. 1973); Khedivial Line, S.A.E. v. Seafarers' International Union, 278 F.2d 49 (2d Cir. 1960); Trans-Continental Inv. Corp., S.A. v. Bank of the Commonwealth, 500 F. Supp. 565 (C.D. Cal. 1980); Cohen v. Hartman, 490 F. Supp. 517 (S.D. Fla. 1980); Valanga v. Metro. Life Ins. Co., 259 F. Supp. 324 (E.D. Pa. 1966); Damaskinos v. Societa Navigacion Interamericana, S.A., 255 F. Supp. 919 (S.D.N.Y. 1966); Lopes v. Schroder, 225 F. Supp. 292 (E.D. Pa. 1963); Upper Lakes Shipping Ltd. v. Int'l Longshoremen's Ass'n, 33 F.R.D. 348 (S.D.N.Y. 1963); Moxon v. The Fanny, 17 F. Cas. 942 (D. Pa. 1793).

[21] *Vencap*, 519 F.2d at 1015 (Friendly J.). "Lohengrin" is the name of an opera by Richard Wagner, involving a mysterious figure who turns out to be a Knight of the Holy Grail.

[22] *See, e.g.*, Dreyfus v. Von Finck, 534 F.2d 24, 31 (2d Cir. 1976) ("[V]iolations of international law do not occur when the aggrieved parties are nationals of the acting state.").

[23] Filartiga v. Pena-Irala, 630 F.2d 876 (2d Cir. 1980).

[24] *Id.* at 880.

[25] *Id.* at 881. One difference between *Filartiga* and *The Paquete Habana* is that *Filartiga* involved in part the interpretation of a statute whereas *The Paquete Habana* involved direct application of international law.

torture was still widespread, but it insisted that the "fact that the prohibition of torture is often honored in the breach does not diminish its binding effect as a norm of international law."[26] The court therefore reasoned that the ATS applied because "[t]his is undeniably an action by an alien, for a tort only, committed in violation of the law of nations."[27]

The court in *Filartiga* also concluded that, even though the suit involved only foreign citizens, it fell within the Article III jurisdiction of the federal courts. "The constitutional basis for the Alien Tort Statute is the law of nations," said the court, "which has always been part of the federal common law."[28] As should be clear from the discussion in Chapter 5, the court's historical assertion about federal common law is incorrect. What is referred to today as "federal common law" is largely a product of the Supreme Court's 1938 decision in *Erie Railroad v. Tompkins*. Before that decision, the law of nations was treated as part of the general common law, which, unlike modern federal common law, probably did not qualify as part of the "Laws of the United States" in Article III.[29] It is possible to argue, of course, that the law of nations should be treated today as federal common law, and perhaps the court in *Filartiga* should charitably be interpreted as making that claim.[30]

Although *Filartiga* was decided by an intermediate court of appeals rather than by the Supreme Court, it was highly significant. It potentially opened U.S. courts to human rights complaints from around the world, as long as personal jurisdiction could be obtained over the defendant.[31] Apparently aware of the significance of its decision, the court in *Filartiga* proclaimed that it was taking "a small but important step in the fulfillment of the ageless dream to free all people from brutal violence."[32] A prominent

---

[26] *Id.* at 884 n.15.

[27] *Id.* at 887.

[28] *Id.* at 885.

[29] *See also* Bellia & Clark, *supra* note 1, at 547 ("The Second Circuit's assertion that the law of nations has always been part of federal common law is anachronistic and lacks a convincing basis in the historical record."). *But see* Dodge, *supra* note 7, 701–11.

[30] *Cf.* Gerald L. Neuman, *Sense and Nonsense about Customary International Law: A Response to Professors Bradley and Goldsmith*, 66 FORDHAM L. REV. 371, 379 (1997) (contending that, in making its claim about federal common law, the court in *Filartiga* "attempted to synthesize cases from all periods of U.S. history").

[31] Most ATS suits have sought damages. A suit for injunctive relief directed at the practices of a foreign government would raise significant comity concerns. *See In re* "Agent Orange" Prod. Liability Litig., 373 F. Supp. 2d 7, 45 (E.D.N.Y. 2005) ("Requests for extraterritorial injunctions often raise serious concerns for sovereignty and enforceability which compel denial.").

[32] 630 F.2d at 890. In a subsequent magazine article, the author of the decision, Judge Irving Kaufman, wrote that "the articulation of evolved norms of international law by the courts" helps "form the ethical foundations for a more enlightened social order" and "is an expression of this nation's commitment to the preservation of fundamental elements of human dignity throughout the world." Irving R. Kaufman, *A Legal Remedy for International Torture?*, N.Y. TIMES MAG. (Nov. 9, 1980), at 44. Several years later, in a law review article on judicial decision-making, Judge Kaufman used the "noteworthy" *Filartiga* case to illustrate his approach to judging and stated that "it is always my hope that my ultimate consideration will be not merely the avoidance of injustice, but what we might call the most just result not only for our place and time, but also for what lies before us." Irving R. Kaufman, *The Anatomy of Decisionmaking*, 63 FORDHAM L. REV. 1, 20–22 (1984).

international law professor and vigorous supporter of the decision analogized it to *Brown v. Board of Education*, the Supreme Court's famous civil rights decision from 1954 that ordered the racial desegregation of public schools.[33]

Cause of Action

To succeed in an ATS case, it is not enough for plaintiffs to establish that the court has jurisdiction. The plaintiffs must also have a cause of action that allows them to seek their requested relief, such as compensatory or punitive damages. The court in *Filartiga* did not resolve the cause of action issue. For purposes of its decision, the court construed the ATS "not as granting new rights to aliens, but simply as opening the federal courts for adjudication of the rights already recognized by international law."[34]

The cause of action issue was highlighted in a case decided in 1984 by the U.S. Court of Appeals for the D.C. Circuit, *Tel-Oren v. Libyan Arab Republic*.[35] In *Tel-Oren*, a group of Israeli citizens and other aliens who were victims of a terrorist attack in Israel sued the Palestine Liberation Organization and others under the ATS, alleging violations of customary international law prohibitions on torture and summary execution. The court dismissed the suit, but the three judges on the panel wrote separate opinions, each relying on a different reason for dismissal. The most noteworthy opinion was by Judge Robert Bork, who argued that the ATS is simply a jurisdictional provision and thus does not itself confer a private cause of action for damages.[36] He also argued that implying a cause of action under this statute for human rights abuses would run counter to Congress's intent in the ATS of avoiding foreign relations conflicts with other nations, since it would allow U.S. courts to adjudicate cases that are likely to cause foreign relations friction. In addition, he expressed concern that the judicial implication of a cause of action would be contrary to the separation of powers, since it would undermine political branch control over U.S. foreign relations. Finally, Judge Bork argued that customary international law does not itself provide a domestic cause of action.[37]

---

[33] Harold Hongju Koh, *Transnational Public Law Litigation*, 100 YALE L.J. 2347, 2366 (1991). For early commentary on the decision, see, for example, Jeffrey M. Blum & Ralph G. Steinhardt, *Federal Jurisdiction over International Human Rights Claims: The Alien Tort Claims Act after* Filartiga v. Pena-Irala, 22 HARV. INT'L L.J. 53 (1981); William T. D'Zurilla, *Individual Responsibility for Torture under International Law*, 56 TUL. L. REV. 186 (1981); Note, *Enforcement of International Human Rights in the Federal Courts after* Filartiga v. Pena-Irala, 67 VA. L. REV. 1379 (1981); Comment, *Torture as a Tort in Violation of International Law:* Filartiga v. Pena-Irala, 33 STAN. L. REV. 353 (1981).

[34] 630 F.2d at 887.

[35] 726 F.2d 774 (D.C. Cir. 1984).

[36] *See id.* at 811 (Bork, J., concurring). *See also, e.g.*, Casto, *supra* note 1, at 479 (arguing that the ATS "clearly does not create a statutory cause of action").

[37] Judge Harry Edwards disagreed with Judge Bork on the cause of action issue, arguing that the Alien Tort Statute itself grants a cause of action for torts in violation of customary international law. Otherwise, Judge Edwards said, the Alien Tort Statute would have essentially no application outside the context of treaties,

If Judge Bork's views had been accepted by other courts, international human rights litigation probably would have come to an end unless and until Congress enacted new legislation authorizing it. In theory, treaties could provide a cause of action. As discussed in Chapter 2, however, the United States did not start joining human rights treaties until the late 1980s, and it has consistently attached non–self-execution declarations to its ratification of these treaties, making them judicially unenforceable. As a result, essentially all ATS cases rely on the law of nations—that is, customary international law—rather than treaties. As Judge Bork argued, however, it seems unlikely that customary international law confers a domestic cause of action.[38]

In fact, this cause of action problem did not materialize, because courts after *Tel-Oren* disagreed with Judge Bork and construed the ATS as implicitly creating a cause of action for damages.[39] As will be discussed, the Supreme Court eventually rejected that construction of the ATS (and thus in effect sided with Judge Bork's view on that point), but this did not occur until 2004. In the meantime, Congress acted to create a cause of action for the two human rights claims that had been at issue in *Filartiga*.

Torture Victim Protection Act

Starting in 1986, apparently in response to *Tel-Oren*, bills were introduced in Congress to create a cause of action for acts of torture and "extrajudicial killing" committed under color of foreign law.[40] When hearings were held on one of the proposed bills in 1989, officials from the administration of George H.W. Bush testified against it, expressing concern that a cause of action directed at the conduct of foreign officials in their own countries would be perceived as improperly extraterritorial and might trigger reciprocal actions targeted at the conduct of U.S. officials.[41]

---

since the law of nations does not itself confer a private right to sue in domestic courts. *See* 726 F.2d at 778–79 (Edwards, J., concurring). But Judge Edwards reasoned that the Palestine Liberation Organization was not a recognized state and that therefore there was no state action involved, something that he concluded was generally required in order for there to be a violation of the law of nations. *See id.* at 791.

[38] The Supreme Court has stated that there is a presumption that even treaties do not confer a private right of action. *See* Medellin v. Texas, 552 U.S. 491, 506 n.3 (2008). *See also* Curtis A. Bradley, *Customary International Law and Private Rights of Action*, 1 CHI. J. INT'L L. 421, 427–29 (2000) (explaining that, in litigation brought by domestic plaintiffs, courts have not been willing to infer a cause of action directly under customary international law).

[39] *See, e.g., In re* Estate of Ferdinand Marcos, Human Rights Litig., 25 F.3d 1467, 1474–75 (9th Cir. 1994).

[40] Senator Arlen Specter first introduced such a bill in 1986, and he reintroduced the bill several times in subsequent years.

[41] *See Torture Victim Protection Act of 1989: Hearing on S. 1629 and H.R. 1662 Before the Subcomm. on Immigration and Refugee Affairs of the Senate Comm. on the Judiciary*, 101st Cong. 8 (1990) (written and oral testimony by John O. McGinnis, Deputy Assistant Att'y Gen., Office of Legal Counsel, U.S. Dep't of Justice, and David P. Stewart, Assistant Legal Advisor for Human Rights and Refugee Affairs, U.S. Dep't of State).

In 1992, however, President Bush signed into law the Torture Victim Protection Act (TVPA). The TVPA, which was codified as a note to the ATS, creates a civil cause of action for damages against any "individual, who, under actual or apparent authority, or color of law, of any foreign nation" subjects another individual to either torture or extrajudicial killing.[42] In signing this legislation, President Bush expressed concern that "[t]here is thus a danger that U.S. courts may become embroiled in difficult and sensitive disputes in other countries, and possibly ill-founded or politically motivated suits, which have nothing to do with the United States and which offer little prospect of successful recovery."[43] As a result, he said that "[i]t is to be hoped that U.S. courts will be able to avoid these dangers by sound construction of the statute and the wise application of relevant legal procedures and principles."[44]

The precise relationship between the TVPA and the ATS is uncertain. The legislative history of the TVPA refers favorably to the *Filartiga* decision.[45] It also notes that Judge Bork had argued in *Tel-Oren* that there must be "an explicit grant by Congress of a private right of action for lawsuits which affect foreign relations," and it states that "[t]he TVPA would provide such a grant, and would also enhance the remedy already available under [the ATS] in an important respect: while the Alien Tort Claims Act provides a remedy to aliens only, the TVPA would extend a civil remedy also to U.S. citizens who may have been tortured abroad."[46] Finally, the legislative history expresses the view that "claims based on torture or summary executions do not exhaust the list of actions that may appropriately be covered by [the ATS]."[47]

It is not clear what weight should be given to this legislative history, because it was not voted upon by the members of Congress. In any event, it is worth noting that the TVPA differs from the ATS in a number of respects. Whereas the ATS refers only to the jurisdiction of the federal courts, the TVPA expressly creates a cause of action for damages. The TVPA thus resolves questions about the source of the cause of action in cases involving alleged torture or extrajudicial killing. By creating a cause of action, the TVPA also removes any uncertainty about the Article III basis for hearing these cases, since federal statutory claims clearly arise under the "Laws of the United States." At the same time, because it is a cause of action statute, the TVPA contains limitations not found in the ATS, most notably a requirement that the claimant have exhausted "adequate and available remedies in the place where the conduct giving rise to the claim occurred," and a ten-year statute of limitations.

---

[42] Torture Victim Protection Act, Pub. L. No. 102–256, 106 Stat. 73 (1992) (set forth in statutory note following Alien Tort Statute, 28 U.S.C. § 1350).
[43] Presidential Statement on Signing H.R. 2092, 28 WEEKLY COMP. PRES. DOC. 465 (March 16, 1992), *reprinted in* 1992 U.S.C.C.A.N. 91.
[44] *Id.*
[45] *See* H.R. REP. NO. 102–367, pt. 1 (1991), *reprinted in* 1992 U.S.C.C.A.N. 84, 85.
[46] 1992 U.S.C.C.A.N. at 86.
[47] *Id.*

Courts are divided over whether plaintiffs can avoid the limitations of the TVPA by bringing a claim for torture or extrajudicial killing under the ATS. One court reasoned that the TVPA "occup[ied] the field" because otherwise its limitations "would be meaningless," since they could be avoided simply by pleading under the ATS.[48] Other courts have disagreed, and have allowed plaintiffs to choose whether to bring claims of torture or extrajudicial killing under either the ATS or TVPA.[49] In any event, for ATS cases that do not involve torture or extrajudicial killing, most courts have held that the TVPA's exhaustion requirement does not apply.[50] By contrast, most courts have held that the TVPA's ten-year statute of limitations does apply to ATS cases, reasoning that ATS claims should be subject to some limitations period and that the TVPA is the most appropriate place from which to borrow such a limitation.[51]

The *Sosa* Decision

The Supreme Court finally addressed the validity of the *Filartiga* line of cases in a 2004 decision, *Sosa v. Alvarez-Machain*.[52] That case concerned the abduction of a Mexican doctor, Alvarez-Machain, in Mexico at the behest of the U.S. Drug Enforcement Agency (DEA), so that he could be tried in the United States on criminal charges. The doctor was suspected of having assisted in the torture and murder of a DEA agent in Mexico, and diplomatic efforts to persuade Mexico to deliver him to the United States had not been successful. The case was reviewed twice by the Supreme Court. In the Court's first decision, which is discussed in Chapter 9, the Court held that the United States had not breached the U.S.–Mexico Extradition Treaty in arranging for the abduction of Alvarez-Machain.[53]

After that decision, the federal trial court that was hearing the criminal case against Alvarez-Machain dismissed the charges for lack of evidence. Alvarez-Machain then brought suit, under the ATS, against both the U.S. government and the Mexican agents who were involved in his abduction. By the time the case reached the Supreme Court the second time, the ATS portion of his case was limited to arbitrary detention claims against one of the Mexican agents, Sosa. The claims against the United States all fell under the Federal Tort Claims Act, which regulates the government's liability for tort claims, and

---

[48] Enahoro v. Abubakar, 408 F.3d 877, 884–85 (7th Cir. 2005).
[49] *See, e.g.*, Aldana v. Del Monte Fresh Produce, 416 F.3d 1242, 1250–51 (11th Cir. 2005).
[50] *See, e.g.*, Jean v. Dorelien, 431 F.3d 776 (11th Cir. 2005); Doe v. Saravia, 348 F. Supp. 2d 1112, 1157–58 (E.D. Cal. 2004).
[51] *See, e.g.*, Chavez v. Carranza, 559 F.3d 486, 492 (6th Cir. 2009); Arce v. Garcia, 400 F.3d 1340, 1345–46 (11th Cir. 2005); Papa v. United States, 281 F.3d 1004, 1012–13 (9th Cir. 2002). For additional discussion of the relationship between the ATS and the TVPA, *see* Philip Mariani, *Assessing the Proper Relationship between the Alien Tort Statute and the Torture Victim Protection Act*, 156 U. PA. L. REV. 1383 (2008).
[52] 542 U.S. 692 (2004).
[53] *See* United States v. Alvarez-Machain, 504 U.S. 655 (1992).

those claims were dismissed by the Supreme Court on the basis of limitations in that particular statute.

The Supreme Court unanimously agreed in *Sosa* that the ATS is a jurisdictional provision that does not create any causes of action. Among other things, the Court noted that the Statute is written in jurisdictional terms and was enacted as part of the Judiciary Act, which concerned federal court jurisdiction, not causes of action.[54] This holding was in accord with part of what Judge Bork had argued in *Tel-Oren.*

A majority of the Court nevertheless concluded that, in light of the "ambient law of the era" in which the ATS was enacted, it was appropriate to allow some modern law-of-nations claims to be brought without a separate cause of action statute.[55] The Court reasoned that the Congress that enacted the ATS would not have viewed it merely "as a jurisdictional convenience to be placed on the shelf for use by a future Congress or state legislature that might, someday, authorize the creation of causes of action or itself decide to make some element of the law of nations actionable for the benefit of foreigners."[56] Instead, the Court thought that Congress likely would have expected that at least a few common law tort claims could have been brought under the Statute without the need for a separate cause of action statute—in particular, the individual law of nations violations recited by Blackstone, that is, claims relating to offenses against ambassadors, violations of "safe conducts" (promises to enemy aliens to come through the territory without impediment), and actions relating to piracy and prize cases.[57] The Court therefore construed the ATS as "underwrit[ing] litigation of a narrow set of common law actions derived from the law of nations."[58]

Applying this interpretation of the ATS, the Court concluded that it would be appropriate to allow a "modest number" of modern law-of-nations claims to be brought under the Statute, subject to what the Court referred to as "vigilant door-keeping" by the federal courts.[59] Because the Court tied the allowance of these claims to the historical expectations of the Congress that enacted the ATS, the Court said that "any claim based on the present-day law of nations [should] rest on a norm of international character accepted by the civilized world and defined with a specificity comparable to the features of the 18th-century paradigms we have recognized."[60] The Court also noted that "the determination

---

[54] 542 U.S. at 713–14. *See also id.* at 729 ("All Members of the Court agree that § 1350 is only jurisdictional.").

[55] *Id.* at 714.

[56] *Id.* at 719.

[57] *Id.* at 715–16, 719–20.

[58] *Id.* at 721. In effect, the Supreme Court attempted to translate what it believed to be the jurisprudential assumptions of the 1789 Congress to modern standards for causes of action and federal common law. *See, e.g.*, Curtis A. Bradley, Jack L. Goldsmith & David H. Moore, Sosa, *Customary International Law, and the Continuing Relevance of* Erie, 120 HARV. L. REV. 869, 873 (2007) (noting this translation point); RICHARD H. FALLON, JR. ET AL., HART AND WECHSLER'S THE FEDERAL COURTS AND THE FEDERAL SYSTEM 720 (7th ed. 2015) (same).

[59] 542 U.S. at 729.

[60] *Id.* at 725.

whether a norm is sufficiently definite to support a cause of action should (and, indeed, inevitably must) involve an element of judgment about the practical consequences of making that cause available to litigants in the federal courts."[61] Although the Court did not specifically say where the cause of action is coming from in these suits, it appears to have had in mind that the ATS is delegating to the federal courts the authority to create a federal common law cause of action for the allowable claims. It noted, for example, that "federal courts should not recognize private claims *under federal common law* for violations of any international law norm with less definite content and acceptance among civilized nations than the historical paradigms familiar when [the ATS] was enacted."[62]

Despite allowing the ATS to be used for modern law-of-nations claims, the Court emphasized the need for "judicial caution."[63] Such caution was appropriate, the Court explained, as a result of a number of considerations: conceptions of the common law, and the role of federal judges in developing it, have changed substantially since the enactment of the ATS; the Supreme Court in recent years has urged a narrow approach to both federal common law and implied rights of action on the ground that the legislative branch rather than the courts should generally make the policy decisions associated with allowing new claims; international law now regulates how nations treat their own citizens, something that would not have been envisioned when the ATS was enacted; judicial scrutiny of the human rights practices of foreign governments has the potential to interfere with political branch management of U.S. foreign relations; and, when the political branches have ratified human rights treaties, they have gone out of their way to make clear that those treaties—which are often cited as the source of law-of-nations human rights norms—are not judicially enforceable.[64]

The Court proceeded to reject Alvarez-Machain's particular claim of short-term arbitrary detention on the ground that it did not involve the violation of a norm of customary international law that was sufficiently well defined to meet the Court's test. In

---

[61] *Id.* at 732–33.

[62] *Id.* at 732 (emphasis added); *see also id.* at 738 ("Creating a private cause of action to further that aspiration [argued by Alvarez-Machain] would go beyond any residual *common law discretion* we think it appropriate to exercise.") (emphasis added); Sarei v. Rio Tinto, PLC, 671 F.3d 736, 751 (9th Cir. 2011) (en banc) ("[W]e read *Sosa* to permit courts to develop the federal common law by incorporating into it certain claims that derive from norms of international law—but only after determining that they meet the *Sosa* standards limiting those norms for ATS purposes."). The Supreme Court therefore appears to have adopted Professor Casto's suggestion that the ATS "though not creating a statutory cause of action, does create a federal forum in which federal judges are given power to implement the law of nations by fashioning appropriate domestic federal remedies." Casto, *supra* note 1, at 480. For an argument that courts are not well positioned to exercise this delegated authority, *see* Julian Ku & John Yoo, *Beyond Formalism in Foreign Affairs: A Functional Approach to the Alien Tort Statute*, 2004 SUP. CT. REV. 153.

[63] 542 U.S. at 725. *See also id.* at 727 ("Since many attempts by federal courts to craft remedies for the violation of new norms of international law would raise risks of adverse foreign policy consequences, they should be undertaken, if at all, with great caution.").

[64] *See id.* at 725–28.

reaching this conclusion, the Court—unlike the court in *Filartiga*—declined to give significant weight to non-binding UN resolutions and non–self-executing treaties.[65] The Court also expressed concern that the consequences of allowing the ATS to be used for claims of short-term arbitrary detention would be "breathtaking" because it "would support a cause of action in federal court for any arrest, anywhere in the world, unauthorized by the law of the jurisdiction in which it took place."[66]

The *Sosa* decision resolved some issues about international human rights litigation but left many other issues unresolved. The decision made clear that some modern customary international law claims would be allowed under the ATS even in the absence of additional implementing legislation. It also made clear that ATS litigation should be limited to a "modest" number of such claims, although the precise implications of this limitation are unclear, and different judges are likely to have different understandings of it.

The Court in *Sosa* did not address the domestic status of customary international law outside the context of the ATS, and its relevance to that broader issue is uncertain. On the one hand, the Court appears to have assumed that the customary international law claims that are allowed under the ATS will have the status of federal common law. On the other hand, the Court emphasized that these claims are authorized by the ATS and did not suggest that they would have had federal law status in the absence of such statutory authorization. In fact, the Court expressly noted that its holding did not necessarily mean that courts could develop common law claims to enforce customary international law in cases not brought under the ATS.[67]

Extraterritoriality

As discussed in Chapter 6, it is generally accepted today that customary international law disallows nations from applying their laws to conduct outside their territory by foreign nationals unless the conduct causes effects within the nation's territory or violates

---

[65] *See id.* at 734 (noting that these instruments "have little utility under the standard set out in this opinion").

[66] *Id.* at 736. Justice Scalia wrote a concurrence that was joined by two other justices. He argued that the reasons that the majority gave for judicial caution were sufficiently strong that modern law-of-nations claims should not be allowed under the Statute absent congressional codification of such claims. *See id.* at 747. Justice Scalia also complained that the Court was in effect allowing the lower courts to engage in judicial lawmaking, "by converting what they regard as norms of international law into American law," in violation of the proper separation of powers between the judiciary and Congress. *Id.* at 750.

[67] *See id.* at 731 n.19. For an argument that *Sosa* implicitly rejects the "modern position" claim that customary international law is automatically federal common law, *see* Bradley, Goldsmith, & Moore, *supra* note 58. For commentary on this article, *see* William S. Dodge, *Customary International Law and the Question of Legitimacy*, 120 HARV. L. REV. F. 19 (2007); Ernest A. Young, *Sosa and the Retail Incorporation of International Law*, 120 HARV. L. REV. F. 28 (2007). *See also Sarei*, 671 F.3d at 752 ("The norms underlying international law torts are not [themselves] part of the 'Laws of the United States' for purposes of Article III until they have been incorporated into the federal common law pursuant to the exacting process articulated in *Sosa*.").

one of a small set of universally accepted norms. Customary international law was even more territorial when the ATS was enacted. Although it was understood at that time that courts might in some cases apply foreign law to adjudicate foreign disputes,[68] prescriptive jurisdiction (the power of a nation to apply its laws to regulate conduct) was viewed as territorially restricted. An influential Dutch scholar, Ulrich Huber, had written in the 1600s that "The laws of each state have force within the limits of that government and bind all subjects to it, but not beyond."[69] Echoing Huber and subsequent commentators, the U.S. jurist Joseph Story would later explain in his conflict of laws treatise that "no state or nation can, by its laws, directly affect, or bind... persons not resident therein," because to do so "would be wholly incompatible with the equality and exclusiveness of the sovereignty of any nation."[70] A potential exception to the territorial nature of prescriptive jurisdiction was for the regulation of a nation's own citizens. As the U.S. Supreme Court stated in the early 1800s, "the legislation of every country is territorial; that beyond its own territory, *it can only affect its own subjects or citizens.*"[71]

Another exception to territorial limitations on prescriptive jurisdiction concerned the prosecution of piracy. At the time the ATS was enacted, it was understood that pirates were *hosti humani generis*—enemies of all mankind. As a result, they could be prosecuted wherever they were found, regardless of their nationality or where their acts of piracy acts took place.[72] In the *Sosa* decision already discussed, the Supreme Court surmised that

---

[68] *See, e.g.*, THE FEDERALIST NO. 82 (Alexander Hamilton), at 491, 493 (Clinton Rossiter ed., 1961) ("The judiciary power of every government looks beyond its own local or municipal laws, and in civil cases lays hold of all subjects of litigation between parties within its jurisdiction, though the causes of dispute are relative to the laws of the most distant part of the globe. Those of Japan, not less than of New York, may furnish the objects of legal discussion to our courts."); 1 ST. GEORGE TUCKER, BLACKSTONE'S COMMENTARIES: WITH NOTES OF REFERENCE, TO THE CONSTITUTION AND LAWS OF THE FEDERAL GOVERNMENT OF THE UNITED STATES app. at 421 (1803) (noting that in diversity cases the rule of decision would be based on "the municipal law of the place where the cause of controversy arises, whether that be one of the United States, or Great Britain, France, Spain, Holland, Hamburg, or any other country").

[69] ULRICH HUBER, DE CONFLICTU LEGUM DIVERSARUM IN DIVERSIS IMPERIIS, cited and quoted in Ernest G. Lorenzen, *Huber's De Conflictu Legum*, 13 ILL. L. REV. 375, 376 & app. at 403 (1919).

[70] JOSEPH STORY, COMMENTARIES ON THE CONFLICT OF LAWS 21 (1834). For an argument, made prior to the Supreme Court's 2013 decision in *Kiobel*, that corporate ATS litigation violated international law limitations on extraterritoriality, *see* Michael D. Ramsey, *International Law Limits on Investor Liability in Human Rights Litigation*, 50 HARV. INT'L L.J. 271 (2009). For an argument that the ATS's reference to "aliens" was intended as a reference to foreign citizens residing in the United States, *see* M. Anderson Berry, *Whether Foreigner or Alien: A New Look at the Original Language of the Alien Tort Statute*, 27 BERKELEY J. INT'L L. 316 (2009).

[71] Rose v. Himely, 8 U.S. (4 Cranch) 241, 279 (1807) (emphasis added); *see also* The Apollon, 22 U.S. 362, 370 (1824) ("The laws of no nation can justly extend beyond its own territories, *except so far as regards its own citizens.*") (emphasis added).

[72] *See, e.g.*, United States v. Smith, 18 U.S. (5 Wheat.) 153, 161 (1820) (referring to piracy as "an offence against the universal law of society, a pirate being deemed an enemy of the human race"); United States v. Klintock, 18 U.S. (5 Wheat.) 144, 152 (1820) (stating that persons committing piracy "are proper subjects for the penal code of all nations"); *see also* Eugene Kontorovich, *The Piracy Analogy: Modern Universal Jurisdiction's Hollow Foundation*, 45 HARV. INT'L L.J. 183, 190 (2004) ("For as long as sovereignty-based jurisdictional principles

one of the tort actions that historically could have been brought under the ATS was an action for piracy.[73] If so, that would suggest that the ATS was not limited to acts occurring within the United States. At the same time, a conclusion that the ATS historically could have been used to address piracy would not necessarily show that the ATS also extended to conduct committed within the territory of a foreign sovereign. At its core, after all, piracy involved conduct on the "high seas" rather than in another state's territorial jurisdiction,[74] and pirate ships were considered to be essentially stateless and thus not under any nation's exclusive jurisdiction.[75]

As discussed in Chapter 6, courts sometimes apply a strict "presumption against extraterritoriality" when considering whether federal statutes apply to foreign conduct. Until recently, however, courts were generally not concerned about extraterritoriality when applying the ATS.[76] ATS cases involve violations of international law, so the perception was that these cases did not raise the same prescriptive jurisdiction issues raised by the extraterritorial application of national law.[77] In addition, some courts pointed out that it is not uncommon to adjudicate even purely domestic law torts that occur abroad,

---

have existed (that is, at least since the early seventeenth century), any nation could try any pirates it caught, regardless of the pirates' nationality or where on the high seas they were apprehended.").

[73] *See* Sosa v. Alvarez-Machain, 542 U.S. 692, 720, 724 (2004).

[74] In the U.S. Constitution, Congress is given the authority to "define and punish piracies and felonies *committed on the high seas.*" U.S. CONST., art. I, § 8, cl. 10 (emphasis added). The federal criminal piracy statute is therefore not surprisingly limited to conduct on the high seas. *See* 18 U.S.C. § 1651. *See also* 4 WILLIAM BLACKSTONE, COMMENTARIES *72 ("The offence of piracy, by common law, consists in committing those acts of robbery and depredation upon the high seas, which, if committed upon land, would have amounted to felony there."). The original federal piracy statute, enacted in 1790, extended not only to the high seas, but also to "any river, haven, basin or bay, out of the jurisdiction of any state." An Act for the Punishment of Certain Crimes against the United States, 1 Stat. 112, § 8 (1790).

[75] *See, e.g.,* United States v. Hasan, 747 F. Supp. 2d 599, 611 (E.D. Va. 2010) ("[U]nlike modern universal jurisdiction crimes, which invoke the doctrine of universal jurisdiction on the basis of the offense's heinousness, piracy was the subject of universal jurisdiction because pirates were stateless actors, able to interfere with global commerce and navigation as a result of the difficulty inherent in policing the high seas."). *See also* Eugene Kontorovich, *Beyond the Article I Horizon: Congress's Enumerated Powers and Universal Jurisdiction over Drug Crimes*, 93 MINN. L. REV. 1191, 1228 (2009) ("The international law of the [period of early U.S. history] did treat pirate ships as having lost their national character or protection.").

[76] For two dissenting opinions arguing that the ATS should not be applied to conduct by foreign citizens in foreign countries, *see* Sarei v. Rio Tinto, PLC, 671 F.3d 736, 809 (9th Cir. 2011) (en banc) (Kleinfeld, J., dissenting); and Doe v. Exxon Mobil Corp., 654 F.3d 11, 30–32, 74–81 (D.C. Cir. 2011) (Kavanaugh, J., dissenting).

[77] *See, e.g., In re* S. African Apartheid Litig., 617 F. Supp. 2d 228, 246–47 (S.D.N.Y. 2009) ("The [ATS] does not by its own terms regulate conduct; rather it applies universal norms that forbid conduct regardless of territorial demarcations or sovereign prerogatives."). *See also* William S. Dodge, *Alien Tort Litigation and the Prescriptive Jurisdiction Fallacy*, 51 HARV. INT'L L.J. ONLINE 35, 37 (2010) ("Courts do not apply U.S. substantive law in ATS cases; they apply customary international law."), *available at* http://www.harvardilj.org/wp-content/uploads/2010/09/HILJ-Online_51_Dodge.pdf. *But see* Ramsey, *supra* note 70, at 298 ("The decision whether to allow individuals to make claims in court, as opposed to offering some other kind of remedy, lies with individual nations. Thus an individual judicial claim based on customary international law depends on a national act to create liability and a right to sue.").

pursuant to the common law doctrine of "transitory torts."[78] When adjudicating foreign torts, however, courts often will apply foreign law rather than U.S. law.[79] Although the court in *Filartiga* entertained that possibility, most subsequent ATS decisions have not, and the Supreme Court in *Sosa* appeared to suggest that the law governing the cause of action in an ATS case is coming from U.S. federal common law, not the law of the place where the tort occurred.

An early opinion by a U.S. Attorney General that mentions the ATS can be read to support some extraterritorial applications of the Statute. The opinion, issued in 1795, concerned the involvement of U.S. citizens in an attack by a French fleet on a British settlement in Sierra Leone.[80] The Attorney General reasoned that, to the extent the conduct occurred in a foreign country, the United States could not exercise criminal jurisdiction over it. He also expressed the view that, to the extent the conduct occurred on the high seas, it might be subject to a U.S. criminal prosecution "in any district wherein the offenders may be found," although he noted that there was some doubt on this point in light of how the relevant federal criminal statute was written. "But there can be no doubt," he said, "that the company or individuals who have been injured by these acts of hostility have a remedy by a *civil* suit in the courts of the United States; jurisdiction being expressly given to these courts in all cases where an alien sues for a tort only, in violation of the laws of nations, or a treaty of the United States." The Attorney General thus appears to have assumed that the ATS could be applied to foreign torts, at least when committed by U.S. citizens.[81]

The Court in *Sosa* did not provide much guidance about whether or to what extent the ATS applies to foreign conduct. In that case, there was foreign conduct (short-term arbitrary arrest), but, unlike most extraterritorial ATS cases, it was connected to actions taken within the United States (directions from the U.S. Drug Enforcement Agency). Moreover, the ATS claim there was rejected on other grounds, so the Court did not need

---

[78] *See, e.g., Exxon Mobil*, 654 F.3d at 24–25 ("Extraterritorial application of the ATS would reflect the contemporaneous understanding that, by the time of the Judiciary Act of 1789, a transitory tort action arising out of activities beyond the forum state's territorial limits could be tried in the forum state."); Filartiga v. Pena-Irala, 630 F.2d 876, 885 (2d Cir. 1980) ("Common law courts of general jurisdiction regularly [have] adjudicate[d] transitory tort claims between individuals over whom they exercise personal jurisdiction, wherever the tort occurred.").

[79] Under the approach of the *Restatement (First) of Conflict of Laws*, the law where the tort occurred would normally be applied, pursuant to the principle of *lex loci delicti*. Under the approach of the *Restatement (Second) of Conflict of Laws*, the law of the place with the "most significant relationship to the occurrence and the parties" would apply. *See Sosa*, 542 U.S. at 707–10 (noting that under both of these approaches foreign law will often be applied). Although the district court in *Filartiga* looked in part to foreign law in adjudicating the tort in that case, *see* 577 F. Supp. 860, 864 (E.D.N.Y. 1984), most subsequent ATS decisions have not done so.

[80] *See* 1 OP. ATT'Y GEN. 57 (1795).

[81] *See* Casto, *supra* note 1, at 502–04. For discussion of the diplomatic context of the Bradford opinion, based on archival research in the records of the U.S. State Department and the British Foreign Office, *see* Curtis A. Bradley, *Attorney General Bradford's Opinion and the Alien Tort Statute*, 106 AM. J. INT'L L. 509 (2012).

to address the issue of extraterritoriality. The Court did appear to accept the validity of the *Filartiga* decision, which involved conduct by a foreign citizen in a foreign country, although the Court did not specifically comment on the extraterritorial aspect of the decision.[82] But in describing some of the reasons for judicial caution in applying the ATS, the Court noted that although modern international human rights law regulates how nations treat their own citizens, "many attempts by federal courts to craft remedies for the violation of new norms of international law would raise risks of adverse foreign policy consequences, [and thus] should be undertaken, *if at all*, with great caution."[83]

The choice-of-law question discussed above intersects with the issue of extraterritoriality. The more that ATS litigation becomes infused with federal common law principles, the more that this litigation appears to involve the projection of American law overseas. As noted in Chapter 6, U.S. courts often presume that federal statutes do not apply to conduct outside the United States. In its briefing in *Sosa*, the executive branch argued that this presumption applied to claims allowed under the ATS and that "[n]othing in [the ATS], or in its contemporary history, suggests that Congress contemplated that suits would be brought based on conduct against aliens in foreign lands."[84] But the Court decided the case on other grounds.

Even if the presumption against extraterritoriality were inapplicable to the ATS, there would be a strong case for applying the *Charming Betsy* canon to limit the scope of ATS litigation. Under that canon, as discussed in Chapter 1, U.S. courts have long construed federal statutes to avoid violations of international law when fairly possible (including violations of international law limitations on extraterritoriality), based on the assumption that courts should not place the United States in breach of international law obligations absent a clear directive from Congress. If anything, this concern with judicial actions that may place the United States in breach of international law without a clear congressional directive has greater force in the context of the ATS, where the claims are grounded in federal common law rather than statutory directive.

As noted in Chapter 6, however, the international law of prescriptive jurisdiction probably allows today for some applications of "universal jurisdiction," at least in criminal cases. In particular, there is significant support for the idea that certain egregious acts, such as piracy, genocide, war crimes, crimes against humanity, slavery, and official torture, can be prosecuted by any nation, regardless of where the conduct occurs.[85] If universal

---

[82] *See* 542 U.S. at 731 ("The position we take today has been assumed by some federal courts for 24 years, ever since the Second Circuit decided Filartiga v. Pena-Irala, 630 F.2d 876 (CA2 1980). . . .").

[83] *Id.* at 727–28.

[84] Brief for the United States as Respondent Supporting Petitioner, at 48, Sosa v. Alvarez-Machain, No. 03–339 (Jan. 2004), *available at* https://www.justice.gov/osg/brief/sosa-v-alvarez-machain-brief-merits. For discussion of how ATS litigation became increasingly infused with federal common law principles, *see* William S. Dodge, *Alien Tort Litigation: The Road Not Taken*, 89 NOTRE DAME L. REV. 1577, 1594–1602 (2014).

[85] *See, e.g.*, INTERNATIONAL LAW ASSOCIATION, COMM. ON INT'L HUMAN RIGHTS LAW AND PRACTICE, FINAL REPORT ON THE EXERCISE OF UNIVERSAL JURISDICTION IN RESPECT OF GROSS HUMAN

jurisdiction applies as well in the civil context (a matter of some debate),[86] then ATS cases involving conduct abroad would not violate international law restrictions on prescriptive jurisdiction in situations in which the conduct falls within universal jurisdiction. This is what the court seemed to suggest in *Filartiga* when it stated that "for purposes of civil liability, the torturer has become like the pirate and slave trader before him *hostis humani generis*, an enemy of all mankind."[87]

Kiobel v. Royal Dutch Petroleum

In its 2013 decision, *Kiobel v. Royal Dutch Petroleum Co.*, the Supreme Court held that the presumption against extraterritoriality applies to claims under the ATS.[88] In *Kiobel*, twelve Nigerian citizens who had obtained political asylum in the United States brought suit against a Dutch oil company and a British oil company. The Nigerian plaintiffs alleged that these companies, through their Nigerian subsidiary, had aided and abetted human rights abuses committed by the Nigerian military in the 1990s. Among other things, the Nigerian subsidiary was alleged to have provided transportation to Nigerian forces, allowed its property to be utilized as a staging ground for attacks, provided food for soldiers involved in the attacks, and provided compensation to those soldiers.

The Supreme Court agreed to review the case after the U.S. Court of Appeals for the Second Circuit held that corporations could not be sued under the ATS, a decision that, as already noted, created a conflict in the circuits. After initially hearing oral argument on the issue of corporate liability, the Supreme Court directed the parties to provide supplemental briefing about whether and to what extent the ATS "allows courts to recognize a cause of action for violations of the law of nations occurring within the territory of a sovereign other than the United States."[89] The Court then proceeded to hold that

---

RIGHTS OFFENCES 4–9 (2000); THE PRINCETON PRINCIPLES ON UNIVERSAL JURISDICTION 29 (2001); RESTATEMENT (THIRD) OF THE FOREIGN RELATIONS LAW OF THE UNITED STATES § 404 (1987).

[86] *See* International Bar Association, *Report of the Task Force on Extraterritorial Jurisdiction* 128 ("Universal civil jurisdiction remains a controversial topic within the area of extraterritorial tort jurisdiction."); Note, *Developments in the Law—Extraterritoriality Law and International Norm Internalization*, 124 HARV. L. REV. 1280, 1282 (2011) ("The legality of this kind of universal civil jurisdiction remains highly contentious."). *See also* Curtis A. Bradley, *Universal Jurisdiction and U.S. Law*, 2001 U. CHI. LEG. F. 323; M.O. Chibundu, *Making Customary International Law through Municipal Adjudication: A Structural Inquiry*, 39 VA. J. INT'L L. 1069 (1999); Donald Francis Donovan & Anthea Roberts, *The Emerging Recognition of Universal Civil Jurisdiction*, 100 AM. J. INT'L L. 142 (2006).

[87] 630 F.2d at 890. For an argument that modern human rights claims are not in fact comparable to the universal crime of piracy, *see* Eugene Kontorovich, *Implementing* Sosa v. Alvarez-Machain: *What Piracy Reveals about the Limits of the Alien Tort Statute*, 80 NOTRE DAME L. REV. 111 (2004).

[88] *See* Curtis A. Bradley, ASIL Insight, *Supreme Court Holds That Alien Tort Statute Does Not Apply to Conduct in Foreign Countries* (Apr. 18, 2013), at http://www.asil.org/sites/default/files/insight130418.pdf.

[89] Kiobel v. Royal Dutch Petroleum Co., 565 U.S. 1244 (2012).

the claims in the case were unduly extraterritorial.[90] All nine justices agreed with that proposition, but they were divided on the reasoning. A five-justice majority held that the general presumption against extraterritoriality applies to the ATS.

While acknowledging that the ATS is potentially distinguishable from federal statutes that expressly create a cause of action, the majority reasoned that "the danger of unwarranted judicial interference in the conduct of foreign policy is magnified in the context of the ATS, because the question is not what Congress has done but instead what courts may do."[91] The ATS was designed to help the United States avoid foreign relations friction, reasoned the Court, such as by ensuring an avenue of redress for foreign officials injured within this country. "Nothing about this historical context," said the Court, "suggests that Congress also intended federal common law under the ATS to provide a cause of action for conduct occurring in the territory of another sovereign."[92] The Court also expressed concern that applying the ATS to foreign conduct can generate rather than avoid foreign relations strife and can create reciprocity problems for the United States. If such "serious foreign policy consequences" are to be triggered, concluded the Court, they should stem from decisions made by the political branches rather than the judiciary.[93]

The majority concluded its analysis by explaining more specifically why the claims in this case should be dismissed:

> On these facts, all the relevant conduct took place outside the United States. And even where the claims touch and concern the territory of the United States, they must do so with sufficient force to displace the presumption against extraterritorial application. . . . Corporations are often present in many countries, and it would reach too far to say that mere corporate presence suffices. If Congress were to determine otherwise, a statute more specific than the ATS would be required.[94]

In addition to joining the majority opinion, Justice Kennedy wrote a one-paragraph concurrence noting that the Court was "leav[ing] open a number of significant questions regarding the reach and interpretation of the Alien Tort Statute."[95] Although Kennedy did not specifically identify those questions, he did observe that cases might arise that are covered neither by the TVPA nor by the reasoning in the majority opinion, "and in those disputes the proper implementation of the presumption against extraterritorial application may require some further elaboration and explanation."[96]

---

[90] *See* Kiobel v. Royal Dutch Petroleum Co., 569 U.S. 108 (2013).
[91] *Id.* at 116.
[92] *Id.* at 124.
[93] *Id.*
[94] *Id.* at 124–25.
[95] *Id.* at 125 (Kennedy, J., concurring).
[96] *Id.*

Justice Alito also wrote a short additional concurrence, joined by Justice Thomas, expressing the view that "a putative ATS cause of action will fall within the scope of the presumption against extraterritoriality—and will therefore be barred—unless the domestic conduct is sufficient to violate an international law norm that satisfies *Sosa*'s requirements of definiteness and acceptance among civilized nations."[97] The majority, however, did not specifically endorse such a requirement.

In a concurrence joined by three other justices, Justice Breyer agreed that the case should be dismissed but disagreed with the majority's reasoning. Breyer argued that, rather than applying the presumption against extraterritoriality, the Court should have limited ATS litigation to three circumstances: when either "(1) the alleged tort occurs on American soil, (2) the defendant is an American national, or (3) the defendant's conduct substantially and adversely affects an important American national interest, and that includes a distinct interest in preventing the United States from becoming a safe harbor (free of civil as well as criminal liability) for a torturer or other common enemy of mankind."[98] Instead of applying a categorical presumption, Breyer thought it appropriate to look to international jurisdictional norms to help determine the proper reach of the ATS, and he noted that these norms sometimes allow for the exercise of prescriptive jurisdiction over foreign conduct. Breyer would have further limited the reach of the ATS to situations in which "distinct American interests are at issue."[99] One of those interests, he contended, is in "not becoming a safe harbor for violators of the most fundamental international norms."[100] Justice Breyer nevertheless agreed that this particular case should be dismissed. Given "the defendants' minimal and indirect American presence," reasoned Breyer, "it would be farfetched to believe . . . that this legal action helps to vindicate a distinct American interest."[101]

In generally disallowing ATS suits for human rights abuses committed abroad, *Kiobel* sharply limited ATS litigation. Its precise implications, however, are a matter of some dispute. In particular, there has been dispute over what is required in order for an ATS claim to, in the words of the Court, "touch and concern the territory of the United States with sufficient force to displace the presumption against extraterritorial application." In light of this standard, it is possible that some ATS cases can still be brought concerning foreign conduct if there is evidence of direction or support of the conduct from the United States.[102] It might also be argued that the touch and concern standard is met if an

---

[97] *Id.* at 127 (Alito, J., concurring).
[98] *Id.* (Breyer, J., concurring in the judgment).
[99] *Id.* at 133.
[100] *Id.*
[101] *Id.* at 140.
[102] For a decision concluding that *Kiobel* disallows all claims "based on illegal conduct that occurred entirely in the territory of another sovereign," *see* Balintulo v. Daimler AG, 727 F.3d 174, 192 (2d Cir. 2013); *see also* Cardona v. Chiquita Brands Int'l, Inc., 760 F.3d 1185 (11th Cir. 2014) (reading *Kiobel* as broadly disallowing claims relating to foreign conduct); Mastafa v. Chevron Corp., 770 F.3d 170 (2d Cir. 2014) (disallowing application of the ATS unless there is conduct in the United States that violates the law of nations or aids and abets

individual defendant commits human rights abuses abroad and then moves to the United States, but the argument does not seem very strong (since the *tortious conduct* would not be connected to the United States), and the lower courts to date have not been receptive to this reading of the decision.[103]

Corporate Human Rights Litigation

Violations of international law, whether customary or treaty-based, generally require state action.[104] This is true even for violations of many international human rights norms, such as the prohibition on torture.[105] Nevertheless, starting in the mid-1990s, ATS suits were increasingly brought against private corporations. The decision that helped pave the way for corporate ATS litigation, *Kadic v. Karadzic*, did not involve a corporate defendant.[106] Rather, it involved a suit by Croat and Muslim citizens of Bosnia-Herzegovina against Radovan Karadzic, the leader of a breakaway Bosnian-Serb republic, for atrocities committed under his command. In allowing the case to proceed, the Second Circuit first noted that the violation of some norms of international law, such as the prohibitions on genocide and war crimes, do not require state action.[107] As for the violations that do require state action, the court reasoned that the breakaway republic might properly be

---

a violation of the law of nations). For a decision finding that claims relating to alleged abuses committed by civilian contractors employed by a U.S. corporation at a U.S. military facility in Iraq sufficiently touched and concerned the United States to overcome the presumption against extraterritoriality, *see* Al Shamari v. CACI Premier Technology, Inc., 758 F.3d 516 (4th Cir. 2014). For a decision allowing an ATS suit to proceed against U.S. corporations that were alleged to have provided financial assistance to cocoa farms in the Ivory Coast that used child slave labor, *see* Doe v. Nestle, S.A., 906 F.3d 1120 (9th Cir. 2018), *amended*, 929 F.3d 623 (9th Cir. 2018). (The Supreme Court subsequently agreed to review this decision during its 2020–21 Term.) In applying the touch and concern test, some courts have considered whether any U.S. conduct alleged in the case falls within the "focus" of the ATS, an approach that is drawn from Supreme Court decisions applying the presumption against extraterritoriality outside the ATS context. (For additional discussion of the "focus" analysis, see Chapter 6.)

[103] *See, e.g.*, Jara v. Núñez, 878 F.3d 1268, 1272 (11th Cir. 2018) ("[A] defendant must have engaged in relevant conduct on American soil before a claim carries sufficient force to displace the presumption against extraterritorial application."); Warfaa v. Ali, 811 F.3d 653, 661 (4th Cir. 2016) ("Mere happenstance of residency, lacking any connection to the relevant conduct, is not a cognizable consideration in the ATS context.").

[104] *See introductory note* to RESTATEMENT (THIRD) OF THE FOREIGN RELATIONS LAW OF THE UNITED STATES, *supra* note 85, ch. 2; 1 OPPENHEIM'S INTERNATIONAL LAW § 6 (Robert Jennings & Arthur Watts eds., 9th ed. 1992).

[105] *See* RESTATEMENT (THIRD) OF THE FOREIGN RELATIONS LAW OF THE UNITED STATES, *supra* note 85, at § 702 & cmt. b. For example, the U.N. Convention against Torture and Other Cruel, Inhuman, or Degrading Treatment or Punishment covers only torture "inflicted by or at the instigation of or with the consent or acquiescence of a public official or other person acting in an official capacity." Convention against Torture and Other Cruel, Inhuman or Degrading Treatment or Punishment, adopted Dec. 10, 1984, S. TREATY DOC. No. 100–20 (1988), 1465 U.N.T.S. 113 (entered into force June 26, 1987).

[106] *See* Kadic v. Karadzic, 70 F.3d 232 (2d Cir. 1995).

[107] *See id.* at 240.

considered a state for these purposes.[108] Even if it was not a state, however, the court concluded that Karadzic's actions could still be considered state action for purposes of liability under the ATS if he had "acted in concert" with the Yugoslav government.[109]

The *Karadzic* decision made clear that nonstate actors could potentially be sued under the ATS. After that decision, numerous ATS suits were brought against a particular type of nonstate actor—corporations—relating to their involvement with abusive foreign governments.[110] For a variety of reasons, corporate defendants were attractive targets for ATS suits: corporations are not thought to benefit from the sovereign immunity doctrines that apply to governmental defendants; most large corporations have a presence in the United States, making it easy to obtain personal jurisdiction over them in this country; they typically have substantial assets that can be reached by U.S. courts; and they have an incentive to settle cases in order to avoid bad publicity. For better or worse, the rise of these corporate cases changed the character of ATS litigation. Whereas the early cases were focused primarily on obtaining symbolic redress and on publicizing human rights abuses, the corporate cases were more centrally focused on monetary compensation.

Most of these suits did not allege that the corporations themselves committed human rights violations. Instead, they alleged that the corporations "aided and abetted" human rights violations by foreign government officials. Outside the context of the ATS, the Supreme Court has stated that, for civil statutes imposing damages liability, "there is no general presumption that the plaintiff may also sue aiders and abettors."[111] This is true even though, as the Court acknowledged, aiding and abetting "is an ancient criminal law doctrine."[112]

The ATS refers to torts "committed in violation of" international law and does not mention secondary liability. Nevertheless, the lower federal courts generally accepted the availability of aiding and abetting liability, largely because such liability has support in international criminal law.[113] There was debate, however, over the proper standard to be

---

[108] *See id.* at 244–45.

[109] *Id.* at 245.

[110] One of the first ATS suits brought against a corporate defendant was *Doe v. Unocal Corp.*, 963 F. Supp. 880 (C.D. Cal. 1997), *aff'd in part and rev'd in part*, 395 F.3d 932 (9th Cir. 2002).

[111] Cent. Bank of Denver v. First Interstate Bank of Denver, 511 U.S. 164, 182 (1994); *see also* Boim v. Holy Land Found. for Relief & Dev., 549 F.3d 685, 689 (7th Cir. 2008) (en banc) ("[S]tatutory silence on the subject of secondary liability means there is none."); Curtis A. Bradley, *State Action and Corporate Human Rights Liability*, 85 NOTRE DAME L. REV. 1823, 1837 (2010) (arguing that "the best conclusion, as a matter of post-*Sosa* federal common law, is that courts should leave the development of aiding and abetting liability to Congress, which can determine both its desirability as well as its appropriate standards and limitations").

[112] *Central Bank*, 511 U.S. at 181.

[113] *See, e.g.*, Doe v. Exxon Mobil Corp., 654 F.3d 11, 30–32 (D.C. Cir. 2011); Khulumani v. Barclay Nat'l Bank Ltd., 504 F.3d 254, 282 (2d Cir. 2007) (Katzmann, J., concurring); *see also* Kiobel v. Royal Dutch Petroleum Co., 621 F.3d 111, 130 (2d Cir. 2010) ("[I]t was only because we looked to international law that we were able to recognize a norm of aiding and abetting liability under the ATS."). Some courts and commentators have also pointed out that a 1795 Attorney General opinion that references the possibility of an ATS suit against U.S. citizens states that the U.S. citizens in question had "voluntarily joined, conducted, *aided, and abetted* a French fleet." Opinion of William Bradford, *Breach of Neutrality*, 1 OP. ATT'Y GEN. 57 (1795) (emphasis

applied for such liability. In particular, there was debate over whether it is sufficient for the plaintiff to show that, in becoming involved with the foreign government, the defendant corporation had knowledge of the government's human rights abuses, or whether there must also be a showing that the corporation acted with the purpose of facilitating the abuses.[114] Courts adopting the stricter purpose test relied heavily on the Rome Statute of the International Criminal Court, Article 25 of which provides for liability if a person "aids, abets or otherwise assists in" the commission or attempted commission of a covered crime "[f]or the purpose of facilitating the commission of such a crime." By contrast, courts adopting the knowledge standard relied on other international law materials or have invoked principles of domestic law.

A central issue in the corporate ATS cases was one of choice of law: In deciding whether the ATS applies to suits against corporations, and also whether there is aiding and abetting liability under the ATS, should courts look to international law or domestic law?[115] The text of the ATS makes clear that, in order for there to be a claim under the Statute, there must be a tort in violation of international law. But it is possible that other issues in ATS litigation, such as the types of tortfeasors that can be sued, the required connection between the defendant and the tort, and the potential defenses that can be asserted, could be resolved by reference to domestic law. (The potential defense of individual official immunity is discussed in Chapter 8.)

One reason this choice-of-law question is potentially significant is that there is little direct support in international law or practice for applying international human rights norms to corporations. International criminal tribunals, starting with the Nuremberg Tribunal, have consistently exercised jurisdiction only over natural persons, not corporations. Although there was a proposal to grant the International Criminal Court jurisdiction over corporations, that proposal was rejected.[116] Moreover, although some treaties

---

added). The U.S. citizens were alleged to be direct perpetrators of the torts, however, and the opinion does not specifically state that mere aiders and abettors could be sued under the ATS. *See also Khulumani*, 504 F.3d at 329 (Korman, J., dissenting) ("[B]ecause the conduct involved direct participation by American citizens, who acted with the intent to make the attack succeed, it seems likely that [the Attorney General] recognized all of the perpetrators as joint tortfeasors, as that term was understood at the time.").

[114] Compare, for example, *Exxon*, 654 F.3d at 39 (knowledge standard), with Presbyterian Church of Sudan v. Talisman Energy, Inc., 582 F.3d 244, 259 (2d Cir. 2009) (purpose standard). *See also* Chimène I. Keitner, *Conceptualizing Complicity in Alien Tort Cases*, 60 HASTINGS L.J. 61 (2008) (discussing possible standards and sources of law for aiding and abetting liability).

[115] For discussion of this question, *see* Ingrid Wuerth, *The Alien Tort Statute and Federal Common Law: A New Approach*, 86 NOTRE DAME L. REV. 1931 (2010).

[116] The treaty for the International Criminal Court limits the Court's jurisdiction to "natural persons." *See* Rome Statute of the International Criminal Court, art. 25(1), opened for signature July 17, 1998, 37 I.L.M. 1002, 1016. The French delegation proposed granting the ICC jurisdiction over corporations and other "juridical" persons, but the proposal was rejected. *See* Albin Eser, *Individual Criminal Responsibility, in* 1 THE ROME STATUTE OF THE INTERNATIONAL CRIMINAL COURT 767, 779 (Antonio Cassese et al. eds., 2002).

specifically refer to corporations and other "legal persons,"[117] human rights treaties do not. As a UN report issued in 2007 noted, "States have been unwilling to adopt binding international human rights standards for corporations."[118]

It is possible to argue, of course, that customary norms of international law apply to corporations even if the jurisdiction of international tribunals and the provisions of human rights treaties do not.[119] But some judges went further and argued that the lack of direct support for corporate liability in international law was beside the point because the issue of whether corporations can be sued under the ATS should be determined as a matter of U.S. domestic law, not international law. These judges distinguished between "conduct-governing norms" and "remedial" norms, arguing that only the former need to be grounded in international law, and that the issue of corporate liability falls into the latter category.[120] Corporate liability is of course an accepted feature of the U.S. legal system and many other domestic legal systems.[121]

Of potential relevance to this issue, the Supreme Court has held that only natural persons may be sued under the TVPA. The TVPA refers to situations in which an "individual"

---

[117] *See, e.g.*, OECD Convention on Combating Bribery of Foreign Public Officials in International Business Transactions art. 2, Dec. 18, 1997, S. TREATY DOC. No. 105–43, 37 I.L.M. 1 (1998) (entered into force Feb. 15, 1999) ("Each state party shall take such measures as may be necessary, in accordance with its legal principles, to establish the liability of legal persons for the bribery of a foreign public official.").

[118] Report of John Ruggie, Special Representative of the Secretary-General on the Issue of Human Rights and Transnational Corporations and Other Business Enterprises, ¶ 44, U.N. Doc. A/HRC/4/35 (Feb. 19, 2007).

[119] *See, e.g.*, Flomo v. Firestone Natural Rubber Co., 643 F.3d 1013, 1019 (7th Cir. 2011) ("It is neither surprising nor significant that corporate liability hasn't figured in prosecutions of war criminals and other violators of customary international law. That doesn't mean that corporations are exempt from that law."). *But see* Julian G. Ku, *The Curious Case of Corporate Liability under the Alien Tort Statute: A Flawed System of Judicial Lawmaking*, 51 VA. J. INT'L L. 353, 355 (2010) ("Customary, as opposed to treaty-based, international law has never recognized the imposition of direct duties on private corporations.").

[120] *See, e.g.*, Doe v. Exxon Mobil Corp, 654 F.3d 11, 41 (D.C. Cir. 2011) (reasoning that "corporate liability differs fundamentally from the conduct-governing norms at issue in *Sosa*, and consequently customary international law does not provide the rule of decision"); *Flomo*, 643 F.3d at 1019 ("We keep harping on criminal liability for violations of customary international law in order to underscore the distinction between a principle of that law, which is a matter of substance, and the means of enforcing it, which is a matter of procedure or remedy."); *Kiobel*, 621 F.3d at 175 n.33 (Leval, J., concurring) ("International law outlaws certain forms of abhorrent conduct and in general leaves to individual nations how to enforce the proscription."). In a much-discussed but cryptic footnote in *Sosa*, the Supreme Court stated that "[a] related consideration [in deciding whether to allow a claim under the ATS] is whether international law extends the scope of liability for a violation of a given norm to the perpetrator being sued, if the defendant is a private actor such as a corporation or individual." 542 U.S. at 732 n.20.

[121] Even in U.S. domestic law, however, corporate liability is not always allowed. For example, although some damage claims can be brought directly under the Constitution against individual federal officials (known as *Bivens* claims), these claims cannot be brought against private corporations even when they are carrying out governmental functions. *See* Correctional Servs. Corp. v. Malesko, 534 U.S. 61 (2001). Without analysis, a U.S. Attorney General opinion in 1907 suggested that a U.S. corporation could be sued under the ATS for a treaty violation. *See* Opinion of Charles J. Bonaparte, *Mexican Boundary—Division of the Rio Grande*, 26 OP. ATT'Y GEN. 250, 253 (1907).

subjects another "individual" to an act of torture or extrajudicial killing, and the Court reasoned that this language is most naturally read as being limited to natural persons.[122] The Court said that this was true "regardless of whether corporate entities can be held liable in a federal common-law action brought under [the ATS]," since, unlike the TVPA, the ATS does not use the term "individuals" to refer to covered defendants.[123] While acknowledging that there are policy arguments for extending liability under the TVPA to other actors, the Court said that "Congress has seen fit to proceed in more modest steps in the Act, and it is not the province of this [Judicial] Branch to do otherwise."[124]

In the *Kiobel* case discussed earlier, the U.S. Court of Appeals for the Second Circuit created a conflict in the circuits by holding that corporations may not be sued under the ATS, even for direct liability.[125] The Supreme Court agreed to review this decision but, as discussed, it ultimately resolved the case on extraterritoriality grounds.[126]

The Court did finally address the issue of corporate liability under the ATS in 2018, in *Jesner v. Arab Bank*.[127] In that case, plaintiffs in a group of ATS lawsuits alleged that a Jordanian bank was responsible for helping to finance terrorist attacks in the Middle East, and they sought damages for the injuries caused by the attacks. The financial activities in question included the channeling of funds through a New York branch of the bank. In rejecting the claims, the Court held that foreign corporations are not proper defendants under the ATS. The Court noted that the *Sosa* decision has insisted on a cautious approach to ATS litigation, and the Court observed that "this caution extends to the question whether the courts should exercise the judicial authority to mandate a rule that imposes liability upon artificial entities like corporations."[128] The Court also explained that the ATS "was intended to promote harmony in international relations by ensuring foreign plaintiffs a remedy for international-law violations in circumstances where the absence of such a remedy might provoke foreign nations to hold the United States accountable," but in ATS cases brought against foreign corporations "the opposite is occurring."[129] The Court concluded: "With the ATS, the First Congress provided

---

[122] *See* Mohamad v. Palestinian Auth., 566 U.S. 449, 454 (2012).

[123] *Id.* at 458.

[124] *Id.* at 461.

[125] *See* 621 F.3d 111 (2d Cir. 2010).

[126] For discussion of some of the costs and benefits of applying the ATS to corporations, and a suggestion that such application "may impose great costs on firms subject to suit in the United States while accomplishing little or nothing to improve human rights," *see* Alan O. Sykes, *Corporate Liability for Extraterritorial Torts under the Alien Tort Statute and Beyond: An Economic Analysis*, 100 GEO. L.J. 2161, 2209 (2012). For a response, *see* Chimène I. Keitner, *Optimizing Liability for Extraterritorial Torts: A Response to Professor Sykes*, 100 GEO. L.J. 2211 (2012).

[127] 138 S. Ct. 1386 (2018).

[128] *Id.* at 1389–90.

[129] *Id.* at 1406.

a federal remedy for a narrow category of international-law violations committed by individuals. Whether, more than two centuries on, a similar remedy should be available against foreign corporations is similarly a decision that Congress must make."[130]

Especially when combined with *Kiobel*, the decision in *Jesner* means that few suits under the ATS are likely to be viable. Suits against natural persons can still potentially be brought for torts in violation of international law committed within the United States, but such cases will rarely arise, and any suits brought against U.S. governmental defendants will face a variety of additional obstacles. In addition, because *Jesner* disallowed only suits against foreign corporations, it is still possible for suits to be brought against U.S. corporations for orchestrating or facilitating human rights abuses abroad, although it is conceivable that the Supreme Court might extend *Jesner* to disallow all corporate liability.[131]

* * *

Although some countries allow for universal criminal jurisdiction, no other country allows for civil litigation over alleged human rights abuses to the extent that had been allowed under the ATS prior to *Kiobel* and *Jesner*.[132] The expansive nature of ATS litigation was due in part to the fact that it had been developed primarily through judicial decisions rather than legislative action, since the U.S. political branches (especially the executive branch) tend to be more reluctant than the courts to assert extraterritorial jurisdiction over human rights abuses. As noted earlier in this chapter, the ATS likely was enacted to reduce foreign relations friction with other countries by allowing certain sensitive tort cases to be heard in the federal courts. This purpose, the Supreme Court

---

[130] *Id.* at 1407. The dissenters in *Jesner* argued that corporations are generally assumed to be liable for torts, and that "[n]othing about the historical background against which the ATS was enacted rebuts the presumption that the statute incorporated the accepted principle of corporate liability for tortious conduct." *Id.* at 1426 (Sotomayor, J., dissenting). The dissenters also contended that "[i]mmunizing corporations that violate human rights from liability under the ATS undermines the system of accountability that the First Congress endeavored to impose." *Id.* at 1437.

[131] As this edition was being prepared for publication, the Supreme Court agreed to review a case that raises the question whether U.S. corporations can be sued under the ATS. *See* Doe v. Nestle, S.A., 906 F.3d 1120 (9th Cir. 2018), *amended*, 929 F.3d 623 (9th Cir. 2018), cert. granted, July 2, 2020.

[132] *See* Ramsey, *supra* note 70, at 305 ("[E]ven the strongest defenders of ATS-style litigation concede that there is essentially no practice of universal civil liability outside the United States."). *Cf.* Caroline Kaeb & David Scheffer, *The Paradox of Kiobel in Europe*, 107 AM. J. INT'L L. 852, 854 (2013) ("Europe does not have an ATS-equivalent per se, but extraterritorial corporate liability exists in Europe.").

perceived in *Kiobel* and *Jesner*, was not being served by expansive assertions of U.S. extraterritorial jurisdiction.[133] There have occasionally been proposals to amend the ATS—for example, to specify and define the claims that can be brought and to place limitations on the claims.[134] The Supreme Court's decisions curtailing ATS litigation may lead to additional calls for legislative action.

---

[133] For discussion of some of the costs and benefits of ATS litigation, *compare* WILLIAM J. ACEVES, THE ANATOMY OF TORTURE: A DOCUMENTARY HISTORY OF FILARTIGA V. PENA-IRALA 159–83 (2007) (generally supportive of the litigation), *with* Curtis A. Bradley, *The Costs of International Human Rights Litigation*, 2 CHI. J. INT'L L. 457 (2001) (generally critical of the litigation).

[134] *See, e.g.*, Alien Tort Statute Reform Act, S. 1874, 109th Cong. (2005) (would have allowed for jurisdiction over claims of "torture, extrajudicial killing, genocide, piracy, slavery, or slave trading," but only if the defendant "is a direct participant acting with specific intent to commit the alleged tort," and imposing requirement of exhaustion, case-specific deference to the executive branch, and a statute of limitations).

8 Sovereign and Individual Official Immunity

THIS CHAPTER DISCUSSES four types of immunity in U.S. litigation: the immunity of foreign governments and their agencies and instrumentalities; the immunity of international organizations; the immunity of foreign diplomats and consular officials; and the immunity of other foreign officials, including heads of state. The United States is a party to treaties that address diplomatic and consular immunity, but it is not a party to any general treaty addressing the other forms of immunity. In 2004, the United Nations promulgated a proposed Convention on Jurisdictional Immunities of States and Their Property, but the Convention has not yet entered into force and has not been ratified by the United States.[1]

As will be discussed, foreign governmental immunity is supported by long-standing norms of customary international law. In addition, it is generally understood that

---

[1] *See* United Nations Convention on Jurisdictional Immunities of States and Their Property, GA Res. 59/508, annex (Dec. 2, 2004), *opened for signature* Jan. 17, 2005, 44 I.L.M. 803 (2005). For a description of the Convention, *see* David P. Stewart, *The UN Convention on Jurisdictional Immunities of States and Their Property*, 99 AM. J. INT'L L. 194 (2005); *see also* THE UNITED NATIONS CONVENTION ON JURISDICTIONAL IMMUNITIES OF STATES AND THEIR PROPERTY (Roger O'Keefe & Christian J. Tams eds., 2013). The Convention will take effect only after it has been ratified by thirty nations, and, as of the time this Third Edition went to press, only twenty-two nations had done so.

customary international law provides governments and officials with some immunity from suit, although there are debates about the current scope of this immunity.[2] Foreign governmental immunity and foreign official immunity thus implicate some of the issues, discussed in Chapter 5, concerning the status of customary international law in the U.S. legal system.

Foreign Governmental Immunity

The recognition by U.S. courts of immunity for foreign governments dates back to the Supreme Court's 1812 decision in *Schooner Exchange v. McFaddon*.[3] In that case, two individuals brought an admiralty action against a French naval vessel that had docked in Philadelphia, claiming that they were the original owners of the vessel and that it had been seized from them unlawfully. In upholding a dismissal of the action, the Court, in an opinion by Chief Justice Marshall, began by noting that "[t]he jurisdiction of the nation within its own territory is necessarily exclusive and absolute" and "is susceptible of no limitation not imposed by itself."[4] As a result, said the Court, "[a]ll exceptions . . . to the full and complete power of a nation within its own territories, must be traced up to the consent of the nation itself."[5] The Court found, however, based on "common usage" and "common opinion," that there was "a principle of public law, that national ships of war, entering the port of a friendly power open for their reception, are to be considered as exempted by the consent of that power from its jurisdiction."[6]

In reaching this conclusion, the Court in *Schooner Exchange* analogized to two well-settled principles of immunity under customary international law: first, "the exemption of the person of the sovereign from arrest or detention within a foreign territory"— what we would today call head-of-state immunity; and, second, "the immunity which

---

[2] For general discussions of the international law of immunity, see, for example, HAZEL FOX QC & PHILIPPA WEBB, THE LAW OF STATE IMMUNITY (3d ed. rev. 2015); and ROSANNE VAN ALEBEEK, THE IMMUNITIES OF STATES AND THEIR OFFICIALS IN INTERNATIONAL CRIMINAL LAW (2008). For the views of the International Court of Justice about the current state of customary international law concerning governmental immunity, see, for example, Jurisdictional Immunities of the State (Germany v. Italy), Judgment, ¶¶ 56–61 (ICJ, Feb. 3, 2012), *available at* https://www.icj-cij.org/files/case-related/143/143-20120203-JUD-01-00-EN.pdf. For the views of the European Court of Human Rights about the current state of customary international concerning the immunity of officials, see, for example, Case of Jones and Others v. The United Kingdom, Judgment, ¶¶ 202–15 (ECHR, Jan. 14, 2014), *available at* https://hudoc.echr.coe.int/eng#{%22itemid%22:[%22001-140005%22]}.

[3] 11 U.S. (7 Cranch) 116 (1812). *See also* Republic of Austria v. Altmann, 541 U.S. 677, 688 (2004) ("Chief Justice Marshall's opinion in *Schooner Exchange* . . . is generally viewed as the source of our foreign sovereign immunity jurisprudence."). For additional discussion of the history of foreign sovereign immunity in the United States, *see* THEODORE R. GIUTTARI, THE AMERICAN LAW OF SOVEREIGN IMMUNITY: AN ANALYSIS OF THE LEGAL INTERPRETATION (1970).

[4] 11 U.S. at 136.

[5] *Id.*

[6] *Id.* at 145.

all civilized nations allow to foreign ministers"—which we would today call diplomatic immunity.[7] (Both of these types of immunity will be discussed.) The Court also appears to have been influenced by the fact that the executive branch had intervened in the case in support of having the case dismissed.[8]

The *Schooner Exchange* was apparently the first national court decision clearly recognizing foreign sovereign immunity.[9] Although the Court had specifically addressed only the immunity of foreign warships from jurisdiction, over time federal and state courts extended sovereign immunity to essentially any suit against a foreign nation.[10] This immunity was viewed as stemming from both considerations of international comity and from principles of customary international law. In dismissing a suit against the government of Mexico in the late nineteenth century concerning its alleged default on bonds, for example, a New York court observed that "[i]t is an axiom of international law, of long-established and general recognition, that a sovereign State cannot be sued in its own courts, or in any other, without its consent and permission."[11] Sovereign immunity during this period was considered to be essentially absolute—if the defendant qualified as a foreign sovereign, then it would have immunity for all of its acts, even those that were purely commercial in nature.[12] At the same time, courts sometimes limited immunity by concluding that certain suits, such as those against state-owned companies or involving state-owned property, were not suits against the state.[13]

Deference to the Executive Branch

In the nineteenth and early twentieth centuries, although U.S. courts gave some weight to the executive branch's views about whether to grant sovereign immunity, the courts

---

[7] *See id.* at 137–39.
[8] *See id.* at 147 ("[T]here seems to be a necessity for admitting that the fact might be disclosed to the court by the suggestion of the attorney for the United States.").
[9] *See, e.g.,* Ian Sinclair, *The Law of Sovereign Immunity: Recent Developments*, 176 RECUEIL DES COURS 113, 122 (1980) (noting that *Schooner Exchange* "is regularly cited as the first judicial expression of the doctrine of absolute immunity").
[10] *See* GAMAL MOURSI BADR, STATE IMMUNITY: AN ANALYTICAL AND PROGNOSTIC VIEW 9–20 (1984); JOSEPH W. DELLAPENNA, SUING FOREIGN GOVERNMENTS AND THEIR CORPORATIONS 3 (2d ed. 2003).
[11] Hassard v. United States of Mex., 29 Misc. 511, 61 N.Y.S. 939 (46 A.D. 1899), *aff'd,* 46 A.D. 623 (1899). *See also, e.g.,* Wulfsohn v. Russ. Socialist Federated Soviet Republic, 138 N.E. 24, 36 (N.Y. Ct. App. 1923) ("[Courts] may not bring a foreign sovereign before our bar, not because of comity, but because he has not submitted himself to our laws. Without his consent he is not subject to them.").
[12] *See, e.g.,* Mason v. Intercolonial Ry. of Can., 197 Mass. 349, 83 N.E. 876 (Sup. Ct. Mass. 1908); Bradford v. Dir. Gen. of R.R.s of Mex., 278 S.W. 251 (Tex. Ct. App. 1925). As these citations indicate, sovereign immunity decisions in the nineteenth and early twentieth centuries were sometimes issued by state courts rather than federal courts. *See generally* Julian G. Ku, *Customary International Law in State Courts*, 42 VA. J. INT'L L. 265, 310–22 (2001).
[13] *See* Note, *The Jurisdictional Immunity of Foreign Sovereigns*, 63 YALE L.J. 1148, 1150 (1954).

ultimately made their own determinations.[14] For example, in a case litigated in the 1920s involving claims against an Italian government-owned steamship relating to its transportation of commercial cargo, the State Department had expressed the view in the district court that government-owned merchant vessels employed in commerce "should not be regarded as entitled to the immunities accorded public vessels of war."[15] Despite those views, the Supreme Court concluded that merchant ships owned and operated by a foreign government have the same immunity as a government warship.[16]

Starting in the late 1930s, courts shifted their approach and began giving absolute deference to suggestions from the State Department about whether to grant immunity in particular cases.[17] In a 1938 decision, *The Navemar*, the Court considered whether to grant immunity in an admiralty case brought against a vessel that Spain alleged to be its public property.[18] The Court explained that "[i]f the claim [to immunity] is recognized and allowed by the executive branch of the government, it is then the duty of the courts to release the vessel upon appropriate suggestion by the Attorney General of the United States, or other officer acting under his direction."[19] In this case, however, the executive branch had declined to submit a suggestion of immunity, and the Court therefore noted that "the alleged public status of the vessel and the right of the Spanish Government to demand possession of the vessel as owner if it so elected, were appropriate subjects for judicial inquiry upon proof of the matters alleged."[20]

In a 1943 decision, Ex parte *Republic of Peru*, the Court confirmed that, because sovereign immunity determinations implicate important foreign relations interests, courts were bound to follow executive suggestions of immunity.[21] Two years later, in *Republic of Mexico v. Hoffman*, the Court went further, stating that even in the face of executive branch silence, U.S. courts should look to "the principles accepted by the [executive branch]."[22] As a result, explained the Court, it is "not for the courts to deny an immunity

---

[14] *See* G. Edward White, *The Transformation of the Constitutional Regime of Foreign Relations*, 85 VA. L. REV. 1, 136 (1999) (explaining that the views of the executive branch about foreign sovereign immunity "were entitled to weight but did not bind the courts").

[15] *See* The Pesaro, 277 F. 473 (S.D.N.Y. 1921).

[16] *See* Berizzi Bros. Co. v. Steamship Pesaro, 271 U.S. 562 (1926). As a result, it is not accurate to suggest, as the Supreme Court has recently done, that executive branch determinations of immunity were treated as binding "[f]or the better part of the last two centuries." Republic of Argentina v. NML Capital, Ltd., 573 U.S. 134, 140 (2014).

[17] *See* Curtis A. Bradley & Jack L. Goldsmith, *Pinochet and International Human Rights Litigation*, 97 MICH. L. REV. 2129, 2162–63 (1999); White, *supra* note 14, at 134–35.

[18] *See* Compania Espanola de Navegacion Maritima, S.A. v. The Navemar, 303 U.S. 68 (1938).

[19] *Id.* at 74.

[20] *Id.* at 75.

[21] 318 U.S. 578, 588–89 (1943).

[22] 324 U.S. 30, 35 (1945).

which our government has seen fit to allow, or to allow an immunity on new grounds which the government has not seen fit to recognize."[23]

It is not entirely clear why the Court shifted toward giving absolute deference to the executive branch in this area. The shift occurred at a time, however, when there was a more general expansion of presidential power, due in part to the broader role of the United States in the world and the advent of the Second World War. As discussed in Chapter 3, for somewhat related reasons, this was also a period in which presidents began making much greater use of executive agreements as an alternative to Article II treaties. Tying immunity to the authority of the executive branch may have also been related to the Supreme Court's 1938 decision in *Erie Railroad v. Tompkins*, discussed in Chapter 1, since the Court's abolition of general common law in that decision would have placed more pressure on the Court to identify a domestic sovereign source for the law of immunity.[24] Whatever the reason, the Court's application of sovereign immunity in this period shifted from direct application of international law and considerations of international comity to an approach grounded more in considerations of domestic separation of powers. As discussed in Chapter 1, a somewhat similar shift occurred in connection with the act of state doctrine.

Tate Letter

By the early twentieth century, a number of nations began moving away from the absolute approach to immunity toward a restrictive approach.[25] Under the restrictive approach, foreign sovereigns are entitled to immunity for public or sovereign acts, but not for private or commercial acts. The basic idea is that when states act like private entities—for example, by entering into a commercial contract—they should be subject to suit like a private entity. Their sovereignty is not infringed by such a suit, it is reasoned, because they are not acting in a sovereign capacity in making the contract. Not surprisingly, this shift started to occur when foreign governments were increasingly engaging in business activities—for example, through state-owned trading companies. The United States was slow to join this shift, although it did enter into a number of bilateral treaties in the early twentieth century that disallowed immunity for commercial activities.[26]

---

[23] *Id.* For an argument that this deference to the executive branch constituted an improper abdication by the courts of their role in determining the international law of immunity, *see* Philip C. Jessup, *Has the Supreme Court Abdicated One of Its Functions?*, 40 AM. J. INT'L L. 168 (1946).
[24] *See* Bradley & Goldsmith, *supra* note 17, at 2163–65.
[25] *See* BADR, *supra* note 10, at 21–62; H. Lauterpacht, *The Problem of Jurisdictional Immunities of Foreign States*, 28 BRIT. Y.B. INT'L L. 220, 221 (1951); Harvard Research in International Law, *Draft Convention and Comment on Competence of Courts in Regard to Foreign States*, 26 AM. J. INT'L L. Supp. 451, 528 (1932).
[26] *See* William W. Bishop, Jr., *New United States Policy Limiting Sovereign Immunity*, 47 AM. J. INT'L L. 93, 96 (1953); *see also* JOSEPH M. SWEENEY, THE INTERNATIONAL LAW OF SOVEREIGN IMMUNITY 42 (State Dept. 1963) (noting that "[f]rom 1948 to 1958, the United States negotiated treaties with fourteen states, each

In 1952, the U.S. State Department formally announced that it supported the restrictive approach. The announcement came in a letter addressed from the State Department's Acting Legal Adviser, Jack Tate, to the Acting Attorney General, and was titled "Changed Policy Concerning the Granting of Sovereign Immunity to Foreign Governments."[27] The Tate Letter explained that "the widespread and increasing practice on the part of governments of engaging in commercial activities makes necessary a practice which will enable persons doing business with them to have their rights determined in the courts."[28] Henceforth, explained the Letter, "the immunity of the sovereign is recognized with regard to sovereign or public acts (*jure imperii*) of a state, but not with respect to private acts (*jure gestionis*)."[29] The Letter concluded with this observation: "It is realized that a shift in policy by the executive cannot control the courts but it is felt that the courts are less likely to allow a plea of sovereign immunity where the executive has declined to do so."[30]

Under the Tate Letter regime, foreign states sued in U.S. courts could seek relief in either of two ways. They could request immunity directly from the State Department, usually by submitting a diplomatic note. If the Department agreed that the foreign state should receive immunity, the Department would send a suggestion of immunity to the Attorney General with a request that it be transmitted to the court, and courts generally treated these suggestions as binding, even if they departed from the approach set forth in the Tate Letter.[31] Alternatively, foreign states could request immunity directly from the court, in which case the court would have to decide how to distinguish between sovereign and commercial acts, albeit often by reference to prior State Department determinations.[32]

This regime, under which the State Department made some immunity determinations and the courts made others, did not always produce consistent decisions.[33] There

---

providing that state enterprises of either party engaged in business activities in the territory of the other are not entitled to immunity").

[27] *See* Letter from Jack B. Tate, Acting Legal Adviser, U.S. Dept. of State, to Gen. Philip B. Perlman, Acting U.S. Att'y (May 19, 1952), *reprinted in* 26 DEPT. ST. BULL. 984, 985 (1952).

[28] *Id.* at 985.

[29] *Id.* at 984.

[30] *Id.* at 985.

[31] *See, e.g.*, Rich v. Naviera Vacuba, S.A., 197 F. Supp. 710, 724 (E.D. Va. 1961); *see also* LOUIS HENKIN, FOREIGN AFFAIRS AND THE UNITED STATES CONSTITUTION 56 (2d ed. 1996) (noting that "if the Executive announced a national policy in regard to immunity generally, or for the particular case, that policy was law for the courts and binding upon them, regardless of what international law might say about it").

[32] *See* Andreas F. Lowenfeld, *Claims against Foreign States—A Proposal for Reform of United States Law*, 44 N.Y.U. L. REV. 901, 909–11 (1969) (describing the approach of courts in this period to immunity issues); *see also* Verlinden B.V. v. Cent. Bank of Nigeria, 461 U.S. 480, 487 (1983) (noting that when the foreign state did not seek a suggestion from the State Department, "responsibility fell to the courts to determine whether sovereign immunity existed, generally by reference to prior State Department decisions").

[33] *Compare* Victory Transport, Inc. v. Comisaria General de Abastecimientosy Transportes, 336 F.2d 354 (2d Cir. 1964) (court concludes, without input from State Department, that a ship chartered by the Spanish government was engaged in commercial activity and thus not entitled to immunity), *with* Isbrandtsen Tankers v. President

were also concerns that it unduly politicized judicial decision-making, and that the State Department was ill-equipped to act as an adjudicatory institution.[34] In addition, the scope of immunity was viewed as too uncertain. It was unclear, for example, whether the nature or the purpose of the activity should be examined in determining if the activity was private or public.

Foreign Sovereign Immunities Act

In 1976, after years of discussion and debate, Congress enacted the Foreign Sovereign Immunities Act (FSIA).[35] The FSIA was designed to codify the restrictive theory of immunity and transfer immunity determinations away from the executive branch to the courts.[36] It provides that foreign states "shall be immune" from the jurisdiction of U.S. courts except as provided in certain specified exceptions.[37] The FSIA contains a variety of exceptions to immunity, including exceptions for waiver, commercial activity, takings of property in violation of international law, noncommercial torts, the enforcement of arbitral awards, and certain admiralty actions.[38] Since 1996, there has also been an exception for suits against certain state sponsors of terrorism,[39] and in 2016 another terrorism-related exception was added.[40] The FSIA does not contain any general exception for violations of international law, and the Supreme Court has noted that "immunity

---

of India, 446 F.2d 1198, 1200–101 (2d Cir. 1971) (granting immunity in factually similar suit brought against Indian government because, although the court was inclined to "find that the actions of the Indian government were . . . purely private commercial decisions," the State Department had determined otherwise).

[34] For criticisms of the Tate Letter regime, see, for example, Monroe Leigh, *Sovereign Immunity—The Case of the "Imias,"* 68 AM. J. INT'L L. 280 (1974); and Andreas F. Lowenfeld, *Litigating a Sovereign Immunity Claim—The Haiti Case*, 49 N. Y.U. L. REV. 377 (1974).

[35] *See* Pub. L. No. 94–583, 94th Cong., 90 Stat. 2891. For discussions of the FSIA and its origins, *see* DELLAPENNA, *supra* note 10, at 26–37; Mark B. Feldman, *The United States Foreign Sovereign Immunities Act of 1976 in Perspective: A Founder's View*, 35 INT'L & COMP. L.Q. 302 (1986); Robert B. von Mehren, *The Foreign Sovereign Immunities Act of 1976*, 17 COLUM. J. TRANSNAT'L L. 33 (1978); and Frederic Alan Weber, *The Foreign Sovereign Immunities Act of 1976: Its Origins, Meaning, and Effect*, 3 YALE J. WORLD PUB. ORD. 1 (1976). *See also* RESTATEMENT (FOURTH) OF THE FOREIGN RELATIONS LAW OF THE UNITED STATES §§ 451–64 (2018).

[36] *See* Republic of Austria v. Altmann, 541 U.S. 677, 691 (2004); Verlinden B.V. v. Cent. Bank of Nigeria, 461 U.S. 480, 488 (1983); H. R. REP. No. 94–1487, at 6–7 (1976).

[37] 28 U.S.C. § 1604. Courts have expressed differing views about whether the FSIA applies in criminal cases. *Compare* Keller v. Cent. Bank of Nigeria, 277 F.3d 811, 820 (6th Cir. 2002) ("[T]he FSIA grants immunity to foreign sovereigns from criminal prosecution, absent an international agreement stating otherwise."), *with* Southway v. Cent. Bank of Nigeria, 198 F.3d 1210, 1214 (10th Cir. 1999) ("If Congress intended defendants . . . to be immune from criminal indictment under the FSIA, Congress should amend the FSIA to expressly so state."). *See also In re* Grand Jury Subpoena, 912 F.3d 623 (D.C. Cir. 2019) (discussing this issue).

[38] *See* 28 U.S.C. § 1605.

[39] *See id.*, § 1605A.

[40] *See id.*, § 1605B.

is granted in those cases involving alleged violations of international law that do not come within one of the FSIA's exceptions."[41]

The FSIA applies only to suits against "foreign states." "Foreign state" is defined to include not only the state itself but also "a political subdivision of a foreign state or an agency or instrumentality of a foreign state."[42] An agency or instrumentality is in turn defined to include "organs" of a foreign state as well as certain corporate entities that have a majority of their shares owned by a foreign state.[43] The Supreme Court has held that the status of an entity under the FSIA is to be determined based on the facts that exist at the time of the suit rather than at the time of the conduct in question, in part because foreign sovereign immunity "is not meant to avoid chilling foreign states or their instrumentalities in the conduct of their business but to give foreign states and their instrumentalities some protection from the inconvenience of suit as a gesture of comity between the United States and other sovereigns."[44]

For the most part, the FSIA does not address the substantive law that will govern whether the foreign state is liable. Rather, it provides that when there is an applicable exception to immunity, foreign states "shall be liable in the same manner and to the same extent as a private individual under like circumstances," except that foreign states other than agencies and instrumentalities shall not be subject to punitive damages.[45] Thus, liability in FSIA cases is often based on state or foreign law rather than federal law. (The terrorism exceptions, however, have their own federal causes of action.)

The structure of the FSIA is complicated because issues of personal jurisdiction, subject matter jurisdiction, and immunity from suit are intertwined. If proper service is made on a foreign state defendant, the FSIA allows for the exercise of personal jurisdiction with respect to any claim for which there is federal subject matter jurisdiction.[46] Federal subject matter jurisdiction in turn exists "as to any claim for relief in personam

---

[41] Argentine Republic v. Amerada Hess Shipping Corp., 488 U.S. 428, 436 (1989). The FSIA contains separate provisions relating to the immunity of foreign states from execution of judgments, and the exceptions to this "execution immunity" are narrower than the exceptions to jurisdictional immunity. See 28 U.S.C. §§ 1610, 1611. The Supreme Court has held, however, that these provisions do not limit discovery proceedings designed to aid in the execution of a judgment. See Republic of Argentina v. NML Capital, Ltd., 573 U.S. 134 (2014).

[42] 28 U.S.C. § 1603(a).

[43] See id., § 1603(b) (defining "agency or instrumentality of a foreign state" to include "any entity—which is a separate legal person, corporate or otherwise, and which is an organ of a foreign state or political subdivision thereof, or a majority of whose shares or other ownership interest is owned by a foreign state or political subdivision thereof").

[44] Dole Food Co. v. Patrickson, 538 U.S. 468, 479 (2003).

[45] 28 U.S.C. § 1606. See also, e.g., McKesson Corp. v. Islamic Republic of Iran, 672 F.3d 1066, 1075 (D.C. Cir. 2012) ("The FSIA is purely jurisdictional in nature, and creates no cause of action.").

[46] It is not clear whether the exercise of personal jurisdiction over foreign state defendants must also satisfy constitutional requirements of due process. See Republic of Argentina v. Weltover, Inc., 504 U.S. 607, 619 (1992) (assuming for the sake of argument that a foreign state is entitled to due process protection but not deciding the issue). For a decision holding that foreign states are not entitled to due process protection, see Price v. Socialist People's Libyan Arab Jamahiriya, 294 F.3d 82, 96–99 (D.C. Cir. 2002).

with respect to which the foreign state is not entitled to immunity."[47] Under this structure, a court must determine whether the foreign state defendant is immune from suit in order to determine whether the court has personal and subject matter jurisdiction. If the court finds that the defendant is immune, the court lacks personal and subject matter jurisdiction. Conversely, if the court finds that there is an exception to immunity, and that proper service has been made, the court automatically has personal and subject matter jurisdiction.[48]

The Supreme Court considered the relationship between this structure and Article III of the Constitution in *Verlinden B.V. v. Central Bank of Nigeria*.[49] In that case, a Dutch corporation was suing a Nigerian government-owned bank for anticipatory breach of a letter of credit. In concluding that a suit between these foreign parties fell within the jurisdiction authorized for the federal courts in Article III, the Court noted that under the FSIA, in order to determine whether a court has subject matter jurisdiction, the court must consider whether a statutory exception to immunity is satisfied. Discerning whether a statutory exception to immunity is satisfied, the Court further reasoned, involves "application of a body of substantive federal law."[50] As a result, said the Court, "a suit against a foreign state under this Act necessarily raises questions of substantive federal law at the very outset, and hence clearly 'arises under' federal law, as that term is used in Art. III."[51]

The Supreme Court has also held that the FSIA provides the exclusive basis for U.S. court jurisdiction over suits against foreign states. In *Argentine Republic v. Amerada Hess Shipping Corp.*, Argentine military aircraft had bombed and destroyed an oil tanker in international waters during the 1982 Falkland Islands War between Great Britain and Argentina.[52] The owner of the tanker and the company that had chartered it—both Liberian corporations—brought suit against Argentina in a New York federal court seeking compensation for the loss of the ship and its fuel. They alleged that Argentina's attack on the neutral tanker violated international law, and they argued that federal courts had jurisdiction over the suit pursuant to the Alien Tort Statute, which (as discussed in Chapter 7) provides that the federal district courts "shall have original jurisdiction of any civil action by an alien for a tort only, committed in violation of the law of nations or a treaty of the United States."[53] The Supreme Court ordered dismissal of the suit, reasoning

---

[47] *See* 28 U.S.C. § 1330(a).
[48] *See generally* Working Group of the American Bar Association, *Reforming the Foreign Sovereign Immunities Act*, 40 COLUM. J. TRANSNAT'L L. 489, 500–506 (2002) (discussing the FSIA's structure).
[49] 461 U.S. 480 (1983).
[50] *Id.* at 497.
[51] *Id.* at 493. After concluding that federal court jurisdiction over the case was proper, the Supreme Court remanded for a determination of whether there was an applicable exception to immunity. *See id.* at 498. The case was settled, however, before the lower courts issued any further decisions.
[52] 488 U.S. 428, 443 (1989).
[53] 28 U.S.C. § 1350.

that "the text and structure of the FSIA demonstrate Congress' intention that the FSIA be the sole basis for obtaining jurisdiction over a foreign state in our courts."[54] The Court also concluded that there were no applicable exceptions to immunity in that case.[55]

The Supreme Court has further held that the FSIA applies to all suits brought against foreign states, even if the suit concerns conduct that predates the FSIA's enactment. In *Republic of Austria v. Altmann*, the Court considered a suit against the government of Austria and its state-owned art gallery, in which the plaintiff alleged that the gallery had acquired stolen paintings from the Nazis.[56] The issue before the Court was whether to apply the FSIA retroactively to conduct that predated the 1952 Tate Letter—a time when the United States still adhered (at least for the most part) to the absolute theory of immunity, subject to deference to the executive branch. Although there is no constitutional bar on applying civil statutes retroactively, normally U.S. courts apply a presumption against such retroactivity, in part because retroactive applications may upset settled expectations. The Court concluded, however, that the presumption had less relevance in the context of the FSIA, since it does not regulate substantive rights. The Court explained that, although foreign governments prior to the FSIA "had a justifiable expectation that, as a matter of comity, United States courts would grant them immunity for their public acts (provided the State Department did not recommend otherwise), . . . they had no 'right' to such immunity."[57] The Court also reasoned that applying the FSIA to all cases brought against foreign states would be consistent with both the text of various provisions in the FSIA as well as the FSIA's purposes of "clarifying the rules that judges should apply in resolving sovereign immunity claims and eliminating political participation in the resolution of such claims."[58]

Even though *Altmann* means that suits against foreign governments can in theory be brought for conduct that occurred long ago, a variety of other limiting doctrines will present obstacles to such suits. As an initial matter, plaintiffs must still satisfy one of the FSIA's exceptions to immunity.[59] Moreover, statutes of limitation are likely to restrict claims under state or federal law. In addition, claims relating to conduct carried out by foreign governments long in the past are more likely to implicate the political question doctrine.[60] The Court in *Altmann* also suggested somewhat cryptically that "should the

---

[54] 488 U.S. at 434.
[55] *See id.* at 438–43.
[56] 541 U.S. 677 (2004).
[57] *Id.* at 694.
[58] *Id.* at 699. *See also* Jurisdictional Immunities of the State (Germany v. Italy), Judgment, ¶ 58 (ICJ, Feb. 3, 2012) (applying the law of immunity that existed at the time of the case rather than at the time of the underlying conduct because "the law of immunity is essentially procedural in nature"), *available at* https://www.icj-cij.org/files/case-related/143/143-20120203-JUD-01-00-EN.pdf.
[59] *See, e.g.*, Garb v. Republic of Poland, 440 F.3d 579 (2d Cir. 2006) (finding no exception to immunity for claims relating to expropriation of Jewish property by Poland after World War II).
[60] *See, e.g.*, Whiteman v. Dorotheum GmbH & Co. KG, 431 F.3d 57 (2d Cir. 2006) (relying on political question doctrine to dismiss claims against Austria and Austrian entities for confiscation of property during Nazi

State Department choose to express its opinion on the implications of exercising jurisdiction over *particular* petitioners in connection with *their* alleged conduct, that opinion might well be entitled to deference as the considered judgment of the Executive on a particular question of foreign policy," while also noting that "[w]e express no opinion on the question whether such deference should be granted in cases covered by the FSIA."[61]

Exceptions to Immunity

The FSIA contains a number of exceptions to immunity, including exceptions for waiver, commercial activity, certain takings of property, and noncommercial torts. There are also exceptions for certain terrorism-related claims.

WAIVER

Under the waiver exception, a foreign state is not immune from suit if it "has waived its immunity either explicitly or by implication."[62] Explicit waivers of immunity, such as a waiver in a treaty or contract, present relatively few problems. Such waiver provisions are commonly included in the legal documents when a foreign state borrows money from a bank or purchases goods or services from a sophisticated company.[63] It is less clear, however, what constitutes a waiver "by implication." The legislative history of the FSIA states as follows:

> With respect to implicit waivers, the courts have found such waivers in cases where a foreign state has agreed to arbitration in another country or where a foreign state has agreed that the law of particular country should govern a contract. An implicit

---

period); Joo v. Japan, 413 F.3d 45 (D.C. Cir. 2005) (relying on political question doctrine to dismiss claims against Japan relating to use of forced prostitution in occupied territories before and during World War II).

[61] 541 U.S. at 702. Retroactive application of the FSIA will not always be advantageous to plaintiffs. Because the Supreme Court has directed that the determination of whether the defendant qualifies as an agency or instrumentality of a foreign state should be determined at the time of the litigation, application of the FSIA to past conduct will be worse for plaintiffs if the defendant currently qualifies as an agency or instrumentality but would not have so qualified when the conduct in question occurred. *See, e.g.*, Abrams v. Societe Nationale des Chemins defer Francais, 389 F.3d 61 (2d Cir. 2004) (upholding dismissal of suit by Holocaust victims and their heirs against a French government-owned railroad because, "[w]hile [the French railroad] was predominately owned by civilians during World War II, it is now wholly-owned by the French government and . . . is an 'agent' or 'instrumentality' of France under the FSIA").

[62] 28 U.S.C. § 1605(a)(1).

[63] *See, e.g.*, Capital Ventures Int'l v. Republic of Argentina, 552 F.3d 289 (2d Cir. 2009); Gulf Res. America, Inc. v. Republic of the Congo, 370 F.3d 65 (D.C. Cir. 2004); *see also* Architectural Ingenieria Siglo XXI, LLC v. Dominican Republic, 788 F.3d 1329, 1338 (11th Cir. 2015) ("For purposes of the FSIA, a foreign state expressly waives its right to immunity only where its intent to do so is clear and unambiguous.").

waiver would also include a situation where a foreign state has filed a responsive pleading in an action without raising the defense of foreign sovereign immunity.[64]

In general, courts have construed the FSIA's implicit waiver exception narrowly, limiting it to situations in which the foreign state defendant has indicated a willingness to be sued in U.S. courts.[65]

Litigants and scholars have sometimes argued that when foreign governments engage in jus cogens violations of international law they should be deemed to have implicitly waived their immunity for purposes of the FSIA.[66] Courts have consistently rejected this argument, reasoning that it is for Congress, not the courts, to fashion additional exceptions to immunity.[67] As one court explained, interpreting the FSIA to have a jus cogens exception would "allow for a major, open-ended expansion of our jurisdiction into an area with substantial impact on the United States' foreign relations."[68] Another court stated more vividly that "something more nearly express is wanted before we impute to the Congress an intention that the federal courts assume jurisdiction over the countless human rights cases that might well be brought by the victims of all the ruthless military juntas, presidents-for-life, and murderous dictators of the world, from Idi Amin to Mao Zedong."[69] Consistent with this approach by U.S. courts, the International Court of Justice has held that, as a matter of customary international law, there is no jus cogens exception to foreign sovereign immunity.[70]

In addition to a general waiver provision, the FSIA contains an exception to immunity for certain counterclaims.[71] Under this exception, foreign states that bring claims in U.S. courts are denied immunity for any counterclaims that either fall within one of the general exceptions to immunity or arise out of the same transaction or occurrence as the foreign state's claim. Moreover, other counterclaims may be asserted against the foreign state "to the extent they do not seek relief exceeding in amount or differing in kind from that sought by the foreign state."[72]

---

[64] H. R. Rep. No. 94–1487, *supra* note 36, at 18.

[65] *See* Restatement (Fourth) of the Foreign Relations Law of the United States, *supra* note 35, § 453 reporters' note 1 ("In U.S. practice, implicit waivers . . . have generally been found only in three situations: when a foreign state agrees to arbitration in the United States; when a foreign state agrees that U.S. laws govern a contract; and when a foreign state files a responsive pleading without raising the immunity defense.").

[66] For an argument along these lines, *see* Adam C. Belsky et al., *Implied Waiver under the FSIA: A Proposed Exception to Immunity for Violations of Peremptory Norms of International Law*, 77 Cal. L. Rev. 365 (1989).

[67] *See, e.g.*, Carpenter v. Republic of Chile, 610 F.3d 776, 779–80 (2d Cir. 2010); Sampson v. Fed. Republic of Germany, 250 F.3d 1145, 1156 (7th Cir. 2001); Smith v. Socialist People's Libyan Arab Jamahiriya, 101 F.3d 239, 242–45 (2d Cir. 1996); Princz v. Fed. Republic of Germany, 26 F.3d 1166, 1174 (D.C. Cir. 1994).

[68] *Sampson*, 250 F.3d at 1156.

[69] *Princz*, 26 F.3d at 1174 n.1.

[70] *See* Jurisdictional Immunities of the State (Germany v. Italy), Judgment, ¶¶ 91–97 (ICJ, Feb. 3, 2012), *available at* https://www.icj-cij.org/files/case-related/143/143-20120203-JUD-01-00-EN.pdf.

[71] *See* 28 U.S.C. § 1607.

[72] *Id.*

COMMERCIAL ACTIVITY

The commercial activity exception is the most litigated exception to immunity and lies at the core of the restrictive theory of immunity codified by the FSIA. This exception provides that a foreign state shall not be immune from the jurisdiction of courts of the United States or of the states in any case:

> in which the action is based upon a commercial activity carried on in the United States by the foreign state; or upon an act performed in the United States in connection with a commercial activity of the foreign state elsewhere; or upon an act outside the territory of the United States in connection with a commercial activity of the foreign state elsewhere and that act causes a direct effect in the United States.[73]

As its language indicates, this exception can be satisfied by any one of three independent nexus requirements, and each nexus requirement uses the term "commercial activity." Another section in the FSIA in turn defines "commercial activity" rather unhelpfully to mean "either a regular course of commercial conduct or a particular commercial transaction or act,"[74] and adds that the "commercial character of an activity shall be determined by reference to the nature of the course of conduct or particular transaction or act, rather than by reference to its purpose."[75]

In *Republic of Argentina v. Weltover, Inc.*, the Supreme Court explained that a foreign state's conduct is commercial in nature if the foreign government "acts, not as regulator of a market, but in the manner of a private player within it."[76] In that case, foreign companies sued the government of Argentina to obtain payment on government-issued bonds,

---

[73] 28 U.S.C. § 1605(a)(2).

[74] As the Supreme Court has observed, the definition of "commercial activity" in the FSIA "leaves the critical term 'commercial' largely undefined." Republic of Argentina v. Weltover, Inc., 504 U.S. 607, 612 (1992).

[75] 28 U.S.C. § 1603(d).

[76] 504 U.S. 607, 614 (1992). For lower court decisions applying the "private player" test, see, for example, Merlini v. Canada, 926 F.3d 21 (1st Cir. 2019) (employment of U.S. citizen as administrative assistant at Canadian consulate without arranging for workers' compensation insurance deemed to be commercial activity); Chettri v. Nepal Rastra Bank, 834 F.3d 50 (2d Cir. 2016) (freezing of bank account as part of an investigation into money laundering not a commercial activity); Embassy of the Arab Republic of Egypt v. Lasheen, 603 F.3d 1166, 1171 (9th Cir. 2010) ("By contracting with a company to manage a health benefits plan and agreeing to indemnify that company, the Egyptian Defendants did not act with the powers peculiar to a sovereign, but instead acted as private players in the market."); Globe Nuclear Servs. & Supply GNSS, Ltd. v. AO Technsabexport, 376 F.3d 282, 289 (4th Cir. 2004) (agreement to supply uranium hexafluoride that was extracted from nuclear weapons held to be commercial activity because "[t]he entrance into a contract to supply a private party with uranium hexafluoride is the very type of action by which private parties engage in 'trade and traffic or commerce' "); and Beg v. Islamic Republic of Pakistan, 353 F.3d 1323, 1326 (11th Cir. 2003) (expropriation of property held not to be a commercial activity because "private actors are not allowed to engage in 'takings' in the manner that governments are").

and the Court concluded that the issuance of bonds constituted commercial activity. The Court explained that it was "irrelevant *why* Argentina participated in the bond market in the manner of a private actor; it matters only that it did so."[77] The Court proceeded to uphold jurisdiction under the FSIA under the third nexus prong of the commercial activity exception: "an act outside the territory of the United States in connection with a commercial activity of the foreign state elsewhere and that act causes a direct effect in the United States." An effect is "direct," explained the Court, if it follows as an immediate consequence of the defendant's activity, regardless of whether the effect is foreseeable or substantial.[78] As a result, the Court found that Argentina's rescheduling of bond payments that were to be made through a New York bank caused a direct effect in the United States, even though the recipients of the payments were not based in the United States. "Money that was supposed to have been delivered to a New York bank for deposit was not forthcoming," noted the Court.[79]

Under the first nexus prong of the commercial activity exception, an action must be "based upon a commercial activity carried on in the United States by the foreign state." The Supreme Court explained in *Saudi Arabia v. Nelson* that a suit is "based upon" "those elements of a claim that, if proven, would entitle a plaintiff to relief under his theory of the case."[80] In that case, Nelson alleged that, after he had been recruited to work in a Saudi Arabian government-owned hospital and had reported safety defects at the hospital, he had been arrested, tortured, and imprisoned. He could not sue under the FSIA's noncommercial tort exception because, as will be explained, it requires that the damage or injury from the tort occur in the United States, whereas Nelson was allegedly injured in Saudi Arabia. Nor could he sue under the third nexus prong of the commercial activity exception (the one at issue in *Weltover*), since that prong requires a direct effect in the United States. Instead, he sued under the first nexus prong, but the Court concluded that his suit was based on the alleged tortious activity, "not the arguably commercial activities that preceded their commission."[81] The Court further reasoned that allowing suit for the conduct at issue in the case would not be consistent with the restrictive theory of immunity that the FSIA attempted to codify because "[t]he conduct boils down to abuse of the power of its police by the Saudi Government, and however monstrous such abuse

---

[77] 504 U.S. at 617.
[78] *Id.* at 618.
[79] *Id.* at 619. The lower courts have differed over how broadly to apply the *Weltover* test for "direct effects," with some requiring a "legally significant act" in the United States (such as failure to make a payment specified in the contract to be made in the United States), but others rejecting such a requirement. *See* Orient Mineral Co. v. Bank of China, 506 F.3d 980, 998 (10th Cir. 2007) (same); Keller v. Cent. Bank of Nigeria, 277 F.3d 811, 817–18 (6th Cir. 2002) (same). For additional discussion of the "legally significant act" requirement, *see* Guirlando v. T.C. Ziraat Bankasi A.S., 602 F.3d 69 (2d Cir. 2010).
[80] 507 U.S. 349, 357 (1993).
[81] *Id.* at 358.

undoubtedly may be, a foreign state's exercise of the power of its police has long been understood for purposes of the restrictive theory as peculiarly sovereign in nature."[82]

The Supreme Court elaborated on the "based upon" requirement in *OBB Personenverkehr AG v. Sachs*.[83] In that case, the plaintiff, a California resident, purchased a European train pass over the Internet from a Massachusetts travel agent. While using the pass to board an Austrian state-owned train in Austria, the plaintiff fell and suffered serious injuries. She subsequently sued the railway for negligence, strict liability, and breach of implied warranty. In concluding that the suit was not "based upon" commercial activity in the United States, the Court explained that, under *Nelson*, "an action is 'based upon' the 'particular conduct' that constitutes the 'gravamen' of the suit."[84] The gravamen of the plaintiff's suit in this case, the Court concluded, "plainly occurred abroad."[85]

TAKINGS OF PROPERTY

The FSIA also has an exception for cases "[i]n which rights in property taken in violation of international law are in issue," and either "that property or any property exchanged for such property is present in the United States in connection with a commercial activity carried on in the United States by the foreign state," or "that property or any property exchanged for such property is owned or operated by an agency or instrumentality of the foreign state and that agency or instrumentality is engaged in a commercial activity in the United States."[86] This was the exception that the plaintiff was relying on in the *Altmann* case discussed earlier.

The legislative history of this provision indicates that the phrase "taken in violation of international law" refers to "the nationalization or expropriation of property without payment of the prompt adequate and effective compensation required by international law," including "takings which are arbitrary or discriminatory in nature."[87] In applying the exception, courts have also relied on the following description of international law set forth in the *Restatement (Third) of Foreign Relations Law*, which states that:

---

[82] *Id.* at 361. Justice White concurred in *Nelson*, arguing that the conduct in question constituted commercial activity because it was "retaliation for whistle-blowing" that was similar to private conduct in the marketplace, but that this activity was not "carried on in the United States" as required by the relevant portion of the commercial activity exception. *Id.* at 365–66, 370 (White, J., concurring).

[83] 136 S. Ct. 390 (2015).

[84] *Id.* at 396.

[85] *Id.*

[86] 28 U.S.C. § 1605(a)(3). There is also an exception to immunity in the FSIA for cases "in which rights in property in the United States acquired by succession or gift or rights in immovable property situated in the United States are in issue." *Id.*, § 1605(a)(4). In *Permanent Mission of India to the United Nations v. City of N.Y.*, 551 U.S. 193 (2007), the Supreme Court allowed the City of New York to bring a declaratory judgment suit under this exception to establish the validity of tax liens imposed on property held by foreign governments for the purpose of housing diplomatic employees and their families.

[87] H.R. REP. No. 94-1487, *supra* note 36, at 19.

A state is responsible under international law for injury resulting from: (1) a taking by the state of the property of a national of another state that (a) is not for a public purpose, or (b) is discriminatory, or (c) is not accompanied by provision for just compensation.[88]

Courts have generally held that it does not violate international law for a foreign government to expropriate the property of its own citizens.[89] Some courts have held, however, that this "domestic-takings rule" may be overcome when it is alleged that the taking was carried out as part of a campaign of genocide.[90]

The Supreme Court has held that a nonfrivolous but ultimately erroneous claim that property was taken in violation of international law is insufficient to sustain jurisdiction against a foreign state under this exception.[91] Rather, in order to establish jurisdiction, a plaintiff "must make out a legally valid claim that a certain kind of right is at issue (property rights) and that the relevant property was taken in a certain way (in violation of international law)."[92]

A number of suits have been brought in recent years against foreign governments and their instrumentalities seeking to recover art and cultural artifacts that were allegedly stolen during the World War II era. There is a process in U.S. law pursuant to which foreign owners of art and other cultural objects can seek a certification from the State Department whereby they can lend the materials to a cultural or educational institution in the United States without having it subject to attachment or seizure.[93] In 2016, Congress went further and provided that the temporary display of art in the United States by foreign governments should not be considered commercial activity under the takings exception if certain conditions are met: (a) "a work is imported into the United States from any foreign state pursuant to an agreement that provides for the temporary exhibition or display of such work entered into between a foreign state that is the owner

---

[88] RESTATEMENT (THIRD) OF THE FOREIGN RELATIONS LAW OF THE UNITED STATES § 712 (1987). *See, e.g.*, Cassirer v. Kingdom of Spain, 616 F.3d 1019, 1027 n.9 (9th Cir. 2010); Siderman de Blake v. Republic of Argentina, 965 F.2d 699, 711 (9th Cir. 1992); Crist v. Republic of Turkey, 995 F. Supp. 5, 10–11 (D.D.C. 1998).

[89] *See, e.g.*, Mezerhane v. Republica Bolivariana de Venezuela, 785 F.3d 545, 549–51 (11th Cir. 2015); Beg v. Islamic Republic of Pakistan, 353 F.3d 1323, 1328 (11th Cir. 2003); Yang Rong v. Liaoning Provincial Gov't, 362 F. Supp. 2d 83, 101 (D.D.C. 2005). *Cf.* Whiteman v. Dorotheum GmbH & Co. KG, 431 F.3d 57, 74 (2d Cir. 2005) (noting that, whether a foreign government's expropriation of the property of its own citizens violates international law "is, at a minimum, a complex and controversial question").

[90] *See, e.g.*, Simon v. Republic of Hungary, 812 F.3d 127 (D.C. Cir. 2016); Abelesz v. Magyar Nemzeti Bank, 692 F.3d 661 (7th Cir. 2012). *See also* Philipp v. Federal Republic of Germany, 894 F.3d 406 (D.C. Cir. 2018) (applying this principle); de Csepel v. Republic of Hungary, 859 F.3d 1094 (D.C. Cir. 2017) (same). (The Supreme Court is reviewing cases raising this issue during its 2020–21 Term.)

[91] *See* Bolivarian Republic of Venezuela v. Helmerich & Payne Int'l Drilling Co., 137 S. Ct. 1312 (2017).

[92] *Id.* at 1316.

[93] *See* Immunity from Seizure Act, 22 U.S.C. § 2459. *See also* Magness v. Russian Federation, 84 F. Supp. 2d 1357 (S.D. Ala. 2000) (applying the Act).

or custodian of such work and the United States or one or more cultural or educational institutions within the United States"; (b) "the President, or the President's designee, has determined ... that such work is of cultural significance and the temporary exhibition or display of such work is in the national interest"; and (c) the notice has been published.[94] There are exceptions in the statute for Nazi-era claims and other situations in which the work "was taken in connection with the acts of a foreign government against members of a targeted group as part of a systematic confiscation or misappropriation of works from members of a targeted and vulnerable group."

NONCOMMERCIAL TORTS

Another exception to immunity under the FSIA is the so-called noncommercial tort exception. This exception removes immunity in any case, not otherwise covered by the commercial activity exception, "in which money damages are sought against a foreign state for personal injury or death, or damage to or loss of property, occurring in the United States and caused by the tortious act or omission of that foreign state or of any official or employee of that foreign state while acting within the scope of his office or employment."[95] The plain language of the noncommercial tort exception requires that the injury or damage occur in the United States and thus by its terms excludes most torts committed abroad. The legislative history of this exception states that it "is directed primarily at the problem of traffic accidents but is cast in general terms as applying to all tort actions for money damages, not otherwise encompassed by [the commercial activity exception]."[96] In part because of this legislative history, courts have generally interpreted the exception as requiring that the tortious act or omission, and not just the damage or injury, occur in the United States.[97]

The noncommercial tort exception does not apply to all torts. In particular, it does not apply to "any claim based upon the exercise or performance or the failure to exercise or perform a discretionary function regardless of whether the discretion be abused."[98] In

---

[94] *See* Foreign Cultural Exchange Jurisdictional Immunity Clarification Act, Pub. L. 114–319 (Dec. 16, 2016), *codified at* 28 U.S.C. § 1605(h). The legislation was in part a response to the decision in Malewicz v. City of Amsterdam, 517 F. Supp. 2d 322 (D.D.C. 2007), in which the court had held that, even when art objects are immune from attachment, their presence in the United States can constitute a sufficient nexus to allow for the assertion of jurisdiction—under, for example, the FSIA's property takings exception.

[95] 28 U.S.C. § 1605(a)(5).

[96] H.R. REP. No. 94-1487, *supra* note 36, at 20–21. *See also* Argentine Republic v. Amerada Hess Shipping Co., 488 U.S. 428, 439 (1989) ("Congress' primary purpose in enacting § 1605(a)(5) was to eliminate a foreign state's immunity for traffic accidents and other torts committed in the United States, for which liability is imposed under domestic tort law.").

[97] *See, e.g.,* Doe v. Fed. Dem. Rep. of Ethiopia, 851 F.3d 7, 9–10 (D.C. Cir. 2017); O'Neil v. Saudi Joint Relief Comm., 714 F.3d 109, 116 (2d Cir. 2013); O'Bryan v. Holy See, 556 F.3d 361, 382 (6th Cir. 2009); Frolova v. Union of Soviet Socialist Republics, 761 F.2d 370, 379–80 (7th Cir. 1985); Persinger v. Islamic Republic of Iran, 729 F.2d 835, 842–43 (D.C. Cir. 1984).

[98] 28 U.S.C. § 1605(a)(5)(A).

addition, it does not apply to "any claim arising out of malicious prosecution, abuse of process, libel, slander, misrepresentation, deceit, or interference with contract rights."[99] The discretionary function limitation on the noncommercial tort exception is modeled on a similar limitation in the Federal Tort Claims Act (FTCA), which sets forth the federal government's immunity from tort claims in U.S. courts, and courts in FSIA cases have looked to precedent under the FTCA when interpreting this limitation.[100] Under this precedent, a function is considered discretionary if it "involves an element of judgment or choice" and if shielding this judgment or choice from liability is consistent with Congress's goal of "prevent[ing] judicial 'second-guessing' of legislative and administrative decisions grounded in social, economic, and political policy."[101] It is not clear whether and to what extent the discretionary function limitation in the FSIA applies to conduct that is illegal under either domestic or international law.[102]

Under the noncommercial tort exception, foreign states can be sued not only for their own torts, but also the torts of "any official or employee of that foreign state while acting within the scope of his office or employment." In determining whether officials or employees were acting within the scope of their employment, courts have looked to the *respondeat superior* law of the state in which the tort occurred.[103] This is what courts would ordinarily do in tort cases brought against private entities, and, as noted, the FSIA indicates that when there is an applicable exception to immunity, foreign states are to be liable to the same extent as private entities. By contrast, the Supreme Court has applied "principles . . . common to both international law and federal common law" to determine the attribution of liability among foreign state entities, since that issue is not addressed in the text of the FSIA.[104]

---

[99] *Id.*, § 1605(a)(5)(B).
[100] *See, e.g.*, Swarna v. Al-Awadi, 622 F.3d 123, 145–46 (2d Cir. 2010); O'Bryan v. Holy See, 556 F.3d 361, 383–84 (6th Cir. 2009).
[101] Berkovitz v. United States, 486 U.S. 531, 536–37 (1988). *See also* United States v. Gaubert, 499 U.S. 315, 322–23 (1991) ("Because the purpose of the exception is to 'prevent judicial "second-guessing" of legislative and administrative decisions grounded in social, economic, and political policy through the medium of an action in tort,' when properly construed, the exception 'protects only governmental actions and decisions based on considerations of public policy.'" (citation omitted)).
[102] *See* Risk v. Halvorsen, 936 F.2d 393, 396–97 (9th Cir. 1991) (holding that the mere fact that the conduct in question was alleged to have violated California criminal law was not enough to prevent it from falling within discretionary function limitation); Liu v. Republic of China, 892 F.2d 1419, 1431 (9th Cir. 1989) ("We hold that the discretionary function exception is inapplicable when an employee of a foreign government violates its own internal law."); Letelier v. Republic of Chile, 488 F. Supp. 665, 673 (D.D.C. 1980) (stating, in case involving assassination in Washington, D.C., that "there is no discretion to commit, or to have one's officers or agents commit, an illegal act").
[103] *See, e.g.*, Doe v. Holy See, 557 F.3d 1066, 1082 (9th Cir. 2009); Liu v. Republic of China, 892 F.2d 1419, 1426–31 (9th Cir. 1989); Joseph v. Office of the Consulate General of Nigeria, 830 F.2d 1018, 1025 (9th Cir. 1987).
[104] *See* First Nat'l City Bank v. Banco Para El Comercio Exterior de Cuba, 462 U.S. 611, 623 (1983).

TERRORISM EXCEPTIONS

In 1996, Congress amended the FSIA to add an exception to immunity for certain suits against "state sponsors of terrorism." The exception allows for suits relating to acts of torture, extrajudicial killing, aircraft sabotage, or hostage taking, or the provision of material support or resources for such acts.[105] The exception applies, however, only to nations included on the State Department's official list of terrorist states at the time of the acts in question or that become later so designated as a result of the acts. As of 2020, only four nations were on the list: Iran, North Korea, Sudan, and Syria.[106] Despite its limited coverage, the State Department initially opposed this exception because of a concern that it would extend the FSIA "beyond established international practice" and have the potential to harm U.S. foreign relations.[107]

Shortly after this exception was added in 1996, Congress passed another statute designed to give plaintiffs in these cases a federal cause of action for damages. This statute, known as the Flatow Amendment, allowed U.S. nationals to sue any "official, employee, or agent of a foreign state designated as a state sponsor of terrorism" for personal injury or death in cases in which the new exception to immunity applied.[108] Large monetary judgments were entered against foreign states under this statute and the immunity exception, and Congress took a variety of steps in an effort to assist plaintiffs in recovering on these judgments.[109] Eventually, however, the U.S. Court of Appeals for the D.C. Circuit

---

[105] The exception was originally codified as a seventh exception to immunity in 28 U.S.C. § 1605(a). In 2008, it was recodified in 28 U.S.C. § 1605A.

[106] Courts have held that it does not offend principles of separation of powers for the executive branch to have the authority to affect federal court jurisdiction through removal of nations from the list of state sponsors of terrorism. *See* Rein v. Socialist People's Libyan Arab Jamahiriya, 162 F.3d 748 (2d Cir. 1998); Price v. Socialist People's Libyan Arab Jamahiriya, 110 F. Supp. 2d 10 (D.D.C. 2000); and Daliberti v. Republic of Iraq, 97 F. Supp. 2d 38 (D.D.C. 2000). If a foreign state that is not on the list commits terrorist acts in the United States, claimants may be able to proceed against the state under the noncommercial tort exception to immunity, assuming they can otherwise meet the requirements of that exception. *See* Doe v. Bin Laden, 663 F.3d 64, 70 (2d Cir. 2011) (concluding that "the terrorism exception, rather than limiting the jurisdiction conferred by the noncommercial tort exception, provides an additional basis for jurisdiction").

[107] *The Foreign Sovereign Immunities Act: Hearings on S. 825 before the Subcomm. on Courts and Administrative Practice of the S. Comm. on the Judiciary*, 103d Cong. 12–15 (1994) (statement of Jamison S. Borek). The International Court of Justice has observed that this exception to immunity "has no counterpart in the legislation of other States." Jurisdictional Immunities of the State (Germany v. Italy), Judgment, ¶ 88 (ICJ, Feb. 3, 2012), *available at* http://www.icj-cij.org/docket/files/143/16883.pdf. *See also* Ronald J. Bettauer, *Germany Sues Italy at the International Court of Justice on Foreign Sovereign Immunity—Legal Underpinnings and Implications for U.S. Law*, ASIL INSIGHT (Nov. 19, 2009) (contending that this exception and related statutory provisions "would be very hard to defend as consistent with the existing state of international law"), *available at* http://www.asil.org/insights091119.cfm. In 2012, however, Canada enacted a similar statute. *See* Justice for Victims of Terrorism Act, S.C. 2012, c. 1, § 2 (assented to Mar. 13, 2012).

[108] Civil Liability for Acts of State-Sponsored Terrorism, P.L. 104–208, Title I, §101(c) [Title V, § 589] (Sept. 30, 1996), 110 Stat. 3009–172, *codified at* 28 U.S.C. § 1605 note.

[109] In 2008, the Congressional Research Service reported that "U.S. courts have awarded victims of terrorism more than $18.5 billion against State sponsors of terrorism and their officials, most of which remains

concluded that the text of the Flatow Amendment allowed for claims only against officials, employees, and agents of foreign states, not the foreign states themselves, and that the state sponsor of terrorism exception to immunity did not itself create a cause of action.[110]

In 2008, Congress recodified the state sponsor of terrorism exception in a stand-alone section and included within the section a cause of action for damages.[111] This cause of action expressly applies to foreign states as well as to officials and employees.[112] The cause of action can be asserted, however, only by U.S. nationals, members of the U.S. armed forces, and employees of the U.S. government or its contractors.[113] In addition, claims under the statute are subject to a ten-year statute of limitations, and claimants are required to give the foreign state "a reasonable opportunity to arbitrate the claim in accordance with the accepted international rules of arbitration."[114]

In 2016, Congress enacted the Justice Against Sponsors of Terrorism Act (JASTA), which creates a new exception to immunity for "any case in which money damages are sought against a foreign state for physical injury to person or property or death occurring in the United States and caused by—(1) an act of international terrorism in the United States; and (2) a tortious act or acts of the foreign state, or of any official, employee, or agent of that foreign state while acting within the scope of his or her office, employment, or agency, regardless where the tortious act or acts of the foreign state occurred."[115] Unlike the state sponsor of terrorism exception in § 1605A, JASTA is not limited to suits against particular foreign nations. A central reason that it was enacted, however, was to facilitate litigation against Saudi Arabia that had been initiated by families of the victims of the September 11, 2001, terrorist attacks.[116]

---

uncollected." Jennifer K. Elsea, *Suits against Terrorist States by Victims of Terrorism* (Cong. Res. Serv., Aug. 8, 2008), *available at* http://www.fas.org/sgp/crs/terror/RL31258.pdf.

[110] *See* Cicippio-Puleo v. Islamic Republic of Iran, 353 F.3d 1024, 1033 (D.C. Cir. 2004).

[111] For an overview, see Elsea, *supra* note 109.

[112] *See* 28 U.S.C. § 1605A(c).

[113] *See id.*

[114] *See id.*, § 1605A(a)(2)(A), 1605A(b).

[115] *See* Pub. L. 114-222 (Sept. 28, 2016), *codified at* 28 U.S.C. § 1605B. The statute also provides that "[a] court of the United States may stay a proceeding against a foreign state if the Secretary of State certifies that the United States is engaged in good faith discussions with the foreign state defendant concerning the resolution of the claims against the foreign state, or any other parties as to whom a stay of claims is sought." Such a stay may be granted for up to 180 days, and the stay can be extended based on a petition from the Attorney General, "if the Secretary of State recertifies that the United States remains engaged in good faith discussions with the foreign state defendant concerning the resolution of the claims against the foreign state, or any other parties as to whom a stay of claims is sought."

[116] In passing JASTA, Congress overrode a veto by President Obama, who expressed concerned that, among other things, the statute might undermine long-standing principles of sovereign immunity and potentially lead to reciprocal actions by other countries to reduce U.S. sovereign immunity. *See* Veto Message from the President—S. 2040 (Sept. 23, 2016), *at* https://obamawhitehouse.archives.gov/the-press-office/2016/09/23/veto-message-president-s2040. Shortly before Obama attempted to veto the legislation, the European Union had sent a letter to the U.S. State Department contending that JASTA "would be in conflict with fundamental

The terrorism exceptions in the FSIA illustrate how Congress sometimes faces domestic pressure to restrict sovereign immunity, even when there may be doubts about the consistency of such restrictions with international law. As this edition was being prepared for publication, another potential illustration of this dynamic arose, as Congress was considering proposals to restrict sovereign immunity in order to facilitate lawsuits against China relating to the spread of the COVID-19 virus.[117]

Immunity of International Organizations

International organizations have immunity from suit in U.S. courts under the International Organizations Immunities Act (IOIA), which was enacted in 1945.[118] The IOIA provides that international organizations "shall enjoy the same immunity from suit and every form of judicial process as is enjoyed by foreign governments, except to the extent that such organizations may expressly waive their immunity for the purpose of any proceedings or by the terms of any contract."[119] The term "international organization" is defined in the IOIA as "a public international organization in which the United States participates pursuant to any treaty or under the authority of any Act of Congress authorizing such participation or making an appropriation for such participation, and which shall have been designated by the President through appropriate Executive order as being entitled to enjoy the privileges, exemptions, and immunities herein provided."[120] The president, however, is authorized "at any time to revoke the designation of any international organization under this section, if in his judgment such action should be justified by reason of the abuse by an international organization or its officers and employees of the privileges, exemptions, and immunities herein provided or for any other reason."[121]

In *Jam v. Int'l Finance Corp.*, the Supreme Court held that the IOIA affords international organizations only the same immunity from suit that foreign governments receive today under the FSIA.[122] In that case, a group of Indian nationals had filed suit against the International Finance Corporation (IFC), an international organization based in Washington, D.C., that is part of the World Bank. The plaintiffs alleged that after the IFC loaned $450 million to an Indian company for the construction of a power plant in

---

principles of international law and in particular the principle of State sovereign immunity." *See* Letter from European Union (Sept. 2016), *at* https://www.washingtonpost.com/news/powerpost/wp-content/uploads/sites/47/2016/09/EU-on-JASTA.pdf.

[117] *See, e.g.*, John B. Bellinger III, Op-Ed, *Suing China Over the Coronavirus Won't Help. Here's What Can Work.*, WASH. POST (Apr. 23, 2020); Chimène Keitner, *Don't Bother Suing China for Coronavirus*, JUST SECURITY (Apr. 18, 2020), *at* https://www.justsecurity.org/69460/dont-bother-suing-china-for-coronavirus/.

[118] *See* 22 U.S.C. §§ 288–288l.
[119] 22 U.S.C. § 288a(b).
[120] 22 U.S.C. § 288.
[121] *Id.*
[122] 139 S. Ct. 759 (2019).

India, the company constructed the plant in a manner contrary to the funding agreement and IFC policy, and that the plant ended up causing environmental and social damage to the surrounding communities. In rejecting the IFC's argument that it was entitled to the essentially absolute immunity that foreign governments would have enjoyed in 1945, the Supreme Court explained that the IOIA's language "seems to continuously link the immunity of international organizations to that of foreign governments, so as to ensure ongoing parity between the two."[123]

In response to the concern that allowing suits against international organizations would unduly interfere with their operation and effectiveness, the Court in *Jam* noted that "the privileges and immunities accorded by the IOIA are only default rules," and if greater protection from suit is needed, "the organization's charter can always specify a different level of immunity."[124] The Court also emphasized that, in order to be able to sue an international organization, plaintiffs would still need to satisfy an exception to immunity in the FSIA, which will not always be possible. Indeed, without resolving the issue, the Court took note of the "serious doubts" expressed by the executive branch about whether the suit in this case would satisfy the FSIA's commercial activity exception, given that the plaintiffs' claims largely concerned tortious activity in India.[125]

Diplomatic and Consular Immunity

Diplomatic and consular immunities were historically regulated by customary international law, but they are now codified in two treaties—the Vienna Convention on Diplomatic Relations ("Diplomatic Convention"), and the Vienna Convention on Consular Relations ("Consular Convention")—both of which the United States has ratified.[126] Under these treaties, the nation that sends the diplomat or consular official is referred to as the "sending state," and the nation that receives the diplomat or consular official is referred to as the "receiving state." The immunity provisions in these treaties are viewed by U.S. courts as self-executing, although there is also legislation implementing the immunity provisions of the Diplomatic Convention.[127]

---

[123] *Id.* at 768.
[124] *Id.* at 771.
[125] *Id.* at 772.
[126] *See* Vienna Convention on Diplomatic Relations, Apr. 18, 1961, 23 U.S.T. 3227, T.I.A.S. No. 7502 [hereinafter Diplomatic Convention]; Vienna Convention on Consular Relations, Apr. 24, 1963, 21 U.S.T. 77, T.I.A.S. No. 6820 [hereinafter Consular Convention]. For general discussions of diplomatic and consular immunity, *see* RESTATEMENT (THIRD) OF THE FOREIGN RELATIONS LAW OF THE UNITED STATES, *supra* note 88, §§ 464–66; and EILEEN DENZA, DIPLOMATIC LAW: COMMENTARY ON THE VIENNA CONVENTION ON DIPLOMATIC RELATIONS (3d ed. 2008).
[127] The 1978 Diplomatic Relations Act provides, among other things, that "[a]ny action or proceeding brought against an individual who is entitled to immunity with respect to such action or proceeding under the Vienna Convention on Diplomatic Relations. . . shall be dismissed," and that "[s]uch immunity may be established upon motion or suggestion by or on behalf of the individual, or as otherwise permitted by law or applicable

Under the Diplomatic Convention, accredited diplomats posted to the United States have broad immunity from both criminal and civil jurisdiction. They are not subject to "any form of arrest or detention."[128] In addition, they have absolute immunity from the criminal jurisdiction of the receiving state.[129] Furthermore, they have immunity from civil and administrative proceedings, with exceptions for certain actions related to immovable property, succession of estates, and nonofficial commercial activities.[130] The commercial activity exception has been read narrowly by U.S. courts, such that it applies only to the conduct of a trade or business, and not to commercial relationships that are incidental to daily life.[131] Members of the family of a diplomat "forming part of his household" shall enjoy the same immunities as long as they are not nationals of the receiving state.[132]

Under the Consular Convention, the immunity of consular officers posted to the United States is more qualified. Consular officers are not subject to arrest or detention "except in the case of a grave crime and pursuant to a decision by the competent judicial authority."[133] They have immunity from criminal and civil jurisdiction, but only "in respect of acts performed in the exercise of consular functions."[134] Even this immunity does not apply with respect to civil actions for certain contract and tort claims where the consular official was not acting expressly in a public capacity.[135] Members of the family of a consular official "forming part of his household," as well as his or her private staff, shall enjoy the same immunities as the consular official.[136]

Diplomatic and consular immunities apply only while the official is serving as a member of the mission. Diplomats have residual immunity after leaving their post, however, for "acts performed by such a person in the exercise of his functions as a member of the mission."[137] Similarly, consular officials have residual immunity after leaving their post

---

rules of procedure." 22 U.S.C. § 254d. Prior to its ratification and implementation of the Convention, the United States had long protected diplomatic immunity through statute. *See* Crimes Act of 1790, § 25, 1 Stat. 112, 117–18 (providing that ambassadors and other public ministers of foreign states, as well as their domestic servants, were immune from arrest and imprisonment, as well from attachment of their goods and chattels, "in any of the courts of the United States").

[128] Diplomatic Convention, *supra* note 126, at art. 29.

[129] *Id.*, art. 31(1).

[130] *See id.* Under the Diplomatic Relations Act, diplomats and diplomatic missions are required to carry liability insurance covering operations of a vehicle, vessel, or aircraft in the United States. *See* 22 U.S.C. § 254e.

[131] *See, e.g.*, Broidy Capital Mgmt. LLC v. Benomar, 944 F.3d 436, 445 (2d Cir. 2019); Tabion v. Mufti, 73 F.3d 535 (4th Cir. 1996); Montuya v. Chedid, 779 F. Supp. 2d 60 (D.D.C. 2011).

[132] Diplomatic Convention, *supra* note 126, art. 37(1). The U.S. State Department has interpreted this language not to include children once they reach the age of twenty-one, except for children still enrolled in school and under the age of twenty-three. *See* United States v. Al-Hamdi, 356 F.3d 564 (4th Cir. 2004).

[133] Consular Convention, *supra* note 126, at art. 41(1).

[134] *Id.*, art. 43(1). *See, e.g.*, Park v. Shin, 313 F.3d 1138, 1141–43 (9th Cir. 2002).

[135] Consular Convention, *supra* note 126, art. 43(2).

[136] *Id.*, art. 53(2).

[137] *Id.*, art. 39(2).

"with respect to acts performed ... in the exercise of [their] functions."[138] The residual immunity of former diplomats and consular officials, in other words, is limited to their official acts.[139]

In addition to the individual immunities discussed, diplomatic and consular properties are protected against interference by the receiving state. Although these properties are not, contrary to popular belief, treated as part of the sending state's territory, they are considered "inviolable" by the receiving state. For diplomatic missions, this means that they cannot be entered by officials of the receiving state "except with the consent of the head of the mission."[140] In addition, the receiving state has a duty "to take all appropriate steps to protect the premises of the mission against any intrusion or damage and to prevent any disturbance of the peace of the mission or impairment of its dignity."[141] For consular premises, officials of the receiving state cannot enter "that part of the consular premises which is used exclusively for the purpose of the work of the consular post except with the consent of the head of the consular post or of his designee or of the head of the diplomatic mission of the sending State."[142] Consent is assumed, however, "in the case of fire or other disaster requiring prompt protective action."[143] As with diplomatic missions, the receiving state has a duty "to take all appropriate steps to protect the consular premises against any intrusion or damage and to prevent any disturbance of the peace of the consular post or impairment of its dignity."[144]

Despite these limitations on its jurisdiction, the receiving state may at any time declare a member of a diplomatic mission or consulate to be *persona non grata*. Once a person is declared *persona non grata*, the sending state must either recall the person or terminate his or her official functions.[145] In addition, both the Diplomatic Convention and the Consular Convention make clear that the immunity of diplomats and consular officials can be waived by the sending state, as long as the waiver is "express."[146] Furthermore, diplomats and consular officials are deemed under these treaties to waive their immunity with respect to counterclaims if they bring suit in the receiving state.[147]

The views of the executive branch can have a significant influence on how these immunity principles are applied by U.S. courts. Courts generally treat as conclusive State

---

[138] *Id.*, art. 53(4).
[139] *See, e.g.*, Swarna v. Al-Awadi, 622 F.3d 123, 135–36 (2d Cir. 2010).
[140] Diplomatic Convention, *supra* note 126, art. 22(1).
[141] *Id.*, art. 22(2).
[142] Consular Convention, *supra* note 126, art. 31(2).
[143] *Id.*
[144] *Id.*, art. 31(3).
[145] *See* Diplomatic Convention, *supra* note 126, art. 9(1); Consular Convention, *supra* note 126, art. 23(1).
[146] *See* Diplomatic Convention, *supra* note 126, art. 32; Consular Convention, *supra* note 126, art. 45.
[147] *See* Diplomatic Convention, *supra* note 126, art. 32(3); Consular Convention, *supra* note 126, art. 42(3). For a decision holding that a waiver of criminal immunity did not entail a waiver of immunity from liability for civil damages, *see* Knab v. Republic of Georgia, 1998 U.S. Dist. LEXIS 8820 (D.D.C. 1998).

Department certifications of a diplomat's status.[148] Courts give substantial but not dispositive weight to executive branch constructions of the Vienna Conventions.[149] Courts also give some weight to the executive branch's views about whether immunity should ultimately be granted in a particular case, although they do not typically treat those views as binding.[150]

Representatives of members of the United Nations and official invitees to the United Nations are also entitled to certain immunities. Under the 1947 Agreement between the United Nations and the United States of America Regarding the Headquarters of the United Nations, also known as the "UN Headquarters Agreement," representatives of member states "shall, whether residing inside or outside the headquarters district, be entitled in the territory of the United States to the same privileges and immunities . . . as it accords to diplomatic envoys accredited to it."[151] The Headquarters Agreement thus incorporates by reference the diplomatic immunity provided for in the Diplomatic Convention. The Agreement also prohibits the imposition of any impediments to transit to or from the headquarters district (a defined area around the United Nations headquarters) by a variety of individuals, including representatives of the UN members as well as "other persons invited to the headquarters district by the United Nations."[152]

The 1946 Convention on Privileges and Immunities of the United Nations, which entered into force with respect to the United States in 1970, provides more specifically that representatives of member states to the United Nations shall "enjoy the following privileges and immunities: (a) immunity from personal arrest or detention . . . ; (b) inviolability for all papers and documents; . . . (g) such other privileges, immunities and facilities not inconsistent [with] the foregoing as diplomatic envoys enjoy."[153] These provisions have been interpreted as in effect conferring diplomatic immunity on even nonresident representatives sent to the United Nations.[154] The Convention also provides that UN officials are "immune from legal process in respect of words spoken or written and all acts performed by them in their official capacity."[155] The immunity specified for the UN Secretary-General and Assistant Secretaries-General is broader, being the equivalent to the immunity granted to diplomats.[156] The immunity of UN officials can be waived by

---

[148] *See, e.g.*, Abdulaziz v. Metro. Dade Cty., 741 F.3d 1328, 1331 (11th Cir. 1984).

[149] *See, e.g.*, United States v. Al-Hamdi, 356 F.3d 564 (4th Cir. 2004); Tabion v. Mufti, 73 F.3d 535, 538 (4th Cir. 1996).

[150] *See, e.g., Knab*, 1998 U.S. Dist. LEXIS at *10 ("Although the Court is not obliged to defer to the State Department's opinion, it finds [the State Department's letter to the court] useful evidence.").

[151] Agreement Regarding the Headquarters of the United Nations, June 26, 1947, art. V, § 15(4), 61 Stat. 3416, 11 U.N.T.S. 11.

[152] *Id.*, art. IV, § 11.

[153] Convention on Privileges and Immunities of the United Nations, Feb. 13, 1946, art. IV, § 11, 21 U.S.T. 1418, 33 U.N.T.S. 261 (entered into force with respect to the United States Apr. 29, 1970).

[154] *See* Tachiona v. Mugabe, 387 F.3d 205 (2d Cir. 2004).

[155] Convention on Privileges and Immunities, *supra* note 153, art. V, § 18.

[156] *Id.*, art. V, § 19.

the UN Secretary-General,[157] and the Secretary-General's immunity can also be waived by the UN Security Council. The Convention also provides that the United Nations itself "shall enjoy immunity from every form of legal process except insofar as in any particular case it has expressly waived its immunity."[158]

Immunity of Heads of State and Other Foreign Officials

It is generally understood that, as a matter of customary international law, government officials are entitled to two types of immunity in foreign courts—status immunity (also called immunity *ratione personae*) and conduct immunity (also called immunity *ratione materiae*).[159] Status immunity protects particular types of government officials from civil suit or criminal prosecution in foreign courts, even for their private conduct, but only while they are in office. This form of immunity applies to "heads of state" (a category that includes presidents, prime ministers, monarchs, and foreign ministers) as well as accredited diplomats. By contrast, conduct immunity protects all government officials who act on behalf of the state from civil suit or criminal prosecution in foreign courts, even after they leave office, but only for the discharge of their functions while in office. This is also the type of immunity that applies to consular officials. As discussed earlier, diplomatic and consular immunity is addressed today by treaty, but there is no general treaty addressing the immunity of other foreign officials.

Before the enactment of the FSIA, there were relatively few decisions by U.S. courts addressing the immunity of individual foreign officials. As discussed, in the *Schooner Exchange* decision, the Supreme Court noted that diplomats and heads of state were entitled to immunity under customary international law. In a handful of decisions in the nineteenth and early twentieth centuries, U.S. courts held that individual officials were immune from suit for their official conduct.[160] The executive branch also seemed to

---

[157] *Id.*, art. V, § 20. *See, e.g.,* United States v. Bahel, 662 F.3d 610 (2d Cir. 2011).

[158] Convention on Privileges and Immunities, *supra* note 153, art. § II, 2. For a decision concluding that this immunity provision is self-executing and thus can be applied by courts even in the absence of implementing legislation, *see* Brzak v. United Nations, 597 F.3d 107, 111–12 (2d Cir. 2010).

[159] *See, e.g.,* Dapo Akande & Sangeeta Shah, *Immunities of State Officials, International Crimes, and Foreign Domestic Courts*, 21 Eur. J. Int'l L. 815 (2010); Curtis A. Bradley & Laurence R. Helfer, *International Law and the Common Law of Foreign Official Immunity*, 2010 Sup. Ct. Rev. 213, 233–36. *See also, e.g.,* Arrest Warrant of April 11, 2000 (Dem. Rep. Congo v. Belg.), 2002 I.C.J. 3, ¶ 54 (Feb. 14) ("[T]he functions of a Minister for Foreign Affairs are such that, throughout the duration of his or her office, he or she when abroad enjoys full immunity from criminal jurisdiction and inviolability.").

[160] *See, e.g.,* Lyders v. Lund, 32 F.2d 308, 309 (N.D. Cal. 1929) ("[I]n actions against the officials of a foreign state not clothed with diplomatic immunity, it can be said that suits based upon official, authorized acts, performed within the scope of their duties on behalf of the foreign state, and for which the foreign state will have to respond directly or indirectly in the event of a judgment, are actions against the foreign state."); Hatch v. Baez, 14 N.Y. Sup. Ct. 596 (Gen. Term 1876) (holding that a former president of the Dominican Republic had immunity for tortious acts done in his official capacity and reasoning that "[t]he fact that the defendant has

suggest this at various times.[161] Because of the relatively low number of cases, however, the scope of this conduct immunity was not explored in any detail.[162]

The Supreme Court endorsed the immunity of foreign officials for their official acts in *Underhill v. Hernandez*.[163] In *Underhill*, a U.S. citizen sued a Venezuelan military commander, whose revolutionary government had been recognized by the United States, for unlawful assault and detention in Venezuela. The decision is most famous for its articulation of the act of state doctrine (discussed in Chapter 1 of this book), pursuant to which "the courts of one country will not sit in judgment on the acts of the government of another done within its own territory."[164] The Supreme Court also recognized, however, "[t]he immunity of individuals from suits brought in foreign tribunals for acts done within their own States, in the exercise of governmental authority, whether as civil officers or as military commanders."[165] Similarly, the lower court in that case noted that "because the acts of the official representatives of the state are those of the state itself, when exercised within the scope of their delegated powers, courts and publicists have recognized the immunity of public agents from suits brought in foreign tribunals for acts done within their own states in the exercise of the sovereignty thereof."[166]

The *Restatement (Second) of the Foreign Relations Law of the United States*, published in 1965, stated that under U.S. common law, a foreign state's immunity extended to an

---

ceased to be president of St. Domingo does not destroy his immunity" because the immunity "springs from the capacity in which the acts were done, and protects the individual who did them, because they emanated from a foreign and friendly government"). At least in the early nineteenth century, foreign official immunity appears to have operated as a defense on the merits rather than as a jurisdictional bar. *See* Chimène Keitner, *The Lost History of Foreign Official Immunity*, 87 N.Y.U. L. REV. 704 (2012).

[161] *See, e.g.*, 1 OP. ATT'Y GEN. 81 (1797) (noting that "it is as well settled in the United States as in Great Britain, that a person acting under a commission from the sovereign of a foreign nation is not amenable for what he does in pursuance of his commission, to any judiciary tribunal in the United States"); 1 OP. ATT'Y GEN. 45 (1794) ("[I]f the seizure of the vessel is admitted to have been an official act, done by the defendant by virtue, or under color, of the powers vested in him as governor, that it will of itself be a sufficient answer to the plaintiff's action; that the defendant ought not to answer in our courts for any mere *irregularity* in the exercise of his powers; and that the *extent* of his authority can, with propriety or convenience, be determined only by the constituted authorities of his own nation."). *See also* 2 JOHN BASSETT MOORE, A DIGEST OF INTERNATIONAL LAW § 179, at 23–32 (1906) (quoting various executive branch and judicial statements in support of individual official immunity); Underhill v. Hernandez, 65 F. 577, 580 (2d Cir. 1895) ("The law officers of the United States have uniformly advised the executive department that individuals are not answerable in foreign tribunals for acts done in their own country, in behalf of their government, by virtue of their official authority."), *aff'd on other grounds*, 168 U.S. 250 (1897).

[162] For additional discussion of the historic scope of the common law of foreign official immunity, *see* Curtis A. Bradley & Jack L. Goldsmith, *Foreign Sovereign Immunity and Domestic Officer Suits*, 13 GREEN BAG 2d 137 (2010); and Chimène L. Keitner, *The Common Law of Foreign Official Immunity*, 14 GREEN BAG 2d 61 (2010).

[163] *See* 168 U.S. 250 (1897).

[164] *Id.* at 252.

[165] *Id. See also* Banco Nacional de Cuba v. Sabbatino, 376 U.S. 398, 340 (1964) (noting that "sovereign immunity provided an independent ground" in *Underhill*).

[166] 65 F. 577, 579 (2d Cir. 1895).

official or agent of a state "with respect to acts performed in his official capacity if the effect of exercising jurisdiction would be to enforce a rule of law against the state."[167] The *Restatement* did not clearly explain, however, when exercising jurisdiction would have the effect of "enforc[ing] a rule of law against the state." As an illustration of such an improper effect, the *Restatement* gave the example of a suit against a foreign official relating to a contract made by the plaintiff with the foreign state. As an illustration of a suit that would not have such an effect, the *Restatement* gave the example of a tort suit against a foreign official relating to a traffic accident in the nation in which the suit is brought.[168] These illustrations suggest that official immunity extends to suits that in effect seek recovery of money from the state and does not extend to suits concerning the tortious acts of foreign officials committed in another country. But the illustrations do not shed much light on other questions, such as whether and to what extent official immunity extends to tortious acts committed by foreign officials in their own country. (As already noted, the FSIA allows suits against foreign governments themselves for torts committed in the United States but not for torts committed abroad.)

As we have seen, starting in the late 1930s, courts began giving essentially absolute deference to the executive branch with respect to foreign sovereign immunity. In some instances, courts appeared to give similar deference concerning the immunity of individual foreign officials.[169] There were few reported cases raising the issue of foreign official immunity, however, which helps explain why Congress did not directly address it in the FSIA. The FSIA refers to suits against "foreign states" and defines this category to include an "agency or instrumentality of a foreign state," which is in turn defined to mean "any entity" that "is a separate legal person, corporate or otherwise" and has certain other characteristics, such as having a majority of its shares owned by a foreign state.[170] This language does not easily accommodate natural persons.

Most courts assumed after the enactment of the FSIA that suits against foreign *heads of state* were not governed by the statute. Instead, at least for suits against sitting heads of state (which under customary international law are entitled to status immunity), courts generally held that there was absolute immunity if suggested by the executive branch.[171]

---

[167] RESTATEMENT (SECOND) OF THE FOREIGN RELATIONS LAW OF THE UNITED STATES § 66 (1965).
[168] *See id.*, cmt. b.
[169] *See, e.g.*, Greenspan v. Crosbie, No. 74 Civ. 4734 (GLG), 1976 WL 481, at *2 (S.D.N.Y. Nov. 23, 1976) ("The Suggestion of Immunity removes the individual defendants from the case."). *Cf.* Waltier v. Thomson, 189 F. Supp. 319, 320 (S.D.N.Y. 1960) (concluding that "[a] consular official is immune from suit when the acts complained of were performed in the course of his official duties"). *See also Sovereign Immunity Decisions of the Department of State*, May 1952 to January 1977, 1977 DIG. U.S. PRAC. INT'L L. 1017 (recounting the practices of the State Department from the issuance of the Tate Letter through the time the FSIA took effect, including practices relating to the immunity of individual foreign officials).
[170] 28 U.S.C. § 1603(a), (b).
[171] *See, e.g.*, Ye v. Zemin, 383 F.3d 620, 625 (7th Cir. 2004); United States v. Noriega, 117 F.3d 1206, 1212 (11th Cir. 1997); Lafontant v. Aristide, 844 F. Supp. 128, 136–37 (E.D.N.Y. 1994); Saltany v. Reagan, 702 F. Supp. 319 (D.D.C. 1988). *See also* Tachiona v. United States, 386 F.3d 205, 220 (2d Cir. 2004) ("We have some doubt

Indeed, when the executive branch suggested it, courts generally extended this head-of-state immunity to other high-level officials and family members.[172] At least one court suggested that the executive also had the ability to preclude head-of-state immunity.[173] There was some uncertainty, however, about what to do when the executive branch was silent.[174]

Courts have generally held that a foreign state may waive a head-of-state's immunity.[175] These courts have reasoned that "[b]ecause it is the state that gives the power to lead and the ensuing trappings of power—including immunity—the state may therefore take back that which it bestowed upon its erstwhile leaders."[176] Courts will only accept a waiver, however, if it comes from a government recognized by the United States.[177] In a number of instances, claims of immunity by former heads of state have been rejected on the ground that their immunity had been waived by the new government. In the absence of a waiver, it is unclear to what extent a former head of state can claim immunity, and to what extent this should be controlled by the executive branch. Some courts have suggested in dicta that former-head-of-state immunity does not extend to private (as opposed to official) acts.[178]

---

as to whether the FSIA was meant to supplant the 'common law' of head-of-state immunity, which generally entailed deference to the executive branch's suggestions of immunity.").

[172] *See, e.g.*, Kline v. Keneko, 535 N.Y.S.2d 303 (Sup. Ct. 1988) (granting immunity to president's wife), *aff'd mem. sub nom.* Kline v. Cordero de la Madrid, 546 N.Y.S. 2d 506 (App. Div. 1989); Kilroy v. Windsor, No. C–78–291, slip op. (N.D. Ohio, Dec. 7, 1978) (unpublished) (granting immunity to Prince Charles of England); Chong Boon Kim v. Kim Yong Shik, 58 AM. J. INT'L L. 186 (Haw. Cir. Ct., Sept. 9, 1963) (granting immunity to foreign minister). *But see* El-Hadad v. Embassy of the U.A.E., 60 F. Supp. 2d 69, 82 n.10 (D.D.C. 1999) (reasoning that head-of-state immunity is limited to heads of state); Republic of Philippines v. Marcos, 665 F. Supp. 793, 797 (N.D. Cal. 1987) (refusing to grant immunity to Philippine solicitor general, despite suggestion of immunity from the State Department).

[173] *See* United States v. Noriega, 117 F.3d 1206, 1212 (11th Cir. 1997) ("[B]y pursuing Noriega's capture and this prosecution, the Executive Branch has manifested its clear sentiment that Noriega should be denied head-of-state immunity.").

[174] Some courts indicated that an executive suggestion was a prerequisite for immunity. *See, e.g.*, Jungquist v. Nahyan, 940 F. Supp. 312, 321 (D.D.C. 1996). Other courts relied on the lack of an executive suggestion simply as a factor weighing against immunity. *See, e.g.*, First Am. Corp. v. Al-Nahyan, 948 F. Supp. 1107, 1121 (D.D.C. 1996). Still other courts reasoned that, when lacking guidance from the executive, a court should decide for itself whether the head of state is entitled to immunity. *See In re* Doe, 860 F.2d 40, 45 (2d Cir. 1988); Abiola v. Abubakar, 267 F. Supp. 2d 907, 915 (N.D. Ill. 2003); *see also* Note, *Interpreting Silence: The Roles of the Courts and the Executive Branch in Head of State Immunity Cases*, 124 HARV. L. REV. 2042 (2011). For additional discussion of head-of-state immunity in U.S. courts, see, for example, Shobha Varughese George, *Head-of-State Immunity in the United States Courts: Still Confused after All These Years*, 64 FORDHAM L. REV. 1051 (1995), and Jerold L. Mallory, Note, *Resolving the Confusion over Head of State Immunity: The Defined Right of Kings*, 86 COLUM. L. REV. 169 (1986).

[175] *See, e.g.*, Doe, 860 F.2d at 44–45; *In re* Grand Jury Proceedings, 817 F.2d 1108, 1111 (4th Cir. 1987); Paul v. Avril, 812 F. Supp. 207, 210 (S.D. Fla. 1992).

[176] *Doe*, 860 F.2d at 45.

[177] *See* Lafontant v. Aristide, 844 F. Supp. 128, 134 (E.D.N.Y. 1994) (declining to recognize waiver by ostensible new government of Haiti because the executive branch had not recognized the new government as legitimate).

[178] *See, e.g.*, Doe, 860 F.2d at 44; Republic of the Phil. v. Marcos, 806 F.2d 344, 360 (2d Cir. 1986); United States v. Noriega, 746 F. Supp. 1506, 1519 n.11 (S.D. Fla. 1990).

A number of circuit courts eventually held that the FSIA applied to suits against foreign officials *other than heads of state* for actions taken in their official capacity. The leading decision was *Chuidian v. Philippine National Bank*.[179] In that case, a Philippine citizen brought suit against a member of a Philippine governmental commission after the defendant had instructed a bank to dishonor a letter of credit that had been issued by a prior government of the Philippines. Noting that foreign officials received common law immunity before enactment of the FSIA, the court reasoned that it would be "illogical" to think that Congress in the FSIA eliminated the application of sovereign immunity to individuals "implicitly and without comment."[180] The court added that "to allow unrestricted suits against individual foreign officials acting in their official capacities ... [would allow] litigants to accomplish indirectly what the Act barred them from doing directly," and "would defeat the purposes of the Act."[181] The court concluded that individual officials who act on behalf of the state can reasonably be considered "agencies or instrumentalities" of the state for purposes of the FSIA. Several other circuit courts subsequently adopted *Chuidian*'s interpretation of the FSIA.[182]

As discussed in Chapter 7, suits brought under the Alien Tort Statute are often brought against foreign officials. After the seminal *Filartiga* decision in 1980, this ATS litigation proceeded for many years without much attention to the issue of individual official immunity. To the extent courts considered the issue, most concluded that when officials committed human rights abuses, they were not acting in an official capacity, although the courts did not always explain why that was the case. Some of these courts referred to foreign law to determine the scope of the official's authority and found that the alleged human rights violations exceeded anything that could plausibly be considered within that authority. Other courts appear to have assumed that human rights abuses are per se unauthorized acts.

Two years after *Chuidian*, Congress enacted the Torture Victim Protection Act (TVPA). As discussed in Chapter 7, the TVPA created a cause of action for damages against individuals who "under actual or apparent authority, or color of law, of any foreign nation" commit acts of torture or "extrajudicial killing." Although the TVPA does not mention immunity, it arguably assumes that foreign officials will not ordinarily be entitled to immunity when sued for acts of torture or extrajudicial killing.

Eventually, greater conflict developed between the *Chuidian* line of decisions and human rights litigation. In several cases alleging war crimes and human rights violations by Israeli officials, courts held that suits against foreign officials for their official acts, even

---

[179] 912 F.2d 1095 (9th Cir. 1990).
[180] *Id.* at 1102.
[181] *Id.*
[182] *See, e.g., In re* Terrorist Attacks on September 11, 2001, 538 F.3d 71, 81 (2d Cir. 2009); Keller v. Cent. Bank of Nigeria, 277 F.3d 811, 815–16 (6th Cir. 2002); Byrd v. Corporacion Forestal y Industrial de Olancho, SA, 182 F.3d 380, 388–89 (5th Cir. 1999); El-Fadl v. Cent. Bank of Jordan, 75 F.3d 668, 671 (D.C. Cir. 1996).

if those acts constituted human rights abuses, were covered by the FSIA.[183] As one court explained, "[a]ll allegations stem from actions taken on behalf of the state and, in essence, the personal capacity suits amount to suits against the officers for being Israeli government officials."[184] Meanwhile, a conflict in the circuits developed over whether the FSIA applied to suits against individual foreign officials, a conflict resolved by the Supreme Court in 2010, in *Samantar v. Yousuf*.[185]

In *Samantar*, the Supreme Court considered a suit by citizens of Somalia against Mohamed Ali Samantar, a former high-ranking official of Somalia, in which they alleged that Samantar was responsible for acts of torture, killing, and arbitrary detention by Somali military forces. The Court rejected Samantar's argument that the suit qualified as a suit "against a foreign state" for purposes of the FSIA. After closely examining the language of the statute, the Court found insufficient evidence that Congress intended to address suits against individual officials. In addition, the Court observed that there were potential differences between a foreign government's immunity and an individual official's immunity, and thus, said the Court, "there is ... little reason to presume that when Congress set out to codify state immunity, it must also have, *sub silentio*, intended to codify official immunity."[186] The Court also noted that, although Congress had sought in the FSIA to shift determinations of foreign governmental immunity away from the executive branch, "[w]e have been given no reason to believe that Congress saw as a problem, or wanted to eliminate, the State Department's role in determinations regarding individual official immunity."[187]

The Court in *Samantar* denied that its holding would allow plaintiffs to avoid the limitations of the FSIA by simply suing foreign government officials. "Even if a suit is not governed by the Act," the Court noted, "it may still be barred by foreign sovereign immunity under the common law."[188] For similar reasons, the Court rejected the argument that its interpretation of the FSIA would place the United States in breach of international law obligations relating to the immunity of foreign officials and thus contravene the *Charming Betsy* canon of construction (which is discussed in Chapter 1 and throughout this book). "Because we are not deciding that the FSIA bars petitioner's immunity but rather that the Act does not address the question," explained the Court, "we need not determine whether declining to afford immunity to petitioner would be consistent with international law."[189]

---

[183] *See* Belhas v. Ya'alon, 515 F.3d 1279, 1284 (D.C. Cir. 2008); Matar v. Dichter, 500 F. Supp. 2d 284, 291 (S.D.N.Y. 2009), *aff'd on other grounds*, 563 F.3d 9 (2d Cir. 2009); Doe I v. State of Israel, 400 F. Supp. 2d 86, 104–105 (D.D.C. 2005).
[184] *Doe I*, 400 F. Supp. 2d at 105.
[185] 560 U.S. 305 (2010).
[186] *Id.* at 322.
[187] *Id.* at 323.
[188] *Id.* at 324.
[189] *Id.* at 320 n.14. The Court's approach can be contrasted with that of the British House of Lords in a much-discussed 2006 decision, in which the House of Lords relied extensively on international law in construing the

The common law of immunity referred to by the Court is presumably *federal* common law, given the strong national interests involved and the connection between this body of law and both the historic executive branch authority over immunity determinations and Congress's regulation of immunity in the FSIA.[190] As a result, this common law of immunity is probably binding on state courts as well as federal courts. The Supreme Court provided little guidance about how the lower courts are to determine the content of this federal common law, so courts have had to work this out over time.[191]

A central issue after *Samantar* is the extent to which courts should defer to the views of the executive branch about whether to grant immunity in particular cases. In suits brought against present and former heads of state, courts after *Samantar* have generally

---

reference to "State" in the United Kingdom State Immunity Act as covering suits against foreign officials for actions taken in their official capacity. *See* Jones v. Ministry of the Interior of the Kingdom of Saudi Arabia, [2006] UKHL 26, [2007] 1 A.C. 270. *See also* Ed Bates, *State Immunity for Torture*, 7 Hum. Rts. L. Rev. 651 (2007) (noting "the Law Lords' clear conclusion that the immunity *ratione materiae* that attached to the State could not be circumvented by claims being brought against individuals who acted on behalf of the State"). For a similar decision from Australia, *see* Zhang v. Zemin, [2010] NSWCA 255, para. 66 (New South Wales Court of Appeal) (construing the Foreign States Immunities Act of Australia to cover individual officials acting on behalf of the state, in part because a contrary interpretation would, "if accepted, render the legislative scheme, and the principles of international law which it was clarifying and implementing, virtually devoid of practical significance"), *available at* https://documents.law.yale.edu/sites/default/files/zhang_243flr299.pdf. *See also* Lori Fisler Damrosch, *Foreign State Immunity at Home and Abroad: Changing the International Law of Sovereign Immunity through National Decisions*, 44 Vand. J. Transnat'l L. 1185, 1188 n.10 (2011) ("Our foreign colleagues could well wonder why the Supreme Court [in *Samantar*] failed to analyze the customary international law principles relevant to individual immunities.").

[190] *See, e.g.*, David P. Stewart, Samantar *and the Future of Foreign Official Immunity*, 15 Lewis & Clark L. Rev. 633, 648–49 (2011) ("Given the national interest in promoting such norms, the need for uniformity in the resolution of such cases, and the sensitive foreign relations context in which the issues necessarily arise, there may be little debate that this area is presumptively one of federal common law."); Ingrid Wuerth, *Foreign Official Immunity Determinations in U.S. Courts: The Case against the State Department*, 51 Va. J. Int'l L. 915, 967 (2011) ("Immunity thus nicely demonstrates the functional need for interstitial lawmaking by the federal courts in cases properly before them: applying state law is a poor alternative, the executive branch does not always weigh in and there are strong functional disadvantages to its complete control of immunity issues, international law is in some respects contested and arguably incomplete, consistency with the federal statute is important, and there are strong federal interests involved."). For a critique of the Supreme Court's invitation of federal common law on this topic, *see* Peter B. Rutledge, Samantar, *Official Immunity and Federal Common Law*, 15 Lewis & Clark L. Rev. 589 (2011).

[191] For discussions of what courts should consider in developing the common law of foreign official immunity after *Samantar*, see, for example, Bradley & Helfer, *supra* note 159; Harold Hongju Koh, *Foreign State Immunity at Home and Abroad: Foreign Official Immunity after* Samantar: *A United States Government Perspective*, 44 Vand. J. Transnat'l L. 1141 (2011); Beth Stephens, *The Modern Common Law of Foreign Official Immunity*, 79 Fordham L. Rev. 2669 (2011); David P. Stewart, Samantar *and the Future of Foreign Official Immunity*, 15 Lewis & Clark L. Rev. 633 (2011); Christopher D. Totten, *Head-of-State and Foreign Official Immunity in the United States after* Samantar: *A Suggested Approach*, 34 Fordham Int'l L. J. 332 (2011); and Wuerth, *supra* note 190.

accorded absolute deference to executive branch suggestions of immunity.[192] On remand in the *Samantar* case itself, however, the U.S. Court of Appeals for the Fourth Circuit expressed the view that absolute deference to the executive branch is warranted only for the immunity of *sitting* heads of state.[193] Such absolute deference is warranted, the court reasoned, because sitting heads of state are entitled under international law to a status-based immunity that is related to the executive's authority to recognize foreign sovereigns.[194] For suits against officials who are entitled only to conduct-based immunity (including former heads of state), by contrast, the Fourth Circuit expressed the view that courts should give only "substantial weight" to the executive's position. The Fourth Circuit also held that conduct-based immunity should not extend to jus cogens violations of international law because such violations "are not legitimate official acts and therefore do not merit foreign official immunity."[195]

There is currently a conflict in the courts on these and related issues. One source of disagreement concerns the implications of Section 66 of the *Restatement (Second) of the Foreign Relations Law of the United States*. As noted, this section states that foreign officials are entitled to common law immunity for acts performed in their official capacity "if the effect of exercising jurisdiction would be to enforce a rule of law against the state."

The U.S. Court of Appeals for the D.C. Circuit interpreted this section narrowly in *Lewis v. Mutond*.[196] In that case, a U.S. citizen sued two high-level officials of the Democratic Republic of the Congo (DRC) for damages under the Torture Victim Protection Act, contending that they were responsible for having him unlawfully detained and subjected to inhumane conditions over a period of six weeks in the DRC. In rejecting the officials' claim of immunity, the court reasoned that conduct immunity, as described in Section 66 of the *Restatement*, applies only when the judgment would be enforceable directly against the state. In this case, however, the court observed that "[d]efendants have not proffered anything to show that Plaintiff seeks to draw on the DRC's treasury or force the state to take specific action, as would be the case if the judgment were enforceable against the state."[197] This was true, reasoned the court, even though the actions concerning which the plaintiff was seeking damages were taken in an official capacity on behalf of the state.

By contrast, the U.S. Court of Appeals for the Ninth Circuit interpreted Section 66 more expansively in *Dogan v. Barak*.[198] In that case, parents of a U.S. citizen killed during an Israeli naval blockade of Gaza sued a former Israeli Defense Minister for damages

---

[192] *See, e.g.*, Doe v. Zedillo, 2014 U.S. App. LEXIS 2873 (2d Cir. Feb. 18, 2014); Manoharan v. Rajapaksa, 711 F.3d 178, 179 (D.C. Cir. 2013); Habyarimana v. Kagame, 696 F.3d 1029, 1032 (10th Cir. 2012); Tawfik v. Al-Sabah, 2012 U.S. Dist. LEXIS 115957 (S.D.N.Y. Apr. 27, 2012).
[193] *See* Yousuf v. Samantar, 699 F.3d 763, 772 (4th Cir. 2012).
[194] *See id.*
[195] *Id.* at 777.
[196] 918 F.3d 142 (D.C. Cir. 2019).
[197] *Id.* at 147.
[198] 932 F.3d 888 (9th Cir. 2019).

under the Torture Victim Protection Act. In concluding that the defendant was entitled to immunity, the court reasoned (among other things) that exercising jurisdiction over the defendant "would be to enforce a rule of law against the sovereign state of Israel" under the standard set forth in Section 66 of the *Restatement*. The court emphasized that "[t]he Complaint's claims for relief state—several times—that [the defendant's] actions were done under 'actual or apparent authority, or color of law, of the Israeli Ministry of Defense and the Government of the State of Israel.'"[199] Thus, unlike the court in *Lewis*, the court in *Dogan* focused on the nature of the acts being challenged as opposed to where the damages award would come from.[200]

* * *

The topic of sovereign and individual official immunity further illustrates the complicated nature of the relationship between international law and U.S. domestic law. Before the enactment of the FSIA, courts in the United States applied international law principles of immunity not as federal law, but rather as part of the now-defunct regime of general common law. Starting in the late 1930s, the courts shifted their approach and grounded their application of immunity at least in part on the authority of the executive branch, with the result that international law often became at most a secondary consideration. Eventually, the president and Senate concluded treaties to address diplomatic and consular immunities, and Congress enacted the FSIA to codify the U.S. position on the restrictive theory of immunity. Some immunity issues have not been addressed by treaty or statute, however, and as a result these issues are still being addressed by the courts through the development of common law—now federal common law rather than general common law. In developing this body of common law, courts have been deferential to the views of the executive branch, and this pattern has continued after the Supreme Court's decision in *Samantar*. By contrast, courts have been more comfortable staking out their own interpretations of the FSIA, in part because they have statutory text to interpret and also because the statute was specifically designed to shift control over foreign governmental immunity away from the executive branch.

---

[199] *Id.* at 894.

[200] The court in *Dogan* also rejected a jus cogens exception to immunity, and it concluded that the Torture Victim Protection Act did not abrogate the common law of foreign official immunity. Unlike in *Lewis*, the State Department had submitted a suggestion of immunity to the court in *Dogan*. The court in *Dogan* said that the suggestion was entitled at least to "considerable weight," but it did not decide whether the suggestion merited absolute judicial deference. *Id.* at 893–94.

9 Extradition and Other Means of Criminal Law Enforcement

ONE CONTEXT IN which international law is frequently applied by U.S. courts is extradition. Extradition is a formal process by which one nation (the "requesting state") can seek to obtain the custody of a criminal suspect located in another nation (the "requested state").[1] Under international law, nations are not obligated to extradite criminal suspects to another nation unless they have an extradition treaty with that nation, although some nations will extradite in the absence of a treaty as a matter of comity.[2]

The United States currently has bilateral extradition treaties with over one hundred countries.[3] It is also a party to a number of multilateral treaties relating to human rights,

---

[1] Extradition is also a process by which one U.S. state can obtain the custody of a suspect located in another U.S. state. Such interstate extradition is governed by the Constitution and a federal statute, *see* U.S. CONST. art. IV, § 2, cl. 2, and 18 U.S.C. § 3182, as well as state law, and is outside the scope of this book.

[2] *See* I.A. SHEARER, EXTRADITION IN INTERNATIONAL LAW 24 (1971); RESTATEMENT (THIRD) OF THE FOREIGN RELATIONS LAW OF THE UNITED STATES 537 (1987) ("[S]tates are not obligated to extradite except as obligated to do so by treaty."); Factor v. Laubenheimer, 290 U.S. 276, 287 (1933) ("[T]he principles of international law recognize no right to extradition apart from treaty.").

[3] *See* 18 U.S.C. § 3181. *See also* Michael John Garcia & Charles Doyle, *Extradition to and from the United States: Overview of the Law and Contemporary Treaties* (Cong. Res. Serv., Oct. 4, 2016), *available at* https://crsreports.congress.gov/product/pdf/RL/98-958. For an account of the history of U.S. extradition practices, see CHRISTOPHER H. PYLE, EXTRADITION, POLITICS, AND HUMAN RIGHTS (2001).

terrorism, and international criminal law that require it to "prosecute or extradite" particular offenders found within its territory.[4] Unlike European nations, however, the United States is not a party to any generally used multilateral treaty on extradition.[5] The terms of bilateral extradition treaties are normally considered self-executing and thus can be enforced by U.S. courts even in the absence of implementing legislation.[6] (The concept of treaty self-execution is discussed in Chapter 2.)

Presidential Power and Extradition

It is well settled that the executive branch does not have the authority to extradite individuals from the United States in the absence of authorization from either a treaty or a statute. This appears to have been the understanding of executive officials in early presidential administrations,[7] and the Supreme Court subsequently stated that the power to extradite "is not confided to the Executive in the absence of treaty or legislative provision."[8] In one instance during the Civil War, President Lincoln extradited an alleged slave trader to Spanish authorities in the absence of a treaty or statute, but his action was anomalous and was criticized in Congress.[9]

Almost all extradition agreements concluded by the United States have been concluded as Article II treaties—that is, with the advice and consent of two-thirds of the Senate. In the 1990s, however, the United States concluded extradition agreements with the international criminal tribunals for the former Yugoslavia and Rwanda as congressional–executive agreements rather than as Article II treaties.[10] In a 2–1 decision, the U.S. Court of Appeals for the Fifth Circuit held that an individual could be extradited pursuant to

---

[4] *See, e.g.*, Convention for the Suppression of Unlawful Acts against the Safety of Civil Aviation, art. 8, Sept. 23, 1971, 24 U.S.T. 564, 974 U.N.T.S. 178 (entered into force Jan. 26, 1973).
[5] The United States is a party to the 1933 Inter-American Convention on Extradition, 49 Stat. 3111, but it has never been used. *See* M. CHERIF BASSIOUNI, INTERNATIONAL EXTRADITION: UNITED STATES LAW AND PRACTICE 96 (6th ed. 2014). In 2010, the United States entered into an extradition treaty with the European Union (EU), but it is implemented through bilateral treaties between the United States and the EU member states. *See* Garcia & Doyle, *supra* note 3, at 2.
[6] *See, e.g.*, Terlinden v. Ames, 184 U.S. 270, 288 (1902) ("Treaties of extradition are executory in their character. . . ."); United States v. Balsys, 119 F.3d 122, 138 n.14 (2d Cir. 1997) ("Extradition treaties are self-executing, and therefore do not require implementing legislation to be binding as law."), *rev'd on other grounds*, 524 U.S. 666 (1998).
[7] *See* 1 JOHN BASSETT MOORE, A TREATISE ON EXTRADITION AND INTERSTATE RENDITION 21–32 (1891).
[8] Valentine v. United States, 299 U.S. 5, 8 (1936).
[9] *See* JOHN G. HAWLEY, THE LAW AND PRACTICE OF INTERNATIONAL EXTRADITION 2–3 (1892); MOORE, *supra* note 7, at 33–35; *see also* QUINCY WRIGHT, THE CONTROL OF AMERICAN FOREIGN RELATIONS 195 (1922) (noting that "the majority of authorities hold that [President Lincoln] here acted in excess of power"). In 1913, President Wilson entered into a sole executive agreement with Great Britain allowing for extradition between the U.S. territorial possessions of the Philippine Islands and Guam and British North Borneo. *See* WRIGHT, THE CONTROL OF AMERICAN FOREIGN RELATIONS, 237.
[10] *See* National Defense Authorization Act for Fiscal Year 1996, Pub. L. No. 104-106, 1342, 110 Stat. 186, 486.

one of these agreements, stating that it was "unconvinced that the President's practice of usually submitting a negotiated treaty to the Senate reflects a historical understanding that a treaty is required to extradite."[11] (The phenomenon of executive agreements, including congressional–executive agreements, is discussed in Chapter 3.)

An early episode involving questions about presidential power in the extradition context concerned Thomas Nash, alias Jonathan Robbins, who was arrested in 1799 in Charleston, South Carolina, and charged with having committed murder during the course of a mutiny aboard a British naval vessel. Britain requested his extradition pursuant to the Jay Treaty of 1794, which included a provision stating the United States and Great Britain were obligated to

> deliver up to justice all persons who, being charged with murder or forgery, committed within the jurisdiction of either, shall seek an asylum within any of the country's of the other, provided that this shall only be done on such evidence of criminality as, according to the laws of the place, where the fugitive or person so charged shall be found, would justify his apprehension and commitment for trial, if the offence had there been committed.[12]

After the matter came before the federal district court in South Carolina, President Adams's Secretary of State, Timothy Pickering, informed the court of Adams's "'advice and request' that [Robbins] may be delivered up to the Consul or other agent of Great Britain" if "such evidence of his criminality be produced, as by the laws of the United States, or of South Carolina, would justify his apprehension and commitment for trial."[13] Notwithstanding this letter, the court reasoned that this was a matter for judicial rather than executive resolution, but it also concluded that Robbins was in fact subject to extradition under the treaty.[14]

After Robbins was delivered to British authorities, he was quickly tried, convicted, and executed.[15] The extradition was highly controversial, in part because Robbins had alleged that he was a U.S. citizen who had been impressed into naval service by the British. There was subsequently a debate in the House of Representatives over whether to censure President Adams for having attempted to interfere with the judicial process. John Marshall, who would go on to become Chief Justice of the U.S. Supreme Court, was at the time a member of the House, and he defended Adams's actions before that body. It was in that context that he famously described the president as the "sole organ

---

[11] Ntakirutimana v. Reno, 184 F.3d 419, 426 (5th Cir. 1999).
[12] Treaty of Amity, Commerce and Navigation between His Britannic Majesty and the United States of America, art. 27, Nov. 19, 1794, 8 Stat. 116, 129, T.S. 105.
[13] Letter from Thomas Pickering to Thomas Bee (June 3, 1799), *reprinted in* 10 ANNALS OF CONG. 516 (1800).
[14] United States v. Rob[b]ins, 27 F. Cas. 825 (D.S.C. 1799) (No. 16,175).
[15] *See* R. KENT NEWMYER, JOHN MARSHALL AND THE HEROIC AGE OF THE SUPREME COURT 136 (2007).

of the nation in its external relations, and its sole representative with foreign nations."[16] He further argued that a treaty is a law, and that the president is obligated under the Constitution to faithfully execute the laws. While conceding that Congress could direct how a treaty was to be executed, he argued that "till this be done, it seems the duty of the Executive department to execute the contract by any means it possesses."[17] Marshall did not assert, however, that the president had the authority to extradite in the absence of a treaty or statute.[18]

U.S. States and Extradition

Article I, Section 10 of the Constitution prohibits U.S. states from engaging in certain foreign relations activities, such as making treaties, waging war, or entering into agreements or compacts without Congress's consent. It does not specifically preclude them from extraditing criminal suspects to other countries or making requests to other countries for extradition. During the first half of the nineteenth century, when there was no federal extradition statute and relatively few extradition treaties, some U.S. states engaged in international extradition.[19]

In an 1840 decision, *Holmes v. Jennison*, the Supreme Court considered the constitutionality of this state practice.[20] In that case, the governor of Vermont, in response to a request from Canadian authorities, had ordered the detention and extradition of an individual accused of committing murder in Canada. A plurality of four justices reasoned, in an opinion by Chief Justice Taney, that Vermont's attempted extradition was a "compact" prohibited under Article I, Section 10 in the absence of congressional authorization.[21]

---

[16] 10 ANNALS OF CONG. 613 (1800). For discussion of the concept of the president as the "sole organ" of the United States in foreign relations, see Chapter 1 of this book.

[17] 10 ANNALS OF CONG. 613 (1800). For an endorsement of Marshall's view of the president's role in extradition, *see* Fong Yue Ting v. United States, 149 U.S. 698, 714 (1893) ("[T]he surrender, pursuant to treaty stipulations, of persons residing or found in this country and charged with crime in another, may be made by the executive authority of the President alone, when no provision has been made by treaty or by statute for an examination of the case by a judge or magistrate."). *But cf. In re* Kaine, 55 U.S. (14 How.) 103, 112 (1853) (plurality opinion of Catron, J.) ("[A] great majority of the people of this country [during the Robbins affair] were opposed to the doctrine that the President could arrest, imprison, and surrender, a fugitive, and thereby execute the treaty himself; and they were still more opposed to an assumption that he could order the courts of justice to execute his mandate, as this would destroy the independence of the judiciary, in cases of extradition, and which example might be made a precedent for similar invasions in other cases; and from that day to this, the judicial power has acted in cases of extradition, and all others, independent of executive control.").

[18] For additional discussion of the Jonathan Robbins affair, *see* PYLE, *supra* note 3, chs. 2, 3; John T. Parry, *The Lost History of International Extradition Litigation*, 43 VA. J. INT'L L. 93 (2002); Ruth Wedgwood, *The Revolutionary Martyrdom of Jonathan Robbins*, 100 YALE L.J. 229 (1990).

[19] *See* MOORE, *supra* note 7, at 53–75.

[20] *See* 39 U.S. (14 Pet.) 540 (1840).

[21] *See id.* at 573–74.

The plurality also reasoned that the exercise of an extradition power by the states would be "totally contradictory and repugnant to the power granted to the United States" to determine whether someone should be extradited, and thus was subject to dormant preemption from the Constitution.[22]

By the late nineteenth century, it was generally assumed that extradition was the exclusive prerogative of the federal government, and this has been the understanding since that time. In a decision in the late 1800s, the Supreme Court approved of Taney's opinion in *Holmes*, stating that "it can hardly be admitted that, even in the absence of treaties or acts of congress on the subject, the extradition of a fugitive from justice can become the subject of negotiation between a state of this Union and a foreign government."[23] In any event, the ability of states to act in the absence of applicable statutes or treaties is much less significant today in light of the existence of a federal extradition statute and numerous extradition treaties.

U.S. Extradition Practice

United States extradition practice has been governed by a federal statute since 1848.[24] As a prerequisite to extraditing someone to another country, this statute normally requires the existence of an extradition treaty with the requesting country. Since 1996, however, the extradition statute has allowed individuals who are not citizens, nationals, or permanent residents of the United States to be extradited even in the absence of an extradition treaty if they have "committed crimes of violence against nationals of the United States in foreign countries" and the Attorney General certifies in writing that "(1) evidence has been presented by the foreign government that indicates that had the offenses been committed in the United States, they would constitute crimes of violence . . . ; and (2) the offenses charged are not of a political nature."[25]

---

[22] *Id.* at 574.

[23] United States v. Rauscher, 119 U.S. 407, 414 (1886). *See also* Valentine v. United States, 299 U.S. 5, 8 (1936) ("It cannot be doubted that the power to provide for extradition is a national power; it pertains to the national government and not to the States."); MOORE, *supra* note 7, at 53 ("It may be regarded as settled doctrine that, in the United States, the extradition of fugitives from the justice of foreign countries is a subject within the exclusive control of the national government, under its constitutional power of conducting foreign intercourse and of making treaties.").

[24] Act of Aug. 12, 1848, ch. 167 (1848). Earlier statutes provided for the return, pursuant to treaty agreements, of foreign seamen who deserted while their ships were in port in the United States. *See, e.g.*, An Act Concerning Consuls and Vice-Consuls, 1 Stat. 254 (1792); Act to Provide for the Apprehension and Delivery of Deserters from Certain Foreign Vessels in the Ports of the United States, 4 Stat. 359 (1829). *See also* Surrender of Deserting Seamen, 6 Op. Atty. Gen. 148, at 17 (1853) (concluding that "the act for the apprehension of deserters from certain foreign vessels, cannot be applied to the case of a Danish mariner, until there be an express provision of treaty between Denmark and the United States, for the restoration of deserting seamen . . . and that, without such treaty, the executive or judicial authorities of the United States have no power to arrest, detain, and deliver up a mariner on the demand of the consuls or other agents of Denmark").

[25] 18 U.S.C. § 3181(b).

The process for extraditing suspects from the United States to other countries operates essentially as follows: When foreign nations seek to obtain custody of a criminal suspect located in the United States, they lodge an extradition request with the U.S. State Department. If the State Department determines that the request is within the terms of the relevant extradition treaty (or falls within the exception noted for crimes of violence against U.S. citizens), it will forward the request to the Department of Justice's Office of International Affairs. If the Department of Justice similarly concludes that the request is proper, it forwards the request to the U.S. Attorney for the judicial district where the person sought is located. The U.S. Attorney then files a complaint with an appropriate judicial officer, seeking an arrest warrant. The suspect may then be detained pending extradition, typically for not longer than sixty days.[26]

A judicial officer, usually a federal magistrate judge,[27] will hold a hearing to determine whether the crime charged is an extraditable crime under the treaty (or falls within the earlier-noted exception), and whether there is probable cause to believe that the person committed the crime. If these requirements are met, the judicial officer will certify to the Secretary of State that the person is extraditable.[28] Upon receiving this certification, the Secretary of State has the discretion to extradite but is not obligated to do so.[29] In some cases, the Secretary of State may decide to impose conditions on extradition. The judicial certification is not directly appealable to another court, but it is subject to collateral challenge through the filing of a habeas corpus petition. If the judicial officer determines that the person is *not* extraditable, the government may not appeal. It may, however, bring another extradition proceeding against the person before a different judicial officer. Unlike some countries, the United States allows its own nationals to be extradited.[30]

The constitutionality of the Secretary of State's role in reviewing judicial determinations of extraditability was challenged in the mid-1990s. Despite the fact that this process had been in place for much of U.S. history, a district court held that it violated Article III of the Constitution because it allowed the executive branch the ability to review and overturn the legal conclusions of a federal court, thereby rendering those conclusions

---

[26] *See* 18 U.S.C. § 3188.

[27] In theory, the judicial officer could be a state court judge, but international extradition hearings are almost never conducted today by state judges.

[28] 18 U.S.C. § 3184.

[29] *See* 18 U.S.C. § 3186.

[30] *See* 18 U.S.C. § 3196; Charlton v. Kelly, 229 U.S. 447, 467 (1913); Neely v. Henkel, 180 U.S. 109, 123 (1901); United States v. Knotek, 925 F.3d 1118 (9th Cir. 2019). Until relatively recently, Israel would not extradite its citizens. This became a point of contention between Israel and the United States when Samuel Sheinbein, an eighteen-year-old Maryland teenager, fled to Israel after committing a grisly murder in Maryland in 1997. Israel controversially refused to extradite Sheinbein to the United States, after determining that he qualified for Israeli citizenship (even though he had never lived in Israel). *See* Melinda Henneberger, *Israel Refuses to Extradite a Murder Suspect*, N.Y. TIMES (Oct. 1, 1997), at A12. Israel has since changed its law to allow for the extradition of its citizens for crimes committed abroad, although if the suspect is a resident of Israel, the law requires that the person serve any prison sentence in Israel.

merely advisory.[31] This decision was vacated on appeal for lack of jurisdiction, however,[32] and other courts have since upheld the constitutionality of the process. One of these courts reasoned that, when a judicial officer makes a determination of extraditability, it is in effect acting as an executive "commissioner" and is therefore not exercising judicial power under Article III of the Constitution.[33]

The process for seeking the extradition *to the United States* of a suspect located in another country typically starts with a request by a federal or state prosecutor to the Department of Justice's Office of International Affairs. That Office forwards the request to the State Department's Office of the Legal Adviser, which forwards it to the U.S. diplomatic representative in the appropriate nation, who then presents it to the foreign government. The foreign government, if it decides to honor the extradition request, is responsible for taking the person into custody and turning him or her over to U.S. authorities.[34]

Common Limitations in Extradition Treaties

There are a number of common limitations in extradition treaties. Extradition is typically limited to serious offenses—for example, offenses punishable by more than one year of imprisonment. Many extradition treaties also contain a "dual criminality" requirement—that is, a requirement that the conduct that serves as the basis for the extradition request be a crime in both the requesting state and the requested state. It is well settled under U.S. practice, however, that the two nations' laws need not be exactly the same in order to satisfy the dual criminality requirement. Rather, they merely need to punish the particular act charged and be "substantially analogous."[35] In addition, there is no lack of dual criminality merely because defenses are "'available in the requested state that would not

---

[31] *See* LoBue v. Christopher, 893 F. Supp. 65 (D.D.C. 1995).

[32] *See* LoBue v. Christopher, 82 F.3d 1081 (D.C. Cir. 1996).

[33] *See* Lo Duca v. United States, 93 F.3d 1100 (2d Cir. 1996). *See also* Lopez-Smith v. Hood, 121 F.3d 1322, 1327 (9th Cir. 1997) (agreeing with *Lo Duca*); *In re* Extradition of Lehming, 951 F. Supp. 505, 509 (D. Del. 1996) (noting that "the balance of federal court decisions support the conclusion that the [extradition] statutes are constitutional").

[34] Extradition proceedings in a foreign country can sometimes take a substantial amount of time. Consider, for example, the case of Ira Einhorn, who was charged with killing his girlfriend in Philadelphia in 1977. The United States requested his extradition from France in 1997. French authorities approved the extradition, but Einhorn was able to delay the extradition through court challenges and appeals to political officials, and he was not extradited until July 2001. *See* Francis X. Clines, *France Sending Fugitive Home to U.S. for New Trial*, N.Y. TIMES (July 20, 2001), at A5. For a more recent high-profile extradition case that has involved extensive court proceedings, *see* Marc Sentora, *Julian Assange Faces Hearing on Extradition to the U.S.*, N.Y. TIMES (Feb. 24, 2020).

[35] *See, e.g.*, Manta v. Chertoff, 518 F.3d 1134, 1141 (9th Cir. 2008); United States v. Saccoccia, 58 F.3d 754, 766 (1st Cir. 1995); *see also* Collins v. Loisel, 259 U.S. 309, 312 (1922) ("It is enough if the particular act charged is criminal in both jurisdictions."); Wright v. Henkel, 190 U.S. 40, 58 (1903) (reasoning that dual criminality requirement was met because the U.S. and foreign statutes were "substantially analogous").

be available in the requesting state, or ... different requirements of proof are applicable in the two states.'"[36] To determine if an act would be criminal if committed in the United States, a court may consult federal law, the state law where the defendant is found, and the law of a preponderance of the states.[37]

Another common limitation in extradition treaties is to disallow extradition when the prosecution is barred by an applicable statute of limitations. Many extradition treaties allow the suspect to invoke both the statute of limitations of the requested state as well as the statute of limitations of the requesting state. When the United States is the requested state, courts will look to federal law rather than state law to determine the appropriate statute of limitations.[38] Some treaties, however, allow the suspect to invoke only the statute of limitations of the requesting state. In that situation, the mere fact that a statute of limitations has expired in the requested state for the analogous crime will not prevent extradition.[39] Statutes of limitation are often tolled when a person is a fugitive or is contesting extradition.[40]

Extradition treaties also typically disallow extradition for "political" offenses. In applying this exception, U.S. courts have distinguished between "pure" and "relative" political offenses.[41] Pure political offenses are acts, such as treason, sedition, and espionage, which are aimed directly at a government and do not violate the private rights of individuals. Courts have typically treated these offenses as non-extraditable. Relative political offenses are common crimes committed in connection with a political act. For those offenses, courts (applying a variety of tests) have examined whether the nexus between the crime and the political act is sufficiently close to warrant treating the crime as non-extraditable. The political offense exception was successfully invoked in several cases in the 1970s and 1980s by alleged members of the Irish Republican Army.[42] These decisions drew protests from the British government, and the United States and Great Britain eventually negotiated a supplemental extradition treaty that expressly excludes from the

---

[36] Gallo-Chamorro v. United States, 233 F.3d 1298, 1307 (11th Cir. 2000) (quoting RESTATEMENT (THIRD) OF THE FOREIGN RELATIONS LAW OF THE UNITED STATES, *supra* note 2, § 476 cmt. d).

[37] *See, e.g.*, DeSilva v. DiLeonardi, 125 F.3d 1110, 1113 (7th Cir. 1997); Yau-Leung v. Soscia, 649 F.2d 914, 918 (2d Cir. 1981). Some extradition treaties also disallow extradition if the person being sought has already been tried by the sending state for the offense that forms the basis for the extradition request. *See, e.g.*, United States v. Trabelsi, 845 F.3d 1141 (D.C. Cir. 2017) (giving deference to Belgium's determination that extraditing an individual to the United States after he had been convicted in Belgium did not violate this provision).

[38] *See, e.g.,* Theron v. United States Marshal, 832 F.2d 492 (9th Cir. 1987).

[39] *See* Murphy v. United States, 199 F.3d 599, 602–603 (2d Cir. 1999).

[40] *See, e.g.*, 18 U.S.C. § 3290 ("No statute of limitations shall extend to any person fleeing from justice.").

[41] *See, e.g.*, Ordinola v. Hackman, 478 F.3d 588, 596–97 (4th Cir. 2007); Vo v. Benov, 447 F.3d 1235, 1240–41 (9th Cir. 2006); Quinn v. Robinson, 783 F.2d 776 (9th Cir. 1986); Eain v. Wilkes, 641 F.2d 504 (7th Cir. 1981).

[42] *See In re* Doherty, 599 F. Supp. 270 (S.D.N.Y. 1984); *In re* Mackin, No. 86 Cr. Misl., app. denied, 668 F.2d 122 (2d Cir. 1981); *In re* McMullen, No. 3-78-1899 M.G. (N.D. Cal. May 11, 1979), *reprinted in* 132 CONG. REC. 16585 (1986).

political offense exception various specified crimes such as murder, kidnapping, and the use of explosives.[43]

Many countries have abolished the death penalty, and some of these countries (such as Mexico, Canada, and most European countries) will not extradite suspects to the United States if the suspects will be eligible for the death penalty.[44] In most cases, extradition is allowed once the relevant state or federal authorities provide an assurance that they will not seek the death penalty.[45] In a 1989 decision, the European Court of Human Rights held that it would violate the European Convention on Human Rights to extradite someone to the United States without an assurance that the person would not face the death penalty, reasoning that the "death row" phenomenon whereby inmates in the United States sometimes await execution for many years while their appeals are being processed constituted "inhuman or degrading treatment or punishment."[46] In a 2003 ruling concerning an extradition by Canada to the United States, the UN committee that administers the International Covenant on Civil and Political Rights concluded that it violates the right to life in the Covenant for an abolitionist country to extradite someone to a death penalty country without an assurance that the death sentence will not be carried out.[47] The death penalty has arisen as a point of contention in some extradition cases relating to the post-September 11, 2001, "war on terrorism."[48]

---

[43] *See* Supplemental Treaty between the Government of the United States of America and the Government of the United Kingdom of Great Britain and Northern Ireland, June 25, 1985, T.I.A.S. No. 12050. In 2003, the United States and Great Britain signed a new extradition treaty, and the Senate gave its advice and consent to this treaty in 2006. *See* Charles Doyle, *Extradition between the United States and Great Britain: The 2003 Treaty* (Cong. Res. Serv., Oct. 10, 2006), *available at* http://www.fas.org/sgp/crs/misc/RL32096.pdf. The new treaty preserves and enlarges the list of crimes that are deemed not to constitute political offenses. For discussion of a politically charged case involving a U.S. effort to have Canada extradite the chief financial officer of a major Chinese company, *see* Dan Bilefsky & Tracy Sherlock, *Huawei Executive Meng Wanzhou's Extradition Fight: What to Know*, N.Y. TIMES (Jan. 19, 2020); Craig Forcese, *Canada and the Rule of Law in the Meng Wanzhou Matter*, LAWFARE (Mar. 7, 2019), *at* https://www.lawfareblog.com/canada-and-rule-law-meng-wanzhou-matter; Chimène Keitner, *Trump, Huawei, and the Politics of Extradition*, FOREIGN AFFAIRS (Jan. 25, 2019). *See also* Tracy Sherlock & Dan Bilefsky, *Extradition of Huawei Executive Clears a Major Legal Hurdle in Canada*, N.Y. TIMES (May 27, 2020).

[44] *See* William A. Schabas, *Indirect Abolition: Capital Punishment's Role in Extradition Law and Practice*, 25 LOY. L.A. INT'L & COMP. L. REV. 581, 604 (2003).

[45] In a case from Italy, however, extradition was denied notwithstanding such assurances from state authorities in Florida. *See* John Tagliabue, *Italian Court Blocks Extradition, Citing Death Penalty in Florida*, N.Y. TIMES (June 28, 1996), at A7. Italy subsequently allowed some of the trial to take place in Florida, albeit under Italian law and with Italian judges.

[46] *See* Soering v. United Kingdom, 11 EUR. CT. H. R. 439 (1989).

[47] *See* Judge v. Canada, Communication No. 829/1998, U.N. Doc. CCPR/C/78/D/829/1998 (2003).

[48] *See, e.g.*, Thomas Michael McDonnell, *The Death Penalty—An Obstacle to the "War on Terrorism"?*, 37 VAND. J. TRANSNAT'L L. 353 (2004); T.R. Reid, *Europeans Reluctant to Send Terror Suspects to U.S.; Allies Oppose Death Penalty and Bush's Plan for Secret Military Tribunals*, WASH. POST (Nov. 29, 2001), at A23. In 2014, the European Court of Human Rights concluded that, in extraditing a criminal suspect to the United States, Belgium had violated the European Convention on Human Rights because the suspect faced the possibility of receiving an

Rule of Non-Inquiry

In considering whether to allow an extradition, U.S. courts apply a rule of "non-inquiry," whereby they will not inquire into the procedures or treatment the suspect will face in the requesting state.[49] The rule stems in part from territorial conceptions about the reach of the U.S. Constitution (a topic discussed in Chapter 6). The Supreme Court has stated, for example, that constitutional provisions "relating to the writ of habeas corpus, bills of attainder, ex post facto laws, trial by jury for crimes, and generally to the fundamental guaranties of life, liberty, and property embodied in that instrument . . . have no relation to crimes committed without the jurisdiction of the United States against the laws of a foreign country."[50] The non-inquiry rule also stems from considerations of judicial competence and separation of powers. As one court explained, "[u]ndergirding this principle is the notion that courts are ill-equipped as institutions and ill-advised as a matter of separation of powers and foreign relations policy to make inquiries into and pronouncements about the workings of foreign countries' justice systems."[51]

In a 1960 decision, the U.S. Court of Appeals for the Second Circuit suggested in dicta that there may be a "humanitarian" exception to the rule of non-inquiry, pursuant to which courts could bar extradition if the suspect would likely face procedures or punishment "so antipathetic to a federal court's sense of decency" so as to compel relaxation of the rule.[52] No court has yet applied such an exception. Although some courts have reserved judgment on the existence of such an exception,[53] other courts have stated that humanitarian considerations relating to the likely treatment of the suspect are proper considerations only for the Secretary of State, not the courts.[54]

---

irreducible life sentence without the possibility of parole. *See* Trabelsi v. Belgium, Judgment (ECHR, Sept. 4, 2014), *at* http://hudoc.echr.coe.int/sites/eng/pages/search.aspx?i=001-146372#{"itemid":["001-146372"]}.

[49] *See, e.g.*, Glucksman v. Henkel, 221 U.S. 508, 512 (1911) ("We are bound by the existence of an extradition treaty to assume that the trial will be fair.").

[50] Neely v. Henkel, 180 U.S. 109, 122 (1901).

[51] United States v. Smyth, 61 F.3d 711, 714 (9th Cir. 1995); *see also* Noeller v. Wojdylo, 922 F.3d 797, 808 (7th Cir. 2019) ("[T]he rule of non-inquiry is intended to prevent extradition courts from engaging in improper judgments about other countries' law enforcement and judicial procedures."); United States v. Kin-Hong, 110 F.3d 103, 110 (1st Cir. 1997) ("It is not that questions about what awaits the relator in the requesting country are irrelevant to extradition; it is that there is another branch of government, which has both final say and greater discretion in these proceedings, to whom these questions are more properly addressed."); United States v. Manzi, 888 F.2d 204, 206 (1st Cir. 1989) ("Courts have chosen to defer these questions to the executive branch because of its exclusive power to conduct foreign affairs."). For additional discussion, *see* John T. Parry, *International Extradition, The Rule of Non-Inquiry, and the Problem of Sovereignty*, 90 B.U. L. REV. 1973 (2010); Jacques Semmelman, *Federal Courts, the Constitution, and the Rule of Non-Inquiry in International Extradition Proceedings*, 76 CORNELL L. REV. 1198 (1991).

[52] Gallina v. Fraser, 278 F.2d 77, 79 (2d Cir. 1960).

[53] *See, e.g.*, Emami v. U.S. District Ct., 834 F.2d 1444, 1453 (9th Cir. 1987).

[54] *See, e.g.*, Hilton v. Kerry, 754 F.3d 79, 87–88 (1st Cir. 2014); Martin v. Warden, 993 F.2d 824, 830 n.10 (11th Cir. 1993); Ahmad v. Wigen, 910 F.2d 1063, 1066–67 (2d Cir. 1990).

In 1994, the United States ratified the Convention against Torture and Other Cruel, Inhuman or Degrading Treatment or Punishment. Article 3 of the Convention states that no state party "shall expel, return ('refouler') or extradite a person to another State where there are substantial grounds for believing that he would be in danger of being subjected to torture." In giving its advice and consent to the Convention, the Senate declared that its terms were not self-executing, and courts have interpreted that declaration to mean that the Convention does not create judicially enforceable rights.[55]

Congress enacted legislation implementing Article 3 of the Convention in 1998 as part of the Foreign Affairs Reform and Restructuring Act ("FARR Act").[56] The FARR Act states that "[i]t shall be the policy of the United States not to expel, extradite, or otherwise effect the involuntary return of any person to a country in which there are substantial grounds for believing the person would be in danger of being subjected to torture, regardless of whether the person is physically present in the United States."[57] The Act also directs heads of the appropriate agencies to "prescribe regulations to implement the obligations of the United States under Article 3" of the Convention.[58] The Act provides, however, that "nothing in this section shall be construed as providing any court jurisdiction to consider or review claims raised under the Convention or this section ... except as part of the review of a final order of removal pursuant to section 242 of the Immigration and Nationality Act."[59] The Department of State subsequently adopted regulations setting out a procedure for the Secretary of State to identify individuals who qualify for relief under Article 3.[60] These regulations nevertheless provide that "[d]ecisions of the Secretary concerning surrender of fugitives for extradition are matters of executive discretion not subject to judicial review."[61]

There has been some disagreement in the courts over whether, in light of this legal framework, the rule of non-inquiry bars judicial consideration of whether an extradition suspect is likely to be tortured in the requesting state. In a 2000 decision in a case involving an extradition request from Mexico, the U.S. Court of Appeals for the Ninth Circuit held that the Secretary of State's application of the regulations enacted pursuant to the FARR Act is subject to judicial review pursuant to the Administrative Procedure Act (APA).[62] The APA provides for review of the final agency decisions "except to the extent that—(1) statutes preclude judicial review; or (2) agency action is committed to

---

[55] *See, e.g.*, Saint Fort v. Ashcroft, 329 F.3d 191, 202 (1st Cir. 2003); Wang v. Ashcroft, 320 F.3d 130, 140 (2d Cir. 2003).
[56] Foreign Affairs Reform and Restructuring Act (FARR Act) of 1998, § 2242, Pub. L. No. 105–277, Div. G, 112 Stat. 2681–822 (Oct. 21, 1998).
[57] *Id.* § 2242(a).
[58] *Id.* § 2242(b).
[59] *Id.* § 2242(d).
[60] *See* 22 C.F.R. §§ 95.1–95.4.
[61] *Id.* § 95.4.
[62] Cornejo-Barreto v. Seifert [*sic*], 218 F.3d 1004 (9th Cir. 2000).

agency discretion by law,"[63] and the court concluded that the FARR Act did not preclude judicial review of the way in which the regulations were applied (as opposed to a challenge to the regulations themselves), and that the duty to implement the FARR Act is nondiscretionary.

In a subsequent decision in the same case, the Ninth Circuit disapproved of the reasoning in the first decision, concluding that neither the Torture Convention nor the FARR Act had displaced the rule of non-inquiry.[64] That subsequent decision was in turn vacated, however, when the Ninth Circuit granted rehearing en banc in the case,[65] and the case was then mooted when Mexico dropped its extradition request, thereby leaving the first decision in place.[66] In 2005, Congress enacted the REAL ID Act, which makes clear that only immigration transferees have a right to judicial review of the likelihood of torture or mistreatment in the receiving country.[67] The U.S. Court of Appeals for the Ninth Circuit has since held that, although individuals being extradited have an enforceable liberty interest in having the Secretary of State actually make the requisite determination, courts are barred by "[t]he doctrine of separation of powers and the rule of non-inquiry" from reviewing the determination.[68]

The rule of non-inquiry also has some application outside the context of a formal extradition request. In a 2008 decision, *Munaf v. Geren*, the Supreme Court held that it would not be proper for U.S. courts to enjoin the transfer, by the U.S. military, of American citizens apprehended in Iraq to Iraqi authorities for criminal prosecution.[69] Invoking the non-inquiry doctrine, the Court explained that such an injunction would unduly interfere with Iraq's sovereign prerogative to apply its criminal law. This was true, reasoned the Court, even though the petitioners alleged that they would be tortured if transferred to Iraqi custody. "Such allegations are of course a matter of serious concern," said the Court, "but in the present context that concern is to be addressed by the political branches, not the judiciary."[70] The Court also noted, however, that the "[p]etitioners here allege only the possibility of mistreatment in a prison facility; this is not a more extreme case in which the Executive has determined that a detainee is likely to be tortured but decides to transfer him anyway."[71]

---

[63] 5 U.S.C. § 701(a).
[64] *See* Cornejo-Barreto v. Siefert, 379 F.3d 1075 (9th Cir. 2004).
[65] *See* Cornejo-Barreto v. Siefert, 386 F.3d 938 (9th Cir. 2004).
[66] *See* Cornejo-Barreto v. Siefert, 389 F.3d 1307 (9th Cir. 2004).
[67] *See* Pub. L. No. 109–13, § 106, 119 Stat. 231, 310 (2005) (*codified at* 8 U.S.C. § 1252(a)(4)). For decisions applying this statute to bar review of torture claims, see Omar v. McHugh, 646 F.3d 13 (D.C. Cir. 2011); Kiyemba v. Obama, 561 F.3d 509 (D.C. Cir. 2009); Mironescu v. Costner, 480 F.3d 664 (4th Cir. 2007).
[68] Trinidad y Garcia v. Thomas, 683 F.3d 952, 957 (9th Cir. 2012) (per curiam). For an analysis of this decision, *see* Stephen I. Vladeck, *Habeas Corpus, Due Process, and Extradition*, 98 CORNELL L. REV. ONLINE 20 (2013).
[69] *See* 553 U.S. 674 (2008).
[70] *Id.* at 700.
[71] *Id.* at 702.

Specialty Doctrine

Under the "specialty doctrine," a requesting state normally cannot try a suspect for a crime different from the one that served as the basis for the extradition request or punish the suspect more severely than was allowed by the law of the requesting state at the time of extradition.[72] The U.S. Supreme Court first recognized this limitation in an 1886 decision, *United States v. Rauscher*.[73] In that case, William Rauscher, the second mate on a U.S. merchant ship, killed one of the crew members on the ship. A U.S. grand jury indicted Rauscher, but he fled to Great Britain before the United States could take him into custody. The United States filed an extradition request with Great Britain in order to try Rauscher for committing murder on the high seas, and Great Britain granted the request pursuant to the 1842 Webster-Ashburton Treaty. Under the tenth article of that treaty, the United States and Great Britain had mutually agreed to extradite suspects "charged with the crime of murder, or assault with intent to commit murder, or Piracy, or arson, or robbery, or Forgery, or the utterance of forged paper."

After receiving custody of Rauscher, the United States attempted to prosecute him for assault and infliction of cruel and unusual punishment, rather than murder. The Supreme Court held that the alteration of the charge was improper under the specialty doctrine. The precise basis for the Court's application of the specialty doctrine was not entirely clear. The Court explained that "according to the doctrine of publicists and writers on international law, the country receiving the offender against its laws from another country had no right to proceed against him for any other offense than that for which he had been delivered up."[74] This might suggest that the doctrine was being applied as a matter of customary international law. But the Court also reasoned that "the enumeration of offences in most [extradition] treaties, and especially in the treaty now under consideration, is so specific, and marked by such a clear line in regard to the magnitude and importance of those offences [specified for extradition], that it is impossible to give any other interpretation to it than that of the exclusion of the right of extradition for any others."[75] This suggests that the doctrine was being applied by implication from the extradition treaty.[76] In a much later Supreme Court decision (which is discussed in the

---

[72] *See* BASSIOUNI, *supra* note 5, at 538–611; RESTATEMENT (THIRD) OF THE FOREIGN RELATIONS LAW OF THE UNITED STATES, *supra* note 2, § 477.

[73] 119 U.S. 407 (1886).

[74] *Id.* at 419.

[75] *Id.* at 420.

[76] The Court also noted that "[i]f there should remain any doubt upon this construction of the treaty itself," the language of the extradition statutes assumed that a person who is subject to extradition "shall not be delivered up by this government to be tried for any other offence than that charged in the extradition proceedings; and that, when brought into this country upon similar proceedings, he shall not be arrested or tried for any other offence than that with which he was charged in those proceedings, until he shall have had a reasonable time to return unmolested to the country from which he was brought." *Id.* at 423.

next section), both the majority and dissent characterized *Rauscher* as having implied the specialty doctrine from the relevant extradition treaty.[77] Many extradition treaties now expressly refer to the specialty doctrine, reducing the need to imply it.

In applying the specialty doctrine, U.S. courts have not required precise uniformity between the charges in the extradition request and the charges in the actual indictment. Rather, as long as the prosecution is based on an offense covered by the extradition treaty (which was not the case in *Rauscher*), U.S. courts merely require that the prosecution rely on the same facts as those set forth in the request for extradition.[78]

Most courts have held that the specialty doctrine does not apply if the sending state specifically consents to the prosecution.[79] Courts are divided over whether the suspect can raise the specialty doctrine when the sending state is silent, with some courts holding that the doctrine may be raised only by the sending state or when it has affirmatively objected to the prosecution,[80] other courts holding that when the sending state is silent a court must guess whether the sending state would object,[81] and still other courts holding that the suspect may raise the doctrine unless the sending state expressly waives this limitation.[82] The specialty doctrine does not apply to offenses committed by the suspect after the extradition takes place, or if the extradited person remains in the requesting state after the extradition offense is resolved and the person has been given a reasonable time to leave.[83] Courts have also held that, when determining the proper sentence for a crime that served as the basis for an extradition request, it does not violate the specialty doctrine to take into account other offenses.[84]

---

[77] *See* United States v. Alvarez-Machain, 504 U.S. 655, 667 (1992) ("In *Rauscher*, we implied a term in the Webster-Ashburton Treaty because of the practice of nations with regard to extradition treaties."); *id.* at 675–78 (Stevens, J., dissenting).

[78] *See, e.g.*, Gallo-Chamorro v. United States, 233 F.3d 1298, 1305 (11th Cir. 2000); United States v. Sensi, 879 F.2d 888, 895 (D.C. Cir. 1989).

[79] *See, e.g.*, Graham v. Young, 776 F.3d 700, 705 (8th Cir. 2018); United States v. Tse, 135 F.3d 200 (1st Cir. 1998); United States v. Puentes, 50 F.3d 1567 (11th Cir. 1995); *see also* United States v. Soto-Barraza, 947 F.3d 1111, 1117 (9th Cir. 2020) ("Because Mexico elected to extradite the defendants on all charges listed in the indictment, the Treaty's principles of specialty and dual criminality are satisfied.").

[80] *See, e.g.*, United States v. Barinas, 865 F.3d 99, 105 (2d Cir. 2017); United States v. Kaufman, 874 F.2d 242, 243 (5th Cir. 1989).

[81] *See, e.g.*, United States v. Andonian, 29 F.3d 1432, 1435 (9th Cir. 1994).

[82] *See, e.g., Puentes*, 50 F.3d at 1575.

[83] *See* BASSIOUNI, *supra* note 5, at 547; RESTATEMENT (THIRD) OF THE FOREIGN RELATIONS LAW OF THE UNITED STATES, *supra* note 2, § 477, cmts. a, e. For a decision holding that the specialty doctrine does not apply when a suspect is delivered to the United States as part of an informal agreement rather than pursuant to the terms of an extradition treaty, *see United States v. Valencia-Trujillo*, 573 F.3d 1171 (11th Cir. 2009). The court there reasoned, among other things, that "[u]nless extradition conditions or restrictions are grounded in self-executing provisions of a treaty, they do not have 'the force and effect of a legislative enactment' that the defendant has standing to assert in the courts of this country." *Id.* at 1181.

[84] *See, e.g.*, United States v. Fontana, 869 F.3d 464 (6th Cir. 2017); United States v. Lomeli, 596 F.3d 496, 501–03 (8th Cir. 2010).

MLATs and Prisoner Exchange Treaties

Since the 1970s, the United States has concluded bilateral Mutual Legal Assistance Treaties (MLATs) with dozens of countries and territories.[85] These treaties provide for intercountry assistance in criminal investigations and prosecutions, relating to matters such as the summoning of witnesses, the production of documents and other evidence, the issuance of search warrants, and the service of process. Under these treaties, each country designates a central authority, usually its justice department, which makes and receives the requests for assistance. The treaties commonly provide that a central authority may deny a request for assistance if (1) the request relates to a political offense, (2) the execution of a request would impair its country's security or other essential interests, (3) the request does not conform to the requirements of the treaty, or (4) the conduct that is the subject of the investigation or prosecution in the requesting party would not constitute a criminal offense under the laws of the requested party and the execution of a request requires a court warrant or other compulsory measure under the laws of the requested party. Although courts have treated the MLATs as self-executing, they have not viewed them as creating judicially enforceable individual rights.[86] Courts have, however, applied the standards in the MLATs when responding to discovery requests from foreign governments relating to criminal proceedings abroad, and they have concluded that the MLATs supersede an earlier federal statute that would otherwise apply to such requests.[87]

The United States also has bilateral treaties with approximately a dozen countries and territories that allow citizens of one country, when convicted in the other country, to be transferred back to their home country in order to serve their prison sentence there.[88] In addition, the United States is a party to two multilateral prisoner exchange treaties, one under the auspices of the Council of Europe and the other under the auspices of the

---

[85] *See* Charles Doyle, *Extraterritorial Application of American Criminal Law* 23 (Cong. Res. Serv., Oct. 31, 2016), *available at* http://www.fas.org/sgp/crs/misc/94-166.pdf; 7 Foreign Affairs Manual § 960 (2018), *available at* https://fam.state.gov/FAM/07FAM/07FAM0960.html; *Contemporary Practice of the United States Relating to International Law: International Criminal Law: Mutual Legal Assistance Treaties with the European Union, Germany, and Japan*, 98 AM. J. INT'L L. 596 (2004).

[86] *See, e.g., In re* Grand Jury Subpoena, 646 F.3d 159, 165 (4th Cir. 2011); United States v. Global Fishing, Inc., 634 F.3d 557, 568 (9th Cir. 2011); United States v. Rommy, 506 F.3d 108, 129–30 (2d Cir. 2007).

[87] *See, e.g., In re* Search of the Premises Located, 634 F.3d 557, 568 (9th Cir. 2011); *In re* Commissioner's Subpoenas, 325 F.3d 1287, 1305–06 (11th Cir. 2003); *In re* Erato, 2 F.3d 11, 15–16 (2d Cir. 1993).

[88] *See* Department of Justice, *International Prisoner Transfer Program*, at https://www.justice.gov/criminal-oia/iptu. The first such treaty concluded by the United States was a 1976 treaty with Mexico. *See generally* Maureen T. Walsh & Bruce Zagaris, *The United States-Mexico Treaty on the Execution of Penal Sanctions: The Case for Reevaluating the Treaty and Its Policies in View of the NAFTA and Other Developments*, 2 SW. J. L. & TRADE AM. 385 (1995). *See also* MICHAEL PLACHTA, TRANSFER OF PRISONERS UNDER INTERNATIONAL INSTRUMENTS AND DOMESTIC LEGISLATION (1993).

Organization of American States.[89] As with extradition, Congress has enacted legislation regulating the prisoner exchange process.[90] Under this legislation, transfers to and from the United States are allowed only pursuant to a treaty, only if the offense for which the individual is sentenced is an offense in both the sentencing and receiving countries at the time of transfer, and only when the offender consents to the transfer.[91] Challenges to the sentence may be made only in the sentencing country, not in the country of transfer.[92] For individuals held in state prisons in the United States, the approval of the state authorities is required for a prisoner transfer, and most states have enacted enabling legislation to allow for such approval.[93] Although constitutional objections have sometimes been raised about the prisoner transfer process (for example, that it can have the effect of ratifying problematic foreign proceedings, or that it does not adequately ensure consent), courts to date have upheld its constitutionality.[94]

International Abductions

Customary international law is widely thought to prohibit one nation from sending its law enforcement personnel into another nation to apprehend a criminal suspect without the other nation's consent.[95] Even though nations sometimes have the authority under international law to apply their criminal laws extraterritorially, direct enforcement of such laws is still limited to a nation's territory, in part because physical incursions into the territory of another nation pose a significant danger of triggering military conflicts. Nevertheless, there have been instances in which nations, including the United States, have abducted criminal suspects from other countries in order to bring them to trial.[96]

---

[89] *See* Council of Europe Convention on the Transfer of Sentenced Persons, Mar. 21, 1983, 35 U.S.T. 2867, 22 I.L.M. 530 (entered into force for the United States July 1, 1985); Inter-American Convention on Serving Criminal Sentences Abroad, June 9, 1993, S. TREATY DOC. NO. 104-35 (1996) (entered into force for the United States June 24, 2001).

[90] *See* 18 U.S.C. § 4100 *et seq.*

[91] *See id.*, §§ 4100, 4107, 4108.

[92] *See id.*, § 3244; Bishop v. Reno, 210 F.3d 1295 (11th Cir. 2000).

[93] *See* David S. Finkelstein, Note, *"Ever Been in a [Foreign] Prison?": The Implementation of Transfer of Penal Sanctions Treaties by U.S. States*, 66 FORDHAM L. REV. 125, 143-45 (1997). When the United States receives a prisoner from another country, the prisoner is held in the federal prison system, regardless of whether the prisoner's offense is one that, if it had occurred in the United States, would have been prosecuted under state law.

[94] *See, e.g.*, Pfeifer v. United States Bureau of Prisons, 615 F.2d 873 (9th Cir. 1980). For a decision holding that courts can review a decision by the executive branch not to transfer a prisoner pursuant to a transfer treaty, but that substantial deference should be given to the executive branch's decision, *see* Sluss v. United States DOJ, 898 F.3d 1242 (D.C. Cir. 2018).

[95] *See* RESTATEMENT (THIRD) OF THE FOREIGN RELATIONS LAW OF THE UNITED STATES, *supra* note 2, § 432(2); Michael Glennon, *State-Sponsored Abduction: A Comment on* Alvarez-Machain, 86 AM. J. INT'L L. 746 (1992).

[96] Probably the most famous government-sponsored abduction was Israel's abduction of the Nazi war criminal Adolf Eichmann from Argentina in 1960. In response to the abduction, the UN Security Council issued a

The Supreme Court considered the legal effect of one of these abductions in a controversial 1992 decision, *United States v. Alvarez-Machain*.[97] In that case, Alvarez-Machain, a Mexican doctor, had allegedly participated in the torture and killing of a U.S. drug enforcement agent in Mexico. After informal negotiations with Mexican officials to obtain custody of Alvarez-Machain were unsuccessful, U.S. officials hired individuals in Mexico to kidnap Alvarez-Machain and bring him to the United States, where he was arrested. Alvarez-Machain subsequently moved to dismiss his criminal prosecution, arguing that the district court lacked jurisdiction to try him because the abduction violated an extradition treaty between the United States and Mexico. The treaty set forth a formal process for obtaining custody of a suspect located in the other country, and Alvarez-Machain argued that, by implication, the treaty prohibited bypassing that process by means of abduction.

Under a U.S. legal doctrine known as the *Ker-Frisbie* doctrine, a prosecution will not ordinarily be dismissed merely because the defendant has been apprehended illegally.[98] In other words, there is no "exclusionary rule of the body." Unlike unlawfully obtained evidence, the physical custody of the defendant is not excluded from trial merely because it was unlawfully obtained. There may be an exception to the *Ker-Frisbie* doctrine, however, for situations in which the defendant was apprehended in violation of a self-executing treaty.[99] In *Alvarez-Machain*, the Supreme Court did not deny the existence of this exception, but rather concluded that the abduction of Alvarez-Machain had not violated the U.S.–Mexico extradition treaty. The Court noted that the treaty neither specifically prohibited abductions nor stated that the extradition procedure specified in the treaty was the exclusive means by which one country could gain custody of a suspect located in the other country.[100] The Court distinguished *United States v. Rauscher* (discussed earlier), in which the Court implied the specialty doctrine from an extradition treaty, as involving an implication from practice relating specifically to extradition, whereas the implication being sought here, said the Court, was from international law more generally.[101]

---

resolution stating that Israel had violated Argentina's sovereignty and requesting that Israel make appropriate reparations. *See* S.C. Res. 138, U.N. SCOR, 15th Year, U.N. Doc. S/4349 at 4 (June 23, 1960).

[97] 504 U.S. 655 (1992).
[98] *See* Ker v. Illinois, 119 U.S. 436 (1886); Frisbie v. Collins, 342 U.S. 519 (1952). *See also* Stefan A. Reisenfeld, *The Doctrine of Self-Executing Treaties and U.S. v. Postal: Win at Any Price?*, 74 AM. J. INT'L L. 892, 893–94 (1980) (explaining the doctrine).
[99] *See* Cook v. United States, 288 U.S. 102 (1933); United States v. Postal, 589 F.2d 862 (5th Cir. 1979).
[100] *Alvarez-Machain*, 504 U.S. at 663–64.
[101] *Id.* at 667–68. The criminal case against Alvarez-Machain was later dismissed for lack of evidence. *See* United States v. Alvarez-Machain, No. CR-87-422-(G)-ER (C.D. Cal. Dec. 14, 1992). Alvarez-Machain then brought a civil suit against the U.S. government and the Mexican nationals who had been involved in his abduction. After many years of litigation, the Supreme Court rejected his claims. *See* Sosa v. Alvarez-Machain, 542 U.S. 692 (2004). (This decision, which involved the Alien Tort Statute, is discussed in Chapter 7.)

Although the Court did not dispute that Alvarez-Machain's abduction violated customary international law, it noted that Alvarez-Machain was arguing that customary international law should "inform the interpretation of the Treaty terms," not that it provided an independent basis for dismissing the prosecution.[102] As discussed in Chapter 5, scholars have debated whether officials in the executive branch have the constitutional authority to violate customary international law, although most lower courts that have addressed the issue have concluded that at least the president and cabinet-level officials have this authority.

The *Alvarez-Machain* decision was heavily criticized by Mexico and other countries.[103] It was also criticized by many academic commentators.[104] In 1992, the Clinton administration negotiated with Mexico an amendment to the U.S.–Mexico extradition treaty that would expressly prohibit "trans-border abductions." For reasons that are unclear, however, the amendment was never submitted to the Senate for its advice and consent. In the absence of such express language, courts will apply the *Ker-Frisbie* doctrine.[105]

Some lower courts have suggested in dicta that severe mistreatment of an abducted suspect might provide another exception to the *Ker-Frisbie* doctrine. The leading case is *United States v. Toscanino*,[106] decided by the U.S. Court of Appeals for the Second Circuit in 1974. In *Toscanino*, a criminal defendant alleged that he had not only been abducted, but also that he had been tortured and otherwise seriously mistreated for more than two weeks, and the court held that dismissal of a prosecution would be required as a matter of due process if the defendant could prove "the government's deliberate, unnecessary and unreasonable invasion of the accused's constitutional rights."[107] In a decision a year later, the Second Circuit made clear that in order for the *Toscanino* exception to be met, a defendant would have to prove "torture, brutality, and similar outrageous conduct" by federal officials.[108] No court has ever applied the *Toscanino* exception to dismiss a prosecution, and some courts have expressly denied the existence of such an exception.[109] In

---

[102] 504 U.S. at 666.
[103] *See* William J. Aceves, *The Legality of Transborder Abductions: A Study of* United States v. Alvarez-Machain, 3 Sw. J. of L. & Trade Am. 101 (1996).
[104] *See, e.g.*, Jonathan A. Bush, *How Did We Get Here? Foreign Abductions after* Alvarez-Machain, 45 Stan. L. Rev. 939 (1993); Andrew L. Strauss, *A Global Paradigm Shattered: The Jurisdictional Nihilism of the Supreme Court's Abduction Decision in* Alvarez-Machain, 67 Temp. L. Rev. 1209 (1994); Douglas J. Sylvester, *Customary International Law, Forcible Abductions, and America's Return to the "Savage State,"* 42 Buff. L. Rev. 555 (1994). *But see* Malvina Halberstam, *In Defense of the Supreme Court Decision in* Alvarez-Machain, 86 Am. J. Int'l L. 736 (1992).
[105] For subsequent decisions relying on *Alvarez-Machain* to hold that extradition treaties were not violated by U.S. government abductions, *see Kasi v. Angelone*, 300 F.3d 487 (4th Cir. 2002), and *United States v. Noriega*, 117 F.3d 1206 (11th Cir. 1997).
[106] 500 F.2d 267 (2d Cir. 1974).
[107] *Id.* at 275.
[108] United States *ex rel.* Lujan v. Gengler, 510 F.2d 62, 65 (2d Cir. 1975).
[109] *See, e.g.*, Matta-Ballesteros v. Henman, 896 F.2d 255, 261–62 (7th Cir. 1990).

addition, it is not clear whether such an exception is consistent with later Supreme Court decisions, including *Alvarez-Machain*.[110]

Extraordinary Rendition

The term "extraordinary rendition" has been used to refer to two practices by the U.S. government: detaining and interrogating suspected terrorists in secret locations outside the United States, and transferring suspected terrorists to other countries for detention and interrogation without the use of judicial proceedings. Although these practices predate the current war on terrorism, they appear to have become more common after the September 11, 2001, attacks. In 2005, allegations surfaced that various countries, including some Eastern European countries, had allowed the Central Intelligence Agency (CIA) to operate secret "black site" detention facilities within their territories, and that other European countries had allowed their airports and airspace to be used by the CIA for the transfer of abducted terrorists.[111] After President Obama took office, he ordered the closure of the secret detention facilities, but the Obama administration continued to engage in rendition of terrorism suspects to other countries.

Extraordinary rendition is highly controversial.[112] Critics have charged that the CIA has used interrogation techniques, such as "waterboarding" (a technique that induces the sensation of drowning), that constitute torture, and that it has turned suspects over to countries known for engaging in torture. (The issue of coercive interrogation is discussed further in Chapter 10.) Extraordinary rendition has been heavily criticized by countries in Western Europe, and some European countries have gone so far as to issue indictments against CIA agents involved in these practices.[113] Although a variety of U.S. laws and treaty commitments may be implicated by extraordinary rendition,[114] to date challenges

---

[110] *See, e.g.*, United States v. Best, 304 F.3d 308, 312 (3d Cir. 2002) ("Subsequent decisions of the Supreme Court indicate that there is reason to doubt the soundness of the *Toscanino* exception, even as limited to its flagrant facts."); United States v. Matta-Ballesteros, 71 F.3d 754, 763 n.3 (9th Cir. 1995) ("Later Supreme Court cases illustrate that the *Toscanino* court was not prescient. The Supreme Court has consistently reaffirmed the *Ker-Frisbie* doctrine, most recently in *Alvarez-Machain*.").

[111] *See* Dana Priest, *CIA Holds Terror Suspects in Secret Prisons*, WASH. POST (Nov. 2, 2005), at A01; *see also* Rebecca Cordell, *The U.S. Carried Out Extraordinary Rendition Flights from 2001 to 2005. Here Are 15 More Countries That Helped*, WASH. POST (Mar. 14, 2017).

[112] *See, e.g.*, Jane Mayer, *The Black Sites: A Rare Look inside the CIA's Secret Interrogation Program*, NEW YORKER (Aug. 13, 2007); Jane Mayer, *Outsourcing Torture: The Secret History of America's "Extraordinary Rendition" Program*, NEW YORKER (Feb. 14, 2005). *See also* Michael John Garcia, *Rendition: Constraints Imposed by Law on Torture* (Cong. Res. Serv., Sept. 8, 2009), *available at* http://www.fas.org/sgp/crs/natsec/RL32890.pdf.

[113] *See* Ian Fisher, *Italy Indicts C.I.A. Operatives in '03 Abduction*, N.Y. TIMES (Feb. 17, 2007); Mark Landler, *German Court Seeks Arrest of 13 C.I.A. Agents*, N.Y. TIMES (Jan. 31, 2007).

[114] The United States ratified the Convention against Torture and Other Cruel, Inhuman or Degrading Treatment or Punishment in 1994, subject to a declaration that its terms are not self-executing. That same year, Congress enacted a statute criminalizing torture committed outside the United States. *See* 18 U.S.C. § 2340A. In December 2005, Congress enacted the Detainee Treatment Act, which, among other things,

in U.S. courts to the practice have been dismissed based on the "state secrets privilege" (a common law evidentiary privilege that allows the government to prevent the discovery of military and state secrets) and the lack of a domestic cause of action.[115]

* * *

The topic of extradition illustrates how treaties can play an important role in the U.S. legal system. In extradition cases, U.S. courts regularly interpret and apply treaties, and the terms of these treaties are generally considered self-executing. At the same time, there are important limitations on the role of the judiciary in this context, including the Secretary of State's ability to decide not to extradite a suspect found by a court to be extraditable, the rule of non-inquiry, and the ability of the executive branch to engage in extraterritorial law enforcement outside the context of extradition. Thus, like many examples in this book, extradition shows how the application of international law in the U.S. legal system is mediated by domestic legal and political considerations.

---

states that "[n]o individual in the custody or under the physical control of the United States Government, regardless of nationality or physical location, shall be subject to cruel, inhuman, or degrading treatment or punishment." Department of Defense, Emergency Supplemental Appropriations to Address Hurricanes in the Gulf of Mexico, and Pandemic Influenza Act, tit. X, § 1003(a). In July 2007, President Bush issued an executive order reauthorizing the CIA's overseas detention and interrogation program on the condition that it not include a variety of practices, including torture and cruel, inhuman, or degrading treatment or punishment. *See* Exec. Order No. 13,440, 72 FED. REG. 40707 (2007). This executive order purported to interpret Common Article 3 of the Geneva Conventions, which the Supreme Court has said applies to the conflict between the United States and the Al Qaeda terrorist organization. *See* Hamdan v. Rumsfeld, 548 U.S. 557, 629–30 (2006). Common Article 3 prohibits, among other things, "cruel treatment and torture" and "humiliating and degrading treatment." Shortly after taking office, President Obama revoked President Bush's 2007 executive order and directed the CIA to close its detention facilities. *See* Exec. Order No. 13491, 74 FED. REG. 4893 (2009).

[115] *See* Mohamed v. Jeppesen Dataplan, Inc., 614 F.3d 1070 (9th Cir. 2010); Arar v. Ashcroft, 585 F.3d 559 (2d Cir. 2009) (en banc); El-Masri v. United States, 479 F.3d 296 (4th Cir. 2007). *See also* Robert M. Chesney, *State Secrets and the Limits of National Security Litigation*, 75 GEO. WASH. L. REV. 1249 (2007); Todd Garvey & Edward C. Liu, *The State Secrets Privilege: Preventing the Disclosure of Sensitive National Security Information During Civil Litigation* (Cong. Res. Serv., Aug. 16, 2011), *at* http://www.fas.org/sgp/crs/secrecy/R41741.pdf.

10 War Powers and the War on Terrorism

THIS CHAPTER CONSIDERS the relevance of international law within the U.S. legal system to the United States' initiation and conduct of war. It also discusses a variety of international law-related issues that have arisen in connection with the "war on terrorism" following the attacks of September 11, 2001.

Much of the interpretation and enforcement of international law in this area occurs outside the courts, especially within the executive branch. As will be seen, courts do not typically enforce the international laws of war directly against Congress or the president. Some aspects of the international laws of war, however, have been incorporated into federal statutory provisions, especially criminal provisions, and these statutes can be enforced by both civilian and military courts. Courts also sometimes take account of international law when construing other federal statutes relating to war. This topic therefore provides yet another example of the indirect, interpretive role of international law in the U.S. legal system.

Even when courts are not involved, the U.S. government gives significant attention to the international laws of war, in part because of concerns about reciprocity with respect to the treatment of U.S. military personnel, but also because of a long-standing commitment to the values reflected in these laws. The government is not a unitary decision-maker, however, and this topic therefore also illustrates how departments within the government often debate both the content and applicability of international law. This is true even within the executive branch itself, as is illustrated by some of the legal debates that have arisen in the war on terrorism.

Modern International Law and Warfare

An extensive body of international law is relevant both to the initiation of war and to how war is conducted. The international law governing the initiation of war is referred to as *jus ad bellum*, and the international law governing the conduct of war is referred to as *jus in bello*.[1] The latter category encompasses what is commonly referred to as the "law of armed conflict" or "international humanitarian law." A variety of treaties and customary norms regulate both areas of international law.

The principal treaty regulating *jus ad bellum* today is the United Nations Charter, to which the United States has been a party since 1945.[2] Under the Charter, nations are allowed to use military force "against the territorial integrity or political independence of any state" in only two circumstances: in individual or collective self-defense, or pursuant to an authorization from the United Nations Security Council.[3] This sharp restriction on the use of force represents a substantial change from how international law historically addressed the initiation of war. At least prior to the formation of the League of Nations after World War I and the adoption of the Kellogg-Briand Pact of 1928, war was understood to be a generally available instrument of foreign policy.[4]

---

[1] Recent treatments of *jus ad bellum* include YORAM DINSTEIN, WAR, AGGRESSION AND SELF-DEFENCE (6th ed. 2017); and CHRISTINE D. GRAY, INTERNATIONAL LAW AND THE USE OF FORCE (4th ed. 2018). Recent treatments of *jus in bello* include YORAM DINSTEIN, THE CONDUCT OF HOSTILITIES UNDER THE LAW OF INTERNATIONAL ARMED CONFLICT (3d ed. 2016); and LESLIE C. GREEN, THE CONTEMPORARY LAW OF ARMED CONFLICT (3d ed. 2008).

[2] *See* United Nations Charter, June 26, 1945, 59 Stat. 1051, T.S. No. 933.

[3] *See id.*, art. 2(4) ("All Members shall refrain in their international relations from the threat or use of force against the territorial integrity or political independence of any state, or in any other manner inconsistent with the Purposes of the United Nations."); *id.*, art. 42 (The Security Council "may take such action by air, sea, or land forces as may be necessary to maintain or restore international peace and security."); *id.*, art. 51 ("Nothing in the present Charter shall impair the inherent right of individual or collective self-defence if an armed attack occurs against a Member of the United Nations, until the Security Council has taken measures necessary to maintain international peace and security.").

[4] *See, e.g.*, 2 CHARLES CHENEY HYDE, INTERNATIONAL LAW CHIEFLY AS INTERPRETED AND APPLIED BY THE UNITED STATES § 597, at 189 (1922) ("It always lies within the power of a State to endeavor to obtain redress for wrongs, or to gain political or other advantages over another, not merely by the employment of force, but also by direct recourse to war."). In the Kellogg-Briand Pact of 1928, a group of nations, including the United States, renounced war "as an instrument of national policy in their relations with one another." Treaty Between the United States and Other Powers Providing for the Renunciation of War as an Instrument of National Policy, Aug. 27, 1928, art. I, 46 Stat. 2343, 94 L.N.T.S. 57. This is not to suggest that there were no efforts before this point to restrict resort to the use of force. For example, some nations (including the United States) agreed in a 1907 treaty not to resort to force in order to recover on contract debt obligations, although even that commitment did not apply if the debtor state failed to arbitrate the dispute. *See* Convention Respecting the

Because the restrictions in the UN Charter on the use of force are directed at the political and military organs of government and concern relations between nations rather than the treatment of individuals, they are probably not "self-executing" in the U.S. legal system.[5] As discussed in Chapter 2, even if non–self-executing treaties are in some sense binding on the executive branch, they are not judicially enforceable. Although customary international law may contain restrictions similar to those in the UN Charter,[6] U.S courts (as we saw in Chapter 5) are unlikely to enforce customary international law against Congress or the president. Indeed, in *The Paquete Habana*, which concerned actions by the U.S. Navy in the Spanish-American War, the Supreme Court noted that customary international law is to be applied in the absence of a "controlling executive or legislative act."[7]

Limitation of the Employment of Force for the Recovery of Contract Debts, Oct. 18, 1907, 36 Stat. 2241, 1 Bevans 607. For an account of the drafting and adoption of the Kellogg-Briand pact and an argument that it helped transform the norms governing the use of force, *see* OONA A. HATHAWAY & SCOTT J. SHAPIRO, THE INTERNATIONALISTS: HOW A RADICAL PLAN TO OUTLAW WAR REMADE THE WORLD (2018).

[5] *See, e.g.*, Flores v. S. Peru Copper Corp., 414 F.3d 233, 250 n. 24 (2d Cir. 2003) ("[A]lthough the Charter of the United Nations has been ratified by the United States, it is not self-executing."); Frolova v. Union of Soviet Socialist Republics, 761 F.2d 370, 373–74 (7th Cir. 1985) ("We have found no case holding that the U.N. Charter is self-executing nor has plaintiff provided us with one. There are, however, quite a few decisions stating that the Charter is not self-executing."); Tel-Oren v. Libyan Arab Republic, 726 F.2d 774, 809 (D.C. Cir. 1984) (Bork, J., concurring) ("Articles 1 and 2 of the United Nations Charter are likewise not self-executing. They do not speak in terms of individual rights but impose obligations on nations and on the United Nations itself."). *Cf.* Medellin v. Texas, 552 U.S. 491, 508–10 (2008) (holding that Article 94 of the United Nations Charter, which obligates nations to comply with decisions of the International Court of Justice, is not self-executing).

[6] *See* Military and Paramilitary Activities in and against Nicaragua (Nicar. v. U.S.), Jurisdiction and Admissibility, 1984 I.C.J. 392, 424 (Nov. 26) ("Principles such as those of the non-use of force, non-intervention, respect for the independence and territorial integrity of States, and the freedom of navigation, continue to be binding as part of customary international law, despite the operation of provisions of conventional law in which they have been incorporated.").

[7] The Paquete Habana, 175 U.S. 677, 700 (1900). *See also,* e.g., Galo-Garcia v. INS, 86 F.3d 916, 918 (9th Cir. 1996) ("[W]here a controlling executive or legislative act does exist, customary international law is inapplicable."); Gisbert v. U.S. Attorney General, 988 F.2d 1437, 1448 (5th Cir. 1993) (agreeing with "other circuits [that] have held in the context of immigration detention that international law is not controlling because federal executive, legislative, and judicial actions supersede the application of these principles of international law"). David Golove contends that the Court's statement simply meant that it would apply customary international law even if there were no legislative or executive act incorporating that law. *See* David Golove, *Military Tribunals, International Law, and the Constitution: A Franckian–Madisonian Approach*, 35 N.Y.U. J. INT'L L. & POL'Y 363, 391–92 (2003). This interpretation ignores the fact that, as the Court itself emphasized, the president had issued orders requiring compliance with the customary laws of war, see *The Paquete Habana*, 175 U.S. at 712, and hence there *was* a controlling executive act that would have supported application of the customary principle applied by the Court. The Court therefore must have been saying that there was no controlling legislative or executive act *barring* the application of the customary international law rule, and that is how most courts and commentators have understood the Court's language. That is also how the dissenting justices in *The Paquete Habana* understood what the majority was saying. *See id.* at 716.

A much wider array of treaties govern *jus in bello*. Some treaties, for example, restrict the types of weapons that can be used in combat.[8] Probably the most important treaties governing conduct in war are the four Geneva Conventions for the Protection of Victims of War that were developed after World War II. These Conventions address the treatment of various categories of individuals during armed conflict, including prisoners of war.[9] The United States ratified the Conventions in 1955, and today essentially all nations in the world are parties to them.[10] Some human rights treaties, such as the Convention against Torture and Other Cruel, Inhuman and Degrading Treatment or Punishment, are also potentially relevant to conduct during war.

It is not clear whether the Geneva Conventions are self-executing. As discussed in Chapter 2, treaty provisions calling for criminal punishment have long been treated in the U.S. legal system as non–self-executing, and some provisions in the Geneva Conventions fall into that category. As for the other provisions in the Conventions, they concern the protection of individuals, a factor that might weigh in favor of self-execution. But the subject matter of the Conventions—conduct during an armed conflict, which often will take place outside the territorial jurisdiction of the United States—might suggest that domestic judicial enforcement was not contemplated. In a 1950 decision, *Johnson v. Eisentrager*, the Supreme Court stated in a footnote that the 1929 Geneva Convention—a precursor to the current Geneva Conventions—was not self-executing. The Court explained:

> It is . . . the obvious scheme of the Agreement that responsibility for observance and enforcement of these rights is upon political and military authorities. Rights of alien enemies are vindicated under it only through protests and intervention

---

[8] *See, e.g.*, Protocol for the Prohibition of the Use in War of Asphyxiating, Poisonous or Other Gases, and of Bacteriological Methods of Warfare, June 17, 1925, 26 U.S.T. 571, 94 L.N.T.S. 65 (entered into force Feb. 8, 1928; for the United States Oct. 4, 1975).

[9] The four Geneva Conventions are (1) the Convention for the Amelioration of the Condition of the Wounded and Sick in Armed Forces in the Field, Aug. 12, 1949, 6 U.S.T. 3114; (2) the Convention for the Amelioration of the Condition of Wounded, Sick and Shipwrecked Members of the Armed Forces at Sea, Aug. 12, 1949, 6 U.S.T. 3217; (3) the Convention Relative to the Treatment of Prisoners of War, Aug. 12, 1949, 6 U.S.T. 3316 [hereinafter Third Geneva Convention]; and (4) the Convention Relative to the Protection of Civilian Persons in Time of War, Aug. 12, 1949, 6 U.S.T. 3516. Each was signed in Geneva on August 12, 1949, and ratified by the United States on July 14, 1955. As of 2020, there were 196 parties to the Conventions. *See* ICRC Humanitarian Law—Treaties & Documents, *at* http://www.icrc.org/ihl.nsf/CONVPRES?OpenView.

[10] There are also two additional protocols to the Geneva Conventions, which were developed in the 1970s. Although the protocols have been widely ratified, the United States is not a party to them. *See* Protocol Additional to the Geneva Conventions of 12 August 1949, and Relating to the Protection of Victims of International Armed Conflicts, June 8, 1977, 1125 U.N.T.S. 3; Protocol Additional to the Geneva Conventions of 12 August 1949, and Relating to the Protection of Victims of Non–International Armed Conflicts, June 8, 1977, 1125 U.N.T.S. 609. Other important treaties governing *jus in bello* include the 1907 Hague Conventions. *See, e.g.*, Convention Respecting the Laws and Customs of War on Land, Oct. 18, 1907, 36 Stat. 2277, 1 Bevans 631.

of protecting powers as the rights of our citizens against foreign governments are vindicated only by Presidential intervention.[11]

The United States ratified the current Geneva Conventions after this decision, and there is no indication in the Conventions that they were intended to provide for a new right of judicial review. Instead, the Conventions provide only for diplomatic mechanisms to resolve disputes under the Conventions.[12]

Regardless of whether the Conventions or other treaties relating to war are self-executing, Congress can incorporate their provisions into U.S. law. It has done so to some extent in the War Crimes Act.[13] As originally enacted in 1996, the Act criminalized the commission of "grave breaches" of the Geneva Conventions when committed either by or against U.S. nationals or armed forces.[14] In 1997, the Act was amended to broaden the definition of war crimes to cover certain violations of other treaties relating to the conduct of warfare, and also to cover any violation (not just "grave breaches") of Common Article 3 of the Geneva Conventions (which provides certain minimum protections for individuals in conflicts "not of an international character").[15] As discussed later in this

---

[11] 339 U.S. 763, 789 n.14 (1950). In *Hamdan v. Rumsfeld*, 548 U.S. 557 (2006), the Court referred to this footnote as a "curious statement" but did not disavow it. *Id.* at 627.

[12] *See, e.g.*, Third Geneva Convention, *supra* note 9, art. 11 (providing that the protecting powers "where they deem it advisable in the interest of protected persons, particularly in cases of disagreement between the Parties to the conflict as to the application or interpretation of the provisions of the present Convention, . . . shall lend their good offices with a view to settling the disagreement"); *id.*, art. 132 ("At the request of a Party to the conflict, an enquiry shall be instituted, in a manner to be decided between the interested Parties, concerning any alleged violation of the Convention."). *See also* Hamdi v. Rumsfeld, 316 F.3d 450, 468 (4th Cir. 2003) ("[W]hat discussion there is of enforcement [in the Geneva Conventions] focuses entirely on the vindication by diplomatic means of treaty rights inhering in sovereign nations."), *vacated and remanded on other grounds*, 542 U.S. 507 (2004). For differing views about whether the Geneva Conventions are self-executing, *compare Hamdi*, 316 F.3d at 468 (holding that the Geneva Conventions are not self-executing), *and* Al-Bihani v. Obama, 619 F.3d 1, 20 (D.C. Cir. 2010) (Kavanaugh, J., concurring) ("[T]he 1949 Geneva Conventions are not self-executing treaties and thus are not domestic U.S. law."), *with* United States v. Hamidullin, 888 F.3d 62, 76 (4th Cir. 2018) (noting that "a self-executing treaty *like the Third Geneva Convention* would . . . preempt common law if the treaty speaks directly to the question") (emphasis added), United States v. Khadr, 717 F. Supp. 2d 1215, 1220 n.4 (Ct. Mil. Comm'n Rev. 2007) ("The Geneva Conventions are generally viewed as self-executing treaties (i.e., ones which become effective without the necessity of implementing congressional action), form a part of American law, and are binding in federal courts under the Supremacy Clause."), *and* United States v. Lindh, 212 F. Supp. 2d 541, 553 (E.D. Va. 2002) ("[T]he [Third Geneva Convention], insofar as it is pertinent here, is a self-executing treaty.").

[13] *See* 18 U.S.C. § 2441.

[14] *See* Pub. L. No. 104–192, 110 Stat. 2104 (Aug. 21, 1996). The Geneva Conventions require parties to criminalize certain "grave breaches" of the Conventions. *See, e.g.*, Third Geneva Convention, *supra* note 9, art. 129 ("The High Contracting Parties undertake to enact any legislation necessary to provide effective penal sanctions for persons committing, or ordering to be committed, any of the grave breaches of the present Convention defined in the following Article."). When the United States ratified the Conventions in 1955, the Senate Foreign Relations Committee expressed the view that U.S. obligations under the "grave breach" provisions in the Conventions were satisfied by existing law and that no implementing legislation was therefore needed. *See* S. Exec. Rep. No. 84–9 (1955), *reprinted in* 84 CONG. REC. 9958, 9970 (1955).

[15] *See* Pub. L. No. 105–118, 111 Stat. 2386, 2436, § 583 (Nov. 26, 1997).

chapter, the Act was amended again in 2006 in response to a Supreme Court decision holding that Common Article 3 applied to the war on terrorism.[16]

Congressional War Powers

The Constitution assigns a variety of war-related powers to Congress. These include the powers to "declare war," to "grant letters of marque and reprisal," and to "make rules concerning captures on land and water."[17] In addition, Congress has the power to "raise and support armies," to "provide and maintain a navy," and to "make rules for the government and regulation of the land and naval forces."[18] Other congressional powers, such as the power to define and punish offenses against the law of nations, are also potentially relevant to war. In addition, Congress has the general authority to make laws "necessary and proper for carrying into execution" not only its own powers but also "all other powers vested by this Constitution in the government of the United States, or in any department or officer thereof," including the war powers of the president.[19]

Academic commentators have disagreed about the implications of the Constitution's assignment to Congress of the power to declare war. At the time of the constitutional Founding, declarations of war served particular functions under international law. Among other things, they would trigger customary international law rules governing conduct such as the seizure of vessels, the shipment of contraband, and the institution of blockades.[20] Some scholars contend that Congress was given only the power to trigger these international law consequences, not control over the United States' initiation of wars.[21] The Constitution provided for war-making to be checked, according to this

---

[16] The Geneva Conventions have also been incorporated into U.S. military handbooks and manuals. *See, e.g.*, FM 6-27, *The Commander's Handbook on the Law of Land Warfare* (Aug. 2019), *at* https://fas.org/irp/doddir/army/fm6_27.pdf.

[17] *See* U.S. CONST. art. I, § 8, cl. 11.

[18] *Id.*, cls. 12–14.

[19] *Id.*, cl. 18.

[20] *See, e.g.*, 3 EMMERICH DE VATTEL, THE LAW OF NATIONS OR THE PRINCIPLES OF NATURAL LAW § 56, at 255 (Charles G. Fenwick Trans., 1916) (1758) ("[P]ublication of the declaration of war is necessary for the instruction and guidance of a State's own subjects, and in order to fix the date from which certain rights belonging to them in virtue of war are to begin, and in order to settle certain effects which the voluntary Law of Nations attributes to formal war.").

[21] *See, e.g.*, John C. Yoo, *The Continuation of Politics by Other Means: The Original Understanding of War Powers*, 84 CAL. L. REV. 167 (1996). A draft of the Constitution would have given Congress the power to "make" war. The word "make" was changed during the Federal Convention to "declare." *See* 2 THE RECORDS OF THE FEDERAL CONVENTION OF 1787, at 318–19 (Max Farrand ed., 1911). For an argument that, in the eighteenth century, war could be "declared by word or action" and that Congress's declare war power therefore gave it the authority to decide whether the United States initiated war, *see* Michael D. Ramsey, *Textualism and War Powers*, 69 U. CHI. L. REV. 1543 (2002). For a response to this argument, *see* John C. Yoo, *War and the Constitutional Text*, 69 U. CHI. L. REV. 1639 (2002), and for a rejoinder, *see* Michael D. Ramsey, *Text and History in the War Powers Debate: A Reply to Professor Yoo*, 69 U. CHI. L. REV. 1685 (2002). *See also* Saikrishna

argument, not through a requirement of advance congressional approval, but rather through congressional control over appropriations for war.[22] Many scholars disagree with this argument, however, contending that the Declare War Clause, along with the Constitution's other grants of war-related authority to Congress, show that the constitutional Founders vested control over war initiation with Congress.[23] These scholars note, among other things, that early U.S. presidents and other political figures appeared to assume, as least in their public statements, that congressional authorization was needed in order for the United States to conduct offensive military operations.[24]

The scholars who maintain that the Constitution requires congressional authorization in order for the president to initiate war do not typically maintain that the authorization must take the form of a declaration of war. Undeclared wars were common before the constitutional Founding,[25] and the United States' first major conflict against another nation after the Founding—a naval war against France at the end of the eighteenth century—was undeclared.[26] In fact, despite being involved in hundreds of military conflicts since its Founding, the United States has declared war in connection with only five conflicts: the War of 1812, the Mexican-American War, the Spanish-American War, World War I, and World War II.[27] Moreover, modern international law, by outlawing

---

Prakash, *Unleashing the Dogs of War: What the Constitution Means by "Declare War,"* 93 CORNELL L. REV. 45 (2007) (arguing that any action by the United States to begin waging war is a declaration of war and thus within the control of Congress, even if another nation has already declared war on the United States by word or action).

[22] *See* Yoo, *supra* note 21, at 295 (contending that "the Framers intended Congress to participate in war-making by controlling appropriations").

[23] *See, e.g.*, JOHN HART ELY, WAR AND RESPONSIBILITY: CONSTITUTIONAL LESSONS OF VIETNAM AND ITS AFTERMATH 3 (1993); LOUIS FISHER, PRESIDENTIAL WAR POWER (3d ed. rev. 2013); FRANCIS D. WORMUTH & EDWIN B. FIRMAGE, TO CHAIN THE DOG OF WAR: THE WAR POWER OF CONGRESS IN HISTORY AND LAW (2d ed. 1989); Charles A. Lofgren, *War-Making under the Constitution: The Original Understanding*, 81 YALE L.J. 672 (1972); William Michael Treanor, *Fame, the Founding, and the Power to Declare War*, 82 CORNELL L. REV. 695 (1997).

[24] *See* Ramsey, *supra* note 21, at 1566 ("As congressional advocates have detailed, Madison, Hamilton, Jefferson, Wilson, Washington, Jay, Marshall, and an array of lesser figures indicated that war power lay primarily with Congress, and no prominent figure took the other side."). *See also* CURTIS A. BRADLEY, ASHLEY S. DEEKS & JACK L. GOLDSMITH, FOREIGN RELATIONS LAW: CASES AND MATERIALS 643–44 (7th ed. 2020) (describing post-Founding statements and practices).

[25] *See* J. F. MAURICE, HOSTILITIES WITHOUT DECLARATION OF WAR: AN HISTORICAL ABSTRACT OF THE CASES IN WHICH HOSTILITIES HAVE OCCURRED BETWEEN CIVILIZED POWERS PRIOR TO DECLARATION OR WARNING: FROM 1700 to 1870 (1883); W. TAYLOR REVELEY III, WAR POWERS OF THE PRESIDENT AND CONGRESS: WHO HOLDS THE ARROWS AND OLIVE BRANCH? 54–55 (1981); Clyde Eagleton, *The Form and Function of the Declaration of War*, 32 AM. J. INT'L L. 19 (1938). *See also* THE FEDERALIST PAPERS, *No. 25: Hamilton*, at 165 (Clinton Rossiter ed., 1961) (noting that "the ceremony of a formal denunciation of war has of late fallen into disuse").

[26] *See* Bas v. Tingy, 4 U.S. (4 Dall.) 37 (1800) (holding that France was an "enemy" for purposes of a statute concerning recapture of vessels even though war had not been formally declared).

[27] *See* Congressional Research Service, *Instances of Use of United States Armed Forces Abroad, 1798–2020* (Jan. 13, 2020), *available at* https://fas.org/sgp/crs/natsec/R42738.pdf.

aggressive war-making and disallowing the changing of legal entitlements through war, has made declarations of war much less relevant than they once were.[28] In part because of these changes in international law, the United States has not issued a formal declaration of war in almost eighty years.[29]

Although Congress has not formally declared war since World War II, it has authorized by statute some of the most significant U.S. military engagements in the post–World War II period, including the Vietnam War, the 1991 Gulf War, the post–September 11, 2001, war in Afghanistan and against Al Qaeda, and the 2003 Iraq War. As will be discussed, however, President Truman initiated the Korean War in 1950 without congressional authorization. Moreover, presidents have initiated a number of smaller-scale military operations in this period (such as in Panama, Somalia, Haiti, Yugoslavia, Libya, and Syria) without specific congressional authorization. As discussed in Chapter 1, historical governmental practice can help inform understandings of the distribution of authority between Congress and the president, so it is not surprising that executive branch lawyers commonly cite to the post–World War II practice as evidence that congressional authorization is not a prerequisite for all presidential uses of force.[30]

As explained elsewhere in this book, Congress has the authority to override both customary international law and earlier-in-time treaties within the U.S. legal system. Thus, as a matter of U.S. law, Congress can authorize war even if the war would violate international law. Consider, for example, the U.S. war in Iraq that began in 2003, after Congress had authorized it in October 2002.[31] It is arguable that this war, because it did not involve defense against an armed attack and was not specifically approved by the UN Security Council, violated international law.[32] Nevertheless, within the U.S. legal system,

---

[28] *See* Paul Kahn, *War Powers and the Millennium*, 34 LOY. L.A. L. REV. 11 (2000).

[29] *See* Jennifer K. Elsea & Matthew C. Weed, *Declarations of War and Authorizations for the Use of Military Force: Historical Background and Legal Implications* (Cong. Res. Serv., Apr. 18, 2014), *available at* http://fas.org/sgp/crs/natsec/RL31133.pdf. *See also* Orlando v. Laird, 443 F.2d 1039, 1043 (2d Cir. 1971) ("The choice, for example, between an explicit declaration on the one hand and a resolution and war-implementing legislation, on the other, as the medium for expression of congressional consent involves 'the exercise of a discretion demonstrably committed to the . . . legislature,' Baker v. Carr, [369 U.S. 186,] 211 [(1962)], and therefore, invokes the political question doctrine.").

[30] *See* Curtis A. Bradley & Trevor W. Morrison, *Historical Gloss and the Separation of Powers*, 126 HARV. L. REV. 411 (2012).

[31] For Congress's authorization of the Iraq war, *see* Authorization for Use of Military Force against Iraq Resolution of 2002, Pub. L. No. 107–243, 116 Stat. 1498 (Oct. 16, 2002).

[32] *Compare* Sean D. Murphy, *Assessing the Legality of Invading Iraq*, 92 GEO. L.J. 173, 256 (2004) ("The legal theory advanced in 2003 by the United States and its allies to justify the invasion of Iraq is not persuasive. Neither the language of the relevant resolutions nor the practice of the Security Council with respect to those resolutions supports the use of force against Iraq, especially in light of the extensive opposition of most of the members of the Security Council over the course of 2002–03."), *with* Christopher Greenwood, *International Law and the Preemptive Use of Force: Afghanistan, Al Qaida, and Iraq*, 4 SAN DIEGO INT'L L.J. 7, 36 (2003) ("[A]lthough it must be recognized that others have taken a different view, the present writer believes that those governments who resorted to force were right to conclude that they could rely on the authorization of military action in [Security Council] resolution 678, read together with resolutions 687 and 1441.").

Congress would have had the authority to approve the war and thereby potentially place the United States in breach of its international law obligations.

Despite Congress's authority to override it, international law is likely to be relevant when discerning the scope and effect of some of Congress's war powers. In addition to the power to declare war, other congressional war powers, such as its ability to issue letters of marque and reprisal and to regulate captures on land and water, directly concern topics that, at the time of the drafting and ratification of the Constitution, would have been regulated by international law.[33] In addition, Congress's authority to define and punish offenses against the law of nations obviously references international law and thus is potentially limited by it. For example, as will be discussed later, when using its define-and-punish power to prescribe crimes by enemy belligerents that can be prosecuted in military commissions, Congress may not be able to go beyond what is considered an offense under international law (although it may have authority outside the define-and-punish power to authorize the prosecution of certain other offenses).

International law is also potentially relevant when interpreting the scope of congressional authorizations of force. If nothing else, a broad authorization of force is likely to be read as conveying the general authority allowed to belligerents under the international laws of war. For example, during the Mexican-American War, for which Congress had formally declared war, the executive branch argued, and the Supreme Court agreed, that the president's exercise of various belligerent rights in occupied California was valid, even in the absence of specific congressional authorization, because the rights were "the belligerent rights of a conqueror" that accorded with "the law of arms and the right of conquest" under the laws of war.[34] Similarly, during the Civil War, which Congress retroactively authorized months after it began, both President Lincoln and the Supreme Court concluded that the president possessed all the authority permitted by the laws of war.[35]

---

[33] For discussion of Congress's power to grant letters of marque and reprisal, *see* Ingrid Brunk Wuerth, *International Law and Constitutional Interpretation: The Commander-in-Chief Clause Reconsidered*, 106 MICH. L. REV. 61 (2007). For discussion of Congress's power to regulate captures on land and water, *see* Ingrid Wuerth, *The Captures Clause*, 76 U. CHI. L. REV. 1683 (2009). *See also* J. Gregory Sidak, *The Quasi War Cases—and Their Relevance to Whether "Letters of Marque and Reprisal" Constrain Presidential War Powers*, 28 HARV. J.L. & PUB. POL'Y 465 (2005).

[34] *See* Cross v. Harrison, 57 U.S. (16 How.) 164, 190 (1854); *see also id.* at 193 (noting that the occupation government "had its origin in the lawful exercise of a belligerent right over a conquered territory"); *id.* at 180–81 (excerpt from brief of the Attorney General).

[35] The executive branch defended Lincoln's blockade of the South on the ground that it was permitted by the laws of war. *See* The Prize Cases, 67 U.S. (2 Black) 635, 660–61 (1863) (quoting argument from Richard Dana, lawyer for the government, that "[t]he function to use the army and navy being in the President, the mode of using them, within the rules of civilized warfare, and subject to established laws of Congress, must be subject to his discretion"). All nine justices in the *Prize Cases*, including the dissenters, accepted this proposition. *See id.* at 672–73; *id.* at 684–85 (Nelson, J., dissenting). Lincoln also justified the emancipation of Southern slaves on the ground that it was a wartime action permitted by the laws of war. *See* Letter from Abraham Lincoln to

The Supreme Court followed a narrower approach to construing congressional authorizations of war in a decision concerning the War of 1812. In *Brown v. United States*, the issue was whether a congressional declaration of war should be construed as authorizing the executive branch to confiscate enemy property located within the United States.[36] A majority of the Court reasoned that, although the United States had a sovereign right to seize the property, modern international practice disfavored such a seizure, and "a construction ought not lightly to be admitted which would give to a declaration of war an effect in this country it does not possess elsewhere."[37] The Court also noted that the Constitution gives Congress the power to make rules concerning captures on land as "an independent substantive power, not included in that of declaring war."[38] In addition, the Court observed that Congress had previously regulated other aspects of the treatment of enemy aliens, which suggested to the Court that such treatment was not addressed by the declaration of war.[39] Finally, the Court reasoned that the determination of the U.S. policy on seizure of enemy property was properly made by Congress because "[t]he rule which we apply to the property of our enemy, will be applied by him to the property of our citizens" and that "[l]ike all questions of policy, it is proper for the consideration of a department which can modify it at will."[40]

Modern assumptions about the scope of congressional authorizations of war appear to be broader than the approach of the Court in *Brown*. As Professor Louis Henkin noted, *Brown* was decided in an era in which presidential war power was "still in its infancy,"[41] and at a time when Congress still micromanaged war-making. Particularly during and after the Civil War, wartime presidents captured and detained prisoners of war, held military trials, and negotiated armistice agreements—all in the absence of specific congressional authorization.[42] That more expansive understanding of presidential wartime

---

James C. Conkling (Aug. 26, 1863), *in* 6 THE COLLECTED WORKS OF ABRAHAM LINCOLN 406, 408 (Roy P. Basler ed., 1953).

[36] 12 U.S. (8 Cranch) 110 (1814).
[37] *Id.* at 125.
[38] *Id.* at 126.
[39] *See id.*
[40] *Id.* at 128–29. Justice Story dissented, arguing that there was a right under customary international law to seize enemy property and that, in declaring war in unlimited terms, Congress had triggered in the executive branch "a right to employ all the usual and customary means acknowledged in war, to carry it into effect." *Id.* at 145 (Story, J., dissenting).
[41] LOUIS HENKIN, FOREIGN AFFAIRS AND THE UNITED STATES CONSTITUTION 104 (2d ed. 1996).
[42] *See, e.g.*, WILLIAM E. BIRKHIMER, MILITARY GOVERNMENT AND MARTIAL LAW 351–55 (rev. 3d ed. 1914) (providing examples of presidential use of military commissions); EDWARD S. CORWIN, THE PRESIDENT: OFFICE AND POWERS, 1787–1984, at 294–95 (Randall W. Bland et al. eds., rev. 5th ed. 1984) (noting examples of presidents concluding armistice agreements); John Yoo, *Transferring Terrorists*, 79 NOTRE DAME L. REV. 1183, 1221 (2004) (surveying U.S. history and concluding that in the Mexican-American War, the Civil War, the Spanish-American War, World Wars I and II, the Vietnam War, the invasion of Panama, and the 1991 Gulf War, Congress "never sought to regulate the disposition of [prisoners of war] or asserted that it has any authority over them").

authority continued through World War II and was reflected in legislation, executive branch practice, and judicial precedent.[43] The approach of the courts to Congress's authorization of force in the war on terrorism, to be discussed, is consistent with this broader understanding.

Presidential War Powers

The Constitution designates the president as the Commander in Chief of the armed forces.[44] Even the scholars who maintain that the Constitution requires congressional authorization when the United States initiates war accept that the president, acting as Commander in Chief, has the authority to order the use of force to respond to attacks on the United States. As the Supreme Court stated in approving a naval blockade that President Lincoln had ordered at the outset of the Civil War, "[i]f war be made by invasion of a foreign nation, the President is not only authorized but bound to resist force by force."[45] It is also generally accepted that the president has some authority to use force to protect U.S. citizens and their property abroad,[46] and presidents and their lawyers have often invoked this power as a justification for military operations. Executive branch lawyers have also claimed that, while seeking to protect U.S. citizens abroad, the president may use force to protect foreign citizens exposed to the same threat.[47]

More broadly, presidents in recent decades have claimed that they have the constitutional authority to use military force if they reasonably determine that it will serve "U.S. national interests" and if the "nature, scope, and duration" of the use of force is such that it does not amount to a "war" for constitutional purposes. This is what the Obama administration claimed in 2011, for example, in using force against Libya, and it was what the Trump administration claimed in 2018 in using force against Syria.[48] The president's

---

[43] *See* CORWIN, *supra* note 42, at 262–97; HENKIN, *supra* note 41, at 45–50; LOUIS WILLIAM KOENIG, THE PRESIDENCY AND THE CRISIS: POWERS OF THE OFFICE FROM THE INVASION OF POLAND TO PEARL HARBOR 55–57, 67–68, 97, 120 (1944); REVELEY, *supra* note 25, at 135–69.

[44] *See* U.S. CONST. art. II, § 2, cl. 1.

[45] The Prize Cases, 67 U.S. (2 Black) 635, 668 (1863). During the drafting of the Constitution, when the phrase "make war" was changed to "declare war," it was noted that this would "leav[e] to the Executive the power to repel sudden attacks." *See* 2 RECORDS OF THE FEDERAL CONVENTION, *supra* note 21, at 318.

[46] *See* Durand v. Hollins, 8 F. Cas. 111 (C.C.S.D.N.Y. 1860).

[47] *See, e.g.*, Memorandum from Jack L. Goldsmith III, Assistant Attorney General, to Alberto R. Gonzales, Counsel to the President, *Deployment of United States Armed Forces to Haiti* (Mar. 17, 2004), 28 OP. OFF. LEGAL COUNSEL 30, 32 (2004); Memorandum from Timothy E. Flanigan, Assistant Attorney General, to William P. Barr, Attorney General, *Authority to Use United States Military Forces in Somalia* (Dec. 4, 1992), 16 OP. OFF. LEGAL COUNSEL 6, 11 (1992).

[48] *See* Memorandum Opinion from Caroline D. Krass, Principal Deputy Assistant Attorney General, Office of Legal Counsel, to the Attorney General, *Authority to Use Military Force in Libya* (April 1, 2011), available at https://fas.org/irp/agency/doj/olc/libya.pdf; Memorandum Opinion from Steven A. Engel, Assistant Attorney General, Office of Legal Counsel, for the Counsel to the President, *April 2018 Airstrikes Against*

lawyers have based this claim in part on long-standing historical practice, noting that prior presidents have often ordered small-scale uses of force without seeking congressional authorization. The "national interests" that have been cited include not only protecting American lives and property, but also preserving regional stability, supporting the credibility of the UN Security Council, providing assistance to U.S. allies, and mitigating humanitarian disasters.[49] As for the "nature, scope, and duration" inquiry, the president's lawyers have explained that this is a highly fact-specific inquiry that does not turn on any one factor. In general, targeted airstrikes that do not involve a significant commitment of grounds troops—even if the strikes are carried out over many days—have been deemed by the president's lawyers to fall below the threshold of when congressional authorization would be required under this test.

Some scholars have argued that the scope of the president's constitutional authority as Commander in Chief is implicitly limited by the international laws of war.[50] To the extent that this is so, it is likely true only of the international law relating to *jus in bello* rather than *jus ad bellum*. As we have seen, international law historically did not place many restraints on the initiation of war. Although modern international law does sharply limit the permissible uses of force, as a matter of practice presidents have exercised the sovereign authority of the United States to decide whether and how to comply with the *jus ad bellum*, and a number of presidentially initiated military operations in the post–World War II period have arguably been inconsistent with it. A noteworthy example is the Kosovo bombing campaign directed by President Clinton in the late 1990s, which neither involved the exercise of self-defense nor was authorized by the UN Security Council and thus did not fall within the two permissible bases for the use of force set forth in the UN Charter.[51] Congress could attempt to impose *jus ad bellum* restrictions on the president by codifying them in statutes, but it has shown no inclination to do so. For example, in its most significant effort to regulate presidential initiation of war—the

---

Syrian Chemical-Weapons Facilities (May 31, 2018), *at* https://www.justice.gov/olc/opinion/file/1067551/download.

[49] For an argument that the "national interests" element of the test imposes no meaningful constraint on presidential uses of force, *see* Curtis Bradley & Jack Goldsmith, *OLC's Meaningless "National Interests' Test for the Legality of Presidential Uses of Force*, LAWFARE (June 5, 2018), *at* https://www.lawfareblog.com/olcs-meaningless-national-interests-test-legality-presidential-uses-force.

[50] *See, e.g.*, Golove, *supra* note 7; David Golove, *The Supreme Court, the War on Terror, and the American Just War Constitutional Tradition, in* INTERNATIONAL LAW IN THE SUPREME COURT: CONTINUITY AND CHANGE 561 (David L. Sloss, Michael D. Ramsey & William S. Dodge eds., 2011). *See also* Wuerth, *supra* note 33, at 64–65 (arguing that international law "is, and has been, attractive to courts, lawyers, and scholars struggling with the Commander in Chief Clause because it can function as a second-order interpretive norm, thereby aiding in the resolution of many of the difficulties associated with the Clause").

[51] For arguments that the Kosovo campaign violated the United Nations Charter, see, for example, MICHAEL J. GLENNON, LIMITS OF LAW, PREROGATIVES OF POWER: INTERVENTIONISM AFTER KOSOVO 13–35 (2001); and Jules Lobel, *Benign Hegemony?: Kosovo and Article 2(4) of the U.N. Charter*, 1 CHI. J. INT'L L. 19 (2000).

War Powers Resolution of 1973 (discussed later)—Congress made no mention of any presidential obligation to comply with international law.

Even with respect to *jus in bello* limitations, the precedent for implied limitations on the commander-in-chief power is limited at best.[52] A more likely way in which *jus in bello* restrictions would bind the president as a matter of domestic law would be if Congress incorporated them into federal statutes. Congress has a variety of powers that it could invoke to do so, including its power to regulate the armed forces and its power to define and punish offenses against the law of nations. Congress does not have the constitutional authority, however, to regulate in a manner that would invade an exclusive presidential power. The scope of the president's exclusive commander-in-chief power is unclear, but at a minimum it probably includes control over the chain of military command,[53] and it might also extend to control over some tactical decisions on the battlefield.[54] In any event, Congress has incorporated aspects of the *jus in bello* into statutory law, such as in the War Crimes Act discussed and in the Uniform Code of Military Justice that regulates the conduct of U.S. military personnel, and these statutory provisions are generally assumed to be constitutional. Congress has also enacted criminal legislation prohibiting torture, as part of the United States' implementation of the Torture Convention.[55] Both the War Crimes Act and the torture statute were the focus of significant discussion in the war on terrorism, as will be discussed.

---

[52] *See* Curtis A. Bradley & Jack L. Goldsmith, *Congressional Authorization and the War on Terrorism*, 118 HARV. L. REV. 2047, 2097 n.220 (2005). *See also* J. Andrew Kent, *Congress's Under-Appreciated Power to Define and Punish Offenses against the Law of Nations*, 85 TEX. L. REV. 843, 930–36 (2007) (questioning the proposition that international law limits the government's constitutional authority).

[53] *See* Youngstown Sheet & Tube Co. v. Sawyer, 343 U.S. 579, 641 (1952) (Jackson, J., concurring) (noting that the Commander in Chief Clause "undoubtedly puts the Nation's armed forces under presidential command").

[54] *See, e.g.,* Derek Jinks & David Sloss, *Is the President Bound by the Geneva Conventions?*, 90 CORNELL L. REV. 97, 171 (2004) ("Commentators generally agree that the President has exclusive authority over battlefield operations, and that Congress's war powers are constrained by the need to avoid interfering with the President's Commander-in-Chief power during wartime."). For a detailed examination of congressional regulation of issues relating to war, and an argument that the president's exclusive commander in chief power extends only to the superintendence of the military chain of command, *see* David J. Barron & Martin S. Lederman, *The Commander in Chief at the Lowest Ebb—A Constitutional History*, 121 HARV. L. REV. 941 (2008); and David J. Barron & Martin S. Lederman, *The Commander in Chief at the Lowest Ebb—Framing the Problem, Doctrine, and Original Understanding*, 121 HARV. L. REV. 689 (2008); *see also* DAVID J. BARRON, WAGING WAR: THE CLASH BETWEEN PRESIDENTS AND CONGRESS, 1176 TO ISIS (2016). For an early decision holding that the seizure of a vessel during the naval war between the United States and France was improper because the seizure did not fall within the scope of a congressional authorization, *see* Little v. Barreme, 6 U.S. (2 Cranch) 170 (1804). For differing views about the significance of *Barreme*, compare MICHAEL J. GLENNON, CONSTITUTIONAL DIPLOMACY 3–8 (1991) (arguing that *Barreme* supports broad congressional authority to control the president during wartime), *with* Sidak, *supra* note 33 (disputing that proposition).

[55] *See* 18 U.S.C. § 2340A.

War Powers Resolution

In 1973, in the wake of the Vietnam War, Congress enacted the War Powers Resolution, over President Nixon's veto.[56] The Resolution begins by expressing Congress's view that the president has the constitutional authority to introduce U.S. military forces "into hostilities or into situations where imminent involvement in hostilities is clearly indicated by the circumstances" only if there is "a declaration of war," "specific statutory authorization," or "a national emergency created by attack upon the United States, its territories or possessions, or its armed forces."[57] The Resolution then proceeds to require that the president consult with and report to Congress concerning the introduction of forces into hostilities.[58] Most dramatically, the Resolution provides that the president normally must terminate the use of armed forces within sixty days unless Congress has either declared war or provided specific authorization for the use of force.[59] The Resolution also makes clear that authorization is not to be inferred from any treaty unless Congress has implemented the treaty with legislation that specifically authorizes the use of U.S. armed forces.[60]

President Nixon argued that the War Powers Resolution was unconstitutional, and other presidents have sometimes raised questions about its validity. Nevertheless, presidents have often submitted reports to Congress about military operations and have stated that these reports are "consistent with" the terms of the Resolution.[61] In addition, when presidents have continued with hostilities beyond the sixty-day cutoff date specified in the Resolution, they have argued that they were acting consistently with the Resolution, not that they could disregard it. Many commentators have expressed the view, however, that the Resolution has not operated as an effective restraint on presidential war-making.[62]

To date, courts have not been willing to adjudicate challenges to purported presidential noncompliance with the War Powers Resolution. As discussed in Chapter 1, the Supreme Court has held that members of Congress generally do not have standing to challenge presidential actions, and lower courts have dismissed congressional efforts to enforce the Resolution on that basis.[63] Other courts have reasoned that the meaning of "hostilities"

---

[56] *See* War Powers Resolution, Pub. L. No. 93–148, 87 Stat. 555 (1973). For President Nixon's explanation of why he vetoed the Resolution, *see* Richard Nixon, *Veto of the War Powers Resolution*, PUBLIC PAPERS 893 (Oct. 24, 1973).
[57] War Powers Resolution, *supra* note 56, § 2(c).
[58] *See id.*, §§ 3, 4.
[59] *Id.*, § 5(b).
[60] *See id.*, § 8(a).
[61] *See* Congressional Research Service, *The War Powers Resolution: Concepts and Practice* (Mar. 8, 2019), *at* https://fas.org/sgp/crs/natsec/R42699.pdf; Richard F. Grimmett, *War Powers Resolution: Presidential Compliance* (Cong. Res. Serv., Sept. 25, 2012), *at* https://fas.org/sgp/crs/natsec/RL33532.pdf.
[62] *See, e.g.*, John Hart Ely, *Suppose Congress Wanted a War Powers Act That Worked*, 88 COLUM. L. REV. 1379 (1988); Michael J. Glennon, *Too Far Apart: Repeal the War Powers Resolution*, 50 U. MIAMI L. REV. 17 (1995).
[63] *See, e.g.*, Campbell v. Clinton, 203 F.3d 19 (D.C. Cir. 2000).

in the Resolution (which does not necessarily track the concept of "armed conflict" under international law) is a nonjusticiable political question that must be worked out by Congress and the executive branch rather than the courts.[64] Still other courts have found particular challenges under the Resolution to be either unripe or moot.[65]

In arguing that it has not violated the sixty-day cutoff provision in the War Powers Resolution, the executive branch has sometimes interpreted the Resolution narrowly. This happened, for example, in connection with the Obama administration's use of force against Libya in 2011. After the Libyan government of Colonel Muammar Qadhafi initiated a violent crackdown against protestors, the UN Security Council authorized nations to "take all necessary measures" to protect civilians there.[66] The United States, operating as part of an international coalition, subsequently launched air strikes against Libyan targets. President Obama submitted a report to Congress about the strikes, which he described as being "consistent with the War Powers Resolution," but he did not seek or obtain congressional authorization for the strikes. The Justice Department's Office of Legal Counsel issued a memorandum arguing that even if the president is constitutionally required to obtain congressional authorization before engaging in "war," the Libyan operation was sufficiently limited in nature, scope, and duration that it did not constitute a war for these purposes.[67] When the operation continued after sixty days, the State Department's Legal Adviser controversially argued that the War Powers Resolution was inapplicable. According to his argument, the United States was not engaged in "hostilities" within the meaning of the Resolution because, among other things, the operation did not involve the use of ground troops and posed little danger to U.S. armed forces.[68] The Legal Adviser did not claim, however, that the president had the legal authority to ignore the Resolution. Indeed, he made clear in an interview that the Obama administration was "not saying the War Powers Resolution is unconstitutional or should be scrapped or that we can refuse to consult Congress."[69]

---

[64] *See, e.g.*, Crockett v. Reagan, 720 F.2d 1355, 1356–57 (D.C. Cir. 1983); Kucinich v. Obama, 821 F. Supp. 2d 110 (D.D.C. 2011); Lowry v. Reagan, 676 F. Supp. 333 (D.D.C. 1987).

[65] *See, e.g.*, Smith v. Trump, 731 Fed. Appx. 8 (D.C. Cir. 2018) (mootness); Conyers v. Reagan, 765 F.2d 1124 (D.C. Cir. 1985) (mootness); Ange v. Bush, 752 F. Supp. 509 (D.D.C. 1990) (lack of ripeness).

[66] *See* S.C. Res. 1973, U.N. Doc. S/RES/1973 (Mar. 17, 2011).

[67] *See* Memorandum Opinion from Caroline D. Krass, Principal Deputy Assistant Attorney General, Office of Legal Counsel, to the Attorney General, *Authority to Use Military Force in Libya* (Apr. 1, 2011), *available at* https://fas.org/irp/agency/doj/olc/libya.pdf. For a critique of the analysis in this memorandum, *see* Michael J. Glennon, *The Cost of "Empty Words": A Comment on the Justice Department's Libya Opinion*, HARV. NAT'L SEC. J. FORUM (2011), *available at* https://harvardnsj.org/2011/04/the-cost-of-empty-words-a-comment-on-the-justice-departments-libya-opinion-2/.

[68] *See Libya and War Powers: Hearing Before S. Comm. on Foreign Relations*, 112th Cong. (June 28, 2011) (statement of Harold Hongju Koh, Legal Adviser, Dep't of State), *reprinted in* 1 J.L. (1 PUB. L. MISC.) 292 (2011). *See also* Trevor W. Morrison, *"Hostilities,"* 1 J.L. (1 PUB. L. MISC.) 233 (2011).

[69] Charlie Savage & Mark Landler, *White House Defends Continuing U.S. Role in Libya Operation*, N.Y. TIMES (June 15, 2011).

The War Powers Resolution is satisfied if Congress has already authorized the use of force, and presidents have sometimes interpreted existing authorizations broadly so that they cover what might appear to be new conflicts. This happened during both the Obama and Trump administrations with respect to uses of force against the Islamic State. These administrations claimed that such uses of force were authorized by either or both the 2001 authorization of force that Congress had enacted in the wake of the September 2001 terrorist attacks and the 2002 authorization of force that Congress had enacted with respect to Iraq in response to concerns that it was developing weapons of mass destruction. Even though these statutes had been enacted many years earlier and had been focused on different targets (Al Qaeda and the Taliban for the 2001 authorization, and the Saddam Hussein regime in Iraq for the 2002 authorization), the administrations interpreted them to confer authority to combat the Islamic State and thereby as rendering inapplicable the War Powers Resolution's sixty-day cutoff provision.[70]

Delegating War Powers

One issue that has arisen in the debates over the constitutional distribution of war authority is whether, assuming congressional authorization is normally required for nondefensive uses of force, authorization from the UN Security Council can serve as a substitute. The United States has been a party to the UN Charter since 1945. Under the Charter, the Security Council, which is composed of five permanent members and ten rotating nonpermanent members, is charged with "primary responsibility for the maintenance of international peace and security."[71] If the Security Council determines "the existence of any threat to the peace, breach of the peace, or act of aggression," and that nonmilitary measures "would be inadequate or have proved to be inadequate," it can authorize "such action by air, sea, or land forces as may be necessary to maintain or restore international peace and security."[72] As a member of the United Nations, the United States has promised in the Charter to "accept and carry out the decisions of the Security Council."[73] Because it is one of the five permanent members of the Council, however, it has a veto power and therefore is in a position to block any decisions by the Council (including authorizations of military force) with which it disagrees.

Some scholars have argued that, even if presidents are normally required to obtain congressional authorization for nondefensive uses of force, they are not required to do so when the use of force has been authorized by the Security Council.[74] These scholars

---

[70] *See* BRADLEY, DEEKS & GOLDSMITH, *supra* note 24, at 773–76.
[71] United Nations Charter, *supra* note 2, art. 24(1).
[72] *Id.*, art. 42.
[73] *Id.*, art. 25.
[74] *See, e.g.*, Thomas M. Franck & Faiza Patel, *UN Police Action in Lieu of War: "The Old Order Changeth,"* 85 AM. J. INT'L L. 63 (1991). *Cf.* David Golove, *From Versailles to San Francisco: The Revolutionary Transformation of the War Powers*, 70 U. COLO. L. REV. 1491, 1492 (1999) (arguing that the president has the authority to use

note that presidents have a constitutional duty to take care that the laws are faithfully executed, and they argue that this duty should encompass the UN Charter, since it is a treaty ratified by the United States. They also contend that, when the United States is using force pursuant to a Security Council resolution, it should not be viewed as engaged in a "war" for purposes of the Constitution.[75]

This sort of argument was made in support of the legality of the Korean War, which was authorized by the Security Council but not by Congress. Senator William Knowland, for example, contended that President Harry Truman had authorization to commit U.S. forces into combat "under the terms of our obligations to the United Nations Charter," and that this action did not require a declaration of war because it was "more in the nature of a police action."[76] More qualified statements along these lines were made in connection with the Gulf War in 1991, which was authorized by the Security Council following Iraq's invasion of Kuwait, although the first President Bush ultimately decided to obtain congressional authorization for that conflict.[77]

Critics of this argument contend that the Security Council is not functionally analogous to Congress with respect to the authorization of the use of force.[78] The Council does not represent the U.S. electorate, and, although the United States has a veto power on the Council, the U.S. representative is appointed by, and subject to the direction of, the executive branch. Moreover, in practice, Security Council resolutions at most authorize

---

force when authorized by the Security Council but that this authority "does not extend to large-scale commitments of the forces of the United States in major military actions").

[75] Earlier in the twentieth century, similar arguments were made in support of various "police actions" initiated by presidents, especially in Latin America. *See, e.g.*, Jean Galbraith, *International Law and the Domestic Separation of Powers*, 99 VA. L. REV. 987, 1019–27 (2013); David Gartner, *Foreign Relations, Strategic Doctrine, and Presidential Power*, 63 ALA. L. REV. 499 (2012). In particular, the claim was that international law is part of the "Laws" referred to in the Take Care Clause and that therefore the president has the authority to use military force to addresses breaches of that law and restore order. The claim is questionable, since even if international law is part of the laws that the president has a duty to faithfully execute, it would not necessarily follow that the president has a general law enforcement power with respect to violations of that law outside of U.S. territory. *See* LOUIS HENKIN, FOREIGN AFFAIRS AND THE CONSTITUTION 55 (1972) (describing the Take Care Clause argument as "clever but not compelling").

[76] 96 Cong. Rec. S9540 (1950).

[77] *See* FISHER, *supra* note 23, at 168–73.

[78] *See* Michael J. Glennon, *The Constitution and Chapter VII of the United Nations Charter*, 85 AM. J. INT'L L. 74, 75 (1991); Jane E. Stromseth, *Rethinking War Powers: Congress, the President, and the United Nations*, 81 GEO. L.J. 597, 639, 663–64 (1993). One of the principal concerns expressed in the Senate concerning the Treaty of Versailles, which established the League of Nations, was that it might impose an obligation on the United States to use military force when called for by the League. To address this concern, Senator Henry Cabot Lodge proposed a reservation to the treaty that would have made clear that the United States would not become involved in the use of force without specific congressional authorization, but President Woodrow Wilson and his supporters in the Senate opposed the reservation. *See* Louis Fisher, *The Korean War: On What Legal Basis Did Truman Act?*, 89 AM. J. INT'L L. 21, 22–23 (1995); Glennon, *supra* note 78, at 75–76. *Cf.* Golove, *supra* note 74, at 1494 (arguing that Wilson accepted the proposition that Congress would have to approve U.S. military operations authorized by the League of Nations).

the use of military force; they do not mandate that nations engage in military action. As a result, there is no inherent conflict between a presidential duty to take care that the laws are faithfully executed and a requirement of congressional authorization. It is also important to keep in mind that the UN Charter was approved by the Senate but not the House of Representatives, whereas the Constitution assigns the power to declare war to the full Congress.

It is noteworthy that, although the Obama administration was acting pursuant to Security Council authorization in conducting military operations against Libya in 2011, it did not claim that Council authorization was a substitute for congressional authorization. Instead, a memorandum from the Justice Department's Office of Legal Counsel reasoned that the military operations were not "sufficiently extensive in 'nature, scope, and duration' to constitute a 'war' requiring prior specific congressional approval under the Declaration of War Clause."[79] Similarly, in a report sent to Congress, the Obama administration argued that "[g]iven the important U.S. interests served by U.S. military operations in Libya and the limited nature, scope and duration of the anticipated actions, the President had constitutional authority, as Commander in Chief and Chief Executive and pursuant to his foreign affairs powers, to direct such limited military operations abroad."[80] The administration did, however, cite to the "longstanding U.S. commitment to maintaining the credibility of the United Nations Security Council and the effectiveness of its actions to promote international peace and security" as a national interest that justified the president's decision to order the use of force.[81] In other words, instead of claiming that the Security Council resolution provided a constitutional alternative to a requirement of congressional authorization, the administration simply claimed that the authorization could help justify the executive branch's use of force in a situation in which congressional authorization was not required.[82]

---

[79] Memorandum from Caroline D. Krass, *supra* note 67, at 10.

[80] *United States Activities in Libya*, at 25 (June 2011), *available at* http://www.foreignpolicy.com/files/fp_uploaded_documents/110615_United_States_Activities_in_Libya_—_6_15_11.pdf. A lawsuit brought by ten members of the House of Representatives challenging the president's constitutional authority to conduct the military campaign in Libya was dismissed for lack of standing. *See* Kucinich v. Obama, 821 F. Supp. 2d 110 (D.D.C. 2011).

[81] Memorandum from Caroline D. Krass, *supra* note 67, at 12.

[82] In 2013, President Obama contemplated using military force against Syria in response to its use of chemical weapons during its civil war, but at the last minute he changed his mind and decided to seek congressional authorization. He explained that, "while I believe I have the authority to carry out this military action without specific congressional authorization," he was "mindful that I'm the President of the world's oldest constitutional democracy" and that "our power is rooted not just in our military might, but in our example as a government of the people, by the people, and for the people." White House, *Statement by the President on Syria* (Aug. 31, 2013), *at* https://obamawhitehouse.archives.gov/the-press-office/2013/08/31/statement-president-syria. Unlike for Libya, the Security Council had not authorized the use of force against Syria. The issue of whether Congress would approve the use of force against Syria became moot in light of a diplomatic resolution of the chemical weapons issue.

Placing U.S. Troops under Foreign Command

Sometimes U.S. military operations are carried out in conjunction with other nations as part of a coalition or international structure. For example, the United States regularly participates in military operations under the auspices of the North Atlantic Treaty Organization or the United Nations. One issue that is implicated by such joint operations is whether it is constitutional to place U.S. troops under foreign command. The Constitution makes the president the Commander in Chief of the armed forces, and also gives him or her the power to appoint officers of the United States, including high-level military officials, subject to the consent of the Senate. It is unclear to what extent these assignments of authority to the president limit the president's ability to delegate command to foreign officers.

In thinking about this issue, it is useful to distinguish between four types of command authority. *Policy command* involves developing general goals that guide the conduct of the military operations. *Strategic command* involves the translation of policies into concrete military plans. *Operational command* involves organizing forces and directing their mission. *Tactical command* involves direct control over troops and their use in combat. In a number of instances in U.S. history, including during both World War I and World War II, U.S. troops have served under the operational command of foreign officers, and sometimes even under their strategic command.[83] Generally, however, the United States has not delegated either policy command or tactical command.

In 1994, after an extensive interagency review process, President Clinton issued Presidential Decision Directive 25, which sets forth guidelines for U.S. participation in multilateral peacekeeping operations.[84] Among other things, the Directive addresses the issue of U.S. soldiers serving under foreign command. According to a White House summary of the Directive, it makes clear that "[t]he President retains and will never relinquish command authority over U.S. forces," and that "[t]he chain of command from the President to the lowest U.S. commander in the field remains inviolate."[85] At the same time, it notes that "the President will consider placing appropriate U.S. forces under the operational control of a competent UN commander for specific UN operations authorized by

---

[83] *See* Michael J. Glennon & Allison R. Hayward, *Collective Security and the Constitution: Can the Commander in Chief Power Be Delegated to the United Nations?*, 82 Geo. L.J. 1573 (1994); David Kaye, *Are There Limits to Military Alliance? Presidential Power to Place American Troops under Non-American Commanders*, 5 Transnat'l L. & Contemp. Probs. 399 (1995); Edward F. Bruner & Nina M. Serafino, *Peacekeeping: Military Command and Control Issues* (Cong. Res. Serv., Nov. 1, 2001), *available at* http://congressionalresearch.com/RL31120/document.php?study=Peacekeeping+Military+Command+and+Control+Issues.

[84] *See* Dep't of State, Bureau of Int'l Org. Affairs, Pub. No. 10161, *The Clinton Administration's Policy on Reforming Multilateral Peace Operations*, reprinted at 33 I.L.M. 795 (1994).

[85] *Id.* at 817.

the Security Council."[86] Even in these situations, however, the United States would retain certain "fundamental elements of the U.S. chain of command":

> U.S. commanders will maintain the capability to report separately to higher U.S. military authorities, as well as the UN commander. Commanders of U.S. military units participating in UN operations will refer to higher U.S. authorities orders that are illegal under U.S. or international law, or are outside the mandate of the mission to which the U.S. agreed with the UN, if they are unable to resolve the matter with the UN commander in the field. The United States reserves the right to terminate participation at any time and to take whatever actions it deems necessary to protect U.S. forces if they are endangered.[87]

In the 1990s, the Clinton administration delegated even tactical command to foreign officers in some multilateral operations.

At least one scholar has argued that such delegations are unconstitutional.[88] A delegation of tactical command, according to this argument, is inconsistent with the Appointments Clause, the unitary nature of the executive branch, and the nondelegation doctrine because it "allow[s] the President or the treatymakers to transfer executive power to individuals independent of presidential control."[89] "If the President delegates command authority over American troops entirely outside of the federal government," the argument runs, "neither Congress nor the public can determine whether foreign or international commanders are exercising their authority according to American standards, nor can they enforce their policy wishes through the usual legal or political methods available when power is delegated within the executive branch."[90]

These concerns seem overstated. As Commander in Chief, the president presumably needs discretion to determine how best to carry out military operations, and in a joint operation sometimes the best course of action may involve delegating responsibility to allies. As long as the president has the ability to decide whether to commit the troops to the operation, and has the ability to terminate the commitment, the commander-in-chief role would seem to remain intact. Moreover, the distinction between operational command and tactical command is somewhat artificial, since all forms of command can be consequential in terms of the risks to U.S. soldiers and the success of the mission. As for accountability, it is unlikely that a presidential allowance of foreign tactical command for

---

[86] *Id.*
[87] *Id.* The Directive has been declassified and is now publicly available. *See* Presidential Decision Directive/NSC-25, *at* http://fas.org/irp/offdocs/pdd/pdd-25.pdf.
[88] *See* John C. Yoo, *Kosovo, War Powers, and the Multilateral Future*, 148 U. PA. L. REV. 1673 (2000); *see also* John C. Yoo, *UN Wars, US War Powers*, 1 CHI. J. INT'L L. 355 (2000).
[89] Yoo, *Kosovo, War Powers, and the Multilateral Future, supra* note 88, at 1714.
[90] *Id.* at 1717.

an operation will eliminate or even reduce presidential accountability for what happens to the U.S. forces. Rather, if the mission does not go well, the president will almost certainly be held responsible for delegating authority to the foreign commander.[91]

Military Detentions in the "War on Terrorism"

On September 11, 2001, nineteen members of the Al Qaeda terrorist network hijacked four commercial airplanes in the United States. The hijackers crashed two of the planes into the World Trade Center in New York and a third into the Pentagon near Washington, D.C. The fourth plane crashed in Pennsylvania after a struggle between the passengers and the hijackers. Thousands of people were killed in the attacks, and they caused billions of dollars in property and economic damage.[92]

A week after the attacks, Congress enacted an Authorization for Use of Military Force (AUMF) that broadly authorized the president to:

> use all necessary and appropriate force against those nations, organizations, or persons he determines planned, authorized, committed, or aided the terrorist attacks that occurred on September 11, 2001, or harbored such organizations or persons, in order to prevent any future acts of international terrorism against the United States by such nations, organizations or persons.[93]

---

[91] At times during the Clinton administration, Congress sought to preclude the placement of U.S. troops under foreign command. In response, the Clinton administration repeatedly insisted that Congress lacked the authority to place such a limitation on the president's discretion as Commander in Chief. In 1996, Congress considered legislation that would prohibit the expenditure of any funds for U.S. armed forces that served under UN operational or tactical command. Commenting on this proposed legislation, the Justice Department's Office of Legal Counsel argued that "[i]t is for the President alone, as Commander-in-Chief, to make the choice of the particular personnel who are to exercise operational and tactical command functions over the U.S. Armed Forces." *See* Memorandum from Walter Dellinger, Assistant Attorney General, to Alan J. Kreczko, Special Assistant to the President and Legal Adviser to the National Security Council, *Placing of United States Armed Forces under Nations Operational or Tactical Control* (May 8, 1996), *available at* https://www.justice.gov/file/20051/download. In other instances during the 1990s in which Congress included restrictions in legislation concerning the placement of U.S. troops under foreign command, President Clinton issued signing statements raising constitutional objections. *See* William J. Clinton, *Statement on Signing the Departments of Commerce, Justice, and State, the Judiciary, and Related Agencies Appropriations Act, 1998*, 2 PUB. PAPERS 1666, 1667 (Nov. 26, 1997); William J. Clinton, *Statement on Signing the Omnibus Consolidated and Emergency Supplemental Appropriations Act, 1999*, 2 PUB. PAPERS 1843, 1847 (Oct. 26, 1998). Shortly after taking office, President Obama issued a similar signing statement. *See* Presidential Statement on Signing H.R. 1105, The Omnibus Appropriations Act, 2009, 1 PUB. PAPERS 216 (Mar. 11, 2009).

[92] For a more detailed description of the attacks, *see* THE 9/11 COMMISSION REPORT: FINAL REPORT OF THE NATIONAL COMMISSION ON TERRORIST ATTACKS UPON THE UNITED STATES (2004).

[93] Authorization for Use of Military Force, Pub. L. No. 107-40, § 2(a), 115 Stat. 224, 224 (2001).

Relying on the AUMF, as well as his authority as Commander in Chief,[94] President George W. Bush responded to the September 11 attacks by, among things, initiating combat operations in Afghanistan, where Al Qaeda had training camps and where its leader, Osama bin Laden, was located.[95] The combat operations were directed against both Al Qaeda as well as the military forces of the Taliban government that ruled much of Afghanistan at the time and had been harboring Al Qaeda. As part of these operations, the United States acquired custody of numerous individuals allegedly connected to Al Qaeda and the Taliban. The United States also obtained custody of alleged members of Al Qaeda apprehended in other locations around the world. Starting in 2002, the United States began housing some of the detainees at the U.S. naval base in Guantanamo Bay, Cuba. As discussed in Chapter 6, the United States has occupied the base since the end of the Spanish-American War and, pursuant to agreements with Cuba, has exclusive jurisdiction and control over the base and the right to remain there indefinitely. Certain high-level Al Qaeda members were initially held by the CIA in secret locations but were eventually moved to Guantanamo.[96]

During the Bush administration, approximately eight hundred detainees were brought to the detention facility at Guantanamo, and the administration eventually released or transferred approximately five hundred of them. Shortly after taking office, President Obama announced an intent to close the Guantanamo detention facility, but, in part because of congressional opposition, this did not happen.[97] President Obama did manage, however, to substantially reduce the number of detainees there by transferring them to other countries. His successor, President Trump, was more supportive of keeping the detention facility open, although he did not move any additional detainees there. When this edition was going to press, there were forty detainees still being held at Guantanamo.[98]

---

[94] Shortly after the September 11 attacks, the Justice Department's Office of Legal Counsel issued a memorandum concluding that the president had the constitutional authority to retaliate not only "against any person, organization, or State suspected of involvement in terrorist attacks on the United States, but also against foreign States suspected of harboring or supporting such organizations," and also the authority to "deploy military force preemptively against terrorist organizations or the States that harbor or support them, whether or not they can be linked to the specific terrorist incidents of September 11." Memorandum from John C. Yoo, Deputy Assistant Attorney General, to the Deputy Counsel to the President, *The President's Constitutional Authority to Conduct Military Operations against Terrorists and Nations Supporting Them* (Sept. 25, 2001), *available at* https://www.justice.gov/file/19151/download.

[95] For an argument that "the laws of war applicable in non-international armed conflict govern the September 11 attacks and that the attacks violated these laws," *see* Derek Jinks, *September 11 and the Laws of War*, 28 YALE J. INT'L L. 1, 9 (2003).

[96] *See, e.g.*, Sheryl Gay Stolberg, *President Moves 14 Held in Secret to Guantanamo*, N.Y. TIMES (Sept. 6, 2006).

[97] *See, e.g.*, Curtis A. Bradley & Jack L. Goldsmith, *Obama's AUMF Legacy*, 110 AM. J. INT'L L. 628 (2016); Aziz Z. Huq, *The President and the Detainees*, 165 U. PA. L. REV. 499 (2017).

[98] *See The Guantanamo Docket*, N.Y. TIMES, *at* https://www.nytimes.com/interactive/projects/guantanamo/detainees/current.

Third Geneva Convention

There was substantial debate within the Bush administration about whether the Geneva Convention Relative to the Treatment of Prisoners of War, also known as the Third Geneva Convention, applied to these detentions. The Convention mandates a variety of protections for "prisoners of war," which it defines in Article 4(A) as including:

(1) Members of the armed forces of a Party to the conflict, as well as members of militias or volunteer corps forming part of such armed forces.
(2) Members of other militias and members of other volunteer corps, including those of organized resistance movements, belonging to a Party to the conflict and operating in or outside their own territory, even if this territory is occupied, provided that such militias or volunteer corps, including such organized resistance movements, fulfil the following conditions:
   (a) that of being commanded by a person responsible for his subordinates;
   (b) that of having a fixed distinctive sign recognizable at a distance;
   (c) that of carrying arms openly;
   (d) that of conducting their operations in accordance with the laws and customs of war.
(3) Members of regular armed forces who profess allegiance to a government or an authority not recognized by the Detaining Power.

Article 5 of the Convention further provides that "[s]hould any doubt arise as to whether persons, having committed a belligerent act and having fallen into the hands of the enemy, belong to any of the categories enumerated in Article 4, such persons shall enjoy the protection of the present Convention until such time as their status has been determined by a competent tribunal."

The Office of Legal Counsel in the Justice Department argued that the Convention did not apply to either Al Qaeda or Taliban detainees. It reasoned that Al Qaeda is neither a nation nor a party to the Convention. It further reasoned that, although Afghanistan is a party to the Convention, Taliban fighters were required to comply with the conditions in Article 4(A)(2) and had not done so.[99] In addition, the Office of Legal Counsel contended that Afghanistan was a "failed state" incapable of fulfilling its

---

[99] *See* Memorandum from Jay S. Bybee, Assistant Attorney General, to Alberto Gonzales, Counsel to the President, and William J. Haynes II, General Counsel of the Department of Defense, *Application of Treaties and Laws to al Qaeda and Taliban Detainees* (Jan. 22, 2002), *available at* https://www.justice.gov/sites/default/files/olc/legacy/2009/08/24/memo-laws-taliban-detainees.pdf; Memorandum from Jay S. Bybee, Assistant Attorney General, to Alberto R. Gonzales, Counsel to the President, *Status of Taliban Forces under Article 4 of the Third Geneva Convention of 1949* (Feb. 7, 2002), *available at* https://fas.org/irp/agency/doj/olc/taliban.pdf.

international obligations, and that the United States therefore had the right to suspend the application of the Conventions to that country. The Legal Adviser's Office of the Department of State, by contrast, took the position that the Third Geneva Convention applied to the conflict in Afghanistan as a whole, although not to the worldwide conflict with Al Qaeda; rejected the "failed states" theory; and argued that the Taliban fighters were entitled to individualized determinations of whether they qualified as prisoners of war.[100] Ultimately, President Bush concluded that the Third Geneva Convention was inapplicable to the conflict with Al Qaeda, even in Afghanistan, and that, although the United States would apply the Convention to the conflict with the Taliban, the Taliban detainees did not qualify for prisoner-of-war status under the Convention.[101] President Bush also concluded that Common Article 3 of the Geneva Conventions—a provision that mandates certain minimum protections for individuals in "an armed conflict not of an international character"—was inapplicable to either Al Qaeda or Taliban detainees because the relevant conflicts were international in scope.

These conclusions regarding the Geneva Conventions were highly controversial. In the view of this author, the president's conclusion that the Third Geneva Convention did not apply to Al Qaeda, even in Afghanistan, was a reasonable legal interpretation. Common Article 2 of the Geneva Conventions provides that the Conventions "shall apply to . . . any . . . armed conflict which may arise between two or more of the High Contracting Parties." Al Qaeda is not a state, much less a high contracting party to the Geneva Conventions.[102] Common Article 2 also applies the Geneva Conventions to a

---

[100] *See, e.g.*, Memorandum from William H. Taft, IV, State Department Legal Adviser, to John C. Yoo, Deputy Assistant Attorney General, Office of Legal Counsel, Department of Justice, *Your Draft Memorandum of January 9* (Jan. 11, 2002), *available at* https://nsarchive2.gwu.edu/torturingdemocracy/documents/20020111.pdf; Memorandum from William H. Taft, IV, *Comments on Your Paper on the Geneva Convention* (Feb. 2, 2002), *reprinted in* 37 Case W. Res. J. Int'l L. 615 (2006).

[101] Memorandum from President George W. Bush to Vice President Dick Cheney et al., *Humane Treatment of al Qaeda and Taliban Detainees* (Feb. 7, 2002), *available at* http://www.pegc.us/archive/White_House/bush_memo_20020207_ed.pdf. For additional discussion of the debates within the Bush administration over these and other issues relating to the war on terrorism, *see* Harold H. Bruff, Bad Advice: Bush's Lawyers in the War on Terror (2009); Jack L. Goldsmith, The Terror Presidency: Law and Judgment Inside the Bush Administration (2007); and John Yoo, War by Other Means: An Insider's Account of the War on Terror (2006). For more general discussions of U.S. policy in the war on terrorism, *see* Peter L. Bergen, The Longest War: The Enduring Conflict Between America and Al-Qaeda (2011); Jane Mayer, The Dark Side: The Inside Story of How the War on Terror Turned into a War on American Ideals (2009); Bob Woodward, Bush at War (2002). For background on some of the events leading up to the September 11 attacks, *see* Daniel Benjamin & Steven Simon, The Age of Sacred Terror: Radical Islam's War against America (2002); Steve Coll, Ghost Wars: The Secret History of the CIA, Afghanistan, and bin Laden, from the Soviet Invasion to September 10, 2001 (2004); and Lawrence Wright, The Looming Tower: Al Qaeda and the Road to 9/11 (2006).

[102] *See also* John B. Bellinger III & Vijay M. Padmanabhan, *Detention Operations in Contemporary Conflicts: Four Challenges for the Geneva Conventions and Other Existing Law*, 105 Am. J. Int'l L. 201, 205 (2011) ("Common Article 2 of the Geneva Conventions, which is the jurisdictional provision for the bulk of the Conventions'

nonparty Power that "accepts and applies the provisions thereof," but even if Al Qaeda is a "Power" within the meaning of Common Article 2 (which it probably is not), it does not accept and apply the Conventions. Nor does it matter, for purposes of Common Article 2, that Al Qaeda may have been fighting in conjunction with the Afghan Taliban forces. Common Article 2 states that "although one of the Powers in conflict may not be a party to the present Convention, the Powers who are parties thereto shall remain bound by it *in their mutual relations*." This provision makes clear that even when two nations fight together against a third nation in a traditional armed conflict, the third nation is bound by the Geneva Conventions only vis-à-vis the enemy that is a party to the Geneva Conventions, not with respect to the enemy that is not a party to the Conventions. At a minimum, the same rule should apply when the nonparty armed forces are members of a terrorist organization.[103]

President Bush's decision to deny prisoner-of-war status to the Taliban fighters is more debatable. On the one hand, the Taliban fighters were the operative military forces of the ruling Afghan government at that time, and the language of Article 4(A)(1) and Article 4(A)(3) seems to suggest that a nation's regular armed forces automatically qualify for prisoner-of-war protection.[104] On the other hand, law of war treaties that predate the Geneva Conventions, and which the Conventions built upon, provide support for the conclusion that the Conventions' reference to the regular armed forces of a party implicitly encompasses the requirements set forth in Article 4(A)(2).[105] In addition to having some historical support, this reading would provide an incentive for regular forces to follow these requirements and thus, for example, adequately distinguish themselves from civilians, which is a fundamental component of the laws of war.[106] Although Article 5 of

---

protections, limits application of the Conventions to conflicts between high contracting parties, which are limited to states. Thus, the Geneva Conventions generally provide regulations governing armed conflicts between nation-states.").

[103] *See also* George H. Aldrich, Comment, *The Taliban, Al Qaeda, and the Determination of Illegal Combatants*, 96 AM. J. INT'L L. 891, 893 (2002) (concluding that "the decision to consider that two separate armed conflicts are being waged is correct").

[104] *See id.* at 895 ("Whether the four conditions applicable under Article 4A(2) to members of militias and other volunteer corps that are not part of the armed forces of a state are also inherent requirements of any of a state's armed forces is a debatable question.").

[105] *See, e.g.*, MICHAEL BOTHE ET AL., NEW RULES FOR VICTIMS OF ARMED CONFLICTS: COMMENTARY ON THE TWO 1977 PROTOCOLS ADDITIONAL TO THE GENEVA CONVENTIONS OF 1949, at 234–35 (1982) ("It is generally assumed that these conditions were deemed, by the 1874 Brussels Conference and the 1899 and 1907 Hague Peace Conferences, to be inherent in the regular armed forces of States. Accordingly, it was considered to be unnecessary and redundant to spell them out in the [Geneva] Conventions."); INGRID DETTER, THE LAW OF WAR (3d ed. 2013) (expressing a similar view); United States v. Lindh, 212 F. Supp. 2d 541, 557 n.34 (E.D. Va. 2002) (same).

[106] *See also* Sean D. Murphy, *Evolving Geneva Convention Paradigms in the "War on Terrorism": Applying the Core Rules to the Release of Persons Deemed "Unprivileged Combatants,"* 75 GEO. WASH. L. REV. 1105, 1125 (2007) ("Although it is clear that Geneva Convention III article 4(A)(3) does not expressly apply the four criteria to 'regular armed forces,' the real question is what is meant by that phrase. Presumably it is not enough that a government merely declare that certain persons are a part of its regular armed forces. If that were the case, then

the Convention mandates status hearings when there is doubt about whether a particular detainee qualifies as a prisoner of war, if the Taliban fighters failed to qualify as a class for this status (as President Bush concluded), then it is not clear that there would be such doubt (although there might be doubt about whether a particular detainee was a member of the Taliban). In any event, concluding that the Bush administration's decision to deny prisoner-of-war protections and status hearings was legally defensible does not mean that it was wise policy, and there is no question that the decision made it more difficult for the United States to persuade other nations of the legitimacy of its detention policy.[107]

Even if the president had concluded that the Third Geneva Convention applied to some or all of the Guantanamo detainees, this would not by itself have precluded the United States from detaining them, since the Convention specifically contemplates military detention. But application of the Convention would have potentially been inconsistent with other aspects of U.S. policy at the time. As will be discussed, the executive branch was reserving the right to try some of the detainees in military commissions for having committed war crimes, and it wanted to have some flexibility in the procedures that would be used in such commissions (such as with respect to the admission of evidence). Article 102 of the Third Geneva Convention, however, states that a prisoner of war can be validly sentenced "only if the sentence has been pronounced by the same courts according to the same procedure as in the case of members of the armed forces of the Detaining Power." In addition, it was evident after September 11 that the acquisition of information was especially vital in combating a clandestine organization such as Al Qaeda, and the executive branch therefore wanted flexibility in interrogating the detainees. Article 17 of the Third Geneva Convention states, however, that prisoners of war are required to give only their name, rank, and a few other pieces of information, and that they may not be subjected to coercive interrogation. Common Article 3 of the Geneva Conventions contains much less stringent restrictions, but there was still potential conflict between the U.S. interrogation and military commission policies and Common Article 3's prohibitions against "cruel treatment and torture" and "the passing

---

any government could designate any persons—whether militias, mercenaries, volunteers, guerrillas, brigands, or pirates—that are willing to attack its enemy as part of its 'regular armed forces,' thereby extending to them a status that the laws of war clearly do not contemplate.").

[107] See Curtis A. Bradley, *The Bush Administration and International Law: Too Much Lawyering and Too Little Diplomacy*, 4 DUKE J. CONST. L. & PUB. POL'Y 57, 64 (2009). *See also* Philip Zelikow, *Legal Policy for a Twilight War*, 30 HOUS. J. INT'L L. 89, 92 (2007) (arguing that the Bush administration, prior to 2006, focused too much on what it *could* do under international law in the war on terrorism and not enough on what it *should* do). Some commentators have argued that if the Al Qaeda or Taliban fighters do not qualify for prisoner-of-war status under the Third Geneva Convention, they must be considered civilians subject to the protections of the Fourth Geneva Convention. *See, e.g.*, ANTONIO CASSESE, INTERNATIONAL LAW 409–10 (2d ed. 2005); Knut Dormann, *The Legal Situation of "Unlawful/Unprivileged Combatants,"* 85 INT'L REV. RED CROSS 45 (2003); Ryan Goodman, Comment, *The Detention of Civilians in Armed Conflict*, 103 AM. J. INT'L L. 48 (2009). For a critique of this claim, *see* Bellinger & Padmanabhan, *supra* note 102, at 216–17; Curtis A. Bradley, *The United States, Israel, and Unlawful Combatants*, 12 GREEN BAG 2D 397 (2009).

of sentences and the carrying out of executions without previous judgment pronounced by a regularly constituted court, affording all the judicial guarantees which are recognized as indispensable by civilized peoples."

Judicial Review of the Detentions

In a 2004 decision, *Hamdi v. Rumsfeld*, the Supreme Court considered the U.S. military's detention authority relating to the conflict in Afghanistan.[108] In that case, Yaser Hamdi, a dual U.S.-Saudi national, had been apprehended in Afghanistan during the fighting there and was eventually moved by the U.S. military to a naval brig in the United States. The military maintained that Hamdi had been serving with the Taliban forces and that he therefore qualified as an "enemy combatant" subject to military detention.

There was no majority opinion in *Hamdi*, but a four-justice plurality opinion written by Justice O'Connor, as well as Justice Thomas in dissent, concluded that the government had the authority to detain Hamdi, assuming that the facts were as the government alleged. For purposes of its analysis, the plurality addressed only the military's authority to detain individuals who are "part of or supporting forces hostile to the United States or coalition partners in Afghanistan and who engaged in an armed conflict against the United States there."[109]

The plurality reasoned that the AUMF, in giving the president the authority to use "all necessary and appropriate force" against the Taliban, implicitly gave him the authority to detain Taliban forces in military custody. In reaching this conclusion, the plurality noted that it is a "fundamental incident of waging war" to detain enemy forces.[110] In describing these incidents of war, the plurality referred both to U.S. historical practice and to international law.[111] The Court further observed that detention serves the important functional purpose of preventing captured individuals from returning to the battlefield.[112] In addressing Hamdi's concern that detention in the "war on terror" could potentially be indefinite, the plurality observed that the international laws of war allow for detention only until the end of active hostilities, and it stated that it understood the AUMF's implicit grant of detention authority as lasting only "for the duration of the relevant conflict."[113] This detention authority, the plurality further reasoned, extends even to U.S. citizens. "A citizen, no less than an alien," said the plurality, can be part of hostile

---

[108] 542 U.S. 507 (2004) (plurality opinion).
[109] *Id.* at 516.
[110] *Id.* at 519.
[111] *See id.* at 518–19.
[112] *Id.* at 518.
[113] *Id.* at 521.

forces and "such a citizen, if released, would pose the same threat of returning to the front during the ongoing conflict."[114]

Despite upholding the military's authority to detain in this situation, the plurality also held that the Constitution's Due Process Clause requires that "a citizen-detainee seeking to challenge his classification as an enemy combatant must receive notice of the factual basis for his classification, and a fair opportunity to rebut the Government's factual assertions before a neutral decisionmaker."[115] It noted, however, that the proceedings could be tailored to alleviate the potential burden on the executive of having to defend its decisions during an ongoing military conflict. In particular, the plurality suggested that it may be proper to allow the introduction of hearsay evidence and to apply a rebuttable presumption in favor of the government's evidence.[116]

Justices Souter and Ginsburg disagreed with the plurality that the AUMF gave the president the authority to detain Hamdi. Although acknowledging that international law allowed for the detention of enemy forces until the end of hostilities, they argued that the military could not invoke international law in support of its detention of Taliban forces because it had not shown that it was complying with international law in carrying out the detentions. In particular, Justices Souter and Ginsburg expressed the view that the military was violating Article 5 of the Third Geneva Convention by failing to hold hearings to determine if Taliban detainees qualified as prisoners of war. Nevertheless, in order to produce a definitive decision, they concurred in the plurality's due process holding.[117]

Although the due process analysis in *Hamdi* was focused on the detention of a U.S. citizen, the U.S. military subsequently adopted a process for the Guantanamo detainees (all of whom have been foreign citizens) that arguably complied with those requirements. In July 2004, the military created Combatant Status Review Tribunals (CSRTs) to ensure that each detainee qualified as an enemy combatant subject to detention.[118] Under the CSRT process, the detainees at Guantanamo were each given notice of the factual basis

---

[114] *Id.* at 519. The plurality reached this conclusion despite the existence of a federal statute, 18 U.S.C. § 4001(a), that provides that "[n]o citizen shall be imprisoned or otherwise detained by the United States except pursuant to an Act of Congress." Pub. L. No. 92–128, 85 Stat. 347 (1971), *codified at* 18 U.S.C. § 4001(a). The plurality did not decide whether this statute applies to military detentions. Even if it does, the plurality reasoned, the AUMF is a sufficient "Act of Congress" to satisfy its terms.

[115] 542 U.S. at 533.

[116] *See id.* at 533–34.

[117] The U.S. government subsequently decided to release Yaser Hamdi and allow him to return to his family in Saudi Arabia, so the hearing mandated by the Supreme Court never took place. *See* Joel Brinkley & Eric Lichtblau, *U.S. Releases Saudi-American It Had Captured in Afghanistan*, N.Y. TIMES (Oct. 12, 2004).

[118] *See* Memorandum from the Deputy Secretary of Defense to the Secretary of the Navy, *Order Establishing Combatant Status Review Tribunal* (July 7, 2004) (emphasis added), *available at* http://www.defenselink.mil/news/Jul2004/d20040707review.pdf; Memorandum from the Deputy Secretary of Defense to the Secretaries of the Military Departments et al., *Implementation of Combatant Status Review Tribunal Procedures for Enemy Combatants Detained at U.S. Naval Base Guantanamo Bay, Cuba* (July 14, 2006), *available at* http://www.defenselink.mil/news/Aug2006/d20060809CSRTProcedures.pdf.

for their detention and an opportunity, with the assistance of a "personal representative" (a military officer who did not act as a lawyer or advocate), to challenge their designation as an enemy combatant. The challenges were heard by panels of three commissioned military officers not involved in the detainees' apprehension, detention, interrogation, or screening. The detainees had the right to call witnesses if reasonably available, question other witnesses, testify, and introduce relevant documentary evidence. Subsequently, in the *Boumediene v. Bush* decision discussed in Chapter 6, the Supreme Court concluded that the CSRT process was not an adequate alternative to habeas corpus review by the federal courts of the legality of the detentions at Guantanamo.

Scope of Detention Authority

The *Hamdi* decision addressed only the detention of individuals captured during the fighting in Afghanistan and did not address the scope of the U.S. military's detention authority with respect to the broader conflict against the Al Qaeda terrorist organization. In 2006, Congress purported to disallow the federal courts from exercising habeas corpus jurisdiction over non-U.S. citizens determined to be enemy combatants in the war on terrorism, while allowing review in the D.C. Circuit of the rulings of the CSRTs. In *Boumediene,* the Supreme Court held that this restriction on habeas corpus review was unconstitutional as applied to Guantanamo. Since that decision, the federal courts in Washington, D.C., have heard a variety of habeas corpus challenges by the Guantanamo detainees and issued a number of important decisions concerning both the scope of the military's detention authority there and the procedures to be used in adjudicating the legality of the detentions.

The courts accepted the executive branch's argument, made first by the Bush administration and then by the Obama administration, that the detention authority conferred by the AUMF extended not only to Taliban fighters, but also to members of Al Qaeda and affiliated groups.[119] One of the key substantive issues in this litigation has been how to determine whether someone is sufficiently affiliated with a covered organization. The courts have applied a case-specific and functional approach to that issue. In applying such an approach, the D.C. Circuit has explained with respect to Al Qaeda:

> That an individual operates within al Qaeda's formal command structure is surely sufficient but is not necessary to show he is "part of" the organization; there may be other indicia that a particular individual is sufficiently involved with the organization to be deemed part of it, ... but the purely independent conduct of a freelancer is not enough.[120]

---

[119] *See, e.g.,* Khan v. Obama, 655 F.3d 20, 23 (D.C. Cir. 2011); Al Odah v. United States, 611 F.3d 8, 10 (D.C. Cir. 2010); Awad v. Obama, 608 F.3d 1, 11–12 (D.C. Cir. 2010).
[120] Bensayah v. Obama, 610 F.3d 718, 725 (D.C. Cir. 2010).

When upholding detention, the courts often cite facts such as the individual having trained in an Al Qaeda training camp or having stayed in an Al Qaeda or Taliban affiliated guesthouse. They also consider facts such as location of capture, routes of travel, and association with known Al Qaeda members. Of course, the detainee's own statements are often probative as well, as is evidence that the detainee carried out commands from Al Qaeda or Taliban leadership. The decisions are highly factual and are often redacted when released to the public in order to shield confidential government information.[121]

Another issue that has arisen in the habeas corpus litigation from Guantanamo is the proper length of detention. As the plurality noted in *Hamdi*, international law contemplates that enemy combatants can be held until the end of active hostilities. That concept may work reasonably well for Taliban fighters apprehended during the conflict in Afghanistan, since active hostilities between the United States and the Taliban will presumably cease at some point in the foreseeable future.[122] In *Hamdi*, for example, the plurality explained that "[i]f the record establishes that United States troops are still involved in active combat in Afghanistan, those detentions [of Taliban fighters] are part of the exercise of 'necessary and appropriate force,' and therefore are authorized by the AUMF."[123] But it is less clear how this "end of hostilities" concept should work with respect to the broader conflict with the Al Qaeda terrorist organization and its affiliate organizations. The plurality in *Hamdi* acknowledged this issue, noting that "[i]f the practical circumstances of a given conflict are entirely unlike those of the conflicts that informed the development of the law of war, that understanding [of the authority to detain until the end of hostilities] may unravel."[124] It further observed that "indefinite detention for the purpose of interrogation is not authorized."[125]

In 2004, the Bush administration created Administrative Review Boards at Guantanamo, which made yearly assessments of whether each detainee should continue to be held, based on an assessment of whether the detainee remained a threat and other considerations.[126] Through that process and other mechanisms, hundreds of detainees were repatriated or released from Guantanamo. In 2011, the Obama administration

---

[121] For a description of the decisions in this area, *see* Benjamin Wittes, Robert M. Chesney, Larkin Reynolds, and Harvard Law Sch. Nat'l Sec. Research Comm., *The Emerging Law of Detention 2.0: The Guantanamo Habeas Cases as Lawmaking* (May 12, 2011), *available at* http://www.brookings.edu/research/reports/2011/05/guantanamo-wittes. *See also* Robert M. Chesney, *Who May Be Held?: Military Detention through the Habeas Lens*, 52 B.C. L. Rev. 769 (2011).

[122] In early 2020, the United States signed an agreement with the Taliban establishing a timetable for a potential withdrawal of U.S. troops from Afghanistan. *See* Mujib Mashal, *Taliban and U.S. Strike Deal to Withdraw American Troops from Afghanistan*, N.Y. Times (Feb. 29, 2020).

[123] 542 U.S. at 521 (plurality opinion).

[124] *Id.*

[125] *Id.*

[126] *See* U.S. Dep't of Def., Order, *Administrative Review Procedures for Enemy Combatants in the Control of the Department of Defense at Guantanamo Bay Naval Base, Cuba* (May 11, 2004), *available at* http://www.defenselink.mil/news/May2004/d20040518gtmoreview.pdf.

established Periodic Review Boards that similarly consider, for each detainee, whether continued detention is "necessary to protect against a significant threat to the security of the United States."[127] To date, the federal courts in D.C. have shown little inclination to regulate the length of detention, instead viewing this as a decision to be made by the political branches of the government. In a 2018 decision, the U.S. Court of Appeals for the D.C. Circuit reaffirmed that the authority to detain under the AUMF was still in effect, noting that "[t]he Executive Branch represents that armed hostilities between United States forces and [the Taliban and Al Qaeda] persist" and that "[t]he record confirms the Executive Branch's representations."[128]

International Law and the AUMF

There has been a dispute among the judges on the U.S. Court of Appeals for the D.C. Circuit over the relevance of international law when interpreting the scope of the detention authority in the AUMF. In a 2010 decision, *Al-Bihani v. Obama*, two of the three judges on the panel reasoned that international law does not limit the executive branch's detention authority under the AUMF.[129] In that case, the issue was whether a paramilitary group in Afghanistan qualified as "associated forces" with the Taliban for purposes of the AUMF. The petitioner there, who had served as a cook in the group, argued that the court should look to the international law principles of "co-belligerency," pursuant to which, he argued, the group should not have been considered an enemy of the United States. In rejecting this argument, the court observed that "[t]here is no indication ... that Congress intended the international laws of war to act as extra-textual limiting principles for the President's war powers under the AUMF."[130] One of the judges on the panel concurred in the denial of relief, but disagreed with the majority's view about the irrelevance of international law, noting that this view "appears hard to square with the approach that the Supreme Court took in *Hamdi*," and that the Obama administration had itself acknowledged the relevance of international law to the interpretation of the AUMF.[131] In declining to grant en banc review of this decision, the full court of

---

[127] *See* Executive Order 13,567, *Periodic Review of Individuals Detained at Guantánamo Bay Naval Station Pursuant to the Authorization for Use of Military Force* § 2 (Mar. 7, 2011), *available at* http://www.whitehouse.gov/the-press-office/2011/03/07/executive-order-periodic-review-individuals-detained-guant-namo-bay-nava. For a decision according substantial weight to the determinations of a Periodic Review Board that a detainee should continue to be held at Guantanamo, see Ali v. Trump, 959 F.3d 364 (D.C. Cir. 2020).

[128] Al-Alwi v. Trump, 901F.3d 294, 299 (D.C. Cir. 2018); *see also* Al-Bihani v. Obama, 590 F.3d 866, 874 (D.C. Cir. 2010) ("The determination of when hostilities have ceased is a political decision, and we defer to the Executive's opinion on the matter, at least in the absence of an authoritative congressional declaration purporting to terminate the war.").

[129] *Al-Bihani*, 590 F.3d at 874.

[130] *Id.* at 871.

[131] *Id.* at 885 (Williams, J., concurring). *See also* Harold Hongju Koh, Legal Adviser, U.S. Department of State, Address at the Annual Meeting of the American Society of International Law: The Obama Administration and

appeals described the decision's reasoning concerning the relevance of international law as "not necessary to the disposition of the merits."[132] That issue was therefore ultimately left unsettled.[133]

In the view of this author, there are good reasons to conclude that international law is relevant in construing the scope of what Congress authorized in the AUMF. The AUMF authorizes a type of conduct—the use of military force—that has long been regulated by international law. The statute also leaves unspecified many of the rules and standards that would govern this use of force. Just as courts consult historical practice, dictionaries, and other background materials to determine what Congress intended, it makes sense—for construing a statute such as the AUMF—to consult the international law backdrop against which Congress legislated. This is particularly true for international law that is reflected in treaties that the United States has ratified and that were in place prior to the enactment of the AUMF, such as the Geneva Conventions. As noted earlier in this chapter, the plurality in *Hamdi* appeared to view international law as relevant when it construed the AUMF to include an authorization of detention until the end of hostilities. If international law is relevant in determining what authority Congress has granted, then logically it should also be relevant in determining what authority Congress has not

---

International Law (Mar. 25, 2010) ("[T]his Administration has expressly acknowledged that international law informs the scope of our detention authority. Both in our internal decisions about specific Guantanamo detainees, and before the courts in habeas cases, we have interpreted the scope of detention authority authorized by Congress in the AUMF *as informed by the laws of war*."), *available at* https://2009-2017.state.gov/s/l/releases/remarks/139119.htm.

[132] 619 F.3d 1, 1 (D.C. Cir. 2010). Each of the three judges from the original panel decision filed an opinion concurring in the denial of rehearing en banc. Judge Brown reiterated her view that "[t]here is no indication that the AUMF placed any international legal limits on the President's discretion to prosecute the war and, in light of the challenge our nation faced after September 11, 2001, that makes eminent sense." *Id.* at 8. Judge Kavanaugh explained at length why, in his view, "[i]nternational-law norms that have not been incorporated into domestic U.S. law by the political branches are not judicially enforceable limits on the President's authority under the AUMF." *Id.* at 9. Judge Williams expressed the view, by contrast, that international law was relevant in interpreting the AUMF. *See id.* at 53–56.

[133] For another case in which international law was potentially relevant to the scope of the detention authority under the AUMF, *see* Al Warafi v. Obama, 821 F. Supp. 2d 47 (D.D.C. 2011). In that case, a Guantanamo detainee claimed that, when he was captured in Afghanistan, he was serving as a medic for the Taliban forces. Under the First Geneva Convention, individuals who operate exclusively as medical personnel are to be detained as prisoners "only in so far as the state of health ... and the number of prisoners of war require," and if they are not needed to take care of other prisoners, they "shall be returned to the Party to the conflict to whom they belong, as soon as a road is open for their return and military requirements permit." Geneva Convention for the Amelioration of the Condition of the Wounded and Sick in Armed Forces in the Field, arts. 28, 30, Aug. 12, 1949, 6 U.S.T. 3114, 75 U.N.T.S. 31. A federal court in D.C. concluded, however, that the detainee had not put forward sufficient evidence to show that he had been operating exclusively as a medic, so the court decided that it did not need to resolve the issue of the relevance of international law. *See* 821 F. Supp. 2d at 54–56. *See also* Al-Hela v. Trump, 2019 U.S. Dist. LEXIS 42717 (D.D.C. Mar. 15, 2019) (looking in part to the international laws of war in discerning what constitutes "substantial support" and "associated forces" for purposes of determining the scope of the government's detention authority under the AUMF).

granted.¹³⁴ Indeed, the plurality in *Hamdi* seemed to recognize this when it observed that "[i]t is a clearly established principle of the law of war that detention may last no longer than active hostilities," and when it concluded from this that "indefinite detention for the purpose of interrogation is not authorized."¹³⁵

Importantly, however, even if international law is relevant in interpreting the scope of the AUMF, this would not mean that Congress in the AUMF has affirmatively prohibited the president from violating international law. The AUMF is a broadly worded authorizing statute that does not have any prohibitory language, let alone prohibitory language referencing international law. Nor does the *Charming Betsy* canon of construction, discussed throughout this book, suggest that the AUMF should be read as having such a prohibitory effect. Under this canon, courts will attempt to construe statutes, when reasonably possible, so that the statutes do not violate international law. It is not clear that the canon even applies in the context of a grant of discretionary enforcement authority to the president, especially when the grant of authority, like the AUMF, overlaps with the president's independent constitutional powers.¹³⁶ Even if the canon does apply, however, it would simply require that the AUMF be construed not to violate international law.¹³⁷ At most, then, application of the canon to the AUMF would yield the interpretation that the AUMF does not authorize the president to violate international law. It would not yield the quite different interpretation that the AUMF affirmatively prohibits the president from violating international law. To put the point differently, nothing in international law, or in the *Charming Betsy* canon, requires that Congress affirmatively prohibit the president from violating international law when authorizing the use of force. The allocation between the domestic legislature and the executive of domestic authority to comply with or violate international law is simply not addressed by international law.

---

¹³⁴ *See* Bradley & Goldsmith, *supra* note 52, at 2094.

¹³⁵ 542 U.S. at 520, 521.

¹³⁶ *See* Bradley & Goldsmith, *supra* note 52, at 2097–98. *Cf.* United States v. Corey, 232 F.3d 1166, 1179 n.9 (9th Cir. 2000) ("These concerns [underlying the *Charming Betsy* canon] are obviously much less serious where the interpretation arguably violating international law is urged upon us by the Executive Branch of our government. When construing a statute with potential foreign policy implications, we must presume that the President has evaluated the foreign policy consequences of such an exercise of U.S. law and determined that it serves the interests of the United States."); *Authority of the Federal Bureau of Investigation to Override International Law in Extraterritorial Law Enforcement Activities*, 13 Op. Off. Legal Counsel 163, 172 (1989) (concluding that the *Charming Betsy* canon was not applicable to "broad authorizing statutes 'carrying into Execution' core Executive powers" (quoting U.S. Const. art. I, § 8, cl. 18)). *But see* Ingrid Brunk Wuerth, *Authorizations for the Use of Force, International Law, and the* Charming Betsy *Canon*, 46 B.C. L. Rev. 293, 333, 339–40 (2005) (arguing that the *Charming Betsy* canon does apply to the AUMF).

¹³⁷ *See* Bradley & Goldsmith, *supra* note 52, at 2099. *See also* Wuerth, *supra* note 136, at 356 ("[I]t bears repeating that if the President is exercising his own authority as Commander in Chief (or some other power granted by the Constitution), then the [*Charming Betsy*] canon is not in play at all."). *But cf.* Ryan Goodman & Derek Jinks, *International Law, U.S. War Powers, and the Global War on Terrorism*, 118 Harv. L. Rev. 2653 (2005) (arguing that the authority granted to the president in the AUMF is implicitly conditioned on compliance with a variety of rules in the international laws of war).

The primary significance of the distinction between interpreting the AUMF not to authorize violations of international law and interpreting it affirmatively to prohibit violations of international law concerns customary international law. As discussed in Chapter 2, the president probably has a duty to comply with treaties that are still in force, on the ground that they are part of the "Laws" that he or she must faithfully execute under Article II. As a result, law-of-war treaties can bind the president independently of the AUMF (although they might not be judicially enforceable). By contrast, as noted, there is a strong argument that the president has the domestic constitutional authority to violate customary international law. If so, then the issue of whether the AUMF incorporates the prohibitions of the customary international laws of war becomes important. If the AUMF does not incorporate these prohibitions, presidential actions in violation of them would fall within the second of the three categories of presidential power outlined by Justice Jackson in his concurrence in the *Youngstown* steel seizure case, in which the president would retain his preexisting authority to violate customary international law.[138] But if the AUMF affirmatively prohibits the president from violating the customary international laws of war, the president's actions in violation of such law would fall within the lowest of the three categories and would be valid only if they involved an area of exclusive presidential authority.[139]

Additional Detention Legislation

In late 2011, Congress enacted legislation, as part of the National Defense Authorization Act for Fiscal Year 2012 (NDAA), that addressed the issue of detention in the war on terrorism.[140] In the NDAA, Congress "affirms that the authority of the President to use all necessary and appropriate force pursuant to the Authorization for Use of Military Force . . . includes the authority for the Armed Forces of the United States to detain covered persons . . . pending disposition under the law of war."[141] It also spells out who can be detained, in terms similar to the standard that had been developed by the federal courts in D.C.:

---

[138] *See* Youngstown Sheet & Tube Co. v. Sawyer, 343 U.S. 579, 637 (1952) (Jackson, J., concurring) (describing as an intermediate category the situations in which "the President acts in absence of either a congressional grant or denial of authority").

[139] *See id.* (noting that "[w]hen the President takes measures incompatible with the expressed or implied will of Congress, his power is at its lowest ebb, for then he can rely only upon his own constitutional powers minus any constitutional powers of Congress over the matter").

[140] National Defense Authorization Act for Fiscal Year 2012, Subtitle D—Counterterrorism, Pub. L. No. 112-81, 112th Cong., 125 Stat. 1298 (2011) [hereinafter NDAA of 2012].

[141] *Id.*, § 1021(a).

(1) A person who planned, authorized, committed, or aided the terrorist attacks that occurred on September 11, 2001, or harbored those responsible for those attacks.

(2) A person who was a part of or substantially supported al-Qaeda, the Taliban, or associated forces that are engaged in hostilities against the United States or its coalition partners, including any person who has committed a belligerent act or has directly supported such hostilities in aid of such enemy forces.[142]

In addition, the NDAA repeatedly refers to detention and disposition "under the law of war," which appears to be a reference at least in part to the international laws of war.[143] This statute thus provides additional grounds for treating international law as relevant to the detention authority. Despite these provisions, the NDAA also states that it is not "intended to limit or expand the authority of the President or the scope of the Authorization for Use of Military Force," and that it should not be "construed to affect existing law or authorities relating to the detention of United States citizens, lawful resident aliens of the United States, or any other persons who are captured or arrested in the United States."[144]

The NDAA also addresses the issue of length of detention, albeit somewhat indirectly. It requires the Secretary of Defense to submit a report to congressional committees setting forth procedures to address various issues relating to the Periodic Review Boards at Guantanamo, including certain "clarifications" sought by Congress.[145] It also states that the procedures should

> ensure that appropriate consideration is given to factors addressing the need for continued detention of the detainee, including—
> (A) the likelihood the detainee will resume terrorist activity if transferred or released; (B) the likelihood the detainee will reestablish ties with al-Qaeda, the Taliban, or associated forces that are engaged in hostilities against the United States or its coalition partners if transferred or released; (C) the likelihood of family, tribal, or government rehabilitation or support for the detainee if transferred or released; (D) the likelihood the detainee may be subject to trial by military commission; and (E) any law enforcement interest in the detainee.[146]

---

[142] *Id.*, § 1021(b).
[143] *See, e.g., id.*, § 1021(c) (referring to "[t]he disposition of a person under the law of war," and "[d]etention under the law of war").
[144] *Id.*, § 1021(d), (e).
[145] *See id.*, § 1023(a).
[146] *Id.*, § 1023(b)(4).

Perhaps most controversially, the NDAA mandates military detention of anyone who is "a member of, or part of, al-Qaeda or an associated force that acts in coordination with or pursuant to the direction of al-Qaeda" and has participated in an attack or attempted attack against the United States or its coalition partners.[147] It exempts U.S. citizens, however, and it mandates detention only "pending disposition under the law of war."[148] It also allows the president to waive the requirement of mandatory detention "if the President submits to Congress a certification in writing that such a waiver is in the national security interests of the United States."[149] President Obama subsequently issued a Policy Directive that prospectively waives mandatory military detention for various situations in which a person has been apprehended by domestic law enforcement, such as when military detention would undermine cooperation with foreign governments or reduce the likelihood of getting cooperation from the detainee.[150]

The NDAA and subsequent appropriations statutes also contained restrictions on the transfer of detainees from Guantanamo, restrictions that President Obama suggested (while signing the statutes into law) might under some circumstances unconstitutionally intrude on his executive authority.[151] In 2014, Obama's release from Guantanamo of five Taliban detainees in return for the Taliban's release of a U.S. citizen, without giving advance notice to Congress as required by the legislation, generated substantial controversy.[152] The Government Accountability Office, an investigative arm of Congress, concluded that the Obama administration had violated federal statutory provisions in making the exchange.[153]

Military Commission Trials

At various times in its history, the United States has used military commissions—that is, criminal tribunals composed of military officers—to try certain classes of individuals.

---

[147] *Id.*, § 1022(a). When signing the legislation, President Obama expressed the view that the mandatory detention provisions were "ill-conceived." *Presidential Statement on Signing the National Defense Authorization Act for Fiscal Year 2012*, 2011 DAILY COMP. PRES. DOC. 978, at 2 (Dec. 31, 2011), *available at* http://www.gpo.gov/fdsys/pkg/DCPD-201100978/pdf/DCPD-201100978.pdf.

[148] NDAA of 2012, *supra* note 140, § 1021(a).

[149] *Id.*, § 1022(a)(4).

[150] *See* Directive on Procedures Implementing Section 1022 of the National Defense Authorization Act for Fiscal Year 2012, 2012 DAILY COMP. PRES. DOC. 123 (Feb. 28, 2012), *available at* http://www.whitehouse.gov/the-press-office/2012/02/28/presidential-policy-directive-requirements-national-defense-authorizatio.

[151] *See, e.g.*, Statement by the President on H.R. 3304 (Dec. 26, 2013), *at* http://www.whitehouse.gov/the-press-office/2013/12/26/statement-president-hr-3304.

[152] *See, e.g.*, Charlie Savage & David E. Sanger, *Deal to Free Bowe Bergdahl Puts Obama on Defensive*, N.Y. TIMES (June 3, 2014).

[153] *See* Memorandum from Susan A. Poling, General Counsel, Government Accountability Office, to the Honorable Mitch McConnell et al., *Department of Defense—Compliance with Statutory Notification Requirement* (Aug. 21, 2014), *at* http://www.gao.gov/assets/670/665390.pdf.

These commissions have been used for three basic purposes: to administer justice in territory occupied by the United States, to replace civilian courts where martial law has been declared, and to try enemy belligerents for violations of the laws of war.[154] They have been used in both formally declared wars and in other military conflicts, such as the Civil War and conflicts with Indian tribes. Military commissions are distinct from "courts-martial," which are the military courts used to try U.S. soldiers for criminal offenses, although the procedures used in military commissions have often been similar to those used in courts-martial. Unlike military commissions, courts-martial have historically been regulated by detailed Articles of War enacted by Congress.[155]

Two months after the September 11 attacks, President Bush issued a Military Order that, among other things, authorized the use of military commissions in the war on terrorism. The Order stated that non-U.S. citizens who were members of Al Qaeda or who otherwise were involved in acts of international terrorism against the United States could be tried by the commissions "for any and all offenses triable by military commission."[156] The decision to use military commissions in the war on terrorism was highly controversial. Among other things, there were concerns that the trials would lack sufficient procedural protections to make them fair and that they would be perceived as illegitimate by the international community.[157]

In subsequently defending the legal validity of such commissions, the Bush administration relied heavily on precedent from World War II, especially a Supreme Court decision from 1942, Ex parte *Quirin*.[158] In *Quirin*, the Court unanimously concluded that President Roosevelt had statutory authority to use a military commission to try a group

---

[154] *See* Curtis A. Bradley, *The Story of Ex parte Milligan: Military Trials, Enemy Combatants, and Congressional Authorization*, *in* PRESIDENTIAL POWER STORIES 93, 95–96 (Christopher H. Schroeder & Curtis A. Bradley eds., 2009); Curtis A. Bradley & Jack L. Goldsmith, *The Constitutional Validity of Military Commissions*, 5 GREEN BAG 2d 249 (2002); *see also* Hamdan v. Rumsfeld, 548 U.S. 557, 595–96 (2006) (plurality opinion); Madsen v. Kinsella, 343 U.S. 341, 346–47 (1952). Military commissions have also been used "when military forces were beyond the jurisdiction of their national courts, but military law did not authorize trying troops for offenses against the local population." David Glazier, Note, *Kangaroo Courts or Competent Tribunal?: Judging the 21st Century Military Commission*, 89 VA. L. REV. 2005, 2023 (2003).

[155] *See* Madsen v. Kinsella, 343 U.S. 341, 348 (1952) ("In the absence of attempts by Congress to limit the President's power, it appears that, as Commander-in-Chief of the Army and Navy of the United States, he may, in time of war, establish and prescribe the jurisdiction and procedure of military commissions, and of tribunals in the nature of such commissions, in the territory occupied by the United States by force of arms.").

[156] Military Order, *Detention, Treatment, and Trial of Certain Non-Citizens in the War against Terrorism*, Nov. 13, 2001, 66 FED. REG. 57833 § 4(a) (Nov. 16, 2001). The Department of Defense subsequently promulgated procedures to be used by the military commissions. *See Procedures for Trials by Military Commissions of Certain Non-United States Citizens in the War against Terrorism*, 32 C.F.R. pt. 9 (2003).

[157] *See, e.g.*, George P. Fletcher, *War and the Constitution: Bush's Military Tribunals Haven't Got a Legal Leg to Stand On*, THE AM. PROSPECT, Jan. 1, 2002, at 26; Harold Hongju Koh, *The Case against Military Commissions*, 96 AM. J. INT'L L. 337 (2002); Anthony Lewis, Editorial, *Abroad and at Home; Right and Wrong*, N.Y. TIMES (Nov. 24, 2001); Aryeh Neier, *The Military Tribunals on Trial*, N.Y. REV. OF BOOKS (Jan. 16, 2002).

[158] 317 U.S. 1 (1942).

of Nazi agents who had surreptitiously entered the United States with plans to carry out acts of sabotage. The Court placed particular emphasis on Article 15 of the Articles of War, which provided that "the provisions of these articles conferring jurisdiction upon courts martial shall not be construed as depriving military commissions . . . of concurrent jurisdiction in respect of offenders or offenses that by statute or by the law of war may be triable by such military commissions."[159] Although Article 15 was phrased as a mere recognition of the president's historical authority to use military commissions, the Supreme Court in *Quirin* construed it as affirmative congressional authorization for such commissions.[160] The Court stated that "[b]y the Articles of War, and especially Article 15, Congress has explicitly provided, so far as it may constitutionally do so, that military tribunals shall have jurisdiction to try offenders or offenses against the law of war in appropriate cases," and the Court further stated that "Congress [in Article 15] has authorized trial of offenses against the law of war before such commissions."[161]

In concluding that Congress had acted constitutionally in authorizing the use of military commissions, the Court in *Quirin* distinguished a famous Civil War–era decision, Ex parte *Milligan*. In *Milligan*, the Court had held that the Union military had acted unconstitutionally in using a military commission to try a group of individuals in Indiana for allegedly conspiring to aid the Confederacy, reasoning that the law of war "can never be applied to citizens in states which have upheld the authority of the government, and where the courts are open and their process unobstructed."[162] The Court in *Quirin* explained that, unlike the case before it, *Milligan* involved the trial of "a non-belligerent, not subject to the law of war save as—in circumstances found not there to be present, and not involved here—martial law might be constitutionally established."[163]

After *Quirin*, Congress recodified Article 15 of the Articles of War in what is now Section 821 of the Uniform Code of Military Justice (UCMJ).[164] Section 821 provides, similar to what had been provided in Article 15, that the UCMJ provisions do not deprive

---

[159] Articles of War of 1916, art. 15, 39 Stat. 650, 653 (1916).

[160] For discussion of the *Quirin* case and the circumstances surrounding it, *see* MICHAEL DOBBS, SABOTEURS: THE NAZI RAID ON AMERICA (2005); LOUIS FISHER, NAZI SABOTEUR ON TRIAL (2d ed. 2005); EUGENE RACHLIS, THEY CAME TO KILL: THE STORY OF EIGHT NAZI SABOTEURS IN AMERICA (1961); and David J. Danelski, *The Saboteurs' Case*, 1 J. S. CT. HIST. 61 (1996). For discussion of why President Bush's decision to use military commissions to try alleged terrorists was much more controversial than President Roosevelt's decision to use a military commission to try the Nazi saboteurs, see Jack Goldsmith & Cass R. Sunstein, *Military Tribunals and Legal Culture: What a Difference Sixty Years Makes*, 19 CONST. COMM. 261 (2002).

[161] 317 U.S. at 28, 29. A few years later, the Supreme Court, relying in part on *Quirin*, again read Article 15 of the Articles of War as explicit congressional authorization for military commissions to try offenses against the laws of war. *See In re* Yamashita, 327 U.S. 1, 46 (1946).

[162] *See* 71 U.S. (4 Wall.) 2, 121 (1866). Four justices in *Milligan* argued that Congress had the constitutional authority to authorize a military commission for this case but had not done so, and that the Court should have rested its decision only on statutory rather than constitutional grounds. *See* 71 U.S. at 136–39 (Chase, J.).

[163] 317 U.S. at 45.

[164] *See* 10 U.S.C. § 821.

military commissions of concurrent jurisdiction with respect to offenders or offenses that by statute or by the law of war may be tried by military commissions. The legislative history of Section 821 indicates that Congress was preserving the language of Article 15 because that language had already been interpreted in *Quirin*.[165] President Bush therefore not surprisingly cited to Section 821 in his Military Order authorizing the use of military commissions.[166]

Several years after Bush issued his Military Order, his administration began initiating military commission proceedings against the Guantanamo detainees, including Salim Hamdan, who allegedly had acted as Osama bin Laden's driver and bodyguard. Hamdan filed a habeas corpus petition challenging the validity of the military commission, and the case eventually went up to the Supreme Court. In a 2006 decision, *Hamdan v. Rumsfeld*, the Court held that the military commission system that President Bush had established was invalid because it violated statutory restrictions in the UCMJ on the use of military commissions.[167] The Court reasoned that "while we assume that the AUMF activated the President's war powers, . . . and that those powers include the authority to convene military commissions in appropriate circumstances," there is nothing in the AUMF indicating that it was intended to expand the president's authority to use commissions beyond what is allowed by the UCMJ.[168]

In particular, the Court in *Hamdan* interpreted provisions in the UCMJ as requiring that military commissions follow the procedures of courts-martial unless shown to be impracticable, and the Court concluded that the government had not made such a showing. The Court relied on, among other things, a reference in Section 821 of the UCMJ to "offenders or offenses that by statute or by the law of war may be tried by military commission," language that the Court interpreted as conditioning Congress's authorization of military commissions on "compliance with the law of war."[169] The laws of war, the Court further reasoned, included the Geneva Conventions, and the Court held that at

---

[165] *See* SEN. RPT. 486, *Establishing a Uniform Code of Military Justice*, 81st Cong., 1st Sess. at 13 (June 10, 1949) ("The language of [Article of War] 15 has been preserved because it has been construed by the Supreme Court. (Ex Parte Quirin, 317 U.S. 1 (1942))."); H. REPT. 491, Uniform Code of Military Justice, 81st Cong., 1st Sess. at 17 (April 28, 1949) (same).

[166] For debate over whether President Bush had the legal authority to establish military commissions, *compare* Bradley & Goldsmith, *supra* note 154 (arguing that he did), *and* John M. Bickers, *Military Commissions Are Constitutionally Sound: A Response to Professors Katyal and Tribe*, 34 TEX. TECH L. REV. 899 (2003) (same), *with* Fletcher, *supra* note 157 (arguing that he did not), *and* Neal K. Katyal & Laurence H. Tribe, *Waging War, Deciding Guilt: Trying the Military Tribunals*, 111 YALE L.J. 1259 (2002) (same).

[167] 548 U.S. 557 (2006).

[168] *Id.* at 594. The Court also reasoned that even if the president has independent constitutional authority to establish military commissions, when exercising this authority, he or she is required to comply with limitations imposed by Congress. *See id.* at 593 n.23. The Court cited Justice Jackson's concurrence in the *Youngstown* steel seizure decision, which is discussed in Chapter 1. *See also id.* at 638 (Kennedy, J., concurring) (relying heavily on the approach set out in Justice Jackson's concurrence).

[169] *Id.* at 628.

least Common Article 3 of the Conventions applied to the conflict between the United States and Al Qaeda.[170] Common Article 3, the Court noted, prohibits "the passing of sentences and the carrying out of executions without previous judgment pronounced by a regularly constituted court affording all the judicial guarantees which are recognized as indispensable by civilized peoples." "At a minimum," concluded the Court, "a military commission 'can be "regularly constituted" by the standards of our military justice system only if some practical need explains deviations from court-martial practice,'" and it found that the government had not shown such a need.[171]

As noted, Common Article 3 applies to conflicts "not of an international character," and the Court interpreted this reference as encompassing a cross-border conflict between a nation and a nonstate terrorist group, on the theory that such a conflict is not between nations and thus is not "international."[172] The Court therefore obviously did not accept the Bush administration's interpretation of Common Article 3, even though, as noted in Chapter 2, courts often give substantial deference to treaty interpretations by the executive branch. The dissent in *Hamdan* argued (with some force, in the view of this author) that "where, as here, an ambiguous treaty provision . . . is susceptible of two plausible, and reasonable, interpretations, our precedents require us to defer to the Executive's interpretation."[173]

The Supreme Court's conclusion that Common Article 3 applied to the conflict with Al Qaeda had potential implications beyond the use of military commissions, especially for interrogation of detainees. Common Article 3 prohibits, for example, "cruel treatment and torture," as well as "humiliating and degrading treatment." Nevertheless, the Bush administration quickly accepted the Court's conclusion: the Deputy Secretary of Defense issued a memorandum directing Department of Defense personnel to ensure that their standards complied with Common Article 3,[174] and President Bush withdrew the portion of his 2002 determination that had stated that Common Article 3 was inapplicable to the conflict with Al Qaeda.[175]

A few months after the decision in *Hamdan*, Congress enacted the Military Commissions Act (MCA) of 2006.[176] The MCA of 2006 specifically authorized the use

---

[170] *See id.* at 629–31.
[171] *Id.* at 632–33.
[172] *See id.* at 630–31.
[173] *Id.* at 719 (Thomas, J., dissenting). *See also* Murphy, *supra* note 106, at 1115 ("A fair reading of the negotiating history suggests that this Common Article 3 paradigm was principally designed to address the situation of an armed conflict internal to a single state.").
[174] *See* Memorandum from Gordon England, Deputy Secretary of Defense, *Application of Common Article 3 of the Geneva Conventions to the Treatment of Detainees in the Department of Defense* (July 7, 2006), *available at* https://fas.org/sgp/othergov/dod/geneva070606.pdf.
[175] *See* Mark Mazzeti & Kate Zernike, *White House Says Terror Detainees Hold Basic Rights*, N.Y. TIMES (July 12, 2006).
[176] *See* Military Commissions Act, Pub. L. 109–366, 120 Stat. 2632 (Oct. 17, 2006) [hereinafter MCA of 2006].

of military commissions to try "unlawful enemy combatants," which Congress defined to include individuals who are "part of the Taliban, al Qaeda, or associated forces."[177] The Act also set forth extensive procedures to be followed by the commissions, and it codified and defined the various crimes that could be prosecuted before the commissions.

The MCA of 2006 contains a number of references to the Geneva Conventions. For example, Congress declared that a commission established in compliance with the requirements it was setting out "is a regularly constituted court, affording all the necessary 'judicial guarantees which are recognized as indispensable by civilized peoples' for purposes of common Article 3 of the Geneva Conventions."[178] It also sought to restrict the use of the Geneva Conventions by detainees in the war on terrorism, providing that "[n]o alien unlawful enemy combatant subject to trial by military commission under this chapter may invoke the Geneva Conventions as a source of rights,"[179] and that "[n]o person may invoke the Geneva Conventions or any protocols thereto in any habeas corpus or other civil action or proceeding to which the United States, or a current or former officer, employee, member of the Armed Forces, or other agent of the United States is a party as a source of rights in any court of the United States or its States or territories."[180]

The MCA of 2006 also limited criminal liability associated with violations of Common Article 3. As already discussed, the War Crimes Act had been amended in 1997 to criminalize all breaches of Common Article 3. The Supreme Court's conclusion in *Hamdan* that Common Article 3 applied to the war on terrorism potentially exposed U.S. officials, such as members of the CIA, to criminal prosecution for breaches of its terms. Congress responded to this development by amending the War Crimes Act to provide that violations of Common Article 3 would fall within the Act only if they constituted "grave breaches" of the Article.[181] The amendment also set forth the acts that would constitute such grave breaches, notably leaving out violations of Common Article 3's prohibitions on "humiliating or degrading treatment" and on "the passing of sentences and the carrying out of executions without previous judgment pronounced by a regularly constituted court, affording all the judicial guarantees which are recognized as indispensable by civilized peoples."[182]

---

[177] *Id.*, § 948a.
[178] *Id.*, § 948b(f).
[179] *Id.*, § 948b(g).
[180] *Id.*, § 5(a).
[181] *See id.*, § 6(d). Salim Hamdan was tried in one of the new commissions and was convicted of providing material support for terrorism, but he received only five months imprisonment beyond the time he had already spent at Guantanamo, and he was released to his home country of Yemen with a month left to serve in his sentence. *See* Robert F. Worth, *Bin Laden Driver to Be Sent to Yemen*, N.Y. TIMES (Nov. 25, 2008).
[182] *See* 18 U.S.C. § 2441(d) (listing conduct considered to be a grave breach of common Article 3 for purposes of the statutes). *See also* Michael John Garcia, *The War Crimes Act: Current Issues* (Jan. 22, 2009), *available at* http://www.fas.org/sgp/crs/intel/RL33662.pdf. For debate over the legal validity of these various restrictions on the use of the Geneva Conventions, *compare* Curtis A. Bradley, *The Military Commissions Act, Habeas Corpus, and the Geneva Conventions*, 101 Am. J. Int'l

In 2009, after President Obama had taken office, Congress enacted a revised Military Commissions Act.[183] The MCA of 2009 refers to "unprivileged enemy belligerents" rather than "unlawful enemy combatants," but the class of individuals covered is similar.[184] The 2009 statute does, however, add to the procedural protections for the detainees, and it makes clear that no statements obtained by either torture or the use of cruel, inhuman, or degrading treatment shall be admissible. It also reduces the restriction on invoking the Geneva Conventions in military commission proceedings: instead of barring their use as "a source of rights," as in the MCA of 2006, it provides that the Conventions cannot be invoked by military commission defendants "as a basis for a private right of action," which seems to allow for the possibility of their use as a defense to prosecution.[185] President Obama initially suspended the use of military commission trials, but he ordered their resumption in 2011.[186]

The government's constitutional authority to use military commissions is not unlimited. At least for the most part, the government can use these commissions only to prosecute violations of the international laws of war.[187] Some of the Guantanamo detainees have therefore challenged military commission charges against them on the ground that these charges do not involve such violations. In *Hamdan*, a plurality of the Supreme Court expressed the view that the crime of "conspiracy" is not recognized under the international laws of war, noting, among other things, that this crime "has rarely if ever been tried as such in this country by any law-of-war military commission not exercising some other form of jurisdiction, and does not appear in either the Geneva Conventions or the Hague Conventions—the major treaties on the law of war."[188] That view was not reflected in a binding majority opinion, however, and Congress in the MCA of 2006 specifically

---

L. 322 (2007) (arguing that they are generally valid), *with* Carlos M. Vázquez, *The Military Commissions Act, the Geneva Conventions, and the Courts: A Critical Guide*, 101 AM. J. INT'L L. 73 (2007) (questioning their validity).

[183] *See* Military Commissions Act, Pub. L. No. 111-84, 123 Stat. 2190, Tit. XVIII (Oct. 28, 2009) [hereinafter MCA of 2009].

[184] *See id.*, § 948a.

[185] *Id.*, § 948b(e).

[186] *See* Scott Shane & Mark Landler, *Obama Clears Way for Guantanamo Trials*, N.Y. TIMES (Mar. 7, 2011).

[187] *See, e.g.,* Ex parte Quirin, 317 U.S. 1, 31 (1942) ("Lawful combatants are subject to capture and detention as prisoners of war by opposing military forces. Unlawful combatants are likewise subject to capture and detention, but in addition they are subject to trial and punishment by military tribunals *for acts which render their belligerency unlawful.*") (emphasis added). To the extent that the prosecutions are based on Congress's power to define and punish offenses against the law of nations, the prosecutions presumably must have some basis in the law of nations; see, for example, Stephen I. Vladeck, *The Laws of War as a Constitutional Limit on Military Jurisdiction*, 4 J. NAT'L SEC. L. & POL'Y 295 (2010), although courts would likely give some deference to the combined judgment of Congress and the president about the content of international law. Based on their other constitutional powers, as well as historical practice, Congress and the president may have the authority to allow military commission trials for certain additional offenses that are not grounded in the law of nations, although this is a matter of some controversy.

[188] 548 U.S. at 603–604.

included conspiracy as one of the offenses that could be prosecuted.[189] The MCA of 2009 similarly includes conspiracy as a chargeable offense.[190] Other crimes listed in those statutes include providing material support for terrorism,[191] and solicitation of another to commit a covered offense,[192] and detainees have argued that those crimes also fall outside the scope of international laws of war.

In 2014, the U.S. Court of Appeals for the D.C. Circuit held that it did not constitute plain constitutional error to try detainees for conspiracy because conspiracy was already a federal crime long before the enactment of the MCA, and because it is not clear that military commissions can try only violations of the international laws of war.[193] In support of the latter point, the court noted that the conspirators involved in the assassination of President Abraham Lincoln as well as the group of Nazi saboteurs apprehended during World War II had been tried in military commissions for conspiracy.[194] The court held, however, that the detainees could not be tried for material support for terrorism or solicitation of others to commit war crimes because these offenses neither involved violations of the international laws of war nor were supported by domestic precedent.[195] The D.C. Circuit subsequently rejected additional constitutional challenges to the conspiracy charge in this case.[196]

Coercive Interrogation

Another topic of controversy that emerged in the war on terrorism was the use by the U.S. government of various coercive interrogation techniques, including most controversially the use of "waterboarding."[197] These techniques implicated U.S. obligations under

---

[189] *See* MCA of 2006, *supra* note 176, § 950v(b)(28).
[190] *See* MCA of 2009, *supra* note 183, § 950t(29).
[191] *See* MCA of 2006, *supra* note 176, § 950v(b)(25); MCA of 2009, *supra* note 183, § 950t(25).
[192] *See* MCA of 2006, *supra* note 176, § 950u; MCA of 2009, *supra* note 183, § 950t(30).
[193] *See* Al Bahlul v. United States, 767 F.3d 1 (D.C. Cir. 2014) (en banc).
[194] *See id.* at 60–66.
[195] *See id.* at 68–80.
[196] *See* Al Bahlul v. United States, 840 F.3d 757 (D.C. Cir. 2016).
[197] Reports indicate that the CIA was authorized to use so-called enhanced interrogation techniques against a number of high-level Al Qaeda detainees, and that these techniques included slapping; forced standing for long periods; light and noise bombardment; and, for several of the detainees, waterboarding. *See* Greg Miller, *CIA Chief Confirms Use of Waterboarding*, L.A. Times (Feb. 6, 2008); Jon Ward & John Solomon, *Interview of the Vice-President*, Wash. Times (Dec. 22, 2008). Waterboarding involves pouring water over a person's face while the person is restrained—for example, by being strapped to a board—in order to induce in the person the sensation of drowning. Less aggressive (but potentially coercive) interrogation techniques, such as manipulation of sleep patterns, were authorized for use at Guantanamo. *See* News Release No. 596-04, U.S. Dept. of Defense, *DOD Provides Details on Interrogation Process* (June 22, 2004), *available at* https://fas.org/sgp/news/2004/06/dod062204.html; Memorandum from the Secretary of Defense for the Commander, U.S. Southern Command, *Counter-Resistance Techniques in the War on Terrorism* (Apr. 16, 2003), *available at* https://legacy.npr.org/documents/2004/dod_prisoners/20040622doc9.pdf.

treaties such as the Geneva Conventions and the Torture Convention, as well as obligations under customary international law. They also potentially implicated statutory provisions that implement these treaty obligations, in particular the War Crimes Act and the criminal statute that implements the Torture Convention.

At the time of the September 11 attacks, the War Crimes Act criminalized "grave breaches" of the Geneva Conventions as well as any violations of Common Article 3 of the Conventions. As already noted, under the Third Geneva Convention, prisoners of war may not be subjected to coercive interrogation. As we have seen, however, the Bush administration concluded that the Al Qaeda and Taliban detainees did not qualify for the prisoner-of-war protections in the Convention. Common Article 3 of the Geneva Conventions prohibits "cruel treatment and torture" as well as "outrages upon personal dignity, in particular humiliating and degrading treatment," but the administration concluded that this treaty provision was inapplicable (a conclusion later rejected by the Supreme Court). Also in place at the time of the September 11 attacks was a statute that implements the Torture Convention by criminalizing acts of torture committed outside the United States.[198] That statute does not address, however, lesser forms of abuse that constitute "cruel, inhuman, or degrading treatment or punishment," even though such conduct is prohibited by the Torture Convention.[199]

In 2002, the Justice Department's Office of Legal Counsel issued a memorandum, which was later leaked to the media, addressing the authority under U.S. law to use coercive methods of interrogation.[200] The memorandum focused in particular on the meaning of the U.S. criminal statute that implements the Torture Convention. When it came to light, the memorandum was highly controversial, both because it adopted a narrow definition of what constituted torture (reasoning that "[p]hysical pain amounting to torture must be equivalent in intensity to the pain accompanying serious physical

---

[198] *See* 18 U.S.C. § 2340A(a).

[199] Article 16 of the Torture Convention provides that "[e]ach State Party shall undertake to prevent in any territory under its jurisdiction other acts of cruel, inhuman or degrading treatment or punishment which do not amount to torture as defined in article 1, when such acts are committed by or at the instigation of or with the consent or acquiescence of a public official or other person acting in an official capacity." Convention against Torture and Other Cruel, Inhuman or Degrading Treatment or Punishment, art. 16, Dec. 10, 1984, S. Treaty Doc. No. 20–100 (1988), 1465 U.N.T.S. 85. When joining the Convention, the United States included a reservation with its instrument of ratification stating that it "considers itself bound by the obligation under Article 16 to prevent 'cruel, inhuman or degrading treatment or punishment,' only insofar as the term 'cruel, inhuman or degrading treatment or punishment' means the cruel, unusual and inhumane treatment or punishment prohibited by the Fifth, Eighth, and/or Fourteenth Amendments to the Constitution of the United States." S. Exec. Rep. 101–30, Resolution of Advice and Consent to Ratification, I(2) (1990). For a discussion of the implications of the Torture Convention for interrogation techniques, *see* Michael John Garcia, *U.N. Convention against Torture (CAT): Overview and Application to Interrogation Techniques* (Cong. Res. Serv., Jan. 26, 2009), *available at* http://www.fas.org/sgp/crs/intel/RL32438.pdf.

[200] Memorandum from Jay S. Bybee, Assistant Attorney General, to Alberto Gonzales, Counsel to the President, *Standards of Conduct for Interrogation under 18 U.S.C. §§ 2340—2340A* (Aug. 1, 2002), *available at* http://www.justice.gov/olc/docs/memo-gonzales-aug2002.pdf.

injury, such as organ failure, impairment of bodily function, or even death"), and because it suggested that the president had the constitutional authority to disregard the torture statute. Independent of its substantive conclusions, the memorandum was criticized for being overly tendentious and for addressing issues not specifically presented. Two years later, the Justice Department withdrew the memorandum and substituted an analysis that was more narrowly drawn.[201] In the meantime, it had been discovered that U.S. soldiers had abused prisoners at the Abu Ghraib prison facility in Iraq.[202] Although these abuses were not directly connected to U.S. interrogation policy in the war on terrorism, their revelation made the issue of coercive interrogation more salient and also triggered concerns that there was slippage between the U.S. approach to the war on terrorism and its approach to the more conventional war in Iraq (where the Geneva Conventions indisputably applied).[203]

In late 2005, Congress acted to restrict coercive interrogation, providing in the Detainee Treatment Act that "[n]o individual in the custody or under the physical control of the United States Government, regardless of nationality or physical location, shall be subject to cruel, inhuman, or degrading treatment or punishment."[204] The Military Commissions Act of 2006 subsequently provided that evidence based on torture would not be admissible in military commission proceedings, and that evidence obtained by cruel, inhuman, or degrading treatment or punishment would not be admissible unless obtained before the enactment of the Detainee Treatment Act.[205] The Military Commissions Act of 2009 goes further and completely disallows the introduction of evidence obtained by cruel, inhuman, or degrading treatment or punishment.[206]

In the meantime, the Supreme Court held in *Hamdan* that Common Article 3 of the Geneva Conventions applies to the war on terrorism. Shortly thereafter, the U.S. Army issued a new Field Manual specifically prohibiting many of the controversial interrogation techniques, including waterboarding.[207] Interrogations by the CIA, however, were not covered by the Manual, and in 2007 President Bush issued an Executive Order

---

[201] Memorandum from Daniel Levin, Acting Assistant Attorney General, Office of Legal Counsel, to James B. Comey, Deputy Attorney General, *Legal Standards Applicable under 18 U.S.C. §§ 2340–2340A* (Dec. 23, 2004), *available at* https://www.globalsecurity.org/security/library/policy/national/doj-dag_torture-memo_30dec2004.pdf.

[202] *See* James Risen, *GI's Are Accused of Abusing Iraqi Captives*, N.Y. TIMES (Apr. 29, 2004).

[203] *See, e.g.*, SEYMOUR M. HERSCH, THE CHAIN OF COMMAND: THE ROAD FROM 9/11 TO ABU GHRAIB (2005). In fact, some of the techniques for degrading prisoners at Abu Ghraib may have been used first at Guantanamo. *See* Josh White, *Abu Ghraib Tactics Were First Used at Guantanamo*, WASH. POST (July 14, 2005).

[204] Detainee Treatment Act of 2005, Pub. L. No. 109–148, Div. A, tit. 10, 119 Stat. 2739, § 1003 (2005).

[205] *See* MCA of 2006, *supra* note 176, § 948r(c).

[206] *See* MCA of 2009, *supra* note 183, § 948r.

[207] *See* Field Manual (FM) 2-22.3, *Human Intelligence Collector Operations*, at 5–21 (Sept. 2006) (specifically disallowing certain conduct in interrogations, including waterboarding), *available at* www.fas.org/irp/doddir/army/fm2-22-3.pdf.

placing less stringent restrictions on the CIA than those that applied to the military.[208] Shortly after taking office, President Obama issued an Executive Order revoking Bush's 2007 Order and limiting interrogation techniques for anyone in U.S. custody to those allowed by the Army Field Manual.[209] Obama later observed critically that, during the Bush administration, the United States had "tortured some folks."[210] President Trump, despite expressing support for coercive interrogation practices when running for president in 2016, did not reinstitute such practices.

Targeted Killing

Although targeted killing of the enemy is not unique to the war on terrorism, there has been significant controversy over the use of this tactic by the United States against alleged members of the Taliban, Al Qaeda, and affiliated organizations. In recent years, these targeted killings have often involved the use of unmanned aerial vehicles, or "drones," although sometimes they have involved more conventional uses of force (such as with the killing of the leader of Al Qaeda, Osama bin Laden, in 2011). The targeted killings have occurred in a number of countries, including Afghanistan, Pakistan, Yemen, Somalia, and Iraq.[211]

The controversy over targeted killings relates to more general disputes about the extent to which members of a nonstate terrorist organization should be considered combatants as opposed to civilians for purposes of the laws of war, the legality of using force within another sovereign state in order to address threats that the state may be unwilling or unable to address itself, and the permissibility of engaging in preemptive self-defense.[212]

---

[208] *See* Exec. Order No. 13,440, *Interpretation of the Geneva Conventions Common Article 3 as Applied to a Program of Detention and Interrogation Operated by the Central Intelligence Agency*, 3 C.F.R. 229 (2007). The Order purported to be consistent with U.S. obligations under Common Article 3 of the Geneva Conventions. *See id.*, § 3.

[209] *See* Exec. Order No. 13,491, *Ensuring Lawful Interrogations*, § 3(b) (Jan. 22, 2009), 74 FED. REG. 4893 (Jan. 27, 2009). Even when based on domestic law, suits brought against U.S. officials for alleged mistreatment in the war on terrorism face a number of legal obstacles. Courts have been reluctant, for example, to infer a damages remedy for violations of the Constitution in this context. *See, e.g.*, Ziglar v. Abbasi, 137 S. Ct. 1843 (2017); Lebron v. Rumsfeld, 670 F.3d 540 (4th Cir. 2012); Arar v. Ashcroft, 585 F.3d 559 (2d Cir. 2009) (en banc); Rasul v. Myers, 563 F.3d 527 (D.C. Cir. 2009) (per curiam). The officials are also entitled to immunity if the law was unclear at the time of their actions. *See, e.g.*, Ashcroft v. al-Kidd, 563 U.S. 731 (2011); Padilla v. Yoo, 678 F.3d 748 (9th Cir. 2012). Statutory restrictions have also barred relief. *See, e.g.*, Ameur v. Gates, 759 F.3d 317 (4th Cir. 2014).

[210] *See* Kathleen Hennessey, *Obama: "We Tortured Some Folks,"* L.A. TIMES (Aug. 1, 2014). In late 2014, the Senate Intelligence Committee released a lengthy report describing and criticizing the CIA's interrogation practices during the Bush administration. *See* Mark Mazzetti, *Panel Faults C.I.A. Over Brutality and Deceit in Terrorism Interrogations*, N.Y. TIMES (Dec. 9, 2014).

[211] *See, e.g.*, Scott Shane, *Targeted Killing Comes to Define War on Terror*, N.Y. TIMES (Aug. 7, 2013).

[212] For discussions of the legality of targeted killing under international law, *see* NILS MELZER, TARGETED KILLING IN INTERNATIONAL LAW (2009); AVERY PLAW, TARGETING TERRORISTS: A LICENSE TO KILL? (2008); TARGETED KILLINGS: LAW AND MORALITY IN AN ASYMMETRICAL WORLD (Claire Finkelstein,

But the controversy also concerns the morality and ethics of engaging in warfare from a distance without much risk of casualties, and whether there is sufficient domestic oversight of this type of lethal force by the executive branch.[213] In addition, concerns were expressed that the Obama administration might be using targeted killings as a way of avoiding the legal and public relations difficulties associated with military detention, although the administration vigorously denied this charge.

In defending the legality of the targeted killings, the Obama administration argued that the United States is in an armed conflict with the Taliban and Al Qaeda and that members of these enemy forces "are belligerents and, therefore, lawful targets under international law."[214] It also argued that nothing in international law "prohibits us from using lethal force against our enemies outside of an active battlefield, at least when the country involved consents or is unable or unwilling to take action against the threat."[215] By contrast, critics contended that the theater of conflict does not extend outside of Afghanistan, and that targeted killings in other locations constitute unlawful assassinations, at least if apprehension is a feasible alternative.[216] The issue has been further complicated by the fact that some of the individuals being targeted are not members of Al Qaeda itself but rather are part of organizations that are affiliated in some way with Al Qaeda.

Unless Congress acted to disallow them, it is unlikely that U.S. courts would review the legality of these targeted killings, at least when conducted against foreign citizens outside the United States. A suit was brought in an effort to stop the U.S. government from targeting Anwar Al-Aulaqi, a dual U.S.–Yemeni citizen who allegedly had an operational role in an organization that is affiliated with Al Qaeda. The court concluded, however, that the targeting decision was a nonjusticiable political question,[217] and Al-Aulaqi was subsequently killed in a drone attack in Yemen.[218] Even if not subject to judicial review,

---

Jens David Ohlin & Andrew Altman eds., 2012); Gabriella Blum & Philip Heymann, *Law and Policy of Targeted Killing*, 1 HARV. NAT'L SEC. J. 145 (2010); and John Yoo, *Assassination or Targeted Killings after 9/11*, 56 N.Y.L. SCH. L. REV. 57 (2011/2012).

[213] *Compare*, for example, Scott Shane, *The Moral Case for Drones*, N.Y. TIMES (July 14, 2012), *with* John Kaag & Sarah Kreps, *The Moral Hazard of Drones*, N.Y. TIMES (July 22, 2012).

[214] Harold Hongju Koh, State Department Legal Adviser, at the Annual Meeting of the American Society of International Law (Mar. 25, 2010), *available at* https://2009-2017.state.gov/s/l/releases/remarks/139119.htm.

[215] John O. Brennan, Assistant to the President for Homeland Security and Counterterrorism at the Woodrow Wilson International Center for Scholars, *The Ethics and Efficacy of the President's Counterterrorism Strategy* (Apr. 30, 2012), *available at* http://www.lawfareblog.com/2012/04/brennanspeech/.

[216] *See, e.g.,* Mary Ellen O'Connell, *Unlawful Killing with Combat Drones: A Case Study of Pakistan, 2004–2009* (July 2010), *available at* http://www.law.upenn.edu/academics/institutes/ilp/targetedkilling/papers/OConnellDrones.pdf.

[217] Al-Aulaqi v. Obama, 727 F. Supp. 2d 1, 46–52 (D.D.C. 2010); *see also, e.g.*, Jaber v. United States, 861 F.3d 241, 247 (D.C. Cir. 2017) ("Put simply, it is not the role of the Judiciary to second-guess the determination of the Executive, in coordination with the Legislature, that the interests of the U.S. call for a particular military action in the ongoing War on Terror.").

[218] *See* Mark Mazzetti, Eric Schmitt & Robert F. Worth, *Two-Year Manhunt Led to Killing of Awlaki in Yemen*, N.Y. TIMES (Sept. 30, 2011); *see also* Charlie Savage, *Secret U.S. Memo Made Legal Case to Kill a Citizen*, N.Y.

press reports have indicated that there is an elaborate process within the executive branch for decisions relating to targeted killings, and that this process even includes the direct involvement of the president.[219] Nevertheless, critics have complained that there is too much secrecy surrounding both the standards used by the government in making targeted killing decisions and the legal justifications for the program.[220]

Assessments of the legality of targeted killing by lawyers in the executive branch illustrate how principles of international law can be intertwined with the interpretation of U.S. statutory and constitutional law. In 2013, a Department of Justice white paper analyzing the legality of targeted killing of U.S. citizens, which had been prepared in 2011, was leaked to the press.[221] The white paper concluded that, when the following three conditions are met, the use of lethal force against a U.S. citizen in a foreign country is permissible: "(1) an informed, high-level official of the U.S. government has determined that the targeted individual poses an imminent threat of violent attack against the United States; (2) capture is infeasible, and the United States continues to monitor whether capture becomes feasible; and (3) the operation would be conducted in a manner consistent with applicable law of war principles."[222] The third condition explicitly links the legality of targeted killing under U.S. law, including U.S. constitutional law, to an assessment of its legality under international law. In addition, the first condition refers to the concept of "imminence," a concept related to the international law right of self-defense, and the white paper adopts a broad conception of the concept for this context, such that it "does not require the United States to have clear evidence that a specific attack on U.S. persons and interests will take place in the immediate future."[223]

TIMES (Oct. 8, 2011). For a debate over the legality of this targeted killing, *see* John C. Dehn & Kevin Jon Heller, *Debate: Targeted Killing: The Case of Anwar Al-Aulaqi*, 159 U. PA. L. REV. 175 (2011).

[219] *See, e.g.,* Jo Becker & Scott Shane, *Secret "Kill List" Proves a Test of Obama's Principles and Will,* N.Y. TIMES (May 29, 2012). For additional discussion of President Obama's involvement in targeted killing decisions, *see* DANIEL KLAIDMAN, KILL OR CAPTURE: THE WAR ON TERROR AND THE SOUL OF THE OBAMA PRESIDENCY (2012).

[220] *See, e.g.,* David Cole, *Killing Our Citizens without Trial,* N.Y. REV. OF BOOKS (Dec. 22, 2011); Steve Coll, Daily Comment, *Kill or Capture,* NEW YORKER (Aug. 2, 2012).

[221] Department of Justice White Paper (Draft Nov. 8, 2011), *at* https://www.justice.gov/sites/default/files/oip/legacy/2014/07/23/dept-white-paper.pdf.

[222] *Id.* at 1.

[223] *Id.* at 7. The paper explains that "certain members of al-Qa'ida (including any potential target of lethal force) are continually plotting attacks against the United States; that al-Qa'ida would engage in such attacks regularly to the extent it were able to do so; that the U.S. government may not be aware of all al-Qa'ida plots as they are developing and thus cannot be confident that none is about to occur; and that, in light of these predicates, the nation may have a limited window of opportunity within which to strike in a manner that both has a high likelihood of success and reduces the probability of American casualties." *Id.* at 8. Attorney General Eric Holder had articulated similar views in a speech in 2012. *See* Department of Justice, *Attorney General Eric Holder Speaks at Northwestern University School of Law* (Mar. 5, 2012), *at* http://www.justice.gov/iso/opa/ag/speeches/2012/ag-speech-1203051.html.

In 2014, the Obama administration released a redacted version of a 2010 memorandum prepared by the Justice Department's Office of Legal Counsel that specifically analyzed the legality of targeting Al-Aulaqi.[224] The memorandum concluded, among other things, that the AUMF's authorization of force "may apply in appropriate circumstances to a United States citizen who is part of the forces of an enemy organization within the scope of the force authorization,"[225] and that the use of force against Al-Aulaqi would not violate other statutory provisions. The memorandum also concluded that a targeted killing of Al-Aulaqi would be consistent with the international laws of war, something that, the memorandum reasoned, "also bears on whether the operation would be authorized by the AUMF."[226] International law would not be violated, according to the memorandum, because the United States was engaged in a non-international armed conflict with Al Qaeda; this conflict now extended to the activities of a group affiliated with Al Qaeda in Yemen, of which Al-Aulaqi was a high-level member involved in planning attacks; and international law allows for the targeting of such a member of an enemy organization.[227]

The Trump administration reportedly lifted some of the Obama administration's restrictions on targeted killings outside of areas of active hostilities. For example, the Trump administration appeared to have designated sections of Somalia and Yemen as areas of active hostilities to which the restrictions did not apply, and to have allowed U.S. forces to target not only high-level militants but also foot soldiers.[228] President Trump also issued an executive order that ended a requirement, imposed by President Obama in 2016, of reporting the number of strikes undertaken by the United States against terrorist targets outside areas of active hostilities and assessing the combatant and noncombatant deaths resulting from those strikes.[229]

Controversy over targeted killing resurfaced in early 2020, when the Trump administration used a drone to target and kill Qassem Soleimani, an Iranian military commander, after he had arrived in Iraq to meet with Iraq's prime minister. The administration offered a variety of legal and policy justifications for the strike, some of which appeared to shift over time.[230] The administration claimed, among other things, that Soleimani was

---

[224] *See* Memorandum from David J. Barron, Acting Assistant Attorney General, to the Attorney General, *Applicability of Federal Criminal Laws and the Constitution to Contemplated Lethal Operations Against Shaykh Anwar al-Aulaqi* (July 16, 2010), *available at* http://justsecurity.org/wp-content/uploads/2014/06/OLC-Awlaki-Memo.pdf.

[225] *Id.* at 23.

[226] *Id.*

[227] *See id.* at 24–27.

[228] *See* Charlie Savage & Eric Schmitt, *Trump Poised to Drop Some Limits on Drone Strikes and Commando Raids*, N.Y. Times (Sept. 21, 2017).

[229] *See* Executive Order on Revocation of Reporting Requirement (Mar. 6, 2019), *at* https://www.whitehouse.gov/presidential-actions/executive-order-revocation-reporting-requirement/.

[230] *See* Chris Cameron & Helene Cooper, *The Trump Administration's Fluctuating Explanations for the Suleimani Strike*, N.Y. TIMES (Jan. 12, 2020).

planning attacks on U.S. embassies and other facilities in Iraq, although the imminence of any such attacks was unclear. For domestic legal authority, the administration cited both the president's commander-in-chief authority as well as a 2002 statute authorizing the use of force in Iraq, which was enacted when Saddam Hussein was still in power in that country. While acknowledging that "the threat posed by Saddam Hussein's regime was the initial focus of the statute," the administration argued that "the United States has long relied upon the 2002 [statute] to authorize the use of force for the purpose of establishing a stable, democratic Iraq and addressing terrorist threats emanating from Iraq."[231] As for the consistency of the strike with international law, the administration claimed that it was a lawful exercise of the U.S. right of self-defense under the UN Charter in response to an "escalating series of armed attacks in recent months" by Iran and Iranian-backed forces on U.S. personnel in Iraq.[232]

* * *

In the United States, the efficacy of international law relating to war, at least in the modern era, is determined in large part by its incorporation and acceptance by the political branches of the government rather than its direct application by the judiciary. Courts are generally deferential to Congress and the executive branch when it comes to issues relating to war, in light of the high stakes involved and the perception that government flexibility is particularly needed in this context, and on some issues the courts are likely to abstain altogether. Moreover, when courts do consider international law as it relates to war powers, they typically apply it only indirectly to help inform their interpretation of political branch actions rather than as a basis for overriding these actions. Nevertheless, as is true with other topics covered in this book, allowing international law an interpretive role can have significant consequences for judicial decision-making.

---

[231] Notes on the Legal and Policy Frameworks Guiding the United States' Use of Military Force and Related National Security Operations, *at* https://www.documentcloud.org/documents/6776446-Section-1264-NDAA-Notice.html. *See also* Robert Chesney & Eric Talbot Jensen, *The Pentagon's General Counsel Defends the Legality of the Soleimani Strike*, LAWFARE (Mar. 11, 2020), *at* https://www.lawfareblog.com/pentagons-general-counsel-defends-legality-soleimani-strike. In response to the strike, Iran launched missiles at two bases in Iraq housing U.S. forces, and, while anticipating a U.S. counter-response, accidentally shot down a civilian airliner shortly after it had taken off from Tehran. *See* Farnaz Fassihi, *Iran Says it Unintentionally Shot Down Ukranian Airliner*, N.Y. TIMES (Jan. 10, 2020).

[232] *See* Hadley Baker, *U.S. and Iran Submit Article 51 Letters on Use of Force*, LAWFARE (Jan. 9, 2020). In July 2020, a U.N. Special Rapporteur on extrajudicial, summary or arbitration executions concluded that the strike was unlawful. *See* Elliot Setzer, *U.N. Special Rapporteur Release Report on Drone Strikes and Soleimani Killing*, LAWFARE (July 9, 2020), *at* https://www.lawfareblog.com/un-special-rapporteur-release-report-drone-strikes-and-soleimani-killing.

It is also worth noting that even if the United States is not always perfectly compliant with the international laws of war, Congress and the executive branch give significant attention to it, in part because the United States has a strong interest in having other nations observe it, but also because it is generally consistent with the country's long-standing values and ideals.[233]

---

[233] For an excellent historical account of the relationship between the United States and the international laws of war, see JOHN FABIAN WITT, LINCOLN'S CODE: THE LAWS OF WAR IN AMERICAN HISTORY (2012).

Conclusion

THE TOPICS ADDRESSED in this book illustrate the rich and varied role that international law plays in the U.S. legal system. Sometimes this role involves direct application of treaties or customary international law by the courts, but often it involves something else: codification by Congress; implementation through executive branch orders or regulations; indirect application through statutory interpretation; or a fusion of international and domestic legal principles in judicially developed common law. Indeed, a central theme of the book is that domestic law and institutions typically mediate the application of international law in the United States and, in doing so, international law is inevitably altered. The international law in the U.S. legal system is not the international law applied by, say, the International Court of Justice. This does not mean that the U.S. legal system always operates as a limitation on international law. At various times, starting at least as far back as the Supreme Court's 1812 sovereign immunity decision in the *Schooner Exchange* case, the application of international law in the U.S. legal system has contributed to its development elsewhere.

To understand how international law operates in the United States, it is necessary to understand the basic structural features of the U.S. constitutional system, particularly the separation of powers among the three branches of the federal government and the federalism relationship between the national government and the states. The separation-of-powers structure means, for example, that some delegations of authority to international institutions will raise constitutional questions for the United States, especially if the delegations entail giving direct domestic effect to the decisions or orders of the institutions. And the federalism structure means, for example, that some issues that might affect foreign relations are addressed by the states in the first instance and that, at least as a matter of political practice, the national government often takes account of state sovereignty when deciding whether and how to conclude international agreements.

The role of the courts with respect to the application of international law is complicated by these structural considerations. As we have seen, because of perceived limitations on their expertise and institutional role, courts generally give deference to the views of the executive branch concerning the content of international law. Moreover, although they sometimes apply international law directly, courts tend not to do so if they perceive that such application is contrary to the wishes of the political branches. Although courts have developed common law doctrines to help resolve foreign relations disputes, these doctrines tend to be informed at least as much by domestic legal and historical considerations as they do by international law. Nevertheless, courts do presume that federal statutes are not intended to conflict with international law, and they more generally seek to avoid creating unnecessary foreign relations friction in their decision-making.

It should be apparent from this book that treaties and customary international law, while of essentially equal weight on the international plane, do not have equal status in the U.S. legal system. Self-executing treaties can override federal statutes, for example, whereas customary international law—whatever its precise domestic status—has a lower position in the hierarchy of American law. Similarly, although courts have often affirmed that treaties can preempt inconsistent state law, there are essentially no judicial decisions giving customary international law such preemptive effect. Moreover, various judicially developed rules such as the act of state doctrine have express exceptions for treaty violations, but they have no such categorical exception for violations of customary international law. This differential domestic status between treaties and customary international law should not be surprising, given that treaties are addressed much more extensively in the U.S. Constitution and engage more directly with U.S. democratic processes.

Even with respect to treaties, international human rights law has posed particular challenges for the U.S. legal system. The rise of this body of law has been one of the most significant developments in the history of international law, but its overlap with sensitive issues of social policy that have historically been regulated at the domestic level (such as capital punishment) poses new questions of self-governance and federalism for the United States. The United States has addressed these questions by selective ratification of human rights treaties and by the use of conditional consent for the treaties that it has ratified, including most notably the frequent use of non–self-execution declarations. The application in the United States of the customary international law of human rights, however, has been managed more by the courts, especially in cases involving the Alien

Tort Statute, and that is part of the reason that the domestic status of customary international law has become so controversial.

The approach of the U.S. legal system to international law has changed over time, as both international law and the place of the United States in the world have evolved. The rise of multilateral, legislative-style treaties, for example, has been paralleled by a more robust use in the United States of the non–self-execution doctrine. The technological and other changes that have made it easier for nations to conclude agreements, along with the more prominent role played by the United States in international affairs, have been paralleled by a significant expansion in the use of executive agreements as an alternative to Article II treaties. The global presence of the U.S. military and frequent involvement of the United States in military operations have been paralleled by the cautionary approach of the United States toward certain international institutions such as the International Criminal Court.

In part because of historical contingency, a final point that should be evident from the book is that many issues surrounding the status of international law in the U.S. legal system are never entirely settled. To take a few examples, the relationship between the treaty power and federalism, the proper scope of executive agreements, and the domestic status of customary international law are all topics of recurring debate and uncertainty. Although the centers of gravity in the debates may appear settled at particular times, changes in other areas of law, or in domestic politics, or in global affairs, can create new bases for contestation. There is in effect a continuing dialogue on these and other topics—among political actors, the courts, the scholarly community, and the public at large. As someone who has written frequently in this area, and who has had the opportunity to provide advice to the government, it has been my privilege to participate in this dialogue.

Table of Cases

A.L.A. Schechter Poultry Corp. v. United States, 295 U.S. 495 (1935), 26–27n.144
Abbott v. Abbott, 560 U.S. 1 (2010), 69n.208, 70, 70–71n.218
Abdulaziz v. Metro. Dade Cty., 741 F.3d 1328 (11th Cir. 1984), 262–63n.148
Abelesz v. Magyar National Bank, 692 F.3d 661 (7th Cir. 2012), 254n.90
Abiodun v. Martin Oil Serv., Inc., 475 F.2d 142 (7th Cir. 1973), 214–15n.20
Abiola v. Abubakar, 267 F. Supp. 2d 907 (N.D. Ill. 2003), 266–67n.174
Abrams v. Societe Nationale des Chemins de fer Francais, 389 F.3d 61 (2d Cir. 2004), 248–49n.61
Adra v. Clift, 195 F. Supp. 857 (D. Md. 1961), 214–15n.19
Agency for Int'l Development v. Alliance for Open Society Int'l., 207 L. Ed. 2d 654 (2020), 179n.23
"Agent Orange" Prod. Liability Litig., *In re*, 373 F. Supp. 2d 7 (E.D.N.Y. 2005), 216–17n.31
Agudas Chasidei Chabad of United States v. Russian Fed'n, 528 F.3d 924 (D.C. Cir. 2008), 165n.103
Ahmad v. Wigen, 910 F.2d 1063 (2d Cir. 1990), 283n.54
Air France v. Saks, 470 U.S. 392 (1985), 69nn.207–08, 70n.217
Al-Aulaqi v. Obama, 727 F. Supp. 2d 1 (D.D.C. 2010), 339–40n.217
Al-Alwi v. Trump, 901F.3d 294, 299 (D.C. Cir. 2018), 322–23n.128
Al Bahlul, United States v., 767 F.3d 1 (D.C. Cir. 2014), 335nn.193–195
Al Bahlul v. United States, 840 F.3d 757 (D.C. Cir. 2016), 335n.196
Al-Bihani v. Obama, 590 F.3d 866 (D.C. Cir. 2010), xi–xiin.7, 322–23n.128, 323–24
Al-Bihani v. Obama, 619 F.3d 1 (D.C. Cir. 2010), xi–xiin.7, 161–62n.87, 297n.12, 323–24n.132
Aldana v. Del Monte Fresh Produce, 416 F.3d 1242 (11th Cir. 2005), 220n.49
Alden v. Maine, 527 U.S. 706 (1999), 30n.161, 63–64nn.175–76
Alexander v. Sandoval, 532 U.S. 275 (2001), 164n.97
Alfred Dunhill of London, Inc. v. Republic of Cuba, 425 U.S. 682 (1976), 12–13n.71, 12–13n.74
Al-Hamdi, United States v., 356 F.3d 564 (4th Cir. 2004), 261n.132, 262–63n.149
Al-Hela v. Trump, 2019 U.S. Dist. LEXIS 42717 (D.D.C. Mar. 15, 2019), 323–24n.133
Ali, United States v., 718 F.3d 929 (D.C. Cir. 2013), 195n.112, 200

Ali Shafi v. Palestinian Authority, 642 F.3d 1088 (D.C. Cir. 2011), 210–11n.5
Allied Bank Int'l v. Banco Credito Agricola de Cartago, 757 F.2d 516 (2d Cir. 1985), 12–13n.72
Allstate Ins. Co. v. Hague, 449 U.S. 302 (1981), 206n.176
Al Odah v. United States, 611 F.3d 8 (D.C. Cir. 2010), 321n.119
Aluminum Co. of Am., United States v., 148 F.2d 416 (2d Cir. 1945), 187–88n.71
Already, LLC v. Nike, Inc., 568 U.S. 85 (2013), 4–5n.18
Al Shamari v. CACI Premier Technology, Inc., 758 F.3d 516 (4th Cir. 2014), 230–31n.102
Alvarez-Machain, United States v., 504 U.S. 655 (1992), 220n.53, 285–86n.77, 289–90
Alvarez-Machain, United States v., No. CR-87-422-(G)-ER (C.D. Cal. Dec. 14, 1992), 289n.101
Al Warafi v. Obama, 821 F. Supp. 2d 47 (D.D.C. 2011), 323–24n.133
Am. Banana Co. v. United Fruit Co., 213 U.S. 347 (1909), 186–87
Am. Baptist Churches v. Meese, 712 F. Supp. 756 (N.D. Cal. 1989), 17n.94
Am. Coalition for Free Trade v. Clinton, 128 F.3d 761 (D.C. Cir. 1997), 122–23n.72
Am. Dredging Co. v. Miller, 510 U.S. 443 (1994), 14–15n.81
Am. Ins. Ass'n v. Garamendi, 539 U.S. 396 (2003), 29, 29n.160, 93–94, 99, 205–6n.175
Am. Ins. Co. v. Canter, 26 U.S. (1 Pet.) (1828), 148–49n.13
Am. Pub. Power Ass'n v. Power Auth., 355 U.S. 64 (1957), 54n.123, 65–66n.187
Ameur v. Gates, 759 F.3d 317 (4th Cir. 2012), 337–38n.209
The Amiable Isabella, 19 U.S. (6 Wheat.) 1 (1821), 50–51n.107
Andonian, United States v., 29 F.3d 1432 (9th Cir. 1994), 286n.81
Ange v. Bush, 752 F. Supp. 509 (D.D.C. 1990), 306–7n.65
Anh v. Levi, 586 F.2d 625 (6th Cir. 1978), 214–15n.20
Animal Science Prods., Inc. v. Hebei Welcome Pharm. Co. Ltd., 138 S. Ct. 1865 (2018), 10n.52
The Apollon, 22 U.S. (9 Wheat.) 362 (1824), 186n.63, 223–24n.71
Aquamar S.A. v. Del Monte Fresh Produce N.A., Inc., 179 F.3d 1279 (11th Cir. 1999), 165–66n.104
Arar v. Ashcroft, 585 F.3d 559 (2d Cir. 2009), 291–92n.115, 337–38n.209
ARC Ecology v. U.S. Dep't of the Air Force, 411 F.3d 1092 (9th Cir. 2005), 18–19n.102
Arce v. Garcia, 400 F.3d 1340 (11th Cir. 2005), 220n.51
Architectural Ingenieria Siglo XXI, LLC v. Dominican Republic, 788 F.3d 1329 (11th Cir. 2015), 249n.63
Argentine Republic v. Amerada Hess Shipping Corp., 488 U.S. 428 (1989), 245–46n.41, 247–48, 255n.96
Arizona v. United States, 567 U.S. 387 (2012), 21–22n.117, 28n.153, 205–6n.173
Arizona State Legislature v. Arizona Indep. Redistricting Comm'n, 135 S. Ct. 2652 (2015), 4n.16
Arjona, United States v., 120 U.S. 479 (1887), 146–47n.5
Arrest Warrant of April 11, 2000 (Dem. Rep. Congo v. Belg.), 2000 I.C.J. 3 (Feb. 14), 264n.159
Asakura v. City of Seattle, 265 U.S. 332 (1924), 44–45n.65, 65n.183
Asarco, Inc. v. Kadish, 490 U.S. 605 (1989), 6n.28
Ashcroft v. al-Kidd, 563 U.S. 731 (2011), 337–38n.209
Assicurazioni Generali, S.P.A., In re, 592 F.3d 113 (2d Cir. 2010), 29n.156, 94n.69
Ass'n of Am. Railroads v. U.S. Dep't of Transp., 721 F.3d 666 (D.C. Cir. 2013), 110n.17
Atamirzayeva v. United States, 524 F.3d 1320 (Fed. Cir. 2008), 179n.22
Att'y General of Canada v. R.J. Reynolds Tobacco Holdings, Inc., 268 F.3d 103 (2d Cir. 2001), 10n.53
Auguste v. Ridge, 395 F.3d 123 (3d Cir. 2005), 40n.44, 46n.75, 53–54n.120
Avena decision *See* Case Concerning Avena and Other Mexican Nationals
Avero Belg. Ins. v. Am. Airlines, Inc., 423 F.3d 73 (2d Cir. 2005), 166n.109
Awad v. Obama, 608 F.3d 1 (D.C. Cir. 2010), 321n.119
Awad v. Ziriax, 747 F. Supp. 2d 1298 (W.D. Okla. 2010), *aff'd*, 670 F.3d 1111 (10th Cir. 2012), 169–70n.129

B. Altman & Co. v. United States, 224 U.S. 583 (1912), 86n.28
Bahel, United States v., 662 F.3d 610 (2d Cir. 2011), 263–64n.157
Bakelite Corp., Ex parte, 279 U.S. 438 (1929), 113n.31
Baker v. Carr, 369 U.S. 186 (1962), 5, 5–6n.25
Balintulo v. Daimler AG, 727 F.3d 174 (2d Cir. 2013), 230–31n.102
Balsys, United States v., 119 F.3d 122 (2d Cir. 1997), 273–74n.6
Balzac v. Porto Rico, 258 U.S. 298 (1922), 177n.5
Banco Nacional de Cuba v. Farr, 383 F.2d 166 (2d Cir. 1967), 14n.79
Banco Nacional de Cuba v. Sabbatino, 376 U.S. 398 (1964), 9n.50, 11–12, 12–13n.72, 12–13n.74, 13–14, 23–24n.121, 28n.152, 155–56, 265n.165
Bannerman v. Snyder, 325 F.3d 722 (6th Cir. 2003), 40n.44
Barclays Bank PLC v. Franchise Tax Board of California, 512 U.S. 298 (1994), 28n.154
Barinas, United States v., 865 F.3d 99, 105 (2d Cir. 2017), 286n.80
Barrera-Echavarria v. Rison, 44 F.3d 1441 (9th Cir. 1995), 159–60n.75
Bas v. Tingy, 4 U.S. (4 Dall.) 37 (1800), 299–300n.26
Baston, United States v., 818 F.3d 651 (11th Cir. 2016), 202–3n.159
Beazley v. Johnson, 242 F.3d 248 (5th Cir. 2001), 40n.44
Beg v. Islamic Republic of Pakistan, 353 F.3d 1323 (11th Cir. 2003), 251–52n.76, 254n.89
Beharry v. Reno, 183 F. Supp. 2d 584 (S.D.N.Y. 2002), *rev'd* 329 F.3d 51 (2d Cir. 2003), 18n.100, 159–60n.77
Belfast, United States v., 611 F.3d 783 (11th Cir. 2010), 201–2n.152, 203–4n.164
Belhas v. Ya'alon, 515 F.3d 1279 (D.C. Cir. 2008), 268–69n.183
Bellaizac-Hurtado, United States v., 700 F.3d 1245 (11th Cir. 2012), 146–47n.5, 203–4n.162, 205
Belmont, United States v., 301 U.S. 324 (1937), 92, 158–59
Benjamins v. British European Airways, 572 F.2d 913 (2d Cir. 1978), 214–15n.20
Bensayah v. Obama, 610 F.3d 718 (D.C. Cir. 2010), 321n.120
Benz v. Compania Naviera Hidalgo, S.A., 353 U.S. 138 (1957), 187–88n.67
Bergman v. De Sieyes, 170 F.2d 360 (2d Cir. 1948), 154
Berizzi Bros. Co. v. Steamship Pesaro, 271 U.S. 562 (1926), 241–42n.16
Berkovitz v. United States, 486 U.S. 531 (1988), 255–56n.101
Bersch v. Drexel Firestone, Inc., 519 F.2d 974 (2d Cir. 1975), 190–91n.87
Best, United States v., 304 F.3d 308 (3d Cir. 2002), 290–91n.110
Bishop v. Reno, 210 F.3d 1295 (11th Cir. 2000), 277n.92
Bi v. Union Carbide Chems. & Plastics Co., 984 F.2d 582 (2d Cir. 1993), 15–16n.88
Bivens v. Six Unknown Named Agents of the Federal Bureau of Narcotics, 403 U.S. 388 (1971), 180n.27
Blackmer v. United States, 284 U.S. 421 (1932), 7n.33, 197
Boim v. Holy Land Found. for Relief & Dev., 549 F.3d 685 (7th Cir. 2008), 232n.111
Bolchos v. Darrel, 3 F. Cas. 810 (D.S.C. 1795), 214–15n.19
Bolivarian Republic of Venezuela v. Helmerich & Payne Int'l Drilling Co., 137 S. Ct. 1312 (2017), 254nn.91–92
Bollinger, United States v., 798 F.3d 201 (4th Cir. 2015), 202–3n.159
Bond v. United States, 572 U.S. 844 (2014), xi, 31, 62–63, 66–67, 111n.20, 115n.40
Bond v. United States, 564 U.S. 211 (2011), 62–63n.167
Boos v. Barry, 485 U.S. 312 (1988), 68
Boots, United States v., 80 F.3d 580 (1st Cir. 1996), 10n.53
Boumediene v. Bush, 553 U.S. 723 (2008), 183–84, 320–21
Bowman, United States v., 260 U.S. 94 (1922), 187–88n.68
Boyle v. United Techs. Corp., 487 U.S. 500 (1988), 9n.50, 154–55n.44

Bradford v. Dir. Gen. of R.R.s of Mexico, 278 S.W. 251 (Tex. Ct. App. 1925), 241n.12
Breard v. Greene, 523 U.S. 371 (1998), 55–56n.126, 63–64n.177, 125
Broidy Capital Mgmt. LLC v. Benomar, 944 F.3d 436 (2d Cir. 2019), 261n.131
Brown v. Board of Education, 347 U.S. 483 (1954), 216–17
Brown v. United States, 12 U.S. (8 Cranch) 110 (1814), 302
Brzak v. United Nations, 597 F.3d 107 (2d Cir. 2010), 263–64n.158
Buckley v. Valeo, 424 U.S. 1 (1976), 111–12nn.25–26
Burnham v. Superior Ct. of Cal., 495 U.S. 604 (1990), 7n.36
Buttfield v. Stranahan, 192 U.S. 470 (1904), 22–23n.120, 202n.156
Byrd v. Corporacion Forestal y Industrial de Olancho, SA, 182 F.3d 380 (5th Cir. 1999), 268n.182

California, United States v., No. 2:19-cv-02142 WBS EFB (E.D. Cal. Mar. 12, 2020), 60n.155
Campbell v. Clinton, 203 F.3d 19 (D.C. Cir. 2000), 4n.15, 306–7n.63
Capital Ventures Int'l v. Republic of Argentina, 552 F.3d 289 (2d Cir. 2009), 249n.63
Cardales, United States v., 168 F.3d 548 (1st Cir. 1999), 198–99n.133, 204nn.168–69
Cardona v. Chiquita Brands Int'l, Inc., 760 F.3d 1185 (11th Cir. 2014), 230–31n.102
Carpenter v. Republic of Chile, 610 F.3d 776 (2d Cir. 2010), 250n.67
Carter v. Carter Coal Co., 298 U.S. 238 (1936), 110n.17
Case Concerning Avena and Other Mexican Nationals, 2004 I.C.J. No. 128 (Judgment), Mar. 31, 2004, 47, 126–27
Case of the S.S. Lotus, 1927 PCIJ, Ser. A, No. 10, 195–96
Cassirer v. Kingdom of Spain, 616 F.3d 1019 (9th Cir. 2010), 254n.88
Cent. Bank of Denver v. First Interstate Bank of Denver, 511 U.S. 164 (1994), 232nn.111–12
Chae Chan Ping v. United States (Chinese Exclusion Case), 130 U.S. 581 (1889), 21–22n.117, 55–56nn.126–27
Champion v. Ames (The "Lottery Case"), 188 U.S. 321 (1903), 202n.156
Chan v. Korean Airlines, 490 U.S. 122 (1989), 69n.210
Charlton v. Kelly, 229 U.S. 447 (1913), 74n.240, 279n.30
Charming Betsy *See* Murray v. The Schooner Charming Betsy
Chavez v. Carranza, 559 F.3d 486 (6th Cir. 2009), 220n.51
The Cherokee Tobacco, 78 U.S. (11 Wall.) 616 (1871), 55–56n.126
Chettri v. Nepal Rastra Bank, 834 F.3d 50 (2d Cir. 2016), 251–52n.76
Chevron, U.S.A., Inc. v. NRDC, Inc., 467 U.S. 837 (1984), 20n.107
Chicago & S. Air Lines, Inc. v. Waterman S.S. Corp., 333 U.S. 103 (1948), 3–4n.12, 114, 114n.35
Chong Boon Kim v. Kim Yong Shik, 58 Am. J. Int'l L. 186 (Haw. Cir. Ct. 1963), 266–67n.172
Chubb & Son, Inc. v. Asiana Airlines, 214 F.3d 301 (2d Cir. 2000), 33–34n.5
Chuidian v. Philippine National Bank, 912 F.2d 1095 (9th Cir. 1990), 268
Cicippio-Puleo v. Islamic Republic of Iran, 353 F.3d 1024 (D.C. Cir. 2004), 257–58n.110
Citizens Ins. Co. of America v. Daccach, 217 S.W.3d 430 (Tex. 2007), 205–6n.172
City of Boerne v. Flores, 521 U.S. 507 (1997), 30n.161, 30n.165
City of Milwaukee v. Illinois, 451 U.S. 304 (1981), 162–63n.90
Clapper v. Amnesty Int'l, 568 U.S. 398 (2013), 3–4n.13
Clark, United States v., 435 F.3d 1100 (9th Cir. 2006), 202–3n.159
Clark v. Allen, 331 U.S. 503 (1947), 44–45n.65
Clearfield Trust Co. v. United States, 318 U.S. 363 (1943), 154–55n.42
Clinton v. City of New York, 524 U.S. 417 (1998), 26–27n.146, 73n.230, 110
Coalition for Fair Lumber Imports v. United States, 471 F.3d 1329 (D.C. Cir. 2006), 122–23n.72
Cohen v. Hartman, 490 F. Supp. 517 (S.D. Fla. 1980), 214–15n.20
Collins v. Loisel, 259 U.S. 309 (1922), 279–80n.35

Commissioner's Subpoenas, *In re*, 325 F.3d 1287 (11th Cir. 2003), 55–56n.129, 287n.87
Comm. of United States Citizens Living in Nicaragua v. Reagan, 859 F.2d 929 (D.C. Cir. 1988), 142
Commodity Futures Trading Comm'n v. Schor, 478 U.S. 833 (1986), 113n.32
Compania de Gas de Nuevo Laredo, S.A. v. Entex, Inc., 686 F.2d 322 (5th Cir. 1982), 14n.79
Compania Espanola de Navegacion Maritima, S.A. v. The Navemar, 303 U.S. 68 (1938), 166–67n.111, 242
Comstock, United States v., 560 U.S. 126 (2010), 21–22n.116, 62n.164
Continental Ore Co. v. Union Carbide & Carbon Corp., 370 U.S. 690 (1962), 187–88n.71
Conyers v. Reagan, 765 F.2d 1124 (D.C. Cir. 1985), 306–7n.65
Cook v. United States, 288 U.S. 102 (1933), 52n.114, 55–56n.128, 56–57n.136, 289n.99
Coolidge, United States v., 14 U.S. (1 Wheat.) 415 (1816), 52n.112, 150n.18
Coplin v. United States, 6 Cl. Ct. 115 (1984), 70–71n.218
Corey, United States v., 232 F.3d 1166 (9th Cir. 2000), 18–19n.102, 325n.136
Cornejo-Barreto v. Seifert [*sic*], 218 F.3d 1004 (9th Cir. 2000), 283–84n.62
Cornejo-Barreto v. Siefert, 379 F.3d 1075 (9th Cir. 2004), 284n.64
Cornejo-Barreto v. Siefert, 386 F.3d 938 (9th Cir. 2004), 284n.65
Cornejo-Barreto v. Siefert, 389 F.3d 1307 (9th Cir. 2004), 284n.66
Correctional Servs. Corp. v. Malesko, 534 U.S. 61 (2001), 234n.121
Crist v. Republic of Turkey, 995 F. Supp. 5 (D.D.C. 1998), 254n.88
Crockett v. Reagan, 720 F.2d 1355 (D.C. Cir. 1983), 306–7n.64
Crosby v. Nat'l Foreign Trade Council, 530 U.S. 363 (2000), 28n.153, 31n.169, 42n.54, 205–6n.173, 205–6n.175
Cross v. Harrison, 57 U.S. (16 How.) 164 (1854), 301n.34
Crowell v. Benson, 285 U.S. 22 (1932), 113n.31
Curtiss-Wright Export Corp., United States v., 299 U.S. 304 (1936), 23–24n.124, 24–25n.133, 26–27n.145, 27–28n.147, 86n.27, 110n.17
Cutting Case, 199

Daimler AG v. Bauman, 571 U.S. 117 (2014), 7nn.34–35
Daliberti v. Republic of Iraq, 97 F. Supp. 2d 38 (D.D.C. 2000), 257n.106
Damaskinos v. Societa Navigacion Interamericana, S.A., 255 F. Supp. 919 (S.D.N.Y. 1966), 214–15n.20
Dames & Moore v. Regan, 453 U.S. 654 (1981), 26n.139, 26n.141, 27–28n.147, 93, 94–95, 99
Darby, United States v., 312 U.S. 100 (1941), 30n.162
Dávila-Reyes, United States v., 937 F.3d 57 (1st Cir. 2019), 204n.169
de Csepel v. Republic of Hungary, 859 F.3d 1094 (D.C. Cir. 2017), 254n.90
DeFunis v. Odegaard, 416 U.S. 312 (1974), 4–5n.18
Delchi Carrier Spa v. Rotorex Corp., 71 F.3d 1024 (2d Cir. 1995), 44–45n.67
Delgado-Garcia, United States v., 374 F.3d 1337 (D.C. Cir. 2004), 187–88n.68, 192–93n.100
DeSilva v. DiLeonardi, 125 F.3d 1110 (7th Cir. 1997), 279–80n.37
Diggs v. Richardson, 555 F.2d 848 (D.C. Cir. 1976), 44n.64, 141–42
Dire, United States v., 680 F.3d 446 (4th Cir. 2012), 165n.101, 200
Doe, *In re*, 860 F.2d 40 (2d Cir. 1988), 266–67n.174, 267nn.175–76, 267n.178
Doe I v. State of Israel, 400 F. Supp. 2d 86 (D.D.C. 2005), 268–69nn.183–84
Doe I v. Unocal Corp., 403 F.3d 708 (9th Cir. 2005), 217n.75
D'Oench, Duhme & Co. v. FDIC, 315 U.S. 447 (1942), 162–63n.92
Doe v. Bin Laden, 663 F.3d 64 (2d Cir. 2011), 257n.106
Doe v. Buratai, 792 Fed. App. 6 (D.C. Cir. 2019), 7–8n.39
Doe v. Bush, 323 F.3d 133 (1st Cir. 2003), 4–5n.20

Doe v. Exxon Mobil Corp., 654 F.3d 11 (D.C. Cir. 2011), 225–26n.76, 225–26n.78, 232–33nn.113–14, 234n.120
Doe v. Fed. Dem. Rep, of Ethiopia, 851 F.3d 7 (D.C. Cir. 2017), 255n.97
Doe v. Holder, 763 F.3d 251 (2d Cir. 2014), 45n.70
Doe v. Holy See, 557 F.3d 1066 (9th Cir. 2009), 256n.103
Doe v. Mattis, 889 F.3d 745 (D.C. Cir. 2018), 185n.59
Doe v. Nestle, S.A., 906 F.3d 1120 (9th Cir. 2018), *amended*, 929 F.3d 623 (9th Cir. 2018), 230–31n.102, 236n.131
Doe v. Saravia, 348 F. Supp. 2d 1112 (E.D. Cal. 2004), 220n.50
Doe v. Unocal Corp., 963 F. Supp. 880 (C.D. Cal. 1997), 232n.110
Doe v. Zedillo, 2014 U.S. App. LEXIS 2873 (2d Cir. Feb. 18, 2014), 270–71n.192
Dogan v. Barak, 932 F.3d 888 (9th Cir. 2019), 271–72
Doherty, *In re*, 599 F. Supp. 270 (S.D.N.Y. 1984), 280–81n.42
Dole Food Co. v. Patrickson, 538 U.S. 468 (2003), 246n.44
Dorr v. United States, 195 U.S. 138 (1904), 177nn.5–7
Dred Scott v. Sandford, 60 U.S. 393 (1857), 55–56n.127
Dreyfus v. Von Finck, 534 F.2d 24 (2d Cir. 1976), 214–15n.22
Duncan v. Louisiana, 391 U.S. 145 (1968), 28n.150
Durand v. Hollins, 8 F. Cas. 111 (C.C.S.D.N.Y. 1860), 303n.46
Durham, United States v., 902 F.3d 1180 (10th Cir. 2018), 202–3n.159

Eain v. Wilkes, 641 F.2d 504 (7th Cir. 1981), 280–81n.41
Edmond v. United States, 520 U.S. 651 (1997), 111–12n.24, 111–12n.27
Edwards v. Carter, 580 F.2d 1055 (D.C. Cir. 1978), 52n.116, 53n.118
Edye v. Robertson (Head Money Cases), 112 U.S. 580 (1884), 55–56n.126
EEOC v. Arabian Am. Oil Co., 499 U.S. 244 (1991), 188–89
El Al Israel Airlines, Ltd. v. Tseng, 525 U.S. 155 (1999), 42n.54, 70–71n.218
El-Fadl v. Cent. Bank of Jordan, 75 F.3d 668 (D.C. Cir. 1996), 268n.182
El-Hadad v. Embassy of the U.A.E., 69 F. Supp. 2d 69 (D.D.C. 1999), 266–67n.172
El-Masri v. United States, 479 F.3d 296 (4th Cir. 2007), 291–92n.115
Emami v. U.S. District Ct., 834 F.2d 1444 (9th Cir. 1987), 282n.53
Embassy of the Arab Republic of Egypt v. Lasheen, 603 F.3d 1166 (9th Cir. 2010), 251–52n.76
Emuegbunam, United States v., 268 F.3d 377 (6th Cir. 2001), 45–46n.73
Enahoro v. Abubakar, 408 F.3d 877 (7th Cir. 2005), 220n.48
Erato, *In re*, 2 F.3d 11 (2d Cir. 1993), 55–56n.129, 287n.87
Erie R.R. v. Tompkins, 304 U.S. 64 (1938), 9, 153, 162–63n.90
ESAB Group, Inc. v. Zurich Ins. PLC, 685 F.3d 376 (4th Cir. 2012), 45–46n.73
Estate of Ferdinand Marcos, Human Rights Litig., *In re*, 25 F.3d 1467 (9th Cir. 1994), 218n.39
Estate of Marcos Human Rights Litig., *In re*, 978 F.2d 493 (1992), 160–61n.78
Ex parte *See name of party*
Extradition of Lehming, *In re*, 951 F. Supp. 505 (D. Del. 1996), 278–79n.33

F. Hoffman-La Roche, Ltd. v. Empagran S.A., 542 U.S. 155 (2004), 190, 195n.111
Factor v. Laubenheimer, 290 U.S. 276 (1933), 70–71n.218, 72n.226
Fed. Treasury Enter. Sojuzplodoimport v. Spirits Int'l B.V., 809 F.3d 737 (2d Cir. 2016), 12n.65
Ferreira, United States v., 54 U.S. (13 How.) 40 (1851), 113–14n.34
Field v. Clark, 143 U.S. 649 (1892), 84n.21
Filartiga v. Pena-Irala, 577 F. Supp. 860 (E.D.N.Y. 1984), 12n.69, 225–26n.79
Filartiga v. Pena-Irala, 630 F.2d 876 (2d Cir. 1980), 157–58, 215–17, 217n.34, 227–28n.87

Financial Oversight and Management Bd. for Puerto Rico v. Aurelius Investment, LLC, 140 S. Ct. 1649 (2020), 111–12n.26, 225–26n.78
First Am. Corp. v. Al-Nahyan, 948 F. Supp. 1107 (D.D.C. 1996), 266–67n.174
First Nat'l Bank of Boston v. Bellotti, 435 U.S. 765 (1978), 4–5n.18
First Nat'l City Bank v. Banco Nacional de Cuba, 406 U.S. 759 (1972), 12–13nn.74–75, 165–66
First Nat'l City Bank v. Banco Para El Comercio Exterior de Cuba, 462 U.S. 611 (1983), 159, 160 nn.107–8, 256n.104
Flomo v. Firestone Natural Rubber Co., 643 F.3d 1013 (7th Cir. 2011), 234nn.119–20
Flores v. S. Peru Copper Corp., 343 F.3d 140 (2d Cir. 2003), 40n.44, 46n.75
Flores v. S. Peru Copper Corp., 414 F.3d 233 (2d Cir. 2003), 295n.5
Foley Bros., Inc. v. Filardo, 336 U.S. 281 (1949), 187–88n.67
Fong Yue Ting v. United States, 149 U.S. 698 (1893), 21–22n.117, 275–76n.17
Fontana, United States v., 869 F.3d 464 (6th Cir. 2017), 286n.84
Forti v. Suarez-Mason, 672 F. Supp. 1531 (N.D. Cal. 1987), 160–61n.80
Foster v. Neilson, 27 U.S. (2 Pet.) 253 (1829), 43–44
Frank, United States v., 599 F.3d 1221 (11th Cir. 2010), 187–88n.68
Friends of the Earth, Inc. v. Laidlaw Envt'l Svcs. (TOC), Inc., 528 U.S. 167 (2000), 4–5n.18
Frisbie v. Collins, 342 U.S. 519 (1952), 289n.98
Frolova v. Union of Soviet Socialist Republics, 761 F.2d 370 (7th Cir. 1985), 45n.68, 255n.97, 295n.5
Fund for Animals, Inc. v. Kempthorne, 472 F.3d 872 (D.C. Cir. 2006), 17–18n.99, 56–57nn.134–35
Furlong, United States v., 18 U.S. (5 Wheat.) 184 (1820), 199–200n.137

Gallina v. Fraser, 278 F.2d 77 (2d Cir. 1960), 282n.52
Gallo-Chamorro v. United States, 233 F.3d 1298 (11th Cir. 2000), 279–80n.36, 286n.78
Galo-Garcia v. INS, 86 F.3d 916 (9th Cir. 1996), 295n.7
Garb v. Republic of Poland, 440 F.3d 579 (2d Cir. 2006), 248–49n.59
Garcia-Mir v. Meese, 788 F.2d 1446 (11th Cir. 1986), 159–60n.75
Garcia v. San Antonio Metro. Transit Auth., 469 U.S. 528 (1985), 61–62n.162
Gaubert, United States v., 499 U.S. 315 (1991), 255–56n.101
Geofroy v. Riggs, 133 U.S. 258 (1890), 65, 72n.226
Georgescu, United States v., 723 F. Supp. 912 (E.D.N.Y. 1989), 17–18n.94
Gerling Global Reinsurance Corp. of Am. v. Gallagher, 267 F.3d 1228 (11th Cir. 2001), 206n.177
Gingery v. City of Glendale, 831 F.3d 1222 (9th Cir. 2016), 29n.160
Gisbert v. U.S. Attorney General, 988 F.2d 1437 (5th Cir. 1993), 159–60n.75, 295n.7
Global Fishing, Inc., United States v., 634 F.3d 557 (9th Cir. 2011), 287n.86
Globe Nuclear Servs. & Supply GNSS, Ltd. v. AO Technsabexport, 376 F.3d 282 (4th Cir. 2004), 251–52n.76
Global Reinsurance Corp. U.S. Branch v. Equitas Ltd., 969 N.E.2d 187 (N.Y. 2012), 205n.172
Glucksman v. Henkel, 221 U.S. 508 (1911), 282n.49
Goldstar (Panama) S.A. v. United States, 967 F.2d 965 (4th Cir. 1992), 45–46n.73
Goldwater v. Carter, 444 U.S. 996 (1979), 4–5n.19, 5–6n.24, 74n.239, 75
Gonzales v. O Centro Espirita Beneficente Uniao do Vegetal, 546 U.S. 418 (2006), 68n.205
Gonzales v. Raich, 545 U.S. 1 (2005), 22–23n.119, 30n.167, 202n.155
Gonzalez, United States v., 776 F.3d 931 (11th Cir. 1985), 198–99n.132
Gonzalez v. Gutierrez, 311 F.3d 942 (9th Cir. 2002), 166n.109
Goodyear Dunlop Tires Operations v. Brown, 564 U.S. 915 (2011), 7n.34
Gordon v. United States, 69 U.S. (2 Wall.) 561 (1865), 8n.35
Graham v. Florida, 130 S. Ct. 2011 (2010), xi–xiin.6, 167–68n.118, 169
Graham v. Young, 776 F.3d 700 (8th Cir. 2018), 286n.79

Grand Jury Proceedings, *In re*, 817 F.2d 1108 (4th Cir. 1987), 267n.175
Grand Jury Subpoena, *In re*, 646 F.3d 159 (4th Cir. 2011), 287n.86
Grand Jury Subpoena, *In re*, 912 F.3d 623 (D.C. Cir. 2019), 245–46n.37
Granholm v. Heald, 544 U.S. 460 (2005), 28n.154
Greenspan v. Crosbie, No. 74 Civ. 4734 (GLG), 1976 WL 481 (S.D.N.Y. Nov. 23, 1976), 266n.169
Gregory v. Ashcroft, 501 U.S. 452 (1991), 30n.161, 42n.52
Grupo Protexa, S.A. v. All Am. Marine Slip, 20 F.3d 1224 (3d Cir. 1994), 12–13n.76
Guaranty Trust Co. v. United States, 304 U.S. 126 (1938), 42n.53
Guaylupo-Moya v. Gonzales, 423 F.3d 121 (2d Cir. 2005), 159–60n.77
Guirlando v. T.C. Ziraat Bankasi A.S., 602 F.3d 69 (2d Cir. 2010), 251–52n.79
Gulf Oil Corp. v. Gilbert, 330 U.S. 501 (1947), 15n.82, 15n.83
Gulf Res. Am., Inc. v. Republic of the Congo, 370 F.3d 65 (D.C. Cir. 2004), 249n.63
Gundy v. United States, 139 S. Ct. 2116 (2019), 26–27n.143, 110n.16
Guy W. Capps, Inc., 204 F.2d 655 (4th Cir. 1953), *aff'd* 348 U.S. 296 (1955), 100n.98

Habyarimana v. Kagame, 696 F.3d 1029 (10th Cir. 2012), 19–20n.105, 166–67n.112, 270–71n.192
Hamdan v. Rumsfeld, 548 U.S. 557 (2006), 26n.139, 58, 70–71n.221, 183n.44, 291–92n.114, 296–97n.11, 328–29n.154, 331–32, 334–35
Hamdan v. United States, 696 F.3d 1238 (D.C. Cir. 2012), 170–71n.130
Hamdi v. Rumsfeld, 542 U.S. 507 (2004), 180–81n.33, 319–21, 322, 324–25
Hamdi v. Rumsfeld, 316 F.3d 450 (4th Cir. 2003), 297n.12
Hamidullin, United States v., 888 F.3d 62 (4th Cir. 2018), 297n.12
Handel v. Artukovic, 601 F. Supp. 1421 (C.D. Cal. 1985), 160–61n.80
Hanson v. Denckla, 357 U.S. 235 (1958), 7–8n.37
Harlow v. Fitzgerald, 457 U.S. 800 (1982), 180n.28
Hartford Fire Ins. Co. v. California, 509 U.S. 764 (1993), 189, 195n.111
Hasan, United States v., 747 F. Supp. 2d 599 (E.D. Va. 2010), 224–25n.75
Hassard v. United States of Mexico, 29 Misc. 511, 61 N.Y.S. 939 (46 A.D. 1899), *aff'd*, 46 A.D. 623 (1899), 241n.11
Hatch v. Baez, 14 N.Y. Sup.Ct. 596 (Gen. Term 1876), 166–67n.110, 264–65n.160
Hawaii v. Mankichi, 190 U.S. 197 (1903), 177n.5
Hayburn's Case, 2 U.S. (2 Dall.) 408 (1792), 113–14
Haywood v. Drown, 556 U.S. 729 (2009), 8n.41
Helicopteros Nacionales de Columbia, S.A. v. Hall, 466 U.S. 408 (1984), 7n.34
Henfield's Case, 11 F. Cas. 1099 (C.C.D. Pa. 1793), 150n.18
Her Majesty the Queen v. Gilbertson, 597 F.2d 1161 (9th Cir. 1979), 10n.53
Hernandez v. Mesa, 140 S. Ct. 735 (2020), 164n.97, 179–80n.26, 180n.29
Hilton v. Guyot, 159 U.S. 113 (1895), 10–11n.57, 15–16n.86
Hilton v. Kerry, 754 F.3d 79 (1st Cir. 2014), 283n.54
Hinderlider v. La Plata River & Cherry Creek Ditch Co., 304 U.S. 92 (1938), 154–55n.41
Hines v. Davidowitz, 312 U.S. 52 (1941), 28n.153, 205–6n.173
Hodgson v. Bowerbank, 9 U.S. (5 Cranch) 303 (1809), 3n.7, 211–12n.8
Holmes v. Jennison, 39 U.S. (14 Pet.) 540 (1840), 59–60n.150, 96n.78, 276–77
Home Ins. Co. v. Dick, 281 U.S. 397 (1930), 206n.176
Hopson v. Kreps, 622 F.2d 1375 (9th Cir. 1980), 52n.113
Howlett v. Rose, 496 U.S. 356 (1990), 8n.41
Hudson & Goodwin, United States v., 11 U.S. (7 Cranch) 32 (1812), 52n.112, 150n.18

Ibarguen-Mosquera, United States v., 634 F.3d 1370 (11th Cir. 2011), 204n.169
Ibrahim v. Dep't of Homeland Security, 669 F.3d 983 (9th Cir. 2012), 179n.22

IIT v. Vencap, Ltd., 519 F.2d 1001 (2d Cir. 1975), 214–15nn.20-21
Illinois v. Milwaukee, 406 U.S. 91 (1972), 154–55n.44
In re *See name of party*
INS v. Chadha, 462 U.S. 919 (1983), 26–27n.146, 27–28n.148, 111
INS v. St. Cyr, 533 U.S. 289 (2001), 180–81nn.31–32
Int'l Shoe Co. v. Washington, 326 U.S. 310 (1945), 7n.31
Isbrandtsen Tankers v. President of India, 446 F.2d 1198 (2d Cir. 1971), 244–45n.33
Islamic Republic of Iran v. Boeing Co., 771 F.2d 1279 (9th Cir. 1985), 100n.97
ITC Ltd. v. Punchgini, Inc., 482 F.3d 135 (2d Cir. 2007), 46n.76
Itoba Ltd. v. LEP Group PLC, 54 F.3d 118 (2d Cir. 1995), 190–91n.87

J. McIntyre Machinery Ltd. v. Nicastro, 564 U.S. 873 (2011), 7–8n.38
J.W. Hampton, Jr. & Co. v. United States, 276 U.S. 394 (1928), 26–27n.142, 84n.21, 109–10n.13
Jaber v. United States, 861 F.3d 241 (D.C. Cir. 2017), 5–6n.24, 339–40n.217
Jam v. Int'l Finance Corp., 139 S. Ct. 759 (2019), xi, 259–60
Japan Line, Ltd. v. Cnty. of Los Angeles, 441 U.S. 434 (1979), 22–23n.120, 28n.154, 202n.156
Japan Whaling Ass'n v. Am. Cetacean Soc'y, 478 U.S. 221 (1986), 5–6n.27, 135n.136
Jara v. Núñez, 878 F.3d 1268 (11th Cir. 2018), 230–31n.103
Jean v. Dorelien, 431 F.3d 776 (11th Cir. 2005), 220n.50
Jesner v. Arab Bank, 138 S. Ct. 1386 (2018), xi, 235–36
Jimenez-Nava, United States v., 243 F.3d 192 (5th Cir. 2001), 45–46n.73
Johnson v. Browne, 205 U.S. 309 (1907), 56–57n.137
Johnson v. Eisentrager, 339 U.S. 763 (1950), 181–82, 296–97
Jones v. Ministry of the Interior of the Kingdom of Saudi Arabia, [2006] UKHL 26, [2007] 1 A.C. 270, 269n.189
Jones and Others v. The United Kingdom, ECHR, Jan. 14, 2014, 239–40n.2
Joo v. Japan, 413 F.3d 45 (D.C. Cir. 2005), 21n.112, 248–49n.60
Joseph v. Office of the Consulate General of Nigeria, 830 F.2d 1018 (9th Cir. 1987), 256n.103
Judge v. Canada, Commc'n No. 829/1998, U.N. Doc. CCPR/C/78/D/829/1998 (2003), 281n.47
Jungquist v. Nahyan, 940 F. Supp. 312 (D.D.C. 1996), 266–67n.174
Jurisdictional Immunities of the State (Germany v. Italy), Judgment (Feb. 3, 2012), 239–40n.2, 248n.58, 250n.70, 257n.107

Kadic v. Karadzic, 70 F.3d 232 (2d Cir. 1995), 231–32
Kaine, *In re*, 55 U.S. (14 How.) 103 (1853), 275–76n.17
Kalamazoo Spice Extraction Co. v. Provisional Military Gov't of Socialist Ethiopia, 729 F.2d 422 (6th Cir. 1984), 12n.68
Kashef v. BNP Paribas S.A., 925 F.3d 53 (2d Cir. 2019), 12–13n.71
Kasi v. Angelone, 300 F.3d 487 (4th Cir. 2002), 290n.105
Kaufman, United States v., 874 F.3d 242 (5th Cir. 1989), 286n.80
Keller v. Cent. Bank of Nigeria, 277 F.3d 811 (6th Cir. 2002), 245–46n.37, 251–52n.79, 268n.182
Ker v. Illinois, 119 U.S. 436 (1886), 152n.28, 289
Khadr, United States v., 717 F. Supp. 2d 1215 (Ct. Mil. Comm'n Rev. 2007), 297n.12
Khan v. Obama, 655 F.3d 20 (D.C. Cir. 2011), 321n.119
Khedivial Line, S.A.E. v. Seafarers' Int'l Union, 278 F.2d 49 (2d Cir. 1960), 214–15n.20
Khulumani v. Barclay Nat'l Bank Ltd., 504 F.3d 254 (2d Cir. 2007), 232–33n.113
Kilroy v. Windsor No. C–78–291, slip op. (N.D. Ohio, Dec. 7, 1978), 266–67n.172
Kin-Hong, United States v., 110 F.3d 103 (1st Cir. 1997), 282n.51
Kinsella v. Singleton, 361 U.S. 234 (1960), 178n.14
Kiobel v. Royal Dutch Petroleum Co., 569 U.S. 108 (2013), xi, 160–61n.79, 191, 228–30

Kiobel v. Royal Dutch Petroleum Co., 621 F.3d 111 (2d Cir. 2010), 232–33n.113, 234n.120, 235
Kiyemba v. Obama, 561 F.3d 509 (D.C. Cir. 2009), 284n.67
Kline v. Keneko, 535 N.Y.S.2d 303 (Sup. Ct. 1988), 266–67n.172
Klintock, United States v., 18 U.S. (5 Wheat.) 144 (1820), 199–200n.137, 224–25n.72
Knab v. Republic of Georgia, 1998 U.S. Dist. LEXIS 8820 (D.D.C. 1998), 262n.147, 262–63n.150
Knotek, United States v., 925 F.3d 1118 (9th Cir. 2019), 278n.30
Kokkonen v. Guardian Life Ins. Co. of Am., 511 U.S. 375 (1994), 2n.1
Kolovrat v. Oregon, 366 U.S. 187 (1961), 70–71n.218
Kontrick v. Ryan, 540 U.S. 443 (2004), 2n.2
Koster v. (American) Lumbermens Mut. Casualty Co., 330 U.S. 518 (1947), 13–14n.81
Kucinich v. Bush, 236 F. Supp. 2d 1 (D.D.C. 2002), 4–5n.20, 73n.235, 75n.247
Kucinich v. Obama, 821 F. Supp. 2d 110 (D.D.C. 2011), 306–7n.64, 310n.80

Lafontant v. Aristide, 844 F. Supp. 128 (E.D.N.Y. 1994), 266–67n.171, 267n.177
LaGrand (Federal Republic of Germany v. United States), 2001 I.C.J. Rep. 466 (June 27), 125–26
Lara, United States v., 541 U.S. 193 (2004), 60–61n.160
Lauritzen v. Larsen, 345 U.S. 571 (1953), 187–88n.69
Lawrence, United States v., 727 F.3d 386 (5th Cir. 2013), 187–88n.68
Lawrence v. Texas, 539 U.S. 558 (2003), 168
Lebron v. Rumsfeld, 670 F.3d 540 (4th Cir. 2012), 337–38n.209
Lee Yen Tai, United States v., 185 U.S. 213 (1902), 56–57n.137
Leija-Sanchez, United States v., 602 F.3d 797 (7th Cir. 2010), 187–88n.68
Letelier v. Republic of Chile, 488 F. Supp. 665 (D.D.C. 1980), 255–56n.102
Lewis v. Mutond, 918 F.3d 142 (D.C. Cir. 2019), 271
Li-Shou v. United States, 777 F.3d 175 (4th Cir. 2015), 5–6n.24
Lindh, United States v., 212 F. Supp. 2d 541 (E.D. Va. 2002), 20n.106, 297n.12
Little v. Barreme, 6 U.S. (2 Cranch) 170 (1804), 305n.54
Liu v. Republic of China, 892 F.2d 1419 (9th Cir. 1989), 255–56n.102, 256n.103
LoBue v. Christopher, 82 F.3d 1081 (D.C. Cir. 1996), 278–79n.32
LoBue v. Christopher, 893 F. Supp. 65 (D.D.C. 1995), 278–79n.31
Locke, United States v., 529 U.S. 89 (2000), 42n.54
Lo Duca v. United States, 93 F.3d 1100 (2d Cir. 1996), 113–14n.34, 278–79n.33
Loewen Group, Inc. v. United States, Case No. ARB(AF)/98/3 (Jan. 5, 2001), 123n.73
Lomeli, United States v., 596 F.3d 496 (8th Cir. 2010), 286n.84
Lopes v. Schroder, 225 F. Supp. 292 (E.D. Pa. 1963), 214–15n.20
Lopez, United States v., 514 U.S. 549 (1995), 22–23n.118, 30n.161, 30n.164, 115n.37, 202n.154
Lopez-Smith v. Hood, 121 F.3d 1322 (9th Cir. 1997), 278–79n.33
Louis Feraud Int'l S.A.R.L. v. Viewfinder Inc., 406 F. Supp. 2d 274 (S.D.N.Y. 2005), 10–11n.58
Louisville & Nashville R.R. v. Mottley, 211 U.S. 149 (1908), 2n.4
Loving v. United States, 517 U.S. 748 (1996), 26–27n.145, 109–10n.14
Lowry v. Reagan, 676 F. Supp. 333 (D.D.C. 1987), 10–11n.64
Lozano v. Montoya Alvarez, 572 U.S.1 (2014), 70n.215
Lujan v. Defenders of Wildlife, 504 U.S. 555 (1992), 3–4n.13
Lujan v. Gengler, United States ex rel., 510 F.2d 62 (2d Cir. 1975), 290–91n.108
Lyders v. Lund, 32 F.2d 308 (N.D. Cal. 1929), 264–65n.160

Mackin, *In re*, No. 86 Cr. Misl., *app. denied*, 668 F.2d 122 (2d Cir. 1981), 280–81n.42
Made in the USA Found. v. United States, 56 F. Supp. 2d 1226 (N.D. Ala. 1999), 86–87n.33, 88
Made in the USA Found. v. United States, 242 F.3d 1300 (11th Cir. 2001), 86–87nn.34–35, 88

Madsen v. Kinsella, 343 U.S. 341 (1952), 328–29nn.154–155
Magness v. Russian Federation, 84 F. Supp. 2d 1357 (S.D. Ala. 2000), 254–55n.93
Malewicz v. City of Amsterdam, 517 F. Supp. 2d 322 (D.D.C. 2007), 254–55n.94
Mannington Mills v. Congoleum, 595 F.2d 1287 (3d Cir. 1979), 189n.82
Manoharan v. Rajapaska, 711 F.3d 178 (D.C. Cir. 2013), 19–20n.105, 166–67n.112, 270–71n.192
Manta v. Chertoff, 518 F.3d 1134 (9th Cir. 2008), 279–80n.35
Manzi, United States v., 888 F.2d 204 (1st Cir. 1989), 282n.51
Maqaleh v. Gates, 605 F.3d 84 (D.C. Cir. 2010), 185nn.57–58
Maqaleh v. Hagel, 738 F.3d 312 (D.C. Cir. 2013), 185n.59
Marbury v. Madison, 5 U.S. 137 (1803), 128
Martin v. Warden, 993 F.2d 824 (11th Cir. 1993), 283n.54
Mason v. Intercolonial Ry. of Can., 197 Mass. 349, 83 N.E. 876 (Sup. Ct. Mass. 1908), 241n.12
Mastafa v. Chevron Corp., 770 F.3d 170 (2d Cir. 2014), 230–31n.102
Matar v. Dichter, 500 F. Supp. 2d 284 (S.D.N.Y. 2009), *aff'd*, 563 F.3d 9 (2d Cir. 2009), 268–69n.183
Matsushita Elec. Indus. Co. v. Zenith Radio Corp., 475 U.S. 574 (1985), 187–88n.71
Matta-Ballesteros, United States v., 71 F.3d 754 (9th Cir. 1995), 290–91n.109
Matta-Ballesteros v. Henman, 896 F.2d 255 (7th Cir. 1990), 290–91n.109
Matusevitch v. Telnikoff, 877 F. Supp. 1 (D.D.C. 1995), 10–11n.58
Ma v. Ashcroft, 257 F.3d 1095 (9th Cir. 2001), 56–57n.134
McBee v. Delica, 417 F.3d 107 (1st Cir. 2005), 187–88n.70
McCullagh, United States v., 221 F. 288 (D. Kan. 1915), 60–61n.157
McCulloch v. Maryland, 17 U.S. (4 Wheat.) 316 (1819), 21–22n.116, 62n.164
McCulloch v. Sociedad Nacional de Marineros de Honduras, 372 U.S. 10 (1963), 187–88n.67, 195n.111
McKesson Corp. v. Islamic Republic of Iran, 672 F.3d 1066 (D.C. Cir. 2012), 160–61n.82, 246n.45
McKessson Corp. v. Islamic Republic of Iran, 539 F.3d 485 (D.C. Cir. 2008), 51n.109
McMullen, *In re*, No. 3-78-1899 M.G. (N.D. Cal. May 11, 1979), 280–81n.42
Mead Corp., United States v., 533 U.S. 218 (2001), 20n.108
Medellin, Ex parte, 223 S.W.3d 315 (Tex. Ct. Crim. App. 2006), 128–29n.102
Medellin v. Texas, 552 U.S. 491 (2008), 24n.128, 26n.139, 29n.157, 46–47, 48–50, 51, 59, 70–71n.218, 70–71n.221, 99, 100n.99, 128–29, 142–43, 163–64n.94, 218n.38, 295n.5
Merlini v. Canada 926 F.3d 21 (1st Cir. 2019), 251–52n.76
Merrell Dow Pharms., Inc. v. Thompson, 478 U.S. 804 (1986), 2n.2
Merryman, Ex parte, 17 F. Cas. 144 (C.D. Md. 1861), 180–81n.33
Mezerhane v. Republica Bolivariana de Venezuela, 785 F.3d 545 (11th Cir. 2015), 254n.89
Microsoft Corp. v. AT&T Corp., 550 U.S. 437 (2007), 189n.78
Midwest Oil Co., United States v., 236 U.S. 459 (1915), 27–28n.147
Military and Paramilitary Activities in and Against Nicaragua (Nicar. v. U.S.), Jurisdiction and Admissibility, 1984 I.C.J. 392 (Nov. 26), 295n.6
Miller v. French, 530 U.S. 327 (2000), 113–14n.34
Milligan, Ex parte, 71 U.S. (4 Wall.) 2 (1866), 330
Mironescu v. Costner, 480 F.3d 664 (4th Cir. 2007), 284n.67
Missouri v. Holland, 252 U.S. 416 (1920), 60–61, 62, 65, 67n.195
Mistretta v. United States, 488 U.S. 361 (1989), 109–10n.12, 110n.15, 113–14n.34
Mohamad v. Palestinian Auth., 132 S. Ct. 1702 (2012), 234–35nn.122–24
Mohamad v. Rajoub, 634 F.3d 604 (D.C. Cir. 2011), *aff'd*, 132 S. Ct. 1702 (2012), 160–61n.82
Mohamed v. Jeppesen Dataplan, Inc., 614 F.3d 1070 (9th Cir. 2010), 291–92n.115
Mondev Int'l Ltd. v. United States, Case No. ARB(AF)/99/2 (Oct. 11, 2002), 123n.74
Montuya v. Chedid, 779 F. Supp. 2d 60 (D.D.C. 2011), 261n.131
Moore v. Mitchell, 30 F.2d 600 (2d Cir. 1929), 10n.54

More v. Intelcom Support Servs., Inc., 960 F.2d 466 (5th Cir. 1992), 45n.70
Morrison, United States v., 529 U.S. 598 (2000), 30n.166, 115nn.37–38, 202n.154
Morrison v. Nat'l Australian Bank Ltd., 561 U.S. 247 (2010), 190–91, 192–93
Morrison v. Olson, 487 U.S. 654 (1988), 73n.231
Mossman v. Higginson, 4 U.S. (4 Dall.) 12 (1800), 3n.7, 211–12n.8
Movsesian v. Victoria Verischerung AG, 670 F.3d 1067 (9th Cir. 2012), 29n.160
Moxon v. The Fanny, 17 F. Cas. 942 (D. Pa. 1793), 214–15n.20
Mt. Crest SRL, LLC v. Anheuser-Busch InBev SA/NV, 937 F.3d 1067 (7th Cir. 2019), 12n.65
Munaf v. Geren, 553 U.S. 674 (2008), 185, 284
Murphy v. NCAA, 138 C. St. 1461 (2018), 63–64n.173, 115n.39
Murphy v. United States, 199 F.3d 599 (2d Cir. 1999), 280n.39
Murray's Lessee v. Hoboken Land & Improvement Co., 59 U.S. (18 How.) 272 (1856), 113n.31
Murray v. The Schooner Charming Betsy, 6 U.S. (2 Cranch) 64 (1804), 16–17, 56–57n.133, 167n.113
Myers v. United States, 272 U.S. 52 (1926), 73n.231

National Fed. of Indep. Bus. v. Sebelius, 567 U.S. 519 (2012), 22–23n.119
Neely v. Henkel, 180 U.S. 109 (1901), 62n.165, 278n.30, 282n.50
Neil, United States v., 312 F.3d 419 (9th Cir. 2002), 199n.135
The Nereide, 13 U.S. (9 Cranch) 388 (1815), 150n.19
New Hampshire v. Maine, 426 U.S. 363 (1976), 60n.153
New York Cent. R.R. v. Chisholm, 268 U.S. 29 (1925), 187–88n.67
New York Life Ins. Co. v. Hendren, 92 U.S. 286 (1876), 152n.28
New York v. United States, 505 U.S. 144 (1992), 63–64n.173, 115n.39
Nielsen v. Johnson, 279 U.S. 47 (1929), 42n.54
NLRB v. Noel Canning, 573 U.S. 513 (2014), 27–28n.147
Noeller v. Wojdylo, 922 F.3d 797 (7th Cir. 2019), 282n.51
Noriega, United States v., 117 F.3d 1206 (11th Cir. 1997), 166–67n.112, 266–67n.171, 266–67n.173, 290n.105
Noriega, United States v., 746 F. Supp. 1506 (S.D. Fla. 1990), 267n.178
Noriega v. Pastrana, 564 F.3d 1290 (11th Cir. 2009), 56–57n.138
Northern Pipeline Const. Co. v. Marathon Pipe Line Co., 458 U.S. 50 (1982), 112–13n.30, 113n.31
NRDC v. EPA, 464 F.3d 1 (D.C. Cir. 2006), 137–38, 142
Ntakirutimana v. Reno, 184 F.3d 419 (5th Cir. 1999), 134, 274–75n.11
Nueci-Pena, United States v., 711 F.3d 191 (1st Cir. 2013), 205n.71
N.Y. State Rifle & Pistol Ass'n v. City of New York, 140 S. Ct. 1525 (2020), 4–5n.18

OBB Personenverkehr AG v. Sachs, 136 S. Ct. 390 (2015), 253
O'Bryan v. Holy See, 556 F.3d 361 (6th Cir. 2009), 255n.97, 255–56n.100
Odeh, United States v., 548 F.3d 276 (2d Cir. 2008), 179n.22
Oetjen v. Central Leather Co., 246 U.S. 297 (1918), 11n.59
Oil States Energy Servs., LLC v. Greene's Energy Grp., LLC, 138 S. Ct. 1365 (2018), 113n.31
Oliver Am. Trading Co. v. Mexico, 264 U.S. 440 (1924), 152n.28
Olympic Airways v. Husain, 540 U.S. 644 (2004), 69n.207, 70n.217
Omar v. McHugh, 646 F.3d 13 (D.C. Cir. 2011), 284n.67
O'Melveny & Myers v. FDIC, 512 U.S. 79 (1994), 9n.5, 164n.96
O'Neil v. Saudi Joint Relief Comm'n, 714 F.3d 109 (2d Cir. 2013), 255n.97
Ordinola v. Hackman, 478 F.3d 588 (4th Cir. 2007), 280–81n.41
O'Reilly de Camara v. Brooke, 209 U.S. 45 (1908), 214–15n.20
Orient Mineral Co. v. Bank of China, 506 F.3d 980 (10th Cir. 2007), 251–52n.79

Orlando v. Laird, 443 F.2d 1039 (2d Cir. 1971), 299–300n.29
Osborn v. Bank of the United States, 22 U.S. (9 Wheat.) 738 (1824), 2n.3
The Over the Top, 5 F.2d 838 (D. Conn. 1925), 51–52n.111, 52n.113
Owen Equip. & Constr. Co. v. Kroger, 437 U.S. 365 (1978), 2n.2
Owner-Operator Independent Drivers Ass'n v. U.S. Dep't of Transportation, 724 F.3d 230 (D.C. Cir. 2013), 17–18n.96, 56–57n.132
Ozanic v. United States, 188 F.2d 228 (2d Cir. 1951), 98n.89

Pacific & Arctic Ry., United States v., 228 U.S. 87 (1913), 187–88n.71
Padilla v. Yoo, 678 F.3d 748 (9th Cir. 2012), 337–38n.209
Palmer, United States v., 16 U.S. (3 Wheat.) 610 (1818), 186nn.60-62
Panama Ref. Co. v. Ryan 293 U.S. 388 (1935), 26–27n.144
Papa v. United States, 281 F.3d 1004 (9th Cir. 2002), 220n.51
The Paquete Habana, 175 U.S. 677 (1900), xiin.12, 151, 295
Park, United States v., 938 F.3d 354 (D.C. Cir. 2019), 62n.165, 203n.161
Pasquantino v. United States, 544 U.S. 349 (2005), 10n.53
Paul v. Avril, 812 F. Supp. 207 (S.D. Fla. 1992), 267n.175
Pendleton, United States v., 658 F.3d 299 (3d Cir. 2011), 202–3n.159
Pennoyer v. Neff, 95 U.S. 714 (1877), 7n.31, 7n.35
People of Saipan v. U.S. Dep't of Interior, 502 F.2d 90 (9th Cir. 1974), 45nn.68–69
Pepe, United States v., 895 F.3d 679 (9th Cir. 2018), 203n.160
Percheman, United States v., 32 U.S. (7 Pet.) 51 (1833), 44n.60, 70n.216
Peretz v. United States, 501 U.S. 923 (1991), 113n.32
Perez v. Brownell, 356 U.S. 44 (1958), 178–79n.18
Perez v. United States, 402 U.S. 146 (1971), 22–23n.118
Perkins v. Benguet Consol. Mining Co., 342 U.S. 437 (1952), 7n.34
Permanent Mission of India to the U.N. v. City of N.Y., 551 U.S. 193 (2007), 165–66n.104, 253n.86
Persinger v. Islamic Republic of Iran, 729 F.2d 835 (D.C. Cir. 1984), 255n.97
The Pesaro, 277 F. 473 (S.D.N.Y. 1921), 241–42n.15
Pfeifer v. United States Bureau of Prisons, 615 F.2d 873 (9th Cir. 1980), 287–88n.94
Pfizer, Inc. v. Gov't of India, 434 U.S. 308 (1978), 23–24n.122
Phillips Petroleum v. Shutts, 472 U.S. 797 (1985), 206n.176
Philipp v. Federal Republic of Germany, 894 F.3d 406 (D.C. Cir. 2018), 254n.90
Pigeon River Improvement, Slide & Boom Co. v. Charles W. Cox, Ltd., 291 U.S. 138 (1934), 56–57n.132
Pike v. Bruce Church, Inc., 397 U.S. 137 (1970), 28n.154
Pink, United States v., 315 U.S. 203 (1942), 23–24n.124, 42n.53, 93, 99n.95
Piper Aircraft Co. v. Reyno, 454 U.S. 235 (1981), 14–15n.81, 15n.82, 15n.83, 15n.84
Plaut v. Spendthrift Farm, Inc., 514 U.S. 211 (1995), 113–14n.34, 114
Poe v. Ullman, 367 U.S. 497 (1961), 4–5n.17
Postal, United States v., 589 F.2d 862 (5th Cir. 1979), 44n.62, 44n.64, 44–45n.66, 45nn.68–69, 289n.99
Power Auth. of N.Y. v. Fed. Power Comm'n, 247 F.2d 538 (D.C. Cir. 1957), 54, 65–66n.187
Presbyterian Church of Sudan v. Talisman Energy, Inc., 582 F.3d 244 (2d Cir. 2009), 232–33n.114
Price v. Socialist People's Libyan Arab Jamahiriya, 110 F. Supp. 2d 10 (D.D.C. 2000), 257n.106
Price v. Socialist People's Libyan Arab Jamahiriya, 294 F.3d 82 (D.C. Cir. 2002), 246–47n.46
Princz v. Fed. Republic of Germany, 26 F.3d 1166 (D.C. Cir. 1994), 18n.100, 160–61n.80, 250n.67, 250n.69

Printz v. United States, 521 U.S. 898 (1997), 63–64nn.173–74, 115n.39
The Prize Cases, 67 U.S. (2 Black) 635 (1863), 301n.35, 303n.45
Puentes, United States v., 50 F.3d 1567 (11th Cir. 1995), 286n.79, 286n.82

Quinn v. Robinson, 783 F.2d 776 (9th Cir. 1986), 280–81n.41
Quirin, Ex parte, 317 U.S. 1 (1942), 52n.112, 329–30, 334–35n.187

Raines v. Byrd, 521 U.S. 811 (1997), 4nn.14–16, 75n.243
Rasul v. Bush, 542 U.S. 466 (2004), 182–83
Rasul v. Myers, 563 F.3d 527 (D.C. Cir. 2009), 337–38n.209
Rauscher, United States v., 119 U.S. 407 (1886), 44–45n.65, 277n.23, 285–86
Regina v. Bow Street Metro. Stipendiary Magistrate, Ex parte Pinochet Ugarte, 2 WLR 827 (HL 1999), 200–1n.147
Reid v. Covert, 354 U.S. 1 (1957), 67–68, 100n.100, 177–78
Rein v. Socialist People's Libyan Arab Jamahiriya, 162 F.3d 748 (2d Cir. 1998), 257n.106
Renkel v. United States, 456 F.3d 640 (6th Cir. 2006), 46n.76
Reno v. Condon, 528 U.S. 141 (2000), 63–64n.173
Republic of Argentina v. City of New York, 250 N.E.2d 698 (N.Y. Ct. App. 1969), 159–60n.74
Republic of Argentina v. NML Capital, Ltd., 573 U.S. 134 (2014), 241–42n.16, 245–46n.41
Republic of Argentina v. Weltover, Inc., 504 U.S. 607 (1992), 246–47n.46, 251–52
Republic of Austria v. Altmann, 541 U.S. 677 (2004), 21n.113, 240n.3, 245–46n.36, 248–49
Republic of the Marshall Islands v. United States, 865 F.3d 1187 (9th Cir. 2017), 45n.70, 46n.75, 165n.103
Republic of Mexico v. Hoffman, 324 U.S. 30 (1945), 166–67n.111, 242–43
Republic of Peru, Ex parte, 318 U.S. 578 (1943), 166–67n.111, 242–43
Republic of Philippines v. Marcos, 665 F. Supp. 793 (N.D. Cal. 1987), 266–67n.172
Republic of the Philippines v. Marcos, 806 F.2d 344 (2d Cir. 1986), 267n.178
Respublica v. DeLongchamps, 1 U.S. (1 Dall.) 113 (1784), 149–50, 213n.14
Retfalvi v. United States, 930 F.3d 600 (4th Cir. 2019), 52n.117
Rice v. Santa Fe Elevator Corp., 331 U.S. 218 (1947), 31n.168, 42n.52
Rich v. Naviera Vacuba, S.A., 197 F. Supp. 710 (E.D. Va. 1961), 244n.31
Risk v. Halvorsen, 936 F.2d 393 (9th Cir. 1991), 255–56n.102
RJR Nabisco, Inc. v. European Community, 136 S. Ct. 2090 (2016), 193
Rob[b]ins, United States v., 27 F. Cas. 825 (D.S.C. 1799), 275n.14
Rock Royal Co-operative Inc., United States v., 307 U.S. 533 (1939), 110n.17
Rodriguez v. FDIC, 140 S. Ct. 713 (2020), 9n.51, 164n.96
Roe v. Wade, 410 U.S. 113 (1973), 4–5n.18
Romero v. Int'l Terminal Operating Co., 358 U.S. 354 (1959), 187–88n.69
Rommy, United States v., 506 F.3d 108 (2d Cir. 2007), 287n.86
Roper v. Simmons, 543 U.S. 541 (2005), xi–xiin.6, 40n.43, 167–68
Rose v. Himely, 8 U.S. (4 Cranch) 241 (1807), 223–24n.71
Ross, *In re*, 140 U.S. 453 (1891), 176–77
Rucho v. Common Cause, 139 S. Ct. 2484 (2019), 5n.23, 6n.29
Ruhrgas AG v. Marathon Oil Co., 526 U.S. 574 (1999), 15n.85

Saac, United States v., 632 F.3d 1203 (11th Cir. 2011), 198–99nn.132–33
Sabbatino *See* Banco Nacional de Cuba v. Sabbatino
Saccoccia, United States v., 58 F.3d 754 (1st Cir. 1995), 279–80n.35
Saint Fort v. Ashcroft, 329 F.3d 191 (1st Cir. 2003), 283n.55

Saldana v. Occidental Petroleum Corp., 774 F.3d 544 (9th Cir. 2014), 5–6n.24
Sale v. Haitian Ctrs. Council, Inc., 509 U.S. 155 (1993), 189n.78
Saltany v. Reagan, 702 F. Supp. 319 (D.D.C. 1988), 266–67n.171
Samantar v. Yousuf, 560 U.S. 305 (2010), 268–69n.185, 269
Sampson v. Fed. Republic of Germany, 250 F.3d 1145 (7th Cir. 2001), 18n.100, 161–62n.87, 250nn.67–68
Sanchez-Llamas v. Oregon, 548 U.S. 331 (2006), 48n.87, 48–49n.92, 50–51, 127–28
Sandberg v. McDonald, 248 U.S. 185 (1918), 187–88n.67
Santovincenzo v. Egan, 284 U.S. 30 (1931), 65n.183
Sarei v. Rio Tinto, PLC, 671 F.3d 736 (9th Cir. 2011), 161–62n.87, 221–22n.62, 225–26n.76
Saudi Arabia v. Nelson, 507 U.S. 349 (1993), 252–53
Schoenbaum v. Firstbrook, 405 F.2d 200, *rev'd*, 405 F.2d 215 (2d Cir. 1968), 190–91n.87
The Schooner Exchange v. McFaddon, 11 U.S. (7 Cranch) 116 (1812), 166–67n.110, 240–41, 264–65, 345
Schooner Peggy, United States v., 5 U.S. (1 Cranch) 103 (1801), 55–56n.128
Sea Breeze Salt, Inc. v. Mitsubishi Corp., 899 F.3d 1064 (9th Cir. 2018), 12n.65
Search of the Premises Located, *In re*, 634 F.3d 557 (9th Cir. 2011), 55–56n.129, 287n.87
Seminole Tribe of Fl. v. Florida, 517 U.S. 44 (1996), 63–64n.173
Sensi, United States v., 879 F.2d 888 (D.C. Cir. 1989), 286n.78
Serra v. Lappin, 600 F.3d 1191 (9th Cir. 2010), 17–18n.98, 160–61n.82
Shauver, United States v., 214 F. 154 (E.D. Ark. 1914), 60–61n.157
Shibin, United States v., 722 F.3d 233 (4th Cir. 2013), 200n.145
Siderman de Blake v. Republic of Argentina, 965 F.2d 699 (9th Cir. 1992), 18n.100, 145–46n.3, 254n.88
Simon v. Republic of Hungary, 812 F.3d 127 (D.C. Cir. 2016), 254n.90
Sinochem Int'l Co. v. Malay. Int'l Shipping Corp., 549 U.S. 422 (2007), 15nn.84–85
Sisal Corp., United States v., 274 U.S. 268 (1927), 187–88n.71
Skidmore v. Swift & Co., 323 U.S. 134 (1944), 20n.109
Skiriotes v. Florida, 313 U.S. 69 (1941), 206n.177
Sluss v. United States DOJ, 898 F.3d 1242 (D.C. Cir. 2018), 287–88n.94
Smith, United States v., 18 U.S. (5 Wheat) 153 (1820), 165n.101, 199–200nn.139–40, 224–25n.72
Smith v. Socialist People's Libyan Arab Jamahiriya, 101 F.3d 239 (2d Cir. 1996), 18n.100, 250n.67
Smith v. Trump, 731 Fed. Appx. 8 (D.C. Cir. 2018), 306–7n.65
Smith v. United States, 507 U.S. 197 (1993), 189nn.78–79
Smyth, United States v., 61 F.3d 711 (9th Cir. 1995), 282n.51
Societe Nationale Industrielle Aerospatiale v. U.S. District Court, 482 U.S. 522 (1987), 15–16n.86
Soering v. United Kingdom, 11 Eur. Ct. H. R. 439 (1989), 281n.46
Sosa v. Alvarez-Machain, 542 U.S. 692 (2004), 53–54n.120, 160–61, 162–63n.91, 162–63n.93, 164nn.98–99, 179n.26, 220–23, 224–25n.73, 225–26n.79, 226–27, 234n.120, 290n.101
Sota, United States v., 948 F.3d 356 (D.C. Cir. 2020), 187–88n.68
Soto-Barraza, United States v., 947 F.3d 1111 (9th Cir. 2020), 286n.79
S. African Apartheid Litig., *In re*, 617 F. Supp. 2d 228 (S.D.N.Y. 2009), 225–26n.77
South Carolina v. Baker, 485 U.S. 505 (1988), 30n.163
Southway v. Cent. Bank of Nigeria, 198 F.3d 1210 (10th Cir. 1999), 245–46n.37
Steel Co. v. Citizens for a Better Env't, 523 U.S. 83 (1998), 15n.85
Steele v. Bulova Watch Co., 344 U.S. 280 (1952), 187–88n.70
Stern v. Marshall, 564 U.S. 462 (2011), 112–13n.30
Stokes, United States v., 726 F.3d 880 (7th Cir. 2013), 179n.22
Strawbridge v. Curtiss, 7 U.S. (3 Cranch) 267 (1806), 3n.5

Stuart, United States v., 489 U.S. 353 (1989), 69n.209
Suerte, United States v., 291 F.3d 366 (5th Cir. 2002), 204n.168
Sullivan v. Oracle Corp., 51 Cal. 4th 1191 (Cal. 2011), 205n.172
Sumitomo Shoji Am., Inc. v. Avagliano, 457 U.S. 176 (1982), 70–71n.218
Sunshine Anthracite Coal Co. v. Adkins, 310 U.S. 381 (1940), 110n.17
Swarna v. Al-Awadi, 622 F.3d 123 (2d Cir. 2010), 255–56n.100, 261–62n.139
Swearingen v. United States, 565 F. Supp. 1019 (D. Colo. 1983), 52n.116, 100n.98
Swift v. Tyson, 41 U.S. (16 Pet.) 1 (1842), 8–9, 152n.27

Tabion v. Mufti, 73 F.3d 535 (4th Cir. 1996), 261n.131, 262–63n.149
Tachiona v. Mugabe, 387 F.3d 205 (2d Cir. 2004), 263–64n.154
Tachiona v. United States, 386 F.3d 205 (2d Cir. 2004), 266–67n.171
Talbot v. Seeman, 5 U.S. (1 Cranch) 1 (1801), 17n.93
Tawfik v. Al-Sabah, 2012 U.S. Dist. LEXIS 115957 (S.D.N.Y. Apr. 27, 2012), 270–71n.192
Taylor v. Morton, 23 F. Cas. 784 (C.C.D. Mass. 1855), 55–56n.127
Tel-Oren v. Libyan Arab Republic, 726 F.2d 774 (D.C. Cir. 1984), 210–11n.5, 217, 295n.5
Terlinden v. Ames, 184 U.S. 270 (1902), 273–74n.6
Terrorist Attacks on September 11, 2001, *In re*, 538 F.3d 71 (2d Cir. 2009), 268n.182
Tex. Indus., Inc. v. Radcliff Materials, Inc., 451 U.S. 630 (1981), 9n.49
Textile Workers Union v. Lincoln Mills, 353 U.S. 448 (1957), 154–55n.43
Theron v. U.S. Marshal, 832 F.2d 492 (9th Cir. 1987), 280n.38
Thomas v. Union Carbide Agric. Prods. Co., 473 U.S. 568 (1985), 113n.32
Timberlane Lumber Co. v. Bank of Am., 549 F.2d 597 (9th Cir. 1976), 189n.82
Toscanino, United States v., 500 F.2d 267 (2d Cir. 1974), 290–91
Trabelsi v. Belgium, Judgment (ECHR, Sept. 4, 2014), 281n.48
Trabelsi, United States v., 845 F.3d 1141 (D.C. Cir. 2017), 279–80n.37
Trans-Continental Inv. Corp., S.A. v. Bank of the Commonwealth, 500 F. Supp. 565 (C.D. Cal. 1980), 214–15n.20
Trans World Airlines, Inc. v. Franklin Mint Corp., 466 U.S. 243 (1984), 44–45n.67, 56–57n.135
Trinidad y Garcia v. Thomas, 683 F.3d 952 (9th Cir. 2012), 284n.68
Triquet v. Bath, 3 Burr. 1478, 97 Eng. Rep. 936 (K.B. 1764), 149–50n.15
Trump v. Hawaii, 138 S. Ct. 2392 (2018), 20–21
Tse, United States v., 135 F.3d 200 (1st Cir. 1998), 286n.79
Turner Ent'mt Co. v. Degeto Film GmbH, 25 F.3d 1512 (11th Cir. 1994), 15–16n.87
Turner v. Am. Baptist Missionary Union, 24 F. Cas. 344 (C.C.D. Mich. 1852), 51–52n.111

Underhill v. Hernandez, 65 F. 577 (2d Cir. 1895), 264–65n.161, 265n.166
Underhill v. Hernandez, 168 U.S. 250 (1897), 11n.59, 155n.46, 265
Ungaro-Benages v. Dresdner Bank AG, 379 F.3d 1227 (11th Cir. 2004), 15–16n.88
United States Steel Corp. v. Multistate Tax Comm'n, 434 U.S. 452 (1978), 60n.153, 96n.78
United States v. *See name of opposing party*
Upper Lakes Shipping Ltd. v. Int'l Longshoremen's Ass'n, 33 F.R.D. 348 (S.D.N.Y. 1963), 214–15n.20

Valanga v. Metro. Life Ins. Co., 259 F. Supp. 324 (E.D. Pa. 1966), 214–15n.20
Valencia-Trujillo, United States v., 573 F.3d 1171 (11th Cir. 2009), 286n.83
Valentine v. United States, 299 U.S. 5 (1936), 274n.8, 277n.23
Van Der End, United States, 943 F.3d 98 (2d Cir. 2019), 204n.168
Verdugo-Urquidez, United States v., 494 U.S. 259 (1990), 178–79
Verlinden B.V. v. Cent. Bank of Nigeria, 461 U.S. 480 (1983), 2n.1, 244n.32, 245–46n.36, 247

Victory Transport, Inc. v. Comisaria General de Abastecimientos y Transportes, 336 F.2d 354 (2d Cir. 1964), 244–45n.33
Vienna Convention on Consular Relations (Paraguay v. United States), Provisional Measures, 1998 I.C.J. Rep. 248 (Apr. 9), 125n.81
Vieth v. Jubelirer, 541 U.S. 267 (2004), 5n.22
Vilar, United States v., 729 F.3d 62 (2d Cir. 2013), 187–88n.68
Virginia v. Tennessee, 148 U.S. 503 (1893), 60n.153
Vo v. Benov, 447 F.3d 1235 (9th Cir. 2006), 280–81n.41
Von Saher v. Norton Simon Museum of Art, 897 F.3d 1141 (9th Cir. 2018), 12n.65

W.S. Kirkpatrick & Co. v. Envt'l Tectonics Corp., 493 U.S. 400 (1990), 12–13n.70, 12–13n.73, 21n.114
W.T. Grant Co., United States v., 345 U.S. 629 (1953), 4–5n.18
Waltier v. Thomson, 189 F. Supp. 319 (S.D.N.Y. 1960), 266n.169
Wang v. Ashcroft, 320 F.3d 130 (2d Cir. 2003), 283n.55
Ware v. Hylton, 3 U.S. (3 Dall.) 199 (1796), 42, 147–48n.8
Warfaa v. Ali, 811 F.3d 653 (4th Cir. 2016), 230–31n.103
Weinberger v. Rossi, 456 U.S. 25 (1982), 86n.28
Weingarten, United States v., 632 F.3d 60 (2d Cir. 2011), 195n.112
Wellness Int'l Network, Ltd. v. Sharif, 135 S. Ct. 1932 (2015), 113n.32
Wheeldin v. Wheeler, 373 U.S. 647 (1963), 9n.51, 164n.96
Whiteman v. Dorotheum GmbH & Co. KG, 431 F.3d 57 (2d Cir. 2006), 21n.112, 248–49n.60, 254n.89
Whitman v. Am. Trucking Assn's, 531 U.S. 457 (2001), 26–27n.143, 110n.16
Whitney v. Robertson, 124 U.S. 190 (1888), 55–56n.126
Wickard v. Filburn, 317 U.S. 111 (1942), 22–23n.119
Wilson v. Girard, 354 U.S. 524 (1957), 82–83n.13, 138n.152
Wright v. Henkel, 190 U.S. 40 (1903), 279–80n.35
WTO Appellate Body, Report: United States—Import Prohibition of Certain Shrimp and Shrimp Products (Recourse to Article 21.5 of the DSU by Malaysia) (Oct. 22, 2001), reprinted in 41 I.L.M. 149 (2002), 121–22n.64
WTO Appellate Body, United States—Standards for Reformulated and Conventional Gasoline (May 20, 1996), reprinted in 35 I.L.M. 603 (1996), 121–22n.64
WTO Appellate Body, Report: United States—Tax Treatment for "Foreign Sales Corporations" (Recourse to Article 21.5 of the DSU by the European Communities) (Jan. 14, 2002), reprinted in 41 I.L.M. 447 (2002), 121–22n.64
Wulfsohn v. Russ. Socialist Federated Soviet Republic, 138 N.E. 24 (N.Y. Ct. App. 1923), 241n.11

Xe Servs. Alien Tort Litig., In re, 665 F. Supp. 2d 569 (E.D. Va. 2009), 161–62n.87
Xuncax v. Gramajo, 886 F. Supp. 162 (D. Mass. 1995), 160–61n.78, 160–61n.80

Yahoo! Inc. v. La Ligue Contre Le Racisme, 433 F.3d 1199 (9th Cir. 2006), 10–11n.58
Yamashita, In re, 327 U.S. 1 (1946), 329–30n.161
Yang Rong v. Liaoning Provincial Gov't, 362 F. Supp. 2d 83 (D.D.C. 2005), 254n.89
Yau-Leung v. Soscia, 649 F.2d 914 (2d Cir. 1981), 279–80n.37
Yen v. Kissinger, 528 F.2d 1194 (9th Cir. 1975), 214–15n.19
Ye v. Zemin, 383 F.3d 620 (7th Cir. 2004), 19–20n.105, 166–67n.112, 266–67n.171
Youngstown Sheet & Tube Co. v. Sawyer, 343 U.S. 579 (1952), 2, 25–26, 27–28n.147, 58–59, 100n.99, 305n.53, 326
Yousef, United States v., 327 F.3d 56 (2d Cir. 2003), 17–18n.98, 159–60n.77, 199n.135, 201–2n.153

Yousuf v. Samantar, 699 F.3d 763 (4th Cir. 2012), 19–20n.105, 270–71nn.193–95
Yunis, United States v., 924 F.2d 1086 (D.C. Cir. 1991), 17–18n.94, 199n.125, 201–2n.153

Zhang v. Zemin, [2010] NSWCA 255 (New South Wales Ct. of Appeal), 269n.189
Zicherman v. Korean Air Lines Co., 516 U.S. 217 (1996), 69n.208
Ziglar v. Abbasi, 137 S. Ct. 1843 (2017), 337–38n.209
Zivotofsky v. Clinton, 566 U.S. 189 (2012), 5n.23, 5–6n.26, 75n.248, 86–87n.35
Zivotofsky v. Kerry, 135 S. Ct. 2076 (2015), xi, 23–24n.121, 23–24n.123, 27–28n.147
Zoelsch v. Arthur Andersen & Co., 824 F. 2d 27 (D.C. Cir. 1987), 190–91n.87
Zschernig v. Miller, 389 U.S. 429 (1968), 29, 205–6n.174

Table of Legislation

An Act Concerning Consuls and Vice-Consuls, 277n.24
Act of Feb. 20, 1792, ch. 7, 84n.18
Act of Aug. 12, 1848, ch. 167, 277n.24
Act to Provide for the Apprehension and Delivery of Deserters from Certain Foreign Vessels in the Ports of the United States, 277n.24
An Act for the Punishment of Certain Crimes Against the United States, 224–25n.74
Agreement between the United States and Great Britain Respecting Naval and Air Bases, 95n.75
Algiers Accords, 93, 96
Alien Tort Statute, xi, 157, 160–61, 160–61nn.79–81, 165n.101, 191, 200, 209–16, 217–18, 219–37, 247–48, 268, 346–47
Alien Tort Statute Reform Act, 236–37n.134
American Servicemembers Protection Act, 131–32, 131–32n.119
Anti-Counterfeiting Trade Agreement, 97
Arms Control and Disarmament Act, 89–90n.43
Articles of Confederation, 41
Articles of War, 328–30
    Article 15, 329–31, 329–30n.159
Authorization for Use of Military Force against Iraq Resolution of 2002, 300–1n.31
Authorization for Use of Military Force (AUMF), 313–14, 313n.93, 319–20, 321, 322–26, 331, 341

Biological Weapons Convention, 139
Boxer Indemnity Protocol of 1901, 98

Case-Zablocki Act, 81–82, 81–82n.10, 101
Chemical Weapons Convention Implementation Act of 1998, 140–41n.164
Civil Liability for Acts of State Sponsored Terrorism, 257–58n.108

Civil Rights Act of 1991, Title VII, 188–89, 188–89n.77, 191–92,
Comprehensive Nuclear Test Ban Treaty, 88–89, 139
Constitution Restoration Act of 2005, 169–70n.126
Convention against Torture and Other Cruel, Inhuman or Degrading Treatment or Punishment, 39–40, 140–41n.164, 176n.1, 204n.165, 231–32n.105, 283, 291–92n.114, 305, 335–37, 336n.199
Convention Between the United States of America and the Republic of Mexico for the Adjustment of Claims, 117n.46
Convention for the Suppression of Unlawful Acts against the Safety of Civil Aviation, Article 8, 273–74n.4
Convention on Combating Bribery of Foreign Public Officials in International Business Transactions, 198n.130, 233–34n.117
Convention on Contracts for the International Sale of Goods, 44–45, 44–45n.67
Convention on Jurisdictional Immunities of States and Their Property, 239, 239n.1
Convention on Privileges and Immunities of the United Nations, 263–64, 263–64n.153, 263–64nn.155–158
Convention on the Civil Aspects of International Child Abduction, 70, 70n.213
Convention on the Prevention and Punishment of the Crime of Genocide, 36–37n.21
Convention on the Prohibition of the Development, Production, Stockpiling and Use of Chemical Weapons and on Their Destruction, 40n.42, 62–63, 62–63n.167, 135–36, 135–36nn.137–141, 139n.157, 139–40
    Article I(1), 135–36n.137
    Article II(2), 135–36n.138
    Article XV(4), 135–36n.139, 136n.141
    Article XV(5)(d), 135–36n.140
    Article VIII(18), 136n.141
Convention on the Rights of the Child, 167–68
Convention Respecting the Laws and Customs of War on Land, 296n.10
Convention Respecting the Limitation of the Employment of Force for the Recovery of Contract Debts, 294n.4
Cuban Liberty and Democratic Solidarity Act of 1996, 196, 196n.118

Detainee Treatment Act, 183n.43, 291–92n.114, 337, 337n.204
Dingley Tariff Act of 1897, 84, 84n.20
Diplomatic Relations Act, 260n.127, 261n.130
Dodd–Frank Wall Street Reform and Consumer Protection Act, 190–91n.90

Federal Rules of Civil Procedure, 6–8
    4(k)(1)(A), 6–7n.30
    4(k)(2), 7–8n.39
    44, 10n.52
Federal Rules of Evidence, 10
Federal Tort Claims Act (FTCA), 179–80, 179–80n.26, 220–21, 255–56
Flatow Amendment, 257–58
Foreign Affairs Reform and Restructuring Act ("FARR Act"), 283–84, 283n.56
    § 2242(a), 283n.57
    § 2242(b), 283n.58
    § 2242(d), 283n.59

Foreign Assistance Act, Second Hickenlooper Amendment, 14, 14nn.79–80
Foreign Corrupt Practices Act (FCPA), 198
Foreign Relations Authorization Act, Fiscal Years 2000 and 2001, §§ 705–06, 131–32n.118
Foreign Sovereign Immunities Act (FSIA), 6–7n.30, 18, 19–20, 100, 160–61n.82, 165–67, 203–4, 245–53, 245–46n.35, 245–46n.37, 264–67, 266n.169, 268–70, 272
Foreign States Immunities Act of Australia, 269n.189
Foreign Trade Antitrust Improvements Act (FTAIA), 187–88n.71

General Agreement on Tariffs and Trade, 120–21
Geneva Conventions for the Protection of Victims of War, 296
    Common Article 3, 58, 70–71, 291–92n.114, 296, 297–98, 315–16, 318–19, 331–32, 332n.173, 333, 336, 337–38
Geneva Convention for the Amelioration of the Condition of Wounded, Sick and Shipwrecked Members of the Armed Forces at Sea, 296n.9
Geneva Convention for the Amelioration of Wounded and Sick in Armed Forces in the Field, 296n.9, 323–24n.133
Geneva Convention Relative to the Protection of Civilian Persons in Time of War, 296n.9
Geneva Convention Relative to the Treatment of Prisoners of War (Third Geneva Convention), 296n.9, 315–19, 336
    Article 2, 316–17
    Article 3, 58, 70–71, 291–92n.114, 296, 297–98, 315–16, 318–19, 331–32, 332n.173, 333, 336, 337–38
    Article 4, 315–16, 317–18, 317–18n.104
    Article 5, 315, 317–18, 320
    Article 11, 297n.12
    Article 17, 318–19
    Article 102, 318–19
    Article 129, 297–98n.14
    Article 132, 297n.12

Hague Convention on the Civil Aspects of International Child Abduction, 70, 70n.213
Hague Convention on the Recognition and Enforcement of Foreign Judgments in Civil or Commercial Matters, 10–11n.56
Hague Conventions, 296n.10, 334–35
Helms-Burton Act, 14n.80, 196, 196n.118

Immunity from Seizure Act, 254–55n.93
Inter-American Convention on Extradition, 273–74n.5
Inter-American Convention on Serving Criminal Sentences Abroad, 287–88n.89
Interim Agreement on Strategic Offensive Arms, 89–90
Intermediate-Range Nuclear Forces (INF) Treaty, 73
International Anti-Bribery and Fair Competition Act of 1998, 198n.131
International Child Abduction Remedies Act, 70n.214
International Claims Settlement Act, 99
International Convention for the Regulation of Whaling, 135, 135nn.132–136
    Article I(1), 135n.134
    Article III(1), 135n.133
    Article V(1), 135n.135
    Article V(3), 135n.136

International Covenant on Civil and Political Rights, 40n.43, 53–54n.120, 56–57n.134
International Emergency Economic Powers Act, 197–98
International Labour Organization Convention No. 87 Concerning Freedom of Association and Protection of the Right to Organize, 36–37n.21
International Organizations Immunities Act, 259–60, 259nn.118–119,
Iran Nuclear Agreement Review Act of 2015, 102n.107

Jay Treaty of 1798, 116, 116n.41, 123–24, 275
Joint Comprehensive Plan of Action (JCPOA), xiv–xv, 102, 102–3n.109
Judiciary Act of 1789, 210, 210n.2, 212, 213–14 , 221, 225–26n.78
Justice Against Sponsors of Terrorism Act (JASTA), 258, 258nn.115–116
Justice for Victims of Terrorism Act (Canada), 257n.107

Kellogg–Briand Pact of 1928, 294, 294n.4
Kyoto Protocol, 88–89

Lanham Trade-Mark Act, 187–88
Law of the Sea Convention, 88–89, 200
Litvinov Assignment, 93

Maritime Drug Law Enforcement Act (MDLEA), 204, 204nn.166–167, 205, 205n.171
McKinley Tariff Act of 1890, 84
Military Commissions Act (MCA) of 2006, 183nn.45–46, 332–33, 332–33n.176, 334–35, 337
§ 5(a), 56–57n.138, 333n.180
§ 6(d), 333n.181
§ 948a, 332–33n.177
§ 948b(f), 333n.178
§ 948b(g), 333n.179
§ 948r(c), 337n.205
§ 950u, 334–35n.192
§ 950v(b)(25), 334–35n.191
§ 950v(b)(28), 334–35n.189
Military Commissions Act (MCA) of 2009, 334n.183, 334–35, 337
§ 948a, 334n.184
§ 948b(e), 334n.185
§ 948r, 337n.206
§ 950t(25), 334–35n.191
§ 950t(29), 334–35n.190
§ 950t(30), 334–35n.192
Montreal Protocol on Substances that Deplete the Ozone Layer, 136, 136n.142, 137, 142
Article 2(9)(c), 136n.142
Article 2(H)(5), 137–38n.149

National Defense Authorization Act for Fiscal Year 1996, 85n.25, 134n.128, 274–75n.10
National Defense Authorization Act for Fiscal Year 2012, 326, 326n.140, 327, 328
§ 1021(a), 326n.141, 328n.148
§ 1021(b), 327n.142
§ 1021(c), 327n.143
§ 1021(d), (e), 327n.144
§ 1022(a), 328n.147

§ 1022(a)(4), 328n.149
§ 1023(a), 327n.145
§ 1023(b)(4), 327n.146
National Defense Authorization Act for Fiscal Year 2020, 73n.236
New Strategic Arms Reduction Treaty, 89–90n.48
New York Convention for the Recognition and Enforcement of Foreign Arbitral Awards, 62*n*176, 143n.174
North American Free Trade Agreement (NAFTA), xiv–xv, 84–85, 86–87, 122–24, 122–23n.68, 123n.73, 123–24n.76, 143
Nuclear Non-Proliferation Treaty, 139
Nuclear Test Ban Treaty, 88–89, 139

Optional Protocol Concerning the Compulsory Settlement of Disputes, 46–47n.82, 124, 124n.80
Optional Protocol to the Convention against Torture and Other Cruel, Inhuman and Degrading Treatment or Punishment, 231–32n.105, 296
Optional Protocol to the United Nations Convention on the Rights of the Child on the Sale of Children, Child Prostitution, and Child Pornography, 203
Optional Protocol to the United Nations Convention Rights of Persons with Disabilities, 88–89
Optional Protocol to the Vienna Convention on Diplomatic Relations, 73

Paris Agreement on Climate Change, xiv–xv, 102–3, 102–3n.109
Patent Cooperation Treaty, 41n.45
Prosecutorial Remedies and Other Tools to End the Exploitation of Children Today (PROTECT) Act, 202–3, 202–3n.158
Protocol Additional to the Geneva Conventions of 12 August 1949, and Relating to the Protection of Victims of International Armed Conflicts, 296n.10
Protocol Additional to the Geneva Conventions of 12 August 1949, and Relating to the Protection of Victims of Non-International Armed Conflicts, 296n.10
Protocol Additional to the Safeguards Agreement between the United States and the International Atomic Energy Association (IAEA), 136–37, 136–37nn.143–144
Protocol for the Prohibition of the Use in War of Asphyxiating, Poisonous or Other Gases, and of Bacteriological Methods of Warfare, 34*n*21, 296n.8
Protocol of the Permanent Court of International Justice (PCIJ), 119, 195–96
Protocol-Spain, Aug. 12, 1898, 95n.74

Racketeer Influenced and Corrupt Organizations Act (RICO), 193, 193n.105
REAL ID Act, 284, 284n.67
Rome Statute of the International Criminal Court, 75, 130–31, 130n.111, 132–33
    Article 5(2), 130n.112
    Article 17, 130n.113
    Article 21, 132–33n.125
    Article 25, 232–33, 233–34n.116
    Article 86, 132–33n.126
    Article 98(2), 131, 131n.116
Rules of Decision Act, 8–9
Rush–Bagot agreement of 1817, 95, 95n.73

Securities Exchange Act of 1934, 190–91, 190–91n.90
Sherman Antitrust Act, 186–87, 187–88n.71, 189, 190
Statute of the International Court of Justice, x–xin.3, 145n.1

Strategic Arms Limitation Agreement, 89–90
Supplemental Treaty between the Government of the United States of America and the Government of the United Kingdom of Great Britain and Northern Ireland, 280–81n.43

Torture Victim Protection Act (TVPA), 203–4, 203–4n.164, 209–10, 219–20, 219n.42, 268, 271–72
Treaty Between the United States and Other Powers Providing for the Renunciation of War as an Instrument of National Policy, 294n.4
Treaty of Amity, Commerce and Navigation between His Britannic Majesty and the United States of America, 116n.41, 275n.12
Treaty of Paris, 41n.46
Treaty of Washington, 117, 118–19n.53
Treaty on Armed Conventional Forces in Europe, 89–90
Treaty on Relations with Cuba, 83n.14
Treaty on the Limitation of Anti-Ballistic Missile Systems (ABM Treaty), 71–72, 73n.235, 75
Twelfth Hague Convention of 1907, 118–19

Uniform Code of Military Justice (UCMJ), 305, 330–32
    Section 821, 330–32
Uniform Foreign Money-Judgments Recognition Act, 10–11
United Kingdom State Immunity Act, 269n.189
United Nations Charter, 294, 294n.2, 295, 304–5, 304–5n.51, 308, 341–42
    Article 2(4), 294n.3
    Article 24(1), 308n.71
    Article 25, 141–42, 308n.73
    Article 42, 294n.3, 308n.71
    Article 51, 294n.3
    Article 94, 47, 48, 50n.105, 119–20, 129
    Article 94(1), 47n.84, 49n.94, 119–20n.57
    Article 94(2), 47n.85
United Nations Headquarters Agreement, 263, 263nn.151–152
U.S. Code,
    1 U.S.C. § 112b(a), 81–82n.10
    5 U.S.C. § 701(a), 283–84n.63
    8 U.S.C. § 1231 Note, 39–40n.40
    8 U.S.C. § 1252(a)(4), 284n.67
    9 U.S.C. § 15, 14n.80
    10 U.S.C. § 821, 330–31n.164
    15 U.S.C. § 78dd-1, 198n.128
    15 U.S.C. § 78dd-2, 198n.129
    18 U.S.C. § 956(a)(1), 197n.122
    18 U.S.C. § 1091(d)(5), 201–2n.150
    18 U.S.C. § 1651, 165n.100, 199–200n.138, 224–25n.74,
    18 U.S.C. § 2340A, 39–40n.40, 201–2n.151, 291–92n.114, 305n.55, 336n.198
    18 U.S.C. § 2441, 297–98n.13, 333n.182
    18 U.S.C. § 2442(c)(3), 201–2n.152
    18 U.S.C. § 3181, 273–74n.3, 277n.25
    18 U.S.C. § 3182, 273n.1

18 U.S.C. § 3184, 278n.28
18 U.S.C. § 3186, 278n.29
18 U.S.C. § 3188, 278n.26
18 U.S.C. § 3196, 278n.30
18 U.S.C. § 3244, 287–88n.92
18 U.S.C. § 3290, 280n.40
18 U.S.C. § 4001(a), 319–20n.114
18 U.S.C. § 4100, 287–88n.90
18 U.S.C. §§ 4100, 4107, 4108, 287–88n.91
19 U.S.C. § 1516a(g)(2), (g)(4)(A), 122–23n.71
19 U.S.C. § 1516a(g)(7)(A–B), 122–23n.71
19 U.S.C. § 3512(a)(1) & (b)(2)(A), 87n.37, 121–22n.65
21 U.S.C. § 959(c), 198–99n.133
22 U.S.C. § 254d, 242n.127
22 U.S.C. § 254e, 261n.130
22 U.S.C. § 271, 85n.24
22. U.S.C. § 286, 85n.24
22 U.S.C. § 288, 259n.118, 259n.120
22 U.S.C. §§ 288a(b), 259n.119
22 U.S.C. § 1621 *et seq*, 99n.93
22 U.S.C. § 2370(e)(2), 14nn.79–80
22 U.S.C. § 2459, 254–55n.93
22 U.S.C. §§ 6081–85, 196n.81
22 U.S.C. § 6085(b), 14n.80
22 U.S.C. §§ 6701–71, 133n.164
22 U.S.C. § 6723(a), (b)(2), 140n.159
22 U.S.C. § 7401(a), 88–89n.42
22 U.S.C. § 7424(b), (c), 131–32n.120
28 U.S.C. § 1257, 3n.9
28 U.S.C. § 1331, 160–61n.80
28 U.S.C. § 1332, 3n.6
28 U.S.C. § 1350, 157n.61, 191n.91, 210n.4, 219n.42
28 U.S.C. § 1441(b), 3n.10
28 U.S.C. § 1441(d), 3n.11
28 U.S.C. § 1603(a), 246n.42, 266n.170
28 U.S.C. § 1603(b), 246n.42, 266n.170
28 U.S.C. § 1603(d), 251n.75
28 U.S.C. § 1604, 245–46n.37
28 U.S.C. § 1605, 257–58n.108
28 U.S.C. § 1605(a)(1), 249n.62
28 U.S.C. § 1605(a)(2), 251n.73
28 U.S.C. § 1605(a)(3), 165n.102
28 U.S.C. § 1650(a)(4), 253n.86
28 U.S.C. § 1650(a)(5), 255nn.95–96
28 U.S.C. § 1605A, 257n.105, 258nn.112–114
28 U.S.C. § 1606, 246n.45
28 U.S.C. § 1607, 250n.71
28 U.S.C. § 2241(a), (c)(1), 181n.34

28 U.S.C. § 2680(k), 179–80n.25
28 U.S.C. § 4102, 10–11n.58
42 U.S.C. § 7676i(9), 137n.148
U.S. Code of Federal Regulations,
    22 C.F.R. §§ 95.1–95.4, 283n.60
    22 C.F.R. § 95.4, 283n.61
    22 C.F.R. §§ 181.1–181.9, 81–82n.10
    22 C.F.R. § 181.7(c), 81–82n.11
U.S. Constitution,
    1st Amendment, 68, 178–79
    4th Amendment, 139n.158, 140–41, 178–79, 179n.22
    5th Amendment, 179n.22, 204
    8th Amendment, 40n.43, 167–69
    10th Amendment, 30, 60–61, 68, 178–79
    14th Amendment, 28, 204, 206
    Article I, § 7, 52n.115,
    Article I, § 8, 21–22nn.115–116, 21–22, 62, 62n.165, 146–47n.5, 224–25n.74, 298nn.17–19, 325n.136
    Article I, § 9, 51–52n.110, 180–81, 180–81n.30, 180–81n.33, 184, 184n.53
    Article I, § 10, 28n.149, 59, 60n.155, 146–47, 276–77
    Article II, 24, 24n.126 , 27–28n.147, 33, 34, 34n.6, 35, 41, 58–59 , 61–62, 67, 67–68n.198, 68–69, 79, 80, 81–83, 81–82n.9, 85, 86–87, 88–91, 89–90n.43, 94–95, 100, 102–3, 111, 111–12nn.23–24, 116, 139–40, 146–47, 159, 274–75, 303, 303n.44, 326
    Article III, 2, 2n.1, 2n.2, 3, 6, 6n.28, 9, 112–14, 112–13n.29, 113–14n.34, 123–24, 123–24n.76, 127–28, 133, 146–49, 151–52, 157–58, 160–61, 211–12, 211–12n.7, 213–14, 216, 228–29n.67, 278–79
    Article IV, 10–11, 10–11n.55, 273n.1
    Article VI, xiin.11, 8, 8n.40, 28n.151, 42, 42n.48, 45–46, 53–54, 57–58, 67, 67n.194, 93, 146–49, 151–52
U.S.-Mexico-Canada Agreement (USMCA), xiv–xv, 84–85, 87, 122–23, 122–23n.69
United States-Mexico-Canada Agreement Implementation Act, 87n.38, 91n.53
U.S.–Mexico Extradition Treaty, 220

Versailles Treaty, 106–7, 309–10n.78
Vienna Convention on Consular Relations (VCCR), 46–47, 46–47n.79, 120, 124, 125n.81, 260, 260n.126
    Article 23(1), 262n.145
    Article 31(2), 262nn.142–143
    Article 31(3), 262n.144
    Article 36, 46–47, 46–47nn.80–81, 48, 50–51, 124, 125–28
    Article 36(1), 124n.78
    Article 36(2), 124n.79
    Article 39(2), 261–62n.137
    Article 41(1), 261n.133
    Article 42(3), 262n.147
    Article 43(1), 261n.134
    Article 43(2), 261n.135
    Article 45, 262n.146

Article 53(2), 261n.136
Article 53(4), 261–62n.138
Vienna Convention on Diplomatic Relations, 260, 260n.126, 262
Article 9(1), 262n.145
Article 22(1), 262n.140
Article 22(2), 262n.141
Article 29, 261n.128
Article 31(1), 261nn.129–130
Article 32, 262n.146
Article 32(3), 262n.147
Article 37(1), 261n.132
Vienna Convention on the Law of Treaties (VCLT), 33–34, 33–34nn.2–3, 69, 70, 81–82, 166, 166n.107
Article 1(a), 79n.1
Article 2(1)(b), 35–36n.15
Article 18, 76, 76n.250
Article 19, 40n.41
Articles 27, 68–69n.206
Article 32, 69n.211
Article 46, 68–69n.206, 81–82n.9
Article 33, 70n.217
Article 53, x–xin.4, 145–46n.3
Article 54, 56, 72n.229
Article 60, 72n.228

War Crimes Act, 297–98, 305, 333, 335–36
War Powers Resolution, 304–8, 306n.56
§ 2(c), 306n.57
§§ 3, 4, 306n.58
§ 5(b), 306n.59
§ 8(a), 306n.60
Warsaw Convention for the Unification of Certain Rules Relating to International Transportation by Air, 44–45, 44–45n.67,
Webster–Ashburton Treaty, 285, 285–86n.77
WTO agreements, 84–85, 86, 87

Index

For the benefit of digital users, indexed terms that span two pages (e.g., 52–53) may, on occasion, appear on only one of those pages.

abductions, international, 288–91
Abu Ghraib prison facility, 336–37
act of state doctrine
    about, 11–14
    congressional override, 14
    customary international law and the, 12
    federal common law, 13–14, 154–57
    human rights norms and, 12
    requirements for doctrine to apply, 12–13
    Second Hickenlooper Amendment, 14
    state courts and the, 155
    treaty violation exception, 7–8
Adams, John, 24–25, 58–59, 92, 275
adjudication and arbitration, international, 116–24
Administrative Review Boards at Guantánamo, 322–23
advisory opinions, 3–4
Afghanistan
    habeas corpus and U.S. detainees in, 159
    U.S. combat operations in, 314
Algiers Accords, 96
Alien Tort Statute litigation
    cause of action, 217–18
    Charming Betsy canon, 227
    choice of law, 233
    corporate human rights litigation, 231–37
    extraterritoriality, 191, 223–28
    the *Filartiga* decision, 157, 214–17
    historical origins, 210–13
    jurisdiction, 157–58
    limitations on, 221–22
    Marbois controversy, 213–14
    relationship with Article III, 211–13
    the *Sosa* decision, 160–61, 220–23
    Torture Victim Protection Act, 218–20
Al Qaeda
    Bush and Obama administrations actions regarding, 314
    detention of members, 314, 321–23
    habeas review, 321
    military commission trials, 328–35
    NDAA and, 326–28
    September 11 attacks, 313
    targeted killings of members, 338–43
    Third Geneva Convention, 315–17

Alvarez-Machain, United States v., 289–90
American Banana Co. v. United Fruit Co., 186–87
American Ins. Ass'n v. Garamendi, 29, 93–94, 99
Anti-Ballistic Missile (ABM) Treaty, 71–72, 75
Anti-Counterfeiting Trade Agreement, 97
arbitration and adjudication, international, 116–24
arms control inspection, 139–41
Article III of Constitution, 2–3, 112–15, 127–28, 132–33, 147–49, 211–13
Articles of Confederation, 41
Atlantic Charter, 101
ATS litigation. *See* Alien Tort Statute litigation

Baker v. Carr, 5
Belmont, United States v., 92, 158–59
Bin Laden, Osama, 314, 338
Blackstone, William, 149–50, 212–13, 221
Bond v. United States, 31, 62–63, 66–67
Boumediene v. Bush, 183–84, 320–21
Bricker Amendment, 38–39
Bush, George H.W., 218, 309
Bush, George W.
  Administrative Review Boards at Guantánamo, 322–23
  AUMF under, 314
  coercive interrogation, 335–38
  detention policy in war on terror, 314
  Geneva Conventions, 315–19
  the ICC and, 75, 130–31, 132
  ICJ and, 47, 127
  Medellín decision, effort to comply with, 47, 59, 128–29
  military commission system under, 58, 328–35
  nuclear weapons cuts and, 89–90
  response to September 11 attacks, 314
  termination of ABM treaty, 75
  "unsigning" of ICC treaty, 75, 130–31

Canada
  extraditions and, 276–77, 281
  NAFTA arbitration and, 122–23
Carter, Jimmy, 39, 93
Case Concerning Avena and Other Mexican Nationals, 47, 126–27
Case-Zablocki Act, 81–82
Central Intelligence Agency (CIA), 291, 314, 337–38

Charming Betsy canon
  Alien Tort Statute, 227
  AUMF, 325
  constitutional interpretation, 168–69
  customary international law and, 167
  executive branch and, 18–19
  extraterritoriality, 186, 189, 190, 195, 200
  FSIA and, 18
  individual official immunity, 269
  overview, 16–19, 56–57
  state law and, 19
  war on terror, 325
Chemical Weapons Convention, 62–63, 135–36, 139
Chevron doctrine, 20
China
  Boxer Indemnity Protocol, 98
  U.S. recognition of, 73, 75
Civil War (U.S.), 117, 180–81, 274, 301, 302–3, 328–29, 330
Clinton, William J., 75, 130–31, 290, 304–5, 311–12
coercive interrogation, 335–38
Combatant Status Review Tribunals (CSRTs), 320–21
comity, international, 10
Commander in Chief power, 23, 303–5
Comprehensive Nuclear Test Ban Treaty, 88–89
conditional consent to treaties, 37–41
Congress. *See* U.S. Congress
Congress of Vienna (1815), 106
constitutional interpretation, foreign and international materials in, xi–xii, 167–70
constitutional powers of Congress and the president, 21–25
Convention on Contracts for the International Sale of Goods, 44–45
Convention on Jurisdictional Immunities, 239
Convention on Privileges and Immunities of the United Nations, 263–64
corporate human rights litigation, 231–37
courts
  act of state doctrine, 11–14
  Charming Betsy canon, 16–19, 56–57, 167, 168–69, 186
  choice of law, 8–11
  customary international law as federal law and the, 159–61
  executive branch deference by, generally, 19–21

Index | 379

forum non conveniens doctrine, 14–16
international comity doctrine, 15–16, 189–90, 194–95
overview of foreign affairs and the, 1–2
personal jurisdiction, 6–8
preemption of state law, 28–31, 42
relationship between Congress and the president and the, 25–28
subject matter jurisdiction and justiciability limitations, 2–6
See also U.S. Supreme Court
criminal law
aiding and abetting, 232–33
assaults on ambassadors, 149–50, 213–14
bribery, 198
Congress's define-and-punish power and, 146–47, 203–4, 213–14, 298
consular immunity, 261
diplomatic immunity, 261
federal criminal liability, 52
FSIA and, 245–46n.37
head of state immunity, 166–67, 266–67
international criminal tribunals, 129–34
jury trial right, 67–68, 133–34
limits on congressional authority, 66–67
military commission trials, 328–35
presumption against extraterritoriality and, 187–88
torture, 39–40
treaties and criminal cases, 52
universal jurisdiction and, 199–200, 227–28
Vienna Convention litigation, 46–51, 124–29
War Crimes Act, 297–98, 336
warrants, 140–41
See also extradition and other means of criminal law enforcement; International Criminal Court (ICC); war on terrorism
Cuba. *See* Guantánamo Bay, Cuba
customary international law
congressional powers regarding, 146–47, 202, 205
Erie Railroad case and, 9, 153–54
and federal common law, 159–64, 216
federal common law challenges, 161–64
Filartiga and the Restatement (Third), 157–59
general common law and, 151–53
overview, 145
"part of our law," 149–51
persistent objection, 145–46

political branch authorization for federalizing CIL, 165–67
Sabbatino case, 11–12, 155–56
statutory interpretation and, 165–66
treaties, comparison with in U.S., 346
treaty interpretation and, 166
uncertainties surrounding, 170–73
U.S. Constitution and, 146–49
See also Alien Tort Statute litigation

Dames & Moore v. Regan, 93, 96, 98–99
death penalty, extradition and the, 281
decisions and orders of international institutions. *See* international institutions
deference to executive branch
discretionary authority and, 20–21
generally, 19–21
immunity issues, 241–43, 266, 270–71
lack of deference, situations involving, 21
statements of interest by executive, 21
treaty interpretation, 20, 70–71
Define and Punish Clause, 146–47, 203–4, 213–14, 298
delegations of authority, 26–27, 105
detentions. *See* military detentions
diplomatic and consular immunity, 260–64
Dispute Settlement Body (WTO), 120–22
Dulles, John Foster, 65–66

enemy combatants, 182–84, 319, 320–21
entanglements with foreign powers, resistance to, xii–xiii
Erie Railroad v. Tompkins, 9, 13–14, 153–54, 216
European Court of Human Rights, 168, 281
exceptionalism, United States, xii–xiii
executive agreements
Anti-Counterfeiting Trade Agreement, 97
C-175 process, 81
Case-Zablocki Act, 81–82
congressional, 84–87
congressional-executive agreements and partial interchangeability with treaties, 88–91
constitutionality, 85–87
extradition and, 274–75
fast-track authority, 85
historical practice, 80, 88–89
interchangeability with treaties, 88–91
legal effect and termination of sole, 100–1

executive agreements (*Cont.*)
    NAFTA, 84–85, 86–87, 122–23
    overview, 80–82
    political or "soft law" agreements, 101–3
    proposed constitutional amendments, 86
    pursuant to treaty, 82–84
    rise of, 80–82
    settlement of claims, 98–99
    sole, 92–97
    State Department guidelines, 81
    termination of, 91, 100
    trade agreements, 84
    types of, 81
    U.S.-Mexico-Canada trade agreement (USMCA), 84–85, 87, 122–23
    World Trade Organization, 84–85, 87
executive branch
    act of state doctrine and, 12–13
    Charming Betsy canon, 18–19
    congressional delegations of authority to, 26–27
    congressional members challenging action by the, 4
    deference to the, generally, 19–21
    diplomacy, conduct of, 24–25
    DSB decisions and the, 120–22
    extradition and the, 274–77
    recognition power, 23–24
    sovereign immunity and the, 241–43
    statements of interest by the, 21
    See also president
exhaustion of remedies, 219
expropriation of property, 12
extradition and other means of criminal law enforcement
    constitutionality, 278–79
    death penalty, 281
    dual criminality, 279–80
    executive agreements, 85
    extraordinary rendition, 291–92
    international abductions, 288–91
    international criminal tribunals, 129–34, 274–75
    Ker-Frisbie doctrine, 289–91
    limitations in extradition treaties, 279–81
    MLATs and prisoner exchange treaties, 287–88
    overview, 273–74
    political offenses, 280–81
    presidential power and, 274–76

rule of non-inquiry, 282–84
specialty doctrine, 285–86
State Department, role of, 278–79
states and, 276–77
statutes of limitation, 280
torture, 283–84
U.S. extradition practice, 277–79
See also criminal law; International Criminal Court (ICC); war on terrorism
extraordinary rendition, 291–92
extraterritorial application of U.S. law
    Charming Betsy canon, 186
    constitutional limits on, 202–5
    consular courts, 176–77n.3
    damage suits against government, 180
    habeas corpus reach, 180–85
    piracy, 199–200, 224–25
    prescriptive jurisdiction, international law limits on, 193–202
    presumption against, 186–93
    state laws and, 205–7
    territorial scope of the Constitution, 176–80
    universal jurisdiction, 199–200, 227–28

federal common law, generally, 9
federal courts
    choice of law, 8–11
    contrast with state courts, 3
    justiciability limitations and, 3–6
    limited jurisdiction, 2
federalism
    ICJ judgments and, 129
    international delegations and, 115
    limited and enumerated powers, 30
    Supreme Court commitment to, 30
    treaties and, 60–64
Filartiga v. Pena-Irala, 157, 214–17
Foreign Corrupt Practices Act, 198
foreign judgments, enforcement of, 10–11
Foreign Sovereign Immunities Act (FSIA)
    about, 245–49
    "based upon," 252–53
    commercial activity, 251–53
    counterclaims, 250
    customary international law and, 165–66, 241
    exceptions to immunity, 165, 249–59
    "foreign state," definition of, 246
    jus cogens norms, suits alleging violations of, 250
    noncommercial torts, 255–56

recovery of art and cultural artifacts, 254–55
relationship to Alien Tort Statute, 247–48
relationship to Article III, 247
retroactivity, 248
structure of statute, 246–47
takings of property, 253–55
terrorism exceptions, 257–59
waiver, 249–50
forum non conveniens doctrine, 15
Foster v. Neilson, 43–44, 70
France
    Louisiana Purchase, 43
    Marbois Controversy, 213–14
    U.S. undeclared war with, 16–17, 299–300
Full Faith and Credit Clause, 10–11

general common law, 8–9, 151–53
genocide, U.S. statute, 201–2
Germany
    German prisoners' habeas petition, 181–82
    LaGrand Case, 125–26
Goldsmith, Jack L., xvi–xvii, 161–62
Goldwater v. Carter, 75
Great Britain
    Alabama Claims Commission, 117
    customary international law in, 149–50
    destroyers for bases agreement, 95
    extradition, 285–86
    Jay Treaty, 38, 116, 123–24, 275
    migratory birds treaty, 60–61
    peace treaty, 41, 67–68
    War of 1812, 150, 299–300, 302
Guantánamo Bay, Cuba
    acquired by executive agreement, 82–83, 182
    Administrative Review Boards, 322–23
    Combatant Status Review Tribunals, 320–21
    detentions, 314
    Geneva Conventions, 318–19
    habeas corpus, 321
    military commissions, 331
    NDAA restrictions, 328
    Periodic Review Boards, 322–23
    U.S. Supreme Court cases regarding, 182–84, 320–21, 331–32

habeas corpus
    CSRT process as alternative to, 320–21
    enemy combatants and, 319, 321
    extradition challenges, 278
    territorial reach of, 180–85

VCCR litigation, 124–29, 142–43
Hague Convention on the Civil Aspects of International Child Abduction, 70
Hamdan v. Rumsfeld, 58, 331–32
Hamdi v. Rumsfeld, 319–20
Hamilton, Alexander, 57–58, 116
Hand, Learned, 154
Headquarters Agreement with UN, 263
Helms-Burton Act, 196
Helsinki Accords, 101
Henkin, Louis, xv–xvi, 39–40, 94–95, 158–59, 302–3
history, relevance of, x, 27–28
Holmes, Oliver Wendell, Jr., 60–61
Hughes, Charles Evans, 65–66
human rights law
    challenges for U.S. legal system, 346–47
    customary international law and, 171, 209
    individual official immunity, 264–72
    jus cogens norms, 145–46, 250
    non-self-execution declarations, 53–54, 162–63, 218
    reservations to treaties, 38–39
    subject matter scope of U.S. treaties, 65–67
    See also Alien Tort Statute litigation; European Court of Human Rights; Inter-American Court on Human Rights

immunity. *See* individual official immunities; Foreign Sovereign Immunities Act; sovereign immunity
individual official immunities
    deference to executive branch, 266, 270–71
    diplomatic and consular immunity, 260–64
    federal common law, 270
    Foreign Sovereign Immunities Act, relevance of, 266–69
    head of state immunity, 166–67, 266–67
    Restatement (Second) of Foreign Relations Law, 265–66, 271
    status and conduct immunity, 264
    Torture Victim Protection Act (TVPA) and, 268
    waiver, 267
    See also Foreign Sovereign Immunities Act; sovereign immunity
Insular Cases, 177
international abductions, 288–91
International Claims Settlement Act, 99

international comity doctrine, 15–16,
    189–90, 194–95
International Court of Justice (ICJ)
    Article 94, United Nations Charter, 47–48
    generally, 119–20
    jurisdiction of the, 46–47, 120
    presidential authority, 59
    VCCR and the, 46–51, 124–29, 142–43
International Criminal Court (ICC)
    American Servicemembers' Protection
        Act, 131–32
    Article 98 agreements, 131
    constitutional concerns, 133
    establishment of, 130
    extradition to, 133–34
    generally, 130–31
    jurisdiction, 130
    jury trial, lack of, 133
    "unsigning," 75, 130–31
international criminal tribunals, 129–34
international institutions
    adjudication and arbitration, 116–24
    Appointments Clause, 111–12, 139–40
    arms control inspection, 139–41
    Article III issues, 112–15
    constitutional principles regarding delegations
        to, 26–27, 108–15
    criminal tribunals, 129–34
    federalism, 115
    individual rights, 115
    international adjudication and
        arbitration, 116–24
    nondelegation doctrine and, 109–11
    non-self-execution of decisions and orders
        of, 141–44
    process issues, 111
    rise of, 106–8
    treaty amendments, 134–38
    Vienna Convention Cases, 46–51, 124–29
International Labour Organization, 137
International Maritime Organization, 134–35
International Monetary Fund, 85
International Organizations Immunities Act
    (IOIA), 259
International Whaling Commission, 135
interrogation, coercive, 335–38
Iran
    hostage crisis, 93
    Iran-United States Claims Tribunal, 122

Joint Comprehensive Plan of Action
    (JCPOA), 102
    targeted killing of Soleimani, 341–42
Iran-United States Claims Tribunal, 122
Iraq
    Abu Ghraib prison facility, 336–37
    American citizens apprehended in, 185
    war in, 309
Irish Republican Army, 280–81

Jackson, Justice, 26, 100
Jam v. Int'l Finance Corp., 259–60
Jay Treaty, 38, 116, 123–24, 275
Jesner v. Arab Bank, 235–36
Jessup, Philip C., 13–14, 153–54
Johnson v. Eisentrager, 181–82
Joint Comprehensive Plan of Action
    (JCPOA), 102
jurisdiction
    international law limits on prescriptive
        jurisdiction, 193–202
    personal, 6–8
    subject matter jurisdiction and justiciability
        limitations, 2–6
jus cogens norms
    customary international law and, 145–46
    FSIA and, 18, 250
    generally, x–xi
Justice Against Sponsors of Terrorism Act, 258
justiciability, 3–6

Kellogg-Briand Pact, 294
Kiobel v. Royal Dutch Petroleum Co., 191, 228–31
Korean War, 25, 58–59, 309
Kosovo bombing, 304–5
Kuwait, invasion by Iraq, 309

League of Nations, 106–7
legislative standing, 4
Libya, air strikes on, 307, 310
Lincoln, Abraham, 180–81, 274, 301, 303, 335
Litvinov Assignment, 92–93
Louisiana Purchase, 43

Madison, James, 57–58, 92, 95
Maritime Drug Law Enforcement Act
    (MDLEA), 204–5
Marshall, John, 17, 24–25, 58–59, 186, 275–76
McKinley, William, 98

Medellin v. Texas, 45, 46–47, 48–50, 128–29, 142–43
Mexican-American War, 301
Mexico
   Claims Commission, 117
   Cutting Case, 199
   DEA agent murder in, 220, 289
   extradition, 289, 290
   ICJ proceedings, 126–27
   NAFTA, 84–85, 86, 122–23
   U.S. abduction of citizen of, 220, 289
   U.S.-Mexico-Canada trade agreement, 84–85, 87
military commission trials, 328–35
military detentions
   AUMF and international law, 323–26
   coercive interrogation, 335–38
   extraordinary rendition, 291–92
   judicial review of, 319–21
   length of detention, 322
   scope of, 321–23
   See also war on terrorism
Missouri v. Holland, 60–61, 90–91
modus vivendi, 97
monism and dualism, xii
Montreal Protocol on Substances that Deplete the Ozone Layer, 136, 137
Mutual Legal Assistance Treaties (MLAT) and prisoner exchange treaties, 55–56, 287–88

NAFTA, 84–85, 122–23
Nash, Thomas (alias Jonathan Robbins), 275
neutrality prosecutions, 150
Nicaragua, U.S. activities in, 120, 142
Nixon, Richard, 306
nondelegation doctrine, 26–27, 109–11
North Atlantic Treaty Organization (NATO), 73n.236, 311
Nuremberg Tribunal, 129–30, 233–34

Obama, Barack
   Anti-Counterfeiting Trade Agreement, 97
   AUMF under, 321
   on closure of Guantánamo facility, 314
   International Criminal Court, 132
   interrogation techniques under, 337–38
   on military commissions trials, 334
   on military detentions, 321
   military operations in Libya, 307, 310
   NDAA, compliance with, 328
   Periodic Review Boards, 322–23
   targeted killings under, 338–43
official immunity. *See* sovereign and official immunity
orders and decisions of international institutions. *See* international institutions
Organization for Economic and Cultural Development (OECD), 198

Palestine Liberation Organization, 217
Paquete Habana, The, 151, 295
Paris Agreement, 102–3
Periodic Review Boards, 322–23
Permanent Court of Arbitration in The Hague, 117–18
Permanent Court of International Justice (PCIJ), 119, 195–96
personal jurisdiction, 6–8
piracy, 165, 186, 199–200, 224–25
political question doctrine, 5–6, 75, 248–49, 306–7, 339–40
Power Authority of New York v. Federal Power Commission, 54
preemption of state law
   dormant, 29
   generally, 28–31, 205–6
   presumption, 31, 42
prescriptive jurisdiction, international law limits on
   corporate affiliates, regulation of, 197–98
   customary international law, 195
   effects within territory, 195–96
   generally, 193–94
   nationals, regulation of, 197
   objective and subjective territorial principles, 197
   passive personality, 199
   prosecute or extradite, 200–1
   protective principle, 198–99
   reasonableness, 194–95
   territorial regulation, 195–96
   universal jurisdiction, 199–200
president
   ambassadors, receipt of, 23
   Commander in Chief, 23
   constitutional powers of, 23
   historical practice and, 27–28, 80

president (*Cont.*)
   nondelegation doctrine and the, 26–27, 109–11
   recognition of foreign governments, 23–24, 74
   relationship with Congress, 25–28
   settlement of claims, 98–99
   sole organ, 24–25
   Take Care Clause, 24, 57–59, 159
   treaties and the, 57–58
   war powers, 303–5
   See also executive branch
presumption against extraterritoriality
   Alien Tort Statute, 191
   antitrust law, 189–90
   Charming Betsy canon, relationship with, 186
   customary international law, status of, 195
   "focus" of a statute, 192–93
   history of, 186
   scholarly critiques of, 188, 191–92
   securities fraud, 190–91
   Supreme Court reaffirmation of, 188–89, 190–91
prisoner exchange and MLAT treaties, 287–88
prisoners of war. *See* military detentions
prize court, 118–19
PROTECT Act, 202–3
public and private international law, x–xi, 146

Rasul v. Bush, 182–83
Rauscher, United States v., 285–86
recognition of foreign governments, 23–24
Reid v. Covert, 67–68, 177–78
Respublica v. De Longchamps, 149–50
Restatements of Foreign Relations Law, xv–xvi, 17–18, 44, 66, 74, 152–53, 156–57, 158, 194–95
Revenue Rule, 10
Rice, Condoleezza, 127
Rome Statute of the International Criminal Court, 75, 130, 133, 232–33
Roosevelt, Franklin D., 92, 95, 329–30
Roper v. Simmons, 167–68
RUDs (reservations, understandings, and declarations), 39–40, 64
Rush-Bagot Agreement, 95

Sabbatino case, 11–12, 154–57
Samantar v. Yousuf, 269–70
Sanchez-Llamas v. Oregon, 50–51, 127–28
Schooner Exchange v. McFaddon, 240–41, 264–65, 345

September 11, 2001 terrorist attack, 313
   See also war on terrorism
soft law or political agreements, 101–3
Sosa v. Alvarez-Machain, 160–61, 220–23
sovereign immunity
   absolute and restrictive theories, 241
   customary international law and, 239–40
   deference to the executive branch, 19–20, 241–43
   international organizations, immunity of, 259–60
   presidential authority to settle claims and, 98–99
   Tate Letter, 243–45
   See also Foreign Sovereign Immunities Act; individual official immunities
Soviet Union
   ABM Treaty, 71–72, 75
   arms control treaties, 89–90
   U.S. recognition of the, 92
Spanish–American War, 95, 151, 182, 295, 314
standing to sue, 3–4
state courts
   choice of law, 8–11, 206
   general jurisdiction, 3
   removal from, 3
state law
   extraterritorial application of, 205–7
   preemption of, 28–31, 41–42
   restricting courts from using foreign, international, or Sharia laws, 169–70
   sole executive agreements and, 92–97
   treaties and, 41–42
states (U.S.)
   compacts or agreements, 59
   constitutional powers and the, 28
   extradition and the, 276–77
   treaty-making prohibition for, 59
   See also federalism
status of forces agreements, 95
Story, Joseph, 59–60, 148–49
Supremacy Clause, 8, 9, 28, 42, 45–46, 53–54, 57–58, 93, 147–48
Supreme Court. *See* U.S. Supreme Court
Swift v. Tyson, 8–9, 152

Taft, William Howard, 118
Taiwan, defense treaty with the U.S., 75

Taliban
    associated forces with the, 323–24
    AUMF and, 319–20
    combat operations against, 314
    detention of, 314, 317–18
    end of hostilities, 322–23
    Geneva Conventions, 315–16, 317–18
    prisoner of war status, 317–18
targeted killing, 338–43
Tate Letter, 243–45
territorial possessions. *See* extraterritorial application of U.S. law
terrorism, sovereign immunity exceptions for, 257–59
torture
    coercive interrogation, 335–38
    Convention Against Torture, 39–40, 200–1, 283
    criminal statute, 201–2
    extradition and, 283–84
    extraordinary rendition, 291–92
    Filartiga case, 157, 215–16
    jus cogens norms, 145–46
    Pinochet case, 200–1
    state action, 231–32
    universal jurisdiction, 227–28
Torture Victim Protection Act (TVPA), 203–4, 218–20, 234–35, 268
treaties
    advice and consent, 35
    amendments to, 134–38
    conditional consent, 37–41
    decline in, 37, 80
    exclusive congressional authority, 51–53
    failure to ratify, 36–37
    federalism and, 60–64
    human rights treaties, 38–39
    individual rights and, 67–69
    interpretation of, 69–72
    last-in-time rule, 55–57
    non-self-execution, 43–46
    non-self-execution declarations, 53–54
    preemption of state law, 42
    the president and, 57–59
    private rights of action, 51
    process for making, 34–37
    proliferation of, xi
    reinterpretation, 71–72
    RUDs (reservations, understandings, and declarations), 39–40

    Senate's role, 35
    signature, 35–36
    states and, 59–60
    subject matter scope of treaty power, 65–67
    supreme federal law, 41–42
    terminating treaty commitments, 72–77
    treaty amendments and international institutions, 134–38
    treaty process, 34–37
    unsigning, 75, 130–31
    VCCR litigation, 46–51, 124–29, 142–43
    withdrawal of reservations, 41
    See also international institutions
troops (U.S.) under foreign command, 311–13
Trump, Donald, xiv–xv, 37, 76, 102–3, 121–22, 132, 196, 303–4, 314, 341–42
Trump v. Hawaii, 20–21

Uniform Code of Military Justice (UCMJ), 330–32
Uniform Foreign Money Judgments Recognition Act, 10–11
United Nations
    Charter of the United Nations, 47, 294–95
    establishment of, 107
    the *Filartiga* decision and resolutions of the, 215–16
    growth in international agreements and the, xi, 171–72
    ICJ rulings and members of the, 47, 119–20
    immunity and the, 263–64
    military operations under the, 131–32, 308
    Security Council, 308–10
    structure of, 107
    treaties, growth of, 80
U.S. Army Field Manual, 337–38
U.S. Congress
    act of state doctrine and the, 14
    appropriations, 51–52, 298–99
    Charming Betsy canon, 16–19, 167, 186
    commerce power, 22–23, 58, 84, 202
    constitutional powers of, 21–22, 51–53
    criminal liability, creation of, 52
    customary international law and, 159–60
    delegations of authority, 26–27, 105
    diplomatic activities, 24–25
    executive branch action challenges by, 4

U.S. Congress (*Cont.*)
　foreign affairs powers, 21–22
　Necessary and Proper Clause, 21–22, 62
　relationship with the president, 25–28
　state law preemption by, 28
　taxation and duties, 52
　war powers, 298–303
U.S. Constitution
　Appointments Clause, 111–12, 139–40, 312
　Article I, Section 10, 59, 276
　Article III, 2–3, 112–15, 127–28, 132–33, 147–49, 211–13, 216, 247, 278–79
　Commerce Clause, 21–22, 84, 202
　customary international law and the, 146–49
　delegations of authority to international institutions and the, 108–15
　Due Process Clause, 7–8, 28, 168, 204, 206, 290–91, 320–21
　Fourth Amendment, 140, 178–79
　Eighth Amendment, 167–68
　habeas corpus reach, 180–85
　individual rights provisions, 67–69, 115
　Necessary and Proper Clause, 21–22, 62
　Supremacy Clause, 8, 9, 28, 42, 53–54, 57–58, 93, 147–48
　Suspension Clause, 180–81
　Take Care Clause, 24, 57–59, 159
　Tenth Amendment, 30, 60–61
　territorial scope of the, 176–80
　treaties and the, 60–69
　Vesting Clause, 24
　war powers (congressional), 298–303
　war powers (presidential), 303–5
U.S. Department of Justice Office of International Affairs, 278, 279
U.S. Justice Department Office of Legal Counsel, 27–28, 111–12, 307, 315–16, 336–37, 341
U.S.–Mexico Claims Commission, 117
U.S. State Department
　art and cultural objects and the, 254–55
　certification of diplomat status, 262–63
　extradition and the, 279
　international agreement negotiations and the, 81
　sovereign immunity determinations, historically, 242, 244–45
　terrorism sovereign immunity exception and the, 257

U.S. territorial possessions, U.S. Supreme Court on, 177
U.S. troops under foreign command, 311–13

Vattel, Emmerich, 96, 212–13
Verdugo-Urquidez, United States v., 178–79
Versailles Treaty, 80, 106–7
Vienna Convention on Consular Relations (VCCR), 46–51, 124–29, 142–43, 260
Vienna Convention Diplomatic Relations (VCDR), 260
Vienna Convention on the Law of Treaties (VCLT), 33–34, 69, 76, 81–82
Vietnam War, 306

war
　congressional authorizations, 300, 308
　declarations of war, 53, 299–300
　enemy combatants, 182–84, 319–21
　foreign command of troops, 311–13
　international law and, 294–98
　presidential war powers, 303–5
　See also war on terrorism; war powers
War of 1812, 150, 302
war on terrorism
　AUMF and international law, 323–26
　Authorization for Use of Military Force (AUMF), 313
　coercive interrogation, 335–38
　Detainee Treatment Act, 336–37
　detention authority scope, 321–23
　detentions and judicial review, 313–21
　detentions and the Third Geneva Convention, 315–19
　detentions in the, 313–14
　extradition and, 281
　extraordinary rendition, 291–92
　Guantánamo Bay, 82–83, 182
　Military Commissions Act (MCA), 332–34
　military commission trials, 328–35
　NDAA, 326–28
　targeted killing, 338–43
war powers
　authorizations of force, 300, 308
　congressional, 298–303
　declarations of war, 298–300
　delegating, 308–10
　Libya, use of force against, 307, 310

modern international law and, 294–98
placing troops under foreign
  command, 311–13
presidential, 303–5
Third Geneva Convention, 315–19
UN Security Council and, 308–10
War Powers Resolution, 306–8
See also war
Ware v. Hylton, 42, 147–48
Warsaw Convention, 44–45
Washington, George, xii–xiii, 35
World Bank, 85, 107
World Trade Organization (WTO)
  agreements, 84–85, 120–21
  Appellate Body, 121–22
  dispute settlement, 120–22
  DSB decisions, 121–22
  U.S participation in, 120–21
World War II
  criminal tribunals regarding, 172
  executive agreements, 80
  German nationals in occupied Germany, 181
  military commissions and, 329–30
  theft of art and cultural artifacts, 254–55
  U.S. war declaration, 299–300
Wright, Quincy, xv
WTO. *See* World Trade Organization

Youngstown case, 25–26

Zivotofsky v. Clinton, 5
Zschernig decision, 29